Taxes and the Economy

Taxes and the Economy

A Survey of the Impact of Taxes on Growth, Employment, Investment, Consumption and the Environment

Willem Vermeend

Faculty of Law and the Faculty of Economics, University of Maastricht, The Netherlands

Rick van der Ploeg

Professor of Economics, University of Oxford, UK and University of Amsterdam, The Netherlands

and

Jan Willem Timmer

Faculty of Law, University of Maastricht, The Netherlands

Edward Elgar
Cheltenham, UK • Northampton, MA, USA

Published by
Edward Elgar Publishing Limited
The Lypiatts
15 Lansdown Road
Cheltenham
Glos GL50 2JA
UK

Edward Elgar Publishing, Inc.
William Pratt House
9 Dewey Court
Northampton
Massachusetts 01060
USA

Paperback edition 2009

A catalogue record for this book
is available from the British Library

Library of Congress Cataloguing in Publication Data

Vermeend, W. A.
    Taxes and the economy : a survey on the impact of taxes on growth,
employment, investment, consumption and the environment / by Willem
Vermeend, Rick van der Ploeg, and Jan Willem Timmer.
        p. cm.
    Includes bibliographical references and index.
    1. Taxation. 2. OECD countries—Economic policy. I. Ploeg, Rick van der.
II. Timmer, Jan Willem, 1980– III. Title.
    HJ2305.V47 2008
    330.9—dc22

                                                        2007039489

ISBN 978 1 84720 115 7 (cased)
ISBN 978 1 84980 016 7 (paperback)

Printed and bound by MPG Books Group, UK

Contents

APPENDICES

Preface

How taxes affect the economy is the key question of this book, which surveys the economic impact of taxation and the political make-up of tax systems and presents tools for tax design. The survey is concerned with taxation in the leading group of OECD economies and focuses in particular on the impact of taxes on growth, employment, investment, consumption and the environment. The idea is not to provide an academic monograph for economic scholars. Instead, the book offers a survey of theory, findings of important academic studies and practical experiences in OECD countries.

The framework provides tools for developing a well-designed tax system that can play a role in promoting sustainable economic growth and employment. We hope that this book will be of particular use to those who are dealing with public finance, fiscal economics and tax law, as well as to policy makers, practitioners and other interested readers.

Willem Vermeend is Professor of European Fiscal Economics in the Faculty of Law and the Faculty of Economics at the University of Maastricht, the Netherlands, and adviser on international taxation with the law firm DLA Piper. In his capacity as State Secretary of Finance and Minister of Social Affairs and Employment in the Dutch government (1994-2002) he gained much experience with the implementation and evaluation of a large number of tax measures, both in the Netherlands as well as in the European Union. He initiated the major Dutch tax reform of 2001 and also co-authored the book Greening Taxes: The Dutch Model (Vermeend and van der Vaart, 1998).

Rick van der Ploeg is Professor of Economics at the Department of Economics, University of Oxford, the United Kingdom, and Professor of Political Economy in the Faculty of Economics and Business at the University of Amsterdam, the Netherlands. He is a specialist in public finance and macroeconomics. He has a wealth of experience in politics, especially as chief financial and taxation spokesperson for the parliamentary Labour Party in the Dutch parliament (1994-98) and later as State Secretary for Education, Culture and Science in the Dutch cabinet (1998-2002).

Jan Willem Timmer studied fiscal economics and tax law at the University of Maastricht, the Netherlands. He has worked in the Faculty of Law and has taught several economics courses at the Faculty of Economics and Business

Administration at the university. Currently, he is employed as tax adviser with the global law firm DLA Piper.

Willem Vermeend
Rick van der Ploeg
Jan Willem Timmer

Introduction

Three objectives of taxation are generally distinguished. First, taxes are levied by governments around the world to finance public expenditure. Taxation that covers such spending relates to the traditional function. Second, taxes are used to alter income and wealth distributions among households. Governments frequently use the tax system for carrying out such income politics. In this context, taxation has a distributional function. Finally, taxation can be employed to realise structurally balanced economic growth or to smooth business cycles.

In the post-Second World War period, OECD countries have increasingly relied on taxation to achieve a variety of economic policy objectives, of which stimulating economic activity and employment are usually the most important.[1] The tax system is also used to create a favourable climate for investment, to spur business innovation and to promote long-term sustainable environmental policy.[2]

This book examines the effect of taxation on the economy and its development. More specifically, it discusses the impact of taxes on growth, employment, investment, consumption and the environment. It aims to provide the reader with the necessary empirical information, while at the same time presenting an overview of the latest theoretical insights. In doing so, many relevant policy issues are touched upon.

We refer to theoretical and empirical studies as well as the practical experiences of various OECD countries. Using a combination of four factors

---

[1] The Organisation for Economic Cooperation and Development (OECD) is an international organisation of 30 developed countries that embrace the principles of democratic government and the free market economy. Its forerunner was the Organisation for European Economic Cooperation (OEEC), which was established in 1948 to administer the Marshall Plan for the reconstruction of Europe after the Second World War. In 1961, the OEEC was re-formed into the OECD. The organisation is based in Paris and includes the following member states: Australia, Austria, Belgium, Canada, the Czech Republic, Denmark, Finland, France, Germany, Greece, Hungary, Iceland, Ireland, Italy, Japan, Korea, Luxembourg, Mexico, the Netherlands, New Zealand, Norway, Poland, Portugal, the Slovak Republic, Spain, Sweden, Switzerland, Turkey, the United Kingdom and the United States. See www.oecd.org.

[2] Two pioneering studies on tax reform are the Meade Committee Report (1978) and the Mirrlees Review which is currently being carried out at the London-based *Institute of Fiscal Studies* and aims to identify the characteristics of a good tax system in the 21st century global economy.

should provide the reader with accurate and current insights as to the potential of the tax system as an instrument for economic policy:

1. the latest theoretical and empirical studies and scientific work;
2. practical experiences of the various countries;
3. an interactive website, www.taxesandeconomy.com kept up to date with the latest developments; and
4. the opportunity for readers to post their own comments, remarks and suggestions on the website.

The emphasis lies on the 1970-2007 period. Besides a general and more theoretical framework, we have examined a sample of countries and included a variety of (specific) tax measures implemented by them. The measures have been adequately examined and evaluated, both *ex ante* and *ex post*, by government or academia in the English language. Furthermore, the practical experiences are our own or have been derived from documents and websites, including in other languages: French, German, Italian, Swedish and Dutch.

THE SELECTION OF COUNTRIES

The selection of countries is guided by two principles. First, the countries must be in the leading group of OECD economies in terms of GDP per capita. Second, the selection should involve countries which have implemented tax measures that are relevant for our survey. The sample thereby comprises: Australia, Austria, Belgium, Canada, Denmark, Finland, France, Germany, Ireland, Italy, Japan, the Netherlands, Norway, Sweden, the United Kingdom and the United States.

With the exception of Australia, Canada, Japan, Norway and the United States, all these countries are members of the European Union (EU). The EU is a supranational and intergovernmental organisation of democratic independent states. It was established in 1992 under the Maastricht Treaty and superseded the European Economic Community (EEC) which was originally established in 1958 with six members. The EU now embraces 27 member states with roughly 500 million people.[3] Table 1 provides an overview of the names and accession dates of EU member states. The EU is relevant as its institutions importantly affect national tax policy conducted by member states.[4]

---

[3] For a statistical overview, see European Commission (2006a). More information on the EU is available at http://europa.eu.

[4] A (statistical) outline of the tax systems of EU member states and developments within is offered in European Commission (2006b).

The most important institutions within the EU are the Council of the European Union, the European Commission, the European Parliament and the European Court of Justice (ECJ). The Council consists of the ministers from the national governments in the relevant policy areas and is responsible for policy and passing legislation. The Commission is based in Brussels and manages the day-to-day affairs. It is responsible for the implementation of EU (spending) policies and ensuring that member states abide by EU law, including tax laws.

There are three types of EU law: treaties; institutional acts such as directives, regulations and decisions; and case law from the ECJ. Within the EU, member states also follow and review the tax policies of other members by means of the so-called 'open coordination method'. This method relies on the creation of guidelines, peer review, best practice, benchmarking and the learning and diffusion of shared beliefs among policy makers.

Table 1   Development of the European Community/Union

Year	Development
1958	EC-6: Belgium, Federal Republic of Germany, France, Italy, Luxembourg and the Netherlands
1973	EC-9: Denmark, Ireland and the United Kingdom join EC-6
1981	EC-10: Greece joins EC-9
1986	EC-12: Spain and Portugal join EC-10
1995	EU-15: Austria, Finland and Sweden join EC-12
2004	EU-25: Czech Republic, Estonia, Cyprus, Latvia, Lithuania, Hungary, Malta, Poland, Slovenia and Slovakia join EU-15
2007	EU-27: Bulgaria and Romania join EU-25

Source: European Commission (2006a).

The European Parliament is made up of 785 members and is elected every five years by the people of the 27 EU countries to represent their interests. Its main job is to scrutinise and approve EU laws. Finally, the ECJ adjudicates on all legal issues and disputes involving Community law. The Court is based in Luxembourg and comprises a judge from each of the member states. The judges are appointed for a period of six years. The ECJ mainly deals with referrals from national courts regarding interpretation of Community law and actions mostly started by the Commission against a member state that is in non-compliance with Community law.

Selection of Tax Measures

We have largely confined ourselves to tax measures that were implemented after 31 December 1989. This is for two reasons: first, the availability of studies is higher for this period - before the 1990s, evaluations were more fragmented and difficult to obtain; and second, research methods have improved greatly in these years due to better insights and greater availability of data. The measures must have had a structural and significant budgetary impact.

It should be stressed that it is not our objective to provide a per country analysis of tax policy. The theory presented and measures examined serve the sole purpose of gaining general insights into the effects of tax policy on the economy. It is inevitable that certain countries will be discussed in greater detail than others. This may be due to a richer history in tax policy making, more extensive evaluation or a combination of both.

In the main text we abstain from any mathematical modelling. In the footnotes we shall occasionally insert the appropriate mathematical formulae and the appendices include some formal models to provide the relevant background for the interested reader. Our main aim is to give a non-technical explanation of the often quite mathematical theories of public finance, thereby equipping the reader with the necessary knowledge to be able to understand and appreciate reform proposals and tax policy, while keeping the text accessible to a broad audience.

THE PATH FORWARD

Chapter 1 begins by discussing a number of key indicators for economic policy. The chapter examines fundamental distortions created by taxation and the marginal cost of public funds, a circular flow model, and equivalence relations and the impact of taxation on economic growth. Chapter 2 continues in a general fashion with a focus on basic principles in tax design. This includes the characteristics of a good tax system, an exposition of the tax base and (effective) tax rates, revenue statistics, the tax expenditure concept and criteria for using the tax system for policy.

Chapter 3 examines tax policy in relation to labour market performance. Encouraging employment and the work effort is a crucial factor in creating (future) economic prosperity. Besides directly affecting both variables, taxes often facilitate generous income-support systems that indirectly affect labour supply. There is an inevitable trade-off between on the one hand stimulating employment and the work effort, and on the other, having social welfare and income support for the poor.

The effects of taxes on capital investment are analysed in Chapter 4. A continuing integration of capital markets on a global scale creates issues that are international in nature. The tax system can be an important factor in the investment decision of companies. There are two ways through which taxes affect the level of investment: first, taxes reduce the return to investment by raising the cost of capital; and second, international variations in statutory and average capital income tax rates affect the location of investment.

Chapter 5 turns to the economic effects of taxes on consumption, and includes a review of the effects of a shift from income- to consumption-based taxation. A consumption-, as opposed to an income-based tax, exempts the return to savings and thus leaves the consumption-savings decision unaffected. This should encourage investment. Academic studies have measured significant effects on economic growth from such a shift. A consumption tax can assume several forms, including the much discussed Hall and Rabushka flat tax proposal which imposes a single rate on taxpayers.

Two vital elements in realising a sustainable economic growth are research and development (R&D) and human capital. The tax system affects both factors, which are examined in Chapters 6 and 7, respectively. Together, this should provide a comprehensive picture of how the tax system can be deployed to the benefit of the economy.

Chapter 8 proceeds with a discussion of international tax competition. In the globalising economy, barriers to trade and factor movements are rapidly being removed, which exposes the allocation of resources more directly to tax differences between countries. To create a sustainable development, governments nowadays more frequently coordinate their tax policies.

Furthermore, at the outset of the 21st century, economic growth can no longer be separated from sound and long-term sustainable environmental policies. Global pollution is increasing rapidly and mobility of traffic is deteriorating. Rising greenhouse gas levels in the atmosphere could under plausible assumptions in the coming 30 years cause an average rise in global temperature of over 3°C. This would have a devastating impact not only on the environment, but also on economic growth and development. Green tax measures can play a role in policy that deals with these issues, a subject that is reviewed in Chapter 9. Tax policy should seek to discourage polluting activities as well as promote the development of environmentally related technologies.

The book concludes with a summary of findings and lessons for tax policy. In the final chapter we also present a simplified concept of a tax system that we refer to as 'second life tax'. The following appendices are included:

A1   the Solow model of economic growth;
A2   the Keynesian model;
A3   microeconomic topics in commodity taxation;
A4   the OECD classification of taxes;
A5   revenue statistics;
A6   relevant web links.

The purpose of Appendices 1-3 is not to provide a comprehensive overview of theory, but rather to provide an introduction to some of the key economic principles and notions that are addressed in the main text.

PART I

Principles of taxation

1. Taxation and economic policy

An individual sacrifice for a collective goal may well be the shortest way of defining taxation.

(Grapperhaus, 1998)[1]

1.1 INTRODUCTION

In studying the effects of government intervention by means of taxation, we should first acknowledge that it is one of the key responsibilities of government to create and maintain a prosperous economy. Many people would agree that the higher their standard of living, the more satisfaction they get out of life. A widely accepted measure to compute economic growth over time is gross domestic product (GDP). GDP measures the aggregate expenditure in an economy, which consists of the sum of consumption, investment, government spending and exports, minus imports during a given period.[2] The calculation of GDP is defined by international guidelines (SNA93).[3]

It should be noted that GDP gives an incomplete picture of economic welfare, which also includes other factors such as health, security, education, employment, poverty and income inequality, housing, leisure and externalities from pollution. A survey of 178 countries that measured such factors showed that people living in European countries are reported to be the happiest in the world (White, 2006). The meta-analysis combined the

---

[1] The quotation is cited from Ferdinand Grapperhaus's appealing book *Tax Tales for the Second Millennium*. The book offers a historical account of taxation and the forming of society in Europe (1000-2000); taxation as a stepping-stone to the formation of the United States of America (1765-1801); and taxation in the Mughal Empire in India (1526-1709).

[2] This can be represented by the following identity $GDP = C + I + G + NX$. Gross, as opposed to net, means that depreciation of capital is not included. Formally, GDP can be measured by one of three approaches: the *expenditure* approach measures the total of the above four factors; the *income* approach measures the total of wage and capital income; whereas the *output* approach measures the total value of goods and services produced in an economy. Except for some technical adjustments, the three methods should sum to the same value.

[3] The System of National Accounts was prepared jointly by representatives of the International Monetary Fund (IMF), the World Bank, the United Nations, the OECD and the EU. The system was originally designed in 1968 and updated in 1993.

findings of over 100 different studies around the world in which 80,000 people were questioned on subjective well-being.[4] Denmark tops the list, followed by Switzerland and Austria (see Table 1.1, below). Other notable results in the top 20 included Iceland (4), Finland (6), Sweden (7), Canada (10), Ireland (11), Luxembourg (12), the Netherlands (15) and Norway (19). UNICEF (2007) obtained similar findings for children. According to the study of 21 rich countries, offspring in the Netherlands are 'happiest', followed by those in Sweden, Denmark and Finland. Children in the UK are 'unhappiest', with the US coming second to last.

GDP growth differentials are nevertheless a root cause for the large discrepancies in the distribution of income, wealth and economic opportunity in the world. Government policy should therefore be aimed at creating an efficient and sustainable economic growth, taking into account the other factors that affect economic well-being.

Less developed countries (LDCs) face a particularly compelling challenge in this area in the decades to come. These countries usually have a small capital stock and thus a high return due to diminishing returns to capital. This should attract investment and enable them to grow faster than richer countries, provided that the quality of institutions and their legal systems is adequate. The World Bank (2006a) has projected that high growth will be responsible for large reductions in extreme poverty in extensive areas around the world, especially in Asia. In 1990 more than 1.2 billion people were living on $1 or less a day. By 2015 this number is estimated to have dropped to approximately 620 million.

BOX 1.1

Economic growth is the primary driver of prosperity in the developed world and the main factor capable of reducing poverty in LDCs with good institutions in an adequate and sustainable manner. Yet, it is not the only contributor to economic welfare. Other factors such as education, employment, health, security, income distribution and the environment are also important.

Only Sub-Saharan Africa will experience an increase in extreme poverty. Even though average growth rates in the region can be considered reasonable, they are insufficient to keep up with population growth so as to actually

---

[4] The 23 December 2006 edition of *The Economist* also emphasised the growing significance of the science of 'happiness', which combines psychology with economics: 'Capitalism can make a society rich and keep it free. Don't ask it to make you happy as well'. In the 21st century, 'happiness' has become an increasingly important issue on the political agenda.

reduce the absolute number of people living in extreme poverty. Overall, the World Bank expects developing nations to experience an average per capita growth of 3.5 per cent up to 2015, compared to 2.4 per cent for high-income countries.

Government Tools in Economic Policy

With the tax system, the government has a powerful instrument in the arsenal of government tools to steer public behaviour. Ever since there has been some organisation of government and taxation, its function has nevertheless been a subject for debate. This is no less true for the government role in economic policy. Former US President Ronald Reagan (1911-2004) once summed up the role of government to merely encompass the following:[5] 'If it moves, tax it. If it keeps moving, regulate it. And if it stops moving subsidize it'. These words, despite being sceptical, have some legitimacy in them. Government involvement is widespread and not always in the interest of the economy. Because the economy is an intricate and dynamic system of interacting markets, numerous factors shape its performance. To give just a few examples, the size of the labour force and capital stock, the level of R&D, educational standards, geographic conditions such as proximity to other economies and natural harbours, and internal and external conflict are all factors that contribute to a high level of output.

These factors can be affected by a wide array of tools that the government has at its disposal, including regulation (for example, minimum wage and price requirements), direct control (for example, government production, quotas and licensing), firm-level legislation (for example, antitrust, environment and safety laws) and subsidies (for example, for health, education, childcare and housing). They also include appropriate monetary and fiscal policies.

The primary concern here is taxation, or the revenue side of fiscal policy. The issue is how to optimise the system of taxation, particularly in view of globalisation and increasing competition in world markets. The current state of globalisation is unprecedented. Economies are increasingly open with rising foreign investment and exports accounting for 30 per cent of global GDP (much of it originating from emerging markets such as China and India).[6] This inevitably affects tax systems.

The concept of taxation can be interpreted in a broad sense. The definition covers the entire tax system used by government to raise revenue and conduct economic policy. This contrasts with the strict definition that merely

---

[5] Ronald Reagan was the 40th President of the United States and in office from 1981 to 1989.

[6] Globalisation is a positive-sum game, but creates both winners and losers. Free trade and investment enhance competition, improve efficiency in the allocation of resources and stimulate firms to innovate. The OECD growth study concludes that a 10 per cent rise in trade openness raises per capita income by 4 per cent on average.

encompasses the bundle of taxes imposed on an individual or legal entity by a state.[7] Today, the lion's share of tax revenue in developed countries is collected by personal income tax, including social security premiums, the corporation income tax and consumption taxes such as the value-added tax (VAT) and excises.

Three Objectives of Taxation

The tax system is used to achieve a variety of purposes. The public finance literature traditionally distinguishes between three major functions of taxation:[8]

1. the *traditional* function of raising revenue to finance government expenditure that cannot be financed through other means;
2. the *distributional* function as an instrument to alter the distribution of income and wealth among households; and
3. the *stabilisation* function, which uses taxation to dampen the business cycle.

An example of the application of taxation for government policy is the raising or lowering of the tax burden on consumption, income, profits and/or wealth. Tax breaks are also employed to promote more-specific policy objectives, for example, for the purpose of increasing the work effort of certain groups of workers (for example, low-skilled or older workers) and to grant all kinds of subsidies (for example, for childcare, housing or healthcare). Tax incentives are also created to stimulate more specific business investment (for example, to the shipping, film or information and communication technology (ICT) sectors). Thus, it is hoped that tax policy will enhance overall efficiency and equity.

Public Opinion and Tax Morality

Taxation is one of the broadest government policy areas in existence and one of the few that contain both considerable legal aspects and economic considerations. In practice, tax systems are strongly shaped by the political considerations of the ruling parties. This typically leads to many special tax breaks and arrangements and complicated tax legislation. The simplicity of tax systems, a much-cited objective by lawmakers, is thereby undermined. In the words of German Chancellor Angela Merkel: 'Everyone wants a more simple tax system. But if this means that certain tax breaks have to be cut,

---

[7] A tax is also referred to as a 'duty' or 'levy'.
[8] See Musgrave and Musgrave (1989), who refer to the allocation, distribution and stabilisation functions of tax and expenditure policy.

people are no longer so enthusiastic'. [9] Political considerations therefore often prevail over legal or economic arguments.

Because taxation is such a powerful instrument, people often view it as an infringement of their lives as autonomous individuals. For revenue collection to be effective, taxes must be compulsory, while there is no direct link between payments made and public goods and services received. It was the credo 'no taxation without representation' that fuelled the revolutionary war in the American colonies between 1775 and 1783. Colonists had been required to pay a variety of taxes without representation in the British parliament before this time. [10] This led to outrage and a series of events such as the famous 'Boston tea party', which culminated in formal independence of the United States of America from Great Britain in 1783.

A proper functioning of the tax system thus requires a certain level of public acceptance, awareness and confidence that a nation's tax laws are easy to understand and fair. Many international poll findings show that the majority of people have an aversion to higher taxes and the introduction of new taxes. At the same time, a large number of taxpayers believe that the ability-to-pay principle should be reflected in income tax. For example, when British Prime Minister Margaret Thatcher introduced the Community Charge in 1990 (more popularly referred to as a poll tax), public resistance was high. [11] The tax transformed local progressive taxes on property into an equal single-rated tax on every UK resident. The measure was very unpopular with voters, caused significant political turmoil and contributed to Thatcher's demise as prime minister.

Traditionally high tax rates in many countries

Before the mid-1980s, top statutory income tax rates of 70, 80 or even over 90 per cent were not uncommon in many European economies, especially the Nordic ones (that is, Denmark, [12] Finland, Norway and Sweden) but also in now low-rate countries such as the UK and the US. In 1979, the UK tax system still featured a top rate of 83 per cent, implemented over 12 tax brackets. Even the US income tax was characterised by a top rate of 91 per cent, with over 24 brackets in 1954. [13]

These high tax rates were typically met with a good deal of public opposition, which clearly has reflected on the way tax systems are designed

---

[9] Quoted from an interview in the *Financial Times*, 20 July 2005. Angela Merkel became the first female Chancellor of Germany on 22 November 2005.

[10] Mainly under the Stamp Tax Act of 1765 and the Townshend acts of 1767.

[11] Margaret Thatcher was Prime Minister of the UK from 1979 to 1990. Because of her steadfast and unwavering political style she is referred to as the 'Iron Lady'.

[12] Denmark is the only sample country with an independent Ministry of Taxation.

[13] Only years later was it reduced to 70 per cent and 15 brackets under the 1964 Revenue Act. US President Ronald Reagan thereafter slashed it further to 50 per cent with the Economic Recovery Tax Act of 1981 and to 28 per cent under the Tax Reform Act of 1986. Of course, US states also levy taxes.

and the way politicians approach the issue of taxation. In the 2008 Republican presidential nomination campaign, candidate and former mayor of New York City Rudy Giuliani simply repeatedly proclaimed: 'I don't like taxes'. But also in more social countries such as Norway we see that in 1973 the 'Progress Party' (FRP) was founded in reaction to an 'unacceptable' high level of taxation, government subsidies and regulation. In 2007 the FRP held 37 seats in the Norwegian *Stortinget* (parliament), making it the second-largest party in the country.

Tax songs (the Beatles and Kinks)
The debate on taxes was not only carried on in politics and academia, but has also been widespread in other areas, including popular culture. In the 1960s, high taxes inspired the Beatles to compose the hit song 'Taxman', which features lyrics such as 'Let me tell you how it will be; there's one for you, nineteen for me ... Should five per cent appear too small, be thankful I don't take it all'.[14] Another memorable hit single was 'Sunny afternoon' by the Kinks, which was very indicative of certain leisurely behaviour induced by taxation: 'The tax man's taken all my dough, And left me in my stately home, Lazing on a sunny afternoon, I can't sail my yacht, He's taken everything I've got, All I've got is this sunny afternoon'.[15] The tax songs echoed public opinion on government involvement in the daily life of people at that time.

Less tax is generally preferred
On the question of the best form of government assistance for the individual, public opinion polls show that less tax is by far the most preferred option. Polls also demonstrate that the majority of taxpayers are of the opinion that income tax is not equitable. The perception exists that high-income citizens are not paying their 'fair share'. Tax morality obviously differs per country but generally speaking there appears to be more acceptance of taxation when the revenues are spent on popular items such as education and health.

For example, a number of Australian polls demonstrated a clear hierarchy in the types of government spending that voters prefer should attract taxpayer money (Grant, 2004). Indeed, health had a high rating, whereas spending on unemployment benefits attracted only a low preference.

---

[14] From the album *Revolver* that was released on 6 August 1966. The Beatles were a world famous British band from Liverpool, featuring the musicians John Lennon, Paul McCartney, George Harrison and Ringo Starr.
[15] The Kinks were a popular UK band during the 1960s until the 1980s. The song 'Sunny afternoon' from the album *All the Hits and More* was a big hit in the summer of 1966 in the UK.

BOX 1.2

The tax system gives the government the power to affect what households and firms care about most: their disposable income. General and tax-specific measures can create incentives or disincentives that affect the choices people make, which affects the performance of an economy in the short and long runs. In practice, the shape of tax systems is not only affected by economic and legal considerations, but it is also strongly influenced by the government (elected officials who represent their electorate) and political debate.

1.2 THE OECD MEMBER COUNTRIES AT A GLANCE

Cross-country Comparisons of GDP

The most widespread indicator used to calculate the size of an economy is gross domestic product (GDP), which measures total output of goods and services in the formal economy during a specific period. The black market is not taken into account, as money spent there is not registered. GDP is typically computed for a country, but also for other geographical areas such as a state, city or continent.

A primary distinction is made between nominal GDP and real GDP. *Nominal* GDP calculates output of goods and services at current prices. Hence, inflation is included. Clearly, when prices increase but total physical output remains the same, the standard of living does not increase. To make a comparison over time, *real* GDP is a more appropriate measure as it computes output at constant prices (that is, corrected for realised inflation from a predetermined year). Additionally, a distinction should be made between total GDP and GDP per capita (that is, per head or inhabitant).

Total GDP of a country may well be higher than that of another country. With $12,397.9 billion, total GDP in the US is the highest in the world and significantly higher than that of Luxembourg, which has a total GDP of $42.5 billion. However, Luxembourg has a population not much greater than 400,000, whereas the US with roughly 300 million inhabitants is the most populous country in the OECD area. With a GDP per capita of $77,860, Luxembourg's per capita income is the highest in the world and over 1.5 times as high as the US GDP per capita.

Table 1.1 Key economic and social statistics for OECD countries, 2006

Country	Total GDP (US$ bn)	Population (thousands)	GDP per Capita (US$)[a]	Average GDP growth rate 1970-2005[b]	General government expenditure (% of GDP)[c]	Income inequality, Gini index (rank)[d]	Subjective well-being (rank)[e]	CCPI (rank)[f]
Australia	737.7	20,605	34,240	3.2	34.9	35.2 (21)	26	-0.45 (27)
Austria	323.5	8,282	36,296	2.6	49.6	29.1 (10)	3	-0.16 (24)
Belgium	394.0	10,479	34,762	2.4	50.1	33.0 (15)	28	0.31 (08)
Canada	1131.8	32,623	34,058	3.2	39.3	32.6 (13)	10	-0.55 (28)
Czech Rep.	143.0	10,251	22,244	1.4	43.9	25.4 (04)	79	0.10 (16)
Denmark	276.2	5,434	36,066	2.2	53.0	24.7 (01)	1	0.52 (02)
Finland	209.6	5,267	33,161	2.9	50.8	26.9 (07)	6	-0.09 (22)
France	2250.0	60,873	31,742	2.5	54.4	32.7 (14)	62	0.35 (07)
Germany	2913.2	82,368	32,222	2.2	46.8	28.3 (09)	35	0.46 (04)
Greece	308.4	11,104	31,647	2.8	46.7	34.3 (17)	84	-0.28 (25)
Hungary	112.9	10,071	18,452	3.0	50.5	26.9 (8)	107	0.45 (05)
Iceland	16.3	304	39,257	3.9	44.5	-	4	0.31 (09)
Ireland	200.4	4,235	38,850	5.3	34.6	34.3 (18)	11	-0.05 (21)
Italy	1850.9	58,435	29,272	2.3	48.2	36.0 (22)	50	0.05 (19)
Japan	4549.2	127,770	30,773	3.0	36.9	24.9 (02)	90	0.08 (17)
Korea	888.0	48,297	23,581	7.0	28.1	31.6 (12)	103	-
Luxembourg	42.5	459	77,860	4.1	43.3	-	12	-0.34 (26)

Mexico	768.0	104,874	11,540	3.7	-	49.5 (28)	51	0.30 (10)
Netherlands	670.3	16,346	37,712	2.5	45.7	30.9 (11)	15	0.06 (18)
New Zealand	110.3	4,140	26,855	2.4	40.6	36.2 (24)	18	0.16 (14)
Norway	335.0	4,670	53,116	3.4	42.9	25.8 (05)	19	0.17 (12)
Poland	340.9	38,132	15,074	3.6	42.8	34.5 (19)	99	0.17 (13)
Portugal	194.6	10,586	20,961	3.2	47.8	38.5 (25)	92	0.18 (11)
Slovakia	55.1	5,391	17,603	4.3	37.7	25.8 (06)	129	0.16 (15)
Spain	1230.6	44,068	28,962	3.2	38.2	34.7 (20)	46	-0.15 (23)
Sweden	383.8	9,081	34,017	2.1	56.4	25.0 (03)	7	0.56 (01)
Switzerland	387.8	7,437	36,282	1.5	36.4	33.7 (16)	2	0.39 (06)
Turkey	403.5	72,974	7,711	4.4	-	43.6 (27)	133	0.01 (20)
UK	2373.5	60,209	34,470	2.4	45.1	36.0 (23)	41	0.52 (03)
US	12397.9	299,399	43,801	3.2	36.6	40.8 (26)	23	-0.59 (29)

Notes:

[a] The GDP data have been adjusted to reflect Purchasing Power Parity (PPP) to eliminate differences in price levels between countries.

[b] For the Czech Republic (1991), Hungary (1992), Poland (1991) and Slovakia (1992) the values have been calculated from different starting years since GDP was not previously available.

[c] Data are for 2005.

[d] Denmark with a Gini index of 24.7 has the smallest inequality, Mexico with a value of 49.54 the highest. The Gini index is a measure of the differences in income or consumption between the richest and the poorest people in a country. The index varies between 0 and 100. It is noted that the underlying household surveys differ in method, year and type of data collected, which makes the data not fully comparable.

[e] The ranking is derived from a study of 178 countries by Adrian White of the University of Leicester cited in Section 1.1.

[f] The climate change performance index (CCPI) is published by Germanwatch, an independent development and environmental organisation which lobbies for sustainable development. The method used for developing the index is based on OECD guidance for creating performance indicators. A 0 indicates the average score of countries. Sweden (0.56) tops the list followed by Denmark (0.52) and the UK (0.52). The statistics are for 2007.

Sources: Compilation from the Electronic database of the OECD, United Nations Human Development Report 2006, White (2006) and Germanwatch.

Table 1.1 below shows that GDP per capita varies considerably. Luxembourg, Norway and the US have the highest per capita incomes, while Turkey, Mexico and Poland have the lowest.[16]

Growth patterns over time

Average growth rates over the 1970-2005 period range between 1.4 per cent in the Czech Republic and 7.0 per cent in Korea. With specific reference to the sample countries, growth has been slowest in Sweden and fastest in Ireland. Noteworthy is that France, Germany and Italy experienced relatively slow average growth over the period and have a low GDP per capita (together they account for over 50 per cent of EU GDP). Economic growth of all 30 OECD countries averaged 3.1 per cent.

Figure 1.1 shows that the EU-15 and Japan lost ground to the US in the 1990s. Initially the economies were converging rapidly after near complete destruction of the European and Japanese infrastructures in the Second World War (European GDP was also below 40 per cent of US GDP before 1950). The European catch-up stagnated in the 1970s, while Japan continued to grow at an admirable pace. This too came to a halt with the financial crisis and its aftermath in 1991, and Japanese GDP per capita has since fallen back to European levels.

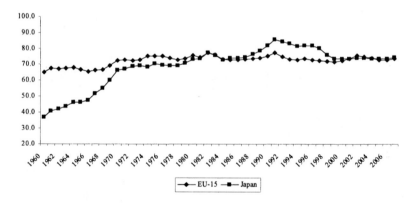

Note: [a] The GDP data have been adjusted to reflect PPPs.

Source: EU Commission, computed from the AMECO database.

Figure 1.1   The development of GDP per capita (US = 100) [a]

---

[16] We regularly draw on the Electronic database of the OECD, but other sources also provide an abundance of economic and tax statistics, including the United Nations, the IMF and the World Bank, the EU statistics office Eurostat, and the US Census Bureau. The websites of the ministries of finance of the individual countries also contain relevant information.

Table 1.2 shows that in this period per capita growth in Japan was on average significantly lower than in Europe and the US. Forecasts for 2007-08 predict growth to slow in the US, while it picks up significantly in Europe and Japan.

Table 1.2   GDP per capita (percentage change preceding year), 1992-2008

	5-year averages							Forecast	
	1992-96	1997-01	2002	2003	2004	2005	2006	2007	2008
US	2.0	2.4	0.6	1.5	2.9	2.2	2.3	1.2	1.7
EU-27	-	2.7	0.9	0.9	2.0	1.3	2.7	2.6	2.4
Japan	1.1	0.3	0.0	1.2	2.7	1.9	2.3	2.4	2.2

Source: European Economy 2/2007: Economic Forecast, Spring 2007.

Although the US is currently the largest economy in the world, China and India are experiencing high structural growth. The US investment bank Goldman Sachs predicts that by 2050, total GDP in China and India will have surpassed that of the US (Poddar and Yi, 2007). In absolute size, the economies will be respectively number one, two and three in the world.

The Size of Government

No country in history has succeeded in attaining a high level of economic prosperity without some form of government. Governments have enacted and enforced laws, established property rights, built infrastructures and schools and provided national defence which all enabled countries to flourish. Yet, there are limits to what can be achieved. A government that is too large has a suffocating effect on the economy by reducing incentives to work, killing the entrepreneurial spirit and exacerbating the problem of 'free riding' whereby people thrive on the efforts of others. The experiences in the former Soviet Union and a comparison of West and East Germany during the Cold War era painfully attest to this.

As such, there is an obvious interrelatedness between the size of government and the tax system. The task of government is to ascertain average voter preferences and, provided that true preferences can be measured, to tax accordingly. Broadly speaking, a country with a large government spending is characterised by high tax rates and many different taxes to finance government expenditure. To illustrate, the fifth column of Table 1.1 shows general government spending ratios per country in the OECD area. Countries such as Belgium, Finland, France and Sweden have large governments, which spent over 50 per cent of their GDP in 2005. Other countries have smaller public sectors, most notably Korea, Australia, Ireland, Japan and the US.

The precise allocation of government spending depends on culture, political preferences and people's tastes, and leads to very different outcomes in each country. Table 1.3 lists the principal components of government spending according to the UN Classification of the Functions of Government (COFOG). Large differences exist between the size and allocation of government spending, of which some are undoubtedly more beneficial to economic growth than others. For example, spending on education is usually considered to be more economically beneficial than spending on social protection and housing and community amenities. Ultimately, government spending is mostly a matter of political preferences, judgement and quibble.

Spending on general public services is relatively high in Europe and Japan. The US spends significantly more on defence, whereas recreation, culture and religion and social protection attract relatively large funds in Europe.[17]

Table 1.3   Categories of government spending as a percentage of GDP, 2005

	EU-15	US	Japan
General public services	6.6	4.9	6.7
Defence	1.6	4.2	0.9
Public order and safety	1.8	2.1	1.4
Economic affairs	3.7	3.7	4.0
Environmental protection	0.7	0.0	1.2
Housing and community amenities	1.0	0.6	0.7
Health	6.6	7.4	7.1
Recreation, culture and religion	1.0	0.3	0.2
Education	5.2	6.2	3.9
Social protection	19.0	7.1	12.1
Total	47.2	36.6	38.2

Source: Compilation from Eurostat and the Electronic database of the OECD.

Optimal government expenditure
On the question whether there is an optimal allocation of government spending, or more generally size of government, there appears to be no straightforward answer. The issue has intrigued many economists over the past decades. The IMF (1995) cites a large number of studies that have attempted to estimate the contribution of certain public expenditures to

---

[17] Most spending on social protection in the EU is directed at old age, sickness and healthcare, disability, family and children and unemployment benefits (European Commission, 2006a).

economic growth. Most studies find only weak links between public investment and economic growth, mainly because of the difficulty in valuing public sector output; independently measuring the impact of financing methods of public expenditures; and differentiating among other factors that affect economic growth.

Others have attempted to approximate the optimal size of government. Barro (1990) argues that there are two main effects at work. First, an increase in government expenditure benefits the economy by raising the marginal productivity of capital and thereby economic growth. So in this context, government spending contributes positively to economic development. Second, however, since every increase in the size of government has to be financed by distortionary taxes (a point to which we shall return later), a larger government at the same time stifles dynamic economic growth. Barro's model shows that the former effect is stronger when government is relatively small, while the latter effect dominates when government is large.

BOX 1.3

In Europe, government spending constituted on average 47.2 per cent of GDP in 2005. In the United States and Japan this was, respectively, 36.6 and 38.2 per cent of GDP.

The optimal size of government has more popularly been estimated by the so-called 'Armey curve'. The Armey curve rests on the assumption that in a state of anarchy output is limited; however, when government is at or near 100 per cent of the economy there is not much production, either.[18] There should be an optimum somewhere in between these two extremes. Table 1.4 shows some empirical insights, which are presented in US Joint Economic Committee (1998) and Pevcin (2004). On this basis, most governments would be oversized from an efficiency point of view, with Ireland being the only exception.

The outcomes should be interpreted with caution. In democratic countries the size of government is the outcome of numerous political decisions in the past, the present and anticipations for the future, which makes it complicated to construct a well-founded or academically sound argument on the matter. There are simply too many factors that shape the final result. Ultimately, a country will have to decide through the process of democratic elections what it wants from government, the level of spending on public programmes and

---

[18] The Armey curve was conceived by US Republican Representative for Texas, Richard Armey (1985-2003). The principle resembles the regularly cited Laffer curve, which is discussed in Section 1.4.

other government services it desires and how they are paid for in terms of tax preferences.

Table 1.4   The optimal size of government, 1996

Country	Actual size of government [a]	Optimal size of government
Italy	44.9	37.1
France	54.7	42.9
Finland	58.7	39.0
Sweden	65.0	57.0
Germany	48.7	38.5
Ireland	39.6	42.3
Netherlands	52.0	44.9
Belgium	53.0	41.9
United States [b]	22.0	17.5

Notes:
[a] The ratios are in terms of GNP except for the US which is compared to GDP.
[b] The ratios are calculated on the basis of federal spending only over the 1947-97 period.

Sources: Compilation from US Joint Economic Committee (1998) and Pevcin (2004).

   Vreymans and Verhulst (2005) examine 25 possible causes of growth differentials between EU-15 member states, such as the level of education, annual working hours, the effect of the age structure, population density, the size of public spending, inequality, and the proportion between direct and indirect tax. Based on a multiple regression analysis over the 1985-2004 period, they claim that excessive government spending and a de-motivating tax structure have a significant impact on economic growth. The analysis showed that trimming public spending by 5 per cent of GDP could raise growth by up to 3 per cent. Ireland is a good example of a country that has successfully demonstrated how cuts in superfluous spending can contribute to rapid economic expansion.[19]

   Four so-called social models are generally distinguished (Sapir, 2006). The *Nordic* model (Denmark, Finland, Sweden, plus the Netherlands) have large public sectors, a relatively heavy tax burden and devote the highest part of expenditure to social protection and universal welfare provision; the *Anglo-Saxon* model (Ireland and the UK) provide relatively large social assistance of the last resort, with cash transfers mainly aimed at working-age people; the *continental* model (Austria, Belgium, France, Germany and

---

[19] Within the EU it has been noted that Ireland was able to carry out these changes solely by significant development aid from the EU. In other words, that the measures were largely financed by the EU, thus by the other member states.

Luxembourg) are characterised by high government interference in an economy and rely on insurance-based, non-employment benefits and old-age pensions; the *Mediterranean* model (Greece, Italy, Portugal and Spain) feature high spending on old-age pensions and allow for considerable differences in entitlements and status.

In the debate over the choice of social model, Vreymans and Verhulst favour the Anglo-Saxon model over the Nordic model, the continental European model and US-style 'laissez-faire' policy.[20] Although the Nordic social model appears promising as well, particularly in view of globalisation, there is uncertainty about whether it is sustainable in the long run (this is also confirmed by the OECD Economic Survey of Denmark (OECD, 2005a).[21]

On the other hand, the Economic Survey of the United States (OECD, 2005d) notes that a small government, a competitive business climate and a flexible labour market have over the years contributed significantly to creating the country's strong economy. As a negative economic development, the report sees the rising income gap between rich and poor, which has widened rapidly over the past 25 years and continues to grow.

Income Inequality, Happiness and the Environment

One flaw of the market economy is that the market cannot guarantee that the fruits of economic growth are distributed equitably. The majority of people in developed countries nowadays agree that there should be some form of social protection. However, there is less agreement about how much. People typically have different ideas about the size and type of spending on social protection and the degree of redistribution. Government practices differ widely, with varying effects on the economy.

To get a rough idea of income inequality in OECD countries, the seventh column of Table 1.1 presents the so-called 'Gini index'. This is a measure of the differences in income or consumption between the richest and the poorest people in a country. The index varies between 0 and 100. A high number indicates large income inequality, while a smaller number indicates a more even income distribution. It shows that countries such as Denmark, Finland and Sweden have relatively little income inequality, whereas Australia, Italy, the UK and the US feature relatively high income inequality. For example, the US ranks 73rd of the 126 countries surveyed by the UN development

---

[20] Becker and Schwartz (2005) are critical of drawing generalisations from a specific model, as defined by national social, economic, and political institutions. They argue that the success factors in previous economic 'miracles' are not easily untangled and that coincidence or random chance have been just as important. A strong housing market turns out to be a particularly important factor for economic growth and employment, not so much wage dampening or costs as is regularly assumed. Moreover, high competitiveness in no way precludes a large welfare state, and success is not synonymous to the US 'deregulation' approach.

[21] Although according to OECD (2006a), the country has been in the process of taking measures, such as the implemented 'tax freeze', which stipulates that taxes cannot rise further.

Programme Report 2006. The richest 10 per cent earn 15.9 times more than the poorest 10 per cent, and the richest 20 per cent earn 8.4 times as much as the poorest 20 per cent.[22]

Table 1.5   Income distribution and share of tax liability in the US, 2005

Distribution of people aged 15 or over		
$ 25,000 or less	47.2%	
$ 25,001 < $ 50,000	29.9%	
$ 50,000 < $75,000	12.5%	
$ 75,000 < $100,000	4.7%	
$ 100,000 or more	5.7%	
Median household income		
Median income of all households	$46,326	
Households with two income earners	$67,348	
Distribution of household income		
Lowest 20%	less than $18,500	
Middle 20%	$34,738-$55,331	
Highest 20%	over $88,030	
Share of the tax liability [a]	Total federal tax	Personal income tax
Lowest quintile	1.1%	-2.7%
Second quintile	5.2%	-0.1%
Middle quintile	10.5%	5.4%
Fourth quintile	19.5%	15.2%
Highest quintile	63.5%	82.1%

Note: [a] Numbers are for 2004

Sources: US Census Bureau and US Government Accountability Office (2005).

To give an example, Table 1.5 provides income distribution statistics among individuals and households in the US for 2005. Almost half of the American people earn less than $25,000, while the median income lies at $46,326. The table also illustrates that 63.5 per cent of the total federal tax and 82.1 per cent of personal income tax is borne by the highest 20 per cent of incomes. The lowest 40 per cent have a negative contribution, implying that they are net receivers.

---

[22] The ratio does not take into account absolute income levels. The poorest people of one country may very well be richer than people with a middle or high income in another country. Cross-country comparisons then become less meaningful.

The degree of inequality lies very much at the heart of the discussion on income redistribution and the role of government. Large governments are often claimed to reduce the incentives to work and invest and ultimately make people worse off. Obviously there is merit to the argument, especially given what was said above on the Armey curve. But matters may be more complex than the sometimes oversimplified debate between 'left-wing' and 'right-wing' political parties and the full adherence to traditional political ideologies within those parties.

Noteworthy is that the top 10 of the 'happiest' countries includes six European countries. Table 1.1 confirms that these countries have a relatively high GDP per capita (between US$31,000 and US$36,000), large government expenditure (on average above 45 per cent of GDP) and a relatively small difference between 'rich' and 'poor'. A roughly similar pattern emerges from the UNICEF (2007) survey research on child well-being in 21 rich countries (see Table 1.6).[23]

Table 1.6 Child well-being in 21 rich countries, 2007

Country	Score	Country	Score	Country	Score
Netherlands	4.2	Italy	10.0	Czech Rep.	12.5
Sweden	5.0	Ireland	10.2	France	13.0
Denmark	7.2	Belgium	10.7	Portugal	13.7
Finland	7.5	Germany	11.2	Austria	13.8
Spain	8.0	Canada	11.8	Hungary	14.5
Switzerland	8.3	Greece	11.8	US	18.0
Norway	8.7	Poland	12.3	UK	18.2

Source: UNICEF (2007).

Denmark with a GDP per capita of US$34,400, public spending of 53 per cent of GDP and relatively little income inequality is the happiest nation on earth. The country also performs high in terms of environmental policy.

The US stands out with a high GDP per capita, a relatively small government, strong average growth of above 3 per cent, ranks 23rd on subjective well-being and has a large difference between 'rich' and 'poor'. A 2006 poll by the US market research bureau Bloomberg also reported that three-quarters of Americans are now concerned about rising income inequality. According to Alan Greenspan, chairman of the US Federal Reserve Board from 1987 to 2006, the key policy tools to address the problem of rising inequality are education and immigration: 'Specially, we

---

[23] The survey measures six dimensions: material well-being, health and safety, educational well-being, family and peer relationships, behaviours and risks, and subjective well-being.

need to harness better the forces of competition that have shaped the development of education in the United States, and we need to make immigration easier for highly skilled individuals' (Greenspan, 2007, p. 400).[24]

Comparative Strengths and Weaknesses of Economies

That a prosperous economy can coincide with a fairly large government, at least under current world market conditions, is confirmed by so-called 'competitiveness rankings'. These rankings take the strong points and weaknesses of an economy, as embodied in several key variables, and unite them into a single index of competitiveness. Well-known rankings are published by the World Economic Forum, the International Institute for Management Development (IMD) and the Economist Intelligence Unit.

The global competitiveness report

The Global Competitiveness Report is a leading competitiveness monitor published by the World Economic Forum.[25] The index identifies over 180 factors that affect its ranking of 117 economies worldwide. These factors range from recession expectations and government debt to the prioritisation of energy efficiency, the level of innovation, the number of cell phones and the degree of brain drain. It also includes a number of tax and fiscal policy variables.

The rankings do not necessarily provide a measure of wealth or economic performance, but in practice politicians use them in order to attune their policies. Furthermore, business leaders create so-called 'shortlists' of the most attractive countries to invest in and scholars use the rankings in their research on various economic variables. But there are also criticisms. For example, it matters a great deal what variables are included and how exactly they are aggregated. Many variables are based on survey research, which makes the data not strictly comparable across countries. Moreover, the composition of the index and countries included has changed over time.

Table 1.7 gives an overview of the development in the rankings of the top 25 most competitive economies over the past 10 years according to the Global Competitiveness Report. It shows that the Nordic countries are currently among the most competitive economies in the world, followed closely by the US, Japan, Germany, the Netherlands and the UK. These countries are also in the top tier of the Business Competitiveness Index 2006, a separate ranking of the World Economic Forum.

---

[24] See also IMF World Economic Outlook (WEO) – Globalization and Inequality, October 2007 (IMF, 2007b).
[25] The World Economic Forum is an annual meeting of prominent CEOs, political leaders and selected academics hosted by Professor Klaus M. Schwab in Davos, Switzerland.

Furthermore, of the 55 economies ranked in the IMD *World Competitiveness Yearbook* of 2007, the US ranks number one, followed by Singapore, Hong Kong, Luxembourg, Denmark, Switzerland, Iceland, the Netherlands, Sweden, Canada, Austria, Norway, Ireland, Mainland China, Germany, Finland, Taiwan, New Zealand and the UK. Japan ranks 24th, Belgium 25th, France 28th, and Italy 42nd.

Table 1.7   Global competitiveness ranking, 1998-2007

Rank	1998-99	2000-01	2002-03	2004-05	2006-07
1	Singapore	US	US	Finland	Switzerland
2	Hong Kong	Singapore	Finland	US	Finland
3	US	Luxembourg	Taiwan	Sweden	Sweden
4	UK	Netherlands	Singapore	Taiwan	Denmark
5	Canada	Ireland	Sweden	Denmark	Singapore
6	Taiwan	Finland	Switzerland	Norway	US
7	Netherlands	Canada	Australia	Singapore	Japan
8	Switzerland	Hong Kong	Canada	Switzerland	Germany
9	Norway	UK	Norway	Japan	Netherlands
10	Luxembourg	Switzerland	Denmark	Iceland	UK
11	Ireland	Taiwan	UK	UK	Hong Kong
12	Japan	Australia	Iceland	Netherlands	Norway
13	New Zealand	Sweden	Japan	Germany	Taiwan/China
14	Australia	Denmark	Germany	Australia	Iceland
15	Finland	Germany	Netherlands	Canada	Israel
16	Denmark	Norway	New Zealand	Arab Emirates	Canada
17	Malaysia	Belgium	Hong Kong	Austria	Austria
18	Chile	Austria	Austria	New Zealand	France
19	Korea	Israel	Israel	Israel	Australia
20	Austria	New Zealand	Chile	Estonia	Belgium
21	Thailand	Japan	Korea	Hong Kong	Ireland
22	France	France	Spain	Chile	Luxembourg
23	Sweden	Portugal	Portugal	Spain	New Zealand
24	Germany	Iceland	Ireland	Portugal	Korea
25	Spain	Malaysia	Belgium	Belgium	Estonia

Source: Global Competitiveness Reports, various.

The Lisbon Agenda for growth and jobs

In addition to the general competitiveness ranking, the World Economic Forum's *Lisbon Review* (2006) offers insights of performance in specific policy areas, as based on the Lisbon criteria or agenda. The Lisbon Agenda was formulated in March 2000 by European leaders in response to mounting concerns over slow growth. The strategy sets out an action plan that should make 'the EU the world's most dynamic and competitive economy' by 2010. It focuses on improving the environment for business and innovation, building an inclusive labour market for stronger social inclusion, developing the knowledge society, and promoting a sustainable environmental policy. So

Table 1.8 Country rankings according to the Lisbon Review benchmark, 2006

	Overall Rank	Information society	Innovation and R&D	Liberalisation	Network industries	Financial services	Enterprise	Social inclusion	Sustainable development
		Score	Score	Score	Score	Score	Score	Score	Score
Denmark	1	5.53	5.15	5.58	6.24	6.28	5.63	5.49	6.17
Finland	2	5.41	5.90	5.58	5.93	6.29	5.24	5.35	6.23
Sweden	3	5.93	5.73	5.43	6.14	6.36	5.07	5.09	6.15
Netherlands	4	5.63	4.82	5.62	6.01	6.23	5.48	5.06	5.87
Germany	5	4.98	5.31	5.71	6.38	6.39	4.69	4.53	6.23
UK	6	5.61	4.82	5.59	5.97	6.47	5.13	4.74	5.69
Austria	7	5.24	4.55	5.35	5.87	6.15	4.43	4.75	6.09
Luxembourg	8	5.05	3.96	5.26	6.16	6.14	4.91	5.05	5.82
France	9	4.91	4.66	5.17	6.18	6.19	4.87	4.25	5.44
Belgium	10	4.44	4.67	5.25	5.84	5.91	4.77	4.83	5.47
Ireland	11	4.55	4.47	5.34	4.95	6.13	5.35	4.82	5.10
Estonia	12	5.49	4.06	4.98	5.01	5.72	5.10	4.37	4.69
Portugal	13	4.06	3.81	4.74	5.37	5.66	4.50	4.10	4.90
Czech Rep.	14	4.10	3.85	4.96	5.16	4.84	3.99	4.44	4.90
Spain	15	3.93	3.89	4.62	5.41	5.65	4.33	3.63	4.48
Slovenia	16	4.50	3.96	4.30	5.07	4.88	3.76	4.02	5.00
Hungary	17	3.74	3.92	4.55	4.80	5.22	4.18	4.16	4.61
Slovakia	18	3.97	3.44	4.82	4.76	4.84	4.33	4.09	4.76
Malta	19	5.22	3.23	4.46	4.64	5.44	3.83	4.35	3.84
Lithuania	20	3.97	3.69	4.18	4.86	4.96	4.57	3.95	4.26
Cyprus	21	3.90	3.30	4.46	5.02	5.12	4.25	4.30	3.86

Latvia	22	3.76	3.63	4.32	4.57	4.79	4.78	3.87	4.29
Greece	23	3.17	3.77	4.32	5.09	5.27	4.14	3.79	3.98
Italy	24	4.06	3.73	4.29	4.82	4.80	3.71	3.54	4.40
Poland	25	3.32	3.57	4.02	3.86	4.23	3.60	3.41	4.10
US	-	5.63	6.01	5.21	5.72	5.97	5.21	4.58	5.26
East Asia[b]	-	5.41	5.23	5.13	5.96	5.54	5.11	4.87	5.02

Notes: [a] East Asia refers to Japan, Hong Kong, Republic of Korea, Taiwan and Singapore.

Source: Blanke (2006, Table 2, p. 6), World Economic Forum at http://www.weforum.org.

far, progress has been disappointing, which can be partly attributed to a high labour tax burden in many EU countries, a colossal government bureaucracy and administrative burden that rests on entrepreneurial activity and innovation.[26]

According to the Lisbon review benchmark, the most competitive economy is Denmark, followed by Finland, Sweden, the Netherlands and Germany (see Table 1.8). The variables included in the ranking are information society, innovation and R&D, liberalisation, network industries, financial services, enterprise, social inclusion and sustainable development. This gives interesting cross-country insights of progress in the individual policy areas, some of which are undoubtedly affected by tax and social safety policies. For example, Germany scores high on R&D, liberalisation, network industries and innovation, but performs poorly on enterprise and social inclusion. The US is by far the leading country in innovation and R&D, but typically underperforms on social inclusion and sustainable development in comparison with many European countries. France, despite having a large welfare state, shows only a mediocre performance on social inclusion.

BOX 1.4

Competitiveness rankings demonstrate that countries can be competitive on world markets despite having a relatively large government. In 2006-07, Finland, Sweden and Denmark ranked second, third and fourth, respectively, in the global competitiveness ranking of the World Economic Forum, while the government spending ratio exceeded 50 per cent of GDP and the levels of taxation 45 per cent. In a globalising world with increasing capital mobility and tax competition, the effect of (high) taxes on competitiveness is nevertheless likely to become more important than it has been thus far.

1.3   TAX DISTORTIONS AND THE COST OF PUBLIC FUNDS

The notion of promoting economic growth by means of carefully conducted tax policy is controversial. Sir Winston Churchill once stated: 'We contend that for a nation to try and tax itself into prosperity is like a man standing in a

---

[26] The Lisbon programme was evaluated in a report by the High Level Group chaired by former Prime Minister of the Netherlands Wim Kok, 1994-2002 (European Commission, 2004a).

bucket and trying to lift himself up by the handle'.[27] Many people would agree with him as they view taxation as worrying. Others argue that taxes merely transfer the spending decision from households to the government. As long as the government carries out its tasks appropriately and keeps up demand, no real effect on the economy should result from it. However, both views ignore the fact that taxes cause behavioural responses and distort economic decisions in both positive and negative ways.

The Excess Burden of Taxation

Tax policy normally starts from the notion that markets clear and that supply and demand are brought in line through price adjustments.[28] Every government intervention whether regulation, direct control, firm-level legislation, subsidies or taxation nevertheless involves a reallocation of resources and gives rise to distortions to choice. Taxes impinge on the economic choice of individuals and firms by altering the relative prices of the factor inputs and goods and services. In general, people purchase less of more heavily taxed inputs and goods and services (and vice versa). The tax system may thereby distort the following choices:

- work and leisure;
- consumption and savings; and
- domestic and foreign investment.

Tax-induced distortions impede an efficient allocation of resources across the economy and lead to a cost over and above the actual revenue collected. Not only does the tax present a cost to the taxpayer, it also creates an additional welfare loss. This welfare loss is also referred to as an 'excess burden' or 'deadweight loss' of taxation. And even if the efficiency cost does not represent a loss of real money, it does make people worse off (for a short review, see Appendix 3).

Lump-sum Taxation

Excess burdens are inherent to taxation and can technically be avoided only by imposing a lump-sum tax. Lump-sum taxation comes in two main forms. A 'retroactive tax' places a one-off (unexpected) levy on past economic

---

[27] Winston Leonard Spencer Churchill was Chancellor of the Exchequer of the UK from 1924 to 1929 and Prime Minister from 1940 to 1955. In 1953 he won the Nobel Prize in literature for his many historical and bibliographical books.

[28] In reality, market failures are plentiful and everywhere. For instance, in the case of an *externality* the behaviour of one individual affects another's welfare in a way that is outside the market; *asymmetric information* where one party to a transaction has more or better information than the other party; or a *monopoly* where there is only one supplier with market power.

choices and activity. There would be no way to escape such a tax, since past actions cannot be reversed. In practice, the tax would be flatly rejected on grounds of fairness, but also because it would add a high degree of uncertainty to an economy. Obviously, such a tax destroys the credibility and trustworthiness of the government.[29]

Second, a 'poll tax' imposes a fixed amount of tax on every citizen. There would be no way to avoid the tax by changing behaviour (except by immigration or death), so the revenue collected exactly equals the burden on the taxpayer. The actual implementation of a lump-sum tax is, however, undoubtedly questionable on equity grounds, as the UK's Prime Minister Margaret Thatcher found to her cost during the 1980s.

Intertemporal Decisions on Leisure, Consumption and Saving

At the same time, the issue highlights an important trait in socio-economic policy making. Whenever government wishes to use taxes for objectives other than raising revenue to finance expenditure, it must do so on the basis of some observable characteristic such as income, consumption and/or wealth. By definition it must discriminate against a certain group of people in favour of another. This offers some taxpayers the opportunity to change their behaviour and act in line with tax-favoured individuals.

Modern tax systems therefore cannot help but produce some efficiency loss. In a world with only labour and physical capital as factors of production, an income tax therefore induces two economic distortions. First, income tax tends to distort the so-called 'intertemporal leisure-consumption' decision by changing people's preference for both factors. Second, it distorts the 'intertemporal saving-consumption' decision of individuals.

The tax on labour income is responsible for the former effect by reducing after-tax earnings. Workers can simply avoid the tax by reducing hours worked in favour of more leisure time. In other words, the opportunity cost of leisure decreases. However, they also become poorer from a wage tax, hence some might choose to work more hours instead. Although the net effect is uncertain, income tax clearly affects the working decision of people.

Capital income tax has similar effects with regard to the saving-consumption decision. A positive tax on the return to savings reduces the price of current consumption relative to the price of future consumption (see Chapter 5 for an example). This may either encourage people to consume now and save less, or stimulate them to save more in anticipation of a given level of future consumption. Again the net effect depends on which force prevails.

---

[29] A third more appealing but none the less impracticable lump-sum tax called 'Tinbergen's talent tax' is discussed separately in Section 3.3 in Chapter 3.

Empirically, the magnitude of these behavioural responses is somewhat undecided, but evidence tends to indicate that income tax reduces overall labour supply moderately, has a slight negative effect on savings and a larger effect on investment. In addition, most income tax systems contain a mixture of different provisions that create complex distortions. Some of these distortions are discussed more extensively in later chapters. The main point we want to highlight for now is that the tax system affects the decisions of economic agents and comes at a welfare cost over and above revenue collected.

BOX 1.5

Taxes cause distortions to economic choices and thereby create an excess burden, which presents a cost to the taxpayer on top of the actual tax revenue collected. Tax distortions can technically be avoided only by imposing a lump-sum tax. Such a tax imposes a fixed rate per individual, but is hard to justify on social and political grounds.

The Marginal Cost of Public Funds

To get a rough idea of the efficiency costs of taxation, we can perform a simple back-of-the-envelope calculation. In the public finance literature the direct cost of taxation and extra welfare cost produced is measured by the marginal cost of public funds (MCPF), first named by Browning (1976). The MCPF is an essential part in any cost-benefit analysis of a public spending programme financed by distortionary taxes. More generally, it affects the optimal size of government.[30]

If one unit of extra revenue is needed, how much does this actually cost the public when behavioural responses are accounted for? Under quite reasonable assumptions the cost is shown to be significant. The calculations typically focus on the effect of taxation on labour supply. Labour is regarded as the relatively immobile factor and therefore presumed to bear much of the burden of taxation. The MCPF depends on the tax rate on labour and the response to it as measured by the uncompensated elasticity of labour supply.[31]

Thus when accounting for labour and consumption taxes, a tax rate of 50 per cent is not unrealistic for many countries. Both reduce the take-home pay

---

[30] The classic theory was developed by Nobel Prize-winning economist Paul Samuelson and later refined further by Stiglitz and Dasgupta (1971) and Atkinson and Stern (1974).

[31] The relationship can under certain conditions be described by $MCPF = 1 / [1 - (t_L / 1 - t_L) \varepsilon_U]$, where ε_U is the uncompensated wage elasticity of labour.

of households and thereby affect the labour supply decision. If we then assume an uncompensated elasticity of supply of 0.4, it is straightforward to establish an MCPF of approximately 1.7.[32] In other words, every additional €1 in revenue spent by government actually costs the taxpayer €1.70.

This is a hefty premium for government services that sometimes may just as easily be supplied by the private sector. The nature of government spending financed by taxation thus matters. Money spent on a road project, public transportation or schools is more beneficial to economic development than spending on public parks, recreational facilities and social protection which tends to affect labour supply negatively. The former raises government intake and decreases the size of the MCPF, while the latter unambiguously increases the MCPF. An MCPF of 1 implies no extra welfare cost. Theoretically, it is possible to obtain a value below unity when taxes create positive behavioural responses that outweigh other costs.

The Nordic countries, despite hefty tax burdens and a large MCPF, also spend heavily on R&D, education and active labour market policies to get the unemployed back to work quickly (we will explore these issues in later chapters). These are crucial factors for creating a strong and competitive economy in the 21st century. The way they allocate expenditures thus partly explains their success.

The absolute size of the MCPF depends on the combination of tax rates, elasticities and productivities. Moreover, if a variety of different tax instruments are used to raise the necessary revenue, optimal policy requires the MCPF to be the same across all types of taxes to minimise distortionary losses. Otherwise, welfare could theoretically be enhanced by switching from more- to less-distorting taxes.

Table 1.9   The marginal cost of public funds

Country	MCFP	Country	MCPF
Austria	1.56	Ireland	1.45
Belgium	2.14	Italy	1.52
Denmark	2.22	Netherlands	1.52
Finland	2.23	Sweden	2.08
France	1.72	UK	1.26
Germany	1.85		

Source: Kleven and Kreiner (2006, Table II).

---

[32] Chapter 3 shows that prime-age males are largely unresponsive to changes in wage rates. However, when additionally accounting for the participation decision, an elasticity of labour supply of 0.4 seems quite reasonable.

Kleven and Kreiner (2006) have approximated the MCPF for a number of European countries, using advanced modelling techniques. The study results are summarised in Table 1.9. The MCPFs in Belgium, Denmark, Finland and Sweden are astonishingly high, but taxation in other countries also entails a considerable excess burden. With relatively low tax rates on labour and small benefit payments, the UK and Ireland are the only countries with a MCPF below 1.5.

1.4   DREAMING ABOUT SELF-FINANCING TAX CUTS

Policy that is successful in increasing the efficiency of the tax system and stimulating economic activity should increase the revenue intake by the treasury. For example, workers may supply more labour and businesses step up entrepreneurial activity and investment and thereby the rate of capital accumulation. Lower taxes typically also induce higher private spending on consumption. These positive behavioural responses raise the tax revenue that is collected from taxes that target these bases, such as personal and corporate income tax and VAT.

The treasury is thus likely to recuperate some of the tax revenue forgone with the tax cut by inducing higher economic activity. Despite initially lowering the revenue intake, a tax cut is thus partly *self-financing*.

The Laffer Curve: Maximising Potential Revenues

The Laffer curve conjecture is closely related to these notions and describes an extreme case of self-financing. The curve was named after US economist Arthur Laffer and describes the theoretical relationship between the level of income taxation and total revenue collected.[33] The Laffer curve is part of 'supply-side' economics, a branch of thought that stresses the importance of supply-side factors in economic policy making. The theories became particularly popular during the Reagan years from 1981 to 1989, after oil shocks and union conflicts in the 1970s had contradicted basic Keynesian theory.

The Laffer curve is depicted in Figure 1.2. The horizontal axis represents the average income tax rate, the vertical axis total revenue collected. Its underpinning can be described as follows. Think of how much revenue government would raise under an income tax of 100 per cent. The answer is probably none or nearly none. A few idealists would keep on working, but

---

[33] Professor Arthur B. Laffer is considered to be a supply-side economist and was political adviser on Reagan's Economic Policy Advisory Board (1981-89). Although the curve is popularly named after him, the concept had already been conceived and described earlier by 19th-century French economist Jules Dupuit (Auerbach, 1985).

the overall majority of people would stop, to enjoy leisure instead, as working does not pay. In other words, such high levels of taxation take away all incentives for people to work, thus leaving the treasury without any source of revenue.

If the income tax rate were set at zero, no revenue would be collected either. It follows that somewhere in the middle of these extremes should lie an optimal point from the perspective of maximal revenue collection. In Figure 1.2 this point is represented by t^*. The exact position may vary across countries and depends inversely on the wage elasticities of labour supply. However, at the point of maximal revenues the marginal cost of public funds, that is, including the excess burden of taxation as discussed above, approaches infinity, so in practice the tax rate will be well below t^*.[34]

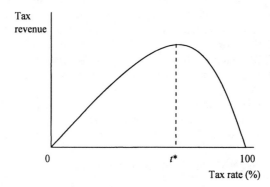

Figure 1.2   The Laffer curve

The implications of the Laffer curve are controversial, since tax revenue could actually be increased by cutting taxes. This occurs when tax rates are to the right of point t^* and positive behavioural responses raise revenue collection over and above the cost of the initial cut. To the right of t^*, the cost of funds is actually negative. On the other hand, to the left of t^* the opposite is the case.

In practice it is difficult to establish at which point on the Laffer curve a country finds itself. For example, when the Reagan administration cut taxes with the Economic Recovery Tax Act of 1981 (ERTA) revenue fell at first.[35] Figure 1.3 shows that in 1982 the percentage growth of tax revenue was even

[34] Maximal tax revenues occur where $t^* / (1 - t^*) = 1 / \varepsilon_U$, where ε_U is the uncompensated wage elasticity of labour. Let the tax revenue be: $T = tW L[(1 - t)W]$, where $L[(1 - t)W]$ is the labour supply schedule. Then $\partial T / \partial t = WL\ tW^2\ \partial L / \partial(-t)W = WL\ [\ 1 - (t / (1 - t)\varepsilon_U]$, where $\varepsilon_U \equiv (1 - t)W\ (\partial L/L) / \partial(1 - t)W$ is the uncompensated wage elasticity of labour supply. Hence, maximal tax revenue will be where $\partial T / \partial t = 0$, that is, when $t^* / 1 - t^* = 1 / \varepsilon_U$.

[35] Under ERTA, marginal statutory rates in each bracket were cut by approximately 25 per cent in three phases from 1982 to 1984. The revenue cost was estimated at 1.5 per cent of GDP.

negative, implying that in absolute terms revenue was lower than the year before, while GDP growth remained steady throughout the period. In a paper on dynamic scoring, a term used when accounting for behavioural reactions in predicting the impact of fiscal policy changes, Mankiw and Weinzierl (2004) estimate that a broad-based income tax cut of both the labour and capital income tax recoups only about 25 per cent of the lost revenue. For a capital income tax cut only the effect would be larger, about 50 per cent of lost revenue, but still significantly below recovering 100 per cent.

In any case, current US income tax rates are relatively low compared to other countries.[36] In Sweden where marginal income tax rate topped well over 80 per cent in the early 1980s, Laffer effects have been measured more clearly (see, for example, Stuart, 1981; and Feige and McGee, 1983).[37]

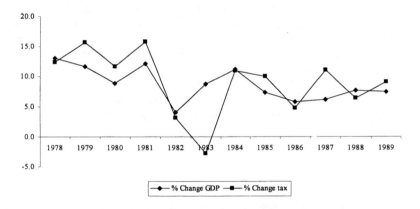

Source: Economic Report of the President (2005). Washington, DC: US Government Printing Office.

Figure 1.3   Percentage change in GDP and tax revenue in the US

Tax Avoidance, Evasion and Fiscal Fraud

High taxes encourage taxpayers to expose a smaller amount of their money to taxation, through either tax avoidance or evasion. High tax rates typically coincide with many exceptions to the tax base and apply at different levels to different sources of income. These tax breaks result in a highly non-uniform

[36] One should be careful to interpret marginal tax rates in the US. The US tax system contains a multitude of different federal, state and local tax rates, which all affect the final tax burden.

[37] Survey research discloses that Swedes are not averse to high taxes on principle, though. Edlund (2000) uses survey data for the 1981-97 period and discerns no long-run trend of discontent. He notes, however, that in the short run there have been some fluctuations in discontent and that in later years tax morality has decreased slightly.

tax treatment of income, which introduces opportunities for tax avoidance and arbitrage of various sorts. There are two basic principles in income tax avoidance (a process that is usually referred to as 'tax planning'). The first is taking advantage of differences in tax rates on different types of income; the second involves postponement of taxes.[38]

Tax planning may involve anything from transforming high-taxed corporate income into low-taxed capital gains, to claiming deductible expenses against fully taxable income to subsequently report it as 'other' preferentially treated income; or postponing capital gains tax on the sale of an asset. In the case, of plain evasion, people simply fail to report taxable income.

Whether these practices are permissible or illegal, lower tax rates can lead people to expose more income to taxation. In the United States, the Internal Revenue Service (IRS) estimates that the net tax gap was at least $257 billion in 2001, where the net tax gap is defined as the difference between taxes legally due and what taxpayers actually remitted to the government or, about 13 per cent of total federal income (US Government Accountability Office, 2005). This has a non-trivial impact on the collection effort and tax system on the whole, since taxpayers who do rightfully remit their due taxes are required to pay higher than normal taxes in the absence of such tax fraud. The economic literature estimates tax fraud to be around €200-250 billion in the EU, or 2.5 per cent of EU GDP.[39]

BOX 1.6

Behavioural responses form an integral part of tax policy making. They account for changes in labour supply, investment and consumer spending as well as participation in tax avoidance and evasion schemes.

The New Tax Responsiveness Literature

To measure behavioural effects, the past two decades have seen some interesting developments in public finance. A new generation of studies combines Laffer-type notions with the fact that high tax rates induce taxpayers to expose less income to taxation, yet in a sophisticated manner. Goolsbee (1999) has called this new branch of literature the 'new tax

---

[38] Postponement of taxes is favourable as a euro is worth more today than it is tomorrow (assuming that there is inflation and tax rates do not rise).

[39] See also the EU Council conclusions on combating VAT fraud within the Union, 2766th Ecofin Council meeting, Brussels, 28 November 2006.

responsiveness' (NTR) literature. The studies demonstrate that behavioural responses can have a measurable impact on revenue collection.

The main idea is that taxation entails a considerable excess burden and that high tax rates do not increase revenue collection from taxpayers at the top of the income distribution. This outcome does not by itself result from reduced labour supply, but may instead arise if high-income earners shift their income out of taxable form. Hence, taxpayers succeed in transforming taxable income into non-taxable income. The excess burden and revenue loss from behavioural responses in such a case may assume similar proportions as under the original Laffer conjecture, even if the elasticity of labour supply is zero.

Natural experiments

Large tax regime changes in the US which involved substantial tax cuts have made it possible to test empirically a number of induced behavioural responses. For example, Lindsey (1987) has found that up to one-quarter of the revenue loss from the 1981 ERTA under Reagan was recovered through positive behavioural responses. The data revealed the revenue-maximising tax rate to lie around 40 per cent.

Bosworth and Burtless (1992) showed that by 1989 the number of hours worked by males had indeed increased by 6 per cent relative to the trend before the Reagan tax cuts, including the Tax Reform Act of 1986. Most of this increase, however, occurred among poor households that were not targeted by the tax measures and therefore remained unaffected. Feldstein (1997) concluded that refraining from enacting 'job protection' legislation and high long-term unemployment benefits improved the US labour markets. Later-implemented minimum wage cuts, taxation of unemployment insurance and work requirements for people on welfare provided further incentives. On the whole, the US labour market therefore functioned more efficiently in the 1980s.

Based on panel data including over 4,000 medium- and high-income married taxpayers, Feldstein (1995) found an elasticity of taxable income with respect to the marginal net-of-tax rate of greater than 1 for the US Tax Reform Act of 1986. Hence, due to positive behavioural responses, disposable income of households increased proportionally more than the tax cut amounted to. The revenue loss encountered was therefore also less.

Similarly, the 1993 tax rise of US President Bill Clinton is another example, yet this time of the reverse.[40] Feldstein and Feenberg (1993) projected revenues to increase by $26.1 billion annually (roughly 0.4 per cent

---

[40] William J. Clinton served as the 42nd President of the United States between 1993 and 2001. The tax package implemented under his administration was formally referred to as the Omnibus Budget Reconciliation Act of 1993 (OBRA-93). The measures increased the top marginal tax rate on income exceeding $250,000 from 36.0 to 42.5 per cent and the middle rate on income between $140,000 and $250,000 from 31.0 to 38.9 per cent (including a Medicare rise).

of GDP) without accounting for any behavioural response. The study revealed that merely a small behavioural response of high-income earners would reduce the revenue intake substantially. A decline in taxable income of 5 per cent due to a decreased labour supply and/or the use of tax-avoidance schemes would lower the revenue intake by an estimated $10 to $16.1 billion; a 10 per cent reduction of income would shrink total revenue collection to a mere $6.6 billion (that is, roughly 0.1 per cent of GDP).

Indeed, a follow-up study based on real IRS data showed that had the 1993 personal income tax measures not been enacted, 7.8 per cent more taxable income would have been reported with the IRS (Feldstein and Feenberg, 1995). The calculations revealed that revenue collection was effectively only half of what it would have been without such a response, or $8.4 billion instead of $19.3 billion.[41] It was also estimated that the resulting excess burden was approximately twice as large as the extra revenue collected ($15.9 billion). The US economy functioned much less efficiently while raising little extra revenue.[42] Feldstein (1999) estimated the total efficiency cost of US personal income tax to range from $181 to $284 billion in 1994.

Finally, Goolsbee (1999) examined six different tax changes in the US since 1922. The study finds behavioural responses largely in line with the above studies for the Reagan tax cuts in the 1980s. For tax changes in the decades before this, the results typically suggest lower responses.

BOX 1.7

Empirical evidence for the US demonstrates that behavioural responses can have a significant impact on the final revenue outcome of a tax measure, both in positive and negative ways. A tax cut may be partly self-financing due to positive responses. By contrast, a tax rise may induce negative behavioural reactions. Estimations show that the tax rise under US President Clinton in 1993 generated only half the revenue projected, or $8.4 billion instead of $19.3 billion.

---

[41] Since the two highest rates were increased, only high-income earners were affected. The study considered only the personal tax rate increase and not the simultaneous rise in Medicare premiums.

[42] Hodge et al. (1996) of the Heritage Foundation, using the Washington University Macro Model (WUMM) calibrated with their own assumptions and input variables, found that only 49 per cent of the predicted revenue by the Congressional Budget Office was actually collected. GDP was reduced by $14, $41 and $66 billion in 1993, 1994 and 1995, respectively (in 1995 dollars) compared to a simulation without the act. In the same period, employment decreased by an equivalent of 867,000 workers and fixed investment by $24 billion.

1.5 THE MODEL OF CIRCULAR FLOWS

The economy can be schematically organised in a circular flow model, which illustrates the major flows of income between households and firms. Consider Figure 1.4. Money flows in a clockwise direction from the firms to the market for factors of production as payments for the use of labour and capital (1). The payments on capital are in turn transferred to the financial markets as business savings (5), or diverted to households in the form of dividend and interest (2). Labour payments such as wages and salaries are also transferred to households (2). Household income is subsequently divided between consumption (3) and savings (6).

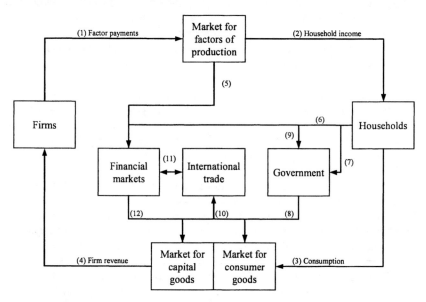

Figure 1.4   Circular flows in the economy

However, first household income is siphoned off by taxes that are transferred to the government (7). In reality taxes are collected at many points in an economy. The single flow from households is a simplifying but none the less realistic assumption. Fundamentally only individuals pay taxes and *not*, as is regularly assumed, legal entities such as proprietorships and corporations (although they remit taxes they do not bear the economic burden). The revenue is allocated to government to finance its spending (8).

If the budget is not balanced, the complementary amount makes up net government saving (9). In the case of a budget deficit government savings are negative. The financial markets then make up the difference. For this, governments issue all sorts of bonds varying from short-term ones with maturities of less than one year, to long-term ones, such as US Treasury Bonds, British Gilts or German *Bunds* with maturities of more than 10 years. If in surplus, the excess is transferred to the financial markets. The financial markets are funded by business, household and government savings (5, 6 and 9), which together with net foreign trade (10) determine total investment (11). The circle is completed if money spent on capital together with that spent on consumer goods and services is re-injected into the firms as revenue (4).

Introducing Taxation into the Model

Abandoning the assumption of a single flow of taxes from household to government (7), we can establish the points in the model where taxes can formally be inserted. As we have seen, the flow at point (1) consists of factor payments for the use of labour and capital. Capital payments are equivalent to firm revenue (4) minus cost of capital. A *corporate income tax* is imposed at this stage. Labour payments are typically targeted by a *payroll tax* or *wage tax*. Household income at point (2) in turn consists of wages and capital income such as dividends, interest and rents. Both factors lie within the remit of a *personal income tax*. The payroll or wage tax, if levied, then generally serves as an advance levy for personal income tax. This is considered to be an effective solution, because the legal liability for collection and remittance lies with firms rather than households.[43]

Money spent by households on the consumption of goods and services at point (3) may be subject to a *personal expenditure tax*, which records annual household income and deducts annual saving to determine private consumption. Firm revenue at point (4) may be subject to a *retail sales tax* or *value-added tax*. A retail sales tax simply adds a certain percentage to the sales price, while VAT is imposed through a more sophisticated process of calculating and taxing value added at each stage of production at the business level. Finally, an *export levy* and an *import levy* can be placed on net exports at point (10).

The model shows that taxes are placed on either the *income* side or the *spending* side in an economy. There is a third possible tax base that cannot be represented in a circular flow model, namely the holding of wealth. Indeed wealth is a stock variable. Compare it to a company's income statement and a balance sheet. The income statement represents a period of time, while the balance sheet represents a specific moment in time. Because wealth is

---

[43] Furthermore, a *dividend withholding tax* or an *interest withholding tax* may be imposed at the firm level. A withholding tax (WHT) is a tax that is withheld or retained at the source by the payer of certain income such as wages, dividends, interest or royalties. The tax is remitted directly to the tax authorities and the payee is given the balance. The primary objective of WHTs is to reduce (international) tax avoidance and evasion.

measured at a *moment* in time, it cannot be included in a *flow* model. A wealth tax is typically used to build further progression into a system.[44]

1.6   EQUIVALENCE RELATIONS

On this basis a number of interesting long-run equivalencies can be observed between certain categories of taxes. For example, a tax on income is conceptually similar to a tax on output, provided that all transactions take place in the formal economy. Also, a tax on firms as producers is equal to a tax on households as consumers. A crucial factor in these equivalence relations is the taxation of interest. Take equation (1.1). [45]

$$Y \equiv W + R \equiv C + S, \tag{1.1}$$

where:

Y = national income;
C = consumption;
S = saving;
W = wage income; and
R = return on capital (both normal and above-normal return).

The identity indicates that national income (Y) in an economy equals total value added in the production ($W + R$), which in turn equals the total of consumption and savings ($C + S$). In essence, a uniform tax on income would thus be equivalent to a uniform or comprehensive tax on firm output. The former is expressed by (Y) and the latter by ($W + R$). It follows that an income tax is equivalent to a comprehensive tax on value added.

VAT as imposed in most countries is nevertheless not comprehensive. Generally speaking, business investment is exempted from the tax base to

---

[44] Another interesting tax is the 'Tobin tax'. Named after the Nobel Prize winner James Tobin, it proposes a small sales tax typically between 0.1 and 0.25 per cent on cross-border currency trades to discourage short-term speculations on exchange rates and thereby stabilise financial markets. Although a small levy, the revenue potential lies in the billions of US dollars due to the sheer size of the tax base (in 2005 estimated to be over $1.8 trillion each day, generating between $100 billion and $300 billion annually). As yet the Tobin tax has to be implemented in reality. In 2004, the Belgian parliament committed its government to implementing the so-called 'Spahn tax' (a Tobin-type of tax) under the precondition that all eurozone countries have adopted a similar measure. This makes implementation highly unlikely.

[45] This subsection draws on Cnossen (2001, pp. 474-6).

prevent 'cascading'.[46] If investment (I) is assumed to equal savings, which is true in the long run, equation (1.1) can be rewritten as follows:

$$C \equiv Y - S \equiv W + R - I. \tag{1.2}$$

Here, investment is deducted from total value added ($W + R - I$), which forms the base for a tax credit or invoice type of VAT as found in over one hundred countries worldwide. At the same time it is equivalent to a direct tax on consumption (C), for example, a retail sales tax.

In addition, a tax on consumption is equal to a tax on income with an exemption for savings ($Y - S$). An often heard criticism of income tax is that it taxes savings twice, which is exactly what happens if S is not exempted. This discourages saving, since the tax on those who consume later in life by raising their current savings is higher than on those who consume their income immediately. In contrast, the present value of a consumption tax is the same regardless of whether consumption takes place now or in the future.

By a different reasoning, a tax on consumption (C) is equal to a tax on labour income (W) and business cash flow ($R - I$). The deduction of investment ensures that the normal return is expensed immediately under a consumption tax, as the investment's acquisition price is determined by the present value of its prospective normal return (where the normal return may be approximated by the risk-free interest rate).[47] The main difference between a tax on consumption and a tax on income is therefore the immediate expensing of the normal return to investment under the former, while it is only depreciated over its effective lifetime under the latter. As a result, the normal return on 'new' investment is double taxed under an income-based tax. Both variants none the less tax above-normal profits as well as the normal return to 'initial' capital which has been fully depreciated.[48]

In practice, the two taxes are obviously not equivalent. Under existing tax structures, income and consumption taxes are imposed on differential bases. VAT is generally broader based. All consumers pay VAT, while the income tax base depends on the level of income and a variety of other factors such as marital status, household composition and extraordinary expenses. VAT is also more difficult to evade than an income tax.

---

[46] That is, a tax on a tax, which occurs if business inputs are not completely relieved of tax. This would lead to a double taxation of that part of value added when it is subsequently sold and taxed again. Chapter 5 elaborates further on this.

[47] Except for certain timing differences and only in the absence of intergenerational transfers.

[48] Auerbach et al. (1997) provide formal proof for these basic equivalencies and extend the analysis to account for open borders. This suggests that a given policy objective may be attained by different routes, some of which may be more politically feasible than others.

BOX 1.8

On a theoretical level, a tax on consumption is similar to a tax on income which exempts the normal return to capital. This equivalency means that many tax systems, although formally income based, are in reality a hybrid of both an income and a consumption tax. This is, for example, due to the existence of tax-exempt saving schemes and pension plans.

1.7 TAXATION AND ECONOMIC GROWTH

Research Methods in Economics

Ever since governments in the 20th century embarked on active tax policies, research has been undertaken into the economic effects of the tax measures. The research can be divided into three broad categories. In the first place, *behavioural* research conducts surveys among target groups to investigate whether a certain tax measure has affected workers, consumers and/or firms in their behaviour and, if so, to what extent? The research may nevertheless include biased responses and the response rate is generally low.

A second branch of research is *statistical* research, which examines macroeconomic time-series and cross-country data to analyse the impact of taxation on economic variables such as economic growth, employment and private investment. Third, *econometric* research is based on complex models to measure the quantitative effects of tax measures on the development of the aforementioned variables. Econometric research often gives an oversimplified view of reality and is out of necessity based on historical data.

Take econometric modelling, which is generally classified along either of two lines. First, macroeconomic models mainly concentrate on business-cycle fluctuations. These models are mostly used by central banks, treasuries and other researchers concerned with monetary and fiscal policy. By contrast, computable general equilibrium (CGE) models typically assume perfectly competitive goods and factor markets, and focus on more structural aspects of production. Thus they analyse the long-term impact of, for instance, a tax reform, trade liberalisation or climate change. The stochastic variants of CGE models are nowadays called 'real business-cycle models' and explain the business cycle by stochastic shocks to technology. The Nobel Prize winners (2004) Edward C. Prescott and Finn E. Kydland have been responsible for this excitingly new branch of economic research.

The models constructed often encompass several hundred or even thousand lines of mathematical formulae to capture the dynamics in an economy. The main problem is that their outcome is highly dependent on the suppositions and parameterisation of the model builder, which will mechanically reflect the outcome. Changing only a small variable may produce very disparate results. The Keynesian models highlight market fairness and involuntary unemployment, while the real business-cycle models argue that markets work and unemployment is voluntary (caused by, say, high benefits or trade union power).

Theoretical and Empirical Studies

Studies are broadly divided into theoretical and empirical ones. The former are mostly econometrical in nature and are carried out through formal growth models. This offers a quantitative measurement of the effects of tax policy changes. Empirical studies typically compare cross-country and time-series data to estimate whether there is a link between taxes imposed and economic growth rates observed. The results differ widely between them.

The outcome critically depends on the parameters chosen and whether growth is exogenous or endogenous.[49] Also, the results seem to be particularly sensitive to the proportion of factor inputs, the applied depreciation schedule and the elasticity of labour supply and intertemporal substitution (Stockey and Rebelo, 1995). Some of these parameters are difficult to estimate. Empirical studies show less variation, but are still subject to significantly different outcomes.[50] However, over time the results have become more pronounced in the sense that taxes indeed affect economic growth.

One of the earliest influential studies on taxes and long-run economic growth was conducted by Harberger (1964), who observed that, based on historical data for the US, the savings rate remained largely unaffected by changes in tax rates. This led him to the conclusion that the effects of tax

---

[49] The difference between both assumptions is explained in Appendix 1. Where exogenous growth models explain long-run economic growth by population growth and an exogenous rate of labour-augmenting technical progress, endogenous growth theory explains growth from 'within' the model by knowledge spillovers, human capital and R&D activity.

[50] According to Auerbach (1996a), there are a number of reasons why it is difficult to measure the impact of tax reform. There is limited time for evaluation. Other factors arise that also alter behaviour. In addition, tax measures are often taken as part of a larger (complex) reform. Different tax measures affect a single economic factor through a variety of interconnected channels. Tax policy is, moreover, endogenous. The question may be asked whether different tax policies cause unequal growth, or whether unequal growth is responsible for different tax policies? Variations in growth can often also be attributed to 'normal' business-cycle fluctuations. Finally, abstract economic notions such as tax-induced excess burdens are simply very difficult to gauge.

changes on welfare were insignificant, at least for the changes observed until then.

Table 1.10 Studies on taxation and economic growth

Study	Coverage and timeframe	Economic impact
Koester and Kormendi (1989)	63 countries over the 1970s	Holding average tax rates constant, a decrease in marginal tax rates of 10%-points, increases per capita income by 7.4%
Engen and Skinner (1992)	107 countries over 1970-85	10%-point increase in taxation reduces growth rates by 1.4%-points
Easterly and Rebelo (1993)	About 100 countries over 1970-88	No discernible relation between taxes and growth
Jones et al. (1993)	Model simulations	Eliminating all distorting taxes increases growth rates by 4-8%
Cashin (1995)	23 OECD countries over 1971-88	1%-point of GDP increase in taxation reduces output per worker by 2%
Engen and Skinner (1996)	Model simulations for US economy	5 and 2.5%-point increase in marginal and average tax rates, respectively, reduces growth by 0.2-0.3%-points
Leibfritz et al. (1997)	OECD countries over 1965-95	10 %-point increase in tax to GDP ratio reduces growth by 0.5-1%-point
Mendoza et al. (1997)	Theoretical and empirical framework	10% tax cut increases investment by 0.5-2%-points; negligible effect on growth
Kneller et al. (1999)	22 OECD countries over 1970-95	1%-point of GDP decrease of distortionary taxes increases the growth rate by 0.1-0.2% per year
European Commission (2000a)	Model simulations by QUEST model	1% of GDP reduction of taxes increases GDP between 0.5 and 0.8%
Fölster and Henrekson (2001)	Sample of 29 rich OECD and non-OECD countries over 1970-95	10%-point increase in tax to GDP ratio reduces GDP growth by 1%-point
Bassanini et al. (2001)	21 OECD countries over 1971-98	1%-point increase in tax to GDP ratio reduces per capita output by 0.3-0.6%
Padovano and Galli (2001)	23 OECD countries over 1950-80	Negative correlation between high marginal tax rates and long-run economic growth
Barton and Hawksworth (2003)	18 OECD countries over 1970-99	1% of GDP increase in distortionary taxation reduces GDP growth by 0.2-0.4%-points
Lee and Gordon (2005)	70 countries over 1970-97	10%-point corporate tax cut increases growth by 1-2%-points

Lucas (1990) also found negligible affects on US growth. He estimated that eliminating the capital tax would change growth by 0.03 percentage points. Using an endogenous growth model, he initially found that eliminating the capital income tax would increase the capital stock by 35 per cent. However, accounting for diminishing returns to capital and the fact that such a capital expansion would entail a long-term reduced consumption in the transitional phase, leads to a trivial overall effect on welfare.

In the beginning of the 1990s endogenous growth theory gained wider acceptance and research started to focus on the parameters used. The quantitative effect on welfare that is predicted by such models is likely to be much larger than with the traditional exogenous models. This is because (tax) policy has the potential to influence growth in these models.

King and Rebelo (1990) estimated that a 10 per cent income tax increase has a welfare impact 40 times larger in a two-sector endogenous growth model and 47 times larger in a simple endogenous growth model, than in the basic neoclassical model. The same study concluded that the effect of taxation on economic growth depends significantly on human capital and how it is produced. Also, the effect of labour mobility should be taken into account, as workers migrate in search of higher wages (Lucas, 1988). Countries with high average tax rates on labour may as a result experience relatively lower growth rates (Rebelo, 1991). Accounting for 'core' capital that can be produced and accumulated regardless of factors that cannot (like land), as such, explains sustained growth.

On the basis of theoretical and empirical research, studies since the 1990s have found measurable effects of taxation on economic growth. Table 1.10 summarises the main studies and their results.

BOX 1.9

Based on theoretical and empirical research, most economists today agree that high taxes affect economic growth negatively.

1.8 BRIEF SUMMARY

This chapter has provided an introduction to taxation and economic policy. The primary purpose of the tax system is to collect revenue to finance government expenditure. The size and function of government to an important extent determine the level of taxation and taxes used, which all affects the behaviour of taxpayers and the economy as a whole by impinging on the incentives to consume, work, invest and save. The tax system also influences a country's competitiveness ranking on world markets.

A widely accepted measure to determine economic prosperity is GDP, which constitutes the sum of consumption, investment, government spending and exports minus imports in a given period. GDP gives an incomplete picture of economic welfare, though. The chapter has shown that several other factors also need to be taken into account, such as health, education, employment, income inequality, housing, leisure and a clean environment. Taking all these factors into consideration, research shows that both adults and children in European countries are the happiest in the world.

Interesting cross-country differences may be observed. For example, Denmark has a relatively high GDP per capita, a large government, a top competitiveness ranking, little income inequality and the happiest people in the world. The US produces one of the highest GDPs per capita, has a relatively small government, large income inequalities between rich and poor and ranks 23rd in terms of happiness. Many of these factors reflect on the size of government and the tax system of a country.

A large government requires high tax rates to raise the required revenues, which create distortions in the choice of economic agents. For example, workers reduce labour supply and businesses lower the rate of investment and thereby capital accumulation. Taxpayers are also encouraged to expose a smaller amount of their income to taxation through the use of tax-avoidance and -evasion strategies. In the EU such tax fraud is estimated to constitute approximately 2.5 per cent of GDP.

Behavioural responses form an integral part of tax policy. Under certain simplifying assumptions, tax distortions from high taxes on labour can be shown to create a considerable welfare loss in countries such as Denmark, Finland, Belgium and Sweden. Here, every euro collected in revenue induces a loss of economic welfare to the taxpayer of over two euros (that is, the marginal cost of public funds exceeds 2). Besides creating an excess burden, these behavioural responses have a measurable impact on the budgetary outcome of a tax measure or reform. A tax cut can be partly self-financing, while a tax rise will generate less revenue than projected under static methods.

Finally, the chapter summarised a large number of theoretical and empirical studies that have found a negative impact from taxes on the economy. From the 1990s onwards, the majority of studies have established negative relationships between high marginal tax rates and economic growth. In a globalising world, with increasing capital mobility and tax competition the effect of (high) taxes on international competitiveness will intensify.

2. The design of tax systems

Every system is perfectly designed to achieve exactly the results it gets.

(Berwick, 2003, p. 449)

2.1 INTRODUCTION

The design of tax systems or of specific tax measures depends on a large number of social, economic and political factors. The previous chapter noted that tax structures in OECD countries have been largely shaped by (past) decision making and political preferences of parties in power. This will certainly remain a dominant influence in any future modification or far-reaching reform of the tax system. Even so, several criteria have been developed over time, which aim to give policy makers an objective framework for designing a high-standard tax system capable of raising the necessary revenues.

Apart from the primary function of collecting tax revenue to finance government expenditure, the design of the tax system depends on the way it is used to accomplish other objectives of government policy. The main taxes used by industrialised nations are personal and corporate income tax and consumption taxes, such as VAT, excise and green taxes.[1] Other objectives of taxation are mostly unconnected to raising revenue for the government treasury. In particular, this includes how and to what extent personal income tax and VAT reflect ability to pay and are used to promote employment, specific business investment and/or prevent socially undesirable consumption such as excessive drinking or smoking. There is also relevancy in achieving environmental objectives.

Against this background, this chapter addresses aspects of tax design. We begin by examining the important 21st-century trends and challenges that affect the design of tax systems and call for an active government position. Some of the main issues are the world of the internet, population ageing, tax

---

[1] Social security contributions (SSCs) are considered to be taxes. The contributions place a heavy burden on labour in most OECD countries. The size and nature of the social systems strongly defines the final burden and effect. The separate economic effects of SSCs are not discussed.

competition and climate change. Next, the characteristics of a good tax system are discussed. This is followed by a categorisation of taxes to obtain a better understanding of the formal tax instruments available to government. This section also includes an overview of OECD revenue statistics. The chapter continues by examining more closely the three variables that make up the final tax liability of the taxpayer: the tax base, the tax rate and tax breaks. Important objectives in tax design are simplicity and transparency and both these principles are considered in turn. Finally, the criteria for using the tax system as a tool of government policy are outlined.

2.2   ECONOMIC AND DEMOGRAPHIC TRENDS AND ISSUES IN THE 21st CENTURY

Tax policy requires a continuous adaptation to reflect changing social, economic and political circumstances. Ongoing globalisation and digitalisation require greater flexibility of domestic product and factor markets. The world is integrating rapidly and with it the interaction between economic institutions of countries. At the same time, a general ageing of the population and deterioration of the environment can be observed that affect the economy, government finances and the tax system. A combination of technological innovation, increasing global trade and cross-country capital flows, and a resilient macroeconomic policy framework and financial institutions have supported strong productivity growth in the past decades. According to the IMF (2007a, p. xvi) 'it is essential that these pillars remain in place, and that trends that could pose challenges to continued strong global performance – such as population ageing and global warming – are adequately addressed'.

A number of key issues and trends are identified that will have to be addressed by governments of OECD countries in the decades to come:

- a globalising world with increasingly borderless economies and high capital and labour mobility;
- an interconnected world driven by technological change and the internet;
- increasing competition on world markets and importance of worldwide economic competitive strength on economic growth;
- human capital as a key productive factor, that is, worldwide demand for creative, smart and high-skilled workers;
- the battle between countries for companies, brains and affluent individuals, mostly the elderly, who have built up wealth over their lifetime;
- population ageing;

- the environment and the fight against climate change in creating and maintaining sustainable economic growth; and
- increasing political attention to relative well-being and the happiness of people and consequences of economic policy.

Due to the global character, governments can do less autonomously to affect developments. These issues will put further pressure on the existing tax arrangements and require adaptation. From a taxation point of view, of particular importance are the world of the internet and e-commerce; population ageing and its effect on labour markets and government finances; intensifying (tax) competition; and climate change.

Taxation, the Internet and E-commerce

The design of tax systems dates back to the time when the internet did not exist. The internet revolution is currently leaving a significant mark on the global economy and the operation of tax systems. Nobel laureate (1976) Milton Friedman has remarked: 'The most important ways in which I think the Internet will affect the big issue is that it will make it more difficult for government to collect taxes'.[2] The internet creates an entirely new dimension for individuals and business to interact. Tax systems need to be adjusted in response to the world of the internet for several reasons.

During the past decade, internet use whether for fun or trade has grown spectacularly. From 1996 to 2007, the number of internet users increased explosively from 36 million (0.4 per cent of the world population) to over 1 billion (16.8 per cent).

Internet commerce principally takes place on websites for online advertising, marketplaces and web shops, an 'industry' that demonstrates strong annual growth. Existing tax systems are designed for traditional trade of goods and services and the availability of (written) information (Muscovitch, 2005). This includes information on the location (that is, country) where the transaction takes place (that is, who has the right to tax), the identity of the taxpayer (that is, who is taxed), the moment of transaction (that is, when does the tax liability arise) and the type of transaction (that is, which tax should be imposed and at what rate).

The development of the internet has adverse consequences for revenue collection, especially from VAT and corporate income tax. Besides national adjustments to the tax system, international coordination regarding the sales and profits of internet commerce is needed to mitigate the loss of tax revenues (see, for example, OECD, 2001 and 2005b).

A major bottleneck for tax authorities is ascertaining the identity of the parties involved. Internet buyers and sellers can be located anywhere in the

---

[2] Quoted on http://quotations.about.com/od/moretypes/a/taxquotes2.htm (8 March 2007).

world, using different computers and assuming any identity. Another difficulty lies in identifying the taxable profits of a web server and the country allowed to levy the tax. Sometimes internet transactions are routed via so-called 'tax havens', which make taxation virtually impossible. Other forms of tax avoidance and evasion wherein the internet plays a role also occur; for example, cigarettes mailed from low-excise tax countries, illegal sales of DVDs and recordings, internet gambling, online auctions and so forth. Tax authorities nowadays scan the internet with special search engines to identify taxable transactions.

The internet has also created virtual worlds such as 'Second Life', which involves thousands of entrepreneurs who on a daily basis with over two million 'inhabitants' from all over the globe form a virtual society and economy.[3] The Second Life economy features service-orientated businesses, but it does not yet have a (virtual) tax system. However, in so far as the economic transactions in the economy generate revenues for participating individuals or companies in official monetary currencies, this can lead to taxation in the real world.

The economic value of the transactions in virtual economies exceeds €1 billion worldwide. The value added is nevertheless produced in a dimension for which existing accounting principles and tax rules have not been written or do not apply. The virtual world leaves a void or formal no man's land to which existing systems need to be adapted to ensure effective revenue collection.

Specific internet taxes are banned in the US
When the number of internet transactions started to rise rapidly in the late 1990s, strategies were voiced in the United States for several forms of internet taxation such as an internet access tax, bit tax, bandwidth tax and e-mail tax. The plans were soon put on hold and have since even led to the introduction of a special law in the US called the 'Internet Tax Freedom Act',[4] which bans all forms of internet taxation. In the EU, politicians have also argued for special internet taxes, but so far these have not been introduced.

Taxation and an Ageing Workforce

Ageing workforces are a reality for Europe and Japan and, to a lesser extent, the United States. The large number of 'baby boomers' are approaching

---

[3] See http://secondlife.com/.

[4] The Internet Tax Freedom Act was signed into law by President Bill Clinton on 21 October 1998. The law has been extended twice. Currently, it is called the Internet Tax Nondiscrimination Act (Public Law No. 108-435), which will expire in November 2007. The law prohibits any federal, state or local tax on the aforementioned taxes, and taxes on e-commerce.

retirement age, which will have a profound impact on fiscal policy. The grey wave inevitably affects the tax burden in order to maintain the rising costs of healthcare, pensions and social security. These costs will in the near future increase by several percentage points of GDP in most OECD countries. At the same time, fewer people work and those who do so work less and retire early. A relatively smaller group of younger workers will have to shoulder the associated costs.

Figure 2.1 shows the actual and projected old-age dependency ratios for 2020, which measure the ratio between the number of elderly persons of an age when they are typically economically inactive (aged 65 and over) and the number of persons of working age (from 15 to 64). In all countries the share of people aged 65 and over increases compared to the labour force. In Finland and Japan there is almost a doubling.

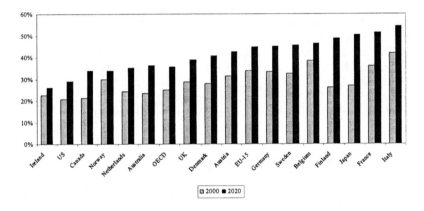

Source: Electronic Database of the OECD.

Figure 2.1   Old-age dependency ratio: people aged 65 and over relative to the labour force

The OECD estimates that by 2050 there could be on average more than 70 older and inactive people for every 100 workers in OECD countries (the figure currently stands at 38). In Europe, this number may even approach 100. For every active worker there will thus be an older non-active person.[5] The development would place enormous pressure on the public finances of countries. In addition, declining workforces and labour participation cause a reduction in labour supply in many European countries, putting upward pressure on wages. In 2007, the EU workforce numbered 194 million workers. By 2050, there will be an estimated labour shortage of 32 million

---

[5] Statistics are obtained from the OECD website on Ageing and Employment Policies.

workers. In Germany and Italy with workforces of 35 and 22 million, respectively, the labour shortage is estimated to reach 8 and 6 million, respectively, by 2050. In France and the UK the problems are less critical with estimated shortages of 1 and 0.5 million workers, respectively.

It is inevitable that existing tax systems will be revised in response. Favourable tax arrangements for early retirement and special tax arrangements for those already retired must be re-examined.[6] Transfer systems not based on earlier contributions should be gradually transformed into more funded systems. It is also critical to bring more people into the workforce by removing disincentives that make it attractive for the unemployed to remain unemployed.

Given the scale of the ageing problem, is it also inevitable that the official retirement age is raised to 67.[7] In addition, a major achievement of modern society is that people live longer and healthier lives, so it seems natural that they should contribute to the related costs. In the 1970s, the US decided to increase the retirement age from 65 to 67 over an extended period. A gradual implementation means that people are able to anticipate and adapt to changes. In 2007, the Chairman of the Federal Reserve Bank (FED), Ben Bernanke, expressed concern before the US Senate that failure to reform the pension system further could severely affect the economy in the long run. If no action is taken, the US social security system will be bankrupt by 2040. Moreover, a further delay of 20 years could result in a 13.7 per cent reduction in private consumption, since lower labour participation leads to a lower income per head of the population.

Given current forecasts on economic growth, government spending and tax revenues, today's policies in most OECD countries are not sustainable and need to be changed. Figure 2.2 shows as an example the long-term fiscal challenge in the US. The costs of social security and the US healthcare system (Medicare and Medicaid) increase markedly. Economic growth alone will not be able to resolve the problem. Projections show that if discretionary spending grows at the same rate as the economy, revenues will be sufficient to cover little more than the interest on US government debt by 2040. In Europe, where ageing is an even greater problem, the debate is also ongoing. Countries such as the UK and Germany have made similar proposals to extend the retirement age. But in too many countries the topic is still taboo.

---

[6] In a number of countries the receipt of retirement benefits leads to higher taxes on income earned after this time due to so-called 'means tests'. It is considered inappropriate to continue working while simultaneously receiving a public pension.

[7] Often the actual or effective retirement age is lower than the legal retirement age. An example is Norway, where the official retirement age already lies at 67, yet the effective age is only 62.3 for women and 63.7 for men (OECD, 2005e).

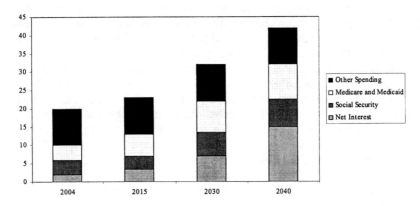

Source: US Government Accountability Office (2005).

Figure 2.2   US federal spending as a share of GDP

Budget policy

The OECD (2007) recommends that national governments strive for budget balance in the face of ageing. A target surplus of 1 per cent to pay down debt would be preferable. Tools to achieve this, according to the OECD 'daunting agenda', include closer adherence to expenditure, deficit and debt targets, greater transparency and a focus on the medium term.[8] Testing the so-called 'tax and spend' and 'spend and tax' hypothesis for nine developed countries, Koren and Stiassny (1998) found that in Austria, France and Italy the expenditure side is a leading driver of budget determination. In Germany, the Netherlands, the UK and the US, the tax side, or equivalently the tax and spend hypothesis, is central to budget policy.

Tax Competition

In many areas of the modern economy, companies are confronted with increasing integration of labour and capital markets and product markets. Trade barriers have been removed and improved means of transportation have resulted in a sizeable expansion of cross-border activity. Goods and services flow around the globe more freely than ever. The internationalisation of economies also opened up capital markets in the 1990s. The trends have increased dynamics and competition on world markets, including in the area of taxation. These issues are explored further in Chapter 8.

ICT and the digital highway have made markets more transparent and accessible. Firms and households are nowadays better informed on

---

[8] See IMF, Guidelines in Public Debt Management (21 March 2001), for responsible public debt management.

alternative investment opportunities and the tax systems of other countries, including specific tax arrangements that may be favourable to them, and this has improved the opportunities for tax planning.

The global developments have generated an entire new industry of ICT and internet companies and thereby reinforced the shift to a service-orientated economy. They have also increased the need for innovation and solid entrepreneurship. Indeed, high capital intensity and economies of scale are no longer analogous to a stable and high rate of return. In the knowledge-based economy of tomorrow, human capital, excellence and skills are crucial factors.

The battle for brains and companies
Governments worldwide have to reckon with the fiscal issues of economic globalisation and the world of the internet. Tax policy and particularly the so-called 'tax package' of a country are of growing significance in the battle for companies and brains. Human capital is a key determinant of labour productivity in the 21st century and competitiveness of economies on world markets. As countries face ageing workforces, the business world, government and academia are increasingly seeking high potential and talent. Not only is there thus a battle for companies, but also, increasingly, a battle for brains. The winners will be the countries with smart, creative and high-skilled workforces and dynamic entrepreneurship. A relatively low tax rate and special tax breaks can be helpful to attract foreign investment, companies and qualified personnel.

The Environment and Climate Change

In recent decades, concern over the global environment has grown rapidly. Never before have the issues surrounding air, water and soil pollution as well as depletion of natural resources and relative living space been as relevant as in contemporary times. Most compelling is perhaps global climate change and rising CO_2 emissions.

Figure 2.3 demonstrates that global temperatures have risen by 0.7°C since 1900. Most scientists now concur that the ongoing climate change is caused by rising concentrations of greenhouse gases in the earth's atmosphere, though some experts are still sceptical and argue that the link is too weak, largely as a result of methodological flaws in the research methods used. The report by the former chief economist of the World Bank, Sir Nicholas Stern (2007), estimates that global warming may shrink the world economy by up to 20 per cent in the long run if governments do not act now.

The UN's Intergovernmental Panel on Climate Change (IPCC, 2007) in its 4th Assessment Report in January 2007 estimated that between then and 2100, global temperatures could rise by over 3°C if no action is taken. The IPCC released further evidence in April 2007 that global warming is already having a discernible impact on all continents and most oceans. In a third report, published on 4 May 2007, the panel calculated that limiting global warming to 2°C by 2030, a critical level after which irreversible damage is done, will cost roughly $300 in annual income per head of the world population.

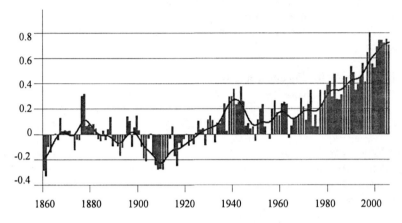

Source: HM Treasury (2006).

*Figure 2.3   Global average near surface temperatures, temperature
            difference (°C) with respect to end of 19th century*

Against this background, Chapter 9 discusses measures that aim to 'green' tax systems. The measures should not just discourage environmentally unfriendly behaviour, but promote the development of sustainable technologies and renewable energies as well.

BOX 2.1

The 21st century raises new issues for government in the area of taxation. The main challenges lie in adapting tax systems to globalisation, the world of the internet, ageing of workforces, rising international tax competition with an intensifying battle between countries for companies and brains, and climate change.

2.3 CHARACTERISTICS OF A 'GOOD' TAX SYSTEM

In 1776, Adam Smith put forward four so-called 'maxims with regard to taxes in general', that is, the 'canons of taxation'.[9] Later economists have added and refined several criteria, but the basics remain the same. The criteria for a good tax system give guidance on how the tax system or a specific measure should be designed to raise a given amount of revenue:[10]

- *Sufficient and stable revenue yield.* The tax system should collect adequate revenues to cover government spending. The revenue collection should be steady and to some degree resistant to business-cycle fluctuations, so as to allow government to implement a consistent financial and economic policy;
- *Efficiency.* The system should be as neutral as possible in achieving the objectives pursued. Taxes alter people's preferences to work, save, invest and consume. A 'good' tax system causes minimal distortions to economic choice and minimises 'excess burdens' that arise as a result. These distortions affect the size of the economy. Hence, enhancing the efficiency of the tax system can create a temporary increase in economic growth;
- *Equity, both vertical and horizontal.* Vertical equity implies that a government redistributes income from high- to low-income households in a manner that is perceived as fair. The tax structure should enable a government to make such a redistribution. Horizontal equity aims at equal treatment of people in a similar position. People in a dissimilar position should as a result be treated unequally. Two closely related principles are 'ability to pay' and 'benefit'. The former implies that individuals should be taxed according to financial capacity to contribute to the public provision of public goods and services. The latter suggests that people who in some way gain from public goods and services should be the ones to pay for them;
- *Minimum costs of administration and compliance.* Administration costs are incurred by government in collecting revenue, for example, the cost of processing tax returns, enforcing payment and providing taxpayer assistance. Compliance costs are incurred by individuals and businesses to meet their tax obligations. These include factors such as time spent on keeping records, learning about laws, and filling out forms oneself or the costs for hiring a tax adviser;

---

[9] Adam Smith was an 18th-century economist and moral philosopher. His classical book 'An Inquiry into the Nature and Causes of the Wealth of Nations' (1776 [2004]) is widely accredited for laying the foundations for the modern free market system.
[10] An elaborate discussion of the principles is offered in the Meade Committee Report (1978).

- *Flexibility, simplicity and transparency.* The political values of individuals and society as a whole alter over time, as do the ruling political parties and their view on the role of government. The tax system should be reasonably able to absorb these changes. A good tax system is transparent and easily comprehensible. Measures that are too complex are difficult to understand and fail to yield the intended effect. Moreover, a very simple tax rule may not be transparent if the rationale is unclear to people; and

- *International adaptability.* The more workers, capital and commodities are able to move freely between countries, the more pressing it becomes that national tax systems can be flexible in responding to international tax issues and rising competition. The tax system should thus enable governments to adapt policy to international economic developments and long-term trends.

BOX 2.2

A 'good' tax system ideally yields sufficient revenue to cover government expenses; deals with issues of efficiency and equity; imposes minimal costs of administration and compliance; is flexible, simple and transparent; and adapts to international economic developments. In practice, however, each tax proposal offers a compromise between conflicting characteristics, which is strongly influenced by the political make-up of a country. In all countries, citizens and elected officials express a wide range of opinions about optimal tax policy.

In practice, every concrete tax proposal strikes a compromise between conflicting criteria. The classical trade-off is between equity and efficiency. Redistribution requires higher taxes on the better-off, which in turn creates an excess burden since a distortion is created in the labour supply decision. But other characteristics conflict as well. Equity raises the costs of administration and many exceptions are created to make the system fairer at the expense of simplicity. Sales taxes, albeit easy to understand, encounter administrative problems when a distinction is made between taxed and tax-exempt commodities. This reduces efficiency. Moreover, some criteria are subjective in nature, such as equity and transparency, while others such as efficiency can be defined more objectively.

Ultimately, tax design is a matter of value judgement on how best to balance efficiency, equity, simplicity and the cost of administration and compliance. The outcome will vary across countries.

2.4 DIFFERENT TYPES OF TAXES

Direct and Indirect Taxes

For a formal definition of the term 'taxes' OECD (2005c), in their Interpretative Guide to the OECD classification of taxes confines it to compulsory and unrequited payments to general government. Fines unrelated to tax offences and compulsory loans paid to government are not included. Since every tax has a different effect on the behaviour of people and the economy as a whole, familiarity of classifications of taxes according to their legal definitions is essential. Such *legal* categorisation differs from the *economic* categorisation, which classifies taxes according to economic function.

A primary distinction is made between *direct* and *indirect* taxes. Direct taxes are typically levied on individuals and corporations. Think of income tax, which is formally divided into a *personal* and a *corporate* component, and also *wealth* and *inheritance* taxes. Indirect taxes are imposed on the spending on goods and services (which is a close proxy for consumption) and are more commonly known as 'consumption' taxes. They mainly consist of *value-added* and *excise taxes*, but also *export levies* and *import tariffs*. VAT, or value-added tax, taxes value added, or the difference between the cost of production and sales price. These taxes are indirect in a sense that the final burden intentionally rests elsewhere than where the tax has been imposed. Figure 2.4 provides a graphical illustration.

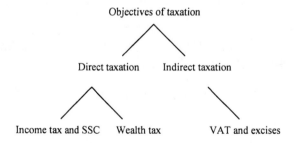

Figure 2.4 Primary categories of taxes

That some taxes are better suited to a particular purpose than others can be illustrated with some examples. For instance, if for environmental reasons the purpose is to discourage the use of cars, it is more efficient to levy an indirect tax on gasoline and tyres than to impose a tax on car owners through the system of income taxation. Although the latter would yield some effect, indirect taxation is much more effective. A scheme of in-work benefits to increase labour supply, in contrast, is carried out more efficiently through income tax. In fact, it would be nearly impossible to introduce such a scheme through an arrangement of indirect taxation. The incentives provided would be much weaker since people do not see a direct link between their working effort and the benefit provided. The two categories also differ in their administrative aspects.

Ad Personam and *In Rem* Taxation

In addition, some scholars distinguish between '*ad personam*' and '*in rem*' taxation (for example, Musgrave and Musgrave, 1989). The definitions resemble closely those of direct and indirect taxes. An *ad personam* tax takes into account the taxpayer's personal situation and his or her ability to pay. A basic condition is that it is imposed on an individual basis. By nature, an *ad personam* tax can be shaped to reflect a taxpayer's ability to pay by a progressive rate structure and special tax allowances. It enables governments to discriminate on the basis of marital status, age or number of children. These taxes are particularly useful when it comes to incorporating equity aspects into the tax system. Examples include personal income tax or expenditure tax. By contrast, *in rem* taxes are levied on activities or objects. Hence, they are independent of the personal situation of a taxpayer. Examples of *in rem* taxes are VAT and a tax on the holding of wealth.

Official Classifications

A more sophisticated classification is provided by the OECD (see Appendix 4). The overview categorises in greater detail most of the taxes that are imposed by government. The OECD publishes its classification of taxes in the annual *Revenue Statistics* (OECD, 2005c).[11] The classification distinguishes between six main subcategories of taxes:

- taxes on income, profits and capital gains;
- social security contributions;
- taxes on payroll and workforce;
- taxes on property;
- taxes on goods and services; and
- other taxes.

---

[11] The IMF also publishes a Classification of Revenue in the Government Finance Statistics Manual (IMF, 2002). The classification makes a primary distinction between taxes and social security contributions, and groups them accordingly.

Many different taxes exist within each category, and the list is by no means exhaustive. This is demonstrated by a country such as Hungary where over 200 different taxes are imposed by government. Because the OECD's electronic tax database is organised along the lines of its classification, it provides a useful reference point in finding relevant data and statistics.

Revenue Statistics and Trends over Time

Noticeable differences exist between the tax to GDP ratios in the surveyed countries. These differ from the government expenditure ratios that were presented in Chapter 1 in that there can be deficit finance. Large ratios often indicate more socially orientated countries with large governments, which is the case for most Western European countries. Low ratios are associated with more liberal or capitalist countries favouring less government involvement, a good example of which is the United States.

Table 2.1 shows that in Sweden, over 50 per cent of national product is allocated to the government, while in the US this is approximately half. In all the countries the total tax burden has increased since 1970. With the exception of Australia, the increase has been relatively modest in the Anglo-Saxon countries, the Netherlands and Germany. More dramatic increases can be found in Belgium, Finland, France and Sweden. Italy tops the list, with an increase of over 16 percentage points in total taxation.

The Tax Mix
By dividing the total tax revenue into separate categories according to the legal definition and expressing them as a fraction of GDP, we obtain insights into the composition of the tax to GDP ratio. SSCs, used by governments to conduct income politics, play a special role.[12] While formally not taxes, they are compulsory and represent a direct cost to the taxpayer. The collection of SSCs does not, however, represent direct government revenue that is freely allocable from the budget.

There are two distinct approaches to classifying SSCs (Messere et al., 2003). The '*Bismarck-Beveridge*' approach treats SSCs as compulsory social insurance premiums for which later benefits are received. Because of this 'link' they are not considered to be taxes. Under the '*Scandinavian-South Pacific*' approach, the revenue accruing from SSCs is used to supplement revenue from income and consumption taxes in financing social security expenditures. This approach considers them to be taxes and has become the accepted model in recent decades.

Redistribution through transfer payments is attained in two ways. First, through *social welfare*, whereby benefits not linked to earlier payments are distributed to the poor. The burden lies on the current labour force, since

---

[12] SSCs are mostly split into an employer and an employee component.

Table 2.1 The development of the tax to GDP ratio, 2005

	1970-74	1975-79	1980-84	1985-89	1990-94	1995-99	2000-05	% change
Australia	22.7	25.6	27.1	28.7	27.4	29.6	30.6	+7.9
Austria	34.9	37.5	39.4	40.4	40.9	43.0	43.0	+8.1
Belgium	35.3	41.2	42.7	43.6	42.6	44.5	45.0	+9.7
Canada	31.0	30.9	32.5	33.7	35.8	36.3	34.1	+3.1
Denmark	40.6	40.5	43.5	48.4	47.0	49.3	48.6	+8.0
Finland	33.5	38.0	37.2	41.2	45.1	46.2	45.4	+11.9
France	33.6	37.1	41.1	42.2	42.4	44.1	43.8	+10.2
Germany	34.2	36.6	36.9	37.0	36.6	36.7	35.6	+1.4
Ireland	28.7	29.6	33.5	35.2	34.0	31.9	29.8	+1.1
Italy	25.5	26.3	32.5	35.4	39.8	41.9	41.6	+16.1
Japan	21.2	22.6	26.4	28.8	27.6	26.9	24.9	+3.8
Netherlands	36.6	40.3	41.6	42.3	42.6	39.7	38.2	+1.6
Norway	37.9	40.7	42.8	43.1	40.9	41.9	43.6	+5.7
Sweden	39.5	46.1	47.5	51.0	48.8	50.6	51.0	+11.5
UK	34.3	34.1	37.2	37.2	34.6	35.6	36.4	+2.1
US	25.9	25.7	26.0	26.1	27.2	28.7	27.2	+1.3
OECD average	28.2	30.9	32.3	33.7	34.8	35.8	36.1	+7.9

Source: Electronic database OECD: Revenue Statistics.

there is no direct link between contributions paid and potential benefits derived (that is, a pay-as-you-go system). Examples include a minimum income guarantee for the unemployed and elderly, or housing subsidies. Second, *social insurance* requires people to pay contributions to social insurance funds. This constitutes an indirect redistribution. For example, health insurance redistributes from the rich to the poor and the young to the old as contributions demand an income, but not old age, while benefits mainly accrue to older people with small pensions.

Figure 2.5 shows the trend in specific tax to GDP ratios in the OECD area for the 1970-2004 period (five-yearly unweighted averages).[13] Only the major sources of revenue are included: personal and corporate income tax, general sales taxes and excises, property taxes and social security contributions. Payroll and 'other' taxes have been left out, since they constitute a small fraction of total revenue. A number of significant changes have occurred.

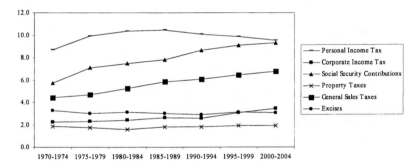

Source: Electronic database OECD: Revenue Statistics.

Figure 2.5 Developments in the composition of the tax to GDP ratio: OECD average

In the 1970s and early 1980s, personal income tax gained in importance, but this stabilised in the mid-1980s. After 1985 a declining trend can be observed. The revenue intake from SSCs has increased steadily and almost doubled. In 2004, SSCs were nearly as high as personal income tax. The reliance on general sales taxation has likewise gained gradually. Corporate income taxes have remained relatively stable, though after 1995 there was an upsurge. The revenue intake from excises has declined slightly compared to 1970, and property taxes have remained roughly equal.

---

[13] Appendix 5 lists the Revenue Statistics for each of the 16 OECD economies considered, the EU-15 and total OECD over the 1970-2004 period.

The *tax mix* shows the relative shares of tax receipts from the legal categories in total tax revenues. Hence, it is derived by dividing the revenues from the separate categories by total revenue collected. Together with the time series of the tax to GDP ratios, the tax mix reveals certain trends. This yields a more sophisticated picture of country practices over time.[14]

Figure 2.6 shows that on average the share of personal income taxation has been reduced by over 5 percentage points since the early 1980s. The trend is accompanied by a steady increase in the importance of SSCs and general sales taxes such as the VAT rate. The share of corporate taxation is more stable, although it has increased somewhat in the past decade. The reliance on excise and property taxes has declined more markedly.

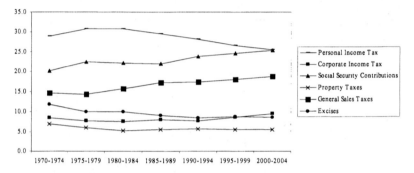

Source: Electronic database OECD: Revenue Statistics.

Figure 2.6   Developments in the tax mix: OECD average

BOX 2.3

The revenue statistics reveal that the OECD area as a whole has experienced a shift from personal income taxation to general consumption taxation in the 1970-2004 period. The importance of property taxation has reduced somewhat, that of excises more markedly. The revenue intake from corporate income tax has not changed much during the past three decades.

---

[14] Note that both variables are complementary in the information they provide. The tax mix reveals shifting between relative shares in the total tax revenue. These shifts might go unnoticed if just a particular tax to GDP ratio were considered. The latter may remain stable over time while the relative share in total tax receipts increases or decreases. At the same time a change in the share of one source of revenue in the tax mix may be compensated by a change in revenue from other sources. This effect can be filtered out by looking at the tax to GDP ratio.

2.5 THE TAX BASE, TAX RATES AND SPECIFIC TAX BREAKS

The first impression of a tax system is obtained by looking at a country's tax code. The tax code is the legal framework that defines tax base, tax rates and specific tax breaks. These three factors together determine the tax liability of a taxpayer.

The Tax Base

Before being able to apply a tax rate, the tax base must be determined. This is a definition of taxable factors, that is, what is taxed. In legal terms a central distinction is drawn between income, consumption and wealth as factors to be subject to taxation. The first two are dynamic or 'flow' variables, and represent transactions. The last is a 'stock' variable, since wealth is measured at a point in time. Because individuals and corporations are considered as separate legal entities under the law, country tax codes typically separate the taxation of income into a personal and a corporate income tax component.

The economic impact of a tax on each of these variables differs substantially in terms of timing, distributional efficacy and behavioural responses provoked. Contrary to the legal definition, economists therefore distinguish a labour (wages and salaries) and a capital (interest, dividends, royalties and capital gains) income component. This enables a separate analysis to be made of the effect of taxation on the main factors of production, labour and capital.[15]

BOX 2.4

According to their legal categorisation, taxes are imposed on income, consumption or wealth. In economic analysis a further differentiation can be made based on different criteria. For example, it is useful to divide income into that derived from the main factors of production labour, and capital. The effective tax liability can be reduced by tax deductions and tax credits.

Tax Rates and Schedule

When the tax base has been determined, the tax rate can be applied. The *statutory tax rate* is the rate as stated in the law. It is imposed on the tax base

---

[15] Note that capital income can be captured under personal and corporate income tax.

according to a specific rate schedule, which specifies the size of a taxable threshold, the number and size of subsequent tax brackets and applicable tax rates. The taxable threshold is the level of income at which the first tax is paid. A tax bracket is characterised as the band of income to which a particular tax rate applies.

If the tax rate is applied uniformly to both the labour and capital income component, we speak of a 'comprehensive' or 'global' income tax. By contrast, if labour and capital income are taxed separately, it is commonly referred to as a 'dual' income tax (see Chapter 4).

Tax Deductions, Credits and Exemptions

The final tax liability is determined by various tax exemptions, tax deductions and tax credits, or tax breaks in short, that are provided with distributive and regulatory purposes. This is illustrated in Figure 2.7. The difference between a tax *deduction* and a tax *credit* is that the former lowers taxable income, while the latter is a unit-for-unit reduction of tax payable. Tax credits can be either refundable so that the tax burden may be reduced below zero (a so-called 'negative' tax), or non-refundable in which case the maximum gain extends to tax payable. Beyond this point, credit is exhausted. An exemption simply precludes an essentially taxable event from the tax base.[16]

| Tax base (taxable income - deductions) | * | Tax rate | - | Tax credits | = | Tax liability |

Figure 2.7   Function for determining the tax liability

Tax breaks aimed at income redistribution
For example, many countries have incorporated into their tax systems a basic allowance of varying generosity. The allowance exempts a given amount of income deemed necessary for subsistence and is thus not taxable. Other common tax breaks are the deductibility of work-related, educational and medical expenses and child and earned income tax credits (EITCs) to support low-income households.[17]

---

[16] For example, with an income tax rate of, say, 40 per cent, a tax deduction or exemption of 20 per cent of income implies a final tax liability of 32 per cent. It is thus equal to a tax credit of 20 per cent of the tax bill, or equivalently 8 per cent of income.
[17] The earned income tax credit (EITC) is believed to promote the work effort of workers. The EITC is discussed in greater detail in Chapter 3.

Tax breaks to induce certain behaviour
All surveyed countries also make use of special tax breaks to induce specific behaviour such as the work effort (for example, participation or hours put in) and (specific) business investment (for example, in new buildings, business assets and energy-saving equipment), with investment tax credits and accelerated depreciation. In some cases an extra deduction for investment costs is allowed from taxable profits.

Introducing Tax Progression

Chapter 1 has already touched upon the issues of income inequality and redistribution. Generally speaking, three types of rate structure are discerned in the debate on the overall fairness of a tax system:

- *progressive tax rates*: the tax liability as a percentage of income increases as income increases;
- *proportional tax rates*: the tax liability as a percentage of income is the same regardless of the size of income; and
- *regressive tax rates*: the tax liability as a percentage of income decreases as income increases.

The rate schedule allows a country to shape the tax system according to its own preferences. Depending on government taste for redistribution, more or less tax progression can be built into a system.

A flat rate income tax
To analyse the concept of tax progression, we start with the most basic case where government imposes a flat rate income tax on total household income. This is illustrated graphically in Figure 2.8A.

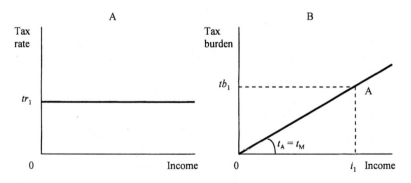

Figure 2.8   Schedule for the basic flat income tax

It can be seen that the same tax rate (tr_1) is imposed throughout the entire range of the income distribution. However, this is a rather stylised way to present an income tax schedule. Figure 2.8B presents an alternative, which is better suited to illustrate the case of tax progression. The function starts in the origin, so at zero income the tax burden is indeed zero. The figure indicates that the tax burden subsequently increases in a linear fashion as income increases. Hence, on every unit of income earned, the same rate of tax applies. The marginal tax rate, that is, the rate of tax paid on the last unit of income earned, is denoted by t_M and measured by the slope of line 0B. The average tax rate is denoted by t_A and is determined by dividing the total tax burden (tb_1) by gross income (i_1). Since both are equal, the tax system does not exhibit tax progression.

A flat rate income tax with basic allowance
Tax progression that aims at redistribution is commonly defined by an increasing *average tax rate* as income progresses and may, in contrast to what is routinely believed by commentators, be achieved with a flat rate income tax in combination with a tax deduction.

Figure 2.9A shows a basic flat tax schedule with a taxable deduction. Up to an income of i_1 the tax rate is zero. After this point the tax rate becomes tr_1. Figure 2.9B shows the alternative illustration. In spite of the flat rate, it can be seen that the system exhibits some progressivity due to the taxable deduction of 0A. The marginal tax rate is denoted by t_M and measured by the slope of line AB. The average tax rate is denoted by t_A and is again determined by dividing the total tax burden (tb_1) by gross income (i_1). It is measured by the slope of line 0B, or equivalently t_M(income – basic allowance), and shows that individuals with gross incomes at A or lower do not pay income tax. From point A on, taxes payable subsequently rise in relative terms as income progresses. Since t_M is typically larger than t_A the tax system exhibits progression.

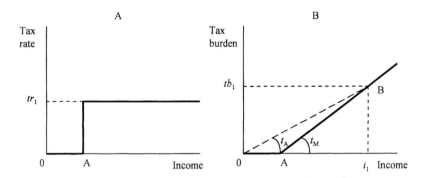

Figure 2.9   A flat income tax with taxable threshold

Indeed, a measure of tax progression is given by $S \equiv (1-t_M) / (1-t_A)$, which measures the percentage change in net income resulting from a 1 per cent change in gross income. With a marginal tax rate of, say, 40 per cent and an average tax rate of 30 per cent, we have $S = 0.86$. With a marginal and average tax rate of 50 and 30 per cent, respectively, $S = 0.71$.

A numerical example is presented in Table 2.2. It shows that people with an income of €10,000 or less do not pay taxes. This is because the tax deduction applies. Above €10,000 in earnings, a statutory tax rate of 30 per cent is imposed. As income subsequently increases, the average tax rate also rises. Eventually it approaches the marginal tax rate of 30 per cent.

Table 2.2   A flat income tax of 30 per cent, with a basic tax allowance of €10,000 and no additional deductions from income

Taxable income	Average tax rate[a] (t_A)	Marginal tax rate (t_M)
€10.000 or less	0	0
€20.000	15.0%	30.0%
€40.000	22.5%	30.0%
€60.000	25.0%	30.0%
€100.000	27.0%	30.0%

Note: [a] The function is linear, but still results in non-proportional taxes. With an equal marginal tax rate and tax allowance at the base of the income schedule, the tax deduction decreases in relative terms with rising income, so the average tax rate increases with the size of the tax base.

The notion thereby differs from what is popularly held to encompass tax progression, namely a rise in *marginal* tax rates. In practice, the size of various tax deductions rises with income, which makes the rate schedule less progressive than would be concluded at first glance. Furthermore, income-related benefit schemes are phased out as income progresses, which means that marginal tax rates for low- and middle-income households rise sharply as income increases. Caps on social security contributions may lead to low-income households facing relatively high marginal tax rates.

An income tax with multiple brackets and rates
By introducing multiple brackets and graduated tax rates, tax progression is increased further. Figure 2.10A demonstrates the rate schedule of an income tax with two tax brackets. It is basically similar to the previous example, albeit an extra bracket is introduced at an income of i_1 with a tax rate of tr_2. Figure 2.10B illustrates the alternative. Compared to the previous examples, the AB line becomes a curve that can be shaped in any desired way. At an income of i_1 the second bracket with a higher marginal tax rate sets in. The

average tax burden thereby also increases, which is indicated by a steeper angle of curve 0C as compared to 0B.

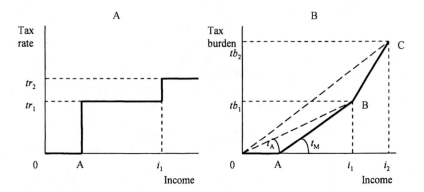

Figure 2.10 An income tax with taxable threshold and two tax brackets

A numerical example is shown in Table 2.3. Obviously, the average tax rate now climbs somewhat faster as income progresses, but only after €40,000. In the case of €100,000 in earnings, it lies well above the basic statutory rate of 30 per cent.

Table 2.3   An income tax of 30 per cent up to €40,000 and 40 per cent above, no additional deductions from income and a basic tax allowance of €10,000

Taxable income	Average tax rate (t_A)	Marginal tax rate (t_M)
€10,000 or less	0	0
€20,000	15.0%	30.0%
€40,000	22.5%	30.0%
€60,000	28.3%	40.0%
€100,000	33.0%	40.0%

In this way the tax burden can be shifted more or less heavily onto specific categories of earners. Commonly distinguished are low-, middle- and high-income earners, but it is of course possible to make any kind of distinction based on a certain income or other observable characteristics. As a corollary, the impact of taxation on economic behaviour is diverse. Making the system more progressive at the upper end of the income distribution implies relatively high marginal tax rates on individuals who fall within this income range. Only a few people pay taxes to raise the necessary revenue. This could decrease the number of hours worked by high-income earners. In contrast, shifting the tax burden to the lower end of the income distribution discourages unemployed low-skilled workers from finding work, particularly if the benefits for low-income households are high.

BOX 2.5

Tax progression is typically defined as a rise in average tax rates as income increases, not a rise in marginal rates as regularly perceived.

Three Measures of Effective Tax Rates

The complexity of modern tax systems means that very little can be said on the basis of the statutory tax rate alone (contrary to what often appears to be believed by many politicians, judging by their actions).[18] In fact, it is not uncommon for the statutory tax rate to deviate substantially from the effective rate of tax. The latter provides an indication of the actual tax burden faced by individuals or firms, thus ideally taking into account all factors that affect its level.[19]

The standard definition of an effective tax rate, as used in the King and Fullerton (1984) approach to taxation of capital, can be formulated as 'the share of the value added generated by an economic decision that is taken in tax' (see Heady, 2004). Two measures are computed: the *average* effective tax rate (AETR) and the *marginal* effective tax rate (METR). The AETR is calculated by dividing a taxpayer's total tax liability by his or her pre-tax income. The METR measures the effective tax burden on an additional unit of pre-tax income. This gives an idea of the incentives for work or investment.

Broadly speaking, the average tax rate provides a measure of the equity of a tax system, while marginal tax rates give an indication of efficiency. In practice, there is no single way of calculating effective tax rates due to the intricacy of modern tax structures and the difficulty of obtaining relevant data. Nevertheless, to get an idea, several approaches have been developed

---

[18] Differences in definition and interpretation under the tax law complicate matters further and have a significant impact on the final outcome in terms of the tax liability. It may also be difficult to evaluate certain earnings for tax purposes, such as fringe benefits.

[19] In some cases *implicit* taxes arise as well, for example, if a lower explicit tax burden on tax-favoured investment raises demand for this investment and leads to a bidding-up of prices. The investor then receives a lower rate of return which can be considered as an implicit tax, or shadow price or virtual tax. The tax is measured as the difference in the before-tax rate of return of a tax-favoured and tax-disfavoured investment. Import controls, licensing and minimum wages are other examples of measures that generate implicit taxes.

that offer insights into the effective tax burden on households and firms. Figure 2.11 gives an overview of the main (categories of) studies.

Effective tax rates	Average	Macro backward looking	Mendoza et al. (1994) (empirical)
		Micro forward looking	Devereux and Griffith (2001) (theoretical) Jacobs and Spengel (1999) (theoretical) OECD taxing wages (theoretical)
		Micro backward looking	Buijink et al. (1999) (empirical) Nicodème (2001) (empirical)
	Marginal	Micro forward looking	King and Fullerton (1984) (theoretical) Devereux and Griffith (2001) (theoretical) OECD taxing wages (theoretical)

Figure 2.11   Methods of calculating effective tax rates

Macro backward looking
The first type of studies relate aggregate data on the collected tax revenue to its corresponding tax base as obtained from the national accounts. The resulting tax ratios measure the effective burden on a macroeconomic level.[20] Because of their character, these studies are referred to as 'macro backward looking'. Commonly calculated are the effective tax burdens on labour and capital income and on consumption. Other ratios that are computed include taxes on corporate profit and a combination of taxes on labour income and consumption (the last two both reduce disposable income of households). A clear advantage of this method is the wide availability of data from which the

---

[20] Different terminology is used for indicating tax ratios that are calculated following the macro backward-looking approach. This may be confusing. Eurostat, for example, uses the term 'implicit tax rates', while other studies refer to 'effective' or 'average tax ratios'. See Volkerink and de Haan (2001) for a discussion on this.

ratios are relatively easy to compute. Since real-life data are used, the approach is empirical in nature.

Micro forward looking

A second set of studies, referred to as 'micro forward looking', design one or more hypothetical investment projects. By applying the project to a tax code, an approximation of the effective tax rate is derived. The approach is theoretical in nature, which at the same time is considered its major shortcoming: tax structures are usually more complex than can be simulated by a hypothetical case, but also behavioural responses are not accounted for. The approach nevertheless offers valuable insights into investment incentives by tax systems. In a similar manner the effective tax burden on households can be calculated.

Micro backward looking

A final category is 'micro backward looking', which use financial statement data to derive tax paid by a company and the corresponding tax base to compute the effective tax rate. Hence, they are empirical in nature. By using financial statements it becomes possible to conduct research on a sectoral or industrial level. Nevertheless, a commonly cited shortcoming of this method is that a certain 'endogeneity' exists. The tax liability as faced by corporations already reflects several provisions in a tax system, which cannot be separated from one another for evaluation. So by itself this reveals little about the specific incentives provided. Moreover, many companies are multinational and the tax liability in part depends on interaction with foreign tax systems.[21]

BOX 2.6

The information provided by the statutory tax rate is limited. Graduated rates and various tax breaks often create an effective tax rate that differs substantially from the statutory rate. Effective tax rates therefore provide a more accurate yardstick of the tax burden and (negative) incentives faced by individuals and companies.

A more detailed review of the three approaches, their pros and cons, is offered in Nicodème (2001). The OECD (2000b) conducts a more general

---

[21] Also see Graham (1996a) for a discussion of a method for calculating effective tax rates used in Shevlin (1990) and Graham (1996b). The method explicitly takes account of the asymmetric tax treatment that results from carrying losses as well as tax credits back and forward and is sometimes used in financial analysis on the cost of capital, financing policy (debt versus equity), corporate hedging and reorganisation, and the pricing of securities.

analysis. Together, both studies offer comprehensive insights and can be consulted for further study.

2.6   REDISTRIBUTON OF INCOME ACROSS HOUSEHOLDS

Income inequality and redistribution have always been a dominant concern to governments of OECD economies. The primary aim of redistribution is to achieve a fairer income distribution across households. Such redistribution aims to provide either (i) basic poverty relief and income support for the poor or (ii) more universal redistribution, including households in the middle bracket of the income distribution. The first system thus primarily focuses on (child) poverty relief; the second on mitigating inequality more generally. Government redistributes income through income transfers and other social spending, minimum wage increases, public control of executive salaries and progressive taxation.

Relative Poverty and Income Inequality

Figure 2.12 shows that relative poverty is still an acute problem in many sample countries, in particular in Italy, Japan and the United States. The Nordic countries (Denmark, Finland, Norway and Sweden) feature relatively little poverty.

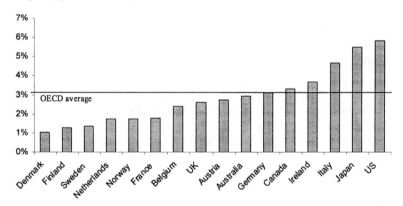

Source: Förster and d'Ercole (2005, Figure 8).

Figure 2.12   Composite measure of relative poverty, 2000

The composite poverty measure multiplies the poverty rate by the poverty gap in these countries. Indeed, not only does the number of people living in poverty matter, but also the average income gap to the poverty line. The measure provides an indication of the size of income transfers necessary to raise all those in poverty up to the benchmark poverty threshold, which is typically set at 50 per cent of median disposable income for the entire population.

There has been a significant change in the income distribution in many OECD countries. Generally speaking, income inequality has increased with the years (Förster and Pearson, 2002; Förster and d'Ercole, 2005). Table 2.4 shows the trends in income inequality for the sample countries from the mid-1970s to the year 2000. Most countries have experienced a small or moderate increase in income inequality.

Table 2.4   Trends in income inequality for the entire population

	Mid-1970s–mid-1980s	Mid-1980s–mid-1990s	Mid-1990s–2000
Moderate decline	Finland Sweden		
Small decline	Canada	Australia Denmark	France Ireland
No change		Austria Canada France Ireland	Australia Germany Italy Netherlands US
Small increase	Netherlands	Belgium Germany Japan Sweden	Austria Canada Denmark Japan Norway UK
Moderate increase	US	Finland Netherlands Norway UK US	
Strong increase	UK	Italy	Finland Sweden

Source: Förster and d'Ercole (2005, Table 1).

Figure 2.13 reproduced from Atkinson (2002), shows tax-based data for four OECD countries of the disposable income accruing to the top 1 per cent of the population as a share of the income of the top decile (that is, highest 10 per cent of incomes). Although declining until the 1980s, this suggests that there has been a steady increase in the income of the richest share of the population in Canada, the UK and the US since then. Hence, even if these countries have a relatively high GDP per capita, this income is increasingly concentrated among the top incomes.

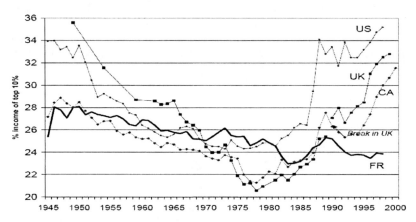

Source: Atkinson (2002)

Figure 2.13 Income accruing to the top 1 per cent as a share of the top 10 per cent of incomes

Why Tax Progression is often Ineffective

Income inequality often rises with economic growth, so income policies are necessary to create a more equitable distribution. Most existing tax systems, however, have limited scope to alter the income distribution.[22] When tax rates rise, tax bases typically tend to shrink. Tax progression is mitigated by a variety of tax deductions that are often concentrated on those with the highest incomes. For example, tax deductions, in contrast to tax credits, favour high-income individuals who benefit from higher marginal tax rates. Examples are the deduction for mortgage interest and vocational expenses, but also non-taxable fringe benefits that are more often enjoyed by medium- or high-income earners.

   Tax progression is also mitigated by caps on social security contributions and income-related social security that is phased out as income progresses. The latter may cause marginal income tax rates to rise sharply for low-income earners as income increases. Furthermore, the tax benefits on

---

[22] See, for example, Papadimitriou (2006) for a discussion of the effects of government spending and taxation on the redistribution of income.

contributions to pension plans tend to primarily favour high-income earners. For example, in the US, in some instances more than 50 per cent of the benefits may accrue to the top 10 per cent of incomes. By contrast, low-income households benefit little from income tax incentives since they contribute little and the gain is low or zero due to low or zero marginal income tax rates.

This is not to say that taxation has a trivial impact on the income distribution. For several countries, statistical evidence suggests that progressive income taxes have had a real and significant impact on the top share of incomes over the last decades (Atkinson and Salverda, 2005). But countries can improve existing arrangements by realising more effective tax progression (which might actually be achieved by lower marginal tax rates). As the above shows, maintaining steep marginal tax progression might compromise economic efficiency, while doing little in terms of equity. Research also shows that relative developments in the income distribution are determined by factors unrelated to the tax system. Changes to the income distribution arise from many autonomous socio-economic-like adjustments to gross wages, the composition of household and demographic changes. Joblessness is also a central reason for poverty.

BOX 2.7

In many countries, tax systems are far less progressive than would appear on the basis of statutory tax rates alone. Tax deductions that disproportionately favour people in high-income tax brackets, social security caps and the phase-out of benefits for low incomes are all factors that reduce the effectiveness of the tax system in achieving a more equitable income distribution.

Moreover, the experiences of various OECD countries show that the objective of achieving a fairer income distribution can be effectively realised by government expenditure programmes such as social benefit payments, family and child allowances, student grants and education, housing subsidies and so forth. A precondition would be that government targets the expenditure programmes appropriately, to support low-income households. We note that many of these expenditures are currently handed out via special tax subsidies (see next section on tax expenditures).

We also emphasise the role of better education systems in helping those individuals whose jobs are affected by 21st-century issues and trends. Greater labour market flexibility and welfare systems that cushion but do not hinder the effect of economic change and a broad, low and simple tax system with effective tax progression (see Chapter 10) can also contribute.

Technological Advancement and a More Individualistic Society

According to the IMF (2007b), technological change has contributed most to
the rise in income inequality in many countries over the past decades.
Financial globalisation, in particular foreign direct investment, has also
played a role in growing income inequality; however, contrary to popular
conviction, increased trade has been associated with a decline in income
inequality. Because of the opposing influences of financial and trade
globalisation, globalisation has had a much smaller overall effect than
technological change on the development of relative incomes. Looking
ahead, the IMF concludes that enhancing educational opportunities and the
access to finance could help improve the overall distribution of income. Also,
policies that facilitate the movement of workers from declining to expanding
sectors of the economy should contribute.

As country borders are fading, the scope for the tax system to alter the
income distribution declines. Governments face moving labour and capital,
rapid technological change, and global competition that raises the demand for
skills and talent. The *skills premium* at the higher end of the occupational
spectrum is likely to grow further. Thus far, supply of high-skilled workers
has been able to offset somewhat the rise in income inequality in many
European countries. But supply of high-skilled labour is not infinite and will
not match higher future demand (see, for example, Nahuis and de Groot,
2003; and Jacobs, 2004). The disparity between low- and high-skilled
workers and the gap between rich and poor thereby widens.

In conjunction with technological change, societies are becoming more
individualistic. A larger variety of social, work and living patterns in modern
economies mean that people can adapt more easily to take advantage of
redistributional arrangements. It becomes harder for government to separate
the 'lucky ones' from the 'needy ones' and achieve redistribution of
resources.

Migration is also enhancing cultural, social and ethnic diversity in
Western states and thereby increasing the heterogeneity of populations. For
countries with traditionally very homogenous populations, high social
solidarity, tax morality and acceptance of state intervention in society, such
as Sweden and Denmark, it will become more difficult to command current
high levels of taxation and welfare spending. These welfare states rely
heavily on the mutual trust and benevolence between state and population.
The system works only if it is not undermined by free riding (especially in
view of the free movement of persons in the EU), which strains the budget
and leads to a loss in productive capacity. Hence, those on a low income are
induced to enter a jurisdiction with a large welfare state because of generous
benefits, while high-income productive workers leave because of the
associated high tax burden. This reduces the effectiveness of the tax system
in achieving intended redistribution and increases the deadweight loss from

progressive taxes, making reform of existing redistributional institutions necessary and urgent.

Andersen (2004) concludes that to preserve present welfare arrangements in Denmark and ensure sustainable public finances, it is inevitable that the already high tax burden on citizens is raised. The permanent revenue rise would have to be in the order of magnitude of 2-3 per cent of GDP annually.

2.7   TAX EXPENDITURES AND GAINS FROM SIMPLICITY

Almost all tax reforms witnessed in OECD countries since the mid-1980s were driven by the principle of broadening tax bases and lowering tax rates. Many reforms aimed at promoting investment, entrepreneurial activity, risk taking, and providing improved work incentives. In the mid-1980s, top statutory income tax rates in most OECD countries surpassed 65 per cent (OECD, 2006a), whereas nowadays most top rates are below 50 per cent. Likewise, the corporation tax in OECD countries typically exceeded 45 per cent at that time, while the OECD average now lies below 30 per cent.[23] A central objective of these reforms has been to reduce tax distortions, which can be considered a significant impediment to economic growth.

The objective in any reform should be to achieve neutrality, in other words to minimise tax discrimination in favour of or against certain economic activities. In practice, this boils down to defining the income and consumption tax bases as broadly as possible and minimising the differentials in tax rates applied to these bases. Such a tax policy adheres to the principles of 'broad, low and simple'. Transparency helps to achieve these objectives by showing policy makers where improvements can be made.

The Tax Expenditure Concept

To enhance the transparency of tax systems, most OECD countries publish an annual 'tax expenditure' overview. According to the OECD, tax expenditures can be defined as the transfer of public resources that is achieved by reducing tax obligations with respect to a benchmark tax, rather than by a direct expenditure.[24] This notion rests on the assumption that tax rates should be applied on a comprehensive definition of the tax base, so as to maximise the revenue intake at any given rate.

Indeed, many tax expenditures constitute an alternative to direct government spending on subsidies to certain categories of taxpayers. They

---

[23] The reforms were started by the major tax system overhauls in the UK in 1984 and the US in 1986 under Thatcher and Reagan, respectively.

[24] See OECD (2004), which provides best-practice guidelines for budgeting tax expenditures.

are considered losses to the treasury. The 'tax expenditure' concept is controversial because tax payments are considered from the viewpoint of the government and not the taxpayer. Ultimately, taxation constitutes taxpayer money that is allocated to the government and not the reverse.

Politicians often tend to be unaware of the implicit costs of tax expenditures. For example, former US speaker of the House, Newt Gingrich (R-A),[25] normally a fierce advocate of stringent federal spending policy, once proposed when addressing the problems of the poor: 'Don't we have to bring the poor with us? Maybe we need a tax credit for poor Americans to buy a laptop'.[26] He later admitted that the remark had been somewhat 'dumb' by failing to recognise the corresponding cost of up to US$25 billion. This cost would make the credit in effect identical to a direct government expenditure programme, for example by the US government procuring a laptop for every poor American.

For this reason, the Assistant Secretary of the US Treasury for Tax Policy, Stanley S. Surrey, proposed drafting a list of tax expenditures in 1967. A main purpose was to gain insight into the potentially large costs of tax breaks and hidden entitlements to build momentum for tax reform.[27] Later the concept gained wide acceptance in other countries. The budgetary impact of tax expenditures lies roughly between 1 and 8 per cent of total income tax receipts in OECD countries.

To give an example of a tax expenditure budget, Table 2.5 lists the top 25 tax expenditures in the US personal and corporate income tax for the fiscal year 2007. The complete tax expenditure budget in the US currently encompasses 163 items, which amount to a cost roughly equivalent to 6.8 per cent of GDP.[28]

If all tax expenditures were repealed in the US, income tax rates could be cut across the board by roughly 25 per cent (McIntyre, 1996). Of course, this is not an entirely realistic supposition. But scaling back many of these tax expenditures can enhance efficiency, reduce sheltering activities and contribute to improving overall fairness of the tax system.

---

[25] Newton Leroy Gingrich joined the Senate in November 1978. Between January 1995 and January 1999 he was Speaker of the US House of Representatives.

[26] Cited from McIntyre (1996, p. 1).

[27] Surrey and McDaniel (1985) have provided a comprehensive account of the tax expenditure concept and how in their view it is best applied.

[28] Since 1974, the US Congressional Budget Office is required to publish annually a list that projects the tax expenditures for each of the following five fiscal years (Section 308(c) of the Congressional Budget Act of 1974).

Table 2.5   Tax expenditures in the United States (millions of dollars), 2007

Rank	Tax provision	Cost
1	Exclusion of employer contributions for medical insurance premiums and medical care	146,780
2	Deductibility of mortgage interest on owner-occupied homes	79,860
3	Accelerated depreciation of machinery and equipment	52,230
4	Capital gains exclusion on home sales	43,900
5	401(k) plans	39,800
6	Employer plans	52,470
7	Exclusion of net imputed rental income	33,210
8	Child credit	42,120
9	Deductibility of charitable contributions, other than education and health	34,430
10	Step-up basis of capital gains at death	32,460
11	Exclusion of interest on public-purpose state and local bonds	29,640
12	Deductibility of non-business state and local taxes other than on owner-occupied homes	27,210
13	Exclusion of interest on life insurance savings	20,770
14	Capital gains (except agriculture, timber, iron ore and coal)	26,760
15	Social security benefits for retired workers	19,590
16	Deduction for US production activities	10,670
17	Deductibility of state and local property tax on owner-occupied homes	12,810
18	Deferral of income from controlled foreign corporations	11,940
19	Keogh plans	10,670
20	Deductibility of medical expenses	5,310
21	Individual retirement accounts	5,970
22	Exclusion of workers' compensation benefits	6,180
23	Exemption from passive loss rules for $25,000 of rental loss	6,230
24	Expensing of research and experimentation expenditures	6,990
25	Earned income tax credit	5,147

Source: Budget of the US Government: Analytical Perspectives, Fiscal Year 2007.

Indeed, the OECD (2005d, p. 15) Economic Survey of the United States concludes: 'the complexity of the personal and corporate income taxes has steadily increased since the last major tax reform in 1986, largely due to the continued proliferation of deductions, exemptions, credits and tax shelters that have substantially narrowed the tax base and created many distortions, several of which harm incentives to save'.

BOX 2.8

Tax expenditures are the cost to government of providing tax breaks. This is based on the assumption that tax rates should be applied on a comprehensive definition of the tax base, so as to maximise the revenue intake at any given rate. The costs of tax expenditures to the treasury typically range between 1 and 8 per cent of GDP in OECD countries.

Many of these expensive tax subsidies are concentrated on the relatively well-off and contribute negatively to the aim of achieving a fairer income distribution. They also raise the efficiency cost of redistribution by forcing governments to impose higher marginal tax rates.

To give an example, the Netherlands employs a large mortgage interest deduction. The tax subsidy totals €7 billion in tax revenue forgone (roughly 1.3 per cent of GDP), which leads to several adverse side-effects. Low costs of owner-occupied housing artificially raise demand for privately owned dwellings and reduce the supply of rental housing. Accordingly, purchase or rental prices are needlessly high. The government is forced to keep rental prices low with housing subsidies, which requires higher taxes that reduce labour market incentives and other economic activity. The deduction itself also narrows the tax base and necessitates higher marginal tax rates. Abolition would facilitate an income tax cut of 2.75 percentage points across the board and create a long-run welfare gain of €1 billion, or 0.2 per cent of GDP (van Ewijk et al., 2006).

A number of countries now periodically evaluate certain tax expenditures on effectiveness. In the case of an insufficient score, the measure is repealed. Such a periodical evaluation is highly recommended. It enhances the overall effectiveness of government spending and the tax system in economic policy.

Tax Complexity Itself is a Kind of Tax[29]

While taxes finance public spending, Chapter 1 demonstrated that high tax rates do not always relate to high tax revenues. As the tax burden increases, the scope for raising additional revenue withers on account of behavioural

---

[29] As was once remarked by US Senator Max Baucus (D-MT).

responses. There are also many bad practices in collecting the required revenue.

A high tax burden coincides with many different taxes, high tax rates and exceptions that erode the tax base. Tax complexity puts compliance at risk as taxpayers do not fully comprehend the system and make mistakes. Others plainly ignore what is asked of them, which often goes unnoticed under systems of voluntary compliance. This forces any committed tax administration to raise audits and thus the cost of administration. Tax collection itself may also be subject to considerable improvement. Estimates indicate that in 2002 the US IRS fell short of collecting no less than $20 billion in taxes legally due, but unpaid by taxpayers (McKinnon, 2002, cited in Rosen, 2005, p. 68). Turning this task over to private debt-collection agencies, it is argued, could recover most of these taxes in a cost-effective manner.

Cutting compliance costs for businesses

The joint study 'Paying Taxes: The Global Picture' by the World Bank (2006b) and the international accounting firm PricewaterhouseCoopers estimates that firms and households in Italy, Japan and the US put in 360, 350 and 325 hours, respectively, to comply with tax rules (see Table 2.6). By contrast, Norway and Ireland have relatively simple tax systems: on average, individuals and corporations spent only 87 and 76 hours on filing tax returns and satisfying other formal requirements.

There are also large differences in the volume of tax codes. With 8,300 pages of primary tax legislation, the UK ranks number one of OECD countries in terms of pages used to collect the required revenue. Australia and Japan come second and third with 7,750 and 7,200 pages, respectively. Countries such as Belgium and Sweden manage to make do with 830 and 700 pages, respectively. There is also substantial differentiation in the number of tax payments between countries. In France, as many as 33 different taxes have to be administered, while in Norway there are only five.[30]

The financial costs of compliance are substantial. The US Joint Economic Committee (2005a) estimates that the US tax code, which currently contains more than 1.4 million words, imposes a cost of compliance of $83 billion annually, or about 0.8 per cent of GDP. Other numbers are also cited. For example, *The Economist* of 15 April 2006 reports that tax returns take up approximately 3.5 billion hours of American households' time, or on average 26 hours per household. In total, approximately $140 billion was spent on compliance. Similar figures have been found for other countries.

---

[30] A salient detail is that businesses in the 175 countries covered file on average 35 pages of tax returns annually. Since there are approximately 250 million registered businesses and a mature tree produces around 85,500 sheets of paper, tax compliance is equivalent to a loss of 100,000 trees annually, even without accounting for households and after accounting for countries where returns can be submitted electronically.

Table 2.6   The number of tax payments and compliance time, 2004

	Tax payment (number per year)				Time to comply (hours per year)			
	Total	PIT	CIT	Other	Total	PIT	CIT	VAT
Australia	11	3	1	7	107	18	35	54
Austria	20	4	1	15	272	96	80	96
Belgium	10	2	1	7	160	40	24	96
Canada	10	3	2	5	119	36	47	36
Denmark	18	2	1	15	135	70	25	40
Finland	19	2	13	4	264	200	16	48
France	33	24	1	8	128	80	24	24
Germany	32	3	15	14	105	35	30	40
Ireland	8	1	1	6	76	36	10	30
Italy	15	1	2	12	360	320	24	16
Japan	15	2	3	10	350	140	175	35
Netherlands	22	12	1	9	250	150	40	60
Norway	3	1	1	1	87	15	24	48
Sweden	5	2	1	2	122	35	50	36
UK	7	1	1	5	105	45	35	25
US	10	3	2	5	325	100	200	25

Source: World Bank (2006b).

Figure 2.14 shows a formula to measure total cost of taxation, including the efficiency cost as discussed in Chapter 1.

Tax liability + Excess burden + Compliance cost = Cost of taxation to the taxpayer

Figure 2.14   Function for determining the cost of taxation to the taxpayer

Small measures may already help to reduce costs. For example, in 1986 the Australian Taxation Office (ATO) abandoned its system of manual assessment of tax returns (occupying roughly a third of the staff with routine scrutiny of yearly returns), replacing it by a system of self-assessment. Individual returns have since been accepted at face value and checked randomly by computer audits and information matching. Simultaneously, taxpayers were granted a fixed deduction of expenses without substantiation below a certain threshold. In the event of an audit, substantiation is required only when claiming expenses above the threshold. The mechanism actually increased revenue for the ATO, as fewer taxpayers claimed expenses in excess of the threshold (Porter and Trengove, 1990).

Simplicity and compliance

With the majority of tax systems collecting well over 40 per cent of GDP, simplicity is an essential feature for an efficient tax system. A simple tax system features fewer exceptions in the tax base and suffices with lower tax rates. This reduces the scope for tax avoidance, evasion and fraud. Regardless of how hard it tries, government is always one step behind in closing a loophole or tax shelter, which may take years due to the legislative procedures, and new tax planning strategies conceived by smart tax lawyers (and unwittingly, it often creates fresh tax-avoidance opportunities in the process).[31]

Simpler tax systems with lower tax rates and progressivity also provoke less resistance with the public and encourage firms and households to leave the underground economy (see, for example, Trandel and Snow, 1999). Tax loopholes and tax shelters erode confidence in the tax system and lead people to believe that the system is unfair. Since the majority of tax systems rely heavily on voluntary compliance, compliance is higher in countries with simple tax legislation and thus so are total tax revenues. By contrast, if taxpayers do not find the tax system credible, then voluntary compliance and tax revenues are likely to decline. This is illustrated in Figure 2.15.

Number of taxpayers	*	Tax liability	*	Compliance rate	=	Total tax revenue

Figure 2.15 Function for determining total tax revenue

BOX 2.9

The existing tax legislation imposes substantial costs on taxpayers. Paying taxes in Italy, Japan and the US demands on average four times as much time as in Ireland and Norway. Simple tax legislation encourages businesses to enter the formal economy, and reduces the number of exceptions that erode the tax base and the scope for tax avoidance. Countries with simple tax legislation therefore typically collect more revenue than those with complex systems.

---

[31] A 'loophole' is a provision of the tax code that allows an individual or company to reduce its tax bill. A 'tax shelter' typically refers to an investment scheme that achieves the same objective.

Three Stylised Examples

Here we consider how the issues discussed work out in three stylised examples. The examples do not take into account behavioural responses.

A personal income tax reform
In an effort to reform the personal income tax system the hypothetical government of country X decides to scrap all exemptions, deductions and graduated rates in favour of an income tax with a basic allowance and a flat rate.[32] Table 2.7 gives some characteristics of the tax system before the reform. In the example, the average tax rate is 30 per cent of the net income tax base and 22.5 per cent of the gross income tax base.

The guiding principle of the reform is to achieve revenue neutrality. Hence, an equal amount of revenue should be collected after as before the reform. There is no budgetary flexibility so the reform is financed solely by the elimination of tax exemptions and deductions. Since the total tax deduction is 200 billion units and there are 40 million taxpayers, a flat rate income of 30 per cent and a basic allowance of 5,000 units for every taxpayer could theoretically be constructed. The taxable base would become 600 billion units (800 billion minus 200 billion). A tax rate of 30 per cent would then generate tax revenues of 180 billion units.

Now consider taxpayer A, who has an annual taxable income base of 4,000 units and no deductions except for the basic allowance. Before the reform he or she pays the low rate of 10 per cent over a tax base of 2,000 units (4,000 minus the basic allowance of 2,000), which amounts to 200 units in taxes payable. After the reform the tax becomes 30 per cent over zero. In other words, he or she does not owe any taxes because taxable income lies below the threshold of the basic allowance.

By contrast, taxpayer B has gross annual earnings of 15,000 units. B is also entitled to the basic allowance of 2,000 units and an earned income allowance of 1,000. Before the reform B pays income tax over a taxable base of 12,000 units (15,000 minus deductions of 3,000). He/she would then be liable for 2,100 units in tax (the sum of 10 per cent over the first bracket of 5,000 units; 20 per cent over the second bracket of 5,000 units; and 30 per cent over the remaining 2,000 units in taxable income). After the reform B pays an amount of 3,000 units in income taxes (that is, 30 per cent over 15,000 minus the basic allowance of 5,000), which is significantly more than 2,100 units.

---

[32] For a comprehensive overview of the advantages of a flat rate tax, see Heath (2006) of the Tax Payer's Alliance (TPA), Britain's independent grassroots campaign for lower taxes. According to the author, flat rate taxes would reduce excess burdens, increase transparency and simplicity, reduce tax evasion, cut back on excessive government and boost economic growth.

Table 2.7   Characteristics of the income tax of country X before tax reform

Number of taxpayers		40 million
Gross tax base without tax deductions and exemptions (a GDP per capita of 20,000 is assumed).		800 billion
Total tax deductions and exemptions		200 billion
Basic allowance of 2,000 per person	80	
Allowance for children	10	
Earned income allowance for workers	45	
Deductible vocational expenses	35	
Deductible pension contributions	10	
Exemptions for certain types of income	10	
Deductible extraordinary expenses	7	
Deductible donations	3	
	200	
Net tax base (800 billion minus 200 billion)		600 billion

The following rate structure applies

Less than 5000	10%
5,000 and less than 10,000	20%
10,000 and less than 20,000	30%
20,000 and less than 40,000	40%
40,000 and less than 80,000	50%
Over 80,000	55%

Total annual tax revenue	180 billion

The main caveat, however, is that such a calculation of the flat tax ignores any *behavioural* reactions in labour supply and capital accumulation. For example, the flat tax may lead to higher (lower) labour supply for those people who face lower (higher) marginal tax rates. In addition, it needs no further explanation that the above sketched reform is politically unrealistic given current sentiments on ability to pay and income equality. The distributional effects would be dramatic and so unevenly spread that no government would dare to take such a step. Voters would simply not accept the outcome.

A corporate income tax reduction
A tax reform is not necessarily revenue neutral. For this reason, it is worthwhile to provide an illustration of a tax reduction. The example

describes three scenarios whereby the government of country X reduces its corporate income tax rate of 30 per cent to 25 per cent. The following conditions apply:

- the total of a country's profit corporate base amounts to 100 billion units;
- the tax base to which the tax rate applies is 80 billion units (which is less than 100 billion because the tax law permits certain tax breaks up to 20 billion, such as accelerated depreciation of capital outlays and tax credits);
- the tax revenue is 24 billion units (30 per cent of 80 billion); and
- the effective tax rate is 24 per cent.

Example 1   A tax reduction that is entirely financed out of general funds. The taxable base remains the same. Lowering the rate from 30 to 25 per cent reduces the revenue intake by 4 billion units and the effective tax rate from 24 to 20 per cent.

Example 2   A tax rate reduction that is fully compensated by a broader tax base. The tax base is broadened with 16 billion units by the following limitations:

- the deduction of depreciation for tax purposes is tightened by 6 billion units;
- exemptions are curbed by 5 billion units;
- deductible expenses are reduced by 3 billion units; and
- the deduction for contingency provisions is limited by 2 billion units.

The tax base of 80 billion units is broadened to 96 billion by these measures. Hence, the rate cut is fully financed:

- 30 per cent on a tax base of 80 billion units equals tax revenue of 24 billion units; and
- 25 per cent on a tax base of 96 billion units equals tax revenue of 24 billion units.

The effective tax rate thus remains 24 per cent.

Example 3   A tax rate reduction is financed by a broadening of the tax base and an increase in environmental levies on households. The tax base is broadened in a similar manner as described above, albeit this time by only 10 billion units. At the same time, the environmental levies are increased so as to generate additional tax revenue of 1.5 billion units. Thus:

- 25 per cent on a tax base of 90 billion units equals tax revenue of 22.5 billion units; and
- an increase of environmental levies equals tax revenue of 1.5 billion units.

This once more generates a total tax revenue of 24 billion units. Since households now pay part of the tax, the effective corporate tax rate has been reduced to 22.5 per cent.

Tax breaks to promote investment

Accelerated depreciation   Accelerated depreciation reduces the effective tax rate on investment by deferring the tax liability. The tax deferral from accelerated depreciation lowers the effective tax rate on investment. The tax advantage depends on the tax rate, the interest rate and the lifetime of the investment. For example, company Y purchases a new building for 15 million units in 2007. According to the standard accounting rules for tax purposes, depreciation takes place on a linear basis. If we assume a depreciation period of 30 years and a residual value of 6 million units, the annual rate of depreciation becomes 300,000 units (15 million minus 6 million divided by the number of years).

If company Y is now allowed to depreciate the building at an accelerated pace of, say, 40 per cent in the first year, depreciation in the first year would amount to 3.6 million units. Compared to the 'normal' situation, an additional deduction of 3.3 million units is allowed (3.6 million minus 300,000). In the remaining years, the company depreciates the residual 5.4 million units as usual on a linear basis (other variants keep the accelerated rate in place in the years after, until annual depreciation falls below 300,000).

In total, the same amount of 9 million units would be deducted from taxable profits in 30 years time. However, because the initial allowance for tax purposes exceeds the standard deduction, accelerated depreciation creates a liquidity and a deferral gain. The liquidity gain arises in the year that the extra deduction from taxable profits is granted, that is, 3.3 million units. The extra deduction reduces the tax bill in that year, which means that the taxpayer has extra cash at his/her disposal. In later years, the deduction for depreciation is automatically lower so the benefit is cancelled out. The gain from deferral arises because the income is at the disposal of the taxpayer for a longer period. It is measured by the difference in the net present value (NPV) of the tax savings that result from accelerated depreciation and the NPV of the tax savings that result from 'normal' depreciation, relative to the acquisition price of the asset. In other words, the implicit return on the tax 'saved' goes untaxed, which reduces the effective rate of tax.

An investment tax credit   Using a hypothetical case we can also demonstrate the workings of an investment tax credit. Suppose that the government of country X wishes to promote investment in energy-saving equipment. The total annual amount of investment without the tax credit is equal to 100 million units per year. The objective is to raise the amount of spending to 120 million units annually. To achieve this, the government designs a credit of 20 per cent of the purchase price of energy-saving equipment. Hence, a business that invests an amount of 100,000 units obtains a credit for 20,000 units from the tax authorities. After five years the credit is repealed by a so-called 'sunset provision', which limits the credit's life span.

Taking the planned amount of 120 million units as a reference point, the government estimates the cost of the credit at 24 million units per year (20 per cent of 120 million). This means that an amount of 24 million units is spent annually to generate 20 million in additional investment.

After enactment of the investment tax credit, the total amount of energy-saving investment assumes the following path (under equal price levels). In 2007 the level of investment is 110 million units; in 2008, 120 million; in 2009, 125 million; in 2010, 110 million; and in 2011 investment falls back to 100 million. Hence, over the 2007-11 period the total cost of the tax credit to the government amounts to 113 million units, while the extra investment is only 65 million. Note that a direct subsidy is likely to have yielded a one-to-one efficacy, so roughly 113 million incremental investment would be generated (there might be some crowding-out).

No sensible government should thus agree to a credit under these terms. The example illustrates that the costs and benefits of the tax stimulus need to be evaluated accurately to ensure effectiveness, which includes a proper *ex ante* and *ex post* analysis. Only then might a government elect a tax measure. Limiting the credit's life span to three years would in this case also have enhanced the cost effectiveness of the credit.

2.8   TAXATION AS AN INSTRUMENT OF ECONOMIC POLICY

The traditional function of raising revenue to finance government spending will remain the primary objective of taxation. Apart from this, the non-revenue-raising function has gained in importance, but not without certain criticism. Using taxation as an instrument of economic policy harms the traditional function and results in an increasing complexity of the system and its enforcement.

However, taxation cannot be seen independently from many other government policy areas. Examples include increasing tax competition whereby countries try to enhance the attractiveness of their tax systems to foreign companies and investors; tax policies that stimulate the labour market; and the incorporation of environmentally related tax incentives into systems. Taxation is also used to conduct income politics. As a tool, it must be carefully evaluated against other government policy instruments.[33]

Such an assessment generally takes into account four criteria: effectiveness, efficiency and whether a tax measure can reasonably be fitted into the existing legislation and structure of administration. In practice, political preferences and compatibility with international law also play an important role. For example, the EU member states are bound by both general and special tax rules with regard to the national tax system.

Effectiveness and Efficiency

Effectiveness relates to the extent to which a measure produces the intended result, regardless of the cost. The decision that needs to be made is whether a tax measure is more effective than any other policy instrument. Taxation is a broad instrument with generic effects. The more specific a measure becomes, the higher the risk for 'leakages' to taxpayers who strictly speaking should not be targeted. This risk can only be taken away by using a different policy instrument than taxation, perhaps a subsidy.

A measure is more efficient if the desired result can be achieved at lower cost. This implies that the preferred measure is one which, with the available means, achieves the largest effect at the lowest cost (including the cost of executing policy). Generally speaking, taxation has the advantage that the existing structure of administration and money flows can be exploited. A measure that avoids additional administration and the filing of tax returns is favoured over measures with equal effectiveness that do not do so.

Compatibility with Existing Arrangements

The final condition which states that a tax measure can reasonably be inserted into the existing tax structure deals with issues of technical feasibility, enforceability, options for audit and susceptibility to evasion. Questions that play a central role in making this assessment include: to what extent does the measure introduce new elements into the existing tax legislation; does the tax administration already possess information that can be used for enforcement;

---

[33] As noted in the introduction to Chapter 1, the most important other financial government instruments are subsidies, state aid and state participations in companies. An economy can also be effected by means of regulation.

and how far can the legal provisions be transferred into clear and workable criteria for conduct?

Equity Considerations

In addition to these criteria, there is the more fundamental issue of horizontal equity. This principle requires that all equal cases be treated as equal, which implies that only on the basis of objective criteria, as opposed to subjective criteria, can it be determined whether a taxpayer is eligible for a certain tax arrangement. Hence, taxation is likely to be an instrument with a broad and generic effect.

To create higher economic welfare, a sustainable economic growth and favourable development of the labour market are essential. The tax system can contribute to achieving this. The above shows that taxation can form an integral part of general economic policy. The decision on whether a tax measure is the appropriate policy instrument can be based on the aforementioned criteria.

BOX 2.10

Regarding only the revenue-raising function of taxation ignores the synergy that arises when using tax instruments for non-tax policy objectives. Many countries have explicitly chosen to use the tax system as an instrument in other areas of government. The main criteria on which to base this assessment are effectiveness, efficiency and whether a tax measure can reasonably be fitted into the existing (tax) legislation.

Transition Rules in Tax Reform

Many OECD countries are, or have been in the past decade or two, in the process of reforming their tax systems to improve efficiency. These systems are based on historical socio-economic developments, often an inadequate political process and, crucially, the coming and going of governments with different political agendas. Tax provisions have regularly been added and removed at will, leaving fragmented and less-effective pieces of tax legislation. These reforms are dynamic processes where the cost of transition must be borne in mind. They also need to provide generous transition times for their proposals to mobilise support for reform.

Of course, the main difficulty in adjusting the tax system to new socio-economic conditions is that the demand for a new tax arrangement has to compete with existing arrangements that already confer specific benefits on certain taxpayers or groups of taxpayers, often with strong political influence.

Every reform inevitably impinges on incomes and causes distributional effects. This creates winners and losers. Hence, so-called 'windfall gains' and 'windfall losses' in tax reform benefit some people, while others become worse off (even closing a loophole is likely to be inequitable, which makes it hard to achieve in practice).

Politicians need to be aware of these income effects, especially taking into account the negative ones. Transitional effects can be mitigated in several ways:

- *grandfather clauses* that provide transitional relief by exempting certain taxpayers from the new legislation. This leads to an unequal tax treatment of taxable activities over time;
- *phase-in period* with gradual implementation to give taxpayers time to adapt and comprehend the new legislation;
- *grandfather clauses and phase-in period* by making certain taxpayers subject to the first, while others are subject to the second; and
- *new and old legislation*, yet another variant that would immediately tax new activities, such as new investment, under the new legislation, while existing assets are subject to phase-in.[34]

Although these measures are advocated on equity grounds, they are likely to reduce the momentum and efficiency of tax reform or a proposed measure. Grandfathering also makes the system more complex in the transition period.

The Argument for Self-financing in the Political Debate

In tax reform or with the introduction of a specific tax measure, the government budgetary office makes an *ex ante* assessment of the cost involved and the overall budgetary impact. This calculation can give rise to a discussion between the Minister of Finance as keeper of the treasury and other ministers. For clarification, we give a simplified example derived from actual experience.

The Minister of Economic Affairs of country X proposes an extra tax subsidy for advanced technological investment that leads to substantial energy savings. The Cabinet of Ministers endorses the measure and commits a yearly amount of 0.5 billion units in the form of a tax credit to companies that invest in energy saving. The amount represents an annual expense to the treasury. On enactment of the tax credit in 2008, the total business spending on the energy-saving investment is 1 billion units. For many companies, however, the return is still too low to make the investment viable.

---

[34] This variant has been outlined by the US Department of Treasury (see US Government Accountability Office, 2005).

The Minister of Economic Affairs expects that the tax credit will induce additional investment, as the credit brings down the acquisition cost and thereby increases the return on investment. Research shows that total investment in 2008 will be 1.8 billion units (that is, 0.8 billion extra due to the credit); a total of 2.0 billion in 2009; and also 2 billion in 2010 and later years. The study also shows that the extra investment will stimulate economic activity. This leads to higher tax revenues of 0.2 billion units in 2008 and 0.3 billion from 2009 on.

The minister then reasons as follows. The government has apportioned 0.5 billion units from the treasury. Since the tax credit additionally induces higher growth, a structural amount of 0.3 billion units may be added to this (that is, the revenue effect from self-financing). Hence, the Minister of Economic Affairs is of the opinion that a total amount of 0.8 billion units can be spent, which allows him to design a tax credit of 40 per cent of the acquisition costs of the energy-saving investment (that is, total investment is approximated at 2 billion from 2009 on). The Minister of Finance chooses a different approach. He thinks it is irresponsible to assume self-financing. The chances of non-realisation are too great. He therefore presumes that an annual amount of 0.5 billion units is available. On the basis of the estimated 2 billion units of investment, he designs a tax credit of only 25 per cent.[35]

In practice, the view of the Minister of Finance as guardian of the treasury is usually adhered to. Prudence requires that budgetary estimations for a tax cut or subsidy do not take into account any prospective self-financing. If the incremental revenue is not collected, the gap in the budget has to be covered by alternative taxes or other sources of finance. In the case of a tax rise, however, governments should account for behavioural responses as was demonstrated in Chapter 1 under the Clinton tax rise, which effectively collected only an estimated $8.4 billion of the projected of $19.3 billion in revenues.

2.9   BRIEF SUMMARY

This chapter has outlined various aspects in the tax design and formal working of a tax system. The primary purpose of the tax system is to collect the revenues needed to fund government. Particularly since the Second World War (1939-45), OECD economies have increasingly used taxation to achieve a variety of economic, social and environmental objectives. As a result, the current tax systems have become overly complex.

---

[35] It should be noted that there is a difference in effectiveness between a tax credit of 40 per cent and a tax credit of 25 per cent. The above example does not make allowance for this.

The chapter started with a discussion of the six main criteria for a well-tailored tax structure. The criteria are also widely accepted for assessing (fundamental) tax reform. In brief, these criteria include:

- a sufficient and stable revenue yield;
- efficiency;
- equity, both vertical and horizontal;
- minimal costs of administration and compliance;
- flexibility, simplicity and transparency; and
- international adaptability.

Ultimately, tax design is a value judgement on how to best balance these criteria. There are a wide variety of views and opinions among citizens and governments about a good tax system. Indeed, there are no single right answers, only approximations and many different interpretations.

In addition to these characteristics, a number of (international) trends and developments will increasingly leave their mark on tax design. Current tax systems are insufficiently equipped to respond to these developments:

- globalisation with increasing competition on world markets;
- the world of the internet and e-commerce;
- the effect of ageing on labour markets and government finances;
- tax competition; and
- environmental developments and climate change.

The chapter subsequently examined different types of taxes and their categorisation. The impact of taxation is assessed mainly against its effect on macroeconomic variables such as labour, capital and consumption. The formal legal framework of tax systems differs from such a categorisation. For example, a tax on capital may take the form of a corporate income tax, a wealth tax or perhaps a tax on the imputed rents from owner-occupied housing. Similarly, the legal definition of a personal income tax covers both a labour and a capital income component and income tax involves both personal and corporate tax. Formal classifications such as those of the OECD help policy makers to get a good overview of the available taxes.

The tax base, tax rate and special tax breaks of a particular tax in turn determine the final liability faced by an individual taxpayer. They also determine the amount of tax progression built into the system. We have noted that the scope of the tax system in achieving a more equitable income distribution is limited by various factors, such as tax deductions that disproportionately favour high incomes, social security caps and the phase-out of benefits for those on a low income. The tax breaks also call for higher marginal tax rates that distort economic choice.

Simplicity is crucial. Existing tax systems are complicated and generate significant costs of administration and compliance to government, households and firms alike. It is best to promote tax compliance by keeping tax rates moderate, rather than to create complex anti-avoidance legislation in response to high tax rates and abuse of tax breaks. Furthermore, a complicated tax regime generates less revenue than a simple tax regime, which leaves less scope for avoidance strategies and encourages businesses to leave the informal and enter the formal economy. Therefore there appears much to be gained from a broader tax base combined with a lower tax rate and a simpler tax arrangement.

Finally, the chapter has set out a number of criteria for using taxation as a tool to accomplish policy objectives other than the primary one of raising revenue. Use of taxation depends on the relative effectiveness and efficiency of a tax measure, compared with other instruments in government. Compatibility with existing arrangements and international law also play a role. The guiding principle in income tax design should be a comprehensive tax base with the least number of exceptions possible (see also the concluding Chapter 10 for a summary of the advantages of broad tax bases). If a specific tax measure is chosen, its design may be subject to any of the following considerations:

- lessons and best practices from other countries with such tax provisions;
- monitoring of tax subsidies by a periodical cost-benefit analysis and by annually publishing a list of tax expenditures;
- prudence in budgetary calculations and reliance on the argument of self-financing; and
- limitation of tax incentives to a specific period if this enhances effectiveness (that is, introduction of sunset provisions). At the end of the period the measure is revoked.

These conditions contribute to an efficient working of the tax structure and specific tax breaks, all the more so against the background of important trends and developments in the 21st century.

PART II

Key macroeconomic variables

3. Taxes, benefits and labour market performance

> The art of taxation consists in so plucking the goose as to get the largest amount of feathers with the least amount of hissing.
>
> (Jean Baptist Colbert)[1]

3.1 INTRODUCTION

Although generally declining in recent years, the effective tax burden on labour is still substantial in many OECD economies. In some countries the labour-tax ratio has risen by well over 10 percentage points since 1975 (Carey and Rabesona, 2004). The resulting high tax burdens adversely affect labour markets.[2] They reduce labour supply as a consequence of lower after-tax wages for individuals and lower labour demand due to the high labour costs to firms. In many countries there has been a general reduction in labour supply and a rise in unemployment rates since the 1970s.

High labour market utilisation forms a central factor in promoting individual and national welfare. This is not only true in a pure economic sense. Employment keeps people engaged and channels energies in constructive directions. Work and income raise people's self-esteem, and offer perspective and a favourable future outlook. It thereby contributes to a more stable living environment for both younger and older workers. British economist Andrew Oswald (1997a) finds that, based on survey research for the US and Europe, since the 1970s economic growth in itself has raised people's happiness only marginally. At the same time, unemployment seems to have been an important cause of unhappiness. Low participation and high unemployment, moreover, constitute a fall in national product and are a primary source of poverty in the developed world.

---

[1] Jean Baptist Colbert (1619-83) served as the French Minister of Finance from 1665 to 1683 under King Louis XIV.

[2] Several studies endorse this. See, for example, OECD (1995), Bovenberg (2006) and van der Ploeg (2006a).

Facilitating high labour market participation and employment is thus an important policy objective. Labour market participation and hours worked should be increased in many of the countries under consideration if it is politically desirable to maintain the provision of public pensions and health in the light of ageing populations. There are no objective criteria for determining what the rate of participation should be. But given current and future labour market developments (for example, ageing workforces) labour market performance should be improved. Second, unemployment is high in many economies. In some countries long-term unemployment accounts for more than half of total unemployment, so it is no longer a temporary phenomenon between jobs or in a recession, but structural in nature. Not only is this a waste of human potential, but it also presents a big burden to the taxpayer.

This chapter looks at how taxes affect labour market performance. It starts with an overview of labour market statistics, including the labour tax wedge which is large in many countries. Then it examines the effect of taxes on labour supply and demand. What follows is a short overview of social policies and reasons why large welfare states do not necessarily imply worse economic performance. Some economists have argued that shifting the tax on labour to other tax bases improves labour market performance, and this is discussed next. The chapter concludes by examining a number of specific income support and labour market strategies that aim to make tax and social security policies less categorical and better targeted to improve work incentives.

3.2   LABOUR MARKETS AND THE TAX SYSTEM

On a macroeconomic level the two indicators to assess the state of a labour market are the *participation* rate and the *unemployment* rate. The former expresses the number of people aged 15 to 64 who are in the labour force; the latter the number of people in the labour force who are out of work but actively looking for a job. Hence, the labour force consists of the total number of people employed and unemployed. Those who are neither, such as retired people or discouraged workers, are not included. To fully capture labour supply, the individual work effort as approximated by the average hours worked per worker should be considered.

The concept of labour supply also includes other elements such as a worker's education, health and motivation, which may all influence the effective labour supply. Education and training improve the quality of labour and thus effectively boost the labour supply.

Participation and Hours Worked

Table 3.1 presents the participation rates, hours worked and productivity levels for the sample countries. Participation typically varies from 63.7 per cent in Italy, implying that less than two-thirds of the working-age population contributes to the production, to 81.6 per cent in Sweden. The average for these countries is 75.6 per cent. The Anglo-Saxon countries, with the exception of Ireland, have participation rates above average. In three of the four Nordic countries labour market participation is even higher, despite the relatively high rates of taxation. Indeed, high employment rates are a distinctive factor in maintaining the welfare state in these countries (public finances are very sensitive to the fraction of the population that is active, as an active population on the labour market implies both higher tax revenue and less expenditure on income transfers).

Hours worked per worker also vary greatly. Whereas workers in the Netherlands put in an average of 1,367 hours, Japanese employees work on nearly 500 hours more with an average of 1,775 hours. Most continental European countries work less than the average of 1,620 hours, with only Austria working more. However, continental European countries stand out with a relatively high productivity of labour per hour worked.

Female participation
Even though there is a rising trend in female participation, it is still less than male participation. This constitutes a great loss of potential. It will help to have a separate treatment of married couples for tax purposes. Many systems have long discriminated against married women and in doing so discouraged female labour force participation. For example, in Germany it is still the case that the spouse's income is added to that of the breadwinner and thus taxed at a relatively high marginal tax rate. It also helps if government provides childcare and nurseries, which encourages (young) mothers to work. The Scandinavian countries have had good experiences with such arrangements.[3]

Sweden introduced separate taxation of women in 1971. Although that was mainly dictated by equity considerations, stimulating female labour supply was also an important motive. Gustafsson (1992) compared the Swedish tax system with the German system using econometric methods and survey data from 8,598 interviews The German system is less individualistic than the Swedish one where income taxation is independent of household composition. Structural dissimilarities between both tax systems were an important contributing factor in the difference in female labour participation between both countries. For example, in 1988 the participation rate in Sweden was 81.8 per cent against 55.0 per cent in Germany. The presence of

---

[3] According to the World Economic Forum (2005) the Nordic countries occupy the top four global positions in terms of female empowerment.

Table 3.1 *Key labour force statistics, 2006*

Country	Participation rate	Hours worked [a]	Output per hour worked $US [a]	Female participation	Elderly participation (55-64 yrs)
Australia	77.5	1,730	40.4	69.9	57.4
Austria	74.5	1,656	41.1	67.6	36.8
Belgium	66.3	1,534	53.5	59.3	32.2
Canada	79.3	1,736	38.5	74.5	58.7
Denmark	81.4	1,574	42.4	77.5	63.2
Finland	75.5	1,718	39.4	73.9	58.4
France	69.3	1,546	49.0	64.2	43.6
Germany	76.0	1,437	45.5	69.3	55.3
Ireland	72.7	1,638	50.3	62.1	54.7
Italy	63.7	1,815	37.4	51.2	33.4
Japan	79.3	1,775	34.6	66.0	67.3
Netherlands	76.6	1,367	51.1	69.8	49.1
Norway	79.7	1,421	66.8	76.0	68.2
Sweden	81.6	1,588	42.2	78.7	73.0
UK	77.7	1,672	41.2	71.5	59.1
US	78.3	1,713	48.3	71.7	63.7
Average	75.6	1,620	45.1	69.0	57.9

Note: [a] Statistics are for the year 2005.

Source: OECD labour force statistics and productivity database.

children deters female participation in Germany, but this is not so in Sweden with its generous childcare arrangements and paid parental leave.[4]

Decomposition of Unemployment

The structural component of unemployment depends on specific labour market institutions.[5] The cyclical component of unemployment is sensitive to the business cycle. This makes the data less stable over time and more critical to the point of measurement (that is, it is less of a structural indicator). With 3.5 per cent, Norway experiences the lowest unemployment rate, while France, Germany and Belgium suffer from the highest unemployment rates.

A careful interpretation of these numbers is vital. Adema (2001) finds that disability spending in Finland and the Netherlands with 3.4 per cent of GDP is highest in the sample countries. In spite of this, unemployment is relatively low. Germany with the highest formal unemployment rate spends a mere 1.4 per cent of GDP. It seems plausible that these discrepancies do not solely originate from differences in disability among workers and that some schemes are ill-defined and poorly managed. Disability is also an attractive way to dispose of a worker; roughly two-thirds of people on disability in the Netherlands had difficult to determine health problems (for example, they claimed to have 'back' or 'psychiatric' problems).

The middle three columns in Table 3.2 show that in Belgium, Germany and Italy approximately half of the unemployed have been so for longer than one year. Other countries such as France, Ireland and the Netherlands have less, but still notable long-term unemployment. Long-term unemployment is structural and imposes a heavy burden on an economy and the taxpayer. Combating it will be a particularly challenging task for continental European countries. Finally, youth unemployment rates are high in many countries: on average, they are more than twice the standard unemployment rates.

Tax Incidence: Who Bears the Labour Tax Burden?

In a competitive economy it does not matter whether the tax is imposed on firms or on workers. Hence, the *legal* incidence of taxes generally differs from the *economic* incidence. To give an example, the burden of a payroll tax on firms is partially shifted on to workers through lower wages, especially if

---

[4] In 2001, the Dutch replaced the tax-free allowance at the basis of the income tax schedule by a tax credit equal for both partners. Since the former allowance was transferable between partners, an implicit tax arose when somebody entered the labour force while the working partner was taxed in a higher bracket. The new arrangement ensures that income by a second earner does not reduce the first earner's basic allowance. By statistically relating employment figures for married women to single ones, the Dutch Central Planning Bureau observed that employment has indeed increased at an accelerated pace among the former group since 2001 (CPB, 2005).

[5] Four 'labour market institutions' are distinguished that may affect labour market performance: generous benefits, union power, taxes and wage inflexibility (Oswald, 1997b).

Table 3.2 Cyclical, structural and youth unemployment rates, 2006 (%)

Country[a]	Standardised unemployment rate[b]	Less than 3 months	3 months - less than 1 year	1 year and over	Youth unemployment (15-24 yrs)
Australia	4.8	54.0	28.2	17.8	10.4
Austria	4.7	35.2	37.6	27.3	9.1
Belgium	8.2	18.2	26.3	55.6	18.9
Canada	6.3	70.0	21.3	8.7	11.6
Denmark	3.9	43.5	36.0	20.4	7.6
Finland	7.7	39.5	35.7	24.8	18.8
France	9.5	22.0	33.9	44.0	23.9
Germany	8.3	14.6	28.2	57.2	13.5
Ireland	4.4	29.0	36.7	34.3	8.4
Italy	6.8	17.7	29.4	52.9	21.6
Japan	4.1	35.6	31.5	33.0	8.0
Netherlands	3.9	19.9	34.9	45.2	7.6
Norway	3.5	53.7	32.2	14.1	8.6
Sweden	7.0	50.7	35.1	14.2	21.3
UK	5.3	39.0	38.9	22.1	13.9
US	4.6	67.6	22.4	10.0	10.5

Notes:
[a] Unemployment duration numbers may not add up to 100 per cent due to rounding errors; [b] Numbers are for 2005.

Source: OECD labour force statistics database.

labour demand is elastic while supply is inelastic. In a sense, inelastic labour supply implies that workers are 'sitting ducks ready to be plucked!'. By the same token an increase in income tax on workers lowers after-tax wages but not by the full amount if firms are forced to pay higher before-tax wages and carry some of the burden of the tax hike. This is particularly so if labour supply is relatively elastic while labour demand is inelastic. Consumption taxes have similar effects, since they too fall on labour (except for a small amount of consumption that is financed out of capital income).

BOX 3.1

Taxes drive a wedge between the gross wage cost to an employer and the corresponding net consumption wage of the employee. The tax wedge consists of payroll taxes, income taxes and consumption taxes. With a relatively small wage elasticity of labour supply and a high wage elasticity of labour demand, the burden of taxation is mostly borne by workers rather than firms.

With the advent of globalisation and the opening-up of markets in Europe and elsewhere, international competition is becoming fiercer and the wage elasticity of labour demand becomes bigger. As many countries are trying to lower taxes on labour, this translates increasingly into higher take-home pay rather than lower wage costs and more jobs.

The Average Tax Wedge

Table 3.3 presents gross wage earnings for an average production worker (APW) and the average tax wedge for six specific subgroups of earners, including average taxes on consumption.[6] The numbers are based on the OECD's annual 'Taxing wages' study, which presents an alternative approach to determining the tax rates on labour (Heady, 2004). This offers better insights into average and marginal tax rates, since both taxes and (cash) benefits are incorporated. There is also information on a variety of households, including 67, 100 or 167 per cent APWs, single or married and with or without children.

---

[6] According to Heady (2004, p. 266). 'probably the most important methodological limitation is the exclusion of taxes on the goods that workers consume. Theoretically a uniform sales tax has the same incentive and distributional effects as a proportional income tax on workers who do not save. Thus the exclusion of sales taxes can be seen as arbitrary'. The main problem is finding detailed consumption tax data (distribution of household consumption, the types of goods consumed and applicable sales tax rates) for all OECD countries.

Table 3.3 Gross wage earnings and the average tax wedge, including effective taxes on consumption, 2004 (%)

Country	Gross earnings before taxes 100% APW ($US)[a]	Single - no children, 67% APW[b]	Single - no children, 100% APW	Single - no children, 167% APW	Single - 2 children, 67% APW	Married - 2 children, P100% APW and S0% APW[c]	Married - 2 children, P100% APW and S67% APW
Australia	38,021	0.38	0.40	0.47	0.16	0.31	0.37
Austria	26,617	0.49	0.55	0.59	0.29	0.41	0.45
Belgium	35,622	0.57	0.63	0.68	0.44	0.48	0.56
Canada	34,038	0.41	0.44	0.45	0.19	0.37	0.42
Denmark	37,582	0.54	0.55	0.62	0.35	0.46	0.51
Finland	29,979	0.51	0.55	0.60	0.40	0.49	0.50
France	25,459	0.46	0.58	0.60	0.39	0.51	0.50
Germany	35,203	0.54	0.58	0.62	0.41	0.43	0.51
Ireland	27,301	0.34	0.40	0.49	0.05	0.26	0.33
Italy	36,303	0.52	0.56	0.60	0.40	0.48	0.52
Japan	31,195	0.34	0.35	0.38	0.32	0.33	0.34
Netherlands	34,062	0.50	0.54	0.52	0.33	0.47	0.49
Norway	33,221	0.47	0.50	0.55	0.33	0.43	0.46
Sweden	26,078	0.60	0.61	0.64	0.52	0.56	0.57
UK	32,896	0.39	0.43	0.45	0.08	0.32	0.37
US	34,934	0.34	0.36	0.41	0.13	0.24	0.30

Notes:

[a] Using purchasing parity power (PPP) exchange rates.

[b] APW is equal to the wage level of an average production worker; 67% AWP lies close to the minimum wage in many countries. Average tax rates for workers with income below 67% APW become less reliable indicators of the tax burden, because several benefit schemes then affect income as well. Similarly, above the 167% APW level, owner-occupied housing and savings are likely to start affecting the tax liability.

[c] P stands for principal earner and S for spouse.

Source: Computed from the OECD electronic database. The average tax wedge is calculated as $(a + c)/(1 + c)$, where a is the tax wedge obtained from the OECD's annual 'Taxing wages' study (which includes income and payroll tax but not indirect taxes) and c is the effective tax rate on consumption as calculated from the 'National Accounts'.

Tax rates vary considerably between countries and over time. For all 30 OECD countries, the labour tax wedge excluding indirect taxes rose on average by 0.2 per cent in 2004 after a declining trend since 1996. According to the OECD, the main causes are higher wages which have pushed workers into higher tax brackets and a different range of tax policy changes per country (OECD, 2005g).

Average tax rates are high in most Western European economies. A worker often has to surrender more than half his/her earnings to the tax authorities. In Sweden the average tax wedge even reaches 60 per cent for three specific categories of earners. In Belgium, Denmark, Finland, France and Germany a single worker earning 167 per cent APW also faces a tax wedge of over 60 per cent. In other words, these people work until September to pay their tax bill before they can start to enjoy their earnings. The Anglo-Saxon countries display smaller tax wedges. Single people with no children are taxed most heavily. Those with two children are taxed at lower rates. This category mainly includes single mothers on a low income. A mix of low taxes and high benefits creates low effective tax rates.

The Marginal Tax Wedge

As a corollary, marginal tax rates faced by these people are typically high. Since benefits are gradually or more abruptly phased out as income increases, these workers pay an implicit tax in the form of benefits forgone. Marginal tax rates may thus even get in excess of 100 per cent (typically low-income people with children, such as single mothers on welfare). This often means that for such people it is not an attractive option to try to earn more by working. They are stuck in a poverty trap.

Table 3.4 indicates that in all countries the marginal tax burden is higher than the average tax burden. Hence, as wages increase, taxpayers surrender a larger portion of their earnings to the tax authorities. It is not uncommon for European countries to impose marginal tax rates above 60 per cent. In Belgium, France and Germany an average production worker can even face a marginal tax rate of 70 per cent or higher. This significantly reduces the incentives to raise the working effort or acquire skills training. In the US or Japan the marginal tax wedge is considerably smaller, typically around 40 per cent of additional earnings.

A Simple Measure of Tax Progression

Labour market (dis)incentives that are created by taxes depend on the tax progression built into a system. Here we measure tax progression according to the residual income progression (RIP). The RIP coefficient is calculated as the percentage increase in net income resulting from a 1 per cent increase in gross income. It decreases with the marginal tax rate and increases with the average tax rate. Typically the RIP coefficient varies across categories of taxpayers.

A higher taxable threshold, keeping the average tax burden constant by increasing marginal tax rates, results in a reduced RIP coefficient and increased progressivity of the tax system. This is one of the most common ways of redistributing income from high to lower incomes. In contrast, if marginal tax rates are kept constant while the tax-free allowance is decreased, the average burden and the RIP coefficient increase. This would make the tax system less progressive.

A closer study of the tax wedges reveals how little progression most tax systems exhibit in practice. The final column of Table 3.4 shows the average RIP-coefficient for the six categories of earners. Belgium and France are the only countries with relatively low values. This is also the case for the UK, but this is mainly caused by high progressivity faced by single parents and one-earner families (due to generous benefits and other tax subsidies that are phased out with rising income). Denmark, Norway and Sweden have RIP-coefficients of over 0.80. Even though the average tax burden in these countries is typically very high, actual tax progression is thus relatively moderate.

3.3   LABOUR SUPPLY: TAXES AND WORKERS

Obviously the effect of taxation on the decision to work or enjoy leisure should be kept minimal.[7] A distortion is nevertheless created if there is a difference between the gross wage cost to the employer and net consumption wage to the employee. The difference represents the tax wedge and equals the tax collected. It accrues to the state. If governments want to avoid tax distortions, they may want to impose individualised lump-sum taxes according to a person's 'income-earning potential'. This would imply that only an individual's ability-to-earn economic rents is taxed, a characteristic that is basically innate.

Such a tax is also referred to as 'Tinbergen's talent tax', named after the first Nobel Prize-winning economist (1961), Jan Tinbergen. In theory, any desired income redistribution could be attained with the talent tax, without distorting the consumption/leisure decision and thus the choice of whether to work.

In history, a number of alternatives have been proposed such as measuring an individual's intelligence with an obligatory IQ test to approximate his/her income-earning potential. However, these measures are far from perfect as people have a strong incentive to underperform on such assessments. Thus in

---

[7] See also Heijdra and van der Ploeg (2002), Chapters 7, 8 and 9, for a discussion of the effect of taxation on labour markets.

Table 3.4 Marginal tax wedge, including effective taxes on consumption, 2004 (%)

Country	Single - no children, 67% APW	Single - no children, 100% APW	Single - no children, 167% APW	Single - 2 children, 67% APW	Married - 2 children, P100% and S0% APW	Married - 2 children, P100% and S67% APW	Average RIP[a]
Australia	0.46	0.46	0.59	0.62	0.62	0.70	0.67
Austria	0.67	0.63	0.68	0.67	0.63	0.63	0.67
Belgium	0.79	0.73	0.76	0.79	0.70	0.73	0.59
Canada	0.47	0.46	0.48	0.65	0.60	0.49	0.79
Denmark	0.56	0.61	0.72	0.56	0.57	0.57	0.82
Finland	0.60	0.64	0.68	0.60	0.64	0.64	0.75
France	0.64	0.73	0.63	0.53	0.69	0.71	0.70
Germany	0.65	0.70	0.70	0.64	0.62	0.67	0.70
Ireland	0.45	0.47	0.61	0.72	0.47	0.47	0.71
Italy	0.61	0.66	0.67	0.61	0.66	0.66	0.74
Japan	0.36	0.39	0.47	0.36	0.37	0.37	0.93
Netherlands	0.64	0.60	0.61	0.61	0.60	0.60	0.75
Norway	0.55	0.55	0.64	0.55	0.55	0.55	0.81
Sweden	0.64	0.64	0.73	0.64	0.64	0.64	0.84
UK	0.51	0.51	0.43	0.78	0.78	0.51	0.68
US	0.40	0.40	0.48	0.37	0.54	0.40	0.82

Note: [a] Residual income progression coefficients are calculated as a simple average for these six categories of earners, where individual coefficients are determined by $(1-t_M)/(1-t_A)$, where t_M indicates the marginal tax rate and t_A the average tax rate. Note that the incomes considered typically range up to 167% of an APW, so earners with incomes above this level are not considered. Tax progression is likely to be higher above this income level.

Source: Computed from the OECD electronic database. The same annotation as under Table 3.3 applies except that the average tax rate has been replaced by the marginal tax rate.

practice it proves impossible to perfectly observe an individual's income-earning potential, as individuals have an incentive to appear less capable in order to pay less tax. Even a Tinbergen tax is thus associated with tax distortions.

In practice, governments use the next best thing, which is the actual income somebody is enjoying. As a result, not only is the ability to earn taxed, but other factors too, such as the work effort and time expended on education and skill training. This distorts the consumption/leisure decision and may encourage people to work less. Thus in addition to the actual burden of the tax, a behavioural response is induced that creates an *excess burden*. If labour supply is inelastic, employees will be largely unresponsive to net wage changes. The distortion to economic choice in such a case is limited. If it is elastic, workers are more inclined to alter labour supply in response to wage changes. The excess burden will be larger.

Income and Substitution Effects in Labour Supply

Average and marginal tax rates may have quite opposite effects on labour supply response. Two separate effects can be distinguished: the *income* effect and the *substitution* effect. Each of these effects operates in the opposite direction and is associated with changes in, respectively, the average and the marginal tax rates on labour.

A higher average tax rate, while keeping tax progression fixed, reduces disposable income and makes people poorer (that is, the RIP remains equal). This induces individuals to increase labour supply at the expense of leisure to compensate for the loss of consumption opportunities. The income effect therefore shows the positive effect of the average labour income tax rate on labour supply. Conversely, if the average tax rate remains fixed but tax progression is increased (that is, the RIP is lowered), the opportunity cost of leisure decreases. Individuals therefore work less and enjoy more leisure at the margin. The substitution effect thus indicates that labour supply is negatively related to the marginal tax rate.

BOX 3.2

The income effect measures the extent to which the work effort is increased to compensate for less income arising from higher average income tax rates, while progression is kept unaltered. In contrast, the substitution effect measures the effect on labour supply of a more progressive income tax but fixed average rate of taxation. This makes leisure at the margin cheaper, so decreases the work effort.

Extensive versus Intensive Margins

The labour supply response can take place along both the extensive and the intensive margins. The distinction is necessary to isolate the effects on, respectively, the incentive to participate in the labour force and the number of hours worked. This gives better insights into the labour effects of tax and welfare policies. Intuitively, for instance, a tax credit would do more for the participation decision of low-income earners than it would for the amount of labour supplied by high-income earners. The opposite could be true for a reduction in the top statutory tax rate.

Empirically, labour supply responses have been found to be larger with regard to the participation decision than the hours-of-work decision (Heckman, 1993). The participation elasticities tend to be very large for certain subgroups in the population, while the hours-of-work elasticities as calculated at the intensive margin seem to lie close to zero for many earners. The extensive responses are strong at the lower end of the income distribution, where high taxes and generous benefits for those out of work may significantly distort the choice to participate in the labour force and find a job.[8]

Intensive responses are found anywhere along the income distribution and depend on the marginal tax rate, including the adverse effects of phasing out benefits where applicable. Because the individual labour supply curve may be backward bending, the associated elasticity can also be negative. Hence, higher taxes at the upper end of the income distribution may actually increase labour supply. The participation elasticity is at all times positive.

Empirical Relationships between Taxes and Labour Supply

Tables 3.1 and 3.2 showed that countries that have high participation rates and low unemployment, such as the Netherlands and Norway, also exhibit relatively low annual hours worked per worker. The variations in hours worked may partly be explained by the particular tax burdens that workers face.

For example, Mendoza et al. (1994) observe a significant negative correlation between the combined labour and consumption tax ratios and total hours worked for six out of seven of the surveyed countries. A combination of high average labour and consumption taxes is thus associated with working fewer hours over time. These results are confirmed by Carey and Rabesona (2004), who also find that Denmark, Finland and Sweden have longer working hours than would be predicted on the basis of the regression.

---

[8] Studies indeed indicate that participation elasticities differ substantially across individuals. They are highest for low-income earners (perhaps over 0.5), while considerably lower for middle-income earners and near zero for high-income earners (Kleven and Kreiner, 2006)

They argue that this may reflect the favourable childcare arrangements in these countries.

In the early 1970s, Western European workers put in as many hours as their colleagues in the US and before the Second World War they worked even harder. Since then the trend in Europe has been downward and nowadays they work around 50 per cent less than Americans. In the Netherlands, Belgium, Germany and France an adult (aged 15-64) works on average 17 to 18 hours a week, whereas in the US people work more than 25 hours per week. Workers in Europe also have significantly more holiday entitlement and retire earlier. The decrease in the work effort of Europeans has slowed down economic growth compared to the US, and lowered welfare.

Others have studied the decline in hours worked and differences in tax rates between countries. Table 3.3 and 3.4 demonstrated that average and marginal tax rates differ markedly between most of the European countries and the US, and they have been diverging markedly in the past 30 years. Davis and Henrekson (2004) examine tax rate differentials among rich countries and find that a tax rise of 12.8 per cent (that is, 1 standard deviation) reduces the hours worked by an adult by 122 per year and causes a 4.9 percentage point drop in the employment-population ratio (furthermore, it increases the black economy by 3.8 per cent of measured GDP).

Typical wage and income elasticities
However, despite all this evidence, taxes cannot be seen as the single most important cause of a relatively low labour supply. The main reason is that most econometric research has shown prime-age male workers to be largely unresponsive at the *intensive margin* to changes in wage and income rates (Pencavel, 1986; Blundell and MaCurdy, 1999; Røed and Strøm, 2002). Table 3.5 illustrates that uncompensated wage elasticities for men are near zero for most observations.[9]

The Nobel Prize-winning economist Edward C. Prescott (2004) therefore argues that the *intertemporal* elasticity of substitution between consumption today and that tomorrow is very low and that this may lead to a very high elasticity of labour supply of nearly 3. For this reason, he assumes that the extra tax revenues flow back in the form of generous benefits through pay-as-you-go social security systems. It is the interaction between high taxes and

---

[9] Uncompensated wage elasticities for women are predominantly positive (see also Killingsworth and Heckman, 1986). The reason is that many women work part-time. While it is difficult to induce people who already work 40 or more hours per week to increase their effort, financial incentives are more effective for people who work fewer hours. The *uncompensated* wage elasticity provides a measure for the total labour supply response as dictated by the labour supply curve. It is contrasted by the *compensated* wage elasticity, from which the income effect has been subtracted and which focuses on the substitution effect.

the social security it finances together with intertemporal substitution that makes people in Europe work less.

Table 3.5   Uncompensated wage and income elasticities

Study	Country	Men		Married women	
		Uncomp. wage elasticity	Income elasticity	Uncomp. wage elasticity	Income elasticity
Arellano and Meghir (1992)	UK	-	-	0.290 to 0.710	-0.130 to -0.400
Arrufat and Zabalza (1986)	UK	-	-	2.030	-0.200
Blomquist (1983)	Sweden	0.080	-0.030	-	-
Blomquist and Hansson (1990)	Sweden	0.080	0.002	0.790	-0.240
Bourguignon and Magnac (1990)	France	0.100	-0.070	1,000	-0.300
Blundell and Walker (1986)	UK	0.024	-0.287	-	-
Blundell et al. (1988)	UK	-	-	0.090	-0.260
Colombino and Del Boca (1990)	Italy	-	-	1.180 to 0.660	0.520
Flood and MaCurdy (1992)	Sweden	0.16	-0.100	-	-
Hausman (1981)	US	0.000 to 0.030	-0.950 to -1.030	0.995	-0.121
Kaiser et al. (1992)	Germany	-0.004	-0.280	1.040	-0.180
Kuismanen (1997)	Finland	-	-	-0.010	0.270
MaCurdy et al. (1990)	US	0	-0.010		
Triest (1990)	US	0.050	0	0.970	-0.330
Van Soest et al. (1990)	Netherlands	0.120	-0.010	0.790	-0.230

Source: Blundell and MaCurdy (1999, pp. 1646-51), also for corresponding references.

On the other hand, Nickell (2003) finds for the 1960-2000 period that a 10 per cent increase in the tax wedge has lowered labour supply by an average of 2 per cent in developed nations. Yet only a small part of the difference in labour supply between the three biggest continental European countries, France, Germany and Italy, and the US can actually be contributed to the difference in the tax wedge. Social safety and other labour market institutions most likely account for the remainder. It seems that the impact of taxes on labour supply is not as strong as is commonly believed.

BOX 3.3

At the extensive margin, taxes have the potential to affect the participation decision, thus the choice of whether to work or not. On the intensive margin taxes affect the number of hours worked and effort put in by people already employed. Participation elasticities are believed to be higher than hours-of-work elasticities, which tend to lie close to zero.

In recent research, Alesina et al. (2005), on the basis of empirical evidence, conclude that factors other than taxation have played a primary role in decreasing labour supply. They point to the increasing power of trade unions in the 1970s and 1980s and part of the 1990s, and to heavy labour market regulation.

In the period under consideration most unions in Europe applied the motto 'work less, so that all can work'. What has become painfully clear since then is that a lowering of labour supply by a reduction of hours worked (the 35-hour week in France, for example), part-time work, longer holidays and early retirement puts upward pressure on wage rates and thus reduces labour demand. Ultimately, the economy slows down, it becomes less strong and it becomes more difficult to finance the welfare state. The 'work less, so that all can work' motto has therefore become known as the 'fallacy of labour' (Layard et al., 2005).

The social multiplier

On a macroeconomic scale, changes in tax rates may have larger effects. The assumption that some sort of social multiplier is at work may imply that people are less inclined to work hard if others around them are also enjoying additional leisure time. The elasticity of labour supply could thus be higher when the economy in considered as a whole and assuming that certain 'complementarities' exist.

For example, people collectively enjoy their two days of leisure on Saturday and Sunday. However, from a viewpoint of capital utilisation and congestion, it would be better for half the labour force to enjoy their leisure days on, say, Sunday and Monday. The argument may apply similarly to hours worked (that is, from 9 to 5) and holidays enjoyed. It is certainly more fun to have a vacation together with friends and family, and indeed many people in Europe arrange their summer holidays in the same weeks of the year. Because more people are inactive at the same time, services associated with leisure and holidays are also more abundantly available in Europe. Therefore, a 'culture of leisure' may have been created that is stronger than in the US.

Evidence has also been found that workers are more productive if others around them are productive. These are so-called 'agglomeration economies in productivity'. By the same token, there seem to be significant differences in labour force participation across demographic subgroups in a particular area. It is less worrisome to be unemployed if others around you are too. High unemployment in closely-knit communities thus impairs morale and reduces labour market performance. An interesting study in this regard was conducted in the Stockholm metropolitan area (Åberg et al., 1999). By examining the behaviour of 20-24 year olds, it was found that the level of unemployment in a neighbourhood negatively affects the social and psychological cost associated with unemployment. Hence, in low unemployment areas, the psychological costs are high. This induces the unemployed to put greater effort into searching for new work. In high unemployment areas the stigma of unemployment is lower, so the unemployed search less intensively for a job. In a sense, unemployment is contagious and it is difficult to get rid of it.

BOX 3.4

Although full-time working males seem to be largely unresponsive to tax changes, it is plausible that through the channel of intertemporal substitution an increase in tax rates makes it less interesting to work and more appealing to enjoy leisure. This increased preference for leisure is strengthened on a macro level by so-called 'social multipliers' that implies that people are less inclined to work hard if others around them are also enjoying additional leisure time.

Overall, these forces seem to carry insufficient weight to explain the large differences in hours worked between Europe and the US. However, according to statistical evidence in Alesina et al. (2005), the increasing power of unions and labour market regulation has been strong enough. The question is whether this role of unions is desirable. Any deviation from an economy's efficient production equilibrium in perfect competition undermines its productive capacity and reduces GDP. Nevertheless, GDP is not the sole determinant of well-being.

Being able to enjoy an increased amount of leisure time could thus be welfare enhancing even if it is at the expense of material consumption. Unions may facilitate this by functioning as a coordination device by collectively standing up to employers. This may be welfare enhancing. On the other hand, if unions prevent workers willing to do extra work from doing so, it is harmful to overall welfare and economic growth. Unfortunately in many countries under consideration this still seems to be the case.

Optimal Tax Theory and Income Redistribution

Considerable efficiency gains can be attained by accurately constructing the tax schedule and finding an appropriate balance with income support programmes. The problem is how to overcome the problem of 'moral hazard'. That is, the problem that taxpayers are not honest and may pretend that they have a lower taxable income than they really have. The theory of optimal income taxation, developed by Nobel Prize laureate James Mirrlees (1971), deals with the question of how marginal income tax rates can be set most optimally, as evaluated against the utilitarian social welfare function of an economy.

The welfare function was so-called by the 19th-century utilitarian political philosophers Jeremy Bentham and John Stuart Mill. Social welfare can be defined as the sum of individual utilities, which is maximised if the marginal utility of income is equal for all individuals in society. As long as utility declines with income, social welfare can be improved by achieving higher redistribution. A second and much debated approach was postulated by 20th-century philosopher John Rawls, and is also referred to as the 'maxi-min criterion'. Here, social welfare depends only on the utility of the individual with the lowest utility which should in turn be maximised. Hence, greater weight is accorded to the welfare of low-income earners, which raises the social benefit from redistribution.

The trade-off between efficiency and equity is central herein. The tension between the two principles arises because the costs of redistribution are high, since the required marginal tax rates are high and the government does not want to discourage the most talented people from earning a good income. They are the ones paying the taxes necessary for redistribution. However, given certain distributional requirements as dictated by a society's preference regarding income inequality, some tax progression is exactly what is needed. The equity aspects that are reflected in a tax system therefore stand in stark contrast to the efficiency objective of minimising the distortion to the work decision.

Mirrlees (1971) identifies three key criteria according to which tax rates ought to be set to optimise labour incentives to attain an optimal income distribution. It is important to note that optimal tax theory is concerned not only with efficiency, but also with redistribution and equity. The three criteria are as follows:

1. *Sensitivity of labour supply to taxes as measured by labour elasticities.* If the elasticities are high, the efficiency costs of taxation are high and thus the government will pursue lower tax rates and less redistribution;
2. *Shape of the income distribution and the associated density of people.* The government does not want to kill the goose that lays the

golden eggs. Hence, the marginal tax rates on the highest-income earners should not be too high. Most of the redistribution should therefore take place via a large deductible sum or tax credit rather than via very high marginal tax rates; and

3. *Government taste for redistribution* (as dictated by society's aversion to income inequality). Obviously, if the government adopts a Rawlsian welfare function, it redistributes more than with a utilitarian welfare function.

The structure of an optimal income tax that follows from simulations turns out to be U-shaped as income progresses (Diamond, 1998; and Saez, 2001). This is indicated by the curve at points II, III and IV in Figure 3.1. However, Mirrlees's analysis and subsequent work was mainly concerned with labour supply responses at the intensive margin and did not incorporate the distortion that taxes produce at the extensive margin. Saez (2002) demonstrates that if the participation decision at the lower end of the income distribution is taken into account, the optimal rate structure follows the pattern from points I to IV. Interestingly enough, many tax systems in reality more or less take this shape.

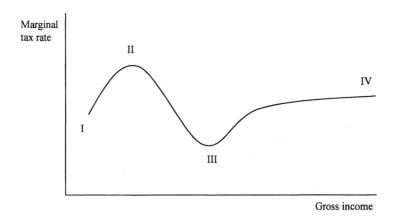

Figure 3.1 The marginal rate structure according to optimal tax theory

The result is by and large arrived at as follows. Low-income earners inevitably face high marginal tax rates if there is to be redistribution. All sorts of income-related benefits and income support that create progression are phased out as earnings increase. This imposes an implicit tax and raises the marginal tax burden (indicated by a rise to the peak at point II). Hence, a low average tax rate at the bottom of the income distribution creates tax progression, but does not imply that the marginal tax rate is low too. Nor does it necessarily imply that marginal tax rates further down the income distribution are high.

Optimal tax theory stipulates that the marginal tax burden should subsequently decline up to point III. Point III occurs around $75,000 in the US according to Saez (2002). The density of taxpayers in this range, that is, those with medium incomes, is large and imposing high marginal tax rates would therefore significantly distort the work/leisure decision and be very inefficient.

Depending on the value the government attaches to redistribution, marginal tax rates on high-income earners would subsequently have to be raised only slightly or more significantly (towards point IV). If a basic income support for low-income households suffices, the marginal burden would not have to be raised much. If, on the other hand, government feels obliged to achieve more wide-ranging income redistribution including to people on middle incomes, marginal tax rates on high-income earners would have to rise more substantially. This reduces labour market incentives for these taxpayers more significantly, although they are relatively small in number.

Finally, so as to not significantly distort the participation decision at the extensive margin, tax rates faced by households at the lower end of the income distribution should be reduced (point I). This can be achieved, for example, by introducing a negative income tax or an earned income tax credit. The workings of both strategies are discussed in Section 3.7.

BOX 3.5

Empirical application of optimal tax theory suggests that most taxpayers should face declining marginal tax rates, that is, up to an annual income of roughly $75,000 in the US. Only after this point should marginal tax rates rise moderately to produce progressivity.

3.4   LABOUR DEMAND: TAXES AND FIRMS

Payroll, income and consumption taxes also impinge on the demand of firms for labour. Most basic macroeconomic models assume that wage costs are influenced by a mix of minimum wage requirements, union bargaining, efficiency wages and taxes.[10] All elements put upward pressures on wage

---

[10] Based on an empirical analysis with data from 20 OECD countries, Nickell et al. (2005) find that approximately 55 per cent of the rise in European unemployment during the 1960-2000

costs, thereby encouraging firms to hire fewer workers than they would otherwise do. The adverse consequences seem to predominantly affect low-skilled workers at the bottom of the income distribution where the bulk of unemployment is concentrated.

The Wage-setting Structure and Unemployment

The role of other labour market institutions is crucial. Daveri and Tabellini (2000) have found a high correlation for continental Europe between labour taxes, which have increased markedly in the past decades, and the level of unemployment. This is mainly caused, they claim, by wage-setting institutions. Workers who are organised in monopolistic trade unions are better able to (partly) shift the labour taxes onto firms. Higher real wages in such a case lead to a reduction in labour demand, thus decreasing employment and increasing unemployment. The capital to labour ratio is also affected because firms will favour investment over hiring relatively more expensive labour. This lowers the rate of return on capital and slows overall economic growth. Smaller correlations are observed for Anglo-Saxon and Nordic countries, which are characterised by competition and coordinated bargaining, respectively.[11]

The conclusions are corroborated by Disney (2000, p. 10) who considers that 'insofar as labor taxes play a role in raising unemployment or slowing economic growth, they do so in a subset of countries classified as intermediate between competition and coordinated bargaining'. In the latter case, the effect of bargaining on overall employment is internalised.

Tax Progression in Non-competitive Markets

Despite an overall detrimental effect of high marginal tax rates, the economic literature shows that tax progression can play a role in moderating wage development and thus improve employment (Lockwood and Manning, 1993). Higher wages have less value to employees if marginal tax rates are high. For this reason, unions are likely to demand lower wages in the bargaining process (for an overview of other studies that confirm these results, see Røed and Strøm (2002)).

---

period can be explained by changes in labour market institutions. The remainder has been cyclical in nature.

[11] The level of centralisation is referred to as the degree of 'corporatism'. The Nordic countries are known to have a high degree of corporatism. A low degree is found in the UK and the US. Countries in between are characterised by decentralised bargaining and include Belgium, France, Germany, Italy and the Netherlands.

BOX 3.6

Unions at a centralised level internalise the effects of higher wages on higher prices. They may thus moderate wages more than decentralised unions, since they realise that higher wages will not lead to much of an increase in purchasing power. They also realise that higher wages push up unemployment and also the level of unemployment benefits, and thus the tax rate. This is another reason why centralised unions moderate wages. Also, centralised unions anticipate that higher wages push up the taxes necessary to foot the bill of higher civil servants' salaries. This is yet another reason for wage moderation. In a competitive labour market, wages are directed to the competitive level.

However, this is only so if wage bargaining is characterised by an intermediate or high level of corporatism. For example Ireland returned to coordinated wage bargaining by the end of the 1980s (Walsh, 2000). In contrast to developments in the UK, which faced equal labour market problems, unions thus remained intact. Government assurances on gradual income tax cuts moderated wage claims and helped to create an internationally highly competitive labour force in the early 1990s. In a competitive environment the tax is shifted onto workers.

BOX 3.7

The economic effects of taxation on labour demand are different in non-competitive (decentralised) labour markets compared to competitive ones. With more tax progression in non-competitive markets, wage increases have less value to employees. This reduces wage demands in the bargaining process and thus increases employment. A rise in the average tax rate yields the opposite result.

Lockwood et al. (2000) provide further insights. Using Danish labour market data, they show that the effect could depend on income. Tax progressivity reduces wage demands for blue-collar workers, and white-collar workers with relatively moderate wages. For white collar workers with high earnings, the opposite is the case. This is explained by the rather individualistic and competitive environment in which the remuneration of these workers is settled, which is usually not part of a coordinated bargaining effort. It also demonstrates that advocating tax progression in non-competitive markets to induce employment does not *per se* conflict with reducing the top statutory rate to stimulate the work effort among high-income earners.

3.5   SOCIAL POLICIES AND LABOUR MARKET PERFORMANCE

Democratic countries with substantial income differentials, and whose citizens tend to believe that getting ahead on the social scale depends on connections, family status or luck, are likely to impose high taxes and have correspondingly large welfare systems. The rise in unemployment in many EU countries has long been ascribed to the build-up of the universal welfare states since the 1970s, along with a reduction in demand for low-skilled workers relative to skilled workers which was driven by technological innovation. Unlike in the US, this shift was not met by a downward adjustment in real wages of low-skilled workers. To finance welfare spending, taxes and social security contributions increased drastically, implying large work disincentives.

A multivariate analysis of post-war OECD economies by Edmund S. Phelps (1994), Nobel Prize laureate of 2006, reveals that the payroll tax that was used to finance much welfare spending is a 'powerful determinant' of the long-term natural unemployment rate. The relative increase of payroll taxes in Europe compared to the US explains much of the steeper rise in unemployment on the European continent.

Gross and Net Social Expenditure

Table 3.6 shows *gross* and *net* social expenditure in the sample countries. Both measures of social spending can in practice deviate significantly from each other, mainly because of the clawback of benefit payments by direct and indirect taxes on consumption by welfare recipients (additionally, as we saw in Chapter 2, the tax system is used to redistribute income through tax breaks with a social purpose). Differences are particularly large in Denmark, Finland, Italy, the Netherlands and Sweden, implying that a great deal of money is pumped around the economy (almost 8 per cent of GDP in Denmark). It also implies larger administration costs. The opposite is true in Australia, Canada, Japan, the UK and the US.

Table 3.6   Gross and net social expenditure as a percentage of GDP, 2001

Country	Gross expenditure	Net expenditure
Australia	20.4	24.0
Austria	29.6	24.8
Belgium	28.0	26.3
Canada	20.4	23.3
Denmark	34.2	26.4
Finland	28.0	22.6
France	33.0	31.2
Germany	30.6	30.8
Ireland	15.3	13.9
Italy	28.3	25.3
Japan	18.5	22.1
Netherlands	24.3	25.0
Norway	27.0	23.6
Sweden	35.1	30.6
UK	25.4	27.1
US	15.7	24.5

Source: Adema and Ladaique (2005, Table 6).

Replacement Rates

Over the years, social security schemes have been introduced in response to all sorts of contingencies (examples include unemployment benefits, social assistance, disability insurance, (early) retirement programmes, housing benefits and family, childcare and single-parent benefits). All these programmes can impinge on worker incentives to supply labour. Hence, not only do high taxes to finance welfare systems imply work disincentives, but the programmes themselves also provoke significant labour market disincentives.

For example, unemployment benefits generally increase unemployment duration since they reduce the effort devoted to job search and raise the so-called 'reservation wage', which is the lowest wage for which people are willing to accept a job. Knowing that there is unemployment insurance can also induce eligible workers to work less hard on the current job, resulting in lower labour supply and, potentially, lay-off. Unemployment benefits also set a floor in wage negotiation, and so push up wages and decrease employment.

On the upside, social safety programmes such as unemployment insurance bring security to people and give the jobless time to search for and find a better job. If this implies that people stay employed longer in a new job, the gains to the individual and to society can be large. There is also evidence that unemployment insurance enables consumption smoothing, which prevents consumption dropping sharply as income falls in unemployment (Meyer, 2002a).

Table 3.7   Net replacement rates in the case of unemployment, 2004

Country	Initial phase of unemployment [a]	Long-term unemployment [b]
Australia	52	51
Austria	70	69
Belgium	72	67
Canada	73	48
Denmark	80	69
Finland	78	69
France	82	60
Germany	77	70
Ireland	59	71
Italy	63	-
Japan	72	59
Netherlands	82	68
Norway	76	56
Sweden	86	67
UK	62	63
US	66	35

Notes:
[a] OECD calculations are based on the unweighted averages for earnings levels of 67% APW and 100% APW for six family types.
[b] Measured in the 60th month of benefit receipt.

Source: OECD website: Benefits and wages: gross/net replacement rates, country-specific files and tax/benefit models (latest update: March, 2006).

The average ratio between out-of-work benefits and in-work earnings, called the 'replacement rate', is sizeable in many countries (see Table 3.7). A person eligible for social assistance typically receives over 70 per cent of his or her potential in-work earnings in a large number of economies. In four European countries (Denmark, France, the Netherlands and Sweden), this is over 80 per cent. In the case of long-term unemployment, the replacement rates decline somewhat, particularly in Canada and the US where they drop below 50 per cent.

High replacement rates create strong disincentives for those out of work to actively look for employment. This is the 'unemployment trap'. Meyer (2002a) finds that an increase in the replacement rate by 10 percentage points raises unemployment duration between 1 and 1.5 weeks (cited in Rosen, 2005). Because many schemes, such as housing benefits, relate eligibility criteria to earnings, raising the work effort or enhancing skills to gain a better position on the labour markets also leads to high marginal taxes in the form of benefits taken away. In other words, high benefits cause low-income workers to suffer from high marginal tax rates as income rises and benefits are phased out, so they are deterred from working longer hours or obtaining skills training to improve their pay. This is the 'poverty trap'.

BOX 3.8

The ratio between out-of-work benefits and in-work earnings is large in European countries, ranging up to 86 per cent in Sweden and 82 per cent in France and the Netherlands. This creates strong disincentives for the unemployed to find employment. Certain schemes also link benefit payments to earnings, so that marginal tax rates are high and workers enter the poverty trap as they are discouraged from increasing their work effort or acquiring skills training to improve pay.

Making unemployment benefits conditional

A key challenge for European economies in the decades to come will be to better target benefits and make them conditional. While unconditional and poorly targeted unemployment benefits destroy jobs, conditional benefits spur job growth. Higher replacement rates raise equilibrium unemployment in both competitive and non-competitive labour markets. However, in non-competitive labour markets, conditional and better-targeted benefits mitigate the adverse effect of unemployment. Granting unemployment benefits only to people who become involuntarily unemployed, but excluding those who quit voluntarily or are dismissed for shirking, can increase employment levels in an economy with efficiency wages (see van der Ploeg, 2006b). Furthermore, limiting the duration of unemployment benefits and making benefits conditional on search effort also encourages people to find new work more swiftly (for example, Shavell and Weiss, 1979). Under these conditions, unemployment benefits could be raised for those who become unemployed through bad luck.

Many OECD countries have over the years introduced stricter conditions for receiving unemployment benefits. However, in many cases failure to enforce and administrate the requirements adequately reduces effectiveness.

Wage indexing

Pissarides (1998) estimates that a cut in payroll taxes by 10 per cent could lower unemployment by as much as 1 percentage point. However, this is only so if unemployment benefits are not indexed to wages. If they are indexed, there tends to be less real wage resistance, so wages are flexible. Labour then absorbs much of the tax cut with little effect on employment and unemployment. Higher average labour taxes thus raise unemployment only if the unemployed in turn manage to escape the additional burden of taxation (or manage to obtain informal and untaxed income). If unemployment benefits are taxed equally, the replacement rate of out-of-work benefits and in-work earnings in the economy is not affected, in which case a tax change is not likely to have much of an impact on employment.

BOX 3.9

Changes in the tax structure reduce unemployment if government succeeds in shifting part of the tax burden onto the unemployed. In this manner the effective replacement rate is lowered, thereby providing an incentive to work. This is only possible if unemployment benefits are not indexed to after-tax wages.

Why Social Policies may be Beneficial to the Economy

Cutting taxes or benefits will not always boost employment (see van der Ploeg, 2006a and 2006c). The traditional idea is that maximising an individual's absolute income is the main factor that raises happiness. However, there is increasing evidence that relative incomes matter much more to people. This effect is popularly referred to as 'keeping up with the Joneses', that is, working excessively hard in order to keep up with the consumption of their peers. Survey research of 5,000 British workers shows that job satisfaction is only weakly correlated with absolute income. Happiness is more significantly reduced if the reference wage of workers in comparable situations increases, thus making the income differential larger (Clark and Oswald, 1996).

In a more recent study, Blanchflower and Oswald (2004) examine developments in the causes of happiness with a sample of 100,000 American and British citizens. Although they find that money buys happiness, relative incomes matter as well and unemployment and divorce have a considerable negative impact. Moreover, the results differed between groups of people. Generally, life satisfaction decreases until the age of 40, after which it rises again. In the US, overall happiness has declined, particularly among white women. The happiness of blacks, on the other hand, has risen. In Britain levels of happiness have remained largely stable.

People thus care about relative incomes and become less happy if others around them earn and consume more. When given the choice in a recent survey, most graduate students of public health at Harvard indicated that they would prefer to be given $50,000 a year if others got half, rather than

$100,000 a year if others got double (Layard, 2003). Hence, they preferred to have less, given that their relative situation is improved. Apparently peer performance is important. Individuals are happier if they outperform their peers, and those who are outperformed feel less happy. It is interesting that the same Harvard students did not show a similar rivalry with regard to leisure time. Asked whether they would prefer either to have 2 weeks of vacation if others have 1 week, or to have 4 weeks if others have 8 weeks, the majority preferred the latter option. Rivalry thus does not extend to leisure. There is also evidence that people who have won the Oscars live on average four years longer than those who were nominated but did not win.

Although these are just a few examples in a vast literature on factors affecting happiness, all of them indicate that people set great store by relative incomes, therefore they work hard and enjoy less leisure in order to improve their relative position on the social scale. Also, a crucial factor is habituation. People quickly get used to a higher standard of living, but have trouble adjusting to a lower standard. At the same time this makes other people feel unhappier. These 'rat races' thus produce adverse externalities which can effectively be corrected by progressive labour taxes that discourage people from working too hard.

Hamermesh and Slemrod (2005) propose a more progressive income tax to correct for the negative spillovers from 'workaholism'. The addiction to work seems to be concentrated among high-ability/high-income workers and causes several internalities and externalities. For example, people who work long hours more often suffer from exhaustion, overweight, stress and high blood pressure. Workaholism also reflects negatively on the partners and children of workaholics. Survey research discloses that workaholism also extends to retirement, which is more likely to be postponed. Using optimal tax theory, the authors argue for a more progressive income tax than would otherwise be appropriate.

Also, many non-tax distortions arise in addition to those induced by tax and benefit policies. This often makes the overall welfare effect of tax distortions uncertain. In a 'second-best' scenario, the adverse effects of a tax and a non-tax distortion may to an extent affect each other, as we have already seen. Greater tax progression, for example, reduces wage pressures and raises employment in non-competitive economies. The real world never suffers from one distortion at a time, but typically has many, ranging from monopoly power in labour markets to high and progressive taxes. It may then well be the case that various distortions cancel each other out, so policy prescriptions based on an ideal world with only one distortion can be very misleading indeed.

Tax progression may also correct a failing insurance market, since it redistributes income from richer older people to younger ones earning less. This reduces the distortions resulting from rationed credit markets. Similarly, tax progression redistributes from the rich to the poor, which partly corrects for the negative effect of credit rationing on the education of students with less-affluent parents. Since insurance markets mostly fall short of fully compensating lost income in the case of illness, work-related injury, disability or unemployment, people also accept less-risky jobs and are willing to undertake less-risky activities. Tax progression mitigates this effect as it redistributes income to those who are less fortunate.

A final consideration is that a higher tax burden facilitates the implementation of government policies that promote growth. And this is exactly what governments in countries with large welfare systems attempt to do. In part it corrects for reduced labour market incentives that arise in non-competitive economies. Examples include so-called 'make work pay' (MWP) and various other active labour market policies. MWP policies seek to mitigate the negative effects of losing benefit payments by providing in-work benefits when locating a job or increasing the work effort. Grauwe and Polan (2003) show that countries that spend most on social security rank highest, on average, in the competitiveness leagues of Lausanne's IMD or the World Economic Forum. They argue that causation is very unlikely to run the other way, so the link going from strong competitiveness to a stronger economy and more funds for the welfare state is weak.

In his pathbreaking historical cross-country study, Lindert (2004) points out that the growth in social spending started in the late 19th century after the right to vote was extended to poorer men and women. It set the stage for the then Prime Minister David Lloyd George's assault on Britain's rich just before the First World War. In addition, extending political voice led to population ageing and income growth, the emergence of comprehensive nationwide social insurance programmes and more spending on public education. The growth in the post-war welfare states was particularly big in countries where the middle and bottom ranks changed places and were ethnically homogenous.

Lindert also argues that there is almost no evidence of a negative effect of a substantial welfare state on GDP. The net national costs of social transfers, and the taxes that finance them, are essentially zero. An important reason is that governments become more efficient, as distortions of higher tax rates are proportionally much higher than lower rates. For example, countries with large welfare states tend to have a more pro-growth and regressive mix of taxes (think of high taxes on vices and low taxes on capital income). Another reason is that those who are unemployed due to the generous welfare states are, typically, less productive and thus the harm to national income is limited. A more fundamental reason is that in advanced market economies with developed welfare states the economics of second best apply. As discussed above, the various distortions of the welfare state tend to wipe each other out, so the burden of the welfare state is much less than simply adding all the distortions one at a time.

The general picture that emerges is that *laissez-faire* advocates have some explaining to do, since neither theory nor empirical evidence suggests that social policies must necessarily harm the economy. However, it can be argued that in tomorrow's globalising economy with a stronger (tax) competition between countries, there will be less room for high taxes and thus state expenditures on social policies.

BOX 3.10

Despite the negative incentives from large welfare systems, there are reasons why social policies and a moderate tax progression can benefit economic welfare. Besides the wage-moderating impacts of tax progression in non-competitive economies, large income differentials impose adverse externalities and higher taxes correct for working too hard. A variety of 'second-best' policy issues related to failing capital and insurance markets may make a case for progressive taxes, which redistribute income from the rich to the poor and encourage risk taking. High taxes also generate funds to facilitate growth-promoting strategies such as MWP policies. We have also noted that in a globalising economy there is less room for high taxes.

3.6   TAX POLICY ALTERNATIVES TO STIMULATE LABOUR MARKETS

Redesigning the Tax Rate Schedule

Improving labour market incentives by tax reform most certainly implies changing the income distribution and/or cutting taxes. This is particularly so in European economies where labour tax burdens are large and non-tax labour market institutions are highly distorting. High effective tax rates on labour, particularly at the lower end of the income distribution, harm labour supply (perhaps not so much for prime-age males, but certainly for part-time workers and married women) as well as labour demand when wage setting is characterised by competition or centralised bargaining.

Disney (2000) provides a review of studies on welfare policies, employment and unemployment. He concludes that lower marginal tax and/or replacement rates increase labour force participation and labour supplied by high-income earners as well as by older workers nearing retirement, low-income families and younger workers entering the labour force. He concludes: 'there seemed to be significant labor supply responses to policy changes for these groups' (p. 35). Whereas high-income earners and older workers respond mainly to lower overall statutory tax rates, participation and labour supply of low-income and younger workers can be stimulated, for example, by an EITC or wage rate subsidy (both labour market strategies are discussed in Section 3.7).

Generally speaking, tax progression is much more efficiently implemented by a large tax deduction or credit that favours low-income households, than by high marginal taxes that reduce work incentives. As such, significant labour market efficiency gains can be achieved by cutting marginal tax rates that could partly be financed by other measures that broaden the tax base. But there are also administrative advantages. These include simplicity in filing tax returns (there would be fewer exceptions to the tax base that often increase administrative requirements), and reduced scope for the use of tax-avoidance schemes and conflict between the taxpayer and the tax authority. These measures should ensure an effective tax progression and revenue collection effort, but it shows that improvements can be made.

Two more rigorous proposals that have been made in recent years include the flat tax and shifting away from labour taxation altogether.

The Flat Tax as a Viable Alternative

The flat tax is an often cited alternative to traditional progressive income taxation by increasing marginal tax rates. Instead, the flat tax is imposed as a single or 'fixed' marginal tax rate. There is a distinction between income- and consumption-type flat taxes and thus whether the return to savings is included in the tax base (see Section 1.6 in Chapter 1 on equivalence relations). There can also be differences in the size of the basic tax allowance granted.[12] The flat tax has the virtue of simplicity, that is, many exceptions to the tax base are eliminated, it stimulates economic activity and it reduces tax distortions and the administrative burden. Since the 1990s, a number of Eastern European countries have switched to flat taxes, including Estonia (1994), Lithuania (1994), Latvia (1997), Russia (2001), Ukraine (2004), Slovakia (2004), Georgia (2005) and Romania (2005). [13]

At the same time, there are inevitably perverse distributional consequences. In fact, most of the burden falls on middle earners who, in Western democracies, comprise the majority of the electorate. This is why the flat tax was a political liability in Germany.[14] In a major report, Britain's

---

[12] The basic flat tax concept was proposed in the US by Hall and Rabushka (1995) and is consumption based. The technicalities of this tax are discussed in Chapter 5.

[13] See Keen et al. (2006) for the applicable tax rates and other specifics.

[14] During the German parliamentary elections of 2005, tax law professor and flat tax proponent Paul Kirchhof's political career was cut short following rising anxieties among German voters on the implementation of a flat tax.

Conservative party also rejected a flat tax as being a step too far if implemented instantaneously:

'While theoretically attractive, moving directly to a 'pure' flat tax in the UK would not in practice be viable. Financing current levels of government expenditure would require a flat tax rate which would entail either undue risk with the public finances or major cuts in expenditure or a steep increase in tax rates for those on low incomes or for middle earners. Nevertheless, many of the features of flatter taxes – simplicity, stability, a broader base, higher thresholds, fewer rates – can and should be actively pursued'. (Tax Reform Commission, 2006, p. 8)

Keen et al. (2006) of the IMF conclude that in none of the Eastern European countries can one actually speak of a pure flat tax. The study demonstrates that actual practices differ widely. For example, in Russia and Ukraine exemptions are reduced over a certain amount of income so that the tax actually becomes progressive. Moreover, it concerns only personal income taxation and not SSCs. In Russia the latter are imposed progressively and at high rates. There has also been no indication of a strong effect on the work effort by the shift. There has been a reduction in revenue, though, and in none of the cases have Laffer effects been measured. In many instances the loss in revenue has been compensated by increases in indirect taxes, such as petroleum taxes and tobacco excises, which even doubled in Russia.

Excessive pay of top executives: a flat tax with a progressive tax
Politicians and the public in OECD countries display a growing uneasiness with and angriness about the extraordinarily high incomes of a select group of top managers. The median pay package of CEOs of the 300 largest corporations in the US was $6.8 million in 2005 and $4.3 million for top executives of the Financial Times Stock Exchange 100 companies in Britain.[15] The salaries plus bonuses no longer seem to reflect efficiency or genuine contributions to productivity or welfare. Nevertheless, practice in the US and Europe shows that the majority of shareholders and supervisory boards are accepting the excessive pay of top executives.

A possible solution to this issue has been proposed by Vito Tanzi, the former director of the IMF's Fiscal Affairs Department.[16] Instead of introducing highly progressive income tax rates or other distorting government intervention (that is, 'replace market failure with government failure'), Tanzi suggests reforming the tax system by combining features of flat-rate taxes with progressive taxes. He favours a steeper rate on the part of

---

[15] Data are from www.corpwatch.org (downloaded on 10 June 2007).
[16] See the *Financial Times* article, 2 March 2007: 'Tax system reform can address unrest over high pay'.

high-income earners exceeding some high threshold, say $1 million in the United States (in the US 240,000 individuals report incomes over this amount).

Given the large and rising share of total income that is enjoyed by top earners (see, for example, Figure 2.13 in Chapter 2), the system would guarantee significantly lower tax rates for workers up to the threshold income, including most high-skilled and mobile workers for whom incentives clearly matter. Similar proposals have been echoed in politics in Belgium, France, Germany and the Netherlands.

Nevertheless, the system would only be effective in mitigating public unrest if executives were to largely or completely bear the additional tax themselves. Seeing that net rather than gross remuneration is often the starting-point in pay-package negotiations on this level (due to the elasticities of labour supply and demand), this is not likely to be the case. International research based on 3,000 pay packages in 17 wealthy nations indeed confirms that countries with higher tax rates also pay top managers higher salaries (Otten, 2007).

To give an example, a top executive has a gross salary of €2.5 million on which he pays 40 per cent in income tax, leaving a net compensation of €1.5 million. If government now enacts a special tax rate of 60 per cent for earnings above €1 million, the executive would pay €1.3 million in income tax (40 per cent over €1 million and 60 per cent over €1.5 million). In practice, the extra income tax of €0.3 million is often compensated by the company, raising gross remuneration to €3.25 million in this case, so that again €1.5 million is left on a net basis (40 per cent over €1 million and 60 per cent over €2.25 million).

To address the issue of excessive pay packages, another option would be to set an (international) benchmark indicating the average compensation (salaries, including pensions and bonuses) of top executives per sector. The data would be published annually. In addition, tax legislation could in turn disallow that part of remuneration above the benchmark from being deducted from corporate tax.[17]

Shifting the Tax Burden away from Labour

Measures aimed at lowering the tax burden on labour have been advocated to stimulate jobs and alleviate the EU unemployment problem. To this end, a number of alternative taxes that feature other tax bases have been put forward. The proposals include a revenue-neutral shift to taxes on other production factors such as capital and energy, a shift to VAT and,

---

[17] Regulation to deal with excessive pay is also an option. In France, President Nicolas Sarkozy has announced legislative measures to prohibit certain excessive compensation packages on discharge (pay for failure).

additionally, a shift from employer-based social security constructions to employee-based social security contributions. It is being argued that each of the tax reforms should help lighten the burden on labour, yet it is not always obvious that this also improves employment. Here we provide a short overview, while the following Chapters elaborate further on the first three proposals.

Since capital is mobile in the long run, a shift to taxation of capital income would cause it to move abroad and reduce capital accumulation with perhaps further detrimental effects. There is much evidence on the sensitivity of (foreign direct) investment to corporate income tax rates (see Chapter 4). Labour would also suffer in the process by reduced productivity, so this is perhaps the least-preferred alternative to labour taxation.

If a higher VAT finances lower labour taxes, employees face a decline in the real value of their wages because consumer prices rise simultaneously. Hence, the labour tax cut is offset by a loss in disposable income due to higher prices. A shift to VAT could nevertheless mitigate the burden on labour, mainly because some consumption is taxed out of capital income. Existing capital at the time of a switch would effectively be taxed twice: once under income tax when the wealth was earned and again under consumption tax when it is spent (a basic condition is thus that the shift is unexpected, otherwise people could anticipate the higher tax and increase current consumption). The shift also redistributes some of the extra burden of ageing from younger workers to capital owners, mostly the elderly who have accumulated wealth over their lifetime. Much of the success of this type of policy depends on the indexation of unemployment benefits to after-tax wages, that is employment increases only if the tax switch manages to reduce the replacement rate indirectly (see Chapter 5).

The effect of a shift from labour taxation to taxes on pollution would depend on whether consumers outside the labour force bear part of the burden – hence, by incomes from income-maintaining transfers or capital income. If so, green tax reform stimulates employment and reduces pollution (see Chapter 9). Moreover, in order not to seriously undermine the competitive position of companies on world markets, international coordination of an energy tax is of crucial importance (CPB, 1996). Otherwise energy-intensive industries would move abroad in response to an energy tax (capital and energy are considered complementary). Since European industries are among the most energy efficient in the world, this could actually increase carbon production. The energy tax could also be restricted to small-scale users. In such a case, the effect on employment is mitigated.

A final option is to increase employee SSCs (which reduce take-home pay), to facilitate a decrease in employer-paid SSCs (which raise employers' gross wage costs of hiring workers). Whether this is so depends on the respective elasticities of labour supply and demand. Some positive short-run effects of such a shift have been observed in OECD countries. Belgium has lowered employer SSC in the 1995-2000 period by on average €1.5 billion annually (or some 0.7 per cent of GDP), while the total labour tax wedge remained roughly the same. Joyeux and Stockman (2003) show that as a result, real wages decreased by 2.6 per cent and employment increased by 1.5 per cent in 2000. Moreover, targeting the tax cuts at low-paid workers maximises the potential effect, since labour supply among these workers is most elastic (OECD, 2003). In the long run the basic equivalency between taxes on labour is nevertheless likely to hold.

3.7 STRATEGIES TO IMPROVE LABOUR MARKET INCENTIVES

Over the years several tax and benefit strategies have been used in OECD countries which have in some way or other aimed to promote employment and/or reduce poverty and to blunt the efficiency versus equity trade-off implicit in most tax and benefit policies. The two conflicting objectives of increasing the work incentive while reducing poverty prove hard to deal with. One thing is certain, a less categorical and piecemeal approach to social security could help to make welfare systems better targeted and more transparent (Haveman, 1996).[18] The income support and labour market strategies that have been used or proposed to this end can be broadly categorised by the negative income tax, credit income tax, basic income guarantee, EITC, earned income allowance, wage rate subsidy and marginal income subsidy.

Income Support Programmes

The negative income tax
The negative income tax (NIT) was first outlined in 1962 by Nobel laureate Milton Friedman and provides cash payments to individuals with income below a certain threshold. In most proposals the threshold lies around the poverty line. Every citizen would file a yearly income tax return on which basis annual earnings are taxed as usual according to the country-specific income tax schedule. Individuals with no earnings, or earnings below the threshold, receive a net benefit payment from the authorities (that is, 'negative' taxes), so a minimum level of income is guaranteed.

For example, assume that a guaranteed income of €5,000 and a tax rate of 25 per cent applies. In this case, an individual with no income receives a

---

[18] Haveman (1996, p. 29) reiterates the iron law that 'an income guarantee assuring all citizens of an "adequate" level of living financed via a personal income tax requires a structure of marginal tax rates implying substantial work disincentive'.

benefit payment of €5,000. For every euro of earnings, 25 per cent would subsequently be taxed away. At an earnings level of, say, €10,000, the person receives a net benefit payment of €2,500 and total income amounts to €12,500. A net benefit is received up to the break-even income of €20,000. After this point, the individual becomes a net taxpayer. In this way, one system replaces many existing social security schemes (for example, pensions, unemployment, disability and sickness benefits, school subsidies and so on).

The NIT is illustrated graphically in Figure 3.2. At the 45° line, net income equals gross income so no taxes are imposed. Point Y^* corresponds to the break-even income below which a government provides a net benefit payment. The guaranteed level of income is measured by the intersection with the y-axis (for example, point A or D). The exact amount may depend on family size, age or other specific characteristics.

If the tax rate is kept constant as income progresses, the structure resembles that in Figure 3.2A. In implementing the system, a distinction can be made between 'low-guarantee' and 'high-guarantee' NIT schemes. The previous numerical example roughly corresponds to line ABC. As one can see, this system provides a low-income guarantee and imposes constant METRs at every level of earnings. Some progressivity might subsequently be built into the system further down the income distribution. The marginal tax rate needed to finance the scheme would be low enough to not significantly affect the work effort of taxpayers. In fact, compared to many current income taxes in the surveyed countries, incentives are likely to be improved considerably (Haveman, 1996). Only a very modest income guarantee would be provided, dealing only with the worst of poverty.

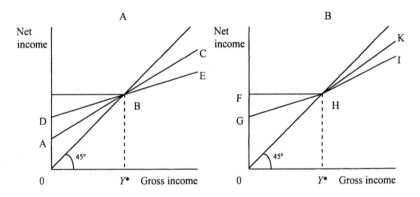

Figure 3.2   The negative income tax with constant and variable METRs

A higher-income guarantee for the same number of people could be characterised by the line DBE (still assuming constant marginal rates).

METRs would have to be increased more significantly to finance the programme, thus lowering the incentives to work.[19]

Under the alternative scenario in Figure 3.2B, METRs are variable across income groups. This is illustrated by line GHK and enables more specific targeting of benefits by government. For example, a relatively high guarantee could be provided but for a smaller number of people. A serious drawback is that individuals with incomes below Y^* face higher METRs, as the relative reduction in benefits with an increase in income constitutes an implicit tax. This creates larger work disincentives at the intensive margin.

The credit income tax
The credit income tax (CIT) operates in an equivalent manner to the NIT. The main difference is that the CIT is incorporated into the existing income tax law, whereas the NIT is implemented as a separate scheme that exists parallel to the existing income tax. The CIT presents a universal tax and benefit system of its own accord. The adoption of a CIT would require a more comprehensive reform, but ultimately would be simpler.

Under the CIT, a refundable tax credit is provided to all residents. Hence, individuals with adequate income and a tax liability that exceeds the allowance would be net taxpayers, while those with insufficient income would receive a net payment from a refundable tax credit. The CIT has similar effects on work incentives as described above for the NIT.

Because the CIT is operated by a single authority, namely the tax authority, and is integrated into the tax system, it is less stigmatising to beneficiaries. No part of the population would be classified as 'welfare recipient or dependent'. As a corollary, people claim the credit sooner, which raises the effectiveness of the social security system. It also makes cross-checks easier, thereby reducing the scope for fraud and enhancing the enforcement effort. On balance therefore, there are a number of additional advantages associated with the CIT.

The basic income guarantee
The basic income guarantee (BIG) ensures a reasonable level of income to all residents independent of other income. The scheme would be the most desirable alternative from an equity point of view. Poverty would be virtually

---

[19] In the US, four federally sponsored NIT experiments were carried out between 1968 and 1982. The programmes were generous, one having an income guarantee of 125 per cent of the poverty line, a tax rate of 50 per cent and a break-even income of 250 per cent of the poverty level. Labour supply was found to decrease considerably. On average, labour supply of married men decreases by the equivalent of 2 weeks of full-time employment; married women by the equivalent of 3 weeks; and youth by roughly 4 weeks (Robins, 1985). Although these responses are large, in continental Europe existing income support and corresponding tax rates are already high. For this reason, the NIT is likely to lead to smaller negative labour supply responses, if at all. On the upside, social safety would become more uniform, transparent and accessible, which are all clear improvements to the current intricate web of social arrangements.

eradicated, provided that the BIG is high enough. The BIG corresponds to line FHI in Figure 3.2B. Hence, for earnings up to Y^* the METR would be 100 per cent. This cancels out all incentives for people with earnings below Y^* to find work or increase effort. Moreover, to be able to finance the system, the METR on people with incomes above Y^* would have to be raised drastically. This would considerably reduce incentives to supply labour and to study and improve skills. The BIG scheme is therefore not an option for countries actively seeking to stimulate employment and increase their labour market performance.

The earned income tax credit

The EITC does not guarantee a certain level of income to all, since eligibility extends only to the working poor. This means that the EITC is a pure in-work benefit programme. Other than that, its functioning is similar to the NIT. The EITC is designed to supplement earnings of workers at the lower end of the income distribution. By making the size of the credit income dependent, workers have an incentive to increase labour supply. Hence, working extra hours raises the total benefit payment that is received. In this manner, poverty is reduced directly by supplementing earnings through the tax credit as well as indirectly by encouraging labour supply.

The structure of the EITC corresponds to line 0AB in Figure 3.3, although several variants are implemented in practice. The earnings supplement is effectuated through an income tax credit or cash payments where the benefit can be made conditional not only on income but also on hours worked (as in the UK).

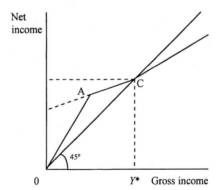

Figure 3.3   The EITC

Earnings are supplemented up to the kink at point A. The steep line indicates that the METR is low for this range, which is commonly referred to as the 'phase-in' range. Higher than usual earnings stimulate people to start working (the extensive margin) or increase their work effort (the intensive margin). This negates the adverse effects of the unemployment and the poverty trap, respectively.

It is infeasible to maintain an earnings supplement for all workers, however, since this would destroy incentives to work. Hence, logically, a 'phase-out' range has to follow. During this phase-out, which is represented by line AC, METRs are high. The credit is still provided but gradually withdrawn as income increases. Beyond point C, earnings are treated as normal again. As a result, some low-income workers are induced to increase labour supply (that is, those with incomes in the phase-in range), while others face reduced work incentives (that is, those in the phase-out range).

Figure 3.4 presents an alternative illustration, which highlights the credits path as income progresses. The EITC implemented in the US has essentially this shape. An intermediate section is inserted where the credit remains steady (from points A to B). The phase-in range is thus not directly followed by a phase-out range. The kinks at points A and B are of special interest.

When targeting a small group of low earners with a generous benefit (corresponding to a steep 0A), strong incentives are created to participate in the labour market and find employment. In other words, labour supply response at the extensive margin is induced. The consequential longer phase-out period will nevertheless have an adverse effect on the hours worked of a large number of low earners already at work.

By contrast, making the programme less generous and available to a larger number of people results in a more gradual phase-in. This encourages the work effort of people at the intensive margin. Even so, a limited response can be expected at the extensive margin as the benefit is inherently low. Hence, the point in the income distribution where the 'kink' is located is important, that is, where the phase-in range is transformed into a phase-out period.

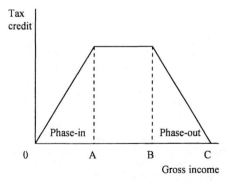

Figure 3.4   Phase-in and phase-out ranges of the EITC

The most effective rate structure and break-even income would have to be determined on the basis of country-specific simulations.[20] But it is generally accepted that, particularly in countries where participation taxes are high with a mixture of high marginal tax rates on those working and generous benefits for those out of work, an in-work scheme such as the EITC presents an effective way to preserve work incentives at the bottom of the income distribution while redistributing money. If it implies that many inactive people find work, the windfall for the treasury could be substantial. Employment implies both more tax revenue and less expenditure on income-maintaining transfers.

United Kingdom   In 1971, the UK adopted an in-work benefit programme that was subsequently replaced by the Family Credit (FC) in 1988 and the Working Families' Tax Credit (WFTC) in 1999. The WFTC was more generous and included the children's tax credit. Where a married couple with one child and no WFTC faced a replacement rate of 143 per cent in the case of part-time employment and 92 per cent in the case of full-time employment, this was reduced by the WFTC to, respectively, 76 and 60 per cent (Ochel, 2001). This has provided strong incentives to find employment. Some 71,000 people participated in the FIS programme in 1971. By 1990, this number had increased to 317,000 and, after the WFTC introduction in 1999, to 1.5 million. The participation effects from introducing the WFTC were estimated to be about 30,000 jobs (Blundell et al., 2000).

The WFTC and children's tax credit were replaced in 2003 by the child tax credit and working tax credit, which together are referred to as the new tax credits.[21] Both tax credits provide an additional £2.7 billion to support low-income families, combat poverty and make work pay. Blundell et al. (2004) estimate that the new system increases single mothers' participation by 3.4 percentage points, reduces that of married mothers by 0.4 percentage points and increases that of married fathers by 0.9 percentage points.

United States   The dynamics in the US EITC programme over time have also allowed evaluation of the effect on labour force participation and hours worked. The Tax Reform Act of 1986 increased the maximum credit from $550 to $851. Eissa and Liebman (1996) find that this raised the participation

---

[20] Saez (2002) concludes that, under conditions of optimal taxation, if labour supply responses are concentrated along the extensive margin, it is efficient to adopt an EITC with a small guaranteed income and transfers that rise with income for those on a low income. If concentrated along the intensive margin a NIT scheme would be optimal with a high level of guaranteed income and a large phase-out range. The participation elasticity is crucial in this consideration.

[21] The UK government also enacted a so-called 'Child Trust Fund' (CTF) to combat child poverty and promote savings up to the age of 18. This is a savings book for every child born on or after 1 September 2002. When the account is opened, the government deposits £250 into it. Family members are subsequently allowed to deposit up to £1,200 per year into the fund. Neither the parents nor the child pays tax on income or gains in the account.

of single women with children from 73.0 to 75.8 per cent, compared to single women without children and therefore no EITC. From the study it could not be concluded, however, that hours worked decreased, something which might have been expected especially for married women already in the labour force. Meyer and Rosenbaum (2001) obtained similar positive results by examining the 1984-96 period.

Eissa and Hoynes (1998) observe a decrease in participation and hours worked by *married* women as a result of credit increases. By examining current population survey (CPS) data from 1984 to 1996, they found that EITC expansions in the period under consideration increased labour force participation of married men somewhat, but reduced participation by married women by 1.2 percentage points. Furthermore, hours worked by married men decreased by between 45 and 47 hours a year and by married women between 13 and 93.

Hence, although the evidence points to a limited labour supply response at the intensive margin, there seem to be unambiguous positive effects on the decision to participate. Interestingly, Meyer (2002b) argues that empirical patterns in the US do not support the theory of reduced hours at the intensive margin either, simply because hours worked have not fallen.[22] The methods used so far may have overstated the labour disincentives along the intensive margins.[23]

The earned income allowance

The earned income allowance (EIA) is slightly different from the EITC. The system operates by allowing a small percentage of earned income to be credited from total taxation with a maximum amount. Hence, the allowance is built up with income typically up to the minimum wage level, after which it remains constant. This means that every worker with sufficient income receives the credit, not just the working poor, and that for most workers it boils down to a fixed amount. The upshot is that the phase-out range with reduced labour incentives as under the EITC is circumvented. However, maintaining a credit for all workers comes at a considerable cost, which most certainly increases marginal tax rates across the board (low incomes gain

---

[22] There could be reasons why the EITC is an effective programme in the US, but not in European countries (Hotz and Scholz, 2000). For example, the US has more flexible employment regulations. Other countries have much more rigid labour markets, making employers reluctant to hire low-skilled workers. The US tax to GDP ratio is also relatively low, so marginal tax rates in the phase-out range are not as high as in high-tax countries. Finally, the US minimum wage is relatively low.

[23] Ireland and Canada also have experience with earnings supplement benefit schemes. In Ireland the Family Income Supplement (FIS) and the Back to Work Allowance (BTWA) are the most important. In 1993, Canada initiated the Self-Sufficiency Project (SSP). These schemes are generally positively evaluated (see Card and Robins, 1996; Michalopoulos et al., 1999; Gradus and Julsing, 2001; and Ochel, 2001;).

disproportionately). In comparison to the EITC, the labour market incentives provided by an EIA are thus significantly lower than those of the EITC.

Labour Market Strategies

A second category of labour market strategies falls under the denominator of active labour market programmes. Active labour market policies are advocated by European lawmakers as an effective way to correct for distortions created by other labour market institutions. They are targeted at disadvantaged, low-skilled individuals with little work experience and/or schooling and aim to promote employment and/or higher wages. They thus try to counter poverty without having to resort to income support.

Public spending on active labour market policies currently ranges between, respectively, 0.2 and 0.3 per cent of GDP in the US and Japan to 1.7 and 1.8 per cent of GDP in Denmark and the Netherlands.[24]

Wage-rate subsidy
The wage-rate subsidy is a labour market strategy which aims to improve labour supply. It operates by setting a target wage rate, which provides a decent income. Since many people are not sufficiently productive to warrant such a wage, they would not find a job unless there is a rate-wage subsidy. An example could be a target wage of 12 units per hour, a subsidy rate of 0.5 units and the actual wage of 8 units per hour. The subsidy received by the worker would than amount to 2 units per hour. If the actual wage were 9 units per hour, the subsidy amounts to 1.50 units per hour. In this manner, the subsidy is slowly phased out up to the target wage. For workers with hourly earnings below this level, higher wages provide a positive incentive to increase the work effort.

This makes the system very similar to the EITC. However, there are some additional economic effects to take into account (see Haveman, 1996):

- the wage-rate subsidy can be used to offset the negative effect of minimum wage requirements. Employers are inclined to hire a large quantity of people even though the productivity of these workers lies below what the minimum wage would call for;
- as labour supply is likely to increase, wages paid by employers tend to decrease because they are effectively bid down (but only if not in conflict with minimum wage policies); and
- a disincentive arises for low-skilled workers to increase their wage rate through investment in skills training and education (in contrast to an increased participation and work effort due to earning supplements).

---

[24] See OECD electronic database on Labour Market Programmes.

Marginal employment subsidy

The marginal employment subsidy focuses on the demand side of the labour market. It encourages employers to hire workers by providing a tax credit to firms that add additional low-skilled workers to their labour force. In this manner, businesses are stimulated to increase output and/or substitute labour for capital. Although the scheme does not provide direct payment to workers, it could lead to a bidding-up of wages so that workers benefit indirectly.

Cherniavsky (1996) shows that an employer-based subsidy is not easy to implement on an economy-wide scale. On a smaller scale they may be successful, but only with adequate provisions that prevent the substitution of workers so as to take advantage of the credit. The New Jobs Tax Credit (NJCT) in the US provided a subsidy of 50 per cent over wages paid in excess of 105 per cent of wage cost in the previous year. It was in place from 1977 to 1979 and was replaced by the Targeted Jobs Tax Credit (TJTC), which aimed only at disadvantaged workers. Here the credit equalled 50 per cent of the first $6,000 of wages paid to an incrementally hired disadvantaged worker. Studies on the overall effectiveness of these programmes produced mixed but overall negative results. The main problems seem to be a low awareness of the existence of the schemes. In addition, the majority of jobs under the TJTC originated from simple replacement of workers (roughly 70 per cent).[25] Survey research also indicated that most workers would have been hired anyway, regardless of the subsidy.

Main drawbacks

Briefly summarised, theoretical studies and practical experiences with these labour market programmes show that:

- the intended effects are small;
- the measures are expensive (cost effectiveness is low);
- the arrangements are complicated and not always understood by people;
- the administrative burden is high;
- programmes can be stigmatising;
- there is substitution of subsidised from non-subsidised labour; and
- the general tax rate could be lower without the subsidy. It is paid for by higher taxes on other workers (there is no such thing as a 'free lunch').

Because of these drawbacks, many of the tax subsidies have been abolished, often against the background of base broadening and rate lowering in income tax. Also, the causes of (temporary) high unemployment among

---

[25] For a similar Canadian scheme, the Employment Tax Credit Program (ETCP), studies found that 63 per cent of the jobs created were by simple transfers from one firm to another.

certain groups of workers have often little to do with the tax system. Labour market strategies then serve as makeshift measures to other factors that distort efficient working of the labour market. Important factors are the minimum wage rate, regulation and employment protection, but also the educational attainment of workers and work seekers, and childcare.

Therefore, partly based on own experiences with these types of tax arrangements, we are not in favour of a broad application of such measures. They also do not fit well within the main trends of the 21st century (see Chapter 2). These trends and issues are calling for a broad, low and simple tax system (see Chapter 10).

3.8   BRIEF SUMMARY

This chapter has shown that taxes and benefits play a positive and significant role in reducing unemployment and promoting employment. Yet, other labour market institutions must play an important role as well: 'The link between taxes and labor-market performance depends crucially on non-tax institutions. In particular, the impact of taxes on wages and unemployment depends on how wages are set and on welfare and unemployment benefits' (Bovenberg, 2006, p. 44).

European welfare systems have grown overly complex and place a heavy burden on labour. Although it is reasonable to prefer more leisure and less work as society becomes more affluent, this becomes more difficult in ageing societies facing growing international competition. The objective is to create a sustainable welfare state by increasing the work effort and extending the retirement age.

Practical experiences with special tax arrangements aimed at improving labour force participation and reducing unemployment show that many of these measures are expensive and have a low cost effectiveness. They are also complicated and impose a high administrative burden. That is why we are not in favour of these types of tax arrangements. Facing the trends and issues of the globalising economy, a broad, low and simple tax system is the best alternative (see Chapter 10). Statutory tax rates can be lowered further in many countries, financed in part by base-broadening measures. This enhances work incentives and simplicity, and reduces the scope for tax-avoidance schemes. The measures should ensure an effective tax progression and revenue collection.

The labour tax cuts could partly be compensated by a shift to consumption taxes such as VAT or green taxes. Further budgetary leeway can be created by modernising social security and making it better targeted. In the process of reforming labour markets, it takes a much greater effort to create a well-functioning welfare state than it takes to dismantle one. The tax system should provide a solid foundation on which labour markets can function efficiently. The challenge is to find a balanced mix of taxes and social safety. Or, in the words of the European Commission (2000b, p. 23): 'an inclusive dynamic society - in which everyone has a fair chance of participating. A Europe of social justice. A caring society. Using, not wasting, society's scarce resources to build sustainable capacity and opportunity for all'.

4. Capital markets, investment and taxation

The results from the academic literature therefore suggest that existing taxes on capital income lose revenue yet generate large efficiency costs and have distributional effects of dubious appeal. The formal models for a small open economy forecast that the optimal tax rate on capital income is simply zero.

(Gordon, 2000, p. 26)

4.1 INTRODUCTION

While taxation of labour income is relatively straightforward and accepted as a reliable source of revenue, capital income taxation is more controversial. Many people intuitively like to tax both factors evenly from an equity standpoint. However, it is not clear whether this should be done from an efficiency point of view. A number of authors even advocate a zero tax on capital income in an open economy, as the above quotation bears out. Hence, not only from an efficiency stance is the desirability of the capital income tax questioned but, on the grounds of redistribution, other tax bases could be preferred as well.

A main reason is high cross-border mobility of capital, compared to more fixed tax bases such as labour or consumption. Efficiency is also compromised because capital income tax distorts investment behaviour and lowers investment and the level of capital accumulation. This affects the interests of non-capital owners as well by lowering labour productivity and thereby raising unit labour costs, reducing employment and economic growth.

Taxing capital income differently from other income would present a clear break with the Schanz-Haig-Simons (S-H-S) concept of a comprehensive income tax, long the accepted criterion for taxing income. Under the S-H-S concept, income is defined as the value of the net accretion to one's economic power during a specific period in time. It comprises the aggregate of consumption and wealth accumulation (Goode, 1990). Thus all income, both in the form of labour earnings as well as that derived from capital, is taxed as it accrues and according to the same tax-rate schedule.

Despite differing views, all developed nations in practice tax capital income. Capital income can be generated by various investments held through a variety of legal forms. This makes capital taxation complex, especially when international issues are brought into the picture. Capital income includes dividends, interest and royalties originating from incorporated and unincorporated businesses, but also, for example, accrued capital gains and imputed rents to owner-occupied housing. Capital taxes are imposed on both a personal and a corporate level through the corporation tax (CT).

This chapter interchangeably addresses issues surrounding capital taxation in general and those of corporations specifically (CT is currently at the heart of the academic and political debate and more than other areas subject to change). This can be done without upsetting the overall structure of the text. First, the chapter surveys existing capital income tax systems and the main investment distortions created. Second, it looks at some considerations in optimal tax theory, which postulates that the long-run efficient tax on capital is simply zero. Next, the chapter turns to consider international aspects in capital income taxation. High capital mobility in modern economies means that investment is increasingly responsive to international taxation variations. We conclude with a discussion of three conceptual approaches to taxing capital income: the allowance for corporate equity, the comprehensive business income tax and the dual income tax.

4.2 CAPITAL INCOME TAX SYSTEMS, INVESTMENT AND TAX DISTORTIONS

Savings that become available on world capital markets ultimately flow into firms as business investment in order to earn the required rate of return by the profits generated. In considering the impact of taxation, a primary distinction is drawn between 'old' and 'new' capital. In other words, between taxes on existing capital assets compared to those on future capital investment.

The distinction is important for two reasons (OECD, 2000b). In the first place, the tax burden on 'old' capital is relevant for assessing equity aspects, while the tax burden on 'new' capital gives an impression of tax-system efficiency. The former measures the current tax burden on capital, while the latter is indicative of the incentives to invest. Second, in many countries the burden on existing capital varies markedly from that on newly produced capital. The effective average tax rate on existing capital may then provide a misleading notion of the tax rate on new capital, which is typically acquired at the margin.

Taxation and the Cost of Capital

The primary channel through which taxes affect investment behaviour is by their impact on the *user cost* of capital, which is defined as the minimum required rate of return that an investment has to earn to be viable. Very much like wages are a cost for employing labour, the cost of capital is thus the expense that a firm incurs for using capital as a production factor. As a broad rule of thumb, a lower cost of capital encourages investment, while a high cost of capital discourages it.

The general consensus in the economic literature is that the effect of the cost of capital on investment is significant. By reviewing much of the empirical literature, Hassett and Hubbard (1997) establish a semi-elasticity of investment with regard to the cost of capital of between -0.5 and -1.0. This implies that a reduction in the cost of capital by 1 percentage point increases capital investment by 0.5 to 1.0 per cent. Thus, in so far as taxation increases the cost of capital, the incentives to invest are adversely affected.

Tax rates and base definitions
Chapter 2 demonstrated that the statutory rate alone gives little indication of the effective tax burden. Indeed, a very high tax rate on a narrow base can generate the same effective burden as a low tax rate on a broad base. The definition of the tax base is thus a key variable.

An investor who comes across an opportunity to undertake a profitable investment project broadly has two means of finance to hand: debt capital, which is obtained from borrowers; and equity capital from new share issues or retained earnings (in practice, typically less than 10 per cent of equity capital is collected by issuing new shares).

A tax system that offers full allowance for the cost of capital (that is, both debt and equity capital) leaves the investment decision unaffected. This is because an investment project can only be commercially undertaken if its net present value (NPV) is zero or positive. The NPV is calculated as the discounted value of 'pure profits' or 'economic rents' that are generated over the investment's effective lifetime.[1] Thus, an investment project that manages to generate a positive return after all the costs of production have been deducted should be undertaken.[2] Given these conditions, an NPV that is positive before tax will remain so after tax, since the tax can never tax away more than the profit. Thus, a tax on pure profits does not interfere with the investment decision. However, if the tax base does include the user cost of

---

[1] The return on capital is divided into a *normal* return that covers the cost of using capital and an *above-normal* return which constitutes 'pure profits' or 'economic rents'.

[2] Firm profits are measured by $Y_R = GP - C - Dep - I - OCE$ (where GP is gross profit, C is labour compensation and material cost, Dep is true economic depreciation, I is interest paid, and OCE is the opportunity cost of equity finance). The definition differs from the usual accounting measure of profit, which does not make an allowance for OCE.

capital, the NPV of an investment project could be positive before tax, but negative after, making the investment commercially unviable.

Besides these general mechanisms, many detailed provisions in a tax code impinge on the cost of capital. An insufficient allowance for depreciation compared to the true economic rate increases the effective cost of acquiring assets and discourages investment. Depreciation spreads an investment's purchase costs by activating an asset on a firm's balance sheet and writing it off in stages. If depreciation for tax purposes is permitted only at a slower pace than actual depreciation, then the asset becomes more expensive to acquire. Likewise, accelerated depreciation effectively lowers the cost of capital and encourages investment, as does an investment tax credit. Indeed, Hall and Jorgenson (1967, p. 391), in one of the first influential papers on investment behaviour, argued: 'The customary justification for the belief in the efficacy of tax stimulus does not rely on empirical evidence. Rather, the belief is based on the plausible argument that businessmen in pursuit of gain will find the purchase of capital goods more attractive if they cost less'. Finally, the prescribed rules for inventory valuation and adjustment for inflation also leave their mark on investment behaviour.

BOX 4.1

As a rough approximation, leaving the tax rate unchanged, a broader tax base including interest and dividends and scrapping investment incentives, raises the cost of capital and harms investment. A narrower tax base, leaving the tax rate unchanged, allowing for a partial or full deduction for the user cost of debt and/or equity finance, reduces the cost of capital.

Standard accounting practices
In practice, all industrialised countries have closely aligned the definition of CT base to general accounting practices for measuring profits. Hence, taxable profits are calculated net of depreciation and interest, but including the opportunity cost of equity capital. This roughly means that the user cost of investment financed by borrowing remains unaffected by CT. On the other hand, the opportunity cost of equity finance cannot be imputed against profits. CT therefore increases the pre-tax return that an investor requires on equity-financed investment, which discourages such investment, while at the same time creating a bias towards investment financed by debt.

Table 4.1 gives an overview of tax rates and base definitions for the sample countries (updated from Cnossen, 2004). CT systems are arranged by the form of *dividend relief* offered, which is explained in the next section.

Table 4.1 General overview of CT regimes, 2005

Country	Top CT rate[a]	Methods and rates (%) of depreciation[b]			Main investment incentives (apart from R&D, see Chapter 6)	Inventory valuation method[c]	Loss carry-over (yrs)		AETRs[d]		METR overall[d]
		Machinery	Buildings	Patents			Forward	Back	Equity	Debt	
Imputation											
Australia	30	Useful life	SL - 2.5	Useful life	Accelerated deductions for certain activities. Tax concession for investment companies that provide equity to SMEs	FIFO	Unlimited	None	26	7	24
Canada	29.1	CCA[e]	CCA[e]	Separate system[e]	Preferential tax rate on manufacturing on first CAD 400,000 of income	Average cost	20	3	28	6	25
UK	30	DB – 25	SL – 4	DB – 25	Exemption real estate investment trusts CT on capital gains	FIFO	Unlimited	1	24	5	20
Schedular PT											
Austria	25	Useful life	SL – 3	Useful life	Favourable treatment private foundations	LIFO	Unlimited	None	22	6	20
Belgium	34	SL – 10/33	SL – 3/5	SL – 20	Accelerated depreciation plant & machinery; 14.5% deduction intangibles	LIFO	Unlimited	None	26	6	22

Denmark	28	DB – 25	SL – 5	SL – 14.3/100	None	FIFO	Unlimited	None	-	-	-
Sweden	28	DB – 30	SL – 5	DB – 30	None	FIFO	Unlimited	None	21	4	16
US	39	DB – 66	SL – 2.5	SL – 6.7	9% deduction for income from qualified domestic production activities	LIFO	20	2	29	6	24
Dividend exemption											
Finland	26	DB – 30	DB – 7	SL – 10	Accelerated depreciation for SMEs for investment in least-developed regions	FIFO	10	None	21	4	17
France	34.4	DB – 41.6	Useful life 20% margin	SL – 20	Conditional exemptions for new companies and regional development incentives. Reduced tax base for headquarters and distribution centres	Average cost	Unlimited	3	25	5	20
Germany	26.4	DB – 20	SL – 4	SL – 15	Accelerated and additional depreciation of tangibles	LIFO	Unlimited	1	32	8	29
Italy	33	SL – 25	SL – 7	SL – 50	Accelerated depreciation tangibles; tax credit for investment in distressed areas	LIFO	5	None	26	3	19

Country	Top CT rate[a]	Methods and rates (%) of depreciation[b]			Main investment incentives (apart from R&D)	Inventory valuation method[c]	Loss carry-over (yrs)		AETRs[d]		METR overall[d]
		Machinery	Buildings	Patents			Forward	Back	Equity	Debt	
Japan	30	DB – 15.2	SL – 2	SL – 12.5	Accelerated depreciation or tax credit for SMEs for certain (energy saving) investment and IT investment incentives	Average cost	5	1	32	8	28
Netherlands	25.5	DB – 20	Limited	SL – 10	Deductions for small-scale investment, energy saving and environment protection	LIFO	9	1	25	6	21
Classical Ireland	12.5	SL – 12.5	SL – 4	Residual life	Special tax regime IFSC until 2010	FIFO	Unlimited	None	11	3	10

Notes:

[a] The CT rates include surcharges in Belgium (3%), Canada (4%), France for large companies (3.3%) and Germany (5.5%). Graduated rates apply in Belgium, France, Ireland, Japan, the Netherlands, the UK and the US.

[b] SL is straight-line; DB is declining balance. Only the most tax efficient possibilities are shown.

[c] LIFO represents the last-in-first-out and FIFO the first-in-first-out methods of inventory valuation. Only the most tax-efficient possibilities are shown.

[d] Data are for 2005. Taxes on shareholder level are not included. The assumed real discount rate is 10%, inflation rate is 3.5%, and depreciation rate is 12.25%.

[e] The capital cost allowance (CCA) system applies to most tangible assets and specific intangible assets. The CCA is calculated on the basis of assets pool classes. For example, office furniture is class 8 and depreciable for DB-20. A separate eligible capital expenditure system applies to intangible capital used directly in business.

Sources: IBFD – European Tax Surveys and PricewaterhouseCoopers Worldwide Tax Summaries. Effective tax rates are updated using methods in Devereux et al. (2002) and can be found on http://www.ifs.org.uk/publications.php?publication_id=3210. Some information may be incomplete or out of date.

Top CT rates range between 12.5 per cent in Ireland and 39 per cent in the United States. In all countries, the acquisition cost of assets is recovered by a selection of straight-line (typically buildings and patents) or declining balance (typically machinery) depreciation methods applying a variety of rates. Inventory valuation rules range between FIFO, LIFO and average cost. According to Cnossen (2004), favourable depreciation rules and LIFO are commonly rationalised as correcting for the negative effects of inflation.

Table 4.1 also shows that loss carry-forward provisions are generous in most countries, while loss carry-back is allowed only in seven and typically limited to 1-3 years. Most countries additionally have a number of investment incentives in place that vary in scope and target qualification.

BOX 4.2

The tax system is likely to affect the cost of capital through the corporate as well as the personal tax. The following are important: the source of finance (new equity capital, retained earnings or debt); the type of investment (long- or short-lived assets, the prescribed depreciation schedule and investment credits); and the type of investor (legal form and domestic or foreign resident).

Effective CT rates

These tax rates and base definitions translate into an effective tax on corporate income that is not easy to measure uniformly (not in the least by timing issues). Despite these difficulties, Devereux et al. (2002) obtain some general insights into effective CT rates by applying a hypothetical investment project to countries' tax codes. The results are reproduced in the final three columns of Table 4.1

The impact of taxes on the cost of capital is estimated through the marginal effective tax rate, that is, the proportionate difference between the pre-tax required rate of return and a corresponding given post-tax required rate of return. A high METR implies a higher required pre-tax rate of return, which lowers the incentive to invest. The METR measures the incentives for a single investment project and does not imply anything about discrete investment choices; in other words, the choice between two or more investment projects. If one of two investments yields a higher return, but faces a higher tax burden, the investment with the lower return may ultimately be undertaken (which could be in another country). This depends on the total amount of tax taken from profits, which is measured by the average effective tax rate.

In all countries marginal investment financed by equity is taxed positively. Canada, Germany, Japan and the US tend to have high effective tax rates, while countries such as Austria, Ireland and Sweden are generally characterised by lower values. The results confirm that debt is highly favoured over equity finance.[3]

Integration of Corporate and Personal Taxes

Why tax corporations?
While CT is often regarded as the backbone of capital income taxation, it is natural to ask why governments impose such a tax in the first place. After all, a personal income tax with a full allowance for the underlying CT would be equivalent to taxing profits once and directly in the hands of the shareholder. And ultimately, only an individual and not a corporation can feel the burden of taxation.

The reasons for corporate taxation are essentially threefold (see Bird, 1996; and Mintz, 1996). In the first place, the tax ensures that corporations pay directly for the provision of public goods and services that improve their profitability. CT also functions as a 'backstop' to personal tax (PT). This ensures a more efficient revenue collection since the tax is levied from relatively few corporate taxpayers instead of from a multitude of shareholders. It also prevents individuals from deferring part of their tax liability on labour income by retaining earnings in a corporation (loans made by the corporation would finance current consumption of the owner/shareholder).

CT gains further application in an international context, since foreign shareholders are typically located beyond the reach of domestic tax authorities. A final motivation is that CT is an efficient tool for capturing economic rents or pure profits, which makes it less distortionary than taxes on other sources of income.

Form of dividend relief
A principal function of CT is thus a withholding one. This means that corporate profits are typically taxed twice and that to fully capture the effects on investment behaviour, PT needs to be considered as well. CT-PT systems are arranged by the form of dividend relief that is provided by the tax law and thus the extent to which double taxation is mitigated. Tax laws either do not integrate PT and CT regimes, leading to full double taxation, or they do, in which case it is a partial or full integration (see Mintz, 2003). The various relief systems are as follows:

---

[3] Bond et al. (1996) have estimated that the bias against equity-financed investment under the UK CT system permanently raises the overall cost of capital by 1-2 percentage points. This reduces the long-run level of corporate investment by up to 5 per cent.

- An *imputation system* provides relief by a full or partial credit for taxes paid by corporations. The relief is calculated by grossing up net dividends with the amount of the imputation credit (if the relief is 100 per cent, this amount is equal to the CT). On this basis the PT rate is applied and the tax credit subtracted. With full imputation, the tax rate on distributed profits thus equals the marginal PT rate on other income. A partial credit results in a higher tax rate. The credit is granted only to domestic shareholders, so the imputation system discriminates against foreign investors;
- A *schedular system* does not tax dividends at the normal marginal PT rate, but instead imposes a separate, typically lower, flat rate. Some countries try to approximate the top PT rate on other income, but mostly a difference exists. As a consequence, investors in high marginal income brackets are favoured relative to those in low brackets;
- An *exemption system* fully or partly refrains from taxing distributed profits at a personal level. Under a full exemption, CT is the final tax imposed. Some countries provide an exemption, for example, for half the dividend; and
- A *classical system* does not provide dividend relief. Distributed profits are first fully taxed at the corporate level and once again in the hands of the shareholder. Dividends are thereby wholly exposed to double taxation.

The extent to which the various systems are equivalent importantly depends on the CT versus the PT rate. If the rates are identical, equivalence between imputation, exemption and a schedular system for dividend relief is straightforwardly established.

A survey of CT–PT systems
To get a basic impression of existing CT-PT systems, Table 4.2 presents an updated review of CT-PT regimes following the methodology by Cnossen (2004). The overview provides only a general outline of such systems, yet brings to light highly divergent government practices.

Three of the 16 countries make use of an imputation system. Of these countries, only Australia provides full relief so that the CT + top PT rate on dividends equals the top PT rate on other income. The UK imputation credit is merely one-ninth, which means that profit distribution is virtually double taxed. Where imputation was a favoured approach by many countries, the trend has been to move away to schedular or dividend exemption systems. Finland, France, Germany, Ireland and Italy have all switched, mainly over concerns of discrimination against foreign investors who do not benefit from the credit. A lower PT rate is used by 5 out of the 16 countries. In Austria, Belgium and Sweden this results in lower tax rates than on other income. In

Table 4.2 Corporation and personal tax systems, 2005

Country	Form of dividend relief	CT rate: retained profits[a]	CT + top PT on distributed profits[b,c]	PT on interest[d]	Top PT rate on other income[e]	PT on capital gains[f]		Personal net wealth tax[g]
						Ordinary shares	Substantial holdings	
Imputation	*Tax credit*							
Australia	3/7 of div	30.0	48.5	48.5	48.5	1/2 of gain	1/2 of gain	-
Canada[h]	1/7.5 of div	29.1	43.0	29.0	29.0	1/2 of gain	1/2 of gain	-
UK[i]	1/9 of div	30.0	47.5	40.0	40.0	10-32	10-32	-
Schedular PT	*PT rate*							
Austria	25	25.0	43.8	25.0	50.0	-	1/2 of gain	-
Belgium	25	34.0	50.5	15.0	53.6	-	-	-
Denmark[j]	28 / 43	28.0	59.0	59.0	59.0	28 / 43	28 / 43	-
Sweden	30	28.0	49.6	30.0	56.5	30	30	1.5
US[k]	15	35.0	44.8	35.0	35.0	15	15	-
Dividend exemption	*Size of exemption*							
Finland[l]	3/10 of div	26.0	40.5	28.0	54.5	28.0	28.0	0.8
France[m]	1/2 of div	33.3	52.8	26.3	58.4	26.3	26.3	0.55-1.8
Germany	1/2 of div	26.4	42.7	44.3	44.3	-	1/2 of gain	-
Italy[n]	3/5 of div	33.0	44.7	27.0	43.6	12.5	2/5 of gain	-
Japan	1/2 of div	30,0	43.0	20	37,0	1/2 of gain	1/2 of gain	-

Netherlands	full	31.5	31.5	-	52,0	25
Norway°	risk-free return	28,0	fluctuates	28	43.5	28
Classical	*PT rate*					
Ireland	none	12.5	49.3	20	42,0	20

Netherlands	1.2
Norway°	0.9-1.1
Ireland	-

Notes:

[a] The tax rate on retained profits does not include personal capital gains taxes, where imposed, since the actual value varies due to deferral.

[b] Calculated as CT + [(1 – CT – Exempt dividend) * PT] – Imputation tax credit where applicable.

[c] A withholding tax (WHT) for dividends paid to residents applies in Austria (25%), Belgium (25%), Denmark (25%), Germany (28%), Ireland (20%), Italy (12.5%), Japan (10-20%) and Sweden (30%). Taxpayers can opt to make the WHT final in Austria, Belgium, Denmark and Italy, and Japan (up to a certain threshold).

[d] A WHT on interest is imposed in Austria (25%), Belgium (15%), Finland (28%), Germany (36.9%), Ireland (20%), Italy (27%), Japan (20%) and the UK (20%). Taxpayers can opt to make the WHT final in Austria, Belgium, Finland, Ireland, Italy and Japan.

[e] PT rates include surcharges in Belgium (average local rate 7-7.5%), Germany (5.5%), Italy (average regional and local rate 1.4%); surtaxes in Australia (Medicare levy 1.5%) and France (CSG 7.5% of which 5.1% is deductible, CRDS 0.5%, Social levy 2.3%); and local taxes in Denmark (33.3%), Finland (varying between 16 and 21%) and Sweden (31.5%).

[f] Only long-term capital gains. Short-term capital gains are typically taxed at higher rates in Denmark, the UK and the US. Several countries exempt small amounts of capital gains and generally roll-over relief is granted.

[g] In Finland, non-resident companies and domestic legal entities other than corporations additionally pay a 1% net wealth tax.

[h] Distributed dividends are grossed up by a fixed rate of 25% for calculating the imputation credit. The official federal CT rate is 38% but a rebate of 10% applies in so far as the income is generated in a Canadian province. As of 2004, however, the rate has been reduced to 21% for most types of income. The effective PT rates on dividends, interest and royalties, thus including provincial tax, typically vary between 39% in Alberta and 53% in Quebec.

[i] The top PT rate on dividends is 32.5%.

[j] Dividends and capital gains are taxed at the 28% rate under DDK43,300 and 43% on any excess. If the total of national and local income taxes exceeds 59%, the top national rate (15%) is reduced by the excess.

[k] Only federal taxes. State personal income taxes come on top of this and typically range between 0 and 25%. Shareholders are subject to an alternative minimum tax (AMT) if the liability as calculated according to this tax exceeds the regular liability. Because this is a 'minimum' tax, it does not detract from the top rates reported in the table.

[l] For the year 2005, the 30% exemption was instead 43%. There is a full exemption for dividends received from a non-quoted company up to an amount of €90,000 (but only for a dividend yield up to 9%).

[m] In 2005, a surcharge of 1.5% applies to the CT, making the effective rate 33.83% (abolished as of 2006). PT on interest and capital gains include social taxes (Contribution Sociale Généralisée (CSG), Contribution pour le Remboursement de la Dette Sociale (CRDS) and Social levy).

[n] The exemption regime applies to shareholders who hold shares in a business capacity or own more than 2% (20%) of the voting power or 5% (25%) of the capital in listed companies (other companies). Ordinary shareholders are subject to a final WHT of 12.5%.

[o] The new system for individual shareholders as of 2006. In calculating capital gains, the acquisitions cost of a share is grossed up annually by a company's retained profits (net of tax and after dividend) that is attributable to that share.

Sources: European Tax Surveys and PricewaterhouseCoopers Worldwide Tax Summaries. Some information may be incomplete or out of date.

the US, where the top PT rate is 'only' 35 per cent, the opposite is true. In Denmark both rates are approximately equal.

Seven governments completely or partly exempt dividends. A popular form is the half-income system, which exempts one-half of the dividend received. The Netherlands is the only country to fully exempt dividends. The new tax system in Norway, effective as of January 2006, presents an interesting alternative by exempting the risk-free return on invested capital (that is, the rate-of-return allowance, or RRA). The excess is taxed at the ordinary progressive rate, while the normal return is taxed at the lower capital income tax rate. If the relief is higher than dividends received the excess can be carried forward. The new system is referred to as the 'shareholder income tax' and replaces Norway's former imputation as well as its RISK system (a Norwegian acronym) for relieving dividends and capital gains from double taxation.[4]

Ireland employs a classical system. Corporation and shareholder are deemed separate entities, fully taxable independently under both CT and PT. While the overall rate on distributed profits because of the low CT rate is still in line with that in other countries, the system does create strong incentives for profit retention.

Distortions under CT–PT systems
The existing CT-PT regimes give rise to several distortions, which critically depend on the respective tax rates on retained and distributed profits, interest, the top PT rate on other income and how they stand in proportion to each other. The treatment of capital gains is also important.

Profit distribution and retention
The tax treatment of distributed profits is determined by the CT in combination with the PT on dividends, corrected for any form of dividend relief. The calculated tax rates for resident investors are shown in the fourth column of Table 4.2 (assuming top rates only). The tax rates on distributed profits range from 31.5 in the Netherlands to 59 per cent in Denmark (not counting Norway, where the rate depends on unknown factors).[5] The tax on dividends is contrasted by that on retained profits, which depends on the CT plus personal capital gains tax (CGT) where levied. The CT rate varies between 12.5 per cent in Ireland and 35 per cent in the US. The exact tax on capital gains is hard to gauge, but it is generally lower than the statutory rate since the effective tax rate declines with deferral of realisation (a point to which we return below). Table 4.2 shows that the CT + top PT rate on distributed profits differs from the CT on retained profits in most countries,

---

[4] The RISK system was used to avoid double taxation of retained profits in conjunction with taxation of realised capital gains on a personal level by permitting shareholders to write up the acquisition price of their shares by retained profits net of CT (Cnossen, 2000).

[5] Six countries impose a net wealth tax to create further tax progression.

including any CGT and particularly when taking account of deferral. The Netherlands is the only exception, with equal marginal CT + PT rates on profit distribution/retention.

The precise impact on the investment decision of this discrepancy gives rise to some controversy in the tax literature. It is relatively straightforward to establish that dividend taxes reduce the return to investment financed by new share issues. Marginal investment financed by new shares requires a future stream of dividends to compensate investors for making available the equity capital. For now familiar reasons, dividend taxes on top of the CT raise the cost of capital and impinge on the decision to invest. The disagreement centres on whether this is also true for investment that is financed out of retained profits.

Two views on dividend taxation   The discussion centres on two 'views' (Sinn, 1991), which concern themselves with the marginal source of finance of investment by *mature* firms that pay dividends. Mature firms contrast with *immature* firms, which are typically small, fast-growing and/or starting-up companies that manage to uncover ample profitable investment opportunities, but do not (yet) generate adequate earnings to pay dividends. All retained earnings of immature firms are reinvested and, if required, any excess investment is financed by issuing new shares. After a while profitable investment opportunities of these firms decline, so the immature firm will transform into a mature one.

The 'old' or 'traditional' view holds that dividend taxes do affect investment financed by retained earnings. That view suggests that shareholders derive a positive benefit from a steady stream of dividends. This could be due to a 'signalling' function. Dividend payouts indicate that the corporation is in good condition and that there is confidence in future developments. Another explanation concerns the so-called 'principal-agent' problem in companies where ownership is separated from management. Dividend payouts then reduce executive discretion over corporate funds and thus the scope for mismanagement. Up to a certain point, these benefits offset the additional 'tax cost' of profit distribution. In other words, companies face a 'minimum distribution constraint' for paying dividends, which means that some investment has to be financed out of new share issues that require future dividend payouts.

The 'new' view differs from the 'old' one by not assuming such a positive benefit implicit in dividend payouts. As long as capital gains are tax favoured, companies use retained earnings to finance investment. An important assumption under the 'new' view is that all equity eventually has to be returned to the shareholder. The only way to achieve this is by paying taxable dividends (and not by share buy-backs). Consequently, the present value of the tax advantage of profit retention is exactly offset by the double taxation of forthcoming dividends (as discounted in the current share price).

As long as the tax rate remains equal dividend taxes therefore do not raise the burden on investment financed with retained earnings.

Although no definite answer has been offered in the literature, most scholars appear to favour the traditional view (Zodrow, 1991).

New share issues Whichever of the two views one chooses to adhere to, Bond (2000) argues that the fraction of new share issues is very limited in practice (typically <10 per cent of investment). When considering buy-backs and cash-financed takeovers with retained earnings, the overall net contribution of new share issuance is generally negative (original estimations stem from Corbett and Jenkinson, 1997). The impact of dividend taxes on the cost of capital could thus be largely unimportant. However, the distortion created can be significant for immature firms that do not generate sufficient earnings to finance investment and have to rely on new share issues.

The treatment of debt versus equity capital
While Table 4.1 demonstrated that debt finance is favoured over equity finance on the corporate level, Table 4.2 demonstrates that this is exacerbated on a personal level. Thirteen out of 16 countries impose lower PT rates on interest than the combined PT + CT rates on distributed profits. In most cases the same is true for the CT + GCT on retained profit.[6] This may have considerable implications for a firm's financial structure and investment behaviour.

The widely acclaimed Modigliani-Miller theorem demonstrates that in a world with no taxes, repackaging a firm's capital structure has no effect on the value of the firm (Modigliani and Miller, 1958).[7] According to the model, introducing financial leverage and increasing the debt to equity ratio does not reflect on company earnings,[8] even if debt finance carries less risk with it. In effect, this lower risk is exactly offset by a higher risk to shareholders of a larger amount of debt in a company, which has priority in the case of bankruptcy. In a world with taxes, however, leveraging increases a firm's value since the deductibility of interest creates a bias against equity finance.

As a corollary, firms opt for a financial structure that deviates from their risk profile. It also compromises tax-base neutrality and efficiency, and creates tax arbitrage opportunities, erodes the tax base and effective revenue collection and discriminates against immature firms. These firms find it

---

[6] Interest is precluded from the CT base, so it may even escape taxation completely because of the existence of tax-exempt institutional investors such as pension funds and life insurance companies. Interest is typically deducted invariably, while not taxed on the receiving end. The return to equity is taxed only at corporate level.

[7] The theory consists of two separate propositions. MM proposition I states that the value of a leveraged firm is exactly equal to the value of an unleveraged firm. MM proposition II asserts that in the absence of taxation the cost of equity capital increases with leverage, since the risk to equity-holders increases in a company with debt.

[8] Leverage denotes the degree of debt that firms use compared to equity to finance operations.

harder to attract debt capital due to low credit ratings; have less scope for providing security (pawn or mortgage) on mostly non-liquid firm-specific business assets; and/or are unable to deduct interest payments as a result of inadequate earnings (see Cnossen, 1996). Tax-disfavoured equity capital remains the only alternative. This critically inhibits young and smaller companies such as biotechnical or internet companies that are often leading in innovation. Indeed, important breakthroughs are made in small unorthodox enterprises, rather than large multinational companies (MNCs) where competition takes place on cost efficiency and economies of scale, yet real innovation and creativity often fail to thrive.

All these considerations are strengthened by the integration of international financial markets and innovation of financial products that makes equity capital more easily substitutable into debt capital.[9] Furthermore, the role of equity capital is likely to become more pronounced with the shift from industrial to service-based sectors and growing knowledge intensity within the economy. Due to the non-material and character of these businesses, little security can be provided to lenders of debt capital. The CT thereby becomes more distortive.

The choice of organisational form

The tax treatment of a self-employed person who is taxed once, usually at the marginal PT rate applicable to the owner,[10] differs conceptually as well as practically from that of incorporated businesses. The precise impact of this breach of neutrality is hard to gauge since the tax rate on non-corporate businesses depends on the bracket in which the owner is taxed. Assuming that the top PT rate applies, tax systems often create a bias against the non-corporate form for doing business (see Table 4.2).

The exact turning-point between both legal forms can depend on personal and corporate taxes on labour earnings, the interest rate and risk premium, financial reserves and provisions and pure profits. Furthermore, compared to most CT systems, income tax regularly exhibits steeper progression. Under most tax systems it is therefore better to be self-employed when having relatively low earnings, while it is more attractive to be incorporated in the case of higher earnings.

Opinions differs on the efficiency gain from achieving a so-called 'global balance' (that is, equal treatment of both organisational forms) in taxing the various legal forms. Gordon and Mackie-Mason (1994) find that removing the differential tax treatment of both forms produces only a slight efficiency gain, suggesting that the responsiveness to taxes in choosing an

---

[9] For example, hybrid loans are loans that are legally characterised as debt (a claim versus liability relationship), but materially function as equity capital by such properties as having a profit-dependent interest rate or no repayment date.

[10] For example, in the case of a sole proprietorship or partnership.

organisational structure is limited. Gravelle and Kotlikoff (1989) report a large gain of over 100 per cent of tax revenue.

BOX 4.3

Existing CT-PT systems distort the profit distribution/retention decision of companies, favour debt over equity-financed investment, and tend to discriminate against unincorporated firms. More uniform capital income limits the scope for avoidance and reduces the overall complexity of the tax system. As a positive side-effect, this stimulates 'immature' firms, often starting up and/or fast growing, which are typically leading in innovation.

Effective Taxation of Capital Gains and the 'Lock-in' Effect

Realisation-based capital gains taxation

As noted, capital gains are difficult to tax in an effective and non-arbitrary manner. Capital gains are commonly taxed according to the form of holding. Most tax systems distinguish between ordinary shares and substantial holdings that signify control (see Table 4.2). All countries except Austria, Belgium, Germany and the Netherlands subject capital gains on ordinary shares to tax, while Belgium also refrains from taxing substantial holdings. Countries that impose capital gains taxation normally use a so-called 'realisation-based' CGT. The gain is calculated by subtracting the acquisition cost from the proceeds of disposal. Hence, a precondition is that the sales price is known and thus, very simply, that the asset has been sold. Only then does liability to pay tax arise.

A drawback of a CGT in this form is that the effective tax burden declines with the holding period of the asset. Because taxation does not take place before sales, an additional return over and above the capital gain is produced. This part effectively goes untaxed. In other words, only the capital gain is taxed but not the return that arises on top of this from not having to pay the tax. When the potential tax liability reaches double-digit percentages, the gain from deferral can be sizeable.

Because sale provokes taxation, a negative incentive is created to dispose of an asset that carries accrued capital gains. This is called the 'lock-in effect'. The lock-in effect becomes more pronounced the higher the tax and frustrates an efficient allocation of capital and portfolio selection as investors accept a lower before-tax rate of return on new capital investment than they would do in the absence of the accrued gains and tax deferral.

Other distortions are created. A realisation-based tax triggers arbitrage opportunities between a given investment project and method of finance. The capital gain on a debt-financed investment can be deferred indefinitely, while the interest can be expensed immediately. This clearly reflects on the risk-taking behaviour of investors.[11] The lock-in effect may also exacerbate stock market fluctuations. During stock market booms investors are encouraged to hold on to their shares to defer realisation, while declining prices stimulate sales in order to realise losses.[12]

To mitigate the adverse effects, the literature has come up with three alternatives. One of these solutions has uniquely been introduced in the Netherlands, and the other two were put forward by the tax literature. Cnossen and Bovenberg (2001) provide an in-depth discussion of the various alternatives of capital gains taxation and their pros and cons. Here we draw on their study to provide a brief description of the approaches.

The presumptive capital income tax

The presumptive capital income tax was put into practice in the Netherlands in 2001. Under the system, a rate of 30 per cent is imposed on a presumptive return of 4 per cent of the value of personally held capital such as bank deposits, stock, bonds and real estate that is not owner occupied. The presumptive return of 4 per cent was approximated by taking the average return on assets over the past 100 years. The Dutch government chose this form because it is relatively robust and easy to administer. Most of the data needed are readily obtainable from banks, insurance companies and other financial institutions. The presumptive return also ensures a relatively steady annual revenue flow to the treasury. But objections exist as well. For example, the fixed return effectively transforms the tax into a net wealth tax of 1.2 per cent so that the capital gain is taxed on an *ex ante* basis instead of *ex post*. Hence, it is not the actual return that is taxed, but an expected return. This implies that highly profitable investment is relatively lightly taxed, while marginal investment that just earns the required rate of return is tax disfavoured.

The retrospective capital gains tax

The retrospective CGT eliminates the lock-in effect by making a correction at the point of sale for the tax advantage that arises from the accrued capital gain. In this manner, the tax still becomes liable on realisation, but the incentive for deferral is effectively taken away. Two basic methods have been developed to this end. Auerbach (1991) proposes to equalise the annual

---

[11] Government may place restrictions on the deduction of capital losses from other taxable income to prevent arbitrage and protect the tax base. This inhibits the demand for risky investments as these are the most likely to generate losses (Stiglitz, 1969).

[12] Stock markets raise the incentives to invest by (i) making the transfer of ownership of assets easier and without disrupting production and (ii) enabling investors to diversify portfolios so that they can spread risk (Levine, 1991). A CGT reduces the expected after-tax resale value of stock and thereby hinders trade, indirectly reducing investment.

appreciation value of the asset to the risk-free interest rate, which subsequently accrues for every year that the asset is retained. The value of the capital gain is thus inferred from the sales price and taxed accordingly with an additional interest on top to compensate for the annuity in deferral. No prior knowledge on the acquisition price is required, just the nominal interest rate and the holding period of the asset. Because taxation still takes place on an *ex ante* basis, the second method proposed by Bradford (1995) also taxes the above-normal return. While more neutral, this raises the administrative complexity.

The accrual-based capital gains tax
The accrual-based CGT, also referred to as a mark to market tax, targets the accretion to an asset's economic value. Hence, capital gains are taxed in full and as they arise on an annual basis. This eliminates the lock-in effect and reduces the scope for avoidance. The scheme is more neutral than the previous proposals, but suffers from other, mainly administrative, shortcomings. The biggest problem lies in valuing assets, particularly non-liquid ones, such as real estate and firm-specific machinery for which there is no everyday market. On the political front the tax also encounters resistance since, as is argued, many households do not have the liquidity to finance the yearly tax without having to sell (some of) the asset (economists are often quick to point out that this can be borrowed at no or little extra cost). Currently, there is none the less some consensus forming that the accrual-based CGT may be applied to stocks, bonds and derivatives for which up-to-date stock market quotations exist. In modern financial markets these securities are also easily transformed into liquidity.

4.3   OPTIMAL TAX THEORY

Tax Shifting within Economies

Chapter 3 showed that the legal incidence of the labour tax can differ markedly from its economic tax burden distribution between employer and employee. In a broader context, taxes may be shifted between the factors of production labour, capital and consumption. The implication of tax shifting is that it is generally not known beforehand whether a capital tax is borne by capital owners through lower after-tax profits, or whether they insist on maintaining a certain after-tax return so that the capital tax is shifted onto workers by reduced wages and/or consumers through higher product prices. Despite a positive revenue intake from CT in every country, it is thus not obvious whether capital owners actually bear any CT.

The difficulty lies in separating the effect of CT solely on owners of corporate capital, from its effect on other parts of the economy. In a celebrated paper, Harberger (1962) has approached the issue by focusing on capital demand. The idea is that a higher demand for capital is associated with a higher after-tax return and vice versa. As such, in partial equilibrium, a higher tax on capital use by firms is partially shifted onto capital providers by lowering the interest rate.

Nevertheless, in general equilibrium, Harberger showed that the interest rate may actually increase. The paper points to two mechanisms at work. The first is the traditionally recognised *substitution* of labour for capital. Higher capital taxes make it more attractive to hire labour than to purchase capital goods, which reduces the demand for the latter. The second occurs between a corporate and a non-corporate sector of production in an economy. Harberger assumed that the non-corporate (service) sector is more capital intensive, which is in line with US evidence, so a *reallocation* of production from the corporate to the non-corporate sector, as induced by a tax, may actually increase the demand for capital. Thus the interest rate can actually increase provided substitution between labour and capital is difficult and the output effect is large.

In a later study, Harberger found that the US CT was indeed largely shifted onto labour as a result.[13]

Cross-border Capital Mobility

In recent years a separate issue has been created by the increasing mobility of capital internationally. Taking into account cross-border capital movement, capital owners will transfer their investment abroad until the after-tax rate of return equals (net-of-tax) world interest rates (see Razin and Sadka, 1991; and Gordon, 2000).[14] Since world prices prevail, firms cannot shift the tax onto consumption through higher product prices. The only way to maintain their returns is thus by lowering wage rates. In a small open economy, the tax is therefore fully shifted onto labour, so the after-tax return to investment remains the same as the return that can be earned elsewhere.

Moreover, if the capital tax is shifted anyway, it can be argued that it is more optimal to tax labour directly. Not only does the entire capital tax burden fall on labour, but so does the excess burden generated by it. For this reason, the long-run efficient tax on capital income is zero.

---

[13] See Hines (2002), who provides a brief yet insightful account of Harberger's major contributions in the field of public finance.

[14] Under the assumption that countries are small enough not to affect the world interest rate.

BOX 4.4

Optimal tax theory concludes that since capital is mobile in the long run the efficient tax rate on capital income is zero. Investment is reduced or transferred abroad up to a point where the after-tax rate of return equates to the world interest rate, so the capital tax is largely if not entirely shifted onto labour (including any excess burden generated by it).

Credibility and Politics

The government itself suffers from a fundamental problem of credibility (referred to as the 'time-inconsistency problem') because it cannot effectively commit to not enacting or raising capital taxes in the future. Consider the following case. To finance a certain public investment project, government decides to impose a one-off tax on capital owners (a so-called 'confiscatory' tax). The tax is imposed only in one year and not to be imposed again. If unanticipated, the tax would be fully efficient because it does not allow taxpayers to alter their behaviour to try to avoid the tax by reducing saving and increasing current consumption.

The problem is that government has an incentive to go back on its promise and in any future year again impose an unexpected 'one-off' capital tax. Taxpayers know this and will reduce their savings in response to the risk of being taxed more heavily in the future, which creates an economic inefficiency.

This mechanism is formally described by the renowned Chamley-Judd model (Chamley, 1986; Judd, 1985), which demonstrates that capital taxes cannot be effectively enforced due to lack of government commitment. Any expected capital tax increase leads capital owners to raise current consumption to circumvent higher future taxes. The longer the anticipation period, the larger this behavioural response and the decline in capital stock that results.

This means that the capital income tax is an inferior alternative for raising the required revenues, also when taking account of redistributive purposes. In fact, if the tax is entirely expected, the burden is fully borne by labour. The optimal long-run tax on capital is therefore zero.

Why Do We Have a Corporate Tax?

In the light of these arguments, it seems legitimate to question why source-based capital income taxes, that is, CTs, have persisted. Are lawmakers simply slow to react, is there political restraint, or are there other reasons?

Gordon (2000) argues that one reason may be that countries implicitly coordinate their tax policies, for example, through the use of crediting arrangements to avoid double taxation (see Section 4.4). In addition, countries may not be full price takers on world markets and may have a certain market power and be large enough to influence world interest rates. Tax policies can then affect the after-tax return received by investors, so the above argument on optimal tax theory and small open economies does not fully apply. Another argument is that capital is simply not as mobile across countries as assumed by the optimal tax literature.

Of these three arguments, the third seems the most relevant. The first effect is not likely to be strong enough, while the second would explain a positive tax on capital but not at levels currently experienced in OECD countries. Gordon et al. (2004) also demonstrate that the issues are far from resolved. By simulating a shift from the current to a consumption-based tax system, the authors estimate that the US capital income tax effectively raised $108.1 billion in tax revenue in 1995.[15] This contradicts the notion that capital owners do not bear any burden of taxation because of tax shifting.

4.4   INTERNATIONAL CAPITAL FLOWS AND TAXATION

The removal of barriers to trade and factor movements in recent decades has exposed the allocation of investment more directly to tax-rate differentials. In an international perspective, two forms of investment are distinguished. *Foreign portfolio investment* encompasses ordinary investment in shares, bonds and bank deposits by relatively smaller investors. The holdings do not signify control in that the investor cannot influence management. *Foreign direct investment* (FDI) consists of investment in assets over which the investor has direct control. Usually a qualified participation exists in the case of 5 or 10 per cent or more of the voting stock of a business.[16]

While countries typically tax portfolio income on the basis of taxpayer residence, direct investment income is taxed at source (that is, by the CT) based on the view that the right to tax real investment accrues to the state that has supported the economic environment for it to flourish. The two taxing principles have varying economic implications for investor behaviour.

---

[15] Note that this can be inferred from the fact that a consumption tax, in contrast to income tax, does not tax the normal return to capital (see equivalence relations in Chapter 1). If the revenue loss of such a shift were zero, no revenue would effectively be raised by the taxation of capital income under the current system.

[16] Investments in reserve assets held by governments and central banks can be considered a third category of foreign investment.

Residence-based Taxation

Because tax rates differ across countries, investors are induced to allocate investment (for example, in a production plant) to low-tax countries in order to optimise the after-tax return. However, this does not necessarily have to be the most efficient place for production. A relatively lower tax may just enable a producer to offer a lower price, while his/her production costs are actually higher than those of his/her competitors at home.

To prevent this circumstance, countries can opt to apply the so-called 'residence' principle under which worldwide capital income of residents is taxed regardless of its source. This is accomplished by granting a full credit for taxes paid on foreign capital income against the domestic tax liability.[17] By taxing all capital income of residents equally, investment is allocated to countries where the before-tax rate of return is the highest (under full capital mobility before-tax rates of return will be equalised). Because an investor faces equal taxes regardless of the location of investment, capital is allocated efficiently. World output and income are thereby maximised. The tax system neither encourages nor discourages capital export, a state which is referred to as achieving 'capital export neutrality'. The tax revenue accrues to the resident country.

Source-based Taxation

Likewise, somebody who is considering undertaking an investment project abroad (for example, a construction job) may be able to do this more efficiently than a competitor who resides in that particular country. However, if the person considering the investment is subject to higher tax rates at home, it might well be that the competitor is able to outbid the firm and gain the contract, while not being the most efficient one in carrying it out.

Under the 'source' principle, countries provide an exemption for taxes paid on capital income generated abroad.[18] Taxation thereby takes place only in the country where the capital income originates and the resident country refrains from taxing foreign capital income. As a result, investment income that arises within a country is subject to equal tax rates, so firms will seek countries for their investment where the *after-tax* rate of return is the highest (when assuming full capital mobility, after-tax rate of returns will be equalised among jurisdictions). This promotes competition within a country as all firms, resident and non-resident, face similar tax rates, a state which is also referred to as achieving 'capital import neutrality'. The tax revenue accrues to the source country.

---

[17] To achieve full neutrality, a refund should be given if foreign taxes exceed domestic taxes. In practice, governments rarely do so, so the credit is restricted to domestic taxes payable.

[18] The source principle is also referred to as the 'territoriality' principle.

Which Alternative is Preferred?

With respect to cross-border capital income flows, both taxing principles have an important characteristic in achieving economic neutrality. At the same time, both cause a distortion. Under capital export neutrality, taxes affect the investment decisions within a country as a domestic investor faces a different rate from a foreign one investing in a certain jurisdiction. Capital import neutrality distorts the investment decisions between countries since two jurisdictions tax investment income differently. Moreover, the revenue allocation differs between governments. It follows that only full harmonisation of tax rates and tax bases guarantees that both export and import neutrality will be achieved at the same time. On a global level this is unlikely to happen, so a trade-off has to be made.

There are arguments in favour of both principles. Residence-based income taxes are generally difficult to enforce and require considerable exchange of information between tax authorities. Otherwise people would simply fail to report foreign investment income on their income tax returns. Foreign countries could also be tempted to raise tax rates to approximate that of the resident country. Most or all tax revenue would thereby be taxed away from the resident to the source country (this is the so-called 'treasury transfer' effect). Source-based taxes on the other hand distort international investment allocation. If this cost is larger than the effect on either the level of savings (which tends to be promoted under capital import neutrality), or the choice of residence (assuming that owners of capital are less mobile than the capital itself), residence-based taxation should be preferred.

4.5   CAPITAL INCOME TAXATION IN AN INTERNATIONAL PERSPECTIVE

The tax system affects marginal investment behaviour not only through the cost of capital, but also by its effect on the discrete investment choices. The overall effect of a CT on investment is thereby equal to the sum of its effect on both influences. Financial capital is nowadays close to being perfectly mobile, and so is much physical capital over the longer term. Generally speaking, investment can generate *firm* - and *location*-specific rents. Only capital that produces firm-specific rents is susceptible to flight. Location-specific rents, for example, due to natural resources, unique markets or seaports, are fixed to one place.[19]

A popular theory on production and FDI is Dunning's OLI paradigm (Dunning, 1981; Markusen, 1995). The theory suggests that firms need at

---

[19] Moreover, a large share of an economy's capital stock consists of real estate, perhaps the most fixed form of capital available.

least an ownership (O), a location (L) and an internalisation (I) advantage to overcome the inherently higher cost of producing abroad. An ownership advantage arises when a firm is able to produce a good or service that other firms cannot produce (for example, as a result of unique production techniques and patents); location advantage relates to the production cost abroad relative to the domestic cost (for example, due to transportation cost and tariffs); and finally internalisation determines whether a company really wants to service a foreign market through a subsidiary instead of, for example, licensing agreements with a foreign producer (for example, in order to keep production technologies in-house). If only the OI advantage is present, a firm generally chooses exports over FDI and when there is only an O advantage some sort of franchising arrangement is usually made. This makes the L advantage crucial for FDI.

There are numerous factors that affect the exact location decision. A few examples are the geographical situation, infrastructure, labour productivity, wage costs, educational standards, the state of science and technology, quality of government, bureaucracy and regulations, and so forth. The list is long and taxation is merely one of them. However, investors and MNCs are generally attracted to friendly tax climates, which they prefer over unfriendly ones in making their investment decisions. European survey research shows that 50 per cent of the managers interviewed indicated that CT is always or often an important factor in the location decision for production branches. For financial institutions this was as high as 80 per cent (Devereux, 1992).[20]

BOX 4.5

The location decision for business investment (FDI) is affected by a myriad of factors such as geographical situation, infrastructure, wage costs, educational standards, the state of science and technology, and quality of government. A country's CT system is one of the factors that managers take into consideration in their investment decisions.

Empirical evidence on the responsiveness of FDI to taxation

In a meta-analysis incorporating 25 studies on taxation and FDI over the 1984–2001 period, de Mooij and Ederveen (2003) establish a median tax rate

---

[20] A high administrative burden, including from taxation, also contributes negatively to the output of corporations and the climate for business investment (see *World Competitiveness Report* of 2007). The administrative burden in the EU is at least 3.6 per cent of the EU GDP, or €340 billion. Calculations show that an EU-wide reduction in red tape by 25 per cent per country leads to a GDP increase of 1.7 per cent (Tang and Verweij, 2004).

elasticity of -3.3. Hence, for every 1 per cent reduction of the domestic tax rate, FDI is increased by on average 3.3 per cent. However, there was a considerable variance in the results of the studies examined, which seemed to differ systematically with the type of FDI considered and tax rates used (that is, statutory, marginal and average tax rates). Table 4.3 provides a summary of semi-elasticities presented. With a value of -9.3 the elasticity seems to be greatest with regard to the AETR, falling to -1.2 with regard to the statutory tax rate.

Table 4.3   Elasticities for a sample of 25 studies on taxes and FDI, 1984-2001

Variable	Elasticity
Elasticity benchmark [a]	-2.4
Alternative tax rate	
Statutory rate	-1.2
METR	-4.2
AETR	-9.3
Alternative FDI	
Property, plant and equipment	-2.0
Plants	-5.7
Mergers and acquisitions	5.1
Number of locations	4.5
Sample year 2002	-3.7

Note: [a] The benchmark case corresponds to the year 1987.

Source: De Mooij and Ederveen (2003).

Gordon and Hines (2002) also report a sizeable tax elasticity for investment of -0.6 for both inward and outward investment. Furthermore, Bellak and Leibrecht (2005) abstract eight factors most likely to affect FDI and empirically examine the effect in Central and Eastern European countries. Pressure on CT rates in the old EU-15 have been mounting with enlargement in 2004 (see Chapter 8; the new member states impose markedly lower CT rates). By statistically contrasting five Central and Eastern European 'host' countries against six EU-15 'home' countries and the US, a semi-elasticity for FDI of -2.93 with regard to the tax variable is obtained.

Gropp and Kostial (2000, p. 5) find strong empirical and econometrical evidence for OECD countries that 'FDI in (out) flows are affected by tax regimes in the host (home) countries'. Countries that provide a tax credit tend to experience less FDI outflow than countries that provide an exemption for foreign source income.[21] The rationale seems straightforward. Investors in countries that provide a credit are generally liable to taxation in the home state regardless of the location of investment, while those in exemption countries benefit if the host country taxes investment lightly or not at all. The incentives to invest abroad are therefore higher in those that exempt foreign source income than in countries that provide a tax credit.

The results also suggest that countries with high corporate taxes and corresponding low FDI inflows and high outflows, show a declining trend in tax revenues from CT. The opposite seems to be the case for low-tax countries due to both a higher investment rate as well as profit shifting into these countries through financial engineering (which is described later).

BOX 4.6

Empirical evidence demonstrates that the tax system is an important factor in the location decision of foreign investment and MNCs. It gives governments an incentive to lower CT rates in the hope of attracting foreign investment.

Reduction of Statutory CT Rates in all Sample Countries

As noted in Chapter 2, the majority of tax reforms in OECD countries since the mid-1980s were characterised by broadening tax bases and lowering tax rates. Table 4.4 shows that top CT rates have been cut in all sample countries during the 1985-2007 period. Cuts have been particularly dramatic in Ireland, Austria and Finland, exceeding 30 percentage points, and less so in Belgium, the UK and the US. CT rates still fell by some 10 percentage points in the latter group.

Less clear-cut is the evidence on the development of effective tax rates. Gorter and de Mooij (2001) observe that effective tax rates on interest, dividend and retained profits in the EU have remained largely stable for the later period, 1990-2000. It follows that the reduction of statutory tax rates has been accompanied by base broadening measures, which has left AETRs unaffected.

---

[21] Exemption countries include: Australia, Austria, Canada, Denmark, Finland, France, Germany, the Netherlands, Sweden and Switzerland (Belgium and Luxembourg were not included in the sample due to problems in gathering the relevant data).

Table 4.4   Reduction of top CT rates, 1985-2007

Country	1985	2007	%-point change, 1985-2007
Australia	50.0	30.0	-20.0
Austria	61.5	25.0	-36.5
Belgium	45.0	34.0	-11.0
Canada	-	36.1	-
Denmark	50.0	28.0	-22.0
Finland	57.0	26.0	-31.0
France	50.0	33.8	-16.2
Germany	61.7	38.3	-23.4
Ireland	50.0[a]	12.5	-37.5
Italy	47.8	37.3	-10.5
Japan	55.4	32.6	-22.8
Netherlands	42.0	25.5	-16.5
Sweden	52.0	28.0	-24.0
UK	40.0	30.0	-10.0
US	49.5	39.3	-10.2
Average	50.9	30.4	-20.4

Note: [a]The high 'standard' rate. A 10% preferential corporate profit tax (CPT) applied to profits from manufacturing and internationally traded services.

Sources: See http://www.econ.ku.dk/pbs/diversefiler/taxcomtables.pdf and Deloitte Worldwide CT rates at http://www.deloitte.com/.

Reasons Why Corporations may be Receptive to Statutory Tax Rates

At first sight, it is not obvious why corporations should prefer low over high statutory tax rates, if the high rate is accompanied by a narrower tax base, and thus the effective rate and company tax bill remain the same as under a low rate and broader tax base. After all, attracting investment seems to work only on the premise that companies, like their individual owners, prefer lower over higher taxes.

As noted before, a tax system that offers full allowance for the cost of capital (that is, both debt and equity capital) leaves the investment decision unaffected. All other things equal, base-broadening measures thus increase the cost of capital and decrease investment.[22] However, more and more evidence is becoming available that in an international setting these results

---

[22] An investment project is only undertaken if its NPV is zero or positive. The NPV is the discounted value of 'pure profits' that are generated over the investment's effective lifetime. A positive NPV before tax will remain so after tax. However, if the tax base includes the user cost of capital, the NPV of investment could be positive before tax, but negative after, making the investment commercially unviable.

may change radically for the reverse. MNCs are increasingly sensitive to the statutory tax rate as well as to the AETR. If the positive effect of a lower statutory tax rate outweighs the negative effect of a broad tax base on capital cost, investment might actually increase.

As such, there are a number of arguments that award a special role to the statutory tax rate alongside the effective tax rate. In the first place, the simple psychology of a low statutory rate counts. A low rate serves as an eye catcher. Corporate boards usually compose so-called 'short lists' of attractive countries in which to invest. Effective tax rates are not easily computed and call for costly research. A high statutory tax rate may cause a country to score a minus on the perceived friendliness of the tax system in the location decision of MNCs, even if the effective tax rate is ultimately internationally competitive. This also follows from the fiscal strategy memorandum of the European Commission (2001a), which finds that overall statutory tax rate differentials in the EU outweigh tax-base differentials. Hence, the leading driver of a country's competitiveness in attracting foreign investment, is not the tax base, but rather the statutory tax rate of the CT.

Second, it is widely held that MNCs engage in active profit shifting to avoid taxation. Revenues are located to low-tax-rate countries, while expenses are allocated to high-rate ones. Such tax planning is carried out mainly by:

- *transfer pricing* which permits MNCs to manipulate the prices related to the transfer of goods, intangibles and services between affiliated entities in different countries;
- *thin capitalisation* which allows corporations to use excessive debt financing to shift interest expenses to be deducted from the tax base in high-tax countries, while payments are made to low-tax ones; and
- *substitution of deductible royalties or interest for dividends* in high-rate host countries, which reduces the overall tax bill of MNCs and often circumvents paying WHTs that are less frequently imposed on royalties.

The first two categories in particular create strong incentives for MNCs to locate in low-tax-rate countries that effectively serve as tax shelters.

A third argument is that a low statutory rate tends to lower the AETRs of highly profitable companies, in proportion to companies that just earn the required rate of return (Bond, 2000). To see why, consider the opposite scenario. If the user cost of capital is fully excluded from the tax base and the tax rate is raised accordingly, marginal investment would not be taxed, but projects earning above-normal profits would be hit comparatively harder. The higher the above-normal profits, the higher the average tax burden. By including the user cost of capital in the tax base, some of the tax burden is shifted onto marginal investment. This lowers the AETR faced by companies earning above-normal returns, which in practice are often highly profitable MNCs.

Empirical evidence on profit shifting is hard to come by as it is conceptually difficult to separate tax-planning effects from real everyday business activity. However, a number of studies produce positive outcomes. Based on a panel of 16 OECD countries, Bartelsman and Beetsma (2003) find that a unilateral CT increase on average does not yield additional tax revenue because the amount of reported profit declines more than proportionally due to avoidance through transfer pricing.[23] Other studies mainly based on the US economy also produce positive evidence on profit shifting. Key contributions include Grubert and Mutti (1991); Hines and Rice (1994); Grubert et al. (1996); and Grubert (1998 and 2001).

BOX 4.7

Besides the effective tax rate, the statutory rate plays a role in attracting foreign investment. For example, MNCs engage in profit shifting, for example, by allocating revenues to low-tax countries and expenses to high-rate ones. This provides a positive incentive to locate in low-tax countries, which in turn benefit from higher foreign investment, reported profits and tax revenue. A low statutory rate also serves as an eye catcher for business managers.

CT Rate Efficiency

Referring to the tax-rate efficiency alone, a good competitive CT rate lies somewhere in the 20-25 per cent region in the coming decade or so. This means there is room for improvement in many countries. Figure 4.1 plots the statutory CT rate against the tax-rate efficiency. The case clearly demonstrates that high-tax-rate countries experience reduced rate efficiencies and vice versa. The only real exception is Norway, in part because benefits from a wealth of natural resources that generate location-specific rents and can easily be taxed away.[24] At both extremes, Ireland's CT collects over five

---

[23] The acuteness of profit shifting can be illustrated with reference to the German carmaker BMW. Because they were able to successfully shift expenses, the company's tax payments in Germany as a percentage of worldwide tax payments fell from 88 per cent to 5 per cent and -16 per cent in 1988, 1992 and 1993, respectively. Remarkably, BMWs CFO openly admitted to the company's efforts to shift expenses to high-tax countries, namely Germany (Bartelsman and Beetsma, 2003).

[24] In 1975, the Norwegian parliament passed a special Petroleum Tax Act. Although amended several times since, currently an additional 50 per cent tax is levied on top of the 28 per cent CT due to the high economic rents associated with producing oil (van den Noord, 2000). This allows

times as much revenue per percentage point of tax as Germany's CT. Countries with above-average CT rates thus seemingly gain from lowering statutory rates. And while the ambiguity on the desirability of active tax competition has not been resolved (see Chapter 8), Figure 4.1 confirms that one needs to at least follow the general trend.

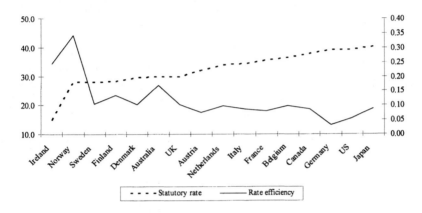

Sources: Computed from OECD Revenue Statistics and the OECD Tax Database.

Figure 4.1   Statutory CT rate vis-à-vis the tax-rate efficiency, 2001-2005

Empirical Insights

Base broadening can limit the budgetary costs of a reduction of the statutory rate. However, a tax-rate cut that is financed by base broadening does not lower the effective tax rate, so economic effects are likely to be smaller. A reduction of the effective CT burden will have a number of positive economic effects:

- a lower average tax burden attracts foreign investment in a way that is much more powerful than a reduction of statutory rates alone;
- a lower effective tax burden stimulates entrepreneurship and risk taking. Firms are inclined to make more (risky) investments if they receive an 'acceptable' net profit in return. This also encourages new companies to enter the market;

---

the government to capture the bulk of oil rents without compromising industry efficiency or competitiveness.

- companies in low-tax countries are better able to be price competitive on international product markets due to a lower cost of capital;
- companies have more financial flexibility, which raises investment indirectly since firms can more often finance their activities internally; and
- a lower effective tax rate stimulates spending on R&D and innovation as these activities are often equity financed.

Finally, Table 4.5 gives a general cross-country overview of the economic effects of a 5 percentage point reduction of effective CT rates, financed by raising the labour tax. We note that many European countries have a heavy tax burden on labour, which is why we are not in favour of raising the labour tax as in Table 4.5. See Chapter 10 for arguments in favour of a shift to consumption taxation.

Table 4.5   A unilateral 5 percentage point CT reduction with labour tax financing

Country	CT revenue	Capital stock	GDP	FDI	Welfare
Austria	-0.22	0.93	0.20	6.42	-0.03
Belgium	-0.19	1.50	0.75	6.52	0.23
Czech Republic	-0.26	1.02	0.22	5.54	-0.09
Denmark	-0.34	1.68	0.52	5.91	0.07
Finland	-0.25	0.89	0.11	5.33	-0.07
France	-0.35	2.24	0.68	5.48	0.21
Germany	-0.03	-0.55	-0.28	5.32	-0.18
Greece	-0.54	1.53	0.78	10.10	-0.10
Hungary	-0.08	-0.03	-0.18	3.26	-0.10
Ireland	-0.24	1.76	0.65	5.00	0.30
Italy	-0.11	0.73	0.15	5.48	-0.02
Netherlands	-0.21	0.99	0.23	5.79	-0.01
Poland	-0.21	0.68	0.08	5.96	-0.19
Portugal	-0.26	1.49	0.35	6.83	0.05
Spain	-0.19	1.31	0.43	6.84	-0.02
Sweden	-0.20	1.57	0.48	9.34	-0.05
UK	-0.14	1.41	0.36	9.03	-0.04

Source: Bettendorf et al. (2006, Table 4.7).

4.6 THREE CONCEPTUAL CORPORATE/CAPITAL INCOME TAXES

Having looked at the main issues in capital taxation, there are three alternative concepts worth considering on a theoretical basis: an allowance for corporate equity (ACE), the comprehensive business income tax (CBIT) and the dual income tax (DIT). As it is unlikely that the 'race to the bottom' in the near future will force tax rates down to zero, and current CT systems are still highly distorting, closer alignment with one of these concepts would create more efficient capital income taxation. The advantages relate to issues of neutrality, tax avoidance and the overall non-complexity.

Allowance for Corporate Equity

One approach to achieve neutrality in the corporate tax base is to introduce an allowance for the opportunity cost of equity-financed investment. Equity capital would be treated in a similar manner as debt capital, that is the user cost of both types of finance would be deductible against corporate profits. Compared to most current tax practices, the tax base would effectively be narrowed. The most commonly cited scheme to accomplish this is the allowance for corporate equity proposal. The ACE was originally conceived by Boadway and Bruce (1984) and for a comprehensive review see IFS Capital Taxes Group (1991).[25]

The allowance is calculated by multiplying shareholders' funds by an appropriate nominal interest rate. The first consists of total equity capital in the corporation (that is, the aggregate of past capital injections minus withdrawals and retained earnings); the second equals a market return that could have been earned if invested elsewhere (and is usually approximated by the risk-free interest rate on government bonds). The allowance is subsequently subtracted from gross profits along with other deductions for tax purposes, such as interest payments and depreciation.

The proposal has attractive economic advantages. In the first place, the ACE reduces the user cost of equity-financed investment and thereby becomes a tax on 'pure profits'. In line with the above discussion, the ACE system therefore does not distort the investment decision. Depreciation rules that deviate from true economic depreciation do not detract from this, which follows from the property that the present value of tax payments over the investment effective lifetime is fixed. For example, if depreciation is set to high relative to the true economic rate, thereby limiting the write-off periods, shareholders' funds and the related tax allowance are too low (and vice versa). Taxes payable would become too high as a consequence. In later

---

[25] Exceptionally, an ACE-type of profit tax was implemented in practice in Croatia from 1994 to 2001 (for a case study, see Keen and King, 2002).

periods, when depreciation is necessarily lower than the true economic rate, the difference is recovered through lower payments. In present value terms the result is the same.[26]

The depreciation schedule affects only the timing of tax payments, not their real value. From an administrative point of view, this is an attractive characteristic as it makes complex anti-avoidance rules and prescribed depreciation schedules redundant. For similar reasons, there is no need to correct for inflation, which is reflected in the nominal interest rate.

Nevertheless, there are also drawbacks to the system. The source of finance decision would still be distorted under PT. Furthermore, since interest and dividends are no longer taxed on a corporate level, foreign investors would be exempt and favoured over domestic ones. To lift these distortions, the current personal income tax would effectively have to be transformed into a personal consumption tax (see Chapter 5 on this). For the time being, this seems a bridge too far, at least in European countries.

Furthermore, budgetary constraints mean that a more narrow tax base needs to be accompanied by a higher statutory rate. This may deter inward foreign investment in a globalising economy, particularly one that is highly profitable. As Lammersen (2002) also points out, the relative benefit of the ACE diminishes with an increasing rate of return of companies (for reasons explained earlier). On the other hand, the statutory rate becomes more important. According to the author, this may explain why countries in the EU have in recent years actually moved away from ACE features in their tax bases to facilitate lower statutory rates.

Comprehensive Business Income Tax

In the light of these considerations, the comprehensive business income tax may present a more optimal arrangement. The tax was proposed by the US Department of the Treasury (1992) with the main aim of introducing single taxation for corporate income. The voluminous report describes four so-called 'integration prototypes'. Unlike the ACE, the CBIT does not create an extra deduction for the opportunity cost of using equity finance. Instead it excludes interest in calculating taxable profits, so the tax base is effectively broadened.

At the same time, taxation of dividend and interest income under PT is abolished. The 'backstop' function of CT is transformed into the final liability, which follows from the basic equivalence between a source-based CT and an equal-rate PT on profits with a full credit for the CT. The structure

---

[26] The basic concept for *pure profit* tax has been discussed in the Meade Committee Report (1978). In the report, it is referred to as the 'R-base business tax' (which is more commonly known as 'cash-flow tax'). Under the scheme business cash flows are taxed directly as they arise (that is, revenues minus current *and* capital expenditures). Investment is thus expensed immediately, with no future allowance for the cost of capital.

of the CBIT means that the CT rate and the top PT rate cannot be too far apart, which makes the tax suited to a country such as the United States where both rates lie close to each other.

The proposal fully eliminates the bias against equity finance. Capital gains on shares would remain taxed, but only in so far as they do not originate from retained earnings on a company level that have already borne the CBIT (that is, the excess of the actual share price over the purchase price supplemented by retained earnings net of CBIT). Technically speaking, the CBIT could cover unincorporated businesses, although the distinction between labour and capital income is harder to make for these entities (see the following subsection on the DIT for such an approach).

A second important benefit comes from the lower statutory rate that is facilitated by a broader tax base. As we have seen, modern economies rely increasingly on low statutory rates to attract foreign capital. A switch to the CBIT would benefit highly profitable companies as this would bring down the AETR faced by these companies, compared to companies earning a marginal return. This is consistent with the empirical finding that MNCs more often succeed in generating above-normal profits.

The proposal leaves intact existing depreciation schedules and other rules for determining taxable profits. Hence, these factors continue to exert an influence on the cost of capital and thus on the investment decision.

Dual Income Tax

A final comprehensive solution to capture capital income is the dual income tax (DIT). All the Nordic countries have a DIT-type tax system, yet they vary in the extent to which their tax systems resemble a 'pure' DIT (the Norwegian system perhaps comes closest). A number of key features distinguish a pure DIT from the global income tax (Cnossen, 2000).

For tax purposes, all income is divided between a labour and a capital income component. Labour income includes wages and salaries, fringe benefits, pensions and social safety income and is taxed at progressive rates. Capital income comprises business profits, dividends, interest, capital gains, rents and rental values. A lower flat or proportional rate applies, which is typically set equal to the lower rate of the labour income tax schedule. Costs associated with earning income are typically only deductible against this lower rate. This reduces the incentive to shift income between the two categories.

Under one variant of the DIT, labour and capital income are subsequently taxed separately at the progressive and proportional rates, respectively. Alternatively, they are taxed jointly at the proportional CT rate, after which further tax progression is added by higher labour income tax rates. This has the advantage that negative capital income can be offset against labour income as well. Under separate taxation, on the other hand, it is straightforward to levy source-based taxes on capital income.

In entities where wages and salaries are actively set by the proprietor (a so-called 'active owner'), profits are separated into a labour and a capital income component by assuming a presumptive return to the firm's capital which is set equal to the interest rate plus risk premium. Earnings above this presumptive return are considered to be labour income and taxed accordingly. Without this rule, labour income could be masked as capital income, which is generally taxed at a lower tax rate. Tax arbitrage is thus prevented,[27] albeit at the expense of increased administrative complexity.

The collection of capital income taxes is guaranteed through withholding at the source, at company level and by other entities paying capital income such as banks and insurance companies (WHT rates should be set equal to the flat CT rate). Payments made to non-residents are mostly not subject to WHT.[28] Double taxation of distributed profits is prevented through an imputation system, or equivalently, dividend exemption. The 'pure' DIT also avoids double taxation of realised capital gains of the shareholder. This is done by permitting a shareholder to write up the basis of a share as a firm's net retained profits that are attributable to that share.

By treating labour separate from capital, the DIT is a schedular rather than a global income tax. The system thereby implicitly recognises the disparity in the elasticities of substitution of labour and capital. This makes the tax practicable in countries with high revenue requirements and ensuing tax burdens. After all, efficiency conditions stipulate that labour should be taxed relatively higher than capital. As such, the DIT strikes a balance between optimal tax theory which dictates a zero rate and the political requirement of a positive tax on capital income. The labour income tax can be set separately in accordance with country-specific efficiency conditions and preferences for redistribution (as discussed in Chapter 3).

A fully-fledged DIT ensures that no particular investment, or certain sources of finance or organisational forms are tax favoured, and the lower rate on capital income mitigates the 'lock-in' effect associated with realisation-based capital gains taxation. A more uniform treatment of capital income limits distortions and opportunities for tax arbitrage and other avoidance behaviour, and ensures a more-efficient revenue collection.

---

[27] In practice this is not entirely true. In 2006, Norway enacted the new 'shareholder income tax' in response to concerns about income shifting. The old income-splitting rules applied only to active owners who own at least two-thirds of a firm, a number that can be manipulated by introducing passive owners into the firm. Between 1992 and 2000, Norway experienced a drop in corporations subject to income-splitting rules from 55 to 32 per cent (Christiansen, 2004).

[28] The extent to which the bias against equity finance remains depends on how interest payments to non-residents are taxed. Note that an interest WHT applied to non-residents likens the scheme conceptually to a CBIT (Cnossen, 2000).

4.7   BRIEF SUMMARY

In modern times with cross-border capital mobility and efficiency high on the political agenda, a capital tax is not an obvious choice. Personal and corporate tax systems (PT-CT systems) adversely affect capital accumulation and create numerous distortions to investor behaviour that should be carefully weighed against the benefits from equity, if any.

Optimal tax theory assumes that the efficient long-run tax on capital income is simply zero. A positive capital tax is detrimental to labour force production efficiency, thus raising unit labour costs. The tax, including excess burden from any investment distortion, is thereby implicitly shifted onto the less mobile factor, labour (indeed, if this is the case, labour is best taxed directly, also on equity grounds). The assumptions made in these studies are nevertheless somewhat rigorous. Capital is held perfectly mobile internationally, which could be true for financial capital, but not with respect to real capital. There are also location-specific rents that may be taxed away without harming efficiency.

Apart from these efficiency considerations, political and budgetary constraints simply dictate a positive tax on capital at least for the time being. In such a case, there are a few considerations to take into account in order to improve the efficiency of PT-CT systems. While the cost of capital is a primary driver of investment demand, much investment these days comes from abroad.

The rules of the game have thereby changed. Lowering the cost of capital through investment tax incentives may no longer be appropriate to generate investment if this implies that the statutory tax rate has to be raised accordingly. There are three main reasons to expect certain sensitivity of internationally operating companies to the statutory tax rate in addition to effective tax rates: first, a low statutory rate serves to catch the eye of business managers; second, there is evidence that companies are quite successful in shifting profits from countries with high statutory tax rates to those with low ones through transfer pricing, thin capitalisation and/or transforming dividends into deductible interest or royalties; and finally, a low statutory rate tends to lower the AETRs of highly profitable companies (mostly multinationals) compared to companies that just earn the required rate of return.

Looking at the tax-rate efficiencies in Figure 4.1, a competitive CT rate in the coming decade should lie somewhere around 20 per cent. To achieve this, lawmakers are bound to pursue a policy of base broadening. By itself, this is compatible with ensuring greater fiscal neutrality in the tax base. Or rather, it presents an opportunity to reduce the tax-system biases against equity finance, the profit distribution decision and/or the choice of organisational form that exists under current CT-PT regimes. Promoting a broad CT base also reduces the complexity of systems, administrative burdens, tax avoidance, the opportunities for aggressive tax planning and conflict between taxpayer and authorities.

Conceptually, the DIT offers an elegant alternative to contemporary global developments, mainly by treating the factors of production, labour and capital, as separate tax bases. The DIT taxes capital positively, yet effectively and not too much. This is good since there is a lot to gain from improved, more-efficient capital income taxation – a gain, to be sure, that accrues to the economy and to society as a whole.

5. Taxes on consumption

But when the impositions are laid upon those things which men consume, every man payeth equally for what he useth; nor is the Commonwealth defrauded by the luxurious waste of private men.

(Thomas Hobbes)[1]

5.1 INTRODUCTION

Consumption as a macroeconomic variable is regarded as one of the least volatile in its fluctuation over time. It is none the less a vital one. By keeping demand up, economic activity in its broadest sense is promoted. Higher consumption and production lead to increased activity in other areas of an economy. Investment is stimulated, somewhat paradoxically, as well as the development of technology. These are important elements in creating economic growth.

The notion of taxing consumption has been around for many centuries. In the 17th century, Thomas Hobbes touched upon several advantages of using consumption as a basis for taxation (see the above quotation). In the first place, it may be considered fairer to tax people on what they take out of the economy, instead of on what they put into it in the form of saving. Those who save contribute to common resources, whereas the opposite is true for dissaving. Second, it is argued that consumption is a truer measure of a person's well-being. Consumption more accurately quantifies what people are really enjoying at a particular moment. If consumption exceeds income, the difference would be targeted under a consumption tax, but not under income tax. And finally, consumption taxation is said to take place on a more voluntary basis since the decision to consume is attributed greater flexibility than the choice to earn income.

These advantages are none the less based on normative arguments of fairness and equality. At the same time, a tax on consumption is inherently regressive in nature as low-income households consume a proportionally larger fraction of their incomes than do high-income households. From an

---

[1] Thomas Hobbes (1588-1679) was a 17th-century British political philosopher who is considered to be one of the most influential men of his time and who had a lasting influence on subsequent political philosophy.

economic standpoint, a consumption tax can nevertheless be favoured because it rejects the income tax discrimination against saving. Therefore it is said to promote investment and economic growth.

This chapter analyses the economic effects and implementation of consumption taxes. It begins by examining the shift from income to consumption-based taxation, which has been a much-cited alternative in discussion on 'fundamental tax reform' in the US and more recently in the EU. Second, higher taxes also lead to a higher price level and a reduction in household consumption, which may cause temporary effects to an economy and certain timing issues. Third, taxes on consumption create a number of distortions in cross-border trade. Sections 5.4 and 5.5 discuss the implementation of different sorts of general and selective consumption taxes, respectively, after which the chapter concludes.

5.2   ECONOMIC EFFECTS OF A SHIFT TO CONSUMPTION-BASED TAXATION

Over the past two decades, there has been a substantial interest, in both academia and the governments of a number of OECD countries, in the substitution of a consumption-based tax for an income tax system based on neutral revenue. The main reason for this attention has been the perceived positive effect of such a reform on the level of savings, which are effectively taxed twice under an income tax.

A simple numerical example demonstrates this (see Meade Committee Report, 1978). Assume an income or in the alternative case a consumption tax of 50 per cent. An individual with 100 units in earnings can either spend his or her income or save it and collect a return of 10 per cent in one year. If all income is consumed there is no difference between either an income or a consumption tax. Under both alternatives the person would be able to spend 50 units. On the other hand, if income is put aside, he or she would be able to save only 50 units under income taxation, while this would be 100 under consumption tax. Hence, the return after one year will be 5 and 10 units under both types of tax, respectively. Assuming that it is consumed afterwards, the return is worth only 2.5 units under the income tax, but 5 under consumption tax. For this reason, income tax discriminates against people who consume later in life (Kaldor, 1977).

Where income tax tends to tilt prices away from future consumption to current consumption and so discriminates against savings, no such distortion is created under a consumption tax (that is, the intertemporal saving-consumption trade-off remains unaffected). For this reason, the long-run savings rate is likely to be higher under a consumption-based tax, which promotes a larger capital stock, output and greater economic welfare. Some economists have also argued that reducing taxes on labour by shifting to an alternative base improves labour market performance.

The Range of Estimated Effects in the US

There is a general consensus among economists that capital accumulation of an economy in the long run benefits from a consumption tax shift. There is less agreement on the extent, mainly due to the widely differing modelling techniques employed and the projections derived.

Gravelle (2002) provides an overview of a number of studies that were carried out for the US economy to measure the effects of such consumption tax reform. For example, the US Joint Committee on Taxation (1997), using both intertemporal as well as reduced form models to simulate the impact of a substitution of a consumption-based flat tax for the current US income tax, found that long-run output would increase between 1.7 and 7.5 per cent by such a shift, with an average increase of approximately 4 per cent. Two other studies by Auerbach (1996b) and Fullerton and Rogers (1996) found that shifting to VAT would increase long-run output by 9.7 and 4.5 per cent, respectively (cited from Gravelle, 2002).

In an updated study, Altig et al. (2001) simulate a shift under five different scenarios of 'fundamental tax reform' in the US, using a sophisticated dynamic life-cycle model.[2] The scenarios include a transition to a proportional income tax, a proportional consumption tax, a Hall-Rabushka flat tax, a flat tax with transitional relief for low-income earners and a so-called 'X-tax'. The X-tax is a concept by Bradford (1986) and is basically similar to the Hall and Rabushka (1995) flat tax, with wages deductible on the business level and taxed on individual level with a large tax deduction. However, instead of taxing labour income at a flat rate, it is taxed at graduated rates up to the single business tax rate (a technical description of both taxes is provided below).

Table 5.1 reproduces the long-run output gains under the respective scenarios. The results were equally positive. A proportional consumption tax yields the largest outcome with a positive output effect of nearly 10 per cent, which is particularly interesting compared to the proportional income tax scenario. Not taxing the return to savings, as under a consumption tax, apparently has a similar growth effect (of roughly 5 per cent) as removing all tax progression of the current income tax system, whether by adopting the proportional income or consumption tax alternative. It is also remarkable that the more progressive X-tax comes second in terms of growth potential. Under transitional relief, the effect is mitigated.

---

[2] The fundamental tax reform discussion assumes full replacement of the existing US corporate and individual income tax systems by a consumption-based tax such as a flat tax. See Zodrow and Mieszkowski (2002) and Gravelle (2004) for a treatment of options and issues.

Table 5.1   Economic effects of fundamental tax reform

Scenario	Output effect (%)
Proportional income tax	4.9
Proportional consumption tax	9.4
Hall-Rabushka flat tax	4.5
Flat tax with transitional relief	1.9
X-tax	6.4

Source: Altig et al. (2001).

BOX 5.1

Simulations for the US economy show that the long-run growth gain from a shift to consumption-based taxation is significantly positive. Output gains range from 1.9 to 9.4 per cent under different model assumptions and policy scenarios.

Caveats to fundamental tax reform

There are three important limitations to these findings. In the first place, the change to a consumption-based tax would confer the equivalent of a one-off wealth tax on the owners of 'old' capital. Existing capital earned by income that has been subject to income tax would be taxed again on consumption in later life. If unanticipated, the consumption tax shift causes a one-off devaluation of 'initial' capital, which is particularly hard on older people who hold a proportionately large share of wealth in the economy. The models indicate that this one-off wealth tax is what contributes importantly to the efficiency gains of fundamental tax reform.

The less expected, the higher the efficiency of the reform since it would not permit capital owners to alter their economic behaviour or choice in response to the tax change. Likewise, any transitional relief alleviates the additional tax burden on existing capital, so the consumption tax would be more or less transformed into a tax on wages during the transitional period, thereby mitigating any positive economic effects.

Second, all scenarios of a full consumption tax shift reflect simulations based on the US economy. However, the tax burden in most EU countries is considerably larger. A revenue-neutral shift in these countries would thus require higher marginal tax rates, making the short-run macroeconomic effects in the transitional phase possibly more severe. The speed with which the adjustment of product prices relative to wages would take place is crucial. Theoretically, the increase in consumption taxes should be offset by a similar reduction of the income tax burden such that household purchasing power remains unaffected. A consumption tax places an additional burden on top of the production price of goods and services, just like the income tax does. Both taxes therefore reduce household disposable income. None the less, since prices and wages are likely to be somewhat sticky in the short run, there could still be a considerable shock to the economy.

Third, consumption taxes have a regressive burden impact as measured against income. Particularly in Europe, the adoption of a consumption-based tax is likely to meet with significant public and political opposition. A one-off across-the-board shift is hardly a realistic alternative here (that is, one big bang).

A Shift to VAT in the EU

As discussed in Chapter 3, a more gradual shift of the income tax burden onto consumption, in particular VAT and green taxes, has been advocated in many EU countries as a solution to address high labour tax burdens. Statutory VAT rates could be raised in many EU countries. Matthews (2003) uses a sample of 14 European countries to estimate Laffer-curve effects for VAT. The estimates indicate an upper bound VAT rate of slightly below 20 per cent, which could serve as a reference point. Erosion of the tax base, evasion and avoidance reduce the revenue intake beyond this point (though tax administrations in Sweden and Norway do not appear to encounter significant enforcement problems with a VAT of 25 per cent).

Statistical research by Hutton and Ruocco (1999) has revealed positive employment effects from such previous VAT shifts. Data for France, Germany, Italy and the UK during the 1985-92 period indicate that gradual VAT increases coincided with lower average income tax rates in all countries except France, where labour income taxes increased. The data showed that in Germany and Italy the shift helped to offset a rise in unemployment, while in the UK it supported an already downward trend. In France, tax policy reinforced a rising unemployment.

Moreover, the European Parliament (2005) reports that a 1 per cent of GDP income tax cut together with an increase in consumption tax of 1 per cent of GDP could generate economic growth exceeding 1 per cent, and the European Commission's QUEST model simulating a tax burden shift from labour to indirect taxes, also produces positive results. The model calibration is set such that the share of indirect taxation constitutes 40 per cent of the tax mix in each EU member state. Hence, the VAT is increased under a simultaneous reduction of the wage tax so that the reform is budget neutral. Table 5.2 presents the results of the simulation, which is performed under three different scenarios.

The simulation highlights the importance of price indexing for the final outcome. Because the VAT is partly levied on consumption by people receiving social benefits and other non-labour income, wage costs are likely to decrease somewhat under a shift. This leads to a positive effect on employment. It can therefore be concluded that the outcome of shifting emphasis to VAT depends crucially on whether such reform succeeds in shifting part of the tax burden away from workers to those outside the labour force. In other words, from the active to the inactive or those receiving income from the informal economy.

Table 5.2   Economic effects of a consumption tax shift such that share of indirect taxation constitutes 40 per cent of the tax mix (% change)

	Scenario 1 No indexation	Scenario 2 Benefits indexed	Scenario 3 Benefits and transfer payment indexed
Labour tax	-4.61	-4.61	-4.61
Debt/GDP	-13.25	-6.54	-1.95
GDP	2.33	1.10	1.10
Employment	2.69	1.26	1.26

Source: Roeger and in 't Veld (downloaded 16 September 2007),
www.cepii.fr/anglaisgraph/communications/pdf/2006/190106/inveld.ppt

Finally, the shift should reduce the export prices of European companies slightly, thereby promoting exports. Firms are expected to reflect some of the (capital) income tax burden in their product prices. For domestic consumers, the net effect would be roughly similar, as higher consumption taxes compensate this. However, exports are free of VAT (that is, zero rated). On the downside, a high VAT raises incentives for ordinary consumers for cross-border shopping. To mitigate these distortions, it has been proposed to coordinate policies whereby countries jointly and gradually increase VAT rates, for example, by 1 percentage point per year under a simultaneous decrease of labour taxes.

BOX 5.2

Simulations with the European Commission's QUEST model indicate that a shift from labour to consumption taxation such that the share of indirect taxation constitutes 40 per cent of the tax mix has significant positive economic effects. The employment increase ranges between 1.26 and 2.69 per cent and of GDP between 1.10 and 2.33 per cent.

Transitional Issue and Timing

Past experiences have shown that shifting to a VAT, or VAT increases, can cause significant short-run shocks to the economy. For example, when the UK in 1979 increased its VAT rate from 8 to 15 per cent to finance a sizeable income tax cut, it added nearly 4 per cent to the consumer price index (CPI) during a time when inflation was already accelerating. Within a few months, the annual inflation rate had soared to over 20 per cent (Dilnot and Kay, 1990). Similarly, Japan raised its VAT rate from 3 to 5 per cent in 1994, at a time when the Japanese economy was just starting to show signs of an early recovery from economic downturn. The rise led to a reduction in consumer spending and slowed down recovery.

Yet VAT increases do not necessarily harm short-run economic activity. On 1 January 2007, the German government increased the standard VAT rate from 16 to 19 per cent. *Ex ante* survey research by the Royal Bank of Scotland (2006) predicted a rise in consumer prices by a 1.2 percentage point from tax-push inflation. This would have a temporary negative effect on consumer spending and impede economic growth.[3] Since Germany is an economic heavyweight in the European Monetary Union (EMU), the VAT hike could raise inflation in the eurozone by approximately 0.35 per cent and prompt the European Central Bank (ECB) to raise interest rates, which is generally not beneficial to economic growth.

Ultimately, prices rose by only 1.8 per cent in January 2007 from 1.4 per cent in December 2006. Hence, inflationary pressures were significantly lower than expected, which shows that timing can be crucial.

5.3   INTERNATIONAL TRADE FLOWS AND TAXATION

International transactions have grown exponentially in the past few decades. Tax-rate differentials between individual jurisdictions as a result increasingly distort consumer behaviour and the allocation of production factors across countries. To prevent double taxation or double non-taxation of goods and services that cross borders, countries make so-called 'border tax adjustments' (BTAs). These corrections are coordinated according to either the *destination* principle or the *origin* principle. Both principles relate to the coordination of indirect taxes, but there is a strong resemblance to the residence and source principles described in Chapter 4.

---

[3] Since not all goods and services are taxed under the standard rate of VAT and not all producers fully pass on the tax to the consumer in the short run, the average price rise is lower than the 3 per cent tax hike. Previous experiences have also shown that in some instances price setters succeed in passing on more than the tax increase. For example, the price of tobacco in Germany increased by 5 per cent in anticipation of the VAT rise.

Destination-based Taxation

Under the destination principle, all goods and services are taxed in the country of consumption (that is, their destination). This means that the revenue accrues to the destination state. In such a case, BTAs involve a rebate of taxes paid in the exporting country and an application of tax in the importing country. For instance, if a commodity is exported from country X to country Y, country X repays all taxes to the exporter collected up to that point (in practice this is mostly done by a tax credit). On import, country Y imposes a tax according to its own tax code and laws. Country Y in turn should also rebate all taxes collected on exports from its territory and so on.

Residents of a certain country thereby face an equal tax rate on both domestically produced and imported commodities. Accordingly, producer prices across countries are unaffected by the tax and, if we assume perfect competition, marginal costs of production are as well. This means that the factors of production are allocated efficiently and output is maximised, a state that is referred to as achieving 'production efficiency'. However, relative consumer prices vary between countries. The price of a commodity in country X will differ from the price of a similar commodity in country Y, since different tax rates apply. Hence, although production efficiency is achieved, consumer choice and trade between countries is distorted.

Origin-based Taxation

The origin principle achieves the contrary by taxing goods and services in the country of production (that is, their origin). This implies exempting imports from tax. Hence, in terms of the previous example, commodities would leave country X still burdened by a tax imposed by country X. Double taxation is prevented by country Y refraining from taxing its imports. As a result, the revenue accrues to the country of production.

Under the origin principle, relative consumer prices are unaffected. A commodity produced in country X will have the same price whether sold in country X or country Z, simply because the tax rate of the origin state applies. Consumer choice and trade are thereby optimised, a situation that is referred to as achieving 'exchange efficiency'. However, because tax rates across countries differ, producer prices are likely to differ as well. Producers in lower-tax countries will have a competitive advantage because their after-tax return is higher. This causes a distortion to the allocation of production factors across countries and undermines production efficiency.

Which Alternative is Preferred?

Countries should adhere to one principle in making BTAs. Only by coordinating their tax policy can double taxation or double non-taxation be prevented. The equivalence theorem states that as long as a uniform tax is applied on a comprehensive base, both the destination and the origin principles achieve neutrality. This is so even if there is an absolute difference in the tax rates, in which case exchange rates or product price adjustments even out the disparity (Robson, 1998).

In other words, as long as both countries apply the same tax principle, recourses are allocated efficiently across borders. This concerns both the allocation of production (investment) and the distribution of commodities (consumption). The reality is nevertheless different. Countries impose a wide variety of tax rates on differential tax bases, so there remain many differences in the way that consumption taxes are implemented. The equivalence theorem therefore holds true only on paper and a trade-off has to be made between the two tax principles.

The destination principle may ultimately be preferred if the cost of inefficient production is likely to be greater than that of inefficient trade (Diamond and Mirrlees, 1971). In addition, it can be argued that if consumers bear the burden of taxation, they should be entitled to receive the government benefits that are financed by it. Hence, the destination principle should apply. A practical objection to the origin principle is the required valuation of imported goods for determining the tax credit, which can be a complex process with high associated cost of administration. Therefore, in its international tax and trading rules, the World Trade Organisation (WTO) officially endorses the destination principle in coordinating indirect taxation.

5.4 GENERAL CONSUMPTION TAX OPTIONS

By definition, a *general* consumption tax imposes an equal rate of tax on the sales of all goods and services. However, usually a number of goods and services are exempt from the main rule. Many countries exclude healthcare or educational services from the tax base and/or tax the basic necessities of life at reduced rates. Despite these inconsistencies, the tax is called general because of its broad character and method of implementation.

In contrast, a *selective* consumption tax targets only specific goods and services, enabling a government to discriminate between commodities and to impose a variety of different tax rates. Selective taxes are especially useful to advance specific policy objectives such as discouraging populations from drinking, smoking and driving. Because of their discriminatory nature, they are by definition distortionary. In the OECD area just over one-third of total consumption tax revenue is collected through selective taxation, leaving two-thirds for general taxation.

Methods of Implementation

Although the basis for a consumption tax is always the same, namely the spending on goods and services, there are several methods to implement a consumption tax. We begin by identifying the factors that determine total spending on goods and services (following Cnossen, 1999):

$$Y \equiv W + R \equiv C + S. \tag{5.1}$$

This identity states that national income (Y) is equal to the sum of wages (W) and return on capital (R), which represents the so-called 'sources' side of an economy. At the same time, national income (Y) is equal to the aggregate of consumption and saving ($C + S$). The proportion of income spent on consumption together with the proportion spent on saving corresponds to the so-called 'uses' side in an economy.

By rewriting equation (5.1) as equation (5.2) we make consumption the dependent variable. In the second part, S has been replaced by I, which is a valid long-run assumption (see also section 1.6 on equivalence relations in Chapter 1):

$$C = Y - S = W + R - I. \tag{5.2}$$

In this form, four general consumption tax bases can be identified that are imposed on any or a combination of the variables. All four taxes are equivalent in that they target consumer spending, yet all have distinct methods for implementation:

- value added tax (VAT);
    - -tax credit-invoice method;
    - -addition method;
    - -direct subtraction method;
- retail sales tax (RST);
- flat tax (FT); and
- cash-flow tax (CFT).

For example, a VAT is imposed on the sum of wages and business cash flow ($W + R - I$), which represents value added at the firm level. Three conceptually different methods for implementing VAT are distinguished. All three target the same value added, but none the less differ substantially when it comes to enforcement and administration. A RST is typically placed on consumption (*C*). Consumers are taxed directly, despite the legal responsibility which lies with the retailers.

The FT also taxes value added, but allows a deduction of wages on the firm level that are subsequently taxed on a personal level. The FT would thus be partly collected from households and partly from businesses. A CFT is levied on annual income minus savings (*Y – S*). Hence, people's consumption is derived indirectly by deducting total annual private saving from income. The FT and CFT are personal taxes and take into account a taxpayer's personal situation. We shall consider the four taxes in turn.

Value-added Tax

While consumption has been taxed for many centuries, VAT is a relatively new idea. The spread of VAT is arguably the most important development in taxation over the last half-century. In the 1950s, France was the first to adopt a VAT scheme, using it to carry out major reform and modernisation of its tax system. Since then about 135 countries have followed suit, making VAT the leading consumption tax in the world. The US is the only OECD country that has not adopted it.

In an early stage, VAT was introduced by all EU member states, for which adoption is a condition of entry. In 1991, Canada also replaced its narrow-based and multiple-rated federal manufacturing sales tax (FST) with the introduction of a VAT-type 10 per cent general sales tax (GST).[4] Norway introduced VAT as early as 1969, but only in 2001 did the country introduce a general liability to pay VAT on services rendered. In addition, the standard VAT rate was increased from 23 to 24 per cent, a reduced rate of 12 per cent on food products was introduced and an investment tax of 7 per cent was abolished.[5] Japan enacted a broad-based VAT in 1989 that was initially levied at a rate of 3 per cent, but in 1994 increased to 5 per cent. The Japanese VAT is not based on invoices but on a subtraction of taxable purchases (elaborated below).[6] Australia has replaced its whole sales tax (WST) by a 10 per cent GST in 2000.[7]

---

[4] Using general equilibrium methods, Hamilton and Whalley (1989) estimated the welfare gain at $672.6 million, or approximately 0.24 per cent of GDP. Although this is relatively small, the authors conclude that this will become bigger when higher future revenue needs are likely to make the tax more efficient.

[5] Bye et al. (2004) estimated that the reform was slightly welfare reducing. Although GDP remains unaffected, consumption decreases by 0.12 per cent. The analysis also reveals that abolishing the investment tax alone would have raised the capital stock and GDP by 0.85 and 0.45 per cent, respectively.

[6] The original structure of the Japanese tax system was introduced in 1949 under the 'Shoup Reform', after the American economist Dr C.S. Shoup who designed it. The structure relied heavily on direct taxation.

[7] The reform was analysed in Dixon and Rimmer (1999) using a dynamic computable general equilibrium (CGE) model (MONASH). Overall it was shown to be slightly welfare reducing

Computation of the VAT base

The tax base of the VAT comprises wage income (W), which is the aggregate of wage payments by firms, and business cash flow ($R - I$). The value added by the capital income part (R) can be split into three individual components: (i) the *normal return* to investment measured by the risk-free interest rate; (ii) the entrepreneur's *risk premium* which depends on the type of business and associated risk profile; and (iii) *above-normal profits* (also called 'rents'). An economically efficient VAT only targets the above-normal return to investment, which comprises the risk premium and above-normal profits. It does not include the normal return to investment, which makes it a pure consumption-based tax.[8]

Although VAT is legally imposed at the business level, the final burden rests with the consumer. The nature of VAT can be illustrated in Table 5.3 by reference to the example of a basic four-stage production process. Production starts with a collection and processing of raw materials (R); then moves to a semi-manufacturer (S); the manufacturer (M); and finally the distributor (D) who sells the product to the consumer. Each of the four stages contributes to added value by labour and capital.

The first stage creates a value added of 40 by the labour force (W) and 10 by the capital stock (R). Total value added equals 50 ($W + R$). The next stages in the production process are computed accordingly, which accumulates a consumer price of 500, exclusive of tax. The entire process shows that, in reverse order, sales price minus purchase price is total value added, which is the aggregate of labour payments and capital income. From an accounting perspective the tax base can thus simply be determined by subtracting purchases from sales.

Table 5.3   A four-stage production process

Details	R	S	M	D	Total
Wages (W)	40	70	160	120	390
Capital (R)	10	30	40	30	110
Transactions (excl. tax)					
Sales	50	150	350	500	-
Purchases	0	50	150	350	-
Total value added	50	100	200	150	500

---

because of a negative terms-of-trade effect (that is, the ratio of a country's export price index relative to its import price index). Because the original WST was highly distorting, export-competing industries benefited from the reform, while import-competing industries suffered.

[8] This is achieved by an immediate expensing of capital expenditures (that is, investment). Indeed, the NPV of an investment equals the capitalised value of the normal returns over its effective lifetime. By immediately expensing investment costs, the normal return is excluded from the tax base. In practice, this is equivalent to granting a full credit for VAT paid on the purchase price of an investment.

In practice, a production process may encompass any number of stages, all contributing to total value added. Because the tax liability is computed at every individual stage, VAT is also referred to as a 'multistage' consumption tax. There are three approaches to taxing value added, as described below.

Tax credit-invoice method

This method taxes all business sales under a full credit for tax paid on purchases, and is illustrated in Table 5.4. The first stage sells its produce at 50 units and has purchases of 0. The supplier is liable for 10 units in tax (that is, 20 per cent of 50). The second stage has sales of 150 units. This amounts to 30 units in tax (that is, 20 per cent of 150); however, a credit is granted for taxes paid on inputs. The net tax payable by the semi-manufacturer therefore totals 20 units. The manufacturer is in turn liable for 40 units in tax and the distributor for 30.

Total tax collected throughout the production process thereby equals 10 + 20 + 40 + 30 = 100, or 20 per cent of the tax-exclusive consumer price of 500 units. The total tax liability is determined by the final chain which sets the consumer price. Because collection takes place throughout the entire production process, the actual remittance lies jointly in the hands of the firms involved.

Table 5.4   Example of the tax credit invoice method

Details	R	S	M	D	Total
Sales	50	150	350	500	-
Purchases	0	50	150	350	-
Tax on Sales	10	30	70	100	210
Tax credit on Purchases	-	10	30	70	110
Tax payable (difference)	10	20	40	30	100

In practice, the tax liability at each individual stage is calculated indirectly and regardless of whether sales and purchases are related. The calculations are based on invoices issued for sales and received on purchases. This results in an interlocking chain of invoices which make compliance easy to verify. Note that although remittance occurs at every stage in the production process, the consumer bears the burden of the tax by a higher retail sales price. The collection procedure of alternating tax and credit also prevents cascading.[9]

Direct subtraction method

A second approach to VAT involves a direct subtraction of purchase costs. The direct subtraction method, also referred to a 'business transfer tax',

---

[9] 'Cascading' refers to the situation where business inputs are not completely relieved of tax which leads to a double tax on that part of value added including a tax on a tax.

allows a deduction of total purchases, including investment goods, from total sales at each individual stage in production. The tax rate is applied to the difference, thereby determining the tax liability directly rather than indirectly as under the credit invoice method. This is illustrated in Table 5.5.

Table 5.5   Example of the direct subtraction method

Details	R	S	M	D	Total
Sales	50	150	350	500	-
Purchases	0	50	150	350	-
Tax on sales – purchases (20%)	10	20	40	30	100

Even if the approach is transaction based, firms have less incentive to register for VAT purposes. There is no credit which reduces the tax liability and whose size depends on taxes already remitted by preceding links (this mechanism is exactly what encourages registration for VAT purposes under the tax credit-invoice method). For similar reasons, it is more difficult to enforce the direct subtraction VAT and administer imports and exports.

Addition method
Under a third approach value added is determined by adding wages and capital income and subtracting the normal return on investment at each individual stage of production. Table 5.6 illustrates the basic characteristics with a numerical example.

Table 5.6   Example of the addition method

Details	R	S	M	D	Total
Wages (W)	40	70	160	120	390
Capital ($R - I$)	10	30	40	30	110
Value added ($W + R - I$)	50	100	200	150	500
Tax on value added (20%)	10	20	40	30	100

The computation is an intricate process. Because the tax is not transaction based but a direct computation, accounting information is needed on employee compensation, the return to investment, depreciation, changes to inventories and so forth. For many firms this is only feasible on the quarterly closing of accounts, which causes unwanted delays in administration, and even if the required data are available, the addition method involves complex calculations and arbitrary estimations.

Zero rating versus exemption
To relieve goods and services of VAT, for example in case of exports or certain basic necessities, government can apply either a *zero rate* or an

exemption. In the case of a zero rate, a business is subject to VAT under the law, that is, there is VAT liability, but remits no tax simply because the rate of tax is zero. However, the good or service is formally part of the tax base so all prior taxes on purchases can still be credited, or if there is no previous VAT to credit against, refunded. On the other hand, under an exemption there is no VAT liability, which precludes taxation of value added and thus the crediting of prior VAT. Any VAT remitted in the production chain prior to the exemption remains intact. The size of such tax depends on the stage in the production chain where a product or service becomes exempt and value added hitherto.

The difference is illustrated in Tables 5.7 and 5.8. In Table 5.7 a zero rate is applied at the manufacturer (*M*) stage. The implication is that the manufacturer is liable for 0 units in taxes on sales. None the less, because there is VAT liability, the manufacturer can claim credit for 30 units in taxes paid at prior stages (by *R* and *S*). The effective total VAT payable throughout the production process therefore is 0 units.

Table 5.7   VAT implications of a zero rate

Details	R	S	M	D	Total
Sales	50	150	350	500	-
Purchases	0	50	150	350	-
Tax non-zero-rated sales	10	30	-	-	-
Tax zero-rated sales	-	-	0	0	-
Tax credit on purchases	-	10	30	0	-
VAT payable	10	20	0	0	0

On the other hand, under an exemption at the same stage, the prior taxes of 30 cannot be credited against sales (see Table 5.8). In total, a tax of 30 units remains intact. An exemption earlier or later in the production process would entail a different outcome depending on value added at that point. If the product does not remain exempted throughout the entire production chain, the VAT liability could end up exceeding the amount that would have been payable without exemption.[10] Obviously, this compromises the efficiency of the VAT.

The tax credit-invoice VAT is less sensitive than other consumption taxes to evasion and issues of product valuation because of the multistage collection effort and trail of interrelated invoices. Over- or undervaluation is likely to be rebalanced at a later stage and, if not, prior-stage taxes have still been collected, thus limiting the damage. Only serious fraud involving the entire production and consumption chain would make total VAT evasion

---

[10] This argument does not apply if the exemption is granted at the beginning of production since no tax has yet been imposed, or at the end because the exemption represents the final relief.

possible. A major second advantage of the credit-invoice type of VAT is the way of dealing with transborder trade. The destination principle prescribes that all exports are zero rated, so trade occurs free of domestic tax. Since the tax liability is calculated on the basis of invoices, BTAs are easily made and verified on both sides of the border (assuming adequate exchange of information).

Table 5.8   VAT implications of an exemption

Details	R	S	M	D	Total
Sales	50	150	350	500	-
Purchases	0	50	150	350	-
Tax before exemption	10	30	-	-	-
Tax after exemption	-	-	-	-	-
Tax credit on purchases	-	10	-	-	-
VAT payable	10	20	0	0	30

Common practices and misconceptions

Despite these considerations, governments regularly prefer an exemption to a zero rate because of the associated simplicity, costs of administration and compliance with international law. Zero-rated firms are still required to register for VAT purposes so administrative obligations remain, while no revenue is effectively collected.

VAT systems incorporate a range of standard exemptions and reduced rates, which are rationalised on egalitarian grounds.[11] A main argument is that people should be protected from being taxed too heavily on so-called 'essential' goods such as food products. Whereas the standard exemptions are commonly applied, most countries only zero rate exports. In addition, an exemption often applies to small businesses. Firms with sales below a registration threshold pay taxes on their purchases, but do not collect taxes on their sales (which are fairly low, anyway). This is considered fair since costs of meeting the VAT obligation are largely fixed and therefore are borne most heavily by small businesses.

A review by Cnossen (2003) concludes that of all VAT systems, Australia and New Zealand come closest to targeting a comprehensive VAT base. The only real exemption in both countries is that of financial transactions, which is tricky to tax under the tax credit-invoice method. The reason is that the banks' intermediation fee, that is, their economic rents, cannot easily be separated from the pure interest rate (only the former should be taxed,

---

[11] Standard exemptions include healthcare, education, governmental services, postal services, cultural and sporting services, charitable work and certain fund-raising events, non-commercial activities of non-profit-making organisations, financial services, insurance and re-assurance, immovable property and betting, lotteries and gambling.

whereas the latter should not). It is argued that there is little reason to exempt many other activities now exempt. Where relief is sought, zero rating is more neutral and efficient.

An interesting second finding is that differentiated rates, that is, those that are standard and reduced, hardly mitigate the regressive character of VAT. This is corroborated in several studies in various countries.[12] Reduced rates are also an administrative nuisance by complicating taxpayer accounting systems, audit and control by tax authorities. These practices would therefore only be distortionary in the light of rising administration and compliance costs. The robustness of the VAT, regularly praised as its strongest trait, is diminished. While lowering the efficiency of the system, it appears that the measures may also be rejected as an effective tool for redistributive purposes.

Labour-intensive services

Reduced VAT rates are also advocated by lawmakers for the macroeconomic objective of stimulating employment in labour-intensive service sectors. Services that are commonly subject to reduced rates include small repairs to bicycles, shoes and clothing, home renovation, house cleaning and domestic care activities, and hairdressing. The measures are generally evaluated as highly inefficient with negative distributional side-effects. According to the European Commission (2003a) a reduction of direct taxes on labour would be 52 per cent more effective in creating employment.

BOX 5.3

Research shows that reduced or zero rates and exemptions are generally an ineffective tool to counter the inherent regressive impact of VAT. The same applies to reduced rates on labour-intensive services, which is frequently advocated by politicians to simulate employment in these sectors. A reduction in direct taxes on labour would be 52 per cent more effective in creating employment.

---

[12] It is useful to reproduce a few findings here. Credit should go to Sijbren Cnossen who makes a convincing case for a more comprehensive and uniform VAT. The OECD's *Taxing consumption* edition of *1988* found that the zero rating of food products (as in the UK), reduced rating (the Netherlands) or even full taxation (Denmark) of food products barely affected the burden distribution. An Australian study revealed that zero rating food products would benefit only 15 per cent of the poorest households (< 20 per cent of total income). In Ireland, a similar zero rate was found to offer twice as many benefits to high-income as to low-income households and a Swedish study showed that 'yuppies' primarily gained from such a measure because they purchase expensive foods, eat out more frequently and throw food away. Finally, a study in the UK showed that eliminating zero rates hardly alters progressivity at all, if higher revenues facilitate an income tax reduction of 1 percentage point in the first bracket.

Moreover, reduced VAT rates aim to weaken the black economy. The impact of a lower rate on tax evasion is nevertheless difficult to measure since, by definition, little is known about these businesses. Second, the primary reason to operate in the black economy is often not to evade VAT, but to avoid any tax, including income tax and social security contributions. The incentive of a lower VAT rate to move out of the black economy is therefore considered limited.

The Retail Sales Tax

The second largest consumption tax in the world is the RST. The tax is primarily employed on a decentralised basis.[13] In the US, the RST offers an independent source of revenue for the majority of its 50 states and over 6,000 local governments. The average rate lies at approximately 5 per cent; this is less than VAT rates in the EU, which without exception reach double-digit percentages. Canada applies a GST on the federal level, which is similar to VAT. In addition, six provinces autonomously apply a provincial sales tax (PST) which functions like an RST. Three provinces impose a harmonised sales tax (HST), which is a combined levy of the GST and PST and is jointly administered on a central level.

In the fundamental tax reform discussion in the US a national retail sales tax (NRST) has frequently been suggested as an alternative. For example, the Fair Tax Act of 2007 is a US Congress proposal for a 23 per cent NRST to replace the federal personal (including social security and Medicare premiums), payroll and corporate income taxes. The fair tax would contain a monthly paid tax rebate to households equal to 23 per cent of annual household poverty-level spending.

The tax base
Instead of collecting the RST throughout the production process like VAT, it is levied at the final consumption stage (C). This includes all sales to end consumers and is not strictly circumscribed in the usual distributional meaning of the term 'retail'. The tax is imposed on final sales, but not on resale. Because the entire tax effort is focused on the last chain in the production-distribution cycle, the RST is a single-stage consumption tax.[14] Holding on to the previous example, Table 5.9 illustrates the workings of the RST.

---

[13] Only a few countries such as Zimbabwe and Namibia still impose an RST on a national level. Many developing countries have over the years made the leap to VAT, including Costa Rica, Honduras, Nicaragua, Paraguay and South Africa.
[14] Other single-stage sales taxes include so-called 'manufacturing' or 'wholesale' sales taxes. They are imposed at different points in the production-distribution chain.

Table 5.9   Example of the retail sales tax

Details	R	S	M	D	Total
Sales	50	150	350	500	-
Tax on retail sales (20%)	-	-	-	100	100

Under most tax laws it is customary to report consumer prices exclusive of tax (under the VAT systems a legal obligation exists to report prices inclusive of tax). The tax is literally added at the cash register. To promote equal pricing policies, tax laws often contain provisions prohibiting retailers from claiming that they will refund or absorb the tax. The tax is thus presumed to end up with the consumer.

Suspension, casual sales and vendor compensation
The US RST operates under three characteristic features of suspension, casual sales and vendor compensation.[15] In an attempt to exempt business inputs, a 'tax suspension' applies to such sales. Taxpayers who make business purchases can obtain a suspension certificate from the tax authorities. The certificate contains the name of the registered purchaser, the product they are allowed to buy and the use of the product. When shown upon purchase, the seller is instructed not to apply sales tax. The collection effort is thus suspended until a producer sells its product to an end consumer.

The scheme places a heavy responsibility in the hands of the seller and is susceptible to abuse. A final consumer can pose as a producer by showing a false certificate or obtain one without legitimate cause, or the retailer can be less strict in applying the tax suspension. In the former case, if the seller has accepted the certificate in good faith, it is the responsibility of the tax authorities to recover the tax from the consumer. In the latter case, the seller becomes liable for the tax. In any case, extensive audit and control is needed, which raises administration costs.

To simplify administration, the RST exempts 'casual sales'. A casual sale is a sale of tangible personal property by a person who is not engaged in the business of selling such goods. Hence, occasional sales do not fall under the system. The exact definition of casual sales differs among jurisdictions. The rule aims to ease administration and compliance. A final measure involves a 'vendor compensation', which is rendered to retailers in compensation for the high administrative responsibility imposed on them. The discount granted typically ranges between 1 and 5 per cent of total taxes collected.

Assuming a well-functioning tax administration, a fairly effective tax collection can be ensured through the workings of the RST. The retail stage is nevertheless considered to be the weakest link in the production-consumption

---

[15] This subsection contains information retrieved from the website of the World Bank at http://www1.worldbank.org/publicsector/pe/tax/retailtax.htm (downloaded on 7 April 2007).

chain. The incentives for evasion are likely to increase as the tax rate increases.

Taxation of services

While taxation on the sale of goods at the retail stage is the general rule, the RST is generally not consistently applied to services. When the RST emerged in the US and Canada in the 1930s, few services were taxed. The main reason for its introduction was revenue collection, and a tax on goods was adequate. Nowadays a number of services are targeted by the RST, but general coverage is not the norm. The reason is not obvious, but could be partly politically motivated. In the US, lobby groups and political action committees (PACs) have considerable influence on political decision making. A few examples of typically taxed services are rental, repair, installation and maintenance for tangible property, contract work, hotel services, utilities and telecommunications, laundry and dry cleaning.

Cascading

To prevent cascading, sales used as business inputs are exempted. The distinction between business inputs and retail sales is nevertheless difficult to make. As a result, commodities are frequently absorbed into the production process, which do not, or not completely, benefit from tax relief. Moreover, many products are considered to be finished and the purchasing firm is regarded as the final consumer. Examples are packaging materials, equipment and machinery as well as fuels and electricity (note that these issues do not arise under VAT).

Estimations on cascading effects for the United States are presented in Ring (1999). The study found that on average only 59 per cent of RST revenue could be attributed to pure consumer spending. A small fraction of the remaining 41 per cent came from sales to government; however, the bulk originated from sales to businesses. In other words, on average about 40 per cent of revenue was collected from business inputs (ranging from 11 per cent in West Virginia to 72 per cent in Hawaii). The results were broadly in line with other studies. The RST thus has significant difficulties in ensuring single taxation.

When the RST system is unable to offer complete tax relief to business inputs, product prices are inflated, including the prices of goods and services sold abroad. This hurts the competitive position of firms relative to firms that operate under a system that guarantees single taxation (an argument that is equally valid with regard to imports as consumers favour imported products not targeted by a cascading tax).[16]

---

[16] Technically speaking, there is no need to make BTAs under the RST since a tax is imposed only at the final retail stage.

BOX 5.4

The tax credit-invoice type of VAT, compared to the RST, is superior in administration and enforcement, both domestically and in cases of cross-border transactions. The VAT is a robust tax and can best be implemented on a broad basis so as to make optimal use of its inherent revenue-raising capacity. The case for reduced rates seems weak as they barely mitigate the regressive impact of VAT measured against income.

The H-R Flat Tax

The main FT proposal was put forward by Robert Hall and Alvin Rabushka (Hall and Rabushka, 1995). The original concept is a combination of a CFT on business income and a tax on workers' earnings with a basic deduction against the latter. Thus, a uniform tax rate applies to value added, which would be calculated by the direct-subtraction method. Because wages are deducted, only business cash flow $(R - I)$ is taxed at firm level. Wage earnings are subsequently taxed at a personal level, taking into account a generous basic allowance.

The H-R FT is thus basically equivalent to a consumption-type, origin-based, direct-subtraction VAT with an additional basic allowance for workers. This is illustrated in Table 5.10.

Table 5.10   Example of a flat tax

Details	R	S	M	D	Total
Sales	50	150	350	500	-
Purchases	0	50	150	350	-
Value added	50	100	200	150	500
Wages (minus)	40	70	160	120	390
Business cash flow	10	30	40	30	110

The original proposal included a basic tax-free allowance of $25,500 for a family of four. Earnings above the allowance would be taxed at a rate of 19 per cent. The same rate would apply to business cash flow. Since no other deductions or exemptions are allowed, the scheme could replace the existing income tax arrangement on a revenue-neutral basis.[17] The only real difference

---

[17] Altig et al. (2001) calculate a tax rate for the H-R FT based on updated revenue requirements of 21.4 per cent for 1997, to be lowered to 21.1 per cent by 2010. The estimation is based on a tax-free allowance of $9,500 per person.

between the H-R FT and a subtraction-method VAT is the tax-free allowance. Where the VAT taxes both wages and the above-normal return to capital at the business level, the FT allows for a deduction for wage payments. These in turn are taxed above the tax-free allowance at the individual level at the same rate.

Proponents of the tax claim that the basic allowance improves the labour force participation of low-income households.[18] The allowance also ensures that millions of US households would no longer be required to pay taxes or even file a tax return, which reduces the administrative burden considerably. Marginal tax rates for middle- and high-income households would also be lowered, raising labour supply among these taxpayers. A broader and more neutral tax base ensures that many existing distortions under personal and corporate income tax are removed. For example, distortions to the type of investment made (including distortions from the classical system of dividend taxation), the choice of organisational form and goods and services consumed. Saving would be stimulated and the CT is effectively reduced to 19 per cent. This encourages investment, entrepreneurial activity and economic growth.

Opponents of the H-R FT mainly focus on deterioration in the position of homeowners. Mortgage interest deduction and the deduction of state and local property taxes would be eliminated. They also point to the reduced progressivity of the scheme and related distributional effects (note that the large tax deduction would bring some progression).

BOX 5.5

The H-R FT proposal forms an attractive alternative in promoting economic growth. The system is said to promote simplicity, compliance, employment and economic growth. This is particularly true in the US where revenue requirements are relatively low, so the flat tax rate could be comparatively low and there is less need for redistribution. For similar reasons, the tax is less of an alternative for European countries.

David Bradford's X-tax features more tax progression (Bradford, 2004). The schematics of the tax are similar to the H-R system, but the X-tax imposes graduated rates on labour income up to the business tax rate. Thus starting at zero over the range of the basic allowance, the tax rate would work itself up through the income distribution until it reaches the flat business tax

---

[18] The flat tax was the central theme in *Fortune* magazine publisher Steve Forbes's campaign for his Republican presidential nomination in the 1996 and 2000 US elections.

rate.[19] The system could be complemented by an EITC to optimise incentives. Technically speaking, the X-tax is not a 'flat tax' but it does contain most FT features, together with stronger equity characteristics.

A Cash-flow Tax

Tax progression to consumption-based taxation can also be introduced via the personal CFT, under which annual consumption is measured indirectly by deducting annual savings from income. The computation of the tax base in this fashion avoids people having to determine their annual consumption through a direct compilation of all annual spending on goods and services. While seemingly simple, the CFT involves a fairly complex and open-ended calculation of total household income and deductible outlays. The scheme could include the following items (Bradford, 1986):

Household income:

- wages, salaries, tips, royalties and so on;
- receipts of pensions, annuities, life insurance cash value, disability compensation, workmen's compensation, and sick pay;
- gifts, inheritances, trust distributions, and life insurance death benefits received;
- gross receipts from unincorporated business enterprises; and
- withdrawals from qualified accounts (including withdrawal of borrowed funds).

Deductible outlays:

- employees' business expenses (including qualified travel expenses, union dues, tools, materials and qualified educational expenses);
- contributions to qualified retirement plans;
- gifts and bequests made to an identified taxpayer or trust with an eligible beneficiary; net life insurance premiums;
- current expenses associated with unincorporated business enterprises, including contributions to employee pensions;
- capital outlays associated with unincorporated business enterprises;
- special items as a matter of policy (for example, charitable contributions, medical expenses); and
- deposits to qualified accounts (including repayment of borrowed funds).

---

[19] This rate is estimated to lie below 30 per cent for the United States.

The necessary information would be largely available from employers, financial institutions and insurance companies and is often already made available to tax authorities. The main advantage is thus a consumption-based tax that is highly adaptable to taxpayers' personal situation. Additional deductions and allowances can be inserted and graduated rates may bring tax progression.

5.5   SELECTIVE CONSUMPTION TAXATION

Selective consumption taxes are more commonly known as 'excise taxes'.[20] They are levied as a fixed amount per item sold, or on an *ad valorem* basis. A *unit* tax simply adds a fixed amount of tax per commodity sold. The price is raised by that value, thus regardless of fluctuations in the relative price level of the commodity. In contrast, an *ad valorem* tax is calculated as a percentage of the retail sales price (RSP), so the amount of tax is levied in proportion to the commodity's market value. Some products, such as a pack of cigarettes, are targeted by both a unit and an *ad valorem* component.

Objectives of Excise Taxation

In history, excise taxes were mainly levied to collect funds for the government treasury. Before the introduction of general consumption taxation during the Great Depression of the 1930s, selective taxes were already responsible for a substantial revenue intake. Since the 1930s general consumption taxes have gradually taken over. With this shift, additional grounds for imposing excise taxes emerged that can be attributed to the high rate and target flexibility of such taxes. The objectives of excise taxation encompass:

- revenue recognition to finance government outlays;
- discouraging undesired consumption;
- correcting for externalities;
- charging user fees on services provided by government;
- taxing luxury goods to increase tax progression;
- protecting domestic industries and agriculture; and
- exporting taxes on goods consumed abroad.

---

[20] Formally selective taxes are defined more broadly than just excises, including profits of fiscal monopolies, customs and import duties, taxes on exports and taxes on investment goods (see the OECD classification in Appendix 4).

In carrying out government policy, excise taxes prove to be an effective tool to regulate behaviour.

The 'Big' Excise Taxes

The lion's share of excise revenue nowadays comes from the three 'big' excise taxes, that is, taxes on alcoholic beverages and tobacco products as well as on mineral oils and vehicles. For a statistical overview of the big excise tax rates applied in the OECD area, see OECD (2005h).

Alcoholic Beverages

Excise duties on alcoholic beverages are subdivided into taxes on beer, wine and spirits. Beer excises usually take the form of a unit tax, after which European countries apply the standard rate of VAT and most American states an RST. Only Mexico and Turkey in the OECD area levy *ad valorem* rate excise taxes. A unit tax imposes a relatively higher burden on cheap products and raw materials, thereby favouring expensive and higher-quality products. As opposed to an ad valorem tax, the tax burden on cheaper products is disproportionately larger. Excises on beer are implemented either per hectolitre per degree Plato or per hectolitre per degree of alcohol.[21] Some countries also impose reduced rates on small breweries with lower production volumes.

Excise taxation of wine is categorised by still and sparkling. Generally speaking, sparkling wine is taxed more heavily than still wine. It is interesting that still wine either is not taxed or is taxed at very low rates in southern European states, while it is taxed heavily in the Nordic countries. This clearly reflects political and cultural differences. Southern states have large wine industries and voters consider it a near necessity of life. Governments in the Nordic countries on the other hand are largely opposed to any consumption of alcohol. Finally, spirits are taxed per litre of pure alcohol in the EU and per gallon in the US.

Behavioural responses

Excessive alcohol consumption imposes large costs on society. The social costs of alcohol range from the direct cost arising from healthcare, alcohol-induced vandalism, road traffic accidents and drinking-related court cases to indirect losses from low productivity by sickness absence at work and unemployment.

Much of the empirical evidence on the effect of alcohol taxes is analysed by Smith (2005). One study he cites has found the elasticities of demand in the US to range between -0.3 for beer, -1.0 for wine and -1.5 for spirits

---

[21] Per hectolitre per degree Plato is a formal measure of sugar content.

(original study by Leung and Phelps, 1993). The price elasticity is expected to be greater in the long run than in the short run. This is because consumption of addictive goods depends on past consumption. Even addicts seem to behave rationally in a sense that they are forward looking and try to maximise utility over time.[22]

Furthermore, moderate drinkers exhibit greater price elasticities than light drinkers, who use alcohol, for example, to relax after a long day's work, and heavy drinkers, who are largely unresponsive (Manning et al., 1995). As to the number of 'heavy-drinking days' reported in survey research, Kenkel (1993) found an average price-elasticity of -0.9 (-0.71 for males and -1.14 for females) over all age groups. For younger people aged 18-21, this value was much higher, -2.24 (-0.95 for males and -3.54 for females). The numbers indicate that alcohol taxes are fairly effective in discouraging drinking and more effective for certain specific categories of drinkers such as younger people.

The social cost of alcohol consumption
Even though alcohol taxes are sizeable, Cnossen (2006) estimates the social cost of alcohol consumption in the EU to still outweigh the size of tax revenue collected. The optimal alcohol excise duty therefore would seem to be higher. Although an alcohol excise tax is a generic instrument that would create welfare losses to non-harmful users, overall welfare could thus be improved. Depending on the price elasticities of demand, the revenues generated could be used to lower other distortive taxes.

Tobacco Products

Cigarettes are the most addictive legally sold consumable goods in the world and extremely hazardous to people's health. On average, a smoker's life span is approximately 10 years shorter than that of a lifelong non-smoker (Doll et al., 2004). For this reason, smokers are taxed heavily across Western economies. Cigarettes account for the bulk of total tobacco consumption (over 90 per cent).

In Europe, cigarettes are targeted by three elements of tax. A pack of cigarettes is first taxed by a specific and an *ad valorem* excise rate, after which VAT is applied. This can lead to a tax burden of up to 400 per cent of the tax-exclusive RSP, as in the UK. In the US, where cigarettes have long been declared 'public health enemy number one', most states impose a specific rate and an RST. The RST is imposed on an excise tax-exclusive basis. This amounts to substantial, but generally lower tax burdens than in Europe.

---

[22] See Becker and Murphy (1988) for the theory of rational addiction.

The empirical evidence on the effect of tobacco taxes is mixed (Cnossen and Smart, 2005). Much recent evidence suggests that the *net* external cost of smoking to society is negligible or small. For example, premature deaths due to smoking reduce the cost of pensions and medical expenses of age-related diseases. Hence, it is not certain high excises on tobacco are warranted on Pigouvian grounds. Furthermore, an argument could be made that as long as consumers are well-informed on smoking-related health hazards, consumer sovereignty requires that taxes should be set no higher than to reflect external costs. On the other hand, Gruber and Mullainathan (2002) report survey evidence for Canada and the US that higher cigarette taxes make smokers happier. Taxes provide a self-control device for smokers who have problems with self-control. And surely non-smokers would not disapprove of such a tax burden shift to smokers.

Behavioural responses
Studies find that excise taxes contribute somewhat to discouraging smoking. The studies principally focus on the impact of cigarette taxes on people's health. For example, higher cigarette taxes have been shown to have a positive impact on the average weight of new-born babies (the probability of a low birthweight being increased by smoking). The price elasticity of smoking participation among pregnant women has thereby been estimated at -0.5 (Evans and Ringel, 1999). Another study examined mortality rates in the US during the 1954-88 period and found that a 10 per cent increase in cigarette taxes would save up to 6,000 lives annually (Moore, 1996). Research also reveals that roughly 90 per cent of adults who smoke started before the age of 18.[23] Since the price elasticity of demand for younger people is twice that of older ones, higher taxes can be an effective tool in discouraging smoking in this group even if the result could take generations to manifest itself.

Master Settlement Agreement (MSA)
The Master Settlement Agreement (MSA) was concluded between 'Big Tobacco' and 50 states in the US.[24] The settlement originated from litigation by states aimed at recovering healthcare costs from the industry. These costs were incurred through the treatment of people who had become ill as a result of smoking. In addition, a large punitive element was included for deceitful industry behaviour by artificially manipulating cigarette nicotine levels to keep people addicted and sales high.

However, what initially started with the aspiration to recoup damage payments from the industry turned out to be nothing more than a disguised

---

[23] See http://tobaccofreekids.org/.
[24] Big Tobacco is a term applied to the largest US cigarette manufacturers and usually refers to Philip Morris, R.J. Reynolds, British American Tobacco, Brown & Williamson and Lorillard.

tax on the consumers of cigarettes. The final settlement that was concluded in 1998 involved among other things the following payments by the industry to state governments: an upfront payment of $12.74 billion; annual payments up to 2025 accumulating to a total of $183.18 billion; a payment to a strategic contribution fund of $8.61 billion; and other payments for miscellaneous purposes involving approximately $1.75 billion. Despite this gigantic sum, Big Tobacco showed little reluctance to settle. Why was this?

The answer lies in the overall elasticity of demand for cigarettes, enabling producers to pass on a large amount of the payment to the consumer. Thus what was meant to be a penalty on the industry was in reality shifted to the consumer. The settlement was to some degree also made dependent on sales volumes, which confirmed that the arrangement resembled more of a tax increase than a settlement for damages. As MIT economist Jonathan Gruber put it: 'Every single cigarette tax ever passed has been paid fully by the consumer. There's no reason to think this will be any different'. (Derthick, 2002, p. 177). However, the MSA shielded Big Tobacco from any future state litigation.

In 1997, cigarette prices averaged around $1.90 per pack (Derthick, 2002). Between 1997 and 2000, market leader Philip Morris raised prices eight times, leading to a price rise of over $1 per pack. In 2001, prices in high excise tax states were about $4 per pack. The settlement also forced states that were initially reluctant to pursue the tobacco industry to participate. At that time it was obvious that the majority of states would settle, so reluctant states would still suffer the price increase, while not sharing in the revenues. Eventually all 50 states took part. What remains unclear is how far the American tobacco industry was able to export the MSA burden to consumers abroad through higher sales prices there.

This case study shows that government needs to be heedful of policy that does not fall directly under the category of taxation. Under the right conditions, measures are easily turned into disguised taxes on households.

Mineral Oil Products and Vehicle Taxes

A variety of fuels are targeted under excise tax schemes. These fuels typically include leaded and unleaded petrol, diesel, heating oil and heavy fuel oil. The excises are imposed as a specific rate on top of which, VAT is levied. Besides general revenue recognition, the taxes are used for environmental purposes. For example, CO_2 emissions are reduced by discouraging fuel use and excise tax differentials can favour the use of unleaded over leaded petrol (albeit the latter is losing significance because of the heavily reduced market share of this type of fuel). In addition, many countries levy a tax on car purchase, ownership and use.

In total, three main tax instruments are used to discourage motoring. These include taxes on *acquisition* such as a registration tax, on *ownership* such as an annual circulation tax and on *motoring* in the form of various fuel taxes. Over the years a better understanding has been developed on the effect of these vehicle taxes, especially in European countries where they are sizeable and widely applied. They account for roughly 4.5 to 10 per cent of total taxation, or between 2 and 3.5 per cent of GDP (European Commission, 2002).

The method traditionally held to be most effective in promoting sustainable transport is a simple raising of excise taxes, mainly because the price elasticities of fuel use are believed to be relatively high. It is standard practice to increase excises if the tax rates in neighbouring countries allow for this, without creating significant cross-border effects. The only general exception is the low excise rate on diesel fuels used by agricultural vehicles, which are thereby subsidised implicitly.

Excise taxes on diesel fuel are typically also lower than on gasoline fuels, which is historically explained by benefiting the road haulage industry. However, the use of diesel in private cars has profited from this differential. Yet given technological standards, diesel is the least environmentally preferred motor fuel. To mitigate this distortion, a special surcharge on the annual vehicle tax is often imposed on privately used diesel cars, but mostly this burden is less than the benefits from the reduced excise rate. It is therefore recommended that the special surcharge should be raised, so that the use of diesel by private cars is discouraged without affecting the road haulage industry. A more rigorous environmental policy would of course discourage road transportation as well.

Behavioural responses to vehicle taxes
The European Commission (2002) finds that the number of cars sold depends crucially on the purchasing power of households (an income rise of 10 per cent increases per capita car demand by 4.1 per cent) and to a lesser extent on the RSP (a 10 per cent reduction in RSP increases per capita demand by 1.1 per cent).

The main elasticities reported by the study are summarised in Table 5.11. The registration tax is significantly more powerful in affecting car prices than is an annual circulation tax. There is only a minor effect on car age from an increase in both taxes (a 10 per cent increase raised car age by 0.28 years). Due to its nature, the registration tax offers better scope to achieve environmental objectives by, for example, differentiating the tax rate according to the environmental qualities of cars sold. The purchase of cars labelled energy efficient by the relevant authorities can thereby be stimulated over large and gas-guzzling cars. The use of LPG (liquefied petroleum gas) cars and electric cars can also be promoted. The former, if equipped with the latest technology, could bring down emissions by about 30 per cent compared to a state-of-the-art gasoline-powered car.

Table 5.11   Typical price elasticities for vehicle taxation

Variable	Fuel price	Annual charges	Vehicle km. charges	Purchase prices
Car stock	0.18 - 0.41	0.04 - 0.08	-	0.25 - 1.60
Fuel consumption	0.20 - 1.00	0.06 - 0.16	-	0.53
Car use	0.05 - 0.55	-0.8 - 0.15	0.1 - 0.8	0.29

Source: European Commission (2002).

BOX 5.6

Excise taxes are used for regulatory purposes other than those that are macroeconomic in nature. Empirical research shows that the three 'big' excise taxes on alcohol, tobacco and motoring contribute positively to discouraging drinking, smoking and driving.

The preferred policy course for vehicle taxation
The number of kilometres driven by private cars has increased steadily in Western countries. Statistically, up to 80 per cent of this increase is explained by an increase in the number of cars rather than by higher mileage per car. Moreover, the average weight of newly purchased cars has risen with, adverse effects on fuel efficiency. The latter factor alone has accounted for a steady increase in CO_2 emissions. The possibilities for green taxes that influence car purchasing behaviour should therefore not be neglected and 'variabilisation', or the raising of excise taxes with a compensating reduction in vehicle taxes, carried too far.

The European Commission is now looking to reduce registration taxes within the EU because of their distorting effect on the internal market. Large tax differences have caused car prices to vary significantly across member states. In setting pre-tax prices, the car industry appears to take into account the levels of taxation. Since this is the relevant variable for consumers willing to buy a car abroad, the neutrality in cross-border trade is jeopardised. From this standpoint, a future shift in emphasis to a circulation tax is thus a preferred policy course, particularly because it provides a more stable source of revenue in the presence of business-cycle fluctuations.

On the other hand, the annual vehicle tax is often related to car weight and should have an impact on consumer preference for smaller cars. A strong linear correlation can be found between vehicle weight and fuel use, suggesting that there is a 0.4 increase in fuel use in litres per 100 kilometres with every 100 kilograms in weight increase (Vermeend and van der Vaart,

1998). Hence, a combination of taxes may be best suited to discourage driving and encourage those who do drive to do so with the least environmental harm. Chapter 9 further elaborates on how negative and positive incentive taxes stimulate environmentally friendly behaviour.

5.6 BRIEF SUMMARY

A growth orientated tax policy is likely to thrive well under a consumption-based tax. Since savings are not 'double taxed', a consumption tax is an attractive choice to collect the required revenue. In terms of distributional efficacy a consumption-based tax is a much less obvious alternative. The burden distribution of a consumption tax measured against income is slightly regressive. There is, moreover, little that reduced rates can do to mitigate this. They are highly distortionary, while the effect on the income distribution is mediocre.

Since taxes on labour and capital factors operate under growing strain from international (tax) competition, greater emphasis on consumption taxation could nevertheless offer a solution. A shift should facilitate a reduction in marginal personal and corporate income tax rates, improve simplicity of tax systems, and trigger economic activity, higher compliance, tax revenues and economic growth. A shift thus offers a viable policy option in ensuring an effective revenue collection in the future.

However, consumption tax reform has to take place along different lines for different countries. In the US, where egalitarian sentiments are less deeply rooted than in European societies, the Hall and Rabushka flat tax could be a realistic alternative to existing personal and corporate income taxation arrangements. The tax would certainly present an improvement in terms of simplicity, compliance and economic incentives. We note that the US has no experience with a multistage VAT, so this would complicate the shift to the flat tax which has essentially the same base.

In European countries the majority of voters regard the flat tax as a tax for the rich. Indeed, it is a bridge too far politically. With it comes a practical objection that the required tax rate would have to be set high to meet revenue needs. This chapter has shown that a gradual rebalancing to VAT constitutes a recommended policy here. Under the assumption of adequate enforcement and international coordination, somewhat higher standard VAT rates in many EU member states could be realistic, ranging up to 25 per cent. Furthermore, elimination of multiple differentiated rates and expansion of the VAT base allows government to take greater advantage of the VAT's inherent robustness and revenue-raising potential. The personal income tax and direct expenditure programmes could subsequently be used to calibrate the redistribution of income to voter preferences.

PART III

Knowledge-based society and economic growth

6. Tax incentives for research and development

There is overwhelming evidence of the vital importance of boosting R&D as a prerequisite for Europe to become more competitive. To fail to act on that evidence would be a fundamental strategic error.

(European Commission, 2004a, p.21)

6.1 INTRODUCTION

Boosting research and development (R&D) stands high on the political agenda of OECD countries. There is broad agreement in the economic literature that R&D is the principal engine of technological progress and hence of improved productivity. In the advent of globalisation and the knowledge-based economy, innovation has become key for companies that operate under growing competitive pressures enforced by world markets and for governments that try to maximise economic growth.

Thus far, progress in acting upon this evidence has been disappointing. Most OECD countries fall short of internationally recognised R&D expenditure spending targets, such as set forth by the Lisbon Strategy for Growth and Jobs (March, 2000). This EU initiative requires an annual R&D expenditure of at least 3 per cent of GDP, of which a minimum of two-thirds should be generated by the business community. A central solution tabled in realisation of this aim is larger tax breaks for companies that engage in R&D activity.

From a competitive stance, too, the stakes are high. The power of innovation and a strong commitment to R&D has already been demonstrated by extraordinary growth rates that Japan and the so-called 'Asian tiger' economies managed to realise in the 1980s and a large part of the 1990s. Nowadays, science and technology is reallocated to emerging markets such as India and China at astonishing rates. These economies offer young, bright and educated scientists who operate in highly advanced research facilities. Failing to maintain and improve standards is thus scarcely an option for developed countries.

A widely accepted problem with R&D investment is that the costs of conducting R&D are considerable and incurred in the short run, while the benefits are reaped only in the long run, if at all, and are typically spread out over several years if not decades. To carry out an R&D investment project successfully takes great planning and rational decision making by business managers and investors. Even then, the associated risks are deemed high. Because the gains of innovation to society are nevertheless also considered high, government intervention to stimulate R&D could be desirable.

This chapter briefly surveys main issues in R&D tax policy, which can be relevant particularly in view of the now frequently advocated shift away from direct government involvement in the economy and the substitution of R&D tax incentives for direct government subsidies. Both measures of course come at a cost to the taxpayer. First, the chapter presents an overview of R&D tax measures currently implemented by the sample countries. Next, it considers why R&D is crucial to economic performance and why government has good reasons to intervene and stimulate R&D. The penultimate section provides an overview of empirical evidence on the effectiveness of R&D tax incentives, and the final section offers a summary.

6.2   CHARACTERISTICS OF R&D TAX INCENTIVES

Tax Provisions for Research and Development

With the introduction of their R&D tax credits in 1962 and 1967, respectively, Canada and Japan were in the vanguard of OECD countries implementing R&D tax measures. It took others more than a decade to follow. In 1981, the United States adopted a credit, followed by France in 1983. Australia's 150 per cent deduction was enacted in 1985 and the Netherlands followed suit in 1994. Despite frequent changes, the basics have remained very similar in many countries. Table 6.1 summarises the measures in place in 2007.

At the time of writing, five sample countries use a tax deduction of some sort (that is, Australia, Austria, Denmark, the Netherlands and the UK), whereas seven countries use R&D tax credits (that is, Canada, France, Ireland, Italy, Norway, Japan and the US). Furthermore, Australia, France and Italy use a combination of both a proportional and incremental allowance: a *proportional* tax allowance is determined relative to the amount of qualified R&D expenditure so that both 'existing' and 'new' investment is tax subsidised; and an *incremental* tax allowance is explicitly designed to induce only 'new' R&D expenditure by granting an allowance on increased spending compared to some previously defined base (for example, average spending in the previous 2 or 3 years).

In contrast to these schemes, the Dutch tax system allows a tax deduction from wage tax for the wage costs of employees engaged in R&D activity. This avoids the risk of tax exhaustion.

Table 6.1   Specific tax incentives for research and development, 2007

Country	R&D investment tax provision
Australia	An R&D tax 'concession' (that is, deduction) of 125%. An incremental concession of 175% applies to companies that have increased R&D expenditure above the average level of the preceding 3 years. Innovative patents can be depreciated in 8 instead of 20 years
Austria	An invention allowance is granted for 25% for R&D expenditure (the development or improvement of inventions valuable to the Austrian economy). Exceptionally, a rate of 35% applies
Canada	A tax credit of 20% for qualifying scientific research activities
Denmark	The ordinary costs of R&D are deductible against profits. The amount is increased to 150% up to DKK 5 million annually if paid by a corporation to a public R&D institution before 31 December 2006
France	An R&D tax credit that consists of 2 parts: first, a 10% credit for all R&D-related expenses; and second, taking into account the annual increase, 40% of the R&D expenses during the year, minus average spending in the previous 2 years adjusted for inflation. The aggregate may not exceed €16 million annually and the credit is only for R&D undertaken in the EU or European Economic Area (EEA) under a tax treaty. There is also a special regime that under certain conditions exempts innovative new companies from CT in the first 3 years
Ireland	A tax credit of 20% is granted for R&D expenditures exceeding €50,000 which is carried out within the EEA. The credit is available until 2008
Italy	A 10% tax credit is granted for R&D costs for the years 2007-09. The credit is increased to 15% if the R&D is conducted by agreement with a public research institute or university. The total cost on which basis the credit is calculated may not exceed €15 million
Japan	An R&D tax credit is calculated by comparing R&D expenses with 'comparative R&D expenses' (the average R&D expenses in the preceding 3 years) and also

	accounting for the corporation's R&D ratio. A higher tax credit applies to small and medium-sized enterprises (SMEs) (that is, corporations with capital of ¥100 million or less). The maximum credit is limited to 20% of the taxpayer's CT liability
Netherlands	Employers' wage tax is reduced with regard to remuneration paid to employees engaged in R&D activities that are organised in the Netherlands. The allowance is 42% of wage cost up to €110,000 and 14% of any excess (up to €8 million per employer). The 42% is increased to 60% for corporations developing technological products
Norway	An R&D tax credit for SMEs of 18 or 20% of expenditure up to NOK 4 million (NOK 8 million if purchases from a university or other research organisation). The research must be approved by the Norwegian research council
UK	Immediate write-off of R&D cost. For SMEs the deduction is increased to 150% of the cost exceeding £10,000. The deduction for qualifying expenditures by large corporations is increased to 125%. Qualifying expenditure by both large corporations and SMEs for the development of certain vaccines by pharmaceutical companies for human use may be deducted at 150%
US	R&D investment can be immediately expensed or amortised over 60 months. Additionally, a 20% credit can be claimed over increased R&D expenditure, where the basis is calculated as a percentage of average gross receipts in the previous 3 years. A 20% credit is also granted for qualified basic research payments

Sources: IBFD – European Tax Surveys and PricewaterhouseCoopers Worldwide Tax Summaries.

R&D tax incentives aim to lower the cost of R&D by reducing the amount of CT paid when undertaking R&D activity. Conceptually, there is no difference between the effect of taxes on the cost of capital for R&D investment and the cost of capital for ordinary investment discussed in Chapter 4.

In practice, however, almost every OECD country permits immediate expensing of R&D related costs, which can be considered as accelerated depreciation, and many accept stepped-up depreciation for capital equipment and machinery used in R&D.[1] There are many other differences in the detail.

---

[1] The latter constitute only a small fraction of total R&D spending, while having been subject unnecessarily to frequent change. Hall and van Reenen (2000, p, 450) argue: 'given that R&D capital expenditure is typically only 10-13 per cent of business R&D, and that the business

To optimally target the incentive, governments define what qualifies as R&D expenditure more broadly or narrowly.[2] This is achieved by, for example, allowing a large or small deduction, high or low rate of credit; imposing a minimum required volume of expenditure; and/or capping the tax relief offered. Systems also differentiate according to firm size, sectors or industries with high growth potential or specific regions with above-average unemployment rates.

The Cost of R&D Tax Incentives

The budgetary cost of these incentives is not straightforwardly verified, but as noted in Chapter 2 most OECD countries nowadays do publish a so-called *tax expenditure* overview to enhance transparency and provide guidance on the revenue lost from having targeted business tax incentives.

For example, the US publishes a comprehensive tax expenditure budget with more than 160 items,[3] and the R&D tax credit cost is estimated at US$29,220 million over the 2007-11 period.[4] While in terms of GDP this seems minor (in the region of 0.2 per cent of GDP), the US CT raised US$450,000 million in 2006. [5] Against this figure, it would make up well over 6 per cent of CT revenues in that year, which is clearly more significant. A simple back-of-the-envelope calculation suggests that such credit has a non-trivial impact on the US corporate tax structure, raising the marginal tax rate by, very roughly, 0.5 per cent.[6]

R&D-GDP ratio is typically 1-2 per cent, implying an R&D capital equipment-GDP ratio of 0.1-0.2 per cent, a remarkable amount of time has been spent in many of these countries tinkering with the expensing and depreciation rules for capital equipment used in R&D activities'.

[2] In 1980, OECD countries jointly established a formal definition of R&D in the OECD's Frascati manual. In practice, many countries depart from the definition, mostly applying a restrictive scope.

[3] Since 1974, the US Congressional Budget Office has been required by law to publish annually a list that projects the tax expenditures for each of the following five fiscal years (Section 308(c) of the Congressional Budget Act of 1974).

[4] Budget of the United States Government: Analytical Perspectives, Fiscal Year 2007, p. 291.

[5] See the Economic Report of the President 2007, p. 328.

[6] If US$29,220 million is divided over five years, the cost amounts to US$5,844 million of a revenue collection of US$450,000 million, or 1.3 per cent. Assuming that a tax rate of 39 per cent applies (see Table 4.1), this yields a change of roughly 0.5 per cent. This calculation is highly simplified. For example, it does not make present value corrections or consider dynamics such as behavioural responses which can be myriad.

6.3   THE ECONOMIC IMPACT OF RESEARCH AND DEVELOPMENT

First and foremost a distinction is made between private and public sector R&D expenditure, which is performed by industry, higher education or government.[7] Table 6.2 shows that business-financed R&D has the prevailing input in most countries. It is interesting that Sweden and Finland traditionally outspend active R&D countries such as Japan and the US in terms of R&D as a percentage of GDP (also referred to as the 'R&D intensity'). Denmark and Austria follow closely. With 1.1 and 1.3 per cent of GDP, respectively, Italy and Ireland invest least in technology.

No more than three countries spend more than the widely accepted 3 per cent of the GDP spending target. In absolute terms the US massively outspends all other countries, which carries over to the full-time equivalent (Fte) (indeed, the R&D sector can be considered highly labour intensive). The OECD area as a whole has experienced a rise in R&D expenditure in recent decades at a rate exceeding the average growth rate. Total OECD spending amounted to approximately US$680 billion in 2003, or on average 2.2 per cent of GDP (OECD, 2005e).

BOX 6.1

Current levels of business R&D spending vary from a little over 1 per cent of GDP in Italy to just below 4 per cent of GDP in Sweden. Only three countries spend more than the widely accepted spending target of 3 per cent of GDP.

Boosting Economic Growth and Competitiveness

While these statistics provide interesting cross-country insights, they give little guidance on the economic effect and desirable level of R&D. R&D investment is an essential ingredient in advancing technologically and thus in creating a higher standard of living and economic prosperity. There is overwhelming evidence of the vital importance of R&D in creating competitive economies and future prosperity.

---

[7] Public R&D is performed within universities, hospitals, or for example, the military. Some funds are additionally invested by non-profit organisations, but this constitutes only a very small share.

Table 6.2   R&D expenditure statistics, 2005

	R&D as % GDP	Million current PPP$	% financed by Industry	% financed by Government	% performed by Industry	% performed by Higher education	% performed by Government	Full-time equivalent
Australia	1.8	11,590	51.6	39.8	53.5	27.2	16.2	81,740
Austria	2.4	7,124	45.8	36.9	67.7	26.7	5.1	28,207
Belgium	1.8	6,205	60.3	23.5	68.3	22.8	7.7	31,880
Canada	2.0	22,702	46.7	33.7	52.4	38.4	8.8	112,624
Denmark	2.4	4,561	59.9	27.1	68.3	23.8	7.2	26,167
Finland	3.5	6,149	69.3	26.3	70.7	19.4	9.3	39,582
France	2.1	40,363	51.7	37.6	61.9	19.5	17.3	200,064
Germany	2.5	61,712	66.8	30.4	69.9	16.5	13.5	268,100
Ireland	1.3	2,015	58.7	32.9	65.3	28.0	6.7	11,151
Italy	1.1	17,920	43.0	50.8	47.8	32.8	17.8	72,012
Japan	3.2	118,026	74.8	18.1	75.2	13.4	9.5	677,206
Netherlands	1.8	9,585	51.1	36.2	57.8	27.9	14.4	37,282
Norway	1.5	3,020	49.2	41.9	54.0	29.9	16.0	21,851
Sweden	3.9	11,385	65.0	23.5	75.7	20.8	3.1	54,041
UK	1.7	32,197	44.2	32.8	63.0	23.4	10.3	157,662
US	2.7	312,535	63.7	31.0	70.1	13.6	12.2	1,334,628

Source: OECD electronic database: Main Science and Technology Indicators (MSTI).

The classical growth accounting literature splits real GDP growth into two components: one attributable to normal factor increases (that is, hard work and ordinary capital investment); and the other resulting from higher factor productivity through R&D (that is, the so-called 'Solow growth residual'). The difference is crucial. Whereas ordinary capital investment triggers only one-off transitory changes to the level of GDP by increasing or decreasing the capital stock,[8] R&D investment improves capital productivity and thereby accounts for sustained GDP growth (see also the Solow growth model in Appendix 1).

Empirical studies demonstrate a significant relationship between R&D and output or productivity growth. For example, regression analysis for the 1966-2002 period indicates that the contribution of total factor productivity to economic growth has been on average one-third in the US and up to two-thirds in the EU-15 (Denis et al., 2004). Guellec and Pottelsberghe (2001) use panel data analysis of 16 OECD countries and find that each extra per cent of business-performed R&D yields on average 0.13 per cent extra productivity growth. Another study estimates that up to 40 per cent of labour productivity rises can be attributed to spending on R&D (European Commission, 2004a). And yet other work finds that a 10 per cent increase in R&D intensity raises per capita output growth between 0.3-0.4 per cent (OECD, 2000a).

The results convincingly underline that the gains of R&D investment are significant and far outweigh those of ordinary investment. R&D is the only factor capable of creating higher productivity and thus sustained economic growth. This is a very important point that could justify the use of targeted R&D tax incentives as an exception to the general base broadening and rate-cutting policy that was discussed in Chapter 4, but only if government believes it is desirable to simulate R&D activity.

BOX 6.2

The potential of R&D in creating economic growth is high by both an output-augmenting effect and, in the global economy of today, maintaining a competitive edge over other economies that become increasingly 'knowledge' based. Between 1966 and 2002, the estimated contribution of total factor productivity to economic growth has on average been one-third in the US and up to two-thirds in the EU-15.

---

[8] If the economy-wide investment rate is higher than depreciation, the capital stock increases in size. Diminishing returns nevertheless eventually cause the economy to settle at a higher level of output where it remains (the so-called 'steady-state level of capital'). Changes to the investment rate therefore cause one-off shifts and cannot explain GDP growth.

Should Government Intervene to Raise R&D Spending?

A widely recognised impediment is that the costs of R&D are large and incurred in the short run, while the benefits are reaped only in the long run, if at all, and typically spread over several decades. Private firms are unable to fully exploit the benefits of the scientific results of R&D investment since they cannot entirely protect their inventions from use by others. Other firms thus profit from an innovation without having to pay their fair share in the costs of R&D leading to the innovation. Furthermore, competition in markets for high-tech products is fierce and near perfect. The gains from R&D are quickly transferred to consumers through lower product prices, leaving a smaller profit margin for firms.

The gap between the private and social return means that we have a private sector underprovision of R&D, and although remedies exist, such as intellectual property rights or the pooling of companies with similar characteristics to jointly conduct R&D, they offer only limited solace in practice. Both ways reduce the scope for unwanted spillovers to other firms in the industry, but do not appear to exert a strong enough influence to fully equate the private and social returns to R&D. In addition, undesirable side-effects are generated by inhibiting knowledge dispersion and preventing firms from building on previous breakthroughs. Indeed, a review by Nadiri (1993) of a large number of studies suggests a substantial underinvestment in R&D activities.

BOX 6.3

Generally speaking, innovations cannot be fully protected from use by other firms, so the social return to R&D deviates from the private return. This leads to an undersupply of R&D investment by the private sector. Government has an incentive to correct this market failure through direct subsidies or tax incentives.

Government Subsidies versus Tax Incentives

The legislature thus has a legitimate reason to step in to correct this market failure. It can do so with a direct subsidy or a tax measure.[9] The choice of

---

[9] In practice, governments look at cross-country data, past trends and overall and specific industry performance to see where it is necessary to induce R&D spending and by how much. Note that any such analysis is complicated by the fact that a certain amount of spending yields a different amount of innovation each time. This may be due to factors such as the quality of scientists, the field of research or just plain luck in making a breakthrough.

instrument hinges importantly on how far tax incentives are sufficiently effective in eliciting extra R&D expenditure. Whenever a tax incentive manages to trigger a proportionate or more than proportionate rise in private R&D expenditure, in other words induce an increase in expenditure on R&D by amounts similar or greater than the forgone tax revenues, they have a number of advantages over direct government subsidies (see Guinet and Kamata, 1996).

First, a tax measure leaves the market in charge of designing and carrying out R&D projects. This permits more-efficient adaptation to market conditions, short-term developments and long-run trends. Business managers are generally in a better position than government officials to take decisions. They are informed, familiar with the playing field and can respond swiftly to changing market environments. Second, administrative burdens associated with tax incentives are likely to be lower than under a bureaucratic and case-by-case assignment of direct subsidies. Firms can simply claim the credit on their annual tax return, instead of going through what is often considered to be an arduous process of filling in application forms, appearing before committees and reporting progress. The nature of a tax incentive is also such that it can be better anticipated by firms. Such incentives are more consistent than periodic and random appropriations from the budget, not least because government tends to reward lobbying.[10]

6.4   R&D TAX POLICY EFFECTIVENESS

Early Studies

The success or failure of R&D tax incentives is evaluated against their effect on the price of R&D as well as on the responsiveness of firms to such a price change. The studies performed either use econometric approaches to approximate the price elasticity of R&D,[11] or survey techniques to measure the responsiveness of firms. Until the 1990s, the case for using the tax system as such did not seem strong.

The foremost drawback was that R&D tax incentives simply failed to induce sufficient additional private sector R&D. Tax price elasticities found by empirical studies were very low and in any case below unity (that is, 1). Every euro in tax revenue forgone thus yielded less than one euro in incremental R&D. The reasoning then should be straightforward. If a tax measure costs more than it delivers in terms of incremental R&D, it is more

---

[10] This point is supported by Cohen and Noll (1991) who give an overview of actual cases of commercial R&D projects in the US that, due to legislative influences, were regularly prolonged well after costs had surpassed potential benefits (cited in Hall and van Reenen, 2000).

[11] The price elasticity of R&D measures the percentage increase in R&D resulting from a percentage decrease in cost.

efficient for government to subsidise directly and appropriate R&D projects to industry, yielding a one-to-one efficacy.

Mansfield (1986) was one of the first to investigate the effect of R&D tax incentives by using a sample of 110 American, 55 Canadian and 40 Swedish firms.[12] The study questioned a random mix of R&D, financial and tax executives and CEOs and showed that R&D spending increased by a meagre 1 per cent or at most 2 per cent in response to the tax measures in all three countries. Government revenue loss was about three times as large, which meant that the effectiveness was seriously questioned. The results largely confirmed those by Mansfield and Switzer (1985), who focused on the Canadian experience alone. The authors also drew attention to the possibility of re-labelling activities as R&D, so as to take advantage of the credit, while reducing the credit's effectiveness.

R&D Price Elasticities of Unity or Higher

With the improvement in basic research methods, the empirical results have become more pronounced in recent years. At the moment, there appears to be consensus that tax incentives are indeed an effective instrument. Table 6.3 summarises some of the results from later studies, revealing a rising trend in R&D price elasticities over time. Moreover, where differentiation is made between the short and the long run, the latter elasticities are twice as high.

Other studies provide insights as well. A remarkable pattern was found by Koga (2003) who investigated the Japanese R&D tax credit over the 1989-98 period. Based on a sample of 904 firms ranging in size from ¥10 million to over ¥10 billion, a tax-price elasticity of 0.68 was found, which is a relatively low value compared to other studies. However, by differentiating firm size he obtains a price elasticity of 1.03 for large firms (that is, those with a capital value above the sample median). One explanation is that larger firms such as MNCs tend to be more institutionalised and less flexible in conducting R&D. Large research centres and departments impose a relatively constant cost, which raises the value of an R&D tax credit for these firms.

By contrast, the Dutch scheme for promoting R&D focuses on wage cost, which may be a sensible policy given the high labour intensity in the sector. The scheme appears to be equally effective. In a robust study using both survey and econometric techniques, Brouwer et al. (2002) obtain an average short-run elasticity between 1.01 and 1.02. The R&D elicited also seemed predominantly incremental in nature, hence in economic parlance, the effect from additionality outweighs the effect from substitution.

In addition to these country-specific studies, Bloom et al. (2002) adopt a cross-country approach using data over the 1979-97 period. The authors focus on the tax policy changes in the treatment of R&D across nine OECD

---

[12] Sweden abolished its R&D allowance in 1984 because of serious doubts on its effectiveness.

countries: Australia, Canada, France, Germany, Italy, Japan, Spain, the UK and the US. This not only captures changes in the tax price of R&D within, but also between countries and enables a better separation of the true effect of the credit from the impact of worldwide macroeconomic shocks. Also, the results obtained for one country may very well not be representative for another. While the short-run elasticity obtained was small, around 0.14, in the long run it increased significantly, approaching unity.

Table 6.3   Typical price elasticities of R&D

Study	Country	Elasticity
Bernstein (1986)	Canada	0.13
Bailey and Lawrence (1987; and 1992)	US	0.75 (0.25)
Bernstein and Nadiri (1989)	US	0.4-0.5
Nadiri and Prucha (1989)	US	Zero
Bailey and Lawrence (1992)	US	1.0
Asmussen and Berriot (1993)	France	0.26 (0.08)
Australia BIE (1993)	Australia	1.0
Berger (1993)	US	1.0-1.5
Hall (1993)	US	1.0-1.5
Hines (1993)	US	1.2-1.6
McCutchen (1993)	US	0.28-10.0?
Mamuneas and Nadiri (1996)	US	0.95-1
Bernstein (1998)	Canada	0.14 (SR) – 0.30 (LR)
Dagenais et al. (1998)	Canada	0.40 (SR) – 0.98 (LR)

Sources: Griffith et al. (1996); and Hall and van Reenen (2000).

BOX 6.4

Empirical evidence points in the direction of a tax price elasticity with regard to R&D investment of around unity (that is, 1) and in some cases higher. This makes tax incentives an attractive policy instrument compared to direct government subsidies to stimulate R&D. Consistent with theory, the elasticities tend to be higher in the long than in the short run.

So what does this do for overall efficiency? Recent work on the UK R&D incentive scheme by the London-based Institute of Fiscal Studies (IFS) on the basis of the above price elasticities concludes that the tax credit is cost effective and pays off (Griffith et al., 2001). Under a range of scenarios, the long-run effect on GDP growth was shown to far outweigh the credit's exchequer costs.

Ensuring Permanence

By implementing a credible and steady policy over time, government can enhance the effectiveness of tax breaks for R&D. From the 1980s on, countries have frequently modified tax legislation and thereby the size of R&D incentives. Hall and van Reenen (2000) present an overview of four countries with the most generous incentives, that is, Australia, Canada, France and the US. All four have experienced considerable fluctuations in the generosity of the tax subsidies for typical R&D investment (see Figure 6.1). Canada has had the most generous tax subsidy in place, except during the 1985-87 period when Australia had the edge.

Regular modifications to the scope of R&D allowances cast uncertainty on firms and business managers. This undermines the effectiveness of R&D tax incentives mainly because the sector is characterised as highly labour intensive. Success may well stand or fall by the quality of the scientists and engineers. Because it takes time to find, hire and discharge researchers, the process requires long-term contracts with high associated (wage) costs. The higher the uncertainty on these expenses, the higher the reluctance of firms to commit and respond to tax incentives. By the same token, the effectiveness of R&D credits is expected to be greater in the long than in the short run.

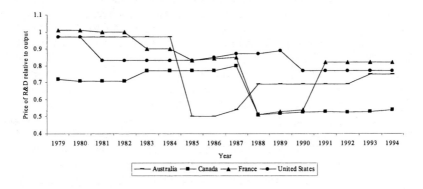

Note: The real interest rate is set at 10 per cent and the user cost is weighted as follows: 90% current expenditure, 3.6% buildings and 6.4% plant & machinery. At 1, the tax system is neutral with regard to the R&D investment decision.

Source: Hall and Van Reenen (2000, p. 454).

Figure 6.1   Development of the tax element of R&D user cost over time

BOX 6.5

Since R&D projects are typically carried out over a long period, frequent changes to the size of the tax benefit creates uncertainty with firms which harms the overall effectiveness of R&D tax incentives.

Proportional or Incremental Tax Incentive?

There is discussion as to what incentives are more effective: proportional or incremental. There appears to be no single answer. The European Commission (2006e) argues that proportional incentives which, as noted at the beginning of the chapter, are based on the total or volume of expenditures, could be more useful in maintaining a certain level of R&D spending where there is a relatively stabilised market demand for R&D. Incremental tax incentives may best be used where the explicit policy objective is to elicit additional R&D and to support dynamic firms or sectors. The next section shows that they are more complicated to design and administer.

Heterogeneity of Impact across Firms

The value of R&D tax incentives varies between firms, depending on the interaction with other provisions in the tax law and whether a firm has a sufficient tax liability to take advantage of the tax break (which is typically not the case for immature firms or those in recession). If not, the tax benefit has to be carried back or forward. As shown in Table 6.1, all tax systems have provisions for this in place. Nevertheless, because the credit's worth is less tomorrow than it is today on account of inflation, its value declines rapidly over time and may be lost entirely if the carry-forward expires.

Altshuler (1988) investigating 5,042 US firms over the 1981-84 period found that on average 23 per cent of the sample firms claimed the US R&D credit, but in any year considered that more than a quarter could not fully offset the credit against their tax liability. Of these firms, roughly 50 per cent had to carry forward their allowances, the remainder using carry-backs. As a result, the average of effective marginal rates of the tax credit was only 2.3 per cent, or less than one-tenth of the statutory rate of 25 per cent at that time. In specific cases the effective rate was even negative, implying a disincentive to invest in R&D.

Eisner et al. (1984) obtained similar findings. Between 14 and 43 per cent of the sample firms could not claim the full credit in 1981. As a result, the effective rate of credit was close to 0 per cent for 1981 and around 4 per cent in 1982. Eisner et al. (1984) also drew attention to another point. If the tax base is determined by a moving average of R&D expenditure in a predefined number of past years (that is, an incremental tax credit), a current increase in R&D expenditure limits future credits because the size of the base is enlarged starting the year after.[13] This may discourage firms from increasing, or even induce them to decrease current spending to benefit from a higher future credit. These perverse effects arise from the incremental nature of the credit and firm-specific characteristics and movements in the tax base. As a remedy, the authors propose pinning down the company-specific tax base to a fixed point in time. Making the credit refundable, though more costly, should also improve effectiveness.

BOX 6.6

The definition of the credit should be carefully chosen, particularly in the case of an incremental credit. The company-specific base should be fixed to a point in time. A refundable credit, although more costly, should also benefit effectiveness.

6.5   BRIEF SUMMARY

The effectiveness of tax incentives as an instrument to stimulate R&D activity has been more or less confirmed by the academic literature in the past two decades. Therefore, the case for R&D tax incentives seems strong. Private firms remain autonomous in the R&D decisions and are not subject to the bureaucracy and uncertainty that is regularly connected to direct subsidies. A tax subsidy can also be better anticipated and creates less uncertainty with business managers. This is likely to increase its effectiveness.

The current trend in OECD economies, in which tax-base broadening is central, does not detract from this. Even though broad-based, low-rate capital taxes may be favoured from an efficiency point of view, this should not become an objective in its own right. If large positive spillover effects are created from R&D, these effects may well outweigh the benefits associated with such broad-based, low-rate taxes. In such a case an exception should be made.

Generally speaking, low statutory tax rates are beneficial to economic incentives, as they exert a positive effect on the location decision of managers, risk taking and entrepreneurial spirit. On its own, this may

---

[13] As a side-effect, inflation may cause nominal expenditure to exceed the credit base, while real expenditure remains equal or is even comparatively lower.

certainly promote R&D investment. A generic rate cut is nevertheless problematic due to high associated revenue costs. In the process, exceptions to the tax base are eliminated. Less-expensive ways to promote R&D from the government side are therefore often sought. These measures could lie outside the tax system, for example specific government assignment of R&D projects and participations or direct subsidies (and despite the above-cited drawbacks).

The government should carefully weigh *all* factors that affect the efficacy of an R&D measure, including any effects from a higher across-the-board statutory tax rate that is required by having costly R&D tax incentives that narrow the tax base. If then a tax measure is preferred, it should be simple to administer, easy to understand and consistent in implementation.

7. Taxes and human capital accumulation

In the progress of society, philosophy or speculation becomes like every other employment, the principal or sole trade and occupation of a particular class of citizens.

(Adam Smith)[1]

7.1 INTRODUCTION

Human capital forms one of the principal pillars in creating prosperity in contemporary society. It is the key feature of economies where the emphasis has shifted from production by traditional factors such as labour, capital and land, to a service-orientated economy with production based on human skills, information and knowledge. Knowledge-based economies can be defined as economies that have a high share of knowledge-intensive jobs; where information sectors are a prerequisite to the functioning of the economy; and intangible capital is dominant over physical capital (Foray, 2004).

This chapter examines the impact of taxes on human capital investment. The topic is closely related to the taxation of labour and capital income and social policies as discussed in Chapters 2 and 3. For example, larger tax progressivity decreases the incentives to invest in education, as do high benefit payments. Investment in human capital is also a direct substitute for that in physical capital. A corporate tax cut that stimulates capital investment should therefore depress human capital investment. At the same time, there is a clear distinction. Whereas issues discussed in Chapter 2 were quantitative in nature (that is, participation, hours worked and unemployment), education, skills and on-the-job training aim to improve the quality of the labour force.

The chapter is structured as follows. Section 7.2 briefly examines the economic gains associated with investment in people through education, from which both the individual and society as a whole benefit significantly. Section 7.3 considers the impact of taxation on human capital accumulation.

---

[1] Quoted from Foray (2004, p. 50). The concept of a knowledge-based society thereby dates back to the time of Adam Smith.

The tax structure distorts the human capital investment decision in particular through four elements: the non-deductibility of direct and indirect cost of education; progressive income taxes; the proportion of labour versus capital income tax; and social policies through endogenous labour supply responses. Section 7.4 sets out a number of government responses to neutralise the negative effects from the tax system. These include education subsidies or, more optimally, a graduate tax or income-contingent loan system. The final section briefly summarises.

7.2   THE HUMAN CAPITAL INVESTMENT PAYOFF

A society where production and diffusion of knowledge are central is closely connected to the development of human capital through education, skills and on-the-job training. Human capital is defined in a broad sense encompassing all productive capital that is embodied in the labour force. As a factor of production, the stock of human capital has been estimated to be up to three times as large as the stock of physical capital in an economy (Davies and Whalley, 1989). When accounting for home production, estimates of human capital even range up to 96 per cent of the total capital stock.

Human capital is acquired in schools and other formal academic institutions, but also on the workfloor through learning by doing and within family homes. The welfare gains from human capital accumulation have been shown to be substantial and accrue to the individual and to society as a whole, hence generating micro- and macro-level returns.

Micro-level Returns

The private internal rate of return (RoR) provides a micro-level measure of the higher earnings that result from human capital investment. The latter can be seen as any ordinary investment with a certain required RoR and cost associated with it. An individual may be induced to obtain some type of formal education by achieving higher productivity, which reflects in higher wages paid by firms. The investment itself represents a direct cost, including cost of tuition, books and travel expenses. But indirect expenses exist as well. The main input in producing human capital is time and time spent on education cannot simultaneously be spent on working. Earnings forgone therefore also represent a cost (or, when obtaining on-the-job training while in employment, loss in output to firms).[2]

Table 7.1 presents the RoR for a number of countries. Provided that education is immediately acquired, the returns are significantly positive and

---

[2] Sometimes spending is also consumptive in nature instead of an investment if, for example, the social status associated with a formal education provides satisfaction to the owner.

well above real interest rates in most countries.[3] If acquired at the age of 40, the returns drop, except for France and Italy.

Table 7.1 *Private internal rates of return for an individual obtaining a university-level degree from an upper secondary and post-secondary non-tertiary level of education* [a]

| | RoR when education is immediately acquired | | RoR when education is acquired at age 40 | | | |
| | | | Forgone earnings are borne by the individual but not direct cost | | Direct cost and forgone earnings are borne by the individual | |
	Males	Females	Males	Females	Males	Females
Belgium	6.1	8.1	1.9	4.2	0.8	2.7
Denmark	4.8	3.4	3.4	0.7	3.3	0.5
Finland	15.8	15.4	11.0	8.6	10.8	8.3
France	8.3	7.2	10.4	7.6	8.6	5.4
Italy	7.6[b]	8.3[b]	13.1	4.5	12.4	3.4
Netherlands	5.3	8.0	0.3	4.6	-0.4	3.1
Norway	10.4	13.0	6.8	6.7	6.6	6.4
Sweden	8.6	7.2	8.5	5.9	7.8	5.1
US	12.6	9.4	11.6	8.4	8.3	3.9

Notes:
[a] For the definitions of the levels of education see the International Standard Classification of Education (ISCED).
[b] For reasons of reliability, the OECD has not used data on earnings for 15-24 year olds in tertiary education. Life income streams are calculated from data for 25-64 year olds.

Source: OECD (2005i).

The OECD (2005i) also calculates that the return to obtaining upper secondary or post-secondary non-tertiary education is 'explosive' in most of the countries in Table 7.1.[4] Females are still treated differentially and earn on

---

[3] Because human capital investment brings risks too, a premium is required (Levhari and Weiss, 1974). Human capital investment is more risky than physical capital investment because it cannot be purchased or sold from or to others. As an asset, human capital is inseparable from its possessor. Hence, diversification of human capital means obtaining a general education and thereby forgoing specialisation. By contrast, investment in physical capital permits specialisation in production in addition to diversification of portfolios across various owners.
[4] Two other micro indicators in the report offer further insights. The *fiscal* internal RoR measures total government expenditure on education and indirect cost from lower income tax revenues (people are in school instead of at work), against the benefits of higher future wages and tax

average only between 60 and 80 per cent of what men earn at a given level of educational attainment.

The table also shows that the return to education declines with the years. The earnings forgone factor becomes more pronounced as workers grow older and receive higher remuneration. But other fundamental factors play a role, too – perhaps an even more important role. For example, research indicates a peak in an individual's ability to acquire skills around the age of 17 to 18, after which time people gradually lose this capacity. People also find it increasingly difficult to apply their skills on the workfloor, lose focus, diligence and so forth. The loss of capacities applies to all humans, both the able and the less able.

Macro-econometric Proxies

There are a number of reasons to believe that returns on an economy-wide scale are even larger than on a personal level. This is due to positive externalities and spillovers.[5] This means that education provides tangible benefits not just to the individual partaking, but to the larger society as well. For example, with better education comes a lower risk of unemployment, higher adaptability to economic change, greater public health, social cohesion and less crime. Workers are better informed and empowered to make 'wiser' choices. This reflects on the political process and participation in democratic institutions. In addition, it has been argued that less-educated workers who are surrounded by more-educated people become more productive, too (Gemmell, 1997).

On the other hand, 'signalling' and/or 'rent seeking' may reduce economy-wide efficiency. Signalling touches on the problem of asymmetric information and occurs if education does not raise productivity, but instead creates value only as an indication to prospective employers of somebody's talents and abilities (Spence, 1973). Rent seeking occurs when individuals manipulate the political or economic spectrum to obtain a larger piece of the cake without increasing productivity and thus making the total cake bigger. This capacity is presumed to increase with the level of education.

Second, therefore, economists try to construct macro indicators that measure the economy-wide social return to human capital investment. Overall, the effects prove hard to capture. Empirical studies are based on proxies such as enrolment rates, literacy scores or years of formal education. As is argued, this fails to take account of factors such as learning by doing within firms, experience or the depreciation of skills. Furthermore, spillovers created from education are simply very difficult to gauge due to causality.

---

revenues. The *social* internal RoR measures the total of private and public benefits against the total cost of schooling and production forgone. Both measures are also significantly positive.
[5] That is, the social return is higher than the private return.

Does education benefit economic growth, or do rich countries simply spend more on education? [6]

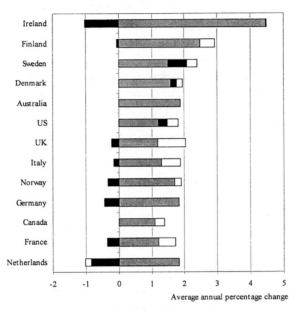

Note:
[a] GDP growth per person employed is composed of the sum of: (1) changes in hourly GDP per efficient unit of labour; (2) changes in average hours worked; and (3) changes in human capital; for Ireland and Germany the years of reference are, respectively, 1990-99 and 1991-2000; and Norway is mainland only.

Source: OECD (2005i).

Figure 7.1　The contribution of human capital to GDP growth per person employed [a]

Despite these complications, each incremental year of schooling is estimated to raise long-term economic growth between 3 and 6 per cent. Figure 7.1 shows that in recent decades, human capital accumulation has contributed substantially to economic growth, in the UK even up to 0.85 per cent. In many countries this has helped offset the negative impact on output

---

[6] What is still puzzling economists is whether human capital is an ordinary factor input and merely adds to the absolute level of GDP, or whether a certain level of human capital has the potential to affect productivity growth rates and thereby explains sustained per capita growth. For an overview of empirical work, see Blundell et al. (1999).

from a reduction in hours worked. Only in the Netherlands has a change in human capital accumulation contributed negatively to growth.

BOX 7.1

Human capital investment is an important driver of economic growth. The return to the individual of obtaining a formal education lies well above the normal return to ordinary capital investment. On an economy-wide scale, lower risk of unemployment, greater public health, social cohesion, less crime, higher adaptability to economic change and production externalities add to the benefits.

Smart, Creative and Skilled Workforces

Before-tax wages depend on a large number of factors, such as labour demand for specific skills, minimum wage requirements, union bargaining and relative experience. There is nevertheless a significant correlation between wage rates and the level of education (OECD, 2005i). Hence, lifelong earnings rise with the level of educational attainment. This can be explained by higher productivity, but also because the supply of high-skilled labour is constrained by differences in endowment. Scholarly aptitude is a scarce resource.

In the US, relative differences in average pay of a person with 4 years of university-level education compared to one without such education has increased from 30 per cent to 90 per cent over the past 30 years. This has contributed to rising income inequality. In the UK similar patterns can be observed. Technological change is often considered to be complementary to high-skilled labour (this is also referred to as 'skill-biased technical change'). Labour demand thus becomes increasingly skills intensive and with it, the skills premium grows. Under plausible assumptions, Jacobs (2004) argues that future demand for skilled workers will increase more rapidly compared to the supply of high-skilled workers, which is likely to increase wage inequality (Nobel laureate Jan Tinbergen once commented that the race between technology and schooling appears to be lost by schooling, since the increase in education levels is too slow compared to the demand for high-skilled workers on account of technological change). Wage inequality between skilled and unskilled workers has increased especially rapidly in the United Kingdom and the United States and less so in continental Europe (Davis, 1992).

Furthermore, the return on an extra year of schooling is high especially at an early age. Best practice therefore seems to raise the level of universal education in society. This should expand the pool of skilled workers and can make a country richer. It should also moderate the wage premium of high-skilled workers and abate rising income inequality in Western economies. Heckman (2000) in fact argues for a reduction in the age of compulsory education to 4-5 when educational investment seems to have a substantial payoff, particularly in terms of subsequent educational attainment of children from disadvantaged backgrounds (a point to which we return later). Moreover, schooling may improve the skill level of some unskilled workers, thereby enhancing their chances of employment and/or pay, but generally these effects are not considered to be great.

7.3   EFFECTS OF TAXATION ON HUMAN CAPITAL ACCUMULATION

The Human Capital Investment Decision

A relevant question to policy makers is whether taxes affect human capital investment, and if so, how human capital formation can be best advanced by the appropriate (tax) policies. The focus is on four consecutive scenarios studied in the tax literature (Nerlove et al., 1993; Trostel, 1993; Heckman et al., 1998; and Jacobs, 2005). These include the effect of a proportional income tax, a progressive income tax, the asymmetric tax treatment of human over physical capital, and social policies under endogenous labour supply.

The basic model
In making the human capital investment decision, a person weighs the marginal return (MR) of education against its marginal cost (MC).[7] On an economy-wide scale, the amount of human capital formation is determined by the point where MR equals MC. This is illustrated in Figure 7.2.

The MR consists of the higher stream of after-tax earnings from obtaining education, discounted by the appropriate interest rate.[8] The return from education increases as the additional remuneration after education is higher, if post-educational labour supply increases, or if the tax rate on future higher earnings from education is lowered (and vice versa). The discount rate has a similar effect. A higher return on physical capital reduces the MR to human capital investment, as does a reduction in the tax on capital. It is assumed that the MR diminishes with the amount of human capital investment.

---

[7] Based on pioneering work by Mincer (1958); Schultz (1963); and Becker (1964).

[8] In mathematical formulae it is represented by: $MR = L(1 - t_h)\Delta w / 1 + r(1 - t_k)$, where L is labour supply; Δw the change in earnings; t_h the tax rate on additional future income; r the return to physical capital, or similarly the interest rate; and t_k the tax rate on this capital.

The MC is a function of the after-tax earnings forgone, the direct cost of education and effort put in.[9] A higher effort raises the cost of human capital investment, but is generally hard to measure in a wealth equivalent. The government can affect the MC by directly or indirectly subsidising the cost of education. The decision to invest is thereby positively affected. An example of a direct subsidy is the provision and finance of public schooling, so tuition costs are kept low. Public grants to students exemplify an indirect subsidy. The MC is assumed to rise with the amount of investment.

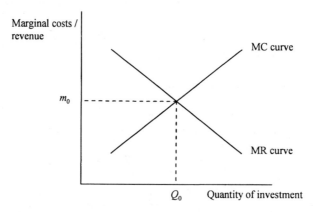

Figure 7.2   The human capital investment decision

Depreciation of human capital

At the same time, human capital wears down and becomes obsolete. Depreciation comprises a *technical* component from changes that originate within workers and an *economic* part from changes in market conditions (van Loo et al., 2001). For example, depreciation of human capital results from ageing, illness or injury. But obsolescence may also be caused by insufficient use of skills due to periods of unemployment, new skill requirements on the job or fewer jobs in the occupation due to changing market conditions.

Two leading studies estimate the rate of human capital depreciation to range between 4-9 per cent and 1-4+ per cent (Trostel, 1993). At retirement, human capital automatically depreciates to zero from an economic stance. Because human capital cannot be transferred, the opportunities to recoup the costs of education are limited in later life. This explains why the return to human capital investment is higher at an early age and diminishes as people

---

[9] Similarly, MC $=f[(1 - t_l)w(1 - s_d), p(1 - s_i), e]$, where t_l is the tax rate on earnings forgone; w stands for earnings; s_d is the percentage of government subsidies on direct cost; p denotes direct cost; s_i government subsidies for indirect cost; and e is effort.

grow older. Spending on human capital investment is thus more cost effectively devoted to younger than to older people.

A Proportional Income Tax

In the basic case, a proportional or flat labour income tax with a full allowance for the cost of education does not distort the human capital investment decision. Future income is taxed at a similar rate as the costs of the investment are now being made deductible. Hence, the costs as well as the return on investment are reduced in the same proportion (the ratio between the MC and the MR remains unchanged). These costs automatically include forgone earnings, but should in addition encompass all other costs associated with obtaining an education. Note that the tax system is simply neutral and whether prospective earnings are higher, lower or equal is unimportant (of course this influences the overall investment decision).

A simple example
Assume a marginal tax rate of 20 per cent and total education costs of 10,000 units. These costs constitute only earnings forgone. In such a case, the net cost to a student is only 8,000 units as he or she 'saves' paying 2,000 units in tax. Now suppose earnings after schooling are 10 per cent higher, that is 11,000 units (assuming equal prices). The tax due on this income is 2,200 units. However, the tax increase from 2,000 to 2,200 units arises exclusively from higher wages, not from higher taxes. The tax system is thus neutral with regard to the investment decision.

If, on the other hand, we assume that half of the costs of human capital investment constitute earnings forgone and the other half, non-deductible tuition cost, the net cost to the student is 9,000 units as he or she 'saves' paying only 1,000 units in tax (that is, 20 per cent of 5000). Hence, the tax cost has risen from 200 to 1,200 units, of which 200 arises from higher wages, and 1,000 from the non-deductibility of tuition. This distorts the investment decision.

Tax breaks for educational expenses
In practice, the direct costs of education are often not deductible, or only limited relief is permitted. Table 7.2 shows that most countries that offer relief fail to alleviate the full cost of education from tax. In all cases, taxable thresholds, caps and other restrictions mean that the taxpayer can be expected to remain burdened with some non-deductible costs. Regardless of the flat

statutory rate therefore, a limited deduction for the cost of education means that future earnings are taxed at a higher effective rate.[10]

Table 7.2   Tax allowances for educational expenses, 2005

Country	Tax subsidy to education
Austria	The costs of education are deductible only if they present an extraordinary burden to the taxpayer, where the amount depends on income. For children living away from home, a fixed deduction is permitted of €110 per month
Canada	Relief for tuition fees, moving expenses, interest paid on student loans and cost of books is offered through a tax credit subject to various conditions and threshold.
France	Parents of children who receive secondary or tertiary education are allowed a credit of €61-183 per child. The exact amount depends on the level of the educational institution
Germany	Expenses related to a first professional education or studies are deductible up to an amount of €4,000 per year (for example, tuition fees, expenses for books, workroom at home and housing).
Italy	A credit of 19% is allowed with regard to expenses for secondary and university education, with a ceiling equal to state tuition fees
Netherlands	Cost with regard to education that aims at a profession can be deducted (not including expenses related to cost of living, travel, workrooms), with a taxable threshold of €500 and a limit of €15,000
UK	Relief is provided for expense of external training courses related to employee's current or future work. Employer contributions to this are not subject to income tax in the hands of the employee. For a self-employed person, costs of training are deductible only if incurred in relation to his or her business or profession
US	Itemised deduction in the category 'miscellaneous' for cost of education that is work related with a floor of 2% of the taxpayer's adjusted gross income (AGI)

Source: Compiled from the Supplementary Service, Section B, to *European Taxation* (looseleaf, Amsterdam: IBFD Publications BV). Some data may be incomplete or out of date.

---

[10] This does not take into account any provisions on carry-back and carry-forward and whether the tax benefit can be offset against tax liability. Students often have little side-income, in which case the value of any allowance is lowered.

Another problem arises because the costs of education are sometimes not easily verified or are difficult to translate into a wealth equivalent. Effort put into obtaining an education cannot be measured accurately, nor can the cost of leisure time sacrificed. Learning is often considered to be a mind-broadening experience and by definition implies discovering new turf. This may be much more stressful than a regular day-to-day job. Hence, psychological costs arise as well. The same is true for the potential benefits. Education creates interesting job opportunities, social status and a more fulfilling life experience overall. These elements are difficult to measure and certainly cannot be taken into account for income tax purposes.

BOX 7.2

A proportional income tax reduces the incentives to invest in human capital because at least a part of educational costs is not deductible from tax. The non-deductibility means that the MC is scaled down relatively less compared to the MR, so a distortion is created.

Trostel (1993) estimates that a proportional income tax rise of 1 percentage point reduces the stock of human capital in the economy by 0.97 per cent over the long term. While this is high, the current consensus in the tax literature appears to be that the effect is less significant because costs mostly comprise earnings forgone.

Progressive Income Taxes

Without exception, all developed countries have a progressive income tax structure aimed at redistribution of resources. This reinforces the distortion caused by a proportional income tax under which at least some educational costs are not deductible from tax. Since students typically obtain schooling when they are in the low tax bracket, tax progression means that higher future earnings are probably taxed in higher brackets. For example, in line with the previous illustration, assume that the 10 per cent wage increase from schooling, or 1,000 units, instead falls into a higher tax bracket of 40 per cent. Then, the marginal return to education is taxed at the 40 per cent level, while the costs are only deductible at the 20 per cent level. The progressive tax thereby imposes an additional tax of 200 per cent (that is, 400 minus the 200 from before). The difference results solely from the fact that the taxpayer has been pushed into a higher tax bracket.

Empirical estimates

The effect of tax progressivity is difficult to gauge though. In deciding how much to invest in schooling, an individual will have to consider the estimated future income streams and expected tax rates that apply over his/her working life. Also, as noted in Chapter 2, most tax systems are typically not as progressive as suggested by their marginal tax rate schedules because of various exceptions in the tax code that can change the final outcome dramatically.

On an economy-wide scale, Heckman et al. (1998) provide some evidence on the impact of progressive taxes. They consider the impact of a revenue neutral shift from the progressive income tax to a flat income tax and a flat consumption tax.[11] Their model is calibrated to the US economy, which is not known for having one of the most progressive income tax systems.[12] This could make it a conservative estimate for other economies as well, but only very roughly. Table 7.3 summarises the key findings (tuition costs are assumed to be not deductible).

Table 7.3   The effects of income tax progression

Variable	Percentage difference from benchmark case with income tax progression	
	Flat income tax	Flat consumption tax
Stock of physical capital	-0.79	19.55
Stock of college human capital	2.82	1.85
Stock of high-school human capital	0.90	0.08
Average wage college graduates	2.60	6.96
Average wage high-school graduates	2.44	6.82
Total output	1.15	4.98
Total consumption	0.16	3.66

Source: Heckman et al. (1998, Table 1).

The results show that progressive taxes indeed reduce the stock of human capital. A switch to a flat rate income tax would raise the stock of college and

---

[11] The authors use a general equilibrium model, which takes account of heterogeneity in age, ability to learn and initial endowment and the economic history of different generations.

[12] See the residual income progression coefficients in Table 3.4 of Chapter 3 for tax progressivity of labour income tax systems.

high-school human capital by 2.82 and 0.90 per cent respectively.[13] This has an overall positive impact on output, in spite of the smaller stock of physical capital associated with such reform. Since a flat rate consumption exempts the normal return to investment, most of the effect on output this time comes from a larger stock of physical capital, and the impact on the stock of human capital is considerably mitigated.

The larger capital stock works through positively on wages, too. Interestingly, the simulation shows that overall wage inequality remains largely unaffected by the switch. This confirms that measures aimed at stimulating capital accumulation could benefit an entire economy through higher wages across the board and not just capital owners.

BOX 7.3

A progressive income tax reduces the incentives to invest in human capital. A US study estimates that a move to a flat income tax or a flat consumption tax would increase output by 1.15 and 4.98 per cent, respectively, without materially affecting overall wage inequality.

Human versus Physical Capital Investment

The results already hint at a fundamental trade-off between promoting human capital and physical capital investment. The trade-off arises because a global income tax targets both a labour and a capital income component (as discussed in Chapter 2).

The capital income tax component reduces the return to physical investment and the rate at which future earnings from human capital investment are discounted. This skews the choice of individuals and encourages them to invest in human capital. Both types of investment can be considered direct substitutes, for that matter. A positive tax on capital income thus creates a distortion that leads to the substitution of human capital away from physical capital. At the same time, the labour income tax lowers the after-tax rate of return to human capital investment by partly taxing away earnings. This discourages human capital investment. Both effects should therefore be theoretically offsetting under a global income tax that targets wages and interest equally.

---

[13] Dupor et al. (1996) investigate the distortions created from tax progression and the non-deductibility of inputs to human capital accumulation under the US tax system. By simulating a shift to a flat tax compared to the 1970 US tax code, they find a modest increase in human capital of 5 per cent. A similar simulation for the 1990 US tax code reveals that a 10 per cent increase in taxes decreases human capital by only 0.2 per cent.

In practice, this property none the less does not hold because, unlike physical capital, human capital cannot be depreciated for tax purposes. Where only the return to physical capital investment is taxed, to the extent that the costs of human capital investment cannot be expensed immediately, both its principal amount and the return are taxed. A global income tax therefore tends to discriminate against the latter kind of investment (Nerlove et al., 1993).

On the other hand, if the tax code does permit immediate and full expensing of the costs of education, the results are rapidly reversed. Human capital investment is essentially taxed on a cash-flow basis. The accounting process of activation and subsequent depreciation of physical assets then creates a relative tax disadvantage for physical capital investment (Nielsen and Sørensen, 1997).

For individuals obtaining full-time education, the difference depends mainly on whether one considers the non-deductible tuition fees to constitute the bulk of costs, or deductible forgone earnings. In developed countries, it may be assumed that the latter situation more closely matches reality, so tax laws tend to discriminate against investment in physical capital. Moreover, on-the-job training is tax advantaged over acquiring a formal full-time education, since in most countries the cost of the former can be immediately expensed under business tax rules, whereas the direct costs of formal education are fully taxed.

Specific tax provisions

The asymmetric treatment of human versus physical capital is reinforced by the structure of existing tax systems. As noted in Chapter 2, these contain a multitude of different tax rates and specific tax breaks applying independently to labour and capital income. The effective rate of tax on each source of income therefore differs markedly in all countries under consideration.

For example, while a positive tax on capital promotes human capital investment, tax subsidies such as generous pension allowances and a mortgage interest deduction for owner-occupied housing reduce the effective tax rate on capital income. Furthermore, younger people less frequently own a house and/or save for a pension. Taxpayers are likely to make use of these tax subsidies later on in life when they have worked a number of years and accumulated financial capital. The tax distortion to acquiring human capital therefore generally increases as the years pass.

Jacobs and de Mooij (2002) calculate that the marginal tax rate on education in the presence of a capital income tax rises from -14 per cent during the first working years to +16 per cent from the age of 41 on.[14] That

---

[14] The calculations are based on a range of simplifying assumptions for the Netherlands. The net return to investment is set at 4 per cent and the interest rate at 5 per cent. The marginal tax rate

is, an individual normally pursues an education only if the discounted value of increased future earnings is higher than the current costs (the NPV). As we have seen, however, the net discount rate depends partly on the effective rate of tax on capital income. A higher (lower) tax then decreases (increases) the return on physical capital and thus increases (decreases) the return on human capital. So the effective tax on capital income is positive early in life, but declines rapidly as people grow older and are better able to take advantage of generous tax allowances for saving. The incentives for becoming more educated automatically diminish.

The Role of Social Policies

People who work less have less opportunity to 'utilise' the acquired human capital. As taxes reduce the time spent on working and lower the so-called 'utilisation rate' of human capital, they indirectly reduce the incentives to acquire human capital, and vice versa. Workers who possess a large stock of human capital are induced to raise labour supply, since higher wages raise the opportunity cost to leisure. There is interaction with other government policy areas that affect labour supply, including social policies, so the decision to acquire human capital is endogenous (Jacobs, 2005). This endogeneity typically worsens the distortion to the learning decision.

For example, high marginal tax rates reduce labour supply and raise the equilibrium unemployment rate in labour markets characterised by decentralised wage bargaining. This lowers employment and reduces the incentives to invest in human capital. Generous benefit payments may have a comparable effect if they are poorly targeted and unconditional. The poverty trap plays a central role. If the stimulus to raise the work effort is meagre, similar negative incentives may be assumed to exist for acquiring an education.

BOX 7.4

The human capital investment decision is endogenous to the labour supply. A low (high) utilisation rate of labour decreases (increases) the return on human capital. Generally speaking, therefore, the spin-off from various social policies is to depress human capital investment.

---

on capital is 30 per cent, but if saved through pensions or owner-occupied housing the effective rate drops to respectively -30 and -55. The working life of an individual is split into two parts, ranging from the ages 23-40 and 41-65, and only in the second period do taxpayers save through tax-advantaged pension schemes or owner-occupied housing.

Labour market strategies such as the negative income tax, earned income tax credit, or wage rate subsidy also impinge on the schooling decision. The measures aim to improve the labour supply of (younger) low-skilled workers and could stimulate schooling among people who would otherwise have been inactive. However, as incomes improve, the indirect cost of forgone earnings also increases so that disincentives to obtain further education and become more highly skilled rise. In a similar vein, the utilisation rate of human capital for older workers is generally low. Particularly in European economies, high inactivity among this group of people diminishes the return to human capital and lowers the incentives to invest. Generous early retirement plans, poorly managed disability and unemployment schemes are all contributing factors.

7.4 GOVERNMENT SUBSIDIES AND SOCIAL STUDY LOANS

As governments impose taxation, they also spend heavily on education (see Table 1.2 in Chapter 1). A primary argument for government subsidies is to internalise externalities associated with education. As argued before, large spillovers exist on a macroeconomic level that an individual fails to take into account in his or her individual decision to take up an educational opportunity. The subsidies are then rationalised on Pigouvian grounds, to mitigate or neutralise entirely the distortions that are created by progressive income taxation.[15] Politicians often also argue that education is a basic right that should thus be available to everyone, regardless of background and free of charge.

At first glance this may appear odd as education subsidies primarily favour high-skilled people who are likely to earn relatively higher wages. A disproportional number of students come from wealthy families and higher social classes. Any subsidy favouring the well-off has a regressive impact, so subsidies for higher education should be fundamentally regressive in nature. Rich individuals (who are likely to be more highly skilled) also have better opportunities to deduct educational costs than do those who are less well-off (and likely to be less skilled).

However, the subsidies also offset the adverse effects from progressive taxes aimed at redistribution. Bovenberg and Jacobs (2005) use a model of optimal income taxation with endogenous human capital and show that the labour tax is more progressive with education subsidies than without. If not all (verifiable) costs of education can be fully deducted at the effective

---

[15] Different studies nevertheless have different costs and social benefits. Contrary to common practices, government should differentiate tuition fees between types of schooling. Studies that create large positive externalities, such as physics or chemistry, should receive higher subsidies than more popular courses such as economics and law (Jacobs and van der Ploeg, 2006).

marginal tax rate on future earnings, government could correct this by providing a subsidy. This reduces the distortion from a progressive income tax, while allowing higher marginal labour tax rates for redistribution. This benefits low-skilled individuals relative to the high-skilled ones who mostly take advantage of the subsidies. For this reason, the authors refer to redistribution of resources and education subsidies as 'Siamese twins'.

But there is another trait. Talent and ability are largely innate. Many countries, especially high-tax ones, provide virtually free admission to educational facilities. A selective group of 'fortunate' people thus have an opportunity to more fully develop their skills and benefit from higher earnings, albeit at the expense of the average taxpayer. As such, it is not unfair that these individuals are taxed at progressive rates. Education subsidies may also correct for capital and insurance markets failing to deliver adequate finance for students to fund their studies.

Education Subsidies in the Sample Countries

When students do not have sufficient income to deduct any direct cost of education, marginal tax rates on future (higher) earnings should equal the marginal subsidy to neutralise the distortion from taxation. So if future earnings are taxed at a marginal tax rate of, say, 40 per cent, the costs of education should be subsidised at the margin by 40 per cent. Figure 7.3 shows that in practice marginal education subsidies are well above marginal tax rates in most countries.

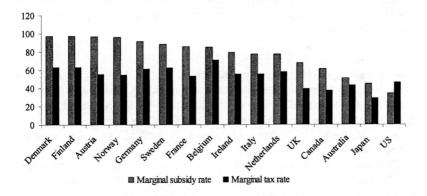

Note: [a]The tax rate applies to a 133% average production worker (APW), the marginal subsidy rate to the total direct costs of tertiary education institutions.

Source: Bovenberg and Jacobs (2005, Table 1).

Figure 7.3 Marginal tax subsidies vis-à-vis marginal tax rates, 2000 [a]

High-tax countries also provide higher subsidies than low-tax ones to eliminate distortions to human capital investment caused by redistributive policies (the correlation between the two variables is 0.77).

BOX 7.5

All sample countries except for the United States have ample government education subsidies in place to compensate for the economic distortions created by (progressive) income taxes.

Hendricks (1999) estimates through a general equilibrium version of a traditional human capital model that a 25 per cent training subsidy increases growth by 0.35 per cent, while the revenue loss of such a measure is fairly modest.

Equity Participation Scheme

Education subsidies may not be the most optimal policy course, though, from either an efficiency or an equity perspective. It is generally believed that a core task of modern government is to provide adequate schooling for all, which includes ensuring accessibility to higher levels of education for those who have the academic capabilities and desire to obtain it. Public systems nevertheless fail to fully achieve this, which typically disadvantages students from poorer backgrounds who receive little financial backing from parents whose income and means are low. Why is this?

Capital market imperfections

Theoretically speaking, human capital investment, just like ordinary capital investment, could be financed by either debt or equity. But since slavery has been formally abolished, human capital cannot be bindingly 'traded' and thus does not make very good collateral for parties wishing to enter into an equity contract. Markets are left with only one viable method to supply the capital needed, which is debt.

This can be problematic if, as has been argued, markets fail to deliver (sufficient) loans to finance human capital investment due to credit rationing, moral hazard and risk aversion among students.[16] For example, financial markets may be reluctant to supply sufficient finance because of 'asymmetric

---

[16] Moral hazard is the name given to the increased risk of 'inappropriate' or 'immoral' behaviour if somebody does not fully suffer the consequences, or may actually benefit, from such behaviour, for example, if a person with car insurance drives more recklessly than one without insurance.

information'. Banks are typically uninformed on the effort and diligence of students during their studies and the probability of success. Nor are they sure of satisfactory participation in the labour market after graduation. These credit market failures hurt in particular disadvantaged students from lower socio-economic backgrounds.

Note that debt contracts attract high-risk investors (that is, students), while equity contracts attract low-risk investors. Stiglitz and Weiss (1981) show that in order to diminish losses from bad loans, it is more optimal for banks to ration the volume of credit, instead of raising the interest rate by demanding a high risk premium. Moreover, if they did raise the interest rate, it would drive out low-risk students who would pay an excessive risk premium. In either case, there is likely to be undersupply of capital.

Likewise, students who do not obtain sufficient finance demand a higher return on education as they have to forgo additional consumption or leisure time during their studies. They thus require extra compensation for the 'sacrifice' made. Risk-averse students may also desire some form of income insurance when undertaking riskier human capital investment. Generally speaking, insurance markets are unable to offer such insurance, because human capital cannot be traded on financial markets. Uncertainty on future wage rates then leads to underinvestment in human capital.[17]

Socio-economic factors that inhibit education

Nobel laureate James J. Heckman (2000) questions whether credit rationing is the central cause of constraining poor students to obtain a higher education. In a statistical examination he shows that ability, or what he calls 'college readiness' has a much more pronounced effect on the decision to take up a formal education. Studies surveyed suggest that this ability depends on parental education and a range of other long-run family and socio-economic factors. Of course, these factors are related to family income, but it demonstrates that government focus should perhaps lie elsewhere. That is, on the underlying family conditions.

The Perry Pre-school programme is one example in a range of fascinating experiments that were carried out in the US. Costing roughly $13,000 per child, the project intervened early on in the lives of a group of children from low socio-economic backgrounds and with low IQ scores of around 80. The 3-4 year olds were provided with comparable care, nurturing and guidance so as to mimic the attention that children in better-off families are given. This included an intensive daily pre-school session of 2.5 hours and weekly visits to the child's home by a teacher. They were read to, played with and so on.

---

[17] Eaton and Rosen (1980) show that these effects are real but can be mitigated by a wage tax. With a wage tax, the government shares in the risk by dampening future wage changes. An individual gains less in the case of a high return, but also loses less in the case of a low return.

At the age of 27 the performance of these children in terms of social responsibility, scholastic and economic success was compared to that of a control group that did not receive such treatment. The outcome was spectacular.[18] Table 7.4 reproduces the key findings.

Table 7.4   The Perry Pre-school project

Variable	Pre-school	No pre-school
Graduation from high school	67%	49%
Employed at age 19	50%	32%
Monthly earnings at age 28	$1,129	$766
Arrested by age 19	31%	51%
5 or more arrests by age 28	7%	35%
Received welfare at age 19	18%	32%
Received welfare at age 28	59%	80%

Source: Heckman (2000). The original study was by Schweinhart et al. (1993).

The benefits in terms of less crime, reduced resort to social welfare, higher employment and wages were so great that they by far outweighed the costs of the programme. The dollar value implicit in these benefits creates an NPV to society as a whole of $95,646 per child invested in and of $19,569 to the participant. Instead of starting education at the regular age of 6-7, Heckman therefore argues that the emphasis in education policy should be shifted to an earlier age of 4-5, where the return to education is likely to be much higher. Early childhood education improves cognitive skills, linguistic competence and social behaviour.

The graduate tax
Despite the legal impossibility, an equity contract is superior to government subsidies and to debt contracts that are either indirect and produce adverse distributional effects or fail to provide sufficient income insurance (Jacobs and van Weinbergen, 2005). An equity contract also permits a degree of risk sharing between the financier and the student. The government is the only institution in modern society that can effectively implement such an equity scheme, given the above remarks on indentured labour. Or, at least it can implement an equivalent measure through a government loan system in combination with a so-called 'graduate tax'.

The system is fairly straightforward. During the time of study, government provides the student with sufficient funds to cover the cost of education.

---

[18] Other early intervention projects yielded less impressive but still considerably positive results: the Mother-Child Home, Head Start and Syracuse programmes and the Yale experiment.

Later when working, the student would 'repay' government through a supplementary graduate tax on his or her earnings on top of the regular labour income tax. The student would thereby be guaranteed an adequate income, without a need for government subsidies. Repayment would depend on the student's success in later life in generating a return on his or her human capital investment. In essence, therefore, the scheme would function just like a standard equity contract where private parties put up risky capital in return for a future stream of dividends depending on earnings.

An equity participation model has important economic advantages. In the first place, it allows everybody to take up an education regardless of credit constraints and family income or wealth. This is achieved without the usual regressive impact of government subsidies, from which primarily the higher educated benefit but which are borne by all taxpayers. In addition, the government bears part of the risk of failure since the return to equity capital depends on the degree of success. Debt servicing on the other hand is fixed and mandatory. This provides stronger incentives for high-risk students to take up education, while at the same time it does not drive out the low-risk ones.

The tax authority is also well equipped to operate a graduate tax at relatively low (transaction) cost and in any case less cost than those incurred by private parties when writing equity contracts. A welcome side-effect would be that students become more cost aware (direct subsidies provided to educational institutions are obscure), which is likely to improve study results and put off those with little potential who enrol under a system of government subsidies. The government could also deny funds to students that fail to perform adequately. As the graduate tax is not based on cost recovery, it entails potentially large resources for the government.[19] Empirical estimates indicate that an equity participation scheme could significantly reduce government outlays for education.

On the downside, the graduate tax on top of income tax suggests larger work disincentives and may delay career choices as payments start when earning income. Government also risks that graduates move abroad and escape the levy (which it may want to avoid by applying an exit tax).

Income-contingent loans
An alternative and perhaps more optimal system that has been advocated for higher education reform is an income-contingent loan (ICL) scheme (see

---

[19] This can lead to the so-called 'Mick Jagger' problem, which was conceived in the academic literature. In his 'younger years', the lead singer of the Rolling Stones studied for a short time at the London School of Economics (LSE). Had the graduate tax applied (and been collected), Jagger's payments for the rest of his life would have seemed exorbitant in relation to the cost of his studies (Chapman, 2005). This example illustrates that the revenue collected may not be in reasonable proportion to the cost incurred.

Chapman, 1997 and 2005; and Jacobs and van der Ploeg, 2006). The scheme can be characterised as a hybrid of both debt and equity financing.

The government would provide the necessary funds to the student to obtain an education (the expenses covered differ under different variants, for example, living costs, tuition fees and so on), but only require them to repay debt including interest after graduation and contingent on a sufficiently high income. Thus, payments take place up to a certain threshold equal to the amount borrowed plus a risk premium for students who are unable to repay. The system thereby offers students a combination of funding and social insurance, which is sought especially by risk-averse students.

Compared to the graduate tax, the ICL system offers less insurance. This is because payments by graduates with high incomes are larger under the graduate tax, which thus features more insurance and redistribution. Because of this, the ICL system offers better work incentives compared to the graduate tax. Furthermore, the repayment tariff of the ICL can be differentiated by study length and size of loan (especially, bigger loans should warrant a higher tariff), which makes the system very flexible in its implementation and in addressing the issue of moral hazard.

BOX 7.6

The government is the only institution that can circumvent the legal prohibition of writing an equity contract for financing human capital investment by enacting a loan system with a so-called graduate tax that is paid on income later in life. This is regarded as both more equitable and economically efficient. An alternative system for higher education reform is an income-contingent loan (ICL) scheme. Government would provide funding, but only require students to repay debt including interest after graduation and contingent on a sufficiently high income. The latter system would offer less insurance and redistribution than the graduate tax and thus have better work incentives.

Public Training Programmes

In an attempt to bridge the gap between low- and high-skilled labour, OECD countries have a variety of public training programmes in place. These programmes are referred to as active labour market policy, a broader categorisation of which they are a part. The programmes involve some form of basic education, classroom training in vocational skills or on-the-job training that typically lasts for a 3-6, or perhaps 12 month period. The common rationalisation of such post-school education is to equip people with the necessary skills and/or work experience to get them into employment or raise earnings.

The efficacy of these programmes is subject to scepticism, though. Heckman et al. (1999) in a comprehensive analysis cover a large number of studies on active labour market policies in countries such as Denmark, France, Germany, the Netherlands, Sweden, the UK and the US. The cost-benefit calculations indicate that in most instances the intended returns are at best mediocre. For younger people the return can even be negative. The individual involved would have been better off working instead of partaking in training. Total lifetime earnings would have been higher.

Moreover, the returns are far below those measured for privately contracted on-the-job training, which are estimated to range between 10 and 20 per cent. Firms are usually not very keen to invest in disadvantaged workers and only spend on high-potential candidates. And this, according to Heckman, is exactly the inherent difficulty with these policies. It is simply very hard to provide an essentially uneducated or illiterate person, of say 20-25 years old, with anything close to the skills of a similarly aged person who has been learning throughout his or her entire life.

BOX 7.7

Empirical research shows that the return on public training programmes in most cases is mediocre and nowhere near the returns on private training programmes within firms. The programmes are unsuccessful in converting low-skilled workers into high-skilled productive workers.

Moreover, labour market issues may not be concentrated around the pool of low-skilled workers, as is regularly believed. MIT economist David Autor challenges the notion that the low skilled largely bear the cost of globalisation and technological change. US labour market data reveal that until the late 1980s the wages of low-skilled workers were indeed under pressure, a trend abetted by falling minimum wages (Autor et al., 2006). At the same time, demand for high-skilled labour was up. This widened the income gap significantly.

Since the beginning of the 1990s, however, this pattern has changed. Where wages at the higher end of the distribution have picked up further, those at the lower end have been rising as well, meaning that the demand for low-skilled jobs has improved. This finding is referred to as the 'polarisation' of the labour market and marks a growth in jobs at the higher and lower ends of the wage and education distribution, relative to the middle segment.

A main explanation for the observed pattern is that routine tasks are rapidly taken over by cheaper computers that make many middle-wage jobs redundant. So where computers complement the non-routine jobs of high-ability people making them even more productive, they are direct substitutes for many tasks traditionally carried out by middle-wage workers. Bookkeeping, financial services, secretarial and other administrative work is increasingly being displaced by digitalisation. By contrast, low-skilled manual occupations, such as cleaners, truck drivers and waiters, are not affected and remain intact.

Thus regardless of the cost effectiveness of public training programmes, it may not be where the real issue lies. Although education improves economic growth and the welfare of people, it is unlikely to significantly alter the relationships within labour markets and by itself create sufficient jobs for every unemployed person. According to Autor, measures such as the EITC are more suited to creating some real financial incentives that induce people to work.

This is not to say that public training programmes should be abolished. Yet government should be selective in targeting the programmes to the right people. Government resources are scarce and should not be diverted away from where the real investment potential lies, namely the very young and universal education. In the future there is likely to be a strong increase in the demand for high-skilled labour in the service sectors. This will put further upward pressures on wages at the upper tail of the income distribution. In the light of the above, it may therefore perhaps be best to tax these people and redistribute the revenues to the poor. But as we have seen this comes at a cost, too.

So if there is a group or community of people that risks ending up in a state of 'learned helplessness', often a stigmatised group, and schooling can get these people into employment, then, even if it were inefficient to society as a whole, government might intervene. But only then. After all, public training programmes do not offer a full-scale remedy to labour market issues at hand. As Heckman (2000, p. 8) puts it: 'invest in the very young and improve basic learning and socialization skills; subsidize the old and severely disadvantaged to attach them to the economy and the society at large'.

7.5   BRIEF SUMMARY

This chapter has demonstrated that taxation can have a non-trivial effect on human capital formation. In an economy where production is carried out solely by unskilled labour and physical capital, then income tax creates two distortions: the intertemporal leisure-consumption choice is affected and also the intertemporal saving-consumption decision. When accounting for human capital accumulation and skilled labour, additional tax distortions occur.

A progressive income tax reduces the stock of human capital and distorts the human versus physical capital investment decision. Social safety policies have a similar effect by reducing labour supply and the return on human capital investment. Ultimately, the question is whether government grants sufficient subsidies for education to mitigate these distortions. However, education subsidies also produce perverse distributional side-effects, by primarily favouring upper-class high-ability people, while they are paid for by the average taxpayer.

One solution to address this deficiency is a so-called 'equity participation' scheme. Under such a scheme the government would lend the required study funds to a person wishing to pursue an education. After graduation the former student would pay a supplementary graduate tax on his or her earnings. The scheme would share the risk between the student and government and make students more cost aware. This creates an efficient platform with an equal prospect for everybody to develop their potential. Estimates show that the graduate tax could reduce government outlays on education significantly. However, the graduate tax on top of income tax also suggests larger work disincentives. An alternative solution, therefore, is an income-contingent loan system, which is a hybrid of both debt and equity financing.

Contrary to what is often believed, it is not low-skilled but middle-wage jobs that are likely to bear the consequences of globalisation and digitalisation. US labour market data reveal that relative wages at the lower end of the income distributions have actually increased over the past decade. Specific public training programmes to bridge the gap between low- and high-skilled labour are likely to be ineffective. An EITC may thus seem more appropriate to provide a real financial incentive to work. Better still would be to raise the general level of education in society. Schooling expands the pool of skilled workers, can make a country richer and mitigates the growing income gap between low- and high-skilled workers that is observed in many OECD economies. Moreover, Heckman (2000) argues convincingly for a shift in emphasis to early childhood education (4-5) where the payoff is high.

PART IV

Sustainable development

8.   Tax competition

> If you create a tax haven for a few people, you condemn the rest to a tax hell.
>
> (Mario Monti, former EU Commissioner for Competition)[1]

8.1   INTRODUCTION

The world economy and interaction between economic institutions in it has changed rapidly since the 1970s. This has serious consequences for workers and companies, which are facing increasing internationalisation. The costs of transportation and communication have declined rapidly, trade barriers have been removed and technological advance has made possible what could only be dreamed of before. Economic areas and agreements have been created that gradually allow more workers to move freely between jurisdictions in pursuit of job opportunities.

Global developments have also heightened dynamics on international capital markets spectacularly. Financial capital is highly mobile, as is most physical capital over the longer term. In the advent of globalisation, the impact of the tax system thus appears to be largest with regard to capital taxation, making it an increasingly problematic task for government. The tax literature discerns two branches of studies which somewhat provocatively assume that the long-run optimal capital income tax is zero. Both achieve this result via slightly different approaches.

Chapter 4 discussed optimal tax theory, which assumes perfect mobility of capital in the long run, so that owners of capital will not bear the burden of a tax. Capital investment is simply reduced or transferred abroad up to the point where the pre-tax rate of return is sufficient to fully compensate for the tax. In other words, the domestic capital stock declines so that due to diminishing returns the marginal return to investment increases (see Appendix 1). In a small open economy, this means that the after-tax return to investment should equate with the fixed world interest rate. In the process, productivity of relatively immobile factors of production falls (that is, labour

---

[1] Quoted on http://civitas.org.uk/eufacts/FSECON/EC3.htm (27 September 2006).

and land), thus implicitly shifting the tax, including any excess burden. The tax competition literature stresses the interaction between countries and their respective tax policies. Governments have an incentive to consistently undercut capital taxes below those in other countries to attract mobile foreign tax bases, in particular capital. This mechanism contributes to a 'race to the bottom' until an effective tax of zero is reached (the so-called 'Nash equilibrium').[2]

This chapter considers some of the key issues of tax competition and whether it is likely that we shall in the future witness a race to the bottom. The chapter starts with a theoretical underpinning of tax competition through a short discussion of the theory of fiscal federalism and Tiebout sorting, which stipulates that households and firms 'vote with their feet' and leave a particular jurisdiction if they feel that the level of taxation is too high. This is followed by an overview of the main (tax) issues encountered in the global economy. Next, comes an evaluation of the different forms of tax competition, that is, acceptable tax competition, harmful tax competition and tax harmonisation. The penultimate section focuses in particular on the EU, where the forces of tax competition are most clearly evident. The chapter concludes with a brief summary.

8.2 THE THEORY OF FISCAL FEDERALISM

Jurisdictions are characterised by different structures of government. Commonly distinguished are the independent nation state, unitary state, federation and confederation, with the first most integrated and the last least so. The form of economic and/or political integration strongly shapes the role of the tax and expenditure system.

The theory of fiscal federalism deals with the question to what levels of government are taxing powers most optimally attributed, a theory pioneered by Richard Musgrave. The relevance of fiscal federalism in economic policy making becomes particularly clear in stabilisation policy and when dealing with issues of tax competition. Despite different constitutional and government structures of countries, the theory provides useful guidelines in assigning powers of taxation. For example, an income tax may be more efficiently imposed at a central government level, whereas a tax on waste disposal is best handled by municipalities.

When it comes to economic policy making, similar considerations come into play. For a precise allocation and attribution of powers to tax income,

---

[2] See Zodrow (2005) for a discussion of capital mobility and taxation in small open economies. The 'race to the bottom' may instead be labelled a 'race to the top' as countries are forced to switch from the use of inefficient taxes to finance government to efficient taxation.

consumption and property, Musgrave (1983) has designed the following criteria, based on the principles of jurisdiction, efficiency and feasibility:

- taxing powers for business-cycle stabilisation should be attributed to a central level. Middle- and local-level taxes should be cyclically stable;
- tax bases that have low mobility between jurisdictions can best be taxed at middle or local levels;
- redistributive taxes should be implemented on a central level;
- progressive personal taxes with a global base should be implemented where this can be done most efficiently. This depends on the specific situation of each country;
- if a relatively unequal distribution of tax bases exists among middle and local jurisdictions, taxation should be implemented on a central level; and
- taxes that are based on the benefit principle and user charges are suitable at every level of government.

These criteria lead to the following attribution of taxing powers to levels of government. At a *central* level, integrated income and expenditure taxes as well as natural resource taxes and user charges can be levied; the *middle* level may impose resident and non-resident income taxes, a destination-type VAT or RST, natural resource taxes and user charges; and on a *local* level property and payroll taxes and user charges are best suited to raise the required revenues.

Tiebout: Voting with Our Feet

The theory of fiscal federalism has been developed further by Charles Tiebout (1956). The idea is that households and firms 'vote with their feet' and leave the jurisdiction of a particular tax authority if they feel they have to pay too much tax in relation to the public goods they enjoy in that jurisdiction. Hence, if culture and tastes differ from one jurisdiction to the next, spending will be different and thus the tax rates may be different.

On a local level, popular preferences can be more adequately reflected in public expenditures than at the federal or national level. This is a fundamental difference with federal or national-level expenditures. At the national level, voter preferences are more or less given and the government does its best to adjust to these preferences, while on a local level revenue and expenditure patterns are more or less fixed and the voter adjusts by moving. The voter picks the jurisdiction that best fits his or her preferences for public goods. The choice process of residents then determines an equilibrium provision of local public goods in accord with the taste of residents.

The Tiebout model is subject to a number of strict conditions. For example, it assumes that voters are perfectly mobile and free to choose their jurisdictions, have full knowledge and information and that there are a large number of jurisdictions where households and firms can choose to live and produce. This model has been shown to be most accurate in suburban areas where there are a large number of different independent communities.

BOX 8.1

The theory of 'fiscal federalism' deals with the question as to which levels of government taxing (and expenditure) powers can best be assigned. The Tiebout model stipulates that households and firms 'vote with their feet' and leave a particular jurisdiction for another if they feel they have to pay too much tax in relation to the public goods they enjoy.

8.3   TAX ISSUES IN AN INTEGRATING WORLD

Tiebout migration specifically refers to local communities and suburbs; however, the theory can be drawn into a wider context of nations as independent jurisdictions. Rapid technological change and growth of international trade have fostered a global integration of markets Enhanced opportunities for transportation and communication increasingly enable workers and companies to move freely between jurisdictions and to make well-informed (fiscal) decisions on such relocation beforehand.

Tax systems become ever more intertwined by interacting markets for production factors, that is, labour and especially capital, and product markets. Many factors complicate the design of tax policy in an economically integrated world. The problems that emerge are threefold (see Slemrod, 1990):

- flight of tax bases abroad as a result of high taxes and tax differentials between countries;
- jurisdiction or tax base entitlement: that is, the country awarded the right to tax and, consequently, where the revenue accrues; and
- enforcement and collection issues with regard to taxes that are imposed on tax bases located abroad.

From a macroeconomic perspective the resulting 'tax competition' is perhaps the most compelling. By consistently undercutting tax rates below those in other countries, governments compete by attracting certain tax bases.

BOX 8.2

Globalisation, that is the liberalisation of domestic and international markets for goods and services, workers, capital and technology leads to increasing international competition in several areas of the economy, including that of taxation. This has created additional concerns in tax design and policy making.

Labour Mobility across Countries

Labour migration in the EU is still limited, despite free movement of workers and a rising trend that can be observed (including the mobility of low-skilled workers, for example in the agriculture, construction and shipping sectors). Factors that impede cross-border movement of labour in the EU are cultural and language barriers, tax system differences, taxation of pension rights and eligibility for social benefits. In the case of secondment, expatriates, and frontier and migrant workers, tax-base allocation problems are usually resolved through bilateral double taxation conventions.[3] With close to 15 per cent of the population moving each year, geographical mobility in the US is much higher (source: US Census Bureau).[4]

Nearly all countries have tax arrangements in place to attract foreign workers and managers with certain specific or scarce skills. The tax breaks involve special tax deductions, partial exemptions and untaxed compensation. These are rationalised as maintaining international business competitiveness.

Foreign managers

To give a few examples, Australia included a measure to exempt foreign source income of temporary residents from its income tax and taxed capital gains on a non-resident basis in its 2005 budget. The Netherlands allows a deduction for foreign managers and expatriates of 30 per cent from income plus the additional compensation from living abroad. And the UK has a

---

[3] The right to levy social security premiums is enshrined in EU law (Regulation 1408/71).
[4] Boeri and Brücker (2005) calculate that a labour migration of 3 per cent from Eastern to Western Europe could increase total EU GDP by 0.5 per cent. These benefits grow over the years, and accrue to both West and East. Having said this, Sweden was the only country to allow full equal treatment of migrant workers in 2006. Denmark, Ireland and the UK also opened up their labour markets, but impose restrictions on employment-related social security.

highly simplified procedure of administration and compliance for internationally mobile employees.

Some countries are reducing the scope of the measures, many of which lead to complicated legislation and high administrative costs. Additionally, there is doubt about the intended efficacy. Experiences in OECD countries show that tax incentives to stimulate profit-related pay and 'employee ownership' can be successful. This involves a large group of ordinary employees who do not hold top positions. According to US studies, employee ownership improves operating profits (Blasi and Kruse, 1991; Rosen and Young, 1991). A more flexible wage base moderates wage demands, improves labour market functioning and increases employment. The European Commission is also a proponent of employee participation in enterprise profit and results (Uvalic, 1991).

Football players
Another field where tax competition practices are evident is the international soccer scene. A 2006 study by the international accountancy firm Ernst & Young found that of the 21 European countries surveyed, Norway is the most attractive for professional soccer players from a tax perspective. The career of professional soccer players is unique in that they typically quit before the age of 35, after which they face reduced earnings. A number of countries therefore have generous pension arrangements in place to safeguard future income. Table 8.1 shows the eight most-attractive countries for soccer players.

Table 8.1   Eight most-attractive countries for soccer players, 2006

Rank	Country	Rank	Country
1	Norway	5	Belgium
2	Netherlands	6	Denmark
3	Spain	7	Portugal
4	UK	8	Italy

Source: Ernst & Young website at http://www.ey.nl.

The UK, which ranked number one during a similar investigation in 2001, fell sharply due to the tightening of generous pension arrangements. This was the result of a new rule, which allows new players to receive pension payments only after the age of 50. The qualification age was previously only 35 years and it is soon to be raised even further to 55.

International Capital Market Integration

Globalisation and ICT have left a significant mark on capital markets in OECD countries. Investors and companies can acquire financial capital, transfer it across countries and change it into other currencies more easily than ever. Capital markets are thus increasingly interconnected and interdependent. Brooks and Catao (2000) have found that the correlation between price developments in European and American stock increased from 0.4 in the mid-1990s to 0.8 in 2000. In other words, 80 per cent of European stock price changes are determined on Wall Street.

But the effects appear to be more far-reaching. Rumours in China of a 20 per cent capital gains tax on stock investments played a role when world stock markets declined sharply at the end of February 2007. The crisis started when the Shanghai Stock Exchange fell by 9 per cent on 27 February following a rumour that the Chinese government could try to dampen stock speculation. The New York Stock Exchange tumbled, with the Dow Jones industrial average experiencing the largest losses (4.3 per cent) since the 11 September 2001.[5] European markets were also affected and dropped by an average of 3 per cent. The fall in stock prices around the world indicate how integrated the world economy already is and how China nowadays is a key player in the global economy.

Rapid increases in foreign investment
An important cause of these international spin-offs and interrelatedness is found in a skyrocketing of FDI in OECD countries in the post-Second World War era. The increase in FDI has been particularly visible since the 1990s, though. Between 1992 and 2005 the total OECD outflow of FDI quadrupled from 186 to 716 billion US dollars, with a peak of US$1,239 billion occurring in 2000. FDI inflow increased from 116 to 623 billion US dollars in the same period and peaked at US$1,239 billion in 2000 (OECD, 2006b).

Due to higher dynamics, investors have become more selective in choosing their investments. As a result, the costs of investment have to be recouped in a shorter period; in other words, investors demand a higher rate of return. The latter is affected by many elements, including systems of personal and corporate income taxation.

For government, the primary concern is the flight of capital that does not produce location-specific rents, that is, those rents are those that are generated by capital 'fixed' to a certain location. This may, for example, be the case for natural resources, a highly developed infrastructure providing access to markets or a specialised labour force. The location of investment importantly determines the distribution of income between countries. A larger capital stock enhances labour productivity, and increases wages as well

---

[5] Instability on the US housing and mortgage markets contributed to the drop of US stock prices.

as tax revenues for the government.[6] Investment abroad generally creates the opposite effects.[7] It gives governments the incentive to keep tax rates low compared to other countries in the hope of attracting FDI.

8.4   TAX COMPETITION IS TAKING PLACE

Tax competition works only if investors and companies are responsive to international taxation variations. If more sensitive to other factors in their location decision, such as market size and distance and skills of workforces, tax competition will not be fully realised. Gorter and Parikh (2000) estimate that an EU country on average increases its FDI position in another EU country by 4 per cent, if the latter country lowers its effective CT rate by 1 percentage point. This is much more than the average of 2 per cent that is obtained in other studies for non-EU countries. Furthermore, on the basis of empirical data, Altshuler and Goodspeed (2002) find that an EU country typically reduces its CT burden by 7.5 per cent in response to a 10 percent lower tax burden in neighbouring countries. This suggests that capital is relatively mobile within the EU and that the pressures from tax competition are real and acute.

Because of this relative mobility of capital, the CT takes centre stage in the discussion on tax competition and fiscal policy. Tax competition takes place principally along two dimensions. A weaker form involves a lowering of statutory CT rates, while a more pronounced form implies cuts in effective tax rates. Countries also compete by means of targeted business tax incentives, ruling practices and their network of bilateral tax treaties.

Statutory Tax Rates

Table 4.3 in Chapter 4 revealed that statutory CT rates have fallen in all sample countries during the 1985-2007 period, in some cases dramatically. The reductions range from a minimum of 10 percentage points in the UK to as much as 37.5 percentage points in Ireland. In line with theory, smaller countries have experienced bigger declines than larger countries (on average 22 percentage points in countries with ≤20 million inhabitants, against 16

---

[6] The case of Ireland is noteworthy. The country lowered its statutory CT rate to 12.5 per cent in 1999. In 1988, *The Economist* still referred to Ireland as the 'poorest of the rich'. Only 10 years later, the same periodical writes that the Celtic tiger serves as a 'shining light' and example to Europe. Of course, factors other than taxes also played a role, such as a relatively easy access to the east coast of the US, an English-speaking skilled labour force and considerable EU aid (see Walsh, 2000).

[7] Total (investment) income of a country may nevertheless increase if investors are able to undertake more-profitable investments abroad than at home. If the market allocates efficiently, this could generate higher returns which would more than offset the loss in wage income.

percentage points in countries with >20 million inhabitants). Smaller countries are presumed to be more susceptible than larger countries to tax competition, since the reallocation of a single investment project increases per capita revenue relatively more. In other words, the elasticity of the tax base is larger, which increases the incentives to undercut tax rates.

Table 8.2 displays similar developments for EU countries. In little more than 10 years, the average statutory tax rate in the old EU-15 has declined from 38.0 to 29.3 per cent. After the accession of the ten new member states, the average tax rate has declined further and currently stands at 24.7 per cent for the EU-25.

Moreover, in May 2007, the German parliament (Bundestag) accepted a proposal to lower the CT rate further to 29.8 per cent. The cost of the package totals €30 billion, of which approximately €22 billion is financed by base broadening and by self-financing from inducing higher compliance and economic activity (Bundesministerium der Finanzen, 2006). The remaining €8 billion is financed from general government funds. The reform should enter into force on 1 January 2008. The 2007 elected French President Nicolas Sarkozy in his campaign also vowed to cut French corporate taxes by €15 billion from 33.8 to 28 per cent.[8]

Effective Tax Rates

The empirical evidence on tax competition by average effective tax rates (AETRs) is mixed. Based on a sample of 60 countries in the EEC, Latin America and Asia, Grubert (2001) finds that AETRs fell by almost 10 percentage points between 1984 and 1992. As noted in Chapter 4, for the later period, 1990-2000, Gorter and de Mooij (2001) establish that effective tax rates on interest, dividend and retained profits have remained largely stable in the EU. Hence, the reduction of statutory rates has been accompanied by a broadening of tax bases and in so doing has left AETRs largely unaffected.

Moreover, despite base broadening, tax systems have become less neutral and did *not* converge. Hence, relative effective tax rates on dividends, retained profits and interest have diverged, largely because of increased overtaxation of dividend income in some countries (Austria, Belgium, Denmark, Ireland and the Netherlands) and overtaxation of retained earnings relative to the other variables in other countries (Finland, France, Germany, Italy, Sweden and the UK). No country overtaxes interest income.[9]

---

[8] In addition to this, he plans to mitigate tax flight of wealthy French with a law that limits the total tax levied on income to 50 per cent.
[9] See also Griffith and Klemm (2004) for a general overview of tax reforms and competition in OECD countries during the last 20 years.

Table 8.2   Corporate income tax rates in the EU-25, 1995-2007

Country	1995	2007	%-point change 1995-2007
Old EU-15			
Austria	34	25	-9
Belgium	40.2	34	-6.2
Denmark	34	28	-6
Finland	25	26	1
France	36.7	33.8	-2.9
Germany	56.8	38.3[b]	-18.5
Greece	40	29	-11
Ireland	40	12.5	-27.5
Italy	52.2	37.3	-14.9
Luxembourg	40.9	29.6	-11.3
Netherlands	35	25.5	-9.5
Portugal	39.6	27.5	-12.1
Spain	35	35	0
Sweden	28	28	0
UK	33	30	-3
New EU-10			
Czech Republic	41	24	-17
Cyprus	25	10	-15
Estonia	26	0	-26
Hungary	19.6	16	-3.6
Latvia	25	15	-10
Lithuania	29	15	-14
Malta	35	35	0
Poland	40	19	-21
Slovakia	40	19	-21
Slovenia	25	25	0
Average			
Old EU-15	38.0	29.3	
New EU-10	30.6	17.8	
EU-25[a]	35.0	24.7	

Notes:
[a] As noted, as of 1 January 2007 the EU encompasses 27 members.
[b] 30 per cent as of 2008.

Sources: European Commission (2004b) and Deloitte's Corporate Tax Rates at a Glance 2006: http://www.deloitte.com/dtt/cda/doc/content/2006_01_23%20Worldwide_CT_Rates_2006%281%29.pdf (downloaded 15 February 2007).

BOX 8.3

Statutory CT rates have been reduced in many countries. In the old EU-15, statutory CT rate on average declined from 38 to 29.3 per cent during the 1995-2007 period. With the accession of the new EU-10 countries, the average tax rate has declined further to 24.7 per cent. Evidence over the 1990-2000 period reveals that AETRs have remained largely stable, however, because of tax base broadening.

For the period after 2000, a number of reforms in EU countries can be observed where in addition to statutory rates, the effective CT burden has declined, for example with the Austrian (2004-05), Dutch (2007) and German (2000 and 2008) CT reforms.

Targeted Business Tax Incentives

Under the broad definition, countries compete not only by offering a favourable tax rate to stimulate investment, but also by granting certain tax allowances. These so-called 'targeted' or 'specific' business tax incentives include exemptions to the tax base, generous tax deductions or credits, favourable treatment of group taxation and/or financing activities. The incentives can have general scope or be targeted at eliciting certain specific investments. There are numerous examples of targeted business tax incentives in countries' tax codes that are frequently subject to change. For a dated overview of specific business tax incentives, see Baker and McKenzie (1999).[10] The Code of Conduct Group (2000) contains an elaborate list of targeted business tax incentives in the EU that were deemed harmful, most of which have now been phased out.

With regard to the incentive effect, a study by the European Communities (1975) concludes that tax incentives for specific investment do have a positive effect on investment volume. The tax incentives serve as a considerable temporary boost to the economy. After a while, other countries are likely to respond with similar incentives, which weaken the effect. The European Commission (2001a) finds that overall statutory tax rate differentials in the EU outweigh differences in the tax base, making the statutory tax rate a more important tax driver than the tax base in assessing a country's competitiveness.

---

[10] The report was commissioned by the Dutch Ministry of Finance and surveys differences in tax rates, tax systems, types of investment, methods of finance, distribution policy, labour intensity, special tax incentives and administrative practices in EU member states.

Ruling Practices of Tax Authorities

The role of MNCs in international trade and business has increased dramatically since the 1970s. In part this reflects the integration of economies and improved means for transport and communication. The difficulty is that the value of many goods, intangibles and services is hard to estimate as a result, so it is often not known where the real value of production accrues. Consider a pharmaceutical company that develops a drug at a research facility in the UK, subsequently produces it at a plant in France and sells it in Italy, while its company headquarters are located in Ireland. In such a setting it is extremely difficult if not impossible to determine where exactly the revenue accrues. The complexity of establishing internal pricing offers opportunities to both MNCs and tax administrations.

The tax climate for business investment is considerably affected by the practices of execution of the law of a country and the attitude of the relevant tax authority therein. A so-called 'advanced tax ruling' (ATR) gives tax authorities the power to enter into specific agreements with taxpayers.[11] When making an investment decision, firms attach great value to getting assurance in advance that a tax provision is applicable in a certain circumstance or not. Moreover, it is well known that some tax authorities have been more relaxed than others in giving such assurances beforehand.

Tax rulings can also be obtained to get assurance on arm's-length transfer pricing. As noted in Chapter 4, transfer prices are charged to settle intra-company transfers of goods, intangibles and services, for example between subsidiaries or branches. Empirical evidence suggests that companies manipulate prices in cross-border situations to shift revenues between related companies.

Tax authorities thus require prices to be calculated at arm's length, as if the companies were unrelated.[12] If the tax authority does not agree with the transfer price used, this may lead to double taxation. A number of countries offer the opportunity of obtaining an advanced pricing agreement (APA) to get assurance beforehand on the calculated price. Obtaining an APA is not mandatory and instead of obtaining an APA, firms may adopt a reporting position on transfer prices. However, the arm's-length nature of the price may then be questioned by the authorities. Firms therefore generally consider it a plus if they can get advanced certainty in a country.

---

[11] Details on ruling practices and conditions under which they are concluded by EU member states are provided in Baker and McKenzie (1999).

[12] Three methods are commonly used to apply the arm's-length principle. The *comparable uncontrolled price* (CUP) method compares the price charged for a commodity or service in a controlled situation to a comparable uncontrolled transaction; the *resale price* method deducts a certain gross margin from the price of a commodity or service sold to an independent party; and the *cost-plus* method which takes the price of a commodity or service purchased from an independent party and adds an appropriate mark-up to this.

Bilateral Tax Treaties between Countries

Finally, a wide and attractive network of tax treaties among countries makes it a viable proposition for companies that operate internationally to reallocate in order to take advantage of the treaty network. Bilateral tax treaties offer legal security and limit the amount of income tax that may be imposed by one treaty partner on residents of the other treaty partner. For example, tax treaties reduce withholding tax (WHT) rates on incoming or outgoing dividend, interest, and royalty payments, or even stipulate the absence of such taxes. Tax treaties also contain provisions that govern the creditability of foreign income tax imposed by a treaty country where certain income originates in calculating the tax owed on such income by residents of the other treaty country.

If country A has no or a less favourable tax convention with country C than country B, it could make sense for a company in country A that does business in country C, to set up a company in country B and have profits flow through there. Such 'treaty shopping' in practice significantly improves the attractiveness of a country in which to locate.

International Tax Planning Practices

To make a well-informed investment decision, companies nowadays more frequently engage in 'tax planning', thus reviewing the tax implications of an international investment decision beforehand, instead of calculating the effective tax burden afterwards. A good tax lawyer is capable of combining opportunities in country tax codes (also called 'loopholes') and so designing a scheme that is legally permissible, but which reduces a multinational's tax bill significantly by shuffling money between (foreign) subsidiaries with no or low tax consequences. The most commonly used vehicles for this purpose include:

- holding companies (for example, to structure foreign assets);
- financial services companies (for example, for on-lending activities); and
- royalty companies (for example, to deal with income from intellectual property).

These companies play an important role in centralising management over (foreign) subsidiaries, structuring internal group services such as financial services, facilitating advertising, managing currency risks and dealing with dividend and royalty payments in a tax-efficient manner.[13]

---

[13] An intermediate foreign holding company is generally established under a trust company, which takes on the management and executive powers of the company and acts on their behalf.

The companies are established in countries with low effective CT rates and/or no or low WHT rates on (outgoing) dividend, interest and royalty payments. Profits then flow through these countries and are subject to very low taxation. Nevertheless, the gains to the domestic economy are sizeable. The sheer volume of the tax base, that is, hundreds or thousands of billions of euros/dollars passing through bank accounts annually, means that despite the low tax rate, the revenues to government are large. The economy also benefits from incremental employment, mainly highly skilled lawyers, tax advisers and accountants, and other economic activity such as in the hotel and catering industry when foreign investors fly in to meet their consultants.

These practices create a highly dynamic playing field where dividends, interest and royalties are funnelled all over the world to wherever tax laws and treaties are most accommodating. The playing field is subject to changes on a daily basis.

The Rolling Stones and Dutch royalty companies

The world famous British rock group the Rolling Stones has managed to keep its tax bill low by channelling royalties through the Netherlands instead of having them directly allocated to the UK. In accordance with its hit song 'Gimme Shelter', the band has paid less than 2 per cent in taxes on nearly $0.5 billion in earnings over the past 20 years. This rate stands in stark contrast to the top British income tax rate of 40 per cent.

Likewise, the Irish rock band U2 is estimated to have accumulated a net worth of nearly $0.9 billion over the years. It has now relocated its headquarters (and its profitable master tapes) from Dublin to Amsterdam. For similar reasons, the giant record label EMI, the Elvis Presley estate and soccer player and icon David Beckham have set up in the Netherlands.[14] MNCs such as Coca Cola, Ikea, Gucci and Nike use similar tax shelter schemes.

The incoming royalties are exempt under most Dutch bilateral tax agreements and the Netherlands does not impose a WHT on outgoing royalty payments (there is no WHT on outgoing interest, either). Hence, the payments flow through the royalty company free of WHT.[15] And although a CT of 25.5 per cent applies, this rate is brought down considerably by requiring only a modest spread (that is, profit margin) on royalty payments that flow through Dutch special companies. The profit margin is reduced

---

The work mainly involves a number of statutory acts such as filing the company's annual statements with the commercial trade register and ordering the audit of the books.

[14] The examples are taken from the New York Times article of 4 February 2007: 'The Netherlands, the New Tax Shelter Hot Spot'.

[15] To be eligible for treaty benefits, Dutch tax law does dictate 'substance requirements'. For example, at least half of the statutory directors need to be resident or situated in the Netherlands; key management decisions must be taken and books and bank accounts maintained in the country.

further by deductible expenses such as trust and director costs, and fees for legal and tax advice and auditing. The companies are usually associated with an offshore company, for example, in the Caribbean, to ensure a tax-efficient outflow of profits.

The favourable tax treatment of intellectual property rights makes it attractive for artists and athletes to settle in the Netherlands.

The Belgian tax call

The Belgian government is currently in the process of phasing out its coordination centres to comply with EU law. The operation has to be completed by 2010. The business tax incentive was enacted in 1982 to restore Belgium's international economic credibility and competitiveness, and offers several tax advantages. The most important is a relaxed profit determination that brings down the effective tax rate to 2 per cent. In 2004, 213 of these centres were still active, generating 18,000 to 20,000 mostly high-skilled jobs. The joint value of capital sheltered in these centres was €147 billion.

In its place, a 'notional interest deduction' (NID) has been introduced to reinforce the country as an attractive location for local and international investors (enacted on 1 January 2006, with an estimated budgetary cost of roughly €500 million). The measure allows companies to offset a certain percentage of equity capital (that is, so-called 'risk capital') against taxable income. The deduction is calculated by multiplying equity by a percentage determined by the government based on the interest rate on 10-year government bonds (as an indication, the basic rate for tax year 2007 is around 3.4 per cent). Depending on the characteristics of a company (that is, financial structure), this should bring down the statutory tax rate of 33.99 per cent significantly. The new rules should also encourage capital-intensive investments and ensure more-neutral treatment of debt and equity finance.

The Belgian authorities are promoting its NID internationally. The NID makes it very attractive to companies with surplus cash to have a financial company in Belgium. Neighbouring countries are feeling the effect: several Dutch, French and German companies have set up in Belgium. The promotion has even extended to Russia, which nowadays is an attractive market for these kinds of tax accommodation. The top 500 wealthiest Russians have accumulated an astounding net worth of roughly €425 billion in little more than a decade.

Swiss tax incentives for companies and private property

In a similar vein, MNCs such as Google, Procter & Gamble, L'Oréal, and Colgate-Palmolive have moved their European headquarters to Switzerland, which traditionally offers a very competitive tax environment and is a well-established location for regional or global MNC headquarters. The Swiss tax structure is characterised by a high degree of decentralisation. A number of Cantons have just revised their tax laws and reduced their CT rates. Local

Cantons such as Zug and Schwyz completely or partially exempt profits generated abroad from tax. Effective CT rates are often well below 10 per cent, which creates strong tax incentives and an attractive fiscal climate for businesses to locate their headquarters, distribution and coordination centres.

The Swiss have also negotiated access to some of the key EU benefits such as the Parent-Subsidiary and Interest-Royalties directive, which reduce WHT on dividend, interest and royalty payments between EU member states and Switzerland to zero. This makes it very lucrative for MNCs to actually locate their headquarters in the country and reduces the need for intermediary holding or finance companies.[16]

The problematic part is that certain company tax regimes of Swiss cantons differentiate between domestic and foreign source income. This discrimination may directly or indirectly affect business competitiveness and distort trade between Switzerland and other countries. This has led the European Commission (2007a) to initiate action against Switzerland. Because the country is sovereign to determine its own tax rates and is not subject to EU law, the Commission has had to take an alternative route by considering the tax regimes as a form of disguised state aid incompatible with a 1972 free-trade agreement between the EU and Switzerland. The Swiss reject the European stance.

Tax migration of rich individuals
The favourable fiscal climate also triggers the migration of the wealthy, mostly older or retired workers. For example, since moving to Switzerland, French pop-star Johnny Hallyday pays less than 10 per cent of the tax bill he faced in France. For similar reasons, singer and composer Phil Collins, Formula one champion Michael Schumacher and Ikea owner Ingvar Kamprad have moved to Switzerland. Revenue losses to national tax authorities are substantial.

8.5   ACCEPTABLE TAX COMPETITION

The fallout from tax competition frequently evokes negative reactions from politicians, particularly in larger economies, which suffer from flight to tax havens. It can affect both physical capital such as production plants and equipment as well as financial capital in the form of savings investment. In an effort to retain these tax bases, governments are induced to undercut taxes to 'competing' countries, leaving them with less revenue for the treasury.

---

[16] Swiss tax law does not mandate substance requirements such as real business activity, personnel or an office. In principle, therefore, the only presence there could take the form of a pure holding company at a trust company's address.

It is generally considered more advantageous to initiate tax competition, than to deal with it in response to developments elsewhere. Countries that initiate tax competition benefit from additional investment until equilibrium is reached again. By itself, tax competition is relatively favourable to capital-exporting countries compared to capital-importing countries (Bovenberg, 1990). Tax competition keeps the tax burden on capital in all countries relatively low, which is especially favourable to those countries with a lot of capital invested abroad.

Moreover, the incentive to undertax is greater for smaller than for larger countries since the relative revenue gain from attracting additional investment is larger for these countries (Kanbur and Keen, 1993). In other words, the elasticity of the tax base is perceived to be higher. Baldwin and Krugman (2001) have also argued that the advantages related to agglomerations and a large 'home' market means that it matters to companies whether a country is in the core of Europe (Benelux, France, Germany and Italy) or in the periphery (Greece, Ireland, Portugal and Spain). As a result, firms are not necessarily inclined to relocate, even if effective tax rates in the periphery are somewhat lower than in the core.

Measures Having a Generic Effect

Not all tax competition is necessarily bad or undesirable, though, and a distinction needs to be drawn between 'acceptable' or 'fair' tax competition, and 'harmful' tax competition.

Each country is sovereign and free to determine its own level of taxation and tax mix used to collect the revenue. Based on voter preferences, one country will choose a high level of government involvement while another will opt for a relatively minor one. This reflects on public goods and services supplied. High-tax countries often have an excellent infrastructure, a skilled labour force and a first class judicial system that guarantees a secure investment climate. All are attractive characteristics to foreign investors.

Hence, an overall high level of taxation does not imply that an economy cannot compete on world markets. As EU Commissioner for taxation László Kovács has pointed out, Finland ranked the most competitive economy in the world in 2005 and did so for three years in a row. Based on the Competitiveness Ranking of the World Economic Forum, the US came second, and Sweden and Denmark third and fourth, respectively. Yet all three Nordic countries have tax to GDP ratios significantly over 40 per cent, Sweden even over 50 per cent.[17] The Commissioner therefore argues: 'it is up

---

[17] Although effective CT rates are ultimately relatively low in these countries, both measured by micro-forward and backward-looking approaches.

to governments to offer the best value for the money of domestic and foreign investors' (Kovács, 2005, p. 3).[18]

Leviathan Monsters?

The literature presents two different views on tax competition (Edwards and Keen, 1996). Under the first view it is argued that tax competition erodes the tax base, leaving no room for government to maximise national welfare. Twenty years ago, Zodrow and Mieszkowski (1986) were already assuming that the 'race to the bottom' would undermine the public provision of goods and services. Since all mobile factors are able to escape taxation by moving abroad, this development could result in the tax burden mostly being shifted onto labour. Ultimately, there should be no room left for the redistributive function of the tax system.

The second view takes quite the opposite stance by claiming that tax competition counterbalances the inclination of governments to increase their spending. This view is held by those who view governments as Leviathan monsters that need to be restrained in their perpetual hunger for more government spending. Tax competition thus forces a more-efficient use of the tax system. Governments around the world increasingly tend to follow this latter view when it comes to tax competition bearing on the overall level of taxation. It should also to some degree enable countries to autonomously compensate for certain competitive disadvantages related to, for example, geographical location, such as remoteness, lack of accessible seaports or fewer natural resources.

BOX 8.4

A certain level of tax competition not only enables governments to follow their individual policy course and to set the required level of taxation, but it could also facilitate a more-efficient distribution in the tax mix used for collecting the required revenue and restrain the tendency for government to be too big.

It is difficult to imagine that international markets will fully clear and allocate efficiently. Numerous imperfections are likely to inhibit the race to the bottom. In that case, a certain tax competition may be desirable since it forces governments to more optimally utilise a number of relatively fixed tax bases that have not yet been fully 'exploited' from an efficiency point of

---

[18] The 21st-century trends and issues discussed in Chapter 2 will nevertheless make it more difficult for countries with a high level of taxation to compete on world markets.

view. Shifting to a consumption tax could in itself be beneficial to economic development. These considerations are reinforced by influential studies that argue that the tax on capital income (where tax competition of course really bites) should be zero on efficiency grounds; this is also seen from the perspective of non-capital owners (see Chapter 4).

8.6 HARMFUL TAX COMPETITION

Tax competition is harmful if measures are specific and targeted at foreign tax bases without affecting the national tax base. The measures create numerous tax distortions and, if left unchecked, lead to a needless erosion of the tax base. Other nations are compelled to adapt their tax system in a way that is detrimental to both national and worldwide economic welfare by having to shift to less-mobile bases such as labour, consumption and property.

Harmful tax practices come in two main categories (OECD, 1998). In the first place there are countries that hardly impose any taxation or offer offshore regimes for non-resident individuals or businesses. They allow non-residents to make use of their territory and financial systems to escape taxation at home. These so-called 'tax havens' have a strong power of attraction on internationally operating companies and wealthy individuals and manage to finance whatever expenditures they make by attracting foreign tax bases.

Since revenue is highly dependent on attracting foreign investment with the favourable tax regime, tax havens have little or no interest in reducing harmful tax practices. A *narrow* definition thus concerns jurisdictions that impose low nominal tax rates or have no taxation at all. Traditionally well-known tax havens are in the Caribbean (for example, Anguilla, Aruba, Barbados, Bahamas, Bermuda, British Virgin Islands and Cayman Islands); and also include the Channel Islands in Europe (Guernsey, Jersey), and Monaco, Liechtenstein and Malta in Europe.

The revenue leakage inflicted by tax havens is difficult to quantify. However, a study by the US Senate estimated that the revenue loss to the IRS could be as large as \$40-\$70 billion (Owens, 2006). This presents a considerable drain of public resources. Irish tax authorities, moreover, recently recovered some €900 million in back taxes from its residents who had been evading taxes by using Channel Island banks. Similarly, the UK expects to collect £1.9 billion from offshore evasion.

A much large number of countries impose a 'normal' rate of taxation, but have special features in their tax systems that can be considered harmful. A *broad* definition of tax competition covers countries with relatively high tax rates, but special tax incentives in place whereby the effective burden on targeted businesses is low or even nil. This also applies to jurisdictions within a federation. A well-known example is the US state of Delaware, which has very favourable tax rules for companies.

Jurisdictions categorised under the broad definition should have an interest in reducing harmful tax practices and partaking in concerted action since they too are exposed to the perils of tax havens and erosion of the tax base.

Perception of Tax Competition in the US

The attitude of US states towards targeted business tax incentives and state aid to attract 'foreign' tax bases and company investment is noteworthy. State aid by governments aims to provide support by granting subsidies or tax benefits only to certain companies. While state aid is generally considered arbitrary and economically undesirable, so that fiscal state aid rules aim to discourage it by imposing quite prohibitive restrictions, it is more or less accepted that US states compete on special business tax incentives.[19]

An interesting example is a Kansas state law that came into effect in 2003 (see Luja, 2006). The law provided a significant tax break for companies that had invested at least $1 billion, would invest another $0.5 billion, create 4,000 new jobs and pay $600 million in wages. The conditions were so strict that only one company fulfilled them, namely Boeing which was planning to build a new plant. In the end the factory was built in the state of Washington, which offered a more favourable deal with a tax break of $250 million for a period of 5 years, to be increased to $3 billion in 20 years. With it came an investment of a couple of hundred million dollars, roughly 17,000 new jobs and thousands of jobs guaranteed.

Specific tax competition can thus be rewarding for local governments. It is also more or less accepted by US legislatures. Moreover, the above example of targeted tax incentives is not an isolated case, and the practice is more widespread (for an overview of incentives, see Smith 1999a and 1999b).

A few individual taxpayers have started to defy these targeted business tax incentives in court by undertaking legal action, for example, in the case of Cuno v. Daimler-Chrysler, where a Miss Cuno challenged a generous tax break granted to the German-American automobile producer Daimler-Chrysler.[20] In anticipation of other such cases, the US Congress has proposed a law that seeks to give US States autonomy to compete with one another and 'provide certain tax incentives to any person for economic development

---

[19] The current debate in the US focuses on reinforcing the competitive position in response to fears that the CT system in itself contributes to a loss of jobs and outsourcing of production activities to the 'exterior' world. The proposals for CT reform are discussed in US Joint Economic Committee (2005b): a consumption-based tax system, integration of individual and corporate income taxes, expensing, a reduction in the CT rate, elimination or reform of the corporate alternative minimum tax or complete elimination of corporate tax.

[20] US Court of Appeals for the Sixth Circuit, *Cuno et al. v. Daimler-Chrysler et al.*, no. 01-3960, 19 October 2004.

purposes'.[21] The law should safeguard the situation whereby US States in the future implement targeted business tax incentives, at their own discretion, aimed at both attracting specific out-of-state business activity and inducing specific in-state companies to stay put.

EU and US Attitudes towards Targeted Tax Competition

Within the EU, the rules of state aid laid down in Article 87 of the EC treaty are more prohibitive when it comes to setting individual tax policies and awarding tax benefits.[22] As a rule, EU countries cannot offer tax advantages to certain enterprises or branches. The ECJ is quick to clamp down on any tax measures that go against the 'four freedoms', that is, free movement of goods, services, persons and capital. The ECJ also guards against (fiscal) state aid in EU countries that hinders fair trade in the internal EU market.

If we compare the EU to the US, American states have much more latitude for using specific business tax subsidies to attract investment. The EU remains far more aloof in this regard. Graetz and Warren (2006) note that experiences with tax competition between US states demonstrate that is it not necessary, or even necessarily desirable, to restrict EU member states in their effort to stimulate their economies by means of targeted tax benefits.

Mainly for budgetary reasons, it is important that both the European Commission and the Council of the EU should make stringent efforts to prevent a 'race to the bottom'.[23] Several EU members are none the less of the opinion that certain exceptions to the tax base are not as harmful as suggested by current EU actions and existing attitudes towards competition by EU institutions. Strict application of the rules of state aid, *per se*, may be detrimental to the long-run economic development of the EU (Vermeend, 1996; Weber, 2006).

In May 2007, Germany published a report on state aid that also argued for more lenient EU policy in permitting member states to grant (fiscal) state aid to new companies and investors. According to the report, globalisation has increased competition on world markets. Since non-EU states have fiscal measures to attract business activity, this means that EU member states will start losing investment to countries outside the EU if they are disallowed from using similar measures. So far, the German plan has received insufficient backing from other member states to be implemented.

---

[21] The Economic Development Act of 2005, S. 1066 / H.R. 2471. The bill has now been referred to the House Subcommittee on Commercial and Administrative Law and is awaiting a number of important Supreme Court rulings on the matter.

[22] See the website of the Commission for a complete overview of past state aid cases at http://ec.europa.eu/comm/competition/state_aid/register.

[23] De Mooij (2005, p. 296) argues that the future of corporate taxation in the EU largely depends on whether it succeeds in coordinating the various systems. If not, 'tax competition will put a severe strain on corporate tax policy and probably even on the effective taxation of capital income more generally'.

The gaming industry in France

To give an example, in November 2006 the European Commission (2006c) opened a formal investigation into the French proposal to grant a tax credit aimed at stimulating video game development. The measure would permit video game parlours a credit of 20 per cent, mainly in response to growing international competition from the US and Asian countries. According to the French government, such a credit should be allowed as it aims to promote culture.[24] The credit would be bound by certain criteria, in particular that the video games satisfy a test of quality, be original and contribute to the expression of European cultural diversity and creativity.

Nevertheless, EU Commissioner for Competition Neelie Kroes has stated: 'we must be sure that the measure will promote only genuine cultural projects and that it will not have the effect of an industrial policy instrument in favour of the video games sector' (ibid.). If the French tax credit were to fall under the rules of state aid, this would most certainly damage the competitive position of the industry, while the economic harm done by the measure to intra-community competition would seem relatively minor.[25]

8.7   COORDINATION OF TAX POLICY ACROSS COUNTRIES

To curb the harmful effects of tax competition in today's increasingly borderless world, it can be more beneficial to coordinate tax policy across countries to reduce economic distortions and permit an efficient revenue collection. Countries are working ever more closely to prevent abuses of global financial and tax systems. This involves making a subtle trade-off between tax competition and harmonisation.

Tax coordination does not necessarily imply full harmonisation. It can take several forms. For instance, a minimum rate may be agreed upon (Kanbur and Keen, 1993). Such a measure was advocated for the EU by German legislators in response to the Irish overall reduction in the CT rate to 12.5 per cent. Countries may also agree to harmonise the tax base, leaving tax rates to fluctuate and adapt to specific revenue needs.[26] In an effort to reduce harmful tax competition, two noteworthy projects have been initiated.

---

[24] Indeed, measures related to culture and heritage conservation are deemed compatible with EU rules if they do not unduly affect competition and trade within the Union.

[25] By the end of 2007, the EU determined the measure constitutes a cultural arrangement and that France is allowed to apply the subsidy.

[26] This is what the 6th directive (77/388/EEC) achieved when harmonising VAT in the EU. The measure was deemed necessary to support the implementation of the internal market. As noted in Chapter 5, with the abolition of border controls in 1992 a so-called 'transitional system' for coordinating cross-border supplies and acquisitions within the EU was adopted. In the US,

The OECD's 'Forum on Harmful Tax Practices'

The OECD's Forum on Harmful Tax Practices has global scope. It was set up following the OECD's 1998 report on harmful tax competition. Its focus lies on harmful tax measures related to the financial and service activities of both OECD and non-OECD member countries. Special attention is given to the harmful tax practices of tax havens. To identify harmful tax measures, similar principles apply as put forward in the EU Code of Conduct (see discussion below).

The forum promotes the implementation of the principles of transparency and exchange of information, although OECD economies retain sovereignty in national tax affairs, and apply their own tax laws. To encourage exchange of information, a special working group has developed a 'Model Agreement on Exchange of Information on Tax Matters'. The document contains two model agreements, which aim to ensure a minimum standard in effective exchange of information and cooperation between participating countries and respective tax authorities in both civil and criminal tax matters.

In an evaluation in 2000, a forum subcommittee identified 47 preferential tax regimes in OECD member states on the basis of the established criteria (OECD, 2000c). The regimes were subdivided into nine categories: Insurance, Financing and Leasing, Fund Managers, Banking, Headquarter regimes, Distribution Centre Regimes, Service Centre Regimes, Shipping and Miscellaneous Activities. The selection was based on self-reviews and cross-examinations by OECD member states. Furthermore, the committee produced a preliminary list of 35 non-OECD member states that met the so-called 'tax haven criteria'. The OECD and participating countries subsequently went to work on this.

In 2004 a progress report was published, which found that 18 of the 47 harmful regimes in OECD member countries had been ended, 14 had been amended so as to take out harmful components and 13 were pronounced not harmful after further evaluation. Moreover, 33 non-OECD countries had by then agreed to greater transparency and committed themselves to an exchange of information (mostly under sanctioning pressures from larger countries such as the US and other 'defensive measures' implemented by OECD member countries). According to the report only five countries remain on the list of 'Uncooperative Tax Havens': Andorra, Liechtenstein, Liberia, Monaco and the Marshall Islands.[27] The OECD is working with these countries to obtain future commitments in the relevant areas.

A progress report in 2006 finally concluded that all 47 potentially harmful tax regimes and preferential tax regimes introduced after 2000 had been

---

concerns have also been expressed on cross-border trade with Canada and Mexico as well as internally between states (for example, regarding interstate cigarette smuggling).

[27] Andorra, Liechtenstein and Monaco have chosen to participate under the EU Savings Directive (see below).

withdrawn or were no longer a threat. The Committee thereby considered that this part of the project had achieved its initial objectives.

The road ahead

However, issues surrounding internationally harmful tax practices are far from resolved. A 2006 OECD Forum conference in Seoul, attended by representatives of the tax authorities of 35 countries, concluded that international (offshore) non-compliance of corporations and aggressive tax planning is of growing concern (Owens, 2006). Consensus was reached that to curb these practices governments need to aim at stricter penalties, strengthen information exchange and enforcement and create awareness with corporate boards of MNCs of the risks attached to hard-line tax planning and their social responsibility.

BOX 8.5

Top management and supervisory boards of international corporations should take on greater direct social responsibility in the use of harmful tax planning strategies and tax havens to reduce their tax bill. Governments should encourage this as well as alertness to (new) harmful tax planning schemes. By communicating concerns with certain schemes, corporate boards become more aware of financial and reputational risks of aggressive tax planning.

The EU 'Code of Conduct for Business Taxation'

In a Code of Conduct for Business Taxation, the EU has developed several criteria for evaluating whether a specific tax measure that imposes an effective level of tax significantly below the general level is considered to be harmful.[28] The document is not legally binding, but it carries some political weight. While it has formally been adopted only by EU member states, the provisions can serve as guidelines elsewhere. The criteria for identifying potentially harmful measures include (European Council, 1998):

- an effective level of taxation which is significantly lower than the general level of taxation in the country concerned;
- tax breaks that are reserved for non-residents or for transactions carried out with non-residents;

---

[28] The Commission is working in the area of transfer pricing. A second EU Code of Conduct on transfer pricing has been adopted to prevent double taxation resulting from member states not accepting each other's arm's length transfer price (European Commission, 2005a).

- the existence of a so-called 'ring-fencing mechanism'. This means that tax advantages are provided for activities that are isolated from the domestic economy and therefore do not affect the national tax base;
- tax advantages that are granted without any real economic activity or economic presence in the country considered;
- accounting rules for profit determination for tax purposes that depart from internationally accepted standards, particularly those approved by the OECD; and
- a lack of transparency, especially when legal provisions can be relaxed at an administrative level in a non-transparent manner.

The first condition speaks for itself. The International Financial Services Centre (IFSC) legislation in Ireland confers tax benefits only to non-residents setting up business in a certain area of Dublin and is illustrative of the second situation.[29] Offshore provisions granting tax advantages to companies that register and locate in a jurisdiction (often a sunny island), but not actually produce there fall under the third condition. Since tax advantages can also be granted if the company presence takes the form of a mailbox, the fourth condition captures the case where not even an administrative or secretarial staff would be present.

The final two criteria mainly cover specific transfer-pricing agreements and ruling practices. It is not uncommon for these agreements to be favourable to foreign firms as compared to standard tax treatments. The ruling practice has been subject to various changes in recent years in an attempt to curb harmful tax practices. With regard to transfer-pricing agreements, guidelines have now been set up by the OECD.[30]

Diaw and Gorter (2002) have suggested that the Code of Conduct may, unintentionally, actually aggravate tax competition between member states. Not allowed to compete through specific tax measures, governments could be forced to use generic CT cuts as an instrument to attract foreign investment. As a result, tax revenue from corporate taxes may ultimately be even lower than without the Code of Conduct (Table 8.2 confirmed that CT rate declined markedly in the period).

---

[29] Under the IFSC tax regime in the 1980s and early 1990s, companies involved in manufacturing activities, established in the IFSC and operating in the Shannon Free Zone, a 2.43 square kilometre international business park benefited from a reduced corporation tax of 10 per cent. The regime was replaced by the introduction of a single CT rate of 12.5 per cent in 1999 and is to be fully phased out by the end of 2005.

[30] See the OECD's 'Transfer Pricing Guidelines for Multinational Enterprises and Tax Administrations 1995/1997'. The transfer-pricing guidelines were first issued in 1979 and have become internationally respected since. They are updated periodically.

Standstill and rollback
Under the Code, EU member states have committed themselves to a 'standstill' with regard to introducing new harmful tax measures (which range from laws and regulations to administrative practices). It also provides for a 'rollback' of existing harmful measures. This process is guided by the Code of Conduct Group.[31] In an effort to identify harmful tax practices, the Group evaluated 271 potentially harmful measures and gave 'a positive evaluation' to 66 them; 40 were implemented in EU member states, three in Gibraltar and 23 in dependencies or associated territories (Code of Conduct Group, 2000).[32] Many have since been or are currently in the process of being phased out.

Banking secrecy and exchange of information
In addition to the Code of Conduct conditions, banking secrecy and the refusal of effective exchange of information in tax-related matters can be considered harmful. Information reporting ensures that governments can enforce their tax law even in the case of cross-border activity. Countries that are reluctant to provide information may be attractive to foreign investors seeking to shield their assets from domestic tax authorities. Banking secrecy often provides a more formal justification for countries to be less than transparent.

A more subtle distinction needs to be made. Reducing harmful tax practices does not mean that countries should not be allowed any form of banking secrecy at all. Banking secrecy may provide valuable protection and guarantees when it comes to privacy matters. As argued above, it falls under a country's sovereignty to choose to observe banking secrecy. Even so, this should not stand in the way of an effective exchange of information in tax-related matters. Judicial systems in developed nations are nowadays fully equipped to ensure the rights of citizens without absolute or unconditional banking secrecy. Moreover, countries such as Switzerland have already amended their banking secrecy policy in the case of criminal conduct and money laundering. By excluding tax-related information from banking secrecy and guaranteeing exchange of information, a level playing field is ensured.

The Savings Directive as a middle way
The Savings Directive (2003/48/EC) was implemented as a compromise between countries favouring exchange of information and those keen on maintaining banking secrecy. Under the directive, EU member states have

---

[31] The Code of Conduct Group is headed by UK Paymaster General Dawn Primarolo, and, hence is referred to as the Primarolo Group.
[32] This shows that the code reaches beyond EU borders. These territories include the islands of Jersey, Guernsey, Aruba, the Netherlands Antilles, Isle of Man and the British Virgin Islands. Many of these jurisdictions are, or were regarded as, tax havens.

committed themselves to adopting a system of information reporting. During a transitional period member states may, however, opt to impose a WHT on interest payments to foreign investors. This obligates them to levy a WHT of 15 per cent in the first 3 years of the agreement, to be increased to 20 per cent in the 3 years thereafter. The rate will finally settle at 35 per cent. The taxpayer can also grant permission for disclosure of the relevant information to the tax administration in his or her resident state. In such a case, no WHT is applied.

The directive also requires that 75 per cent of the associated revenue collected is to be remitted to the resident state of the investor (the remaining 25 per cent serves as compensation to the non-resident state for the cost of administration). The WHT of 35 per cent approaches the domestic tax rate in many countries, thereby reducing the incentive for investors to transfer their assets to countries 'protected' by banking secrecy. Only Austria, Belgium and Luxembourg have opted for the WHT regime. Other countries have chosen to apply the system of information sharing. So far non-EU member countries Switzerland, Andorra, Liechtenstein, Monaco and San Marino have also chosen to adopt equivalent measures as laid down in the directive.

Ultimately, full exchange of information will be more efficient than a WHT arrangement (Keen and Ligthart, 2004). This ensures that taxpayers fall within the scope of the tax system in the resident state, which is likely to impose higher taxes than under a WHT regime. Residence-based taxation also promotes an efficient allocation of investment, but only if all countries are participating.

The Process of Harmonisation in the EU

The above discussion demonstrates that cooperation in the form of exchange of information can yield positive results. While tax competition enables governments to set their policies independently, tax coordination allows them to better enforce their tax laws in spite of cross-border activity. More effective revenue collection means that countries can shift their attention to policies that promote economic growth and employment.

The work of the OECD has diminished the threat of harmful tax competition for the US on an international scale. The US economy was relatively large and thus vulnerable to the adverse effects of tax competition from smaller states. In Europe, the issues are of a different nature. The EU is currently making considerable progress in several areas of the Internal Market. According to Commission President José Manuel Barroso (2006), the main aim is to create economic growth and jobs. While the process of integration continues, the interaction between tax policies of member states becomes more compelling.

However, in the case of direct taxation, matters are still principally in the hands of the individual member states. MNCs face up to 27 different tax authorities in meeting their tax obligations. This creates several economic distortions and inefficiencies. All 27 member states are geographically close and well connected to one another, so on a macroeconomic level relatively large capital flows may be set in motion by tax differentials.

BOX 8.6

   Progress has been made by both the OECD and EU in eliminating harmful tax practices by working together and jointly applying political force to jurisdictions that are less inclined to reduce harmful practices (tax havens). Tax evasion is discouraged and the use of tax-planning and tax avoidance schemes is reduced. A level playing field is thereby created for more 'fair' tax competition. The so-called 'tax package' whereby countries compete becomes more important. Central factors are the total tax burden; the tax mix; statutory and effective tax rates; specific tax incentives for businesses and workers; advanced tax rulings between taxpayer and tax authority; and the network of tax treaties with other countries (see Chapter 10 for a summary of issues).

The Bolkestein Report

The European Commission (2001a and 2001b) has carried out an extensive study on corporate taxation in the EU, known as the 'Bolkestein' Report.[33] This report computes the effective CT rate of member states according to the Devereux and Griffith method. It also identified the main tax obstacles to cross-border activity to be the requirement to use arm's length profit allocation rules through transfer pricing, limited or no loss offsetting for related companies in other member states, group restructuring which often provokes capital gains taxation, and double taxation that results from overlapping tax rights in the case of cross-border income payments.

   The Bolkestein Report has pointed to the high cost of compliance and administration. MNCs that operate in the EU deal with up to 27 different tax regimes and systems of financial reporting. This is a major difference with the US where one system of generally accepted accounting principles (US GAAP) applies uniformly. All EU member states have different administrative arrangements, reporting requirements and intricate networks of tax treaties. The differences in formal procedures impose a significant burden on internationally operating businesses. The requirements of transfer

---

[33] Frits Bolkestein was former EU Commissioner for the Internal Market (1999-2004). The Bolkestein report followed up on the Ruding Committee (1992) which examined CT differentials and the related distortions within the Internal Market. On this basis, the committee recommended implementing a minimum rate for corporate taxation in the EU.

pricing complicate matters further. The high cost of compliance and risks that come from observing the requirements of two or more tax codes can be particularly discouraging to SMEs.

Other efforts by the EU concentrate on enforcing national tax treatment of non-resident EU and EEA taxpayers and foreign-source income, reducing tax fraud and avoidance by exchange of information, mutual assistance in enforcing tax claims, coordination of the tax treatment of dividend distributions, and creating a favourable climate for investment by SMEs.

The institutional structure of the EU

The Commission needs to take account of the political constraints set by the institutional structure of the EU, which is characterised as an economic union with political features that resemble a confederation. This includes striking the right balance between a certain level of tax coordination and the 'principle of subsidiarity'. This principle constitutes a central factor in EU law-making practices and states that the Community should take action only when something cannot be achieved adequately by the individual member states. This applies mostly in the case of scale effects and when preferences are fairly homogeneous. Moreover, since the rule of unanimity applies in direct tax matters, every member state can veto whatever measure is being proposed.

Four comprehensive solutions of the Bolkestein Report

A main objective is thus to devise a system that is acceptable to all member states. This requires significant political manoeuvring and bargaining.[34] Formally, not all states have to participate even though this should be the guiding principle. Under a step-by-step approach some states (that is, at least eight) could take the lead, allowing others to follow later when they believe the time is right. Europe would be characterised by two or more tax integration speeds, thus *Europe à la carte fiscale* (Terra and Wattel, 2005). The Bolkestein report has tabled four comprehensive solutions, each proposing a certain degree of harmonisation: [35]

---

[34] Bottlenecks have already been tackled through separate pieces of legislation or 'remedial measures': the Parent-Subsidiary Directive (2003/123/EC) eliminates taxes on dividend distributions between related companies within the EU, the Interest and Royalties Directive (2003/49/EC) does the same for interest and royalty payments and the Merger Directive (2005/19/EC) prevents capital gains taxation in the case of intra-EU sale or transfer of shares.

[35] See also the proposal by Morris Tabaksblat arguing for a supranational CT over the consolidated EU profits of companies that operate in more than one EU country (Tabaksblat, 1993), a similar proposal by Plasschaert (1997), the Home State Taxation proposals by the Stockholm Group (Lodin and Gammie, 1999), the proposals of the Centre for European Policy Studies (CEPS) for an EU Corporate Income Tax (for example, Klemm and Radealli, 2001), and a Common Base Taxation proposal by the Confederation of European Business (UNICE).

- *Home state taxation (HST)*. Under this approach the tax base is computed according to the tax rules of the country in which the headquarters of an MNC is located. Other countries where the company operates in turn automatically adopt and mutually recognise the tax code and principles of the 'home state' for determining the taxable base. This ensures that an MNC faces only one system for financial reporting, namely that of the 'home state'. Formulary apportionment would allocate the profits to the individual member states, where they are subject to domestic tax rates;[36]
- *Common consolidated corporate base taxation (CCCBT)*. A separate EU tax base would be devised and exist parallel with the national system of profit determination. The separate system would operate throughout the EU. The MNC would be free to use the EU or the national system for determining profits. Formulary apportionment would again allocate the profits to individual states if the EU system is chosen;
- *European Union corporate income tax (EUCIT)*. A separate EU CT system would be constructed. Either the national tax authorities could administer the tax or a single EU administration would be created to do so. The revenue would subsequently be allocated to the EU to finance its expenditure. Initially, the system was thought to be compulsory for large MNCs, but it could also be optional and exist alongside the national systems; and
- *Compulsory 'harmonised tax base' (HTB)*. The final alternative would create an EU-wide system and tax code for corporate taxation to replace the national systems. The system would not be optional and would apply to all corporations in the Union. National authorities could still be responsible for administering the tax, or alternatively, a separate EU institution would be created.

The approaches vary in the degree of encroachment on national sovereignty. In the EU political harmony is at present hard to find, so it is difficult to reach consensus on any form of harmonisation. As noted, every single member state can veto whatever proposal the Commission makes in the area of direct taxation. A single EU system of corporate taxation therefore seems a long shot.

---

[36] Formulary apportionment allocates profits according to a common formula, which specifies the factors that are part of the equation and their relative weight in the end result. Commonly employed factors are payroll, property and sales (see Weiner, 2002, and European Commission, 2005b). The US and Canada already have considerable experience in using formulary apportionment to allocate profits to their states and provinces.

The preferred course of action

The proposal most likely to pass internal constraints within the EU is the common consolidated corporate tax base. From the viewpoint of the Internal Market, the CCCBT is an improvement compared to current arrangements. A common tax base reduces administrative requirements for companies, contributes to simplicity and thereby induces economic growth. EU Commissioner for taxation László Kovács has spoken out in favour of a CCCTB with formulary apportionment (Kovács, 2005). The Commissioner also points out that a difference of 6 to 8 per cent between tax rates of member states is justifiable on the grounds of relative distances and transport costs.

The Commission is expected to come up with legislative measures within three to four years.[37] Whether the proposal for the CCCTB will succeed, remains to be seen. Lack of enthusiasm of some member states became particularly evident during the Ecofin summit of April 2006 (that is, the monthly meeting of EU finance ministers). Most prominent opponents were Estonia, Ireland, Slovakia and the UK. The main objections of member states are that they fear the common tax base will reduce revenue collection. Second, they believe that the CCCBT is a first step in the direction of a fully harmonised European CT, with decision making at the central level as well as the revenue allocated to it. Also, the CCCTB is believed to diminish tax competition and with it the pressure to make current systems more efficient (note that for other people, tax competition and the adverse pressures it puts on government revenue collection, is an argument for the CCCTB).

Others have pointed out that the claimed administrative gains are overstated. Member states will have to develop an entirely new set of rules and run two parallel systems. Moreover, competitive economies need a tax system that is flexible and can rapidly adapt in response to changing conditions on world markets. Since changing the CCCTB would in principle require the approval of all 27 member states, any changes to the system in the near future are close to impossible. The system could therefore drive investment out of the EU to jurisdictions with more flexible and competitive tax systems.

Commissioner Kovacs proposes to implement the CCCBT in stages with a smaller group of countries taking the lead. Success or failure will then depend on the experiences of these countries.

---

[37] To create a legal framework, a high-level study group has so far addressed a number of issues such as the treatment of assets and tax depreciation, liabilities, reserves and provisions, capital gains and group taxation. Only limited attention has been paid to the harmonisation of accounting conventions and financial reporting standards for tax purposes. For a list of possible issues encountered, see European Commission (2003b). In addition, in January 2006 the Commission decided to go ahead with a voluntary five-year home state taxation probe for SMEs (European Commission, 2006d).

What do the models show?

The above analysis demonstrates that member states have reduced their statutory CT rates during the last two to three decades, yet effective tax rates have remained relatively stable. It suggests there may be more to undercutting neighbours' tax rates than just a 'race to the bottom'.

Bettendorf et al. (2006) demonstrate that domestic distortions in tax systems are highly relevant for the incentives to engage in tax competition.[38] A country benefits from a lower CT rate by attracting foreign investment. But if the tax cut cannot be financed from general funds, alternative sources of finance may too be expensive.

Figure 8.1 shows the calculated output gains per country from CT reform when financed by labour and consumption tax increases or a reduction in transfer payments. This outcome confirms that only five countries have an incentive to engage in tax competition if labour taxes finance a CT cut. Lowering transfer payments yields the largest result, but would be unacceptable to many governments. In any case the boost to employment and the economy would be mainly the result of a cut in benefits. Financing CT reform by a shift to consumption taxation boosts output in all but two countries. Hence, the consumption tax is less distortive than the labour tax.

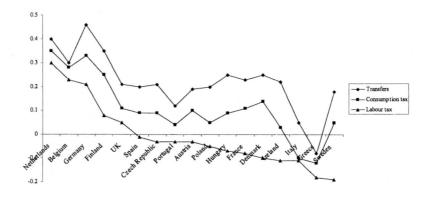

Source: Bettendorf et al. (2006, Figure 4.5)

Figure 8.1   Percentage GDP gain from CT reform by alternative sources of finance

---

[38] The analysis is based on the applied general equilibrium model *CORTAX*. The model is tailor-made to the situation in the EU and builds on the *OECDTAX* model developed by Sørensen (2004).

The model simulations unambiguously indicate that, at current tax levels, CT harmonisation would hardly be welfare enhancing to the EU as a whole.[39] The capital stock expands slightly by 0.14 per cent, while GDP reduces by a negligible 0.02 per cent. Setting a minimum CT rate of 30 per cent to remedy tax competition would not be particularly welfare enhancing, either. If harmonisation took place at a rate of 20 per cent, the welfare loss is even more negative, with a GDP reduction of approximately 0.3 per cent. Only Germany and the Netherlands would gain, whereas the other member states lose. This means that the EU has very few economic incentives to harmonise. However, these models typically do not take account of the gains associated with reduced red tape, enforcement and lower compliance and administrative burdens for companies and government, which can promote entrepreneurial activity in the EU.

BOX 8.7

The harmonisation of corporate tax in the EU would hardly enhance welfare to the EU as a whole. The overall stock of capital would increase by only 0.14 per cent and GDP is reduced by 0.02 per cent.

8.8 BRIEF SUMMARY

Global developments in the past decades have increased the dynamics on international markets for labour, capital and goods and services. This has been accompanied by growing global competition, including in the area of taxation.

First, the chapter discussed the theory of fiscal federalism, which deals with the question of what levels of government taxing powers are most optimally attributed. Commonly distinguished are central, middle and local levels of government. The theory has been refined further by the Tiebout model, which shows that households and firms 'vote with their feet' and leave the jurisdiction of a particular tax authority if they feel they have to pay too much tax.

There are several dimensions in which governments compete over tax bases. As evidence of ongoing tax competition, this chapter has shown that statutory CT rates have declined markedly in many OECD countries. The evidence on tax competition by effective tax rates is more mixed. Effective capital income tax rates have remained largely stable in the EU over the

---

[39] The tax rate is calibrated to 33 per cent, the average in the year 2002.

1990-2000 period. Thus the reduction of statutory rates was accompanied by base broadening. Since 2000, a few countries have been or are in the process of reducing effective tax burdens as well (for example, Austria, Germany and the Netherlands).

A second dimension in which countries compete is by means of targeted business tax incentives such as exemptions to the tax base, generous tax deductions or credits, and favourable treatment of group taxation and/or financing activities. In the EU, action has been taken with the Code of Conduct for Business Taxation and ECJ rulings to curb harmful business tax incentives. US legislation offers greater autonomy for states to design specific business tax incentives. It is accepted that jurisdictions compete according to measures bearing on the overall level of taxation.

There are also jurisdictions that impose low nominal tax rates or refrain completely from any taxation. These 'tax havens' have a strong power of attraction on internationally operating companies and wealthy individuals. Such practices are considered harmful. In addition, a large number of countries impose a 'normal' rate of taxation, but have discriminatory features in their systems that create low effective taxation for certain companies. The OECD's Forum on Harmful Tax Practices has been successful in curbing harmful practices by tax havens and preferential tax regimes in OECD member states.

What it perhaps ultimately boils down to is the policy mix needed to create a sustainable and solid budgetary basis, given future global dynamics. International tax competition curbs the scope for independent policy and flexibility of policy makers in tax design. The specific blend of tax competition, coordination or certain types of harmonisation will in the future become more important on the international agenda in enhancing the overall efficiency of the tax system or of elements within. The process in the EU stands exemplar. On the other hand, we may also conclude that, given the current situation, it is likely that 21st-century trends and issues will tend to intensify tax competition between (EU) countries.

9. Greening tax systems

We can no longer afford to view global warming as a political issue - rather, it is the biggest moral challenge facing our global civilization

(Al Gore, 2006)[1]

9.1 INTRODUCTION

Environmental concerns have become compelling in the past decades. Never before have the issues surrounding air, water and soil pollution as well as the depletion of natural resources been as relevant as in contemporary times. The threat from climate change is of utmost concern to all. The Kyoto agreement (1997) presents a modest, yet remarkable achievement of joint effort made thus far.[2] Over 160 countries have ratified the protocol.[3]

In the years after the agreement, the public debate on climate change has intensified. Most scientists nowadays agree on the link between human activities and rising global surface temperatures (but sceptics still exist). The UN Intergovernmental Panel on Climate Change (IPCC) has established a 90 per cent chance that human activity is the main cause of global warming. Consulting over 600 experts, the 'best estimate' of the IPCC is a global temperature rise of at least 3°C by 2100.

A variety of measures on a global scale are needed to curb greenhouse gas emissions and develop a sustainable platform for economies to function on. Sir Nicholas Stern's (2007) impressive report confirms this. The former chief

---

[1] Quoted from the documentary film 'An inconvenient truth' where the former US Vice President (1993-2001), presidential candidate (2001) and Nobel laureate (2007) argues for drastic action to combat climate change.
[2] The Kyoto protocol was negotiated in December 1997 in Kyoto, Japan, and entered into force on 16 February 2005 after ratification by Russia. The treaty signatories commit themselves to reducing CO_2 emissions and 5 other greenhouse gases. The agreement functions as a 'cap and trade' system whereby so-called 'carbon credits' are traded among countries or individual companies. Hence, energy-intensive companies are issued permits for the amount of CO_2 emissions they are allowed to produce each year. If they desire to produce more, they must buy permits from cleaner businesses with spare allocation.
[3] Notable exceptions are the United States and Australia. China and India have ratified the protocol, but are not yet obliged to curb emissions under the agreement.

economist of the World Bank and his team of experts estimate that global warming is set to shrink the world economy by up to 20 per cent if governments worldwide fail to act now. Given the nature of the problem, a global approach is needed with a focus on market-based instruments.

Since these alarming reports, a political race can is on to be the 'greenest country', especially among European countries. The public response can be multifaceted, such as taking regulatory measures (pollution standards) and standards, issuing tradable pollution rights, and entering into agreements with energy-intensive industries; direct subsidies to stimulate environmentally friendly activities; adopting green taxes and charges that create positive and negative financial incentives with the same objective; and R&D programmes and information instruments.

There are important caveats, though. Environmental measures and in particular green tax levies may impair economic activity. Price increases reduce consumer spending and worsen the competitive position of firms on world markets. The costs of a cleaner environment are often considerable and accumulate in the short run, while the long-run benefits are uncertain and dependent on a variety of factors. Even so, under the right conditions and appropriate rate, environmental taxes do not necessarily impede economic growth.

This chapter explores the use of green taxes in environmental policy. First, we look at some environmental trends. Greenhouse gas emissions from a variety of sources are large in a number of countries and rising rapidly in others. Next, the chapter discusses a number of specific characteristics of green taxes and their economic effects. We present the 'carrot and stick' model, the criteria for the appraisal of a green tax option and an analysis of the 'double dividend' conjecture. The remainder of the chapter is directed at experiences and best practices in 'green tax' countries and a selection of tax measures that aim to green country tax systems, such as the carbon tax and more specific measures that induce investment in a cleaner environment.

9.2   GROWING PROSPERITY AND THE ENVIRONMENT

A growing affluence and world population place an ever-larger strain on the environment. The World Bank projects the global population to increase from approximately 6 billion in 2005 to nearly 9 billion by 2050.[4] While some environmental problems are domestic in nature, the majority have a worldwide effect. Resolving these issues and working towards a more sustainable future requires close international cooperation and coordination.

Effective climate policy requires a global approach. Industrialised countries need to take the lead and develop a joint climate policy and

---

[4] See the Health, Nutrition and Population data platform at www.worldbank.org.

promote the development of clean technologies. There is simply no other option as national or regional climate policy is insufficiently effective and distorts international competitive positions. Furthermore, to persuade countries such as China and India to participate, it is essential to make available to these countries the most advanced clean energy technologies.

National government policy can none the less make an important contribution to realising the targets set (for example, Kyoto targets). The main criteria for appraising potential measures in the context of such a policy are efficiency and effectiveness. The objective should be to achieve the optimal balance between simplicity, cost effectiveness, environmental gain, public support, adherence to the polluter-pays principle, administrative costs and income effects and to maintain international competition.

The emphasis should be on *market-based* instruments: taxes, concessions and tradable CO_2 emission rights. These instruments generally have the advantage that the environmental objective is achieved at the lowest cost. They stimulate technological innovation ('cleantech'), particularly in the area of energy efficiency and renewable energies (wind and solar power, geothermal energy and so on). One way in which emission markets and taxes reduce pollution is by providing incentives to find new technologies, which saves firms money. An important objective in global climate policy is thus to establish an international price for CO_2, which provides guidance in choosing technologies. But it is left up to the market to decide which technologies are developed to attain a given climate objective. Government policy can also grant (tax) subsidies to encourage businesses to make specific investments.

Greening is an Integral Part of Growth-orientated Policy

The potential of economies to develop over the long term will increasingly depend on maintaining a clean and healthy environment. Some 70 years ago, US economist Simon Kuznets recognised that:

'[T]he welfare of a nation can scarcely be inferred from a measure of national income. If the GDP is up, why is America down? Distinctions must be kept in mind between quantity and quality of growth, between costs and returns, and between the short and long run. Goals for more growth should specify more growth of what and for what'. [5]

The significance of the environment for well-being and economic growth can no longer be denied. People derive a vast number of resources and other

---

[5] Nobel Prize laureate (1971) Simon Kuznets developed the uniform set of national accounts for the US, which form the basis of GDP. Kuznets has always remained apt to point out the shortcomings of GDP as an indicator of economic welfare. The quotation is from Kuznets's first report to the US Congress in 1934 and is cited on the web-based encyclopaedia Wikipedia at http://en.wikipedia.org/wiki/Gross_domestic_product (downloaded on 16 January 2007).

(economic) benefits from the environment, both directly and indirectly. Clean air, water and soil can be seen as a commodity, just like any other, characterised by scarcity, and the scarcer these commodities become, the greater the value people attach to them.

The Environmental Kuznets Curve

Despite bleak prognoses, emissions of certain air pollutants such as sulphur dioxide, nitrogen dioxide, carbon monoxide and particulate matter in the US have been declining as a percentage of GDP since the 1950s (Brock and Taylor, 2004). Environmentalists are normally not keen to hear of such findings and claim that this implies nothing about the absolute growth of emissions. Since GDP has grown steadily, on average by roughly 3 per cent per annum, the level of pollution has as well.

It is interesting, therefore, that the absolute level of many emissions and air pollutants in the US did rise at first, but has actually declined in subsequent years, with a peak occurring around the 1970s. This pattern can also be observed in other developed countries. Apparently economic growth first coincides with increasing and later with decreasing pollution. This phenomenon is also known as the 'environmental Kuznets curve' (EKC).

The environment and air quality deteriorates at first with economic development, but then improves again. Economists offer several explanations for the observed pattern. For example, pollution clean-up is subject to increasing returns to scale. Average costs decline over the years. There also seems to be a starting threshold for cleaning up the environment. However, the data for most pollutants do not support such an explanation since the peak in the level of emissions comes at a much later stage than the decline in emissions relative to GDP. In addition, expenditures on cleaning up environmental pollution have stayed roughly stable over the period considered, at approximately 1.5 per cent of GDP.

Other explanations include the economy-wide shift from energy-intensive industrial sectors to services-orientated sectors such as banking, insurance, ICT, education and healthcare. Yet another argument suggests that people initially focus on satisfying the necessities of life, and then start spending on other things such as the environment only after sufficient economic development has occurred.

The 'Green Solow Model' and the Role of Technological Innovation

Brock and Taylor (2004) find these explanations inconclusive. By constructing a 'green Solow model' they argue that the real foundation of the EKC lies in a progressing technological innovation for cleaning up pollution and achieving a more environmentally friendly production. Hence, initially pollution increases despite the decline of emissions as a percentage of GDP.

This is also because poorer countries such as China and India are growing at an accelerated rate. Eventually the positive effects of environmentally friendly technological innovation start to dominate, particularly when convergence with more developed nations sets in and growth rates start to decline.

The emission of pollutants therefore ultimately declines, even though environmental-related spending as a percentage of GDP remains unchanged. Like economic growth rates, emission rates of developing countries should eventually converge to those of developed ones.

BOX 9.1

The environmental Kuznets curve (EKC) describes an empirically observed pattern that economic growth is first associated with increasing and later with decreasing levels of pollution. A central explanation is the relative effect of the development of environmentally friendly technologies in richer countries relative to developing countries.

What Is at Stake?

Table 9.1 shows CO_2 emissions for the largest economies in the world. The US tops the list.[6] In the coming decades, China and India will develop into economic giants. This process coincides with a staggering increase in global pollution. Where the major pollutants on a global scale have so far been the US, EU-15 and Japan with populations of 300, 380 and 130 million inhabitants, respectively,[7] China and India number 1.3 and 1.1 billion inhabitants, respectively. Projections show that Asian economies (including China, India, Indonesia and Vietnam) will be responsible for 50 per cent of world greenhouse gas emissions by 2030, up from 23 per cent in 2007.

---

[6] The US with approximately 300 million inhabitants consumed 25 per cent of world energy production in 2004. The country uses over 20 million barrels of the roughly 80 million barrels of oil produced a day and operates 102 nuclear power plants. Compared to Europe, per capita consumption is more than 1.5 times as high. Industrial production in Europe is on average more energy efficient. Americans also drive larger cars which use relatively more fuel, whereas Europeans walk more often or use a bicycle for transportation. In summer, air conditioning in the US drives temperatures below levels produced by heating in winter.

[7] After the expansions in 2004 and 2007, the EU-27 has roughly 480 million inhabitants.

Taxes and the Economy

Table 9.1 CO_2 emissions for the largest economic areas, 2007

Country	Million tons	Tons per inhabitant	Annual % increase CO_2 1992-2004	Annual % population increase 1992-2004	Number of inhabitants (millions)
US	6,120	20.4	1.4	1.2	300
EU-15	3,572	9.4	0.2	0.3	380
Japan	1,274	9.8	0.7	0.3	130
China	5,010	3.9	3.7	0.9	1,300
India	1,343	1.2	4.3	1.7	1,100

Note: The million tons in the first column have been extrapolated from the tons per inhabitant on the base of total inhabitants.

Sources: Stern Report (2007, ch. 7) and for updated statistics http://www.ipcc.ch; http://www.unfc.int; http://www.unep.org/geo; and http://www.carbonplanet.com/home/country.

Figure 9.1 shows that the sources of CO_2 emissions are diverse. The main categories are industry, power, transport, buildings, land use, agriculture and waste. Of these categories, agriculture, land use and waste are the only non-energy sources. CO_2 emissions from land use originate mainly from deforestation, that is, the burning of forests to prepare the land for agriculture. These emissions are highly concentrated in a few countries around the world, with roughly 30 per cent originating in Indonesia and a further 20 per cent in Brazil. The category 'buildings' includes fuels burned for heating and cooking in commercial and residential property and 'agriculture' refers to emissions from fertilisers and livestock. Overall, some 22 per cent of emissions stem from non-energy sources, against 78 per cent from energy sources. Energy use is thus a key factor in climate policy and roughly 80 per cent of the solution to climate change has to be found in energy politics.

BOX 9.2

In per capita terms the United States is by far the largest emitter of greenhouse gases in the world. Per capita emissions are more than twice those of Europe and Japan. Yet, the biggest hazard emanates from fast-growing economies such as China and India. Both are on track to developing into strong economies in the decades to come. As a result, global pollution is likely to increase at a staggering rate.

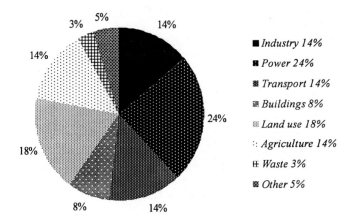

3% 5%
14%
14%
18%
8% 14%
24%

■ *Industry 14%*

▣ *Power 24%*

▒ *Transport 14%*

▒ *Buildings 8%*

▒ *Land use 18%*

∴ *Agriculture 14%*

Ⅱ *Waste 3%*

▩ *Other 5%*

Source:　Stern Report (2007, Figure 7.1, p. 171) at http://www.hm-treasury.gov.uk.

Figure 9.1　Total greenhouse gas emissions by source, 2000

The Ongoing Debate

While these figures speak for themselves, the debate on global warming nevertheless continues and mainly focuses on whether greenhouse gases are indeed the root cause for higher temperatures on earth.

A recent study commissioned by the US Congress shows that the earth has indeed heated up by 0.7°C over and above 'regular' fluctuations in surface temperatures (Committee on Surface Temperature Reconstructions, 2006). The research covered the last 2000 years and aimed to validate earlier findings by Mann et al. (1998, 1999). These researchers were among the first to establish a sharp rise in the earth's surface temperatures in the 20th century, using data over a period of a thousand years. The study was particularly controversial because accurate instrumental temperature records are available only for the past 150 years or so. Hence, it was partly based on an investigation of tree rings, the rationale being that in warmer years trees grow faster, thereby making the distance between rings larger.[8]

The main results of the Mann et al. study are depicted in Figure 9.2. Because of its shape, the graph is also referred to as the 'hockey stick graph' in climatology. The study revolutionised insights into climate change in the late 1990s.

---

[8] Other techniques used to approximate past global temperatures include ice core drilling on Antarctica, Greenland or high mountain glaciers to study ice crystals from thousands of years ago on, for example, carbon dioxide, methane and nitrous oxide concentrations, or examination of sediment layers.

Temperature
Anomaly (°C)

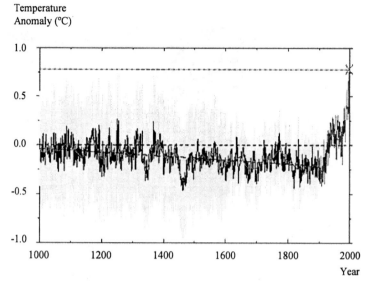

Source: Mann et al. (1999, Figure 3, p. 761).

Figure 9.2   The 'hockey stick' graph

The research method was criticised in later years, mainly in McIntyre and McKitrick (2003) and a number of subsequent studies by these authors. The criticism is based on asserted methodological flaws in the use of proxy data and has been reinforced by a report by Edward J. Wegman (2006) of George Mason University and a team of statisticians. The latter report was ordered by the US Congressional Committee on Energy and Commerce. In addition to these academic influences, numerous other parties influence the environmental policy debate such as the energy lobby and environmental groups, key think-tanks and the anti-globalisation movement.[9]

---

[9] A short list of prominent environmental groups includes: Greenpeace, Friends of the Earth, the Nature Conservancy, the Sierra Club and the Climate Institute. Important think-tanks in the US include the Brookings Institution, the conservative American Enterprise Institute and Heritage Foundation and the more liberally orientated Institute for Policy Studies and Center for American Progress. The Cato Institute is known to be libertarian. The anti-globalisation movement was strongly influenced by Naomi Klein (a Canadian journalist and writer of the book *No Logo*), Vandana Shiva (ecologist, feminist and writer of the book *Biopiracy*), Susan Sontag (an American writer and activist) and Arundhati Roy (mainly known for her opposition to an Indian hydroelectric dam project and nuclear power). Economists that have had a significant impact on the anti-globalisation movement with their writings include James Tobin, Amartya Sen, George Soros and Joseph E. Stiglitz.

Opponents and sceptics in the debate on global warming point out the following:[10]

- the current concentration of CO_2 in the earth's atmosphere is normal from a geological point of view;
- human CO_2 emissions shrink into insignificance compared to emissions from natural sources such as volcanic activity, oceans and land;
- climate models (computer simulations) are unreliable and depend on too many uncertainties; and
- satellite measurements disprove warming of the earth.

According to the UN's IPCC, these objections have now been sufficiently rebutted. There is enough evidence that the earth is heating up mainly as a result of human activity. In its 4th Assessment Report of 2007 the IPCC projects that between now and 2100, global temperature may rise by well over 3°C (see Figure 9.3). The report was produced by 600 authors in over 40 countries and reviewed by over 620 experts.

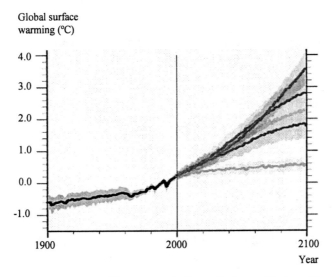

Note: [a]The solid lines represent different scenarios in the simulations. The lowest line is for the experiment where CO_2 concentrations are kept constant at 2000 levels.

Source: United Nations IPCC (2007, Figure SPM-5, p. 14) at http://www.ipcc.ch.

Figure 9.3 Predicted surface temperatures by the year 2100 [a]

---

[10] See Lomborg (2007) (www.lomborg.com; and www.anti-lomborg.com).

The panel established a chance of at least 90 per cent that human activities are the cause of global warming since 1950 (even in a previous IPCC report in 2001, this chance was still estimated to be at least 66 per cent).

On 6 April 2007, the IPCC released additional observational evidence from all continents and most oceans that climate change and temperature rises are already changing natural habitats, thus giving discernible evidence that global warming is affecting the environment. Some of the demonstrated results cited in the IPCC report are enlargement of (the number of) glacial lakes, earlier timing of spring events, changes to the abundance of algae and plankton, losses of coastal wetlands and mangrove swamps, and poleward and upward shifts in ranges in plant and animal species.

In a third report on 4 May 2007, the panel calculated that climate change abatement will cost roughly €225 or $300 in annual income per head of the world population. The report showed that without investment, emissions will continue to rise, but that otherwise there is a 50 per cent chance of reversing the trend and mitigating global warming to 2°C by 2030. The technologies to accomplish this already partly exist and partly can be developed and marketed in time, if CO_2 is reflected in product prices.[11]

A Sense of Urgency: The Stern Report

The former chief economist of the World Bank, Sir Nicholas Stern (2007), also predicts a bleak future if we continue on the current path. The report was commissioned by the British government and puts into perspective the economic consequences of climate change. After publication, the UK government vowed to lead the international response to tackle climate change and is to be advised by the former US presidential candidate Al Gore (who negotiated the Kyoto treaty in 1997 and which President George W. Bush repudiated in 2001), in an effort to draw the US back into international negotiations.

Stern calculates that global warming could shrink the global economy by a staggering 5 to 20 per cent in the long run.[12] Merely a few examples of human, economic and environmental cataclysms caused are floods displacing up to 100 million people; melting glaciers that cause water shortages for 1 in 6 people; extinction of up to 40 species of wildlife; and droughts that create tens of millions of climate refugees. Furthermore, rising sea levels due to melting ice caps could permanently flood over 4 million square kilometres of land, home to about 5 per cent of the world's population. This includes major

---

[11] See UNFCCC (2007) (http://unfccc.int/).

[12] It should be noted that the results are extremely sensitive to the choice of discount factor. The Stern Review has been criticised for having a much too low discount factor, in which case the gains from mitigating climate change now are overstated compared to the cost of taking action in the future (see, for example, Nordhaus, 2006).

metropolitan areas such as Amsterdam, Buenos Aires, London, Miami, New York, St Petersburg, Shanghai and Tokyo.

The Stern review urges better cooperation between the major industrial countries Australia, Europe, Japan and the United States. To stabilise climate change, CO_2 emissions must decline by an estimated 60 per cent by 2050, requiring a significant investment of 1 per cent of global GDP (or approximately \$350 billion annually).

The report effectively removes two of the three most frequently heard arguments by people who oppose government policy to curb emissions: first, the contested link between greenhouse gas emissions and rising surface temperatures; and second, the argument that green measures come at the expense of economic activity and growth. What remains is the well-known free-rider problem, which gives an incentive to countries to unilaterally fail to comply with any multilateral agreement on curbing emissions, thus giving them a short-term competitive advantage over countries that do comply.

BOX 9.3

The bulk of scientific evidence convincingly points to a global climate change and warming up of the earth that is due to human activity. By 2100, global temperatures are projected to increase by 3°C under a variety of scenarios.

Global Temperatures and Energy Use: Reversing the Trend

Without action, primary global energy demand is set to increase by 52 per cent by 2030 according to the International Energy Agency's *World Energy Outlook* of 2006. Some 70 per cent of this rise will come from developing countries such as China and India (China will have surpassed the US in absolute terms as the world largest emitter by 2008). On a brighter side, by acting now through a so-called 'alternative policy scenario', which assumes that governments implement the key measures they are currently contemplating, future prospects can be significantly improved, according to the IEA (2006).

This once again underscores that climate change is not irreversible and that CO_2 concentrations in the air can effectively be reduced. According to the IPCC, this will be enough to avert the most serious consequences of climate change. However, all evidence indicates that governments need to act within 10 to 15 years to reverse the trend. The R&D agenda should centre on developing the newest so-called 'second-generation' technologies (that is, technologies that go beyond current methods and approaches) in the areas of:

- energy saving and efficiency;
- renewable/alternative energies (for example, geothermal energy and wave and tidal power; bio-fuels and biomass; and solar, wind, and hydropower);[13]
- cleaner and lighter transport (for example, cars and trucks); and
- hydrogen and fuel cells.

Another frequently cited option is underground carbon capture and storage (CCS). However, carbon storage is primarily an option for the power generation sector, which is responsible for 'only' 25 per cent of greenhouse gas emissions. The IPCC calculates that of all measures, energy efficiency and saving measures are the most promising to combat climate change. Moreover, R&D investment in CCS technologies comes at the cost of R&D investment in other promising technologies. 'A cost curve for greenhouse gas reduction', a report by the high-level consulting firm McKinsey & Company, estimates that the most cost-effective abatement measures are building insulation, fuel efficiency in (commercial) vehicles, air conditioning, water heating and bio-fuel (Enkvist et al., 2007). The CCS costs are more than twice as high.

Figure 9.4 shows what may reasonably be achieved by cleaner technologies and the development of renewable energies. And although there are initial costs involved, high energy prices experienced from the year 2005 onwards also make energy investment more viable.

Climate Change Performance Index (CCPI)

According to the Climate Change and Performance Index (CCPI) of the international environmental group Germanwatch, Sweden, the UK and Denmark are doing the most in the fight against climate change (see Table 9.2).[14] The CCPI ranks the 56 top CO_2-emitting nations.[15] Together the countries make up 90 per cent of global CO_2 emissions. The index takes into account the emission levels, emission trends and government climate policy.

---

[13] Germany has a very progressive renewable energy policy. On 25 February 2007, the German Parliament adopted the Renewable Energy Law (REL), which aims to raise the share of renewable energy in the electricity market to 10 per cent by 2010. Wind turbines currently generate some 55,000 megawatts (MW) of electricity worldwide. About 20,000 MW is produced by wind turbines in Germany, representing almost 6 per cent of total electricity generated in the country. See also Kutscher (2007) on tackling climate change in the US. The study covers six renewable energies and energy efficiency in buildings, transport and industry, and calculates that these technologies can displace roughly 1.2 billion tons of carbon emissions by the year 2030 (according to the IPCC, sufficient to prevent the most serious consequences of climate change).

[14] Germanwatch is a non-profit organisation that focuses on environmental and trade issues. See also the Climate Action Network at http://www.climnet.org, a group of more than 300 non-governmental organisations that together work to combat climate change.

[15] See also the Carbon Disclosure Project for up-to-date data on relative performance of countries in the fight against climate change (http://www.cdproject.net).

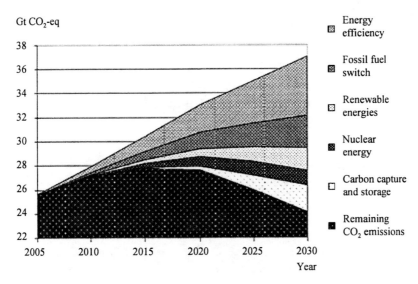

Source: European Commission (2007b, Graph 1, p. 9) at http://europa.eu.

Figure 9.4 Contribution of alternative measures in reducing CO$_2$ emissions

---

BOX 9.4

Energy use is the key factor in climate policy. The only long-term viable solution to the problem of global climate is investing in energy-efficient technologies, renewable and alternative energies such as wind and solar power and switching away from fossil-fuel use. R&D to this end can be stimulated and partly financed by green taxation.

The United States: Waking Up[16]

The United States, a highly developed country, has long been hiding behind feeble arguments of asserted harmful effects on the economy in failing to implement a responsible environmental policy. However, there are signs that environmental concerns are growing here, too. For example, in 2006 twelve American states led by the state of California opposed the Bush administration's environmental policy by demanding with the US Supreme

---

[16] *The Economist* of 2 February 2007 devoted an edition to the greening of America. The magazine concluded that the US is 'waking up and catching up'.

Table 9.2 Climate Change Performance Index, 2007

CCPI rank	Country	Score	CCPI rank	Country	Score	CCPI rank	Country	Score
1	Sweden	0.56	20	Norway	0.17	39	Austria	-0.16
2	UK	0.52	21	Slovakia	0.16	40	Cyprus	-0.18
3	Denmark	0.52	22	New Zealand	0.16	41	Greece	-0.28
4	Malta	0.49	23	Slovenia	0.16	42	Russia	-0.29
5	Germany	0.46	24	Bulgaria	0.10	43	Indonesia	-0.31
6	Argentina	0.46	25	Czech Rep.	0.10	44	Ukraine	-0.33
7	Hungary	0.45	26	Japan	0.08	45	Luxembourg	-0.34
8	Brazil	0.44	27	Poland	0.08	46	South Africa	-0.36
9	India	0.41	28	Singapore	0.06	47	Australia	-0.45
10	Switzerland	0.39	29	Netherlands	0.06	48	South Korea	-0.48
11	Latvia	0.36	30	Estonia	0.05	49	Iran	-0.49
12	France	0.35	31	Italy	0.05	50	Thailand	-0.49
13	Romania	0.32	32	Turkey	0.01	51	Canada	-0.55
14	Iceland	0.31	33	Ireland	-0.05	52	Kazakhstan	-0.56
15	Belgium	0.31	34	Croatia	-0.07	53	US	-0.59
16	Mexico	0.30	35	Algeria	-0.09	54	China	-0.65
17	Lithuania	0.21	36	Finland	-0.09	55	Malaysia	-0.74
18	Morocco	0.20	37	Belarus	-0.12	56	Saudi Arabia	-0.78
19	Portugal	0.18	38	Spain	-0.15			

Source: Germanwatch, at http://www.germanwatch.org (downloaded on 22 April 2007).

Court that the federal government now curbs greenhouse gas emissions. The ambitious course of the state of California deserves follow-up. The seventh economy in the world is developing alternative strategies and solutions for high energy use and introducing innovation in renewable energies for a more efficient fuel use. This sends a strong signal to the federal administration.

In his 2007 State of the Union address, President Bush for the first time acknowledged 'the serious challenge of global climate change' and proposed the 'Twenty in Ten' package, which aims to reduce US gasoline usage by 20 per cent in the next 10 years. The goal should be achieved by (i) increasing the supply of renewable and alternative fuels by raising the mandatory fuels standard and (ii) modernising corporate average fuel economy standards for cars and light trucks. The first measure aims to displace 15 per cent of annual projected gasoline use; the second should reduce projected annual gasoline use by a further 5 per cent.[17] During the United Nations Climate Change Conference in Bali, Indonesia, December 2007, the US also agreed on a two-year timetable to negotiate a successor treaty to the Kyoto Protocol and, in addition, President Bush signed into law the "Energy and Security Independence Act" on 19 December 2007, which calls for a cut in energy use by 7 per cent by 2030 and should lead to a 9 per cent reduction in CO_2 emissions.

Clinton Climate Initiative

In addition to governmental action, admirable non-governmental initiatives such as the Clinton Climate Initiative (CCI) led by former US President Bill Clinton can have a profound impact on curbing emissions. In 2006, Clinton started a campaign to reduce CO_2 emissions and formed an alliance with 40 of the largest cities in the world, including Buenos Aires, New Delhi, Cairo, Johannesburg, London, Melbourne, Moscow, Paris, Rotterdam, Sao Paulo, Tokyo and New York City under the motto 'from big apple to green apple'. Urban areas account for roughly 75 per cent of worldwide CO_2 emissions.

'Greening' has also led to many voluntary initiatives by companies that are in the process of enhancing visibility on environmental issues and climate change and integrating them into their daily business. For example, the Japanese car manufacturer Daihatsu delivers its cars CO_2 neutral by planting trees. The Visa Company has introduced a green card, which compensates for CO_2 emissions arising from items purchased. Thus, 40 litres of gasoline is offset by the planting of 6.75 trees, or a pair of jeans by 5.5 trees.[18] Other initiatives include company statements on responsibilities and actions to tackle climate change, endeavours to make business operate on a carbon-neutral basis, and public reporting on climate objectives achieved.

---

[17] See www.whitehouse.org.
[18] See, for example, www.treesfortravel.nl and www.econsoc.be. A growing forest in Europe absorbs on average 6 tons of CO_2 per hectare, a rainforest about 10 tons of CO_2 per hectare.

The European Stance

Europe has seriously taken to heart the issue of climate change and the Kyoto protocol. At the Climate Summit in March 2007, German Chancellor Angela Merkel even declared 'It's not five minutes to midnight. It's five minutes after midnight'. The summit was preceded by the announcement of an extensive package of measures in January 2007 to limit climate change to no more than 2°C, beyond which point the risks of irreversible and potentially catastrophic impact increase greatly according to the scientific world (European Commission, 2007b). The measures should reduce CO_2 emissions by 30 per cent by 2020 compared with 1990 levels.

According to the Commission, the challenges of climate change need to be tackled effectively and urgently. The package explicitly recognises the importance of R&D in combating climate change and contains measures that should limit transport emissions (that is, aviation and shipping) and emissions from residential and commercial buildings, encourage developing countries to cut emissions (for example, from deforestation) and strengthen the emissions trading scheme (ETS).

The ETS is the largest cap-and-trade company scheme around. It entered into force in 2005 and is mandatory. It covers heavy industry and power generation and includes 12,000 sites across the EU-25. There are also voluntary cap-and-trade schemes such as the Chicago Climate Exchange (CCX) and the UK ETS, which was the first such economy-wide scheme in the world. The UK scheme was launched in 2002 and allows companies to reduce their emissions in return for incentive payments.

In addition, plans have been made to bring the aviation industry into the carbon trading scheme by 2011. Currently, kerosene is not taxed under most excise tax schemes. Taxing aviation has been prohibited by an international treaty that dates back to the 1944 Chicago convention which aimed to encourage air travel, at that time still a nascent industry. The UN's governing body for international air traffic regulation, the International Civil Aviation Organisation (ICVO), has rejected any tax on kerosene until at least 2007. Flying is nevertheless a main source of greenhouse gas emissions, which have risen by 87 per cent in the EU since 1990. Bringing aviation under the ETS could lead to a 46 per cent reduction in flight-related CO_2 by 2020.

Market pull and technology push

With the ETS, the EU has opted for a course that provides strong incentives for businesses to switch to environmentally-friendly technologies in the short run (2007-20). As early as October 1991, the Commission proposed a harmonised carbon tax scheme aimed at stabilising CO_2 emissions in the EU in the medium term. However, the proposal was not implemented due to political opposition. In its place, a renewed proposal was adopted in 1997 based on the current system of excise duties on energy products.

In the long run (2050 and beyond), this so-called 'market-pull' approach adopted with the ETS is not sufficient and needs to be supplemented by a 'technology-push' strategy (EurActiv, 2007). This approach relies on the large-scale deployment of ambitious and heavily funded R&D programmes as in the US, where belief in a market driven technological solution to reverse climate change is strong. Huge budgets are allocated for this purpose. In 2006, 14 per cent of risk capital was allocated to the cleantech sector (this was only 1 per cent in 2000). The programmes aim to develop clean technologies ('cleantech') and renewable energies to reduce pollution and fight climate change. In the EU, member states have their individual research programmes on energy. By changing policy, acting jointly and integrating efforts, research effectiveness can improve markedly.

Ultimately, a mixture of short- and long-run policies should champion climate change. The next section demonstrates that the tax system can play an integral role in promoting long-run R&D programmes.

9.3   GREEN TAXES IN COMBATING CLIMATE CHANGE

Several countries have already individually implemented environmentally-related taxes. An ambitious environmental policy is currently being pursued by the UK. Britain is striving to put itself at the forefront of international effort with a demanding long-term strategy to tackle climate change. In 1997, HM Treasury published a 'Statement of Intent on Environmental Taxation' on the role that the tax system can play in environmental policy. A task force headed by Lord Marshall of Knightsbridge was set up to evaluate economic instruments and the business use of energy. In 2002, HM Treasury (2002) published an extensive report on the use of tax instruments in environmental policy.

The UK has put in place several measures to improve the quality of the environment. Examples are the Climate Change Levy (CCL) which stimulates businesses to reduce CO_2 emissions; the Green Technology Challenge (GTC) to further promote climate-friendly technologies; the earlier mentioned UK ETS; measures to encourage energy efficiency at home; and a variety of transport levies. A Cambridge study has estimated that the CCL alone reduced CO_2 emissions by 3.1 Mton, or 2 per cent, in 2002 and 3.6 Mton in 2003. This reduction will have increased to 3.7 Mton, or 2.3 per cent in 2010 (Cambridge Econometrics, 2005). In March 2007, the British government announced the draft Climate Change Bill. It plans to enact the law in 2008. The draft law proposes a legally binding carbon target of a 60 per cent cut in carbon emissions by 2050.[19] Also, an important report from the Confederation of British Industry (CBI) recently showed that shifting to low carbon sources of electricity and improving energy use in buildings can each contribute to some 30 per cent of the additional cuts necessary (the remaining 40 per cent coming from transport and industry). The report calls for a shift to an economy in which carbon becomes a 'new currency', so consumers and businesses have and incentive to make the right choices.[20]

Environmentally Related Taxes

Green taxes are part of a wider array of government tools that can be used in environmental protection policies. Yet, they form an integral part. The basic framework on environmental tax statistics was created jointly by the OECD, the IEA and the European Commission.

An environmental tax is defined as a tax on tax bases deemed to be of particular environmental relevance. Included are taxes on energy products, motor vehicles, waste, measured or estimated emissions, natural resources and so forth. Excluded is VAT on environmentally harmful tax bases.[21] Table 9.3 shows the size of revenue collected by green taxation in the sample countries. Denmark relies most heavily on green taxes both in terms of GDP and in its tax mix. The Netherlands comes second and Finland (GDP) and Ireland (tax mix) come third. The Nordic countries and the Netherlands have the highest per capita tax burden. The bulk of environmentally related tax revenue is collected from energy and transport taxes, which comprise well over 90 per cent of total tax revenue.

Figure 9.5 illustrates that the main tax bases are unleaded and leaded petrol, diesel oil and taxes (recurrent) on motor vehicles. Furthermore, to give an indication of the wide variety of taxes used, Table 9.4 summarises other non-energy and transport taxes applied in the sample countries. Some of these taxes are applied only in certain states, provinces or other localities.

Green tax shift in the EU

In the EU, a shift from labour to green taxation or a so-called relative 'green tax shift' can be observed during the 1980-2001 period (Eurostat, 2003). Governments have apparently increasingly relied on green taxes to compensate the cost of labour tax cuts in tax reforms. Examples are found in reforms in Denmark, Finland, the Netherlands, Sweden and later the UK.

---

[19] See http://www.hm-treasury.gov.uk/.

[20] See 'Climate change: Everyone's business' at http://www.cbi.org.uk

[21] An environmental database jointly administered by the OECD/IEA offers statistics on 375 green taxes (150 energy product taxes, 125 motor vehicle taxes, about 50 taxes related to waste management and some 50 or so other taxes). In OECD countries, environmentally related taxes include more than 1,150 tax exemptions and several hundred refund mechanisms and other tax arrangements (OECD, 2006c).

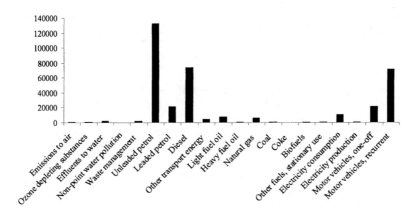

Source: OECD (2006c, Figure 2.4, p. 30).

Figure 9.5   Distribution of tax revenues across the tax base (million $US), OECD average 1995

Table 9.3   Environmentally related tax revenues, 2003

Country	As per cent of GDP	As per cent of total tax revenues	Per capita in $US
Australia	1.9	6.0	500
Austria	2.7	6.3	800
Belgium	2.2	4.9	650
Canada	1.3	4.0	350
Denmark	5.0	10.3	1,950
Finland	3.2	7.4	1,000
France	2.1	4.9	600
Germany	2.7	7.4	750
Ireland	2.4	8.0	950
Italy	2.9	6.7	750
Japan	1.7	6.6	550
Netherlands	3.5	8.9	1,150
Norway	3.0	6.9	1,450
Sweden	3.0	5.8	1,000
UK	2.7	7.6	800
US	0.9	3.5	300

Source: OECD/IEA Electronic database.

Table 9.4 Environmentally related levies other than energy and transport

Country	Tax provisions
Australia	Waste levy, oil recycling levy, aircraft noise levy, ozone protection and synthetic greenhouse gas levy
Austria	Waste deposit levy
Belgium	Packaging charge, groundwater tax, tax on waste dumping and burning, manure tax, water pollution tax, and a tax on waste collection
Canada	Battery tax, logging tax, mining tax, tyre tax, tax on lead acid batteries, federal air conditioner tax, non-deposit containers tax, and alcoholic beverage container tax
Denmark	Duty on raw materials, chlorinated solvents, certain retail containers and on CFC, HFC, PFAC and SF_6, duty on disposable tableware, electric bulbs and fuses, duty on nitrogen, pesticides, waste-sealed NoCd batteries, carrier bags, tyres, polyvinyl chloride and phthalates, duty on waste water, excise duty on antibiotics and growth promoters, and a tax on water quantity
Finland	Oil damage levy, oil waste levy, excise on disposable beverage containers, and a tax on waste
France	General tax on polluting activities
Ireland	Plastic bag levy[a]
Italy	Aircraft noise taxes, charges on air pollution, tax on plastic bags, and a tax on waste disposal
Netherlands	Levy on water pollution, tax on groundwater extraction, tax on tap water, waste tax and tax on the pollution of surface waters
Norway	Tax on final treatment of waste, product tax on beverage containers, basic tax on non-refillable beverage containers, tax on lubricating oil, tax on pesticides and tax on trichloroethane and tetrachloroethane
Sweden	Tax on waste, natural gravel tax, tax on pesticides and artificial fertilisers
UK	Aggregate levy and landfill tax
US	Examples of a number of state-imposed taxes only. Severance tax, waste tyre fee, landfill closure and contingency tax, public community water system tax, spill compensation and control tax, litter control tax and mining severance tax

Note: [a]The Irish tax on plastic bags was introduced in 2002 and helped to reduce their use by over 90 per cent.

Source: OECD (2006c, Table 2.1, p. 27).

More generally, it has resulted from efforts such as embodied in the EU Lisbon Agenda, which stress the use of green taxes as an instrument, not only to create an environmentally sustainable future, but also to increase competitiveness and growth by reducing the tax burden on labour. In 2003, energy taxes in the EU-25 constituted around 76 per cent of total green taxation, transport taxes around 23 per cent, and pollution and resource taxes the rest (Eurostat, 2007).

Figure 9.6 shows the fraction of energy taxes by sector in the EU-15. While businesses account for over 70 per cent of final energy consumption, household energy taxes are by far the largest in share of revenue. They have declined by roughly 5 percentage points over the 1995-2003 period, thereby shifting the relative burden to the business sector. The change has largely been borne by the transport, storage and communication sector.

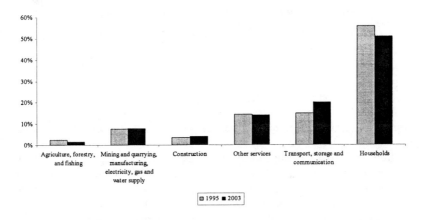

Source: Eurostat (2007, Figure 1, p. 1).

Figure 9.6   EU-15 share of total energy taxes by industry, 1995 and 2003

Figure 9.7 shows that the share of transport taxes on households has increased by over 5 percentage points from 1995 to 2003. This has been accompanied by a slight reduction in transport taxes in the other sectors, with the exception of agriculture, forestry and fishing.

Taxes as an Instrument in Environmental Policy

Practical experiences in OECD countries in the last decade have shown that well-designed green taxes can be an effective and efficient instrument in tackling environmental problems and climate change (OECD, 2006c). Green taxes raise prices, so the cost of pollution is taken into account when making production and consumption decisions. Taxes on polluting were first advocated by Pigou (1932). Environmental damage occurs because those responsible are not the ones who bear the consequences. Specially designed taxes enable the government to align the private and social cost of polluting, thus so-called 'externalities' are internalised (see Appendix 3).

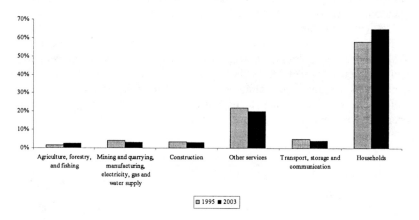

Source: Eurostat (2007, Figure 2, p. 1).

Figure 9.7   EU-15 share of total transport taxes by industry, 1995 and 2003

However, given the scope of the problem, a global approach is needed. On an international level, tax differences can have far-reaching consequences for business competitiveness and distort relative prices and an efficient allocation of consumption. For example, the US has comparatively low energy taxes and high energy consumption. This keeps the price of energy in world markets relatively high. If the US were to increase its energy taxes to levels experienced in the EU, US energy demand would certainly drop, causing a relative shift in energy consumption from the US to high green-tax countries (Bovenberg, 1990). One could also say that, by keeping their own energy demand down, high-tax countries implicitly subsidise the energy consumption of net-importing countries.

Why use taxes?
European efforts have not been without environmental merit, however. Sterner (2007) shows that energy taxes serve an important role for the environment. Often fuel demand is held to be rather inelastic, so energy taxes are believed to be relatively ineffective in achieving environmental aims. However, the study shows that this is true only in the short run. In the long run, research evidence reveals that price elasticities of fuel demand are actually quite high. In fact, had Europe followed the course of the United States and not implemented the currently high levels of fuel taxation, fuel

demand would have been twice that of today. Estimations for different tax scenarios show that taxes 'are the single most powerful climate policy instrument implemented to date – yet this fact is not usually given due attention in the debate' (ibid.).

Taxes are generally a cost effective and an efficient tool in aligning the private and social costs of polluting. They give firms the flexibility to adapt and change their behaviour to avoid paying the tax in the future. Hence, taxes leave the market in charge. The time necessary to make technological adjustments typically varies between firms. Those that adapt quickly and can cut emissions cheaply do so, while those that have high costs and need time to make energy-saving investment pay the tax initially.

In contrast, while government regulations provide some certainty as to the environmental effect and emission reduction (though this strongly depends on stringency), they also affect all firms equally, regardless of relative differences in pollution-control costs. Nevertheless, firms and households are typically heterogeneous, which reduces the economy-wide efficiency of regulation. Indeed, rules apply similarly to all, whereas taxes are based on firm-specific cost curves.

Vollebergh (2007) argues that market-based financial instruments such as taxes also provide stronger incentives than regulation to adopt more efficient energy-saving technologies. By itself, there is no reward for exceeding the requirements set by regulation, whereas a system of taxation enables firms to perform better to lower their tax bill even more. Hence, firms are continually induced to make improvements. According to the author, the financial incentives trigger clearly observable changes in innovation and diffusion of technologies.

Compared to a cap and trade scheme, a CO_2 tax may achieve much the same effect if the tradable permits are sold instead of given away freely as under the European Trading Scheme (ETS) (in the latter case, energy-saving firms who manage to sell excess or 'unused' permits gain the benefit from the system, instead of the government). Under the assumption that they are sufficiently scarce, tradable permits can establish a carbon price, which offer an indication to firms making production and technology decisions (some have argued that the emission of permits itself should be subject to tax to improve the environmental effectiveness and reduce the costs to government of operating the scheme).

The cap-and trade-system is often considered more politically feasible than taxes. This is unfortunate as a CO_2 tax may have important benefits. For example, a CO_2 tax is less sensitive to fraud than a system of tradable permits, which monitors 'invisible' CO_2 emissions. The production volume of fossil fuels is easier to control than the magnitude of CO_2 emissions. Moreover, the allocation of permits does not make adjustment for recession, in which case firms typically pollute less.

BOX 9.5

Research shows that had Europe followed the course of the US and not implemented the currently high levels of fuel taxation, fuel demand would have been twice that of today.

The carrot and stick model

To tackle climate change, a market-orientated approach based on a 'carrot and stick' model has attractive characteristics: rewarding good behaviour, while simultaneously punishing bad behaviour. The original reference is to a mule that is reluctant to pull a cart; he is induced to move by dangling a carrot in front of him ('positive' incentive taxes), assuming he likes it and walks towards it, or hitting him with a stick ('negative' incentive taxes), assuming he dislikes this and walks away from it.

This is both a matter of principle and a pragmatic choice. The principle is that one should convey to citizens and enterprises that environment is not just about higher taxes, but that there are rewards for environmentally sound behaviour. This will enlist support for the environment and not just provoke anxiety. Positive incentives are also more 'activating' than taxes by themselves. Positive incentives point in a practical manner to what is desired and, market forces supplying the products and services thus facilitated endeavours in their own interest to expand the reach of the programme. The pragmatism is that it works and has fewer repercussions on international competitiveness.[22]

Apart from discouraging polluting, governments in already industrialised nations should speed up the advance of environmentally friendly technologies. Clear-cut and carefully designed government policies can stimulate investment in environmentally related R&D. Activating R&D policy generates investment opportunities as new markets are uncovered and the competitiveness of businesses that produce in an ecologically sustainable manner is enhanced. This creates positive spillovers that are beneficial to employment and growth. Furthermore, developing nations will eventually adopt these technologies as their economies grow and pollution increases. Promoting technological innovation thus offers clear benefits to the environment as well as to the economy.

---

[22] Often small is still beautiful. For example, a measure in the Netherlands to promote company bicycles perhaps does as much for the public perception of the government's readiness to protect the environment as does a major green tax. The Dutch environmental planning bureau in 2007 estimated that forgoing car use for all drives up to 7.5 kilometres, using a bicycle instead, could reduce CO_2 emissions by up to 2.4 Mton annually. This reduction corresponds to one-eighth of the Kyoto target.

Measuring the environmental effect

The relative lack of irrefutable evidence makes the public debate on greening tax systems difficult. Models do show effects, *ceteris paribus*, and certainly these models are well founded on empirical data. Unfortunately *ceteris paribus* never becomes reality. A few years after an excise tax rise, energy statistics will show that fuel consumption has again risen. We have become richer and just spend more on driving. In the political debate it is then difficult to defend that the excise rise was nevertheless beneficial to the environment, because fuel consumption would have been even higher in the absence of the excise tax rate. Such a conditional tense does not work well.

Appraising a green tax measure

Expanding existing or introducing new green taxes has to conform to a strict set of requirements. Green tax measures have potentially far-reaching distributional consequences and can hurt business competitiveness and the economy as a whole. The political process that leads to a tax measure thus has to be undertaken carefully. Figure 9.8 presents a decision tree.

In considering a green tax option there has to be a clear environmental benefit. Otherwise the proposal is simply rejected. Second, the measure must have adequate revenue potential. Measures raising little or no revenue are likely to be inefficient from an administrative point of view. In the third place, a green tax measure needs to be compatible with international, or when applicable, EU law. If not, it will be overruled. Administrative feasibility is a fourth check. Many green measures are impossible to enforce because they cannot be effectively controlled or monitored (for example, polluting by very small users).

Tax measures must also not have a significant adverse impact on any key macroeconomic variables. If they do produce negative side-effects, compensatory measures could be considered. If such measures are impractical, however, the proposal should again be rejected. The same is true in the case of severe income or distributional effects. Studies generally reveal a direct regressive impact of the burden distribution of energy taxes. Because low-income households save a relatively large fraction of income, they are hit comparatively hard by an energy tax. As a guiding principle, the purchasing power of all individuals and firms should not be affected unduly.

In relation to this, building acceptance for a green tax option should be emphasised. Whether the public accepts a green tax importantly depends on awareness of the environmental issue at hand. Acceptance can be improved by creating a common understanding of the problem and why the issue needs to be addressed. This also strengthens political support and tends to weaken political opposition. Greater public awareness also helps increase effectiveness. By providing information on a harmful economic activity and the tax applied, the price elasticity of the economic activity in question can increase.[23]

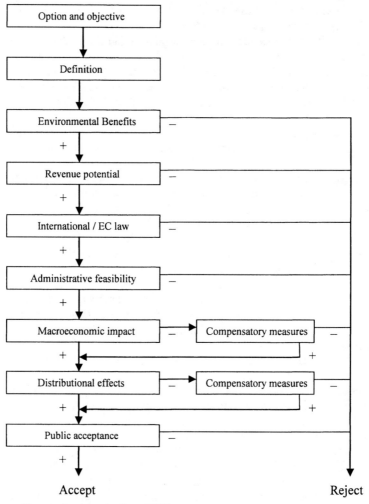

Source: Vermeend and van der Vaart (1998).

Figure 9.8   A decision tree for green tax measures

---

[23] For a discussion on the political economy of environmental taxes, examples and practical policy suggestions to make environmental taxes acceptable to industry, politicians and voters, see Wallart et al. (1999).

Finally, the UK government's *Green Book* contains criteria for public bodies on how to judge new green tax projects before committing significant public funds (HM Treasury, 2003). The book gives elaborate guidance in setting objectives, appraising the options and developing and implementing a well-tailored solution. This includes a long list of relevant issues on, for example, financial arrangements and affordability, commercial and partnering arrangements and information management and control.

Lessons from OECD experiences

Extensive evaluation of a number of *ex post* case studies by the OECD (2006c) reveals that lawmakers should ensure that competitiveness pressures are addressed adequately. Countries are confronted with a deterioration of competitiveness on world markets as companies choose to locate elsewhere or, because of the extra costs, are less efficient in competing on world markets. Moreover, compensatory measures should not mitigate or offset the abatement incentive. By making the tax base as broad as possible, the cost effectiveness of a green tax measure is ensured. In practice, OECD countries by and large appear to have followed this strategy. Broad-based taxes that apply to many instead of a few also tend to facilitate public acceptance and create political support. An OECD-wide energy tax as such would achieve a 'significant' global reduction in carbon emissions (ibid.).

BOX 9.6

The trend in future environmental policy should be towards properly balancing 'negative' and 'positive' incentives (that is, carrot and stick model). The former discourage polluting activities, while the latter encourage environmentally friendly behaviour. Well-designed positive incentive taxes are less detrimental to economic development. A drawback is that they impose a burden on the average taxpayer, which can have an adverse effect on economic activity. Green taxes allocated for this purpose are likely to attract broader public support than green taxes that flow into the treasury.

The Double Dividend Conjecture

Green taxes do not necessarily impede economy activity, if the revenue from green taxation is used to strengthen the budget balance. A so-called 'double dividend' occurs whenever higher green taxes improve the environment, while simultaneously facilitating a cut in other taxes, such as the labour tax, so that employment is improved. Although empirical evidence is relatively scarce and mostly not supportive of the double dividend conjecture, it is worthwhile to briefly consider the theoretical aspects.

A main motive why green taxes may be preferred to regulatory measures is that the benefit accrues to the government instead of to private firms. Regulating a market by limiting production or emissions leads to higher prices as supply is decreased below what it would have been in the absence of regulation. The benefit of higher prices in such a case accrues to the producing firm. In contrast, taxes attain a similar result, except that the benefit of higher prices is transferred to the government in the form of tax revenue. When green tax revenues are used to reduce other more distortionary taxes, the economy may benefit. A double dividend arises from (i) an improvement in the environment due to higher green levies, which are (ii) used to lower other distortionary taxes.

Goulder (1995) distinguishes three categories of the double dividend hypothesis:

- a *weak* form which implies that the efficiency costs of a tax system are lower if green tax revenues are used to reduce other distortionary taxes, compared to the situation where the extra tax revenue is refunded to taxpayers as a lump sum. Hence, there is a relative gross benefit from green taxes since they facilitate reductions in other distortionary taxes (as opposed to regulatory measures);[24]
- an *intermediate* form where the green tax revenue is used to replace an existing distortionary tax so that individual welfare in terms of utility from consumption is actually increased. The substitution involves a zero or negative cost for at least one existing tax; and
- a *strong* form with equal properties, but this time the substitution involves a typical or representative tax (for example, a labour tax) with zero or negative cost.

Numerical simulations confirm that the weak form indeed holds up. The two stronger forms are harder to defend, both on a theoretical basis and based on numerical results. Bovenberg (1999) extends the analysis using a general equilibrium model and finds that only in very specific cases is a double dividend produced. A general precondition is that the government at the outset employed a suboptimal tax structure. Hence, only if the tax system was

---

[24] This is best described by an individual's utility function, which includes utility from environmental quality u_1 and utility from normal consumption of goods and services u_2. Goulder defines *gross benefits* as changes of u_1 and *gross cost* as the negative of changes in u_2, both measured by the wealth equivalents.

already inefficient from a non-environmental viewpoint, may efficiency gains be achieved and also facilitate improvement in environmental quality.[25]

Another branch of studies has focused explicitly on producing a double dividend by reducing labour taxes. The second dividend would in such a case be the reduction of unemployment. This is particularly relevant for European economies where labour taxes are high. Bovenberg and van der Ploeg (1998) simulate the effect of a shift from labour to green taxes under imperfect labour market conditions. The model assumes a small open economy where labour hiring costs cause structural unemployment.

The model shows that a double dividend is achieved only if the labour income tax burden in the formal sector can be (partly) shifted onto the unemployed. This should moderate wage claims and raises employment, but only if unemployment benefits are not indexed. Green taxes achieve this if the unemployed gain income from the informal sector or the black economy. Here, green taxes reduce income though a decrease in labour productivity, while the simultaneous reduction in labour taxes leaves them unaffected since they pay no labour taxes. Moreover, employment increases only if the overall burden imposed by green taxes is not too heavy. Otherwise, economic activity overall would decline too significantly.

BOX 9.7

A double dividend in green tax reform occurs if higher green taxes lead not only to an improved environment but also to a more efficient tax system. The conditions for a double dividend prove to be very strict, but evidence indicates that at least a weak form can be achieved.

9.4 SELECTION OF MEASURES AIMED AT GREENING TAX SYSTEMS

Environmental Effectiveness of Carbon Taxation

In past decades, there has been broad experimentation with green tax measures to reduce CO_2 emissions. This encompassed both negative and positive incentive taxes. Negative incentive taxes are placed on consumption or production, while positive incentives are incorporated into the personal and corporate income tax. Negative incentive taxes discourage

---

[25] If the initial tax system is not optimal from a non-environmental point of view, the green tax reform could reduce the overall welfare loss from taxation. See Bovenberg (1999) for a number of examples where this may be the case.

environmentally undesirable activity by increasing prices and succeed in raising considerable government revenue. Estimates show that short-run elasticities range between -0.13 and -0.26, while long-run elasticities are typically higher and range between -0.37 and -0.46 (OECD, 2000d).[26]

Taxation of energy use

Fuels may be chosen as a tax base because they provide a general link with the 'polluter-pays' principle. A great deal of pollution (particularly air pollution and the noise nuisance caused by traffic) is the direct result of fuel consumption. There is also an indirect linkage, namely that fuel use is a rough indicator of activities which result in pollution. The revenue raised by the fuel tax may be used for environmental-related purposes and policy or be part of the general government revenues.

The tax is collected on energy sources which are used as fuels. Use as raw material or feedstock is generally not subject to this tax. Residuals which are used in the chemical and petroleum industries (petroleum cokes, liquid residuals, gaseous residuals) are taxed provided that the volumes exceed a certain amount. Electricity is not taxed directly, but indirectly via the tax paid on fuel inputs (but only if generated by any of the fuels that are taxed under the system).

The tax rate for the individual fuels can be set according to the energy and/or carbon content (that is, emissions of CO_2). Examples of fuels taxed include gasoline, light fuel oil, gasoil or diesel, heavy fuel oil, coal, coal gasification, LPG, natural gas, petrocokes, liquid residuals and gaseous residuals.[27] In an efficient system, taxes on coal will be higher than on oil and for oil higher than on gas due to the differences in carbon content.

While several methods of collection exist, general arrangements are as follows. The tax on mineral oils is levied on those who are liable for excise duties and is collected together with the excises. The tax on coal is levied on parties who extract, produce or import the coal and subsequently use it as fuel or transfer it to others for domestic use as fuel. The tax on gas is levied on those who extract gas and subsequently use it as fuel, those who produce or import gas and use it as fuel, those who receive gas from the party who extracted it and subsequently use it as fuel, and parties who produce or import gas and subsequently transfer it to others for domestic use. Finally, the tax on petrocokes, and liquid and gaseous residuals used as fuels in petroleum or chemical plants is levied on the plant operator. If markets function properly the tax is passed on to the consumer.

---

[26] The Scandinavian countries were in the forefront of countries implementing carbon taxes (Finland first adopted a CO_2 tax in 1990). For a comprehensive overview of 68 studies conducted on the economic impact and environmental effectiveness, see Andersen et al. (2000).

[27] Uranium used in nuclear power installations to generate electricity can be included in the tax base, even though this source does not produce carbon emissions.

The regulatory energy tax

The regulatory energy tax focuses on small-scale energy consumption by households and SMEs. It is implemented in many countries. The tax avoids the economic risks that result from unilateral imposition of an energy tax on large industrial energy users. Other policy instruments are proving effective in inducing large energy consumers to save energy, such as the carbon tax and trading arrangements. The tax may be levied on natural gas, electricity, light fuel oil, heating oil and LPG. Fuels used to power road vehicles are not subject to the regulatory tax.

A volume ceiling on the taxable energy use focuses the tax on smaller users of energy such as households and small commercial establishments such as restaurants and shops, office buildings, schools and so forth. These are precisely the target groups that are difficult or impossible to reach with policy instruments such as long-term agreements or environmental permits. Larger energy-intensive industries pay only a relatively small amount of tax.

Energy use is taxed only above a certain floor amount per user. The taxable event in the case of natural gas and electricity is the delivery of energy to the final user. In a strictly formal sense, the tax is paid by the company that distributes the energy. The tax is then passed on to customers in the form of a higher price. In practice, the tax is therefore borne by all consumers of energy. Hence, both business and households pay tax unless their total energy use is less than the tax-free allowance. The tax on mineral oil products may be levied on those liable for excise duties.

The existence of a tax-free floor reduces the amount of tax that individuals and firms have to pay. However, it does so without reducing the incentive created by the tax, which exists on the margin. Since it is difficult if not impossible to administer a tax-free allowance for the non-metered mineral oil products, this has been set at zero. The applicable tax rates can be lowered accordingly. The ceiling is set depending on the country-specific situation. Calculations will indicate when it is desirable to tax additional consumption.

Accelerated depreciation of environmental investment

Accelerated depreciation benefits firms liable for personal or corporate income taxation that are reporting positive income, by offering businesses an immediate financial advantage. The scheme allows an entrepreneur to write off equipment at will. Usually it is therefore immediately expensed in the year of purchase. The magnitude of this advantage depends on the tax rate, the interest rate and the lifetime of the investment. All entrepreneurs liable for personal or corporate income tax would be eligible for the scheme.

The measure aims to speed up technological innovation and to facilitate the diffusion of new environmental technologies. Such investments often still yield below-market rate of returns, which make it unviable for businesses to undertake. Since the potential benefits to society are none the less high, government may find it worthwhile to provide an additional incentive.

The equipment should not have been used before, so it has to be new. Only the best available state-of-the-art technologies that have not penetrated the market qualify. The exact technologies that qualify should be identified on a so-called 'environmental list' that is updated continuously, for example by the Ministry of Finance. This process ensures that only the latest technologies are included, so the government does not waste taxpayers' money on old investment that either has become commercially viable or is unlikely to ever become so. The mechanism would have a similar effect to so-called 'sunset provisions', which limit the duration of a specific business tax incentive, and is generally held to improve cost effectiveness.

Energy investment tax credit

The energy investment tax credit allows firms to credit against tax a certain percentage of investment in energy-friendly technologies. The percentage may be dependent on the size of the investment according to a specific rate schedule. An absolute upper limit may be set for the annual aggregate energy investment sum permitted. The energy investment tax credit can be incremental to normal depreciation.

In many cases the investment would also be eligible for free depreciation as described above. The investment costs can then be expensed immediately for the full amount, which in combination with the credit would create a significant financial incentive to invest. Eligible investment projects should have been identified on a separate environmental list by the responsible authorities. The same criteria would apply as discussed above under the accelerated depreciation scheme. Hence, the list should be updated continuously to include only the newest technologies.[28]

Both energy-saving equipment and equipment for the generation of renewable energy can be bought under the credit scheme. The investment may be categorised according to the field of application such as: buildings, processes, buildings and processes, transport and renewable energy. Hassett and Metcalf (1995) using US panel data find that a 10 percentage point in the tax price of energy investment could lead to an increase of 24 per cent in the probability of homeowners making residential conservation investment.

Green Funds: Tax-free Income

Income tax can incorporate a favourable provision for investment in so-called 'green investment funds' to combat environmental pollution. Individuals who invest in the fund receive tax-free income from the fund in the form of

---

[28] In the Netherlands, requests for application of the energy investment tax credit in 2006 totalled €3.7 billion. Farmers in particular invested massively in installations to generate electricity from biomass (in total €892 million). The machines cost between €400,000 and €800,000, which will be recovered within 4 to 8 years because of the energy investment tax credit.

dividends, interest and/or capital gains. The green investment funds invest in designated green projects approved by the public authorities.

BOX 9.8

Accelerated depreciation of environmental investment and the energy investment tax credit provide an incentive to businesses to invest in latest state-of-the-art environmentally friendly technologies, which may otherwise not yet be commercially viable. The qualifying technologies are identified on an 'environmental list' that is updated on a continuous basis. This process guarantees that only the newest technologies (that is, so-called 'second-generation technologies') are promoted which enhances the cost effectiveness of the measures.

The aim of the tax concession is to encourage investment in major environmental projects, involving forests and nature areas, sustainable energy supply and environmental technology. In the Netherlands, green funds have been a resounding success. Most major banks now have green investment funds with assets of €3.6 billions, financing 3,200 green projects. The tax benefit is approximately 2 per cent of the investment amount up to an investment of €50,000 per individual taxpayer. The funds are subject to CT; however, a special tax rate of 0 per cent applies. As noted, all income derived is tax exempt under PT.

The rationale is that by offering fiscal incentives, extra funds are made available for green projects. Such projects prove difficult to finance, since they typically generate below-market rates of return. By ensuring that the return to investors is untaxed or low taxed, a level playing field is created compared to regular investments that are subject to standard tax. As such, the green projects not only offer a sound environmental yield, but they also provide a reasonable financial return.

The activities of green investment funds must primarily be the provision of funds to green projects. As a basic requirement, a substantial share of total assets of the green investment funds should be invested in green projects, for example, at least 70 per cent. The green investment funds would not be allowed to run green projects themselves. The projects have to be new, though a fundamental improvement to an existing project can also be regarded as a new project. The type of projects eligible can be predefined and should primarily include those that cannot be funded commercially. A few examples are:

- projects in the fields of nature, forestry, landscape and organic farming;

- projects in the field of sustainable energy;
- housing, for example built from environmentally friendly materials. Owners can then obtain a so-called 'green mortgage';
- farming, such as 'green label' animal housing and greenhouses;
- soil sanitation;
- cycle lanes; and
- other projects satisfying the criteria employed, which can be put forward and assessed on an individual basis.

The implementation of the scheme is straightforward. If a project falls into one of the categories, those seeking funding can apply to a green investment fund, frequently run by a bank. If the investment fund is prepared to provide the necessary financing, it applies for a green statement for the project in question with the authorised government agency. On this basis the institution can subsequently award tax-free payments from the return on the investment in the project. Green investment funds thus have a number of advantages:

- the market is in charge of investment projects that are beneficial to the environment;
- they attract new players to the environmental team: bank managers in search of green projects;
- they create greater public support and awareness: green investment becomes 'fun'; and
- they generate potentially large funds for environmental purposes.

Promoting sustainable transport
In addition, a number of small-scale measures contribute to the reduction of CO_2 emissions and may be especially constructive in improving public awareness for the environment and climate change:

- *Commuting.* Within limits, income tax allows employers to reimburse free of tax the costs to employees of commuting by public transport. Alternatively, an employee may deduct the cost from his or her taxable income. The amount that is set as a maximum for the tax-free reimbursement or tax deduction can be derived from the costs of public transport. For example, an average amount per kilometre travelled with a minimum distance. Or it could simply be based on public transport tickets submitted to the employer;
- *Carpooling.* Carpooling can be stimulated by, for instance, allowing employers to pay a distance-related amount tax free as a carpool bonus to each employee taking part in the scheme. The carpool bonus would ideally not affect the already available standard possibilities for reimbursing employees tax free for the costs of

commuting or for deducting the costs. A number of conditions can be set for receiving a carpool bonus, such as a minimum travelling distance that is shared by at least two people (driver and one passenger) during a minimum number of days a year;

- *Teleworking.* The dominant method of teleworking in a digitalising economy involves working at home for at least a few days a week. Car use for commuting is avoided on these days. To encourage teleworking, employers can supply an employee with a home computer free of tax up to a certain value. A tax-free reimbursement of the costs for such a computer is also possible;

- *The company bicycle.* In many European countries cycling is the dominant method of commuting smaller distances. Although a small-scale measure, there is clearly an environmental benefit in trying to encourage bicycle use for short-distance commuting. A tax-favourable treatment is provided by allowing employers to supply a bicycle free of tax to employees, for example, once every three years; and

- *Taxing aviation.* Currently, kerosene is untaxed under most excise tax schemes. The introduction of a kerosene tax or ticket tax should discourage flying, especially if it approaches the level of excise tax rates on 'ordinary' fuels. The tax would be passed on to the consumer by higher ticket prices or fuel surcharges, by means of which airlines nowadays frequently rationalise high energy prices.

These measures are a mixed blessing, though. Generally speaking, they present exceptions to broad-based taxation, and increase the complexity and administrative burden of the tax system. As noted, moreover, when considering a green tax measure in environmental and climate policy, the measure must be appraised against the decision model presented in Figure 9.7. Of all the factors that play a role in the selection process, effectiveness in reaching the intended objective comes first (that is, the environmental gain).

For example, most proposals for ticket and kerosene taxes are unlikely to pass the test. The environmental gain of aviation taxes is at best mediocre. The levies are transferred to passengers, though price increases have thus far been moderate in countries that have implemented such levies. The tax revenues flow into government treasuries, without materially affecting air traffic behaviour and the number of flights. In addition, aeroplanes are responsible for a large quantity of greenhouse gas emissions during taxiing and so-called 'parking flights'.

Environment Compensation Fund

A higher environmental gain may be achieved by using the green tax revenues not to finance general government expenditure, but instead by allocating the funds to an environment compensation fund (ECF). Green taxes often encounter more public resistance than other taxes. An aviation tax, for example, raises ticket prices, yet fails to produce a significant effect. With the EFC money, compensatory measures are implemented both domestically and worldwide, such as planting and maintaining forests that absorb CO_2. Air travellers typically show less opposition to such a compensation levy than when the revenue flows into general government funds. The environmental gain is also greater.

Climate Investment Funds

Inspired by the green investment fund, we suggest that tax-free climate funds should be set up. Such funds would have the following characteristics:

- no CT would be levied from the fund;
- dividends, interest and capital gains received by individual taxpayers would be free from PT up to a maximum investment participation of, for example, €100,000; and
- at least 70 per cent of the assets are allocated to fund investment projects that seek to slow, stop or reverse climate change.

The projects would centre on energy saving and efficiency and renewable and alternative energies.

A simplified example of a climate fund would be as follows. Country X has a CT rate of 30 per cent and an income tax with three brackets of 20, 30 and 40 per cent. The climate investment fund is established by a bank and listed on the stock exchange where participations can be traded. To benefit from the tax break the fund must invest at least 70 per cent of its assets in climate projects that contribute to reducing greenhouse gas emissions. The projects are earmarked as such by the government, which issues a climate certificate.

In practice, these investments will be insufficiently undertaken by the market as the (short-term) return is inadequate. Hence, the tax break offers the fund and individual investors a form of compensation and thereby stimulates climate projects. Primarily, the investments constitute loans to climate projects and equity participations in companies with a climate certificate. Table 9.5 shows an example balance sheet of a climate fund.

Net profit from the investments in 2007 is 21 million units. The profits and shareholder distributions are free of corporate and personal income tax. Suppose a participant on 1 January 2007 contributed 10,000 units to the fund and after one year receives 300 units in dividends, so his or her return is 3 per cent (transaction and administration costs are assumed to be zero). Because of the tax advantage there is an additional gain of 120 units (that is, assuming that the top rate applies, 40 per cent of 300 units). The implicit return is therefore 420 units, or 4.2 per cent.

Table 9.5   Balance sheet of tax-free climate fund on 31 December 2007 (before profit distribution in millions)

Shares in climate companies	150	
Loans		
Wind energy	170	
Bio energy	30	
Solar energy	50	
CO_2-neutral commercial and residential buildings	200	
Other assets	100	
Total equity capital		700
	700	700

BOX 9.9

Tax-free green and climate funds are uniquely designed to encourage green investments by smaller portfolio investors. The funds offer a tax-free alternative to ordinary investment and can succeed in attracting significant finance for green investment projects that may otherwise not be undertaken or only later. The funds finance projects in areas of energy saving and efficiency and renewable and alternative energies. The funds boost innovation and contribute to crafting a lasting change in traditional methods of production and transitioning to an entirely new low-carbon economy.

9.5   BRIEF SUMMARY

This chapter has shown that green tax policy is a promising and worthwhile undertaking. The evidence reveals that at current levels of taxation at least a strong single dividend can be achieved. That is, an improvement in the environment with no or a negligible adverse effect on the macro economy. Experience in the last decade or so has demonstrated that well-designed green taxes can be efficient instruments, especially when the tax base is broadly

defined, which improves the cost effectiveness of a green tax measure
(OECD, 2006c).

World prosperity and population are increasing rapidly, putting ever
greater pressure on the earth's atmosphere and natural resources. Since this
development is not sustainable in the long run, economic policy can no
longer be separated from the implementation of a sound and responsible
environmental policy. To tackle climate change effectively, a global
commitment is necessary. Furthermore, given the scope of the problem and
projections for the future, negative (tax) incentives will not be sufficiently
effective to stop or reverse global warming and need to be complemented by
market-based instruments that encourage technological innovation. Briefly,
the following observations can be made with regard to environmental policy:

- the current consensus appears to be that the emphasis should lie on a
  worldwide trade of emission rights (based on market value) that not
  only discourage polluting activities, but also promote the
  development of clean technologies;
- government should focus not so much on stimulating the
  implementation of existing technologies, but instead on the newest
  so-called 'second-generation' technologies (that is, technologies that
  go beyond current methods and approaches) for energy saving and
  efficiency; renewable and alternative energies; and hydrogen and
  fuel cells;
- innovations should be transferred to developing countries such as
  China and India, which is necessary to get these countries
  committed to the environmental cause and offers domestic
  businesses an opportunity to access these booming markets; and
- greening tax systems has a prominent auxiliary role in
  environmental policy and combating climate change.

Green tax measures should be used on the basis of positive evaluation by a
decision tree (see, for example, Figure 9.9). To tackle global warming, we
favour an approach that is based on the carrot and stick model. The model is
market based and features the following 'negative' and 'positive' incentive
tax measures:

- a gradual increase in green taxation up to 5 per cent of GDP in the
  tax mix;
- a carbon tax for households and firms. EU member states, the US
  and Japan are setting an example and have started implementing
  these types of levy (the tax base is energy or carbon content);
- introduction or increase of existing taxes on polluting or energy-
  intensive installations;

- promoting green energy such as solar and wind power by means of fiscal incentives and a purchase/production obligation for renewable energies for consumers and energy suppliers;[29]
- a lower vehicle tax for smaller and cleaner cars and lower excise rates for cleaner fuels;
- an energy investment tax credit or accelerated depreciation for enterprises. A portfolio of technologies will be required to deliver the necessary savings in greenhouse gas emissions. The shift to a low-carbon global economy can be promoted by introducing an energy investment tax credit for investing in new lower-carbon technologies and switching away from high-carbon goods and services to low-carbon alternatives.
- introduction of tax-free green and climate investment funds, which can be set up in the market sector throughout the world, for example, by banks. As a condition for establishment, these funds should invest at least 70 per cent of their money in green investment programmes that are important to the environment, help to tackle climate change and improve air quality. Households that invest in these funds are free from tax on dividends, interest and capital gains derived;
- introduction of a national environment compensation fund. Green tax revenues should (partly) flow into these funds instead of into the treasury. An ECF produces a higher environmental gain by allocating the money to 'green compensation projects' such as planting trees and maintaining forests; and
- more generally, governments should work on improving public awareness of and support for the environmental cause by creating a direct and visible relationship between green taxes and the use of proceeds for improving the environment. Broadly speaking, the public does not consider taxes that flow directly into the treasury as supporting the environmental cause. Instead, they are viewed as an ordinary tax rise.

This policy blend creates a framework whereby individuals and companies in society are not just discouraged from polluting, but are also stimulated to invest in environmentally friendly behaviour and technologies. Thus, sustainable economic growth is created, balanced by sound environmental policy providing s healthy living environment.

---

[29] Examples can be found in Austria, Belgium, Germany, Sweden and the UK.

PART V

Lessons for tax policy

10. Summary of findings and recommendations

To tax and to please, no more than to love and to be wise, is not given to men.

(Edmund Burke)[1]

10.1 21st-CENTURY TRENDS AND ISSUES

Taxes are needed to finance the goods and services provided by government. At the same time, taxes affect the incentives to work, consume, save and invest and have a profound impact on the economy as a whole, both today and tomorrow. This has persuaded many governments to use taxation as an instrument in economic policy, for example, in an effort to stimulate sustainable economic growth and employment, and to achieve a more balanced income distribution and a healthy environmental climate.

There are clear limits to what can be attained. The tax system affects the economic behaviour of taxpayers differently. Broadly speaking, taxes on income and consumption create a distortion in the choice to work, consume, save and invest. High marginal tax rates are inevitably accompanied by many exceptions to the tax base that create distortions and raise opportunities for tax planning and avoidance strategies. This undermines the principle of simplicity and revenue-raising capacity of the tax system. These distortions also reduce economic efficiency (that is, create an excess burden or costs over and above revenue collected) and can have adverse effects on economic growth and employment. Most studies on taxation and OECD economies endorse the notion that high marginal tax rates harm economic growth (see Table 1.10 in Chapter 1).

These issues are reinforced by 21st-century developments that will increasingly leave their mark on tax policy. The most important ongoing economic and (demographic) issues, trends and economic challenges are:

---

[1] Edmund Burke (1729-97) was an 18th-century Irish political philosopher and British statesman.

341

- a globalising world with increasingly borderless economies and high capital and labour mobility;
- an interconnected world driven by technological change and the internet;
- increasing competition on world markets and importance of worldwide economic competitive strength on economic growth;
- human capital as a key productive factor, that is, worldwide demand for creative, smart and high-skilled workers;
- the battle between countries for companies, brains and affluent individuals, mostly the elderly who have built up wealth over their lifetime;
- population ageing;
- the environment and the fight against climate change in creating and maintaining sustainable economic growth; and
- increasing political attention to relative well-being and the happiness of people and the consequences of economic policy.

As noted, governments have various instruments at their disposal besides taxation to conduct economic policy. Examples are regulation (for example, prohibition of harmful products or restrictions on CO_2 emissions), direct government control (for example, government production and licensing), firm-level legislation (for example, antitrust and safety laws), and direct subsidy programmes (for example, for social security, education and health). In order to realise a certain policy aim, careful consideration should be given as to the instrument to use. This can be based on a decision tree and measured against best practices such as in Figure 9.8 in Chapter 9. The outcome could be a tax measure, but also another government instrument.

Key Indicators in Economic Policy

An accepted measure of economic growth is the development of GDP over time. GDP per capita is a primary indicator of economic welfare of a country (see Chapter 1). In addition, we have seen that many other factors affect economic well-being, such as adequate provision of education, healthcare, social safety and public order and security. The gap between 'rich' and 'poor' also contributes to relative happiness, where high inequality typically leads to less happiness. Both in academia and in politics there is rising interest in what actually makes people happy.

Against this background, there are some notable differences in an international comparison of countries in terms of GDP per capita, size of government, the tax burden, international competitive strength, well-being and happiness, and the income gap between rich and poor (see Table 10.1). Noteworthy is that countries with a relatively large government and heavy

Table 10.1 Cross-country comparison of key policy statistics (sample ranking)

Country	GDP per capita (high)	Average growth rate, 1970-2005 (high)	Size of government (small)	Total tax burden (small)	Global competitive-ness (high)	Income inequality (low)	Subjective well-being (high)	Climate change index (high)
Australia	9	4	2	4	13	13	10	14
Austria	5	8	11	10	11	7	2	13
Belgium	7	11	12	14	14	11	11	6
Canada	10	5	5	5	10	9	5	15
Denmark	6	14	14	15	3	1	1	3
Finland	12	7	13	13	1	5	3	12
France	14	10	15	11	12	10	15	5
Germany	13	15	9	6	6	6	12	4
Ireland	3	1	1	3	15	12	6	11
Italy	16	13	10	9	16	14	14	10
Japan	15	6	4	2	5	2	16	8
Netherlands	4	9	8	8	7	8	7	9
Norway	1	2	6	12	9	4	8	7
Sweden	11	16	16	16	2	3	4	1
UK	8	12	7	7	8	15	13	2
US	2	3	3	1	4	16	9	16

Sources: Tables 1.1, 1.6, 1.7 and 10.2.

total tax burden score high in terms of GDP per capita, competitiveness and happiness and feature relatively low in income inequality.

Denmark is an example: it has a relatively high GDP per capita (6), is highly competitive (3), has low income inequality (1), a happy population (1) and a high performance in terms of addressing climate change (3), yet a large government (14) and high tax burden (15). It also experienced relatively low average growth (14) over the 1970-2005 period. The US has the second largest GDP per capita (2), has experienced high growth (3), a small government (3), low total tax burden (1) and is competitive (4). The country has high income inequality (16) and the US population is fairly happy (9), although its children appear to be less so (14). In terms of performance in tackling climate change it ranks last (16).

The table also demonstrates that countries with a relatively small government score well in terms of average growth: Ireland (1), Norway (2), the United States (3), Australia (4), Canada (5) and Japan (6).

Further Tax Reform is Needed

Particularly in the post-Second World War era, the use of the tax systems in OECD countries to accomplish a variety of policy objectives intensified. This was accompanied by a steady rise in government expenditures and marginal tax rates, sometimes exceeding 80 per cent in income tax. This led to narrow tax bases, relatively high marginal rates, complicated tax legislation, conflict between tax authority and taxpayer, and tax avoidance and evasion. It also diminished the distributional efficacy of the tax system.

The period from 1980 to 2007 saw a series of major reforms in OECD countries, both to personal and to corporate income tax. These reforms were characterised by sometimes dramatic tax cuts. Often though, these tax cuts were accompanied by base-broadening measures, so ultimately effective tax rates did not change much. In some cases, effective tax rates have also diminished. At the same time, the general introduction of and/or increases in VAT has been observed in many countries.

Our survey demonstrates that despite major reforms most tax systems are still complex, place a high burden on labour and score insufficiently on the characteristics of a good tax system as discussed in Chapter 2:

- a sufficient and stable revenue yield;
- efficiency;
- equity, both vertical and horizontal;
- minimal costs of administration and compliance;
- flexibility, simplicity and transparency; and
- international adaptability.

All tax systems need to be equipped for key developments, issues and trends in the 21st century. The fiscal challenge centres around:

- globalisation with increasing competition on world markets and high mobility of workers and companies;
- the world of the internet and e-commerce;
- the effect of ageing on labour markets and government finances;
- tax competition; and
- environmental developments and climate change.

We have concluded that a well-designed tax system increasingly contributes to sustainable economic growth and additional employment in the global economy of today and tomorrow (see in particular Chapters 2, 3 and 4). Empirical evidence and practical experiences convincingly point in one direction. Tax reform should centre in particular on broadening tax bases, cutting marginal tax rates, simplification, bringing a shift to consumption-based taxation and greening tax systems. Only then can 21st-century challenges be met effectively.

10.2   A GROWING IMPORTANCE OF THE 'TAX PACKAGE'

Although dynamics in a tax system are the outcome of a myriad of factors, global trends and developments increasingly leave their mark on domestic markets and economies. As a consequence, the tax system becomes a more pronounced determinant in an economy's performance and competitiveness. The 'tax package' whereby countries compete on world markets contains a number of elements:

- the total tax burden;
- the tax mix;
- statutory tax rates;
- effective tax rates;
- specific tax incentives for businesses and workers;
- advanced tax rulings between taxpayer and tax authority; and
- a network of tax treaties with other countries.

Under current global developments, the significance of the tax package will grow further. As part of economic policy, countries should periodically test the attractiveness of the tax package to other (neighbouring) countries. Such comparative analysis enables governments, in the interest of economic efficiency, to proactively react with competitive improvements to developments abroad.

The Total Tax Burden

Table 10.2 shows the tax to GDP ratio for the 16 sample countries in 2004. The overview reveals large differences in the size of respective governments. High-tax countries are Sweden, Denmark and Belgium. Relatively low-tax countries are the United States, Japan and Ireland.

Table 10.2   The tax to GDP ratio, 2004

Country	Tax to GDP ratio	Country	Tax to GDP ratio
Australia	31.2	Ireland	30.1
Austria	42.6	Italy	41.1
Belgium	45.0	Japan	26.4
Canada	33.5	Netherlands	37.5
Denmark	48.8	Norway	44.0
Finland	44.2	Sweden	50.4
France	43.4	UK	36.0
Germany	34.7	US	25.5

Source: Electronic database OECD: Revenue Statistics.

The total level of taxation has increased substantially, that is, 7.9 percentage points in the OECD area in the period from 1970 to 2005 (see Table 2.1 in Chapter 2). A high level of taxation is not by definition harmful to an economy. An attractive mix of a developed infrastructure, a high-skilled labour force, competitive wage rates, flexible labour markets, a stable political climate, a reliable judicial system, low bureaucracy and administrative burden, adequate social and cultural provisions, a clean living environment, and a tax burden that is not considered too high or obstructive are *all* factors that contribute to a favourable environment in which citizens and companies can live and operate.

Countries with a relatively high level of taxation can thus be attractive locations for business investment if they score high on other points. High-tax countries such as Finland, Denmark and Sweden are currently among the most competitive economies in the world (see the competitiveness rankings in Chapter 1). The heavy tax burden is shouldered by an active population in the labour market. Likewise, countries with a relatively low tax burden will not automatically be attractive locations if they perform poorly in other areas, such as those just mentioned.

Whether a high tax burden like that in the Nordic countries is sustainable given 21st-century developments is questionable. The OECD Economic Survey of Denmark (2005) confirms this (OECD, 2005a). As labour is becoming more mobile, high-skilled workers tend to leave high-tax jurisdictions, while high welfare spending attracts low-skilled workers. According to the OECD's Tax Policy Analysis, Denmark is nevertheless in the process of taking measures, such as the implemented 'tax freeze' which stipulates that taxes cannot rise further (OECD, 2006a).

The Tax Mix

Since the 1970s, the tax mix in many countries has changed (see Chapter 2). The OECD average shows a steady increase in general sales taxation, such as VAT, while the revenue intake from excise taxes has diminished. PT has lost in significance, but this has been accompanied by a rise in social security contributions. And although the share of CT has declined since the 1970s, there has been a small upsurge over the past 10 years.

Furthermore, a number of governments have shifted to rely more heavily on environmental levies in their tax mix. Besides improving the environment, the revenue generated has been used to lower labour taxes and to create a more stable revenue intake. Examples of these shifts can be found in income tax reforms in Denmark, Finland, the Netherlands, Norway and Sweden.

Statutory Tax Rates

A closer look at personal and corporate income tax rates reveals large differences between countries (see Appendix 6 for a full overview). A high statutory tax rate in no way implies that the effective tax rate is high too. Several countries impose comparatively high marginal tax rates, while the effective rate is ultimately relatively low due to generous tax breaks. A high tax rate on a narrow base results in a low effective burden. The rates bark, but do not bite. These tax breaks also loom very large on the budget. So-called 'tax expenditures' account for up to 7 or 8 per cent of GDP in OECD countries. As a corollary, marginal tax rates are high to raise the necessary revenue (see Chapter 2 for an overview).

Main drawbacks of high marginal tax rates
A comparison of a tax code with high PT rates and a narrow base with a system that imposes a similar effective burden by lower tax rates and a broader base, reveals several shortcomings of the former. Roughly summarised, tax structures with high marginal tax rates and many exceptions to the tax base encounter the following objections:

- complex tax legislation with multiple exceptions to the tax base;

- high cost of administration and compliance;
- taxpayers seeking tax shields, tax shelter transactions and other strategies that reduce the tax bill;
- tax avoidance, evasion and fraud;
- tax flight of high income earners for a more favourable fiscal climate; and
- negative effects on labour supply and human capital accumulation;

These drawbacks have persuaded many governments to revise PT structures from the mid-1980s on, with the main aim of cutting marginal tax rates, broadening the tax base and simplifying the system. Similar trends, though more pronounced, have been observed for CT.

CT developments in the EU are illustrative

Table 10.3 shows that with a few exceptions, all countries in the EU have lowered statutory CT rates since 1995. Between 1995 and 2007, the average CT rate in the old EU-15 has declined from 38 to 29.3 per cent. The accession of the 10 new Eastern European member states on 1 May 2004 has put more pressure on the average CT rate, which thereby declined further to 24.7 per cent. The tax cuts were partly driven by forces from tax competition. We also point to the significant forthcoming 2008 German tax reform that will further reduce the CT rate to just below the 30 per cent mark. The total package is estimated to cost €30 billion, of which €25 billion is financed by base-broadening measures and self-financing. French President Nicolas Sarkozy in his 2007 election campaign also promised to cut the French CT by €15 billion to 28 per cent.

As noted, many countries have financed the cuts by base broadening, so effective tax rates remained roughly similar. As a rule, a reduction in the statutory tax rate financed by base broadening should not generate similar positive effects as a reduction in the statutory rate with the tax base unchanged. But even if there is insufficient budgetary leeway to fully finance a rate cut, there are on average advantages associated with lower statutory tax rates paid for by base broadening. Some of these advantages have been summarised before (that is, the contra arguments against high tax rates).

In addition, decision makers within international corporations in practice first look to the statutory rate when assessing the tax factor (besides other factors relevant for the investment decision), and not, as one might expect, the effective tax rate. The effective tax rate is not easily determined and calls for costly research. Managers therefore first compose a so-called 'short list' of attractive countries to invest in.

Table 10.3   CT rates in the old EU-15 and new EU-10

Country	1995	2007	%-point change 1995-2007
'Old' EU-15			
Austria	34	25	-9
Belgium	40.2	34	-6.2
Denmark	34	28	-6
Finland	25	26	1
France	36.7	33.8	-2.9
Germany	56.8	38.3[b]	-18.5
Greece	40	29	-11
Ireland	40	12.5	-27.5
Italy	52.2	37.3	-14.9
Luxembourg	40.9	29.6	-11.3
Netherlands	35	25.5	-9.5
Portugal	39.6	27.5	-12.1
Spain	35	35	0
Sweden	28	28	0
UK	33	30	-3
'New' EU-10			
Czech Republic	41	24	-17
Cyprus	25	10	-15
Estonia	26	0	-26
Hungary	19.6	16	-3.6
Latvia	25	15	-10
Lithuania	29	15	-14
Malta	35	35	0
Poland	40	19	-21
Slovakia	40	19	-21
Average			
Old EU-15	38.0	29.3	
New EU-10	30.6	17.8	
EU-25[a]	35.0	24.7	

Notes:
[a] As noted, as of 1 January 2007 the EU encompasses 27 members.
[b] 30 per cent as of 2008.

Sources: European Commission (2004b) and Deloitte's Corporate Tax Rates at a Glance 2006 http://www.deloitte.com/dtt/cda/doc/content/2006_01_23%20Worldwide_CT_Rates_2006%281%29.pdf (downloaded on 15 February, 2007).

A high statutory tax rate can cause a country to score a 'minus point' in the location decision of an MNC, even if the effective tax rate is internationally competitive.[2] By contrast, a low rate serves as an eye-catcher. Only after the composition of the short list is further research conducted on effective tax rates. It is thus important to be on the short list first.

Effective Tax Rate

The fourth element in an attractive tax package is the effective tax rate, which is particularly important as a determinant of discrete investment choices by firms. Most studies find significantly positive tax price elasticities with regard to FDI. Governments therefore pay close attention to the effective tax rates in neighbouring states. The effects may be strong. One study of EU member states reported that a 10 per cent reduction in the capital tax burden in surrounding countries, on average triggers a 7.5 per cent lower tax burden in a European country (see Chapter 4). Such a significant response confirms that tax competition is taking place.

Within the EU, member states review tax policy of other members by means of the so-called 'open coordination method'. This leads to greater awareness and swift reactions to a tax cut in a competing member state. To give a few examples, note the CT reforms in Belgium (2003), Portugal (2004), Austria (2005), Greece (2005), the Netherlands (2006) and Germany (2007).

According to optimal tax theory and the tax competition literature, the effective CT burden should decline as capital mobility increases. Razin and Sadka (1991) even forecast a 'race to the bottom' whereby corporate taxes eventually spiral down to zero. However, current trends do not yet reveal such a pattern. Studies show that effective tax rates on capital have hardly been reduced in recent years. Within the EU this development may be partly explained by a culturally determined 'stay-close-to-home' mentality (in spite of relatively high capital mobility) and by EU regulation against harmful tax competition, EU rules against fiscal state aid and ECJ (tax) rulings. For now, however, there still seems to be leeway to finance rate cuts by base broadening.

Partly due to increasing tax competition, prudent government policy should nevertheless anticipate a period of sweeping CT cuts. Even if the CT raises relatively little revenue, nobody can refute that lower revenues from such a corporate tax would put a significant strain on government finances, which are often already under severe pressure.

---

[2] This also follows from the fiscal strategy memorandum of the European Commission (2001a), which found not the tax base, but rather the statutory tax rate of the CT to be the leading driver of a country's competitiveness in attracting foreign investment.

In the absence of coordination, EU member states simply have few alternatives. Tax competition by targeted business tax incentives in the tax base is increasingly problematic. The autonomy of national governments has been significantly reduced and in many instances such tax arrangements are no longer practicable. The tax measures fall within the scope of EU regulations on state aid, or the EU Code of Conduct for Business Taxation or are not allowed on the basis of the ECJ rulings in direct tax affairs. We note that in the US there is greater flexibility for states to compete by way of specific business tax incentives, while any negative side-effects do not (yet) seem to warrant much concern (Graetz and Warren, 2006).

Specific Tax Incentives for Business and Workers

Countries incorporate a variety of specific or targeted tax incentives into their tax systems that aim to induce certain behaviour, such as a greater work effort or higher investment. For example, targeted business tax incentives seek to attract international investment.

Many of these arrangements have been found in contradiction with the WTO agreement or accepted practices by the OECD. Furthermore, in the EU a large number of specific business tax arrangements have been phased out or are currently in the process of being phased out.[3] As argued, this is mainly under the influence of the efforts of the European Commission and the ECJ.

In special cases, business tax incentives can none the less have a useful function in attracting foreign investment and boosting economic activity in particular industry sectors. Mostly, however, the effects are of a temporary nature. As the tax measure continues over time, its effectiveness is reduced as competing countries introduce counter measures. In many cases, moreover, a thorough *ex ante* and *ex post* evaluation of the measure is omitted. Such analysis is essential for adequate tax policy. It can therefore be useful to bind tax incentives to sunset provisions if this enhances effectiveness. These provisions already determine the date of repeal on introduction and may thereby prevent unnecessary prolongation of an inefficient tax measure.

Advanced Tax Rulings between Taxpayer and Tax Authority

The tax climate for business investment of a country is likewise determined by practices of implementation or execution of the law and the attitude of the relevant tax authority therein. For firms it is of great importance to obtain advance clarity and certainty from the tax inspector in tax affairs. So-called 'advance tax rulings' or 'advance pricing agreements' offer advance certainty

---

[3] Examples include the Irish International Financial Service Centre (Dublin), the Belgian 'coordination centres', and the Dutch arrangement for international financing activities. For a complete list, see Code of Conduct Group (2000).

on whether a tax provision is applicable in a certain circumstance and in what manner. Firms attach great value to having such assurances beforehand when making an investment decision. Tax authorities in many countries offer this opportunity.

The Network of Tax Treaties with Other Countries

The final feature of an attractive 'tax package' is the network of tax treaties that one country has concluded with other countries. Bilateral tax conventions offer legal security, confer specific tax benefits to certain workers and mitigate withholding taxes on cross-border capital income payments such as dividends, interest or royalties. A country with a large network of tax treaties is thus an attractive country in which to locate MNCs.

10.3   REFORMING TAX SYSTEMS TO MEET FUTURE CHALLENGES

In facing 21st-century challenges, tax reform is needed. The costs of social security, pensions and healthcare will in the coming decades rise by several percentage points of GDP in many OECD countries (see Chapter 2). Larger labour market flexibility and moving production factors in an era of globalisation and high competition in world markets make higher taxes a very unattractive alternative to raise the required revenue. High-skilled workers are better able to determine for themselves the amount of labour they supply, so distortions from labour taxation will increase. Furthermore, a growing wage gap due to skill-biased technical change can be observed between high- and low-skilled labour. In many countries wage premiums for educated people and income inequality will increase as a result.

Personal Income Tax

Personal income taxation that takes into account the ability-to-pay principle dates back to the beginning of the 20th century. The principle is expressed though a progressive rate structure and tax breaks for costs that reduce a taxpayer's financial capacity to pay, such as childcare and healthcare costs. High marginal tax rates combined with a narrow tax base not only exerts a negative effect on the economy, it also triggers arbitrage opportunities between different types of income and increases the use of tax shields, and encourages the flight of taxpayers abroad and simple tax evasion.

All these factors erode the tax base and diminish the effectiveness of the tax system in achieving a more-balanced income distribution. In addition, the intended   redistribution   is   frustrated   by   many   tax   breaks   that disproportionately favour the highest incomes and present a significant cost to the average tax payer.

The ideal tax rate?

As noted, marginal tax rates have been reduced in many OECD countries in response. In view of 21st-century challenges, further tax cuts may be desirable. It needs no explanation that it is difficult to put forward a well-founded argument on the 'ideal' income tax rate. Ideal rates do not exist, only a wide variety of differing views and assumptions that support particular opinions. Surveys indicate that each level of taxation to some extent triggers behavioural responses, if not outright opposition. But if government decides that a low rate is worth pursuing, then given current revenue needs, marginal tax rates can be lowered further in many OECD countries by stretching the tax base and curbing tax expenditures, a consumption tax-base shift and greening of tax systems.

Creating effective income tax progression

From a socio-economic standpoint, it would be advisable to revise income tax such that the system is simpler and robust. A regularly advocated proposal to achieve this is a flat rate tax and a basic allowance, which would create moderate tax progression. The flat tax would reduce excess burdens, increase transparency and simplicity, cut back on excessive government and boost economic incentives and growth.

Reality nevertheless dictates that a flat tax is difficult to achieve and cannot be accomplished instantaneously in one large reform (that is, one big bang). Depending on the existing income tax schedule and distribution, the shift would require a minimum of two or three steps. The legislation process in OECD countries is arduous and the constant need to obtain ample parliamentary support proves to be one of the biggest challenges. In addition, Chapter 1 highlighted that the majority of taxpayers in OECD countries believe that the ability-to-pay principle should be reflected in the tax system. The most important obstacle, therefore, is the ensuing income effect of the tax changes, which inevitably creates winners and losers.

Insufficient leeway within government finances and the budget can also be an impediment. Base-broadening measures typically generate inadequate funds so that a budgetary retrenchment is required. Otherwise, the tax rate would have to be set higher, which mitigates much of the positive economic effects of the flat tax. Furthermore, there are a number of arguments that speak in favour of a moderate effective progressive income tax (see Chapter 3). These arguments can be summarised as follows:

- wage dampening in non-competitive labour markets by reducing the value of higher wages to employees, which lowers wage demands in the bargaining process;

- reducing income differentials that cause grievance to people on relatively lower incomes (that is, the effect of 'keeping up with the Joneses);
- limiting the scope for rat races, whereby people work hard and forgo leisure time to improve their relative status, yet ultimately become unhappier;
- correcting for failing capital markets and credit rationing by redistributing income from richer older people to younger people on lower incomes;
- correcting for the negative effect of credit rationing on education for students with less-affluent parents by redistributing income from the rich to the poor; and
- correcting for failing insurance markets that fall short of fully compensating income loss if workers become ill, disabled or unemployed, so people are less willing to undertake risky activities.

A precondition would be to introduce effective tax progression, not high marginal tax rates, while average rates climb only modestly with income as under the 'old' progressive tax systems. Maintaining steep marginal tax progression might frustrate economic efficiency, while doing little in terms of equity. Tax progression is more efficiently achieved with a large tax credit or tax deduction as under the Hall and Rabushka consumption-based flat tax (see Chapter 5). It also simplifies the filing of returns, which is often considered to be a difficult and arduous task by many, especially low-income households.

The Corporation Tax

Tax efficiency and administration
Many existing CT systems contain special tax breaks to accommodate corporations. Chapter 4 has demonstrated that the arrangements, sometimes including personal taxes, typically produce a highly non-uniform tax treatment of capital with systematically varying tax rates across different assets, source of finance (that is, debt or equity) and the choice of organisational form. Likewise, there are complex timing issues related to CGT. This creates distortions to capital markets, markets for real estate and portfolio investment choices, all at the cost of reduced efficiency of the allocation of investment.

There is also a greater need for tax legislation that is resistant to tax planning and sheltering strategies. Hence, the call for anti-avoidance legislation increases. Such anti-avoidance provisions are as a rule complicated and cause conflict between taxpayer and tax authority, which often results in court action.

Tax authorities in high-tax countries also face the prospect of MNCs seeking ways to relocate taxable profits. These companies have subsidiaries and branches in two or more countries and use transfer-pricing methods and thin capitalisation to shift deductible expenses to high-tax countries. Taxable profits are allocated to low-tax countries (see Chapter 4). Because governments are afraid to see some of the tax base locating abroad, additional anti-avoidance rules are introduced that, paradoxically, create new unforeseen opportunities for avoidance strategies. This also increases the wage bill of personnel employed by the tax authorities.

Curbing deductible expenses

Globalisation and a growing international (tax) competition will in the coming decades exert downward pressure on CT rates. Based on trends in the EU and Figure 4.1 in Chapter 4, we foresee a competitive CT rate in the coming decade of close to 20 per cent in Europe. To achieve this level, tax reform will have to focus on broadening the profit tax base to compensate for the revenue loss due to reductions in tax rates. This is also compatible with achieving greater neutrality in the tax base, or rather, it presents an opportunity to reduce tax distortions and improve efficiency, since CT systems often discriminate between activities.

Tax deductions will need to be reconsidered. In virtually all countries these items, that is, specific tax incentives, depreciation and interest expenses on corporate loans, generous carry-back and carry-forward and long-term provisions for fiscal reserves and contingencies, constitute the larger component of cost deduction entries.[4] Curbing these costs can generate the means to finance further reductions of the statutory CT rate.

Even if the effective tax rate does not decline by a conversion of deductable expenses for a lower statutory tax rate, on balance there are still advantages related to such an operation. These have already been highlighted. Furthermore, the financial means for a rate cut can be generated by an increase in other taxes, such as taxes on consumption and green taxes. In interest of simplicity, government bureaucracy and conflict between taxpayers and tax authorities, it is also advisable to carry out such operations as soon as possible.

The tax impact indicator

More generally, a high tax rate and burden has a negative effect on business investment and the international climate for business location. Countries with high tax rates cope with businesses that relocate to countries or undertake

---

[4] Restriction or elimination of the deduction for interest reduces the complications and distortions with regard to equity finance (of which a deduction for the opportunity cost *is not* allowed) and debt finance (of which a deduction for interest cost *is* allowed). Some countries such as Belgium have mitigated this issue with the introduction of a deduction for a fictitious or imputed interest over equity.

their new investment elsewhere. This is confirmed by a large number of studies (see Tables 4.3 and 4.4 in Chapter 4). To measure the effects of a CT cut, Table 10.4 presents a 'tax impact indicator' for the corporation tax. The indicator is based on academic studies and demonstrates that a CT rate cut has positive economic effects, however much they differ in size.

Table 10.4   Tax impact indicator

Country	Study	Revenue cost (% GDP)[a]	Total rate change (%)	Economic impact
Australia	Econtech (1999)	0.10	36-30	GDP +1.6%
Austria	Breuss et al. (2004)	1.10	34-25	GDP +0.43 Gross investment +0.51
Germany	Sørensen (2002)	0.24	51.6-38.6	GDP +0.8% Capital stock +1.5
Ireland	Gropp and Kostial (2000)	-0.83	EU mean rate of 35	FDI -1.33% of GDP
Norway	Holmøy and Vennemo (1995)	0.5	50.8-28	Welfare +0.76 GDP +0.35 Consumption +0.71 Real investment -0.04
Netherlands	CBP (2002)	1.0		GDP +1.0 Investment +3.0 Employment +1.1
Sweden	Auerbach et al. (1995)	0	57-30	Negligible
US	Jorgenson and Yun (1990)	0		GDP +2.8%

Note: [a] A zero indicates revenue neutrality.

The General Consumption Tax

A consumption tax is an attractive alternative to income tax. This is because, in its basic form, the consumption tax creates a distortion only to the intertemporal leisure-consumption decision and not, like under income tax, to the intertemporal saving-consumption decision. In other words, the consumption tax does not target the return to capital and is thus believed to promote investment and growth. A consumption-based flat tax has frequently been put forward in the discussion on fundamental tax reform in the US.

Contrary to what is presupposed in this discussion, a one-off full-scale shift to a consumption tax is hardly realistic in most countries, from either a political or a practical standpoint. Revenue needs in European countries are high and public scepticism towards these proposals is large. Even more problematic are the ensuing income effects. The shift would create a permanent increase in the burden on mainly low-income households and owners of 'old' capital. Hence, although from an economic and administrative standpoint a flat rate tax is worth pursuing, in practice the proposal is unrealistic, especially because of the associated strong negative income effects on mainly low incomes.

Utilising the full revenue-raising capacity of VAT

There may nevertheless be scope to improve existing systems in EU countries, by more gradually tilting the burden from income tax towards VAT. Standard exemptions, and reduced or zero rates serve to mitigate the VAT burden on basic necessities and other essential goods and services. The idea is that everybody should have access to food, books, healthcare and so forth. Although this argument carries weight, the exceptions are often enacted with general redistributive intent to counter the inherently regressive burden distribution of VAT. In such a case, the argument has dubious appeal.

The question may legitimately be asked, if VAT is not an effective tool in addressing equity concerns, whether it should be used for this purpose. A number of studies demonstrate that reduced rates have only a small impact on the income distribution. Even if richer people spend a relatively smaller proportion of their income on consumption, they also spend relatively more, much of it on expensive products and luxuries. These households therefore contribute comparatively more to revenue collection. Governments have other much more effective instruments at their disposal, such as expenditure policies and a well-designed income tax progression.

The focus should shift to taking full advantage of the intrinsic qualities and robustness of VAT (primarily due to its multistage collection process). Based on technical restrictions, only a limited number of standard exemptions are required, most notably of financial services (see Chapter 5). The remainder of goods and services that are exempt, are so for political reasons. Furthermore, countries that impose multiple VAT rates create an administrative nuisance and sizeable compliance burden on businesses. Reduced rates hardly mitigate the regressive impact of VAT measured against income.

A large number of exceptions also entail a higher standard rate of tax, or alternatively, every deviation from a comprehensive and uniform tax pushes up the standard rate of VAT.

A gradual shift to consumption-based taxation

High wage costs are a key problem in many OECD economies. This is reinforced by a substantial income tax burden that either directly or indirectly falls on labour. A gradual step-for-step rebalancing of the tax mix with greater emphasis on VAT could be a sensible policy from an economic point of view (or in the US the introduction of a Hall and Rabushka flat tax or national VAT as discussed in Chapter 5). A number of EU countries are already in the process of making a shift.

Under the assumption of a well-functioning tax administration, 25 per cent is a realistic target rate in many European countries. Countries such as Norway or Sweden with standard VAT rates of 25 per cent do not appear to encounter significant enforcement problems. As noted in Chapter 3, the economically efficient solution would be a single-rated VAT; however, in view of the need to elicit ample public and political support, the standard VAT rate could be complemented by one reduced rate to give relief to the basic necessities (that is, food products). Briefly, with a shift to VAT the tax system would:

- be less distortionary to economic choice, in particular the decision between saving and consumption;
- be simple and with a low cost of perception;
- leave less scope for avoidance and evasion (no matter how hard they try, tax authorities are always one step behind in reacting to new opportunities for tax planning and closing loopholes);
- supply a steady flow of revenue throughout the year and be less sensitive to business-cycle fluctuation;
- be aimed not only at domestic products, but also at imported goods and services; and
- be broad based, that is, all consumers would contribute, including the inactive and those who derive income from the black economy.

Economic models show that a partial shift contributes positively to employment and economic growth. Table 10.5 reproduces the results from an EU study that simulated an increase in consumption taxation to 40 per cent of the tax mix, while reducing the labour tax burden accordingly.

Table 10.5   Economic effects of a consumption tax shift, percentage change

	Scenario 1	Scenario 2	Scenario 3
	No indexation	Benefits indexed	Benefits and transfer payment indexed
Labour tax	-4.61	-4.61	-4.61
Debt/GDP	-13.25	-6.54	-1.95
GDP	2.33	1.10	1.10
Employment	2.69	1.26	1.26

Source: Roeger and in 't Veld (downloaded 16 September 2007),
www.cepii.fr/anglaisgraph/communications/pdf/2006/190106/inveld.ppt.

If unanticipated, the shift also imposes a one-off levy on existing capital owners, mostly the older generation in a high-income bracket, who have already been taxed on income previously earned and would be taxed again when spending their earnings. Even if models show a strong decline in economic effect in the case of full anticipation or transitional relief, the above list demonstrates that there are still benefits associated with a shift to consumption-based taxation. Along with a change in the emphasis of the redistributional effort of government to effective income tax progression and well-designed direct expenditure programmes, a more efficient tax structure would be created capable of raising the required revenues, while preserving a fair income distribution.[5]

For many EU countries, reform along these lines would contribute to achieving the Lisbon goals (see Chapter 1). And although detached from the Lisbon Agenda, for non-EU countries such as the US and Japan, similar considerations apply.

Tax Concessions Aimed at Sustainable Development

Promoting innovation and human capital

In Chapters 6 and 7 we examined a number of measures that play a role in R&D policy and human capital accumulation. R&D activity is widely held to create large positive spillovers. The tax system can play a role in stimulating R&D through specific tax incentives, which have been shown to be cost effective. The amount of R&D generated equals at least the cost of revenue forgone (that is, a tax price elasticity of unity or higher). However, since the

---

[5] As noted in Chapter 3, a steeper tax rate on the part of high income earners exceeding some high threshold, say 1 million euros, could be an efficient way to address public uneasiness with excessive pay. The tax can finance tax cuts for people in the middle-high, middle and lower brackets of the income distribution, for whom such incentives are likely to matter.

measures are costly, they should at all times be subject to *ex ante* and *ex post* cost-benefit analysis. The measures depart from the general base-broadening tenet, which is a desirable purpose for other reasons (as discussed above) and might be placed above other objectives. The government should thus carefully weigh *all* factors that affect the efficacy of an R&D measure. Similarly, the development of human capital can be encouraged by providing adequate education (tax) subsidies.

Smart, creative and skilled workforces

Technological change is often considered to be complementary with high-skilled labour (that is, skill-biased technical change). Future demand for skilled workers is likely to increase more rapidly compared to the supply of high-skilled workers. The already rising wage inequality will thereby increase further. People whose jobs are affected by global trends are helped in particular by better education systems (IMF, 2007a and 2007b). Schooling may bring some unskilled workers up to the mark, thereby improving their chances of employment and/or pay, although cost effectiveness should be carefully considered. Targeting schooling at existing vacancies and job openings can be more effective, as experiences in Denmark show.

More generally, the return on an extra year of schooling is widespread. Best practice appears to be the raising of the level of universal education in society. This expands the pool of skilled workers, raises incomes and makes a country richer. It should also moderate both the wage premium of high-skilled workers and rising income inequality in Western economies. Studies surveyed by Heckman (2000) also suggested that the return to educational investment is high around the age of 4-5, which argues for a reduction in the age of compulsory education to this age. Early childhood education improves cognitive skills, linguistic competence and social behaviour.

Carrot and stick: greening tax systems

Finally, our survey has demonstrated how green taxes can contribute to reducing pollution and discouraging greenhouse gas emissions, which are widely held to be responsible for the ongoing global climate change. Energy is the key factor in climate policy. Given the scope of the problem, a global and market-based approach is needed. The current consensus appears to be that the emphasis should rest on a worldwide trade of emission rights that would not only discourage polluting activities, but also promote the development of clean and energy-efficient technologies and renewable energies.

A prominent auxiliary role is laid down for green taxes. Experiences in OECD countries demonstrate that well-designed green taxes can be effective instruments, especially when the tax base is broadly defined which improves cost effectiveness (OECD, 2006c). Green tax measures are attractive as they can create both negative and positive incentives. Positive incentives promote

R&D in the newest so-called 'second-generation' technologies (that is, technologies that go beyond current methods and approaches) for energy saving and efficiency; renewable and alternative energies; cleaner and lighter transport (for example, cars and trucks); and hydrogen and fuel cells.

Green tax measures should be used after positive evaluation (see, for example, the decision tree in Figure 9.9). To tackle global warming, we favour an approach based on the carrot and stick model, which is market based and features the following 'negative' and 'positive' incentive tax measures:

- a gradual increase in green taxation up to 5 per cent of GDP in the tax mix;
- a carbon tax for households and firms. EU member states, the US and Japan are setting an example and have started implementing these types of levy (the tax base is energy or carbon content);
- introduction or increase of existing taxes on polluting or energy-intensive installations;
- promoting green energy such as solar and wind power by means of fiscal incentives and a purchase/production obligation for renewable energies for consumers and energy suppliers;[6]
- a lower vehicle tax for smaller and cleaner cars and lower excise rates for cleaner fuels;
- an energy investment tax credit or accelerated depreciation for enterprises. A portfolio of technologies will be required to deliver the necessary savings in greenhouse gas emissions. The shift to a low-carbon global economy can be promoted by introducing an energy investment tax credit for investing in new lower-carbon technologies and switching away from high-carbon goods and services to low-carbon alternatives;
- introduction of tax-free green and climate investment funds, which can be set up in the market sector throughout the world, for example, by banks. As a condition for establishment, these funds should invest at least 70 per cent of their money in green investment programmes that are important to the environment, help to tackle climate change and improve air quality. Households that invest in these funds are free from tax on dividends, interest and capital gains derived;
- introduction of a national environment compensation fund (ECF). Green tax revenues should (partly) flow into these funds instead of into the treasury. An ECF produces a higher environmental gain by

---

[6] Examples can be found in Austria, Belgium, Germany, Sweden and the UK.

allocating the money to 'green compensation projects' such as planting trees and maintaining forests; and

- more generally, governments should work on improving public awareness of and support for the environmental cause by creating direct and visible relationships between green taxes and the use of proceeds for improving the environment. Broadly speaking, the public does not consider taxes that flow directly into the treasury as supporting the environmental cause. Instead, they are viewed as an ordinary tax rise.

The measures reduce CO_2 emissions and consequently the harmful effects from climate change. They also promote the development of environmentally friendly and energy-saving technologies ('cleantech') and renewable energies. These technologies can in turn be exported to countries such as China and India, which offer fresh markets and business opportunities for domestic firms and the economy.

10.4 'BROAD, LOW AND SIMPLE', AND A SHIFT TO CONSUMPTION TAXATION

The ultimate goal of economic policy should be to boost future economic productivity and the growth rate in a responsible, fair and sustainable manner. Our survey has underscored that the tax system can play a role in advancing these high-rank objectives. Without question this will require a significant overhaul of existing tax structures, perhaps more significantly than any structural tax reform thus far.

The objective should be a simpler tax arrangement, with a greater emphasis on consumption taxation, in particular VAT and green taxes. A shift from income to consumption taxation, that is from workers and economic activity to consumption, enhances the overall incentives to work, save and invest. Empirical and theoretical studies and experiences in the OECD area confirm that lowering the tax burden on labour (that is, income tax and social security premiums) can stimulate employment and economic growth. However, such reform succeeds only if part of the tax burden can be shifted away from workers to those outside the labour force. Hence, from the active to the inactive or those receiving income from the informal economy. Besides structural improvement, ageing of populations and tighter labour markets sanction such a reduction. Both factors require higher labour force participation and wage premiums for high-skilled labour.

The European Commission has also studied a shift towards reducing the labour tax burden, which is substantial in many European countries. According to the Commission, a reduction in income tax of 1 per cent of

GDP together with an increase in consumption tax of 1 per cent of GDP could generate growth exceeding 1 per cent. This could be part of a broad strategy to change the financing of the social model (European Parliament, 2005).

To mitigate political opposition and ease implementation, the shift to VAT could take place by annual increases of 1 per cent up to the desired rate, under a simultaneous reduction of the labour tax burden. However, as noted, anything short of a full unanticipated shift reduces the economic effects emanating from it. Apart from stimulating economic activity, the shift would imply simpler tax legislation with fewer exceptions to the tax base, higher compliance and tax revenues. The framework thereby adheres to what should be the guiding principle in any future tax reform: 'broad, low and simple'.

Generally speaking, broad, low and simple has the following advantages to the government, households and firms alike:

- lower tax rates are accompanied by fewer exceptions to the tax base, more effective tax progression, tax-induced distortions to choice and a more efficient allocation of resources across the economy. The broader the tax base, the lower (distorting) marginal tax rates can be set, assuming revenue neutrality;
- simple tax legislation and higher revenues. A comprehensive tax base leaves less room for tax breaks. These arrangements erode the tax base and call for intricate anti-avoidance legislation. Simple tax legislation reduces the scope for tax-avoidance strategies, the underground economy and tax flight;
- simple tax legislation leaves less room for interpretation and reduces the number of disputes between taxpayer and tax authority. These conflicts are also less frequently referred to court. The government thus make do with a smaller tax administration;
- a broader tax base with a lower rate implies lower cost of compliance for households and companies. A relatively narrow tax base with many exceptions leads to a significant burden, especially to corporations. In addition, there is the physiological effect that a lower rate provokes less opposition;
- a broad tax base features lower marginal tax rates, which can lead to wage dampening in economies characterised by competition or centralised wage bargaining.
- a low rate functions as a focal point or eye-catcher in the location decision for international operating companies;
- a relatively low marginal tax rate benefits from profit shifting. By way of transfer pricing and other financial engineering, MNCs have an incentive to shift taxable profits from high- to low-rate countries. This creates a larger taxable base in low-rate countries;

- a lower administrative bill to companies. Research shows that red tape contributes negatively to production and economic growth. A reduction improves the environment for entrepreneurial activity and international business investment; and
- a benefit for human capital as the economic driver of labour productivity (creative, smart and high-skilled workforces).

A 'broad, low and simple' tax system is optimally designed to accommodate solid entrepreneurship, innovation, higher employment and growth.[7]

10.5   SECOND LIFE TAX IN NOWHERE LAND

Main Features of SLT

Here we present a simplified concept of a universal tax structure for the hypothetical country Nowhere Land. The concept incorporates the findings from our survey. We call the concept tax structure: second life tax (SLT).[8] Compared to the majority of existing tax systems in OECD countries, SLT is characterised by relatively low statutory tax rates and a broad tax base for direct taxes (personal and corporate income taxes), a low direct tax burden on labour and a high burden on consumption (mainly VAT).

SLT, including social security contributions, features three tax brackets, with a top rate of 35 per cent. The statutory CT rate is 20 per cent. The SLT corporate tax has no additional deductions from tax or credits or exemptions. Hence, there is no deduction for interest. The SLT VAT has a standard rate of 25 per cent and a reduced rate of 5 per cent for basic necessities (food products).

Table 10.6 shows that the SLT tax burden on labour constitutes 14 per cent of GDP. This is 6 per cent lower than the EU-15 average. The tax burden on consumption is 20 per cent of GDP, while in the EU-15 it is 11.5 per cent.

Total SLT Tax Revenue

Nowhere Land is characterised by total tax revenues of 40 per cent of GDP. With 40 per cent, the tax burden in SLT averages that of the EU-15, but as Table 10.2 shows, is higher than in countries such as Ireland (30.1 per cent of GDP), the UK (36 per cent), Japan (26.4 per cent) and the US (25.5 per cent).

---

[7] Generally speaking, most economic models do not reflect the positive side-effects of a broad, low and simple tax system.

[8] The name was inspired by the virtual internet society 'Second Life' at http://secondlife.com.

Chapter 1 has shown that the nature and size of government spending are importantly influenced by the political tastes in countries.

Table 10.6   Nowhere Land tax structure by economic function

	Consumption	Labour	Capital	Total
Nowhere Land	20.0	14.0	6.0	40.0
EU-15	11.5	20.0	8.5	40.0
Austria	12.0	24.0	7.0	43.0
Belgium	11.0	25.0	10.0	46.0
Denmark	16.0	27.0	6.0	49.0
Finland	14.0	24.0	7.0	45.0
France	12.0	23.0	9.0	44.0
Germany	10.0	25.0	5.5	40.5
Ireland	11.0	11.0	8.0	30.0
Italy	10.5	20.5	12.0	43.0
Netherlands	11.0	20.0	9.0	40.0
Sweden	13.0	32.0	6.0	51.0
UK	13.5	14.0	8.5	36.0

Note: Numbers have been rounded to 0.5.

Source: European Commission (2006b).

Nowhere Land chooses an expenditure package that reflects a strong commitment to education. Healthcare and social protection also draw a fair amount of spending. This choice rests on the consideration that countries with such spending patterns score high in terms of GDP per capita and rankings on relative happiness, have relatively little income inequality and are highly competitive economies (see Chapter 1). Education (and innovation) are crucial factors for maintaining a strong and competitive economy in 21st-century world markets. Table 10.7 demonstrates that 26.5 per cent of GDP is allocated to these categories of spending.

Total spending (39 per cent) in Nowhere Land is 1 per cent lower than tax revenues (40 per cent of GDP). This allows the country to strengthen its budgetary position in response to ageing.

Broad, Low and Simple

For direct taxation, the focus is on an as broadly defined tax base as possible. This implies no tax deductibles and other tax breaks that erode the tax base. A broad base in combination with greater emphasis on consumption taxation not only benefits simplicity, but also facilitates lower tax rates. Low marginal tax rates have many advantages over high marginal tax rates. See Chapters 1 and 2 for further elaboration on this.

Table 10.7   Categories of spending as a percentage of GDP

	Nowhere Land	EU-15	US	Japan
General public services	5.0	6.8	4.8	6.1
Defence	1.5	1.7	4.0	1.0
Public order and safety	1.5	1.8	2.1	1.4
Economic affairs	3.5	3.9	3.9	4.4
Environmental protection	-	-	0.0	1.4
Housing and community amenities	0.5	1.0	0.6	0.8
Health	7.0	6.4	7.3	6.9
Recreation, culture and religion	0.5	1.0	0.3	0.2
Education	7.5	5.3	6.4	4.1
Social protection	12.0	19.2	7.3	12.0
Total	39.0	47.1	36.7	38.3

Source: Table 1.2 in Chapter 1.

The majority of people in OECD countries believe that ability to pay should be reflected in the income tax schedule. The SLT is characterised by the following income tax rates and brackets:

15%	15,000 or less
25%	between 15,001 and 50,000
35%	50,001 or more

Compared to most OECD countries, Nowhere Land has low statutory tax rates. A low rate tax system is sooner perceived as fair and less likely to incite public resistance. The system requires fewer tax deductions and other expenditures, the compliance rate is relatively high and so are tax revenues (see Chapter 2). SLT has two tax credits: a *basic* allowance of 1,000 units for every taxpayer and an *earned income* allowance for workers of 1,500 units. Table 10.8 shows the ensuing income tax progression in SLT for workers.

Higher equity and public support for the tax system may further be realised by a special tax rate for taxpayers with exceptionally high incomes (see Chapter 3). Compensation received by top-income earners would be taxed at a steeper rate above a certain threshold; for example, a special tax rate of 45 per cent on earnings above €1 million.

Table 10.8   Income tax progression in SLT

Annual income	Average tax burden workers (%)	Marginal tax burden (%)
10,000	0	15
15,000	0	15
25,000	9.0	25
50,000	17.0	35
100,000	26.0	35
500,000	33.2	35

Three Typical Taxpayers

Here we calculate the tax liability under the SLT system for three typical taxpayers. An unemployed person with an annual taxable income of 12,000 units pays 800 in income tax:

15%	over 12,000	1,800
Total		1,800
Basic allowance		-1,000
Tax liability		800

A worker with an annual income of 20,000 units pays 1,000 in income tax:

15%	over 15,000	2,250
25%	over 5,000	1,250
Total		3,500
Basic allowance		-1,000
Earned income allowance		-1,500
Tax liability		1,000

A worker with an annual income of 100,000 units pays 26,000 in income tax:

15%	over 15,000	2,250
25%	over 35,000	8,750
35%	over 50,000	17,500
Total		28,500
Basic allowance		-1,000
Earned income allowance		-1,500
Tax liability		26,000

Emphasis on Consumption Taxation

The revenue generated by VAT and other consumption taxes amounts to 22 per cent of GDP in SLT. The choice is motivated by a number of economic advantages of VAT over direct taxes including SSC, which were discussed earlier. The argument is reinforced by the effect of ageing on many OECD economies. The number of elderly is rising in proportion to the working-class population, as is government expenditure on social security, pensions and healthcare. The trend will put a significant pressure on future government finances and inevitably lead to a higher tax burden on labour. The shift to a consumption-based taxation, including green taxation, would partially mitigate these pressures by placing a one-off levy on existing capital (see Chapter 5). The baby boom generation which holds much of this capital thereby contributes to the costs of ageing.

In the political debate, the fundamental objection to a consumption-based tax such as VAT is that low-income households pay a disproportionately large share in tax revenue. Indeed, research shows that, compared to income, consumption taxes are moderately regressive. However, high-income households not only spend more on consumption, but also spend more on luxuries. These goods and services are taxed at the high standard rate in many OECD countries (ranging up to 25 per cent in Norway and Sweden). Furthermore, our survey has highlighted that existing income tax schedules are not as progressive as often presumed.

Table 10.9 shows that in absolute terms, high-income households contribute comparatively more to revenue collection. The standard rate of VAT is set at 25 per cent. The reduced rate is 5 per cent.

Average total household expenditure is 24,100 units, of which 4,000 is spent on the necessities of life (NoL). In the lowest decile (that is, the lowest 10 per cent of the income distribution), total consumption (exclusive of VAT) is on average 16,300 units, of which 2,850 is spent on essentials. In the highest decile (that is, the upper 10 per cent of the distribution), average expenditure equals 43.400 units, of which 6,800 is spent on necessities. The top three deciles 8, 9 and 10 pay nearly 45 per cent of the total VAT collection, while the lowest three deciles 1, 2 and 3 contribute 19 per cent.

In countries where a shift from income tax to VAT has taken place, low incomes have in many cases been compensated by allowances in income tax. Apart from taxation, direct expenditure programmes, if necessary and properly administered, may also be used to support low-income families. As such, the strategy could be part of a broader reform of the financing of the European social model, which is now mainly funded by direct taxes and social security premiums. In view of globalisation, ageing and increasing tax competition, this would certainly be a desirable policy course to take.

Table 10.9 Distribution of average consumption expenditure of households

	Income distribution (deciles)					
	1st	2nd	3rd	4th	5th	6th
NoL	2,850	2,250	2,650	3,100	3,550	3,800
Other	13,450	11,450	12,650	14,100	17,650	20,000
Total	16,300	13,700	15,300	17,200	21,200	23,800
VAT[a]	3,405	2,975	3,295	3,680	4,590	5,190
Total	19,705	16,675	18,595	20,880	25,790	28,990

	7th	8th	9th	10th		Average
NoL	4,550	4,950	5,450	6,800		4.000
Other	22,250	24,250	29,050	36,600		20,100
Total	26,800	29,200	34,500	43,400		24,100
VAT[a]	5,790	6,310	7,350	9,490		5,225
Total	32,590	35,510	41,850	52,890		29,325

Note: [a]This highly simplified example is based on consumption data of the Netherlands and calculated by applying a standard rate of VAT at 25 per cent and a reduced rate at 5 per cent.

Table 10.10 Tax revenue as a percentage of GDP

	Indirect tax	Direct tax	Social security	(Green)	Total
Nowhere Land	20.0	10.0	10.0	(5.0)	40.0
EU-15	14.0	13.5	13.5	(2.5)	41.0
Austria	15.0	13.5	14.5	(2.5)	43.0
Belgium	14.0	17.5	14.5	(2.5)	46.0
Denmark	17.5	30.0	1.5	(4.5)	49.0
Finland	14.0	19.0	12.0	(3.0)	45.0
France	16.0	11.5	16.5	(2.0)	44.0
Germany	12.5	11.0	17.0	(2.5)	40.5
Ireland	13.0	12.5	4.5	(2.5)	30.0
Italy	15.0	15.0	13.0	(3.0)	43.0
Netherlands	13.0	12.0	15.0	(4.0)	40.0
Sweden	17.0	20.0	14.0	(3.0)	51.0
UK	14.0	16.0	6.0	(3.0)	36.0

Source: European Commission (2006b).

Finally, it should be noted that if VAT differentials between (neighbouring) countries become too large, consumers in border regions will be increasingly inclined to engage in cross-border shopping. To mitigate these distortions, countries could opt to coordinate policy whereby they jointly agree to gradually increase VAT rates, for example, by 1 percentage point annually and under a simultaneous decrease in labour taxes.

Environmental Taxes (Green)

In view of global warming and climate change, greater emphasis should be put on green taxes. In SLT, the total intake from green taxation (particularly on energy and transport) is 5 per cent of GDP. Table 10.10 shows that in 'real life', of the EU-15 countries, Denmark and the Netherlands come closest to this percentage. The average in the EU-15 is 2.5 per cent of GDP. In this area too, it is important to agree on a joint approach or strategy to mitigate border effects.

A system that is broad, low and simple, and includes a consumption tax-base shift and greening taxes (that is, a lower tax burden on labour) implies enhanced opportunities for growth and employment. The system is effective and fair and optimally equipped to anticipate global developments in the 21st century. This includes ongoing globalisation and digitalisation, ageing of populations and workforces and larger tax competition. Together with responsible environmental policies, it offers a solid budgetary basis and fair income distribution to stimulate economic growth and jobs.

Appendix 1 Economic growth

A1.1 INTRODUCTION

The most influential model to explain long-run economic growth is the Solow growth model (Solow, 1956), named after Robert M. Solow who pioneered the study of economic growth in the 1950s and received the Nobel Prize for his contributions in 1987.

The Solow growth model describes how a combination of saving, population growth and technological innovation causes the GDP of an economy to increase over time. The model shows how the accumulation of capital through investment leads to a larger capital stock and output. It becomes clear, however, that higher investment by itself cannot explain a sustained growth in GDP over time, just transitional shifts to a higher or lower level of output by increasing or decreasing the capital stock. By raising the productive capacity of an economy, population growth does explain sustained GDP growth, but not a sustained growth in GDP per capita. For this, technological innovation is needed which, by enhancing capital efficiency, enables the labour force to produce additional output per head of the population.

Since the development of the Solow growth model, additional work has been conducted under the common denominator of 'endogenous growth theory' (Romer, 1986; Lucas, 1988). This new growth theory has greatly improved the insights into economic growth. The Solow model none the less still serves as a reliable basis for much research into economic growth. For this reason, we begin with an exploration of the model. Later we shall briefly consider some properties of endogenous growth theory (also referred to as 'new' growth theory), which explains economic growth from 'within' the model. To do so, factors such as competition, government and human capital are integrated into the model.

Like every model, the Solow growth model relies on a set of assumptions to make its forecasts on the economy. These assumptions are not always considered to be realistic. For example, the basic model holds that the rate of saving is fixed in proportion to income. Yet, in reality savings fluctuate noticeably. Many factors affect the savings rate, including the tax system. The assumption on technological innovation is awkward as well. Solow takes it as exogenous. Hence, the model does not explain technological change with or within the model. Some people find this a serious shortcoming, after all, the model stipulates that only technological innovation can cause a sustained growth in output per capita over time, but others accept it and appreciate the model for the insights it provides into the factors and their interaction that affect economic growth.

For the purpose of our analysis, a fixed rate of technological progress also presents a problem. Technically speaking, the Solow model cannot be used to explain the effects of taxation on growth. Technological innovation is assumed to be exogenous and is unaffected by other variables. This includes tax policy. We have nevertheless chosen to use the model because it offers a good representation of the interaction between the three variables that affect economic growth. The basic thoughts can be extended to include tax policy. [1]

A1.2   FIVE WAYS FOR TAXES TO AFFECT GROWTH

From the Solow model, technically speaking, five channels can be derived through which taxes can affect the level of output and output growth rates (see also Engen and Skinner, 1996). First, taxes alter the size of capital stock by encouraging or discouraging investment. Second, taxation affects labour supply (that is, participation rates, unemployment and the work effort) and the choice to acquire education and skills training. Third, taxes have the potential to influence the level of R&D and thereby the rate of technological innovation.

The final two ways are less obvious but are none the less very real. Under normal market conditions, capital is allocated to where it is most efficient as measured by the marginal product of capital (MPC). However, in the case of unequal tax rates, capital may be allocated from high-taxed but nevertheless productive sectors or countries to low-taxed sectors or countries with lower productivity. So by distorting capital allocation, taxes reduce overall productivity. Likewise, human capital may be employed inefficiently if high taxes discourage employment in high social productive jobs.

The Level of Output and Growth Rates

The structure of the Solow model shows that there is a difference between the effect of taxation on the overall level of output and that on output growth rates. A country with high output growth rates will ultimately be more prosperous than one with relatively lower rates. Differences in relative growth rates have in history marked some extraordinary catch ups (for example, Ireland). However, growth rates do not provide the whole picture.

---

[1] We also refer to Heijdra and van der Ploeg (2002), Chapter 14, for an advanced discussion of theories of economic growth.

Even if economic growth rates between nations are equal, starting-points in terms of absolute level of output may not have been. The country with the highest initial level of output will in the end be even more prosperous.

To illustrate this, consider Table A1.1. The example includes two countries: Italy has a GDP per capita of $29,272 and Norway a GDP per capita of $53,116 (that is, respectively the lowest and highest values in the sample countries). Assuming that there is no inflation and both countries henceforth succeed equally in realising growth of 3 per cent per annum, the absolute difference between Italy's GDP per capita and that of Norway more than doubles from $23,844 to $49,924 in 25 years. Of course, this is because 3 per cent on a higher base level generates more output than on a lower base level. The effect is amplified by an exponential component that can be very powerful over the years.

Table A1.1   A simple example of economic growth

Country	GDP per capita US$, 2005	Growth rate	GDP per capita US$, 2030
Italy	29,272	1.03^25	61,289
Norway	53,116	1.03^25	111,213
Difference	23,844		49,924

Source: Table 1.1 in Chapter 1.

Ideally, government policy should thus focus on optimising both the absolute level of GDP by an efficient allocation of labour and capital as well as GDP growth rates through innovation and human capital accumulation. How this in theory is achieved, is explored in greater detail below.

A1.3   THE BASIC SOLOW MODEL

The Production Function

To see how the Solow model works, we start by examining the Cobb-Douglas production function of an economy. The production function describes in a formal manner the relationship between the long-run output (Y) of an economy and the factors inputs, being capital (K) and labour (L). Y represents the supply of goods and services; K includes all physical capital ranging from production plants, machinery and equipment to highways and airports; L corresponds to the supply of labour. The production function takes the following form:

$$Y = F(K, L). \tag{A1.1}$$

The function states that a combination of the two factor inputs yields a certain amount of output. Hence, if either K or L rise, or both do, output increases by an amount specified by the production function.[2]

The Solow model assumes that the production function exhibits *constant* returns to scale. This means that if both L and K are increased by an equal percentage, output will change by the same percentage. If a production function shows *increasing* returns to scale, output changes by more than the percentage change of both input variables. Similarly, if a production function exhibits *decreasing* returns to scale, output changes by less than the percentage change in both inputs. A production function exhibits a constant return to scale if:

$$\lambda Y = F(\lambda K, \lambda L). \tag{A1.2}$$

for any positive number of λ.

The assumption of constant returns to scale in the Solow model is critical and in practice proves to be a realistic one. It allows the production function to be rewritten so that output and capital are expressed relative to labour, that is, in per capita terms. This is done by substituting $1/L$ for lambda (λ) into equation (A1.2) (that is, everything divided by L), which creates equation (A1.3):

$$Y/L = F(K/L, 1). \tag{A1.3}$$

In this form, one can measure the effect of a capital change on output since both output and capital are expressed relative to labour (1 is a constant and can be discarded). Hence, the output/labour ratio (Y/L) of an economy depends solely on the capital/labour ratio (K/L).

By defining $y = Y/L$ and $k = K/L$ the production function can be simplified further into what is called its 'intensive form' (see equation (A1.4)):

$$y = f(k). \tag{A1.4}$$

The advantage of the production function in its intensive form is that it shows how an increase in the capital stock causes a rise in output. Thus, by keeping the size of the labour force constant, an increase in output is directly responsible for an increase in GDP per capita. A graphical interpretation of the intensive form production function is given in Figure A1.1.

This figure shows that, as explained, the output to labour ratio depends only on the capital to labour ratio in an economy. It can also be observed that, as the capital to labour ratio increases, the curve of the production function

---

[2] The availability of natural resources also affects the level of output of a country. Since these are more or less fixed, they are not incorporated into the model.

gets flatter. This universal property of the production function can be attributed to the principle of 'diminishing marginal productivity of capital'.

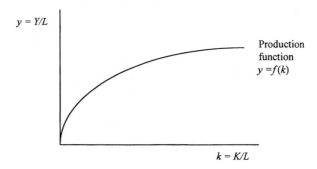

Figure A1.1   Production function in intensive form

The principle can be illustrated with reference to equation (A1.1). Suppose that labour is kept constant and the capital stock is increased by 1 unit. Output increases too. The precise amount by which Y increases is referred to as the marginal product of capital (MPK). The MPK is equal to the ratio between the change in output and change in capital, or $\Delta Y/\Delta K$. However, such output augmentation is limited in scale. As the capital stock expands, less and less labour is available to handle the capital. This reduces the relative rise in output and makes production less efficient. Hence, each time the capital stock grows under a given labour force, the amount with which output increases falls, which makes capital subject to diminishing returns.

The factor labour is subject to the same considerations. Just as for capital, labour becomes less productive as the labour to capital ratio increases. The Solow model thus has diminishing returns to labour and capital separately, and constant returns jointly.

Investment, Depreciation and the Steady State of Capital

Apart from the production function which determines the supply of goods and services, the Solow model incorporates long-run demand in an economy, which is determined by equation (A1.5). Hence, on the spending side of an economy, output (Y) produced is either consumed (C) or invested (I) in new capital:

$$Y = C + I. \tag{A1.5}$$

The function implicitly assumes that the government budget and foreign trade are in balance. In the long run, these assumptions can be considered to be realistic. Government spending is merely a redistribution of resources and any trade imbalances eventually cancel out as exchange rates adjust or debt is repaid.

On the income side of an economy, aggregate household income (Y) is used for consumption (C) and the remainder for saving (S):

$$Y = C + S. \tag{A1.6}$$

Under these assumptions, the economy-wide long-run output is identical to long-run income. Both functions can be used to account for savings in the Solow model. By setting the rate of investment equal to the level of savings (which is a valid proposition in the long run) and assuming that saving constitutes a fixed proportion of income, the relationship between income and new capital investment can be derived. In other words, if savings is assumed to constitute a fixed proportion of income, we can rearrange equation (A1.6) and obtain $C = (1 - s)Y$ (where s is the fixed savings rate). Substitution into equation (A1.5) then gives $Y = (1 - s)Y + I$, or by rewriting it gives the savings function (A1.7).

$$I = sY. \tag{A1.7}$$

As before, this function may be transformed to a per capita form with the first term equal to I/L and the second term equal to $s(Y/L)$. We then arrive at equation (A1.8):

$$I/L = s(Y/L). \tag{A1.8}$$

Or, equivalently, by defining sy as I/L and $sf(k)$ as $s(Y/L)$ in intensive form in equation (A1.9):

$$sy = sf(k). \tag{A1.9}$$

We now have two functions in intensive form: $f(k)$ and $sf(k)$. The first determines total output at a given level of capital and the second determines the allocation of the output between consumption and savings at that level. The rate of saving in turn determines the level of investment in new capital.

Depreciation
At the same time as new investments raise the capital stock, existing capital becomes obsolete and depreciates. The depreciation rate (δk) depends on the time it takes for capital to wear out. Naturally this rate varies between assets, but for the overall economy it can be viewed as an average constant per year. The larger the stock of capital, the higher the amount of depreciation.

It follows that any change to the capital stock on a macroeconomic level is thus determined by the rate of investment in new capital minus the rate of

depreciation of old capital. This relationship is represented by equation
(A1.9), from which it can be inferred that if the depreciation rate is higher
than the rate of investment, the capital stock is shrinking. Likewise, when
investment is higher than depreciation, there is a positive accumulation of
capital:

$$\Delta k = sf(k) - \delta k. \tag{A1.9}$$

Capital accumulation and the steady state
The production function $f(k)$, together with the savings curve $sf(k)$ and
depreciation δk curve can be combined graphically to examine the interaction
between the three variables (see Figure A1.2). The x-axis denotes the capital
to labour ratio, or capital intensity, the y-axis the output to labour ratio. Since
the production function exhibits diminishing returns, the production curve
becomes flatter as the capital to labour ratio increases. Likewise, savings
constitutes a fixed fraction of income, thus exhibits a similar pattern.
Depreciation increases proportionally with the capital to labour ratio.

The capital stock where investment in new capital ($sf(k)$) intersects with
the depreciation curve (δk) is called the 'steady-state level of capital', or
balanced growth path. At the steady state, which is represented by k^* in
Figure A1.2, output per worker is constant. It is called the steady state
because an economy always equilibrates to it.

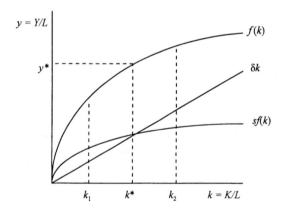

Figure A1.2   The steady-state level of capital

To see why, consider the case where capital intensity is below the steady
state at point k_1. At this point, the savings rate or $sf(k)$ curve is greater than
the depreciation rate (δk). Hence, savings and investment is greater than
depreciation and the capital per worker is increasing. The capital stock will
keep growing until it reaches point k^*. Here saving equals depreciation. On

the other hand, if the level of capital is above $k*$ at point k_2, investment is smaller than depreciation. In this case, the capital stock diminishes until it reaches point $k*$, where investment again equals depreciation.

The steady state therefore represents a long-run equilibrium of the capital stock in an economy. From it, the total output of goods and services can be derived by extending the dotted line at point $k*$ to the production curve, that is, the level of output $y*$ associated with this particular capital stock.

Savings and the Golden Rule Level of Capital

So far we have established that the amount of savings in an economy determines the level of investment. This in combination with the rate of depreciation causes an economy to equilibrate to its steady state. The capital stock related to this point determines the output of goods and services. It becomes clear that the rate of savings plays a distinct role in determining an economy's production and that by changing it the steady state can be altered. In other words, if government policy manages to induce a rise in private saving, or increases public savings, the rate of investment will rise. This causes the economy to equilibrate at a higher steady-state level of capital and output associated with it.

Figure A1.3 illustrates what happens. Suppose the rate of savings is increased successfully so that the savings curve $sf(k)$ is raised to $sf'(k)$. At this rate and capital stock (that is, $k*$), investment is larger than the rate of depreciation. This causes the capital stock to expand, which continues until it reaches the point where capital accumulation is equal to depreciation again. The new steady-state level of capital sets in at point k_1 and output grows from point $y*$ to point y_1.

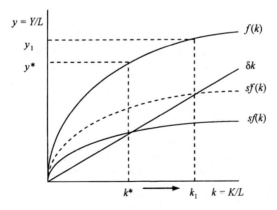

Figure A1.3   A shift of the savings rate

The figure makes it clear that by raising the rate of saving, production can be raised. However, this increase does not represent sustained growth. The economy will eventually settle at a new steady state, albeit with a larger capital stock. After the initial rise, however, output remains fixed at the higher level. The increase thus represents a one-off shift. The same applies in the reverse situation. If saving decreases, the steady state sets in at a lower level of capital with a smaller amount of output associated with it. Once again, only a one-off shift occurs.

Optimal savings

So why then not keep increasing the rate of saving so as to maintain a sustained growth in output over time? After all, income increases every time output increases. Because saving is assumed to be a fixed proportion of income, its increase diminishes as the production curve flattens due to diminishing marginal returns. By contrast, depreciation is proportional to capital and does not decline with marginal productivity.

This implies that larger capital accumulation is needed to keep up with depreciation every time the steady state is raised. Ultimately, all output would be reinvested in new capital, that is, total production would equal depreciation, thereby reducing consumption to zero. Of course, this is not a desirable state. There would be no satisfaction gained from the production of goods and services if all, or a large part of it, is immediately reinvested. The question therefore is how much income households should sacrifice to maintain an optimal level of capital stock and output.

The optimal steady state in an economy is determined by the golden rule level of capital, which states that for consumption to be maximal, and this is what creates satisfaction, the marginal product of capital should equal the rate of depreciation. This is stated by equation (A1.10):

$$MPK = \delta \qquad\qquad\qquad (A1.10)$$

To grasp the principle underlying the golden rule, consider Figure A1.4. By setting the rate of savings so that it corresponds to the capital stock at k^*, the distance between the $sf(k)$ curve and the $f(k)$ curve is maximised. The difference represents consumption. At this point the slope of the production function equals the rate of depreciation, which is the condition required by equation (A1.9).

Only one level of saving is associated with the consumption-maximising steady-state. At this point the economy optimises the allocation of total output between a maximally attainable portion of consumption and a rate of savings that enables the corresponding steady state to be arrived at. Government policy should ideally be aimed at reaching this particular golden rule level of saving.

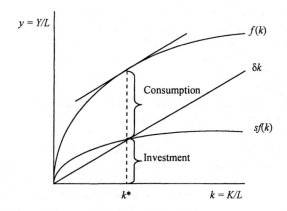

Figure A1.4   The golden rule level of capital

Approaching the golden rule level of capital

When the level of capital is below the golden rule steady state, the economy is said to be 'dynamically efficient'. The majority of economies in the world find themselves in a state of dynamic efficiency. Transition to the golden rule will be more demanding than under the opposite scenario where the steady state is above the golden rule level. People have to save a larger share of their income, which they will be reluctant to do. Increased saving means that the current generation will have to refrain from some consumption, in order for future generations to consume at an efficient level.

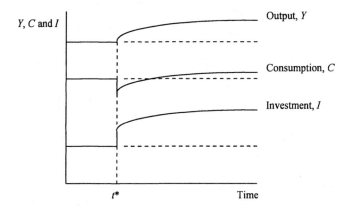

Figure A1.5   Transient paths between steady states under dynamic efficiency

Figure A1.5 illustrates what happens to the level of consumption, investment and output in the transitional phase, that is, between steady states. Assuming that the implemented policy is successful at point t^* in time, investment is increased by the amount necessary to reach the golden rule level of capital. At the same time, consumption decreases by a similar quantity. This is the sacrifice that the current generation makes. As the capital stock grows gradually, output grows as well until the new steady state is reached. At this new steady state, output, consumption and investment are at a higher level than in the previous steady state.

On the other hand, if the savings rate and the capital stock are above the golden rule steady state, the economy is said to be 'dynamically inefficient'. Because there is too much investment in new capital, policy should aim to reduce savings. Figure A1.6 demonstrates the consumption, investment and output paths in the transient phase. Again at point t^* policy is successfully implemented. Savings and thus investment are reduced to a lower level. As a consequence, consumption jumps in the opposite direction by the same amount. At this point the economy is no longer in its steady-state equilibrium. Investment is lower than depreciation, which causes the capital stock to diminish. Output decreases too. In due course the economy reaches the new golden rule steady state with a relatively lower level of output and investment, yet a higher level of consumption.

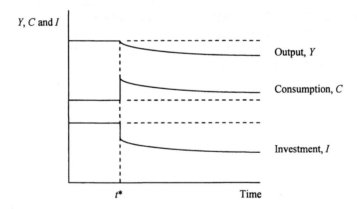

Figure A1.6   Transient paths between steady states under dynamic inefficiency

Accounting for Population Growth

Up to this point, the discussion of the Solow model has implicitly assumed that population size is fixed. Of course, this is not an entirely realistic supposition. The world population increases each day and in many economies by astonishing numbers. With it, labour supply rises as well. To create a more realistic representation of reality, the model will thus have to be adapted to take account of population growth.

When a population grows, it is straightforward to establish that output has to increase by a proportional amount for GDP per capita to remain the same. Hence, if a country desires to realise economic growth, output has to increase by a higher percentage than population growth. Historically, all developed countries have succeeded in achieving this. For less developed countries (LDCs) with high population growth rates, it has been a more daunting task.

Let *n* represent the growth rate of the population. Previously it was shown that in the steady state an economy's depreciation rate (δk) equals the rate of capital accumulation $sf(k)$. In the case of a growing population, additional investment is needed to supply the incremental labour with the necessary capital to sustain a fixed capital to labour ratio in the economy. With some basic reasoning, population growth can be included in the model. The change in capital can be determined by entering *n* into equation (A1.9), which gives equation (A1.11):

$$\Delta k = sf(k) - (\delta + n)k. \tag{A1.11}$$

Again $sf(k)$ represents the investment that increases the capital stock. However, this time both depreciation (δ) and population growth (n) decrease the relative capital stock. Given these new constraints, the economy again converges to its steady-state equilibrium as described before. The capital per worker is now determined by three variables:

- saving (or investment) per worker;
- population growth – higher population growth decreases capital per worker; and
- depreciation, causing the capital stock to decline.

When the savings rate is greater than the population growth rate plus the depreciation rate, capital per worker is increasing. This is known as 'capital deepening'. When, on the other hand, capital is increasing at a rate just enough to keep pace with population growth and depreciation, it is known as 'capital widening'. If saving is below both variables, capital per worker is decreasing.

The effect of population growth on the capital stock is depicted graphically in Figure A1.7. A higher population growth rate lowers the steady-state capital stock and vice versa. If *n* is increased to *n'*, the steady state moves accordingly from k^* to k_1. This implies that countries with high population growth generally have lower levels of output per inhabitant than countries with lower population growth rates. Empirical data confirm a strong correlation between high population and low growth and GDP per capita.[3]

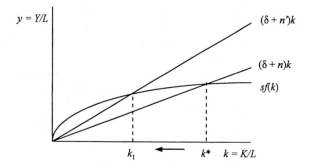

Figure A1.7   Population growth

The condition set forth by equation (A1.10) on the golden rule level of capital is still applicable, though *n* should be added into the equation. The marginal product of capital now equals depreciation *plus* the population growth rate:

$$MPK = \delta + n. \tag{A1.12}$$

With the inclusion of population growth in the Solow model, a sustained growth in the capital stock and output is explained, that is, at the rate of population growth. Not, however, in output per capita.

The labour force and long-run unemployment
By relaxing the assumption of a proportional labour force, the model may be adapted to comprise variations in labour supply. For example, tax policy can create incentives to increase labour force relative to the size of the population (once again this would constitute only a one-off shift). Stimulating the work effort is effective only when there is sufficient labour demand.

Generally it is believed that long-run unemployment is determined by the 'natural rate of unemployment', which consists of two kinds of unemployment: frictional and wait unemployment. *Frictional* unemployment arises because of a time lag between job separation and job finding. The time span in job search can be prolonged by factors such as generous unemployment benefits that induce people to be more relaxed about seeking

---

[3] See Burda and Wyplosz (2005) for scatter plot using Penn World Table 6.1 data.

employment. *Wait* unemployment arises if trade unions and minimum wage requirements prevent labour supply and demand from equilibrating.

The long-term natural rate of unemployment is thus presumed to be equal to the lowest level of unemployment where the labour market is in equilibrium. Lowering unemployment below this natural rate, for example, by artificially increasing labour demand, will cause inflationary effects. For this reason, the natural rate of unemployment is also referred to as the 'non-accelerating inflation rate of unemployment', or NAIRU.

Technological Progress

The question can be raised why if all parameters such as savings (s), depreciation (δ), population growth (n), capital intensity (k) and per capita income (y) grow at the same constant rate of zero, how then can the model explain economic growth? The answer is through technological progress, whereby the production function curve is shifted upward. Only technological progress therefore explains an increase in the capital-labour and output-labour ratios and thereby sustained growth in GDP per capita over time.

By enhancing the efficiency of the capital stock, technological innovation improves production by enabling the labour force to achieve higher output with the same amount of capital. As such, technology cannot be considered to be a factor of production, but merely an influence on a factor of production. The model incorporates technological change by adding a measure of the state of technology to the production function, as represented by A in equation (A1.13):

$$Y = F(K, AL). \tag{A1.13}$$

AL is said to be a measure of effective labour; the higher its value, the more sophisticated the state of technology and the larger the size of output generated per worker. As noted, the Solow model assumes A to be exogenous and that it takes place at a fixed rate per year. The rate by which technology improves annually is denoted by g.

The variable is included by adding it to the population growth rate n, which determines the total growth in effective labour. The computation of $n + g$ is incorporated into equation (A1.9), which gives in equation (A1.14):

$$\Delta k = sf(k) - (\delta + n + g)k. \tag{A1.14}$$

Using the same reasoning as before, the golden rule level of capital including technological innovation is now determined by equation (A1.15).

$$MPK = \delta + n + g. \tag{A1.15}$$

Graphically the relationship between the steady-state level of capital and output is depicted in Figure A1.8.

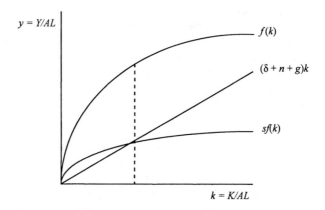

Figure A1.8   Technological innovation

The model thereby accounts for technological progress and explains why output per capita can grow permanently.

In its fully fledged form, the Solow model identifies capital accumulation, population growth and technological progress as the three sources of GDP growth. Capital accumulation alone cannot account for sustained growth due to diminishing marginal returns. Population growth can sustain growth in GDP, but not in GDP per capita. Technological progress therefore is the key to advancing economically and achieving a higher standard of living.

A1.4   CONVERGENCE BETWEEN ECONOMIES OVER TIME

Unconditional Convergence

A key prediction of the Solow model is that economies with roughly similar steady-state equilibria, but different starting-points in terms of initial capital to labour ratios, 'catch up' with economies that have larger capital stocks. Inasmuch as technical change is exogenously given, this technology must be available to any country. Hence, the A term in the production function of countries is the same. An economy with a smaller capital stock should then experience a high return due to diminishing returns to capital. This should stimulate (an inflow of foreign) investment relative to countries with already large capital stocks.

Poorer countries should thus experience a period of rapid growth and eventually 'converge' to richer countries. The property can be derived from Figure A1.2. Because the production function becomes flatter, countries with a smaller capital stock initially experience higher growth rates than countries with a larger capital stock. Theoretically speaking, assuming similar savings and population growth rates, developing nations would eventually attain the same level of output as developed economies.

Empirical evidence reveals that economies with approximately similar rates of saving and technology indeed converge (Mankiw et al., 1990). The evidence is stronger for convergence within countries. Convergence is often observed between regions and states with comparable preferences, cultural and political backgrounds. For example, per capita levels of GDP of southern US states have tended to converge to levels of northern states. The OECD area is also considered to display roughly similar conditions for economic growth.

Conditional Convergence

Empirical evidence nevertheless shows that developing countries in particular have difficulty in catching up. This suggests that matters are not simple. The growth literature therefore distinguishes between unconditional or absolute convergence and conditional convergence (Barro and Sala-i-Martin, 2004). As noted, the steady-state condition is not similar for all countries if they vary in their saving propensities. Because income per capita is low, developing countries are required to allocate a large fraction of their GDP to consumption to the detriment of saving (people first satisfy primary living requirements). This includes countries such as China and India. The conditions for convergence thereby differ between developing and developed countries.

A1.5   ENDOGENOUS GROWTH THEORY

Largely on account of the criticism of the Solow model mentioned in the introduction, research into economic growth has continued and new models have been developed. These new models can be classified under the common denominator of endogenous growth theory. In contrast to the Solow growth model, endogenous growth theory tries to explain economic growth from within the model. To do so, it includes factors such as competition, government regulation and human capital accumulation. The research into endogenous growth theory is extensive and inherently complex. We shall refer to it briefly.

A simple model change enables one to observe how different assumptions are made, particularly that the shape of the production function can change the overall outcome. As explained in Figure A1.1, the Solow model assumes diminishing marginal productivity of capital. If this assumption is abandoned, the results may change markedly (see Figure A1.9). The production function does not exhibit diminishing, but rather a constant marginal productivity of capital. Savings are still fixed to income, and depreciation is a percentage of capital.

Under the new assumption, the model demonstrates that if savings are higher than depreciation, output grows infinitely. For example, at point k_1 saving outweighs depreciation by the distance AB. This causes a capital increase from k_1 to k_2. At k_2, output is higher and thus the savings rate is measured by CD (savings are assumed to be a fixed fraction of income). This again raises the amount of capital and so on. Thus by altering the assumptions on the production function, the model explains sustained growth without requiring exogenously given technological progress.

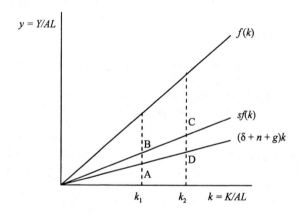

Figure A1.9   Constant marginal productivity of capital

The question is whether it is realistic to deviate from the assumption of diminishing productivity of capital. It could be if K includes not only all physical capital, but also human capital. For example, education of workers and on-the-job training increases knowledge and innovation. This in turn creates more output of goods and services as well as new knowledge and innovation (in which learning by doing plays a central role).[4] As this process continues, it could explain constant or even increasing returns to scale.

---

[4] An important aspect is the protection of knowledge and innovation through intellectual property rights. Generally, knowledge and innovation are non-excludable, non-rival, more or less public goods. By being able to exclude other users, the costs can be recovered making it more attractive to invest in both factors. Knowledge is often supposed to be cumulative. This property, together with non-excludability and non-rivalry, can create a 'combinatorial explosion' (Foray,

Some people have argued that this is what happened in the 1990s in what has been called the 'new' economy. The development of ICT and the internet caused production to shift from the creation of physical capital to the creation of intangible capital such as new concepts and ideas. In this context, it is more plausible that a production function has a constant rather than diminishing marginal productivity. ICT has transformed production processes into creating value by satisfying more intricate and far-reaching customer demands. Whether this takes place between businesses or between business and consumer is of less concern. Studies show ICT production to (still) be subject to increasing returns.

A1.6   SUMMARY

The models we have described employ different assumptions in explaining economic growth. In general, the Solow model assumes diminishing marginal productivity of capital, while endogenous growth theory under certain conditions argues for a constant marginal productivity of capital. We have seen that assumptions made by both models are plausible in certain settings or contexts.

The Solow growth model combines savings, population growth and technological innovation to explain sustained output growth. These factors can to some degree be influenced by government policy.

The model specifies that without population growth and technological innovation, an economy equilibrates to a steady state, after which output remains constant. This is because of the property of diminishing marginal returns to capital. The steady state corresponds to the level where new investment equals depreciation. By a changing rate of savings, the steady state level of capital and size of output is altered in the same direction.

By accounting for population growth, a constant increase in output can be explained. The incremental labour force provides additional productive capacity and output. Technological innovation makes capital more efficient and thereby creates a sustained increase in output per capita.

Where technological progress is an exogenous variable in the Solow model, endogenous growth theory endeavours to explain it from within the model. It does so by including factors such as knowledge spillovers, human capital and R&D activity. The new growth literature assumes that the production function exhibits constant marginal returns, which creates sustained economic growth.

2004). This is a good that can be used without limit to produce other knowledge that also exhibits these three characteristics.

Appendix 2   Keynesian economics

A2.1   INTRODUCTION

The history of taxation goes back a long way. Archaeologists have found artifacts they believe may be a record of taxation taking place long before man developed writing or an abstract conception of numbers.[1] The first known tax system dates back to ancient Egypt where extensive records were kept to counter tax evasion, but also to forecast revenues. Surpluses were accumulated in good times to protect people against famine in worse times, already indicating some form of fiscal management taking place.

The first income taxes were introduced in the 18th-century by the Batavian Republic (1797) and Britain (1799). With the coming of the industrial age at the beginning of the nineteenth century, the academic and public debate, mainly in France and Britain, started to focus on policy issues regarding equity and efficiency aspects of taxation. Before this time these had never played a significant role. Throughout the century theories on taxation were put forward, advocating how it should be employed to the benefit of the economy.

But it was not until the 1930s with the introduction of *The General Theory of Employment, Interest, and Money* by British economist John Maynard Keynes (1936) that the theory of fiscal policy as we know it today really took shape. The condition of a balanced government budget was abandoned. Instead it was advocated that in an economic downturn with high unemployment, policy should aim at stimulating demand by cutting taxes and/or increasing government spending. That government ran a deficit in the process was considered to be of less importance. In economically good times revenues would automatically rise so that debt could be repaid.

Even if Western economies experience an overall economic growth over the long run, fluctuations in GDP growth do exist. The focus in this appendix is shifted to short-term macroeconomics and Keynesian stabilisation policy. Broadly speaking, long-term economics centre on supply-side factors, while short-term stabilisation policy is more demand-side orientated. This difference can have important policy implications. For example, on the

---

[1] See Webber and Wildavsky (1986), who provide a comprehensive overview of the history of taxation and expenditure in the Western world.

supply side high labour costs discourage firms from hiring workers, while short-run unemployment can result from low spending by households and firms. The first phenomenon is structural; the second is demand driven or cyclical in nature.

In the short run therefore, it can be more appropriate to deviate from the long-run prescribed levels of saving and consumption (conditional on the properties of the Solow model in Appendix 1). According to Keynes, government should intervene if effective demand, which establishes an economy's actual output, falls short of achieving the level of output that would exist if there were full employment (that is, potential output). Since economic performance is the result of multiple interacting factors, the economy as a whole may in the short run have trouble adjusting to changes. This causes shocks that drive output away from its long-run natural level. The magnitude of the fluctuations can be dampened by government intervention, making the economy function more smoothly and efficiently.

A2.2 NATIONAL INCOME ACCOUNTING

To analyse these short-run macroeconomic effects, we start by decomposing effective demand, also called aggregate expenditures, into individual categories of spending on final product. Aggregate expenditures consist of the sum of consumption, investment, government spending and net exports (exports minus imports). Thus it is the immediate determinant of national income, or output, which allows us to write it formally as:

$$GDP = C + I + G + NX. \tag{A2.1}$$

The identity is essentially similar to equation (A1.5) in Appendix 1, but extended to include government spending and net exports. These variables are considered fixed over the long term. In the short run, their fluctuations nevertheless become real and need to be accounted for.

It should be noted that GDP does not capture net factor income received from and sent abroad. Indeed, it is a measure of *domestic* income. Factor income consists of dividend and interest payments received by residents from FDI and portfolio investments and of wage earnings received by residents who work in another country. It is lowered by such payments abroad. The measure gross national product (GNP) therefore contains net factor income (*NI*). Although GDP is most commonly cited as a measure of an economy's income, GNP provides a more comprehensive picture. It is computed by adding net factor payments (*NI*) to equation (A2.1), which gives equation (A2.2):

$$GNP = C + I + G + NX + NI. \tag{A2.2}$$

The distinction between GDP and GNP as such is reasonably straightforward. An alternative is to measure GNP by the manner in which income is spent:

$$GNP = C + S + T. \qquad (A2.3)$$

Equation (A2.3) determines that GNP can also be computed as the aggregate of consumption, private saving and net tax payments (that is, total taxes received minus transfer, interest and subsidy payments) made to the government. It allows us to rewrite equations (A2.2) and (A2.3) to arrive at equation (A2.4):

$$I = S + (T - G) - NX - NI. \qquad (A2.4)$$

This shows how investment, savings, the government budget, the trade balance and capital income flows are interrelated variables. For example, if government runs a budget deficit, either private or public savings have to increase or the country will experience a trade deficit.

International Trade and Capital Flows

The magnitude of international trade and capital flows is identified by the 'balance of payments' (BoP), which contains accounts such as the frequently cited *trade* account, which records the mutations in exports and imports. The *current* account includes the trade account *plus* net income payments abroad (NI). It is balanced by the *capital* account which records all changes in the assets held by residents abroad and by foreigners in the country under consideration. Apart from a statistical discrepancy and unilateral transfer payments such as foreign development aid, the current and capital accounts should sum up to zero.

Normally, a country's investment in physical assets, equity or debt is financed out of its savings. If domestic investment exceeds domestic saving, the country must resort to foreign borrowing to finance the difference. Foreign investors then finance the excess domestic investment. If domestic savings are higher than domestic investment, the surplus is lent abroad. It follows that net foreign borrowing should be equal to the difference between investment and saving. This property is represented by equation (A2.5):

net foreign borrowing = investment − saving.   (A2.5)

Alternatively, a country could run a trade deficit. The difference of the value of imports over the value of exports then finances the excess of domestic investment over saving. A trade deficit is therefore accompanied by a capital inflow, while a trade surplus results in an outflow of capital. This is shown by equation (A2.6):

net foreign borrowing = net exports – net investment income.   (A2.6)

Accordingly, if investment is larger than savings, the excess must be balanced either by increased foreign borrowing or by a trade deficit.

A second approach would be to focus on output, which is generally allocated to three different uses. Goods and services produced may be (i) consumed at home or (ii) invested at home, or (iii) exported abroad. Hence, if a country produces more than it consumes and invests domestically it will have to export the surplus. On the other hand, if domestic consumption and investment are higher than production, the country must offset the shortage with imports from abroad.

The distinction between consumption and investment goods is vital. In the case of a trade surplus, the net exporting country essentially lends the excess of exports over imports to the net importing country, but only if the surplus consists of consumption goods. If the surplus arises from the export of investment goods, these goods would essentially be owned by the investors in the exporting country. Hence, a country that experiences a trade deficit must either resort to foreign borrowing to pay for imports or sell some of its assets, or if the deficit arises from the import of investment goods, the assets would be owned by investors in the exporting country.

A trade deficit is thus not by definition undesired or a bad thing. If it arises from the import of investment goods, future output will be higher, so foreign debt can be repaid without current and future consumption being affected. In contrast, if the trade deficit arises from increased consumption, there will be no additional production to repay debt incurred, including accumulated interest. Current generations then benefit from higher consumption at the expense of future generations.

A2.3   SHORT-RUN BUSINESS-CYCLE FLUCTUATIONS AND FISCAL POLICY

Keynes's ideas were inspired by the Great Depression of the 1930s. Starting in the United States and rapidly spreading to Europe and other parts of the world, the Great Depression was a period of severe economic downturn.[2] At its low point in 1933, real GDP in the US had decreased by over 25 per cent. Unemployment soared by a similar percentage and poverty was high. Many

---

[2] An economy with decreasing or even negative growth rates is said to be in a 'recession'. A prolonged recession is known as a 'depression'. Formally, this is the case for two consecutive quarters of negative growth.

economists who have studied the Great Depression agree that poor government policies and inadequate intervention by the Federal Reserve Bank (FED) exacerbated economic downturn. It also showed that in times of severe economic crisis, the right policy measures should kick start the economy in order to get it back on its feet.

The Business Cycle

Fluctuations in output are to some extent a normal macroeconomic phenomenon. In the long run, markets are flexible and prices adjust to bring demand in line with a given level of supply as determined by the production function (see equation (A1.1) in Appendix 1). In the short run prices are more 'sticky' and wages are inflexible downward, for example, due to long-term (union) contracts, minimum wage laws, imperfect market information and menu cost (that is, the cost of changing prices). According to Keynes, this is a main reason why the economy as a whole has trouble adjusting to macroeconomic shocks. In periods of low aggregate demand, firms insist on wage and/or price cuts, instead of reacting by discharging or laying off workers and/or reducing output.[3]

Hence, the short-run macroeconomic equilibrium between supply and demand does not necessarily occur in the long-run natural rate of output, but fluctuates around it. This is illustrated graphically in Figure A2.1.

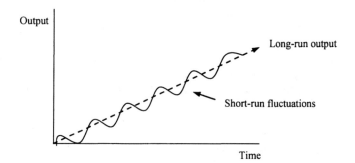

Figure A2.1   Cyclical fluctuations around long-term growth

In recent history, OECD economies have experienced GDP growth rates of as much as 7 or 8 per cent, while at other times GDP growth has been negative.

---

[3] Also see Heijdra and van der Ploeg (2002), Chapters 1 and 2, for an advanced treatment of the Keynesian model and dynamics in aggregate demand and supply.

Expansionary and Contractionary Fiscal Policy

Keynes's explanation of business cycles associated a high level of employment with a high level of output, if all households were spending their income. Hence, when the economy is running smoothly, the circular flows of money in an economy ensure that household spending on goods and services is transformed into firm revenue and that a firm's spending on employment and investment in turn becomes household earnings.

If consumer confidence is harmed for some reason, households react by raising their savings to weather the anticipated bad times. Households thus hoard money, instead of spending it on goods and services. This lowers firm revenue, so firms respond by cutting back on expenditures. In practice, this implies cutting jobs, which further reduces household income and ends up in a vicious circle of low demand, deflation and unemployment. Households hoard money in times of economic hardship, while hard times become harder when households hoard money.

To break this circle, Keynes argued that the central bank should intervene by expanding the money supply. By doing so, consumers would have additional money to spend, thereby restoring effective demand and consumer confidence. However, such a monetary policy works only on the premise that consumers actually spend the additional money – and this is what went wrong in the Great Depression. Beyond a certain point, consumer confidence had dropped so far that people hoarded their money at home (the collapse of many banks in the Great Depression led to panic and widespread distrust in the US banking system). This state is referred to as the 'liquidity trap' and occurs when the interest rate is close or equal to zero, so there is no additional savings and investment because households keep their money 'under the pillow'. This makes the recession even more severe.

If monetary policy no longer works, government should step in and resort to more rigorous fiscal policy thus taking spending into their own hands (Keynes called this 'priming the pump'). On the downside of the business cycle, this means applying *expansionary* fiscal policy through boosting government spending and/or cutting taxes. Higher consumption and investment leads to higher output and income. In this manner, the loss of demand from a lack of spending by the private sector is compensated.

That a government ran a budget deficit in the process was considered to be less important. In fact, Keynes advocated that to keep people employed, government has to run a deficit in the case of a stagnating economy because the private sector does not consume and invest enough to maintain demand and reverse recession. When the economy has recovered, tax revenue would automatically rise and debt incurred in the recession could be repaid.

Likewise, on the upside of the business cycle, an economy should be slowed down. Such *contractionary* fiscal policy involves the opposite measures of those applied in expansionary policy to avoid a serious contrary reaction. Recession resulting from an overheated economy tends to be severe and long lasting. Hence, government should cut spending and raise the tax burden.

A2.4   AGGREGATE DEMAND AND OUTPUT

The IS-LM Model

Although the original theory is ascribed to Keynes, many economists have contributed to 'Keynesian economics'. A leading interpretation of Keynes's theory is given by the so-called 'IS–LM model', which was developed by Sir John Hicks and Alvin Hansen only one year after the publication of the *General Theory*. It captures a large part of short-run Keynesian macroeconomics in a sophisticated, yet understandable, manner. The model is depicted in Figure A2.2. The horizontal axis represents national income or output. The vertical axis corresponds to the interest rate.

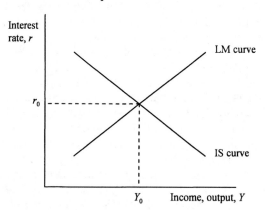

Figure A2.2   The IS-LM model in equilibrium

The IS curve (investment and saving) is a downward-sloping curve that represents equilibrium in the market for goods and services (that is, the real economy). Along the curve, total spending on consumption, planned investment, government purchases and net exports equal an economy's total output. Hence, there is no unplanned inventory accumulation, a point to which we shall return later. The negative relationship indicates that a lower interest rate is associated with higher output and income and vice versa.

The LM curve (liquidity preference and money supply) is an upward-sloping curve that shows potential points of equilibrium in the money market (that is, the nominal economy).[4] The shape of the curve is determined by liquidity preferences of people and the transaction demand for money. The larger the economic income or output, the more households and firms trade with each other. This means that households desire to hold more money to facilitate this trade. At a more or less fixed supply of money by the central bank, a higher output and income is thus associated with a higher demand for money and equilibrium interest rate.

The combination of both curves therefore represents the interface between the 'nominal' and the 'real' economy. In equilibrium, the curves explain short-run fluctuations in aggregate demand.

The Consumption Function and the Keynesian Cross

Private consumption is determined by total household income and the level of taxation. The direct effect of a tax is a reduction in *disposable* income of households. Hence, disposable income is measured as gross household income (Y) minus taxes imposed by government (T). Although T comprises many different taxes, it can be viewed as one lump-sum tax that decreases household purchasing power. The income after taxes have been deducted is divided between consumption and saving.

The ratio between consumption and saving is determined by the *average* propensity to consume (APC). If the APC is high, much income is spent on consumption, less on saving. A smaller APC involves higher saving and a lower consumption. By similar reasoning, the *marginal* propensity to consume (MPC) describes the consumption change when disposable income rises or falls by one unit. The MPC thus provides a measure of the change in consumption in response to a change in disposable income. This relationship is represented in the *consumption function* in equation (A2.7):

$$C = MPC(Y - T). \tag{A2.7}$$

By entering the consumption function into the national income accounts equation (A2.1), it becomes clear that by changing the tax burden, government can affect household consumption and, accordingly, national income. The larger the MPC, the greater the effect of a tax rise or cut on consumption and on income. But this is not all. On top of the direct income effect, comes a *multiplier effect*. The multiplier effect measures the ultimate effect on income of a change in spending, which is larger than the direct effect, or the MPC times the tax change.

The multiplier effect can be explained with the help of the so-called 'Keynesian cross' displayed in Figure A2.3. The Keynesian cross model

---

[4] Since the functioning of the LM curve lies in the monetary policy sphere, we refer to it only briefly below.

determines the equilibrium income where actual expenditure equals aggregate planned expenditure. In other words, output equals demand.

The 45° line denotes *actual* expenditure. The interpretation is straightforward. The line shows that aggregate actual expenditure on, or demand for, goods and services is equal to income. Any point above the 45° line implies that demand exceeds output. At any point under the line, demand falls short of output. The *aggregate planned* expenditure line shows the desired level of expenditure by households and firms at each level of income. Its shape is determined by the consumption function. A larger MPC is associated with a steeper aggregate planned expenditure curve and vice versa. The difference between the origin and intercept with the vertical axis is fixed, at least for now, by total spending on investment, government spending and net exports.

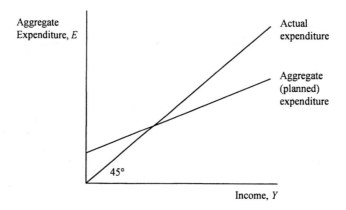

Figure A2.3   The Keynesian cross

The difference between both curves lies in expectations and consumer confidence (indeed, the Keynesian system is said to be based on a subjective psychological approach). The key idea is that, whenever the economy is not in equilibrium, inventory investment deviates from what is actually sold so that firms experience unexpected changes to inventory. In other words, actual expenditure may differ from planned expenditure if firms sell less or more than they anticipated and consequently experience positive or negative inventory accumulation.

Now consider what happens if government cuts taxes. The direct effect is a rise in disposable income and thus consumption by an amount equal to the MPC times the tax change (that is, $MPC*\Delta T$). The increase in consumption possibilities results in a vertical shift of the aggregate planned expenditure curve for the distance that corresponds to such an amount (see Figure A2.4).

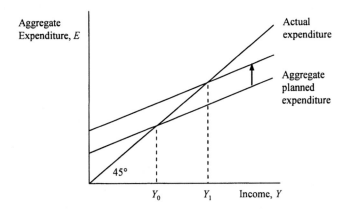

Figure A2.4   Actual and planned household expenditure

Even so, the actual effect on income is larger. That is, the horizontal shift from Y_0 to Y_1 is larger than the upward shift of the aggregate planned expenditure curve. This acceleration effect can be explained as follows. Because the tax cut raises disposable income, consumption is increased (in line with equation (A2.7)). The increase in consumption in turn causes income to rise (equation (A2.1)). This again leads to increased consumption, which causes a rise in income and so forth. The multiplier effect would thus take over and expand the effect on initial spending. Eventually it dies off, but in aggregate it is quite relevant.[5] The total income change in response to a tax change can be calculated by Equation A2.8:

$$\Delta Y = -MPC * \Delta T / (1 - MPC). \tag{A2.8}$$

Investment and the IS-Curve

After consumption, the second key factor in the aggregate expenditure function (A2.1) for maintaining demand is investment. According to Keynes, the rate of investment depends on the prospective returns on the investment, which is determined by the value of output generated during the asset's lifespan minus the running costs (that is, wages and material costs). Because the current value of these future income streams is reduced by a higher interest rate, the level of investment is negatively related to the interest rate. Thus, if the real interest rate goes up, it becomes more expensive to finance

---

[5] Sophisticated contemporary Keynesian econometric models reveal an expenditure multiplier between 2.2 and 2.7 for the United States (Brue and Grant, 2007).

investment. This reduces the rate of investment, as demonstrated in Figure A2.5.

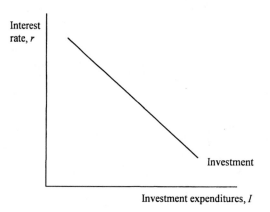

Figure A2.5   The investment demand curve

The IS curve can also be derived from the Keynesian cross. As noted, the IS curve relates the interest rate to national income, as illustrated in Figure A2.5. Consider what happens if the interest rate decreases. Based on the above, the reduced rate will lead, *ceteris paribus*, to a rise in the level of investment in the economy. This gives rise to an upward shift of the aggregate planned expenditure curve, see Figure A2.6A (remember that the difference between the origin and the vertical intercept of the aggregate planned expenditure curve is determined by spending on investment, government spending and net exports). The shift boosts equilibrium from Y_0 to Y_1. By relating the interest rate reduction from r_0 to r_1 to the subsequent rise in equilibrium income from Y_0 to Y_1, Figure A2.6B gives the IS curve.

For any combination of the interest rate and the level of income along the IS curve, the market for goods and services is in equilibrium. All spending is desired or planned and there is no unplanned inventory accumulation or decumulation. Moreover, planned investment equals saving.

Liquidity preference and the LM curve
Contrary to most classical economists before his time, Keynes did not believe that saving depends exclusively on the interest rate, but on the liquidity preference of households. In his view, the motives for saving are threefold:

- *transaction demand* of money as a means to buy goods and services;
- *precautionary demand* to save for a rainy day; and
- *speculative demand* to anticipate interest rate rises that set off a fall in, for example, bond and stock prices.

If the interest rate is low, the liquidity preference, or the desire of people to hold cash balances for speculative purposes, is high. This is because the opportunity cost of holding cash instead of interest-bearing bank deposits or bonds is thought to be low. This can be explained as follows. When the interest rate is low, people may expect it to rise. A rise in the interest rate sets off a fall in bond and stock prices, so that those who hold bonds and stock incur a loss. As a result, people's willingness to hold cash balances is larger when the interest rate is low. By contrast, if the interest rate is high, bond- and stockholders might expect to make a profit from declining interest rates.

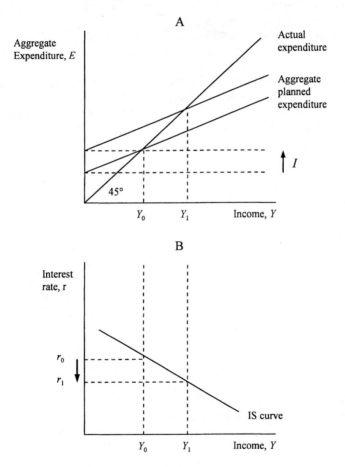

Figure A2.6   Deriving the IS curve from the Keynesian cross

This gives rise to Figure A2.7A. The money curve L is downward sloping because at a lower interest rate households desire to hold more cash balances.

Money supply is fixed by the central bank which translates into a vertical money supply curve M. The intersection of the money supply curve M and the money demand curve L determines the equilibrium interest rate. The liquidity preference function is supposed to become flat below some low interest rate (this is not shown). If the rate of interest is very low, people will become indifferent between holding their wealth in terms of cash or bonds. This is called the liquidity trap. Further increases in the money supply will just be hoarded and will not lower the interest rate and raise investment.

The theory of liquidity preference is used to derive the LM curve. The larger the national income, the more households and firms trade with each other. This means that the transaction demand for money increases. With a more or less fixed supply of money by the central bank, a higher income is thus associated with a higher demand for money and equilibrium interest rate.[6]

This is demonstrated in Figure A2.7B where a rise in income from Y_0 to Y_1 shifts the money demand curve to the right. This raises the equilibrium interest rate from r_0 to r_1. On the other hand, if the central bank expands the money supply, the money supply curve shifts to the right, lowering the interest rate and raising the equilibrium income.[7]

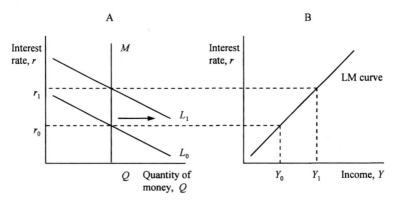

Figure A2.7   Liquidity preferences and the LM curve

For any combination of the interest rate and the level of income along the LM curve, the market for money is in equilibrium.

---

[6] A higher interest rate lowers money demand, so output or income must be higher to boost money demand back to the unchanged level of money supply.

[7] The effectiveness of increasing income depends on the elasticity of investment demand. If it is inelastic, there is only a limited effect of a fall in the interest rate on investment and thus income.

Government Spending on Goods and Services

The third variable that constitutes aggregate demand, government spending, has a very similar impact as a tax cut. Both fiscal policy measures come at a cost to the government budget, either indirectly or directly. If government unfolds its spending potential, there is a direct increase in demand. The effect is to trigger an upward shift of the planned aggregate expenditure curve (as in Figure A2.4) and so achieve a higher equilibrium income, or output. The opposite occurs in the case of a spending cut.

Like a tax cut, an expansion of government spending is subject to a multiplier effect. The corresponding effect on income, or output, is determined by:

$$\Delta Y = \Delta G / (1 - MPC). \tag{A2.9}$$

The magnitude of the effect from a boost in government spending is different from a tax cut. For example, government intends to stimulate the economy for which it allocates 1 billion units. Further assume an MPC of 0.6. By applying equation (A2.4), it can be estimated that income, including the multiplier effect, is raised by $1 / 0.4 = 2.5$ billion units. Yet, an identical tax cut would result in an income rise of only $-0.75 * -1 / 0.4 = 1.875$ billion units. The reason is that not all income gained from a tax cut is spent on consumption. Depending on the MPC, part of it is saved. Every additional unit of government spending none the less causes a boost in demand by that amount.[8]

Fiscal policy and changing equilibrium income

Figure A2.8 shows what happens to the IS curve when government makes a fiscal policy adjustment. For example, a tax cut or government spending increase raises aggregate demand by an amount specified by the multiplier equations (A2.8) and (A2.9), respectively. This prompts an upward shift of the planned aggregate expenditure curve, so that equilibrium income increases by a similar amount from Y_0 and Y_1 (as in Figure A2.4). The IS curve shifts to the right accordingly.

Such fiscal policy also drives up the interest rate from r_0 to r_1. This is because higher income raises money demand while money supply stays fixed (see Figure A2.7). If for some reason a higher interest rate is considered to be unwelcome, the central bank can opt to simultaneously ease the money supply. This is called 'accommodating' monetary policy, whereby the LM

---

[8] If tax revenue does match expenditure, government has to resort to borrowing to finance the budget gap. This higher demand for money puts upward pressure on the interest rate and can lead to a *crowding out* of investment and hence a smaller capital stock in the long run.

curve shifts to the right to LM',[9] lowering the interest rate back to its original level. None the less, the economy operates above its long-run natural capacity, which is sustainable only for a short period.

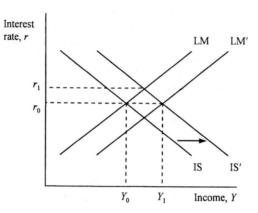

Figure A2.8   A shift of the IS curve

Net Exports: A Variable or Fixed Interest Rate

Economies in the world nowadays are predominantly open. To examine the effect of fiscal policy on exports and imports, we first briefly consider a large open economy, such as the US, which has the power to affect world interest rates. We then turn to examining the effects in a typical economy in the European Monetary Union (EMU). Here, individual countries are still largely free to conduct fiscal policy, while trade is governed by a central exchange rate regime of the European Central Bank (ECB).[10]

Figure A2.9 demonstrates the interaction between the IS-LM model, the interest rate and net exports.[11] Before, it was shown how expansionary fiscal policy shifts the IS curve to the right whereby income rose from Y_0 to Y_1. This is once more illustrated in Figure A2.9B.

By itself, part of the higher income will be spent on imports (that is, it leaks abroad), which raises the demand for foreign currency and the exchange rate. However, the income rise also drives up the interest rate from r_0 to r_1, which makes it more attractive for households to save domestically than abroad. Net foreign investment therefore decreases from NFI_0 to NFI_1 (see also national income accounting in Section A2.2). This lowers the

---

[9] If investment demand is inelastic, there is little effect on income, so the LM curve shifts down instead.

[10] The Maastricht criteria put some restraint on national governments by imposing an upper limit of 3 per cent of GDP for the annual budget deficit.

[11] This graphical interpretation is adopted from Mankiw (2003, Annex to Chapter 12).

demand for foreign currency, which more than fully offsets the initial boost due to increased imports. Figure A2.9C shows that the exchange rate appreciates because of an increased demand for foreign currency. Because the exchange rate appreciates, goods and services become more expensive to consumers abroad, which lowers net exports from NX_0 to NX_1. Hence, the effect of expansionary tax policy is partially cancelled out by lower net exports. [12]

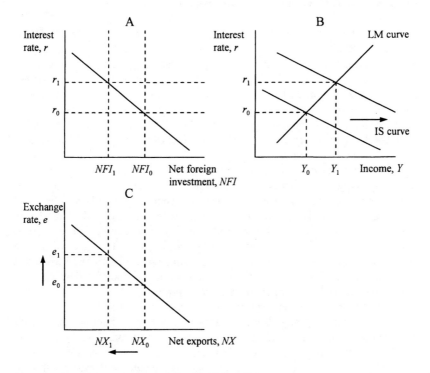

Figure A2.9   Net exports and the IS-LM model

For a typical economy in the EMU, the effect is somewhat different. Again income is stimulated through expansionary fiscal policy. This time the rise in the interest rate is less pronounced because the impact of one country on total EMU money demand is not as significant (even negligible for the smaller countries). The lower rise of the interest rate leads to a smaller appreciation of the euro and a lower decline in net exports. The domestic

---

[12] If imports exceed exports, there is a trade deficit. Expansionary tax policy may then give rise to a *twin deficit* whereby a budget deficit coincides with a trade deficit. The former is caused by expansionary tax policy and reduces domestic saving. A country has to resort to foreign borrowing so that net foreign investment decreases. This lowers net exports further.

effect of expansionary tax policy is thus larger. In particular, the smaller countries, whose share in the aggregate is not significant, are subject to an exchange rate that is determined by the trade balance of all EMU countries. The end result will depend on the fiscal policy simultaneously pursued by other EMU economies. If they, too, are applying expansionary policy, the interest rate could rise more significantly due to the aggregate effect.

Relating the IS Curve to Aggregate Demand

The IS curve shows all possible points where there is equilibrium in the goods market. It also gives an interpretation of the effect of fiscal policy on income and the interest rate. A tax cut or increase in government spending is represented by a shift of the IS curve to the right. The opposite occurs in the case of a tax rise or a cut in government spending. Whenever investment is affected, the interest rate changes to equilibrate investment with savings. This is represented by a move along the IS curve. The IS curve in combination with the LM curve explains the ultimate effect of policy on national income and the interest rate (Figure A2.8).

The model can be used to derive the aggregate demand (AD) curve of an economy. Aggregate demand is represented in a downward-sloping curve, which expresses the negative relationship between output and the price level (see Figure A2.9). The AD curve can be derived from the IS-LM model by assuming that the demand side of the economy is in equilibrium if there is simultaneous spending and money market equilibrium. In other words, the AD curve summarises all possible combinations where the IS and LM curves intersect, that is, those combinations of output and price level for which there is equilibrium in the spending and money market.

Now consider what happens in the case of a price rise. Because money supply is fixed, the interest rate increases.[13] A higher interest rate causes investment to decrease, which leads to a lower demand for goods and services. This shifts the AD curve inward and reduces output. On the other hand, if government spending is raised or taxes are cut, the IS curve shifts out and income in an economy increases. This causes the AD to shift outward.

A2.5   AGGREGATE SUPPLY AND INFLATION

The AD curve together with the aggregate supply (AS) curve determines equilibrium output and price level in an economy. See Figure A2.10, which makes a distinction between long-run and short-run aggregate supply. The

---

[13] The real value of money declines. Money balances are a measure of money supply divided by prices M/P. If M remains equal but P increases the value of M/P decreases, which puts pressure on the interest rate and shifts the LM curve upwards.

long-run AS curve is vertical, indicating that prices are fully flexible and the level of output is set by fixed supply as determined by the production function and state of technology. The short-run AS curve is horizontal because prices are sticky in the short run. Contrary to the long-run natural rate of output, output in the short run is able to fluctuate. That is, manufacturers are to some extent flexible to raise or lower production for short periods in response to changing demand.

Aggregate supply together with aggregate demand establishes short-run equilibrium between output and the price level. Section A2.3 showed that when output is below its long-run natural rate on the downside of the business cycle, government should conduct expansionary fiscal policy. This effect is illustrated in Figure A2.10. A tax cut or higher government spending will shift the AD curve to the right from point 1. If policy is conducted accurately, the AD curve shifts to point 2 where the economy is in equilibrium at its natural long-run position. This is indicated by the crossing of the three curves. The mechanism also works the other way around (this is not shown). If output lies above its natural rate on the upside of the business cycle, contractionary tax policy shifts the AD curve to the left. Output decreases as a result.[14]

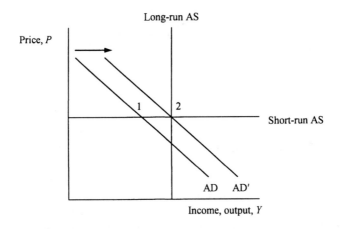

Figure A2.10   Aggregate demand and stabilisation policy

In reality, a flat short-run AS curve to express price stickiness proves a bit inaccurate. Where the long-run AS curve remains vertical, the short-run AS

---

[14] It takes time for government to respond to shocks and for the economy to adjust to implemented policy. This is why policy is not always successful and may even run pro-cyclically. Two kinds of delay are distinguished: the *inside lag* describes the time interval between a shock and government reaction; and the *outside lag* describes the time for implemented policy to become effective, that is, the adjustment time.

curve is somewhat upward sloping, as shown in Figure A2.11. Hence, an increase of income, or output, is associated with inflation. Economists have offered different explanations for the upward-sloping shape of the AS curve. Some emphasise that inflation arises because wages and prices adjust slowly; others ascribe inflation to the market which is generating imperfect information, thus misleading people in their expectations; yet others believe that workers mistake changes in real and nominal wages in response to short-run unexpected price rises (the inflation-unemployment trade-off is dealt with below).

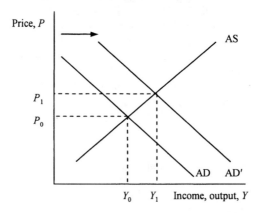

Figure A2.11   Stabilisation policy under an upward-sloping supply curve

Here, a higher demand equilibrates with aggregate supply at a higher price level. And indeed expansionary tax policy often causes inflationary pressures.

Output and Unemployment

Unemployment is a central factor in business-cycle fluctuations. Keynes assumed that there is a significant correlation between income and the level of employment in the short run. One needs employment to create effective demand. During times of recession, slack aggregate demand for goods and services induces firms to discharge or lay off workers, rather than cut wages. Higher unemployment rates in turn amplify the reduction of aggregate demand and employment. This continues until economic recovery, when higher economic activity facilitates an increase in employment.

This countercyclical fluctuation of unemployment with output is illustrated in Figure A2.12. Like capital, the production factor labour is subject to diminishing returns. Labour is a direct input in the production process, so employment increases as output increases and vice versa. Since the unemployment rate is the mirror image of the employment rate (both add up to one), the relationship between output and unemployment is negative.

Output fluctuations cause what is called 'cyclical unemployment', or the deviation of the unemployment rate from its natural long-run level.

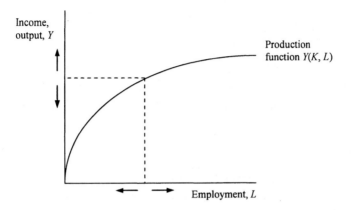

Figure A2.12   The output-employment relationship

Okun's law
The negative relationship between output and unemployment was empirically studied by the economist A.M. Okun (1983). His findings are based on observations for the American economy and formulated in 'Okun's law', which gives the following relationship:

$$U - U_n = -g(Y - Y_{LR}).$$ (A2.10)

The function associates fluctuations of output (Y) around its long-run growth path (Y_{LR}) to fluctuations of the unemployment rate (U) around its long-run natural rate (U_n). The relationship is a negative one. Based on the US economy, Okun originally found a value for g of 1/3. In other words, a 1 per cent decrease in the unemployment rate is coupled to an economic growth of 3 per cent above its long-run trend. Although this specific relationship was found for the American economy and is based on old data, the law can serve as a rule of thumb.

Hysteresis
Although these relations are strictly short run, some economists have argued that the fluctuations could leave more long-lasting marks on output and employment. 'Hysteresis' describes the circumstance where the natural rate of unemployment depends on past unemployment. The unemployed may experience difficulty in finding work after being unemployed in a recession,

even if jobs are now sufficiently available, as skills become obsolete if not used. The long-term unemployed also adopt a different attitude to employment and they lose motivation, self-confidence and/or the discipline needed to be a productive worker in the labour force. Generous unemployment benefits and unions that only consider the interests of the employed in the bargaining process over wages also contribute to hysteresis. In part, governments thus face the implications of past policy decisions and the effect of bad policy can carry on over an extended period.

The Unemployment – Inflation Relationship

In 1958, economist A.W.H. Phillips (1958) found a negative relationship between inflation and unemployment. The theory was transformed into the 'Phillips curve'. The curve is depicted in Figure A2.13 and demonstrates the trade-off between inflation and unemployment in the short term. Phillips based his curve on a sample of nominal wage and unemployment rates in the UK during the 1861-1957 period. Subsequent empirical research showed that the relationship could be observed in other countries too.

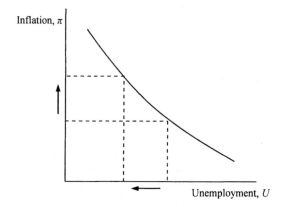

Figure A2.13   The Phillips curve

The theoretical underpinning of the observed relationship can be formulated in a few words: if employment increases, unemployment decreases and labour becomes more scarce. According to the Phillips theory, this causes a rise in wages, which in turn is reflected in product prices and the inflation rate. There was thus a policy trade-off in stimulating employment and combating inflation. Both are equally undesired symptoms. However, whereas in the 1950s and 1960s the Phillips curve appeared to predict adequately, the relationship more or less broke down with the oil shocks of the 1970s and early 1980s.

The expectations augmented Phillips curve

From its conception, the Phillips curve had been subject to criticisms, most notably by Nobel Prize-winning economists Milton Friedman and Edmund Phelps (winning the prize in 1976 and 2006, respectively), who found it atypical that nominal values such as wage rates and price inflation affected real values such as unemployment and output. These concerns were confirmed by later developments in the 1970s and early 1980s, when data no longer supported the traditionally observed inflation and unemployment patterns.

During these years, both unemployment and inflation increased, that is, the problem of 'stagflation' (economic stagnation and sharp rises in inflation occurring at the same time). The Keynesian solution to economic problems no longer presented a viable alternative. The stagflation phenomenon, not observed as such before, meant a simultaneous implementation of expansionary policy (to combat recession) and contractionary policy (to combat inflation).

In response, the expectations augmented Phillips curve was developed, which renewed insights into the relation between short- and long-run effects of economic policy. Thus far, the model seems to describe the inflation and unemployment relationship accurately. The relationship is as follows:

$$\pi = \pi^e - b(U - U_n) + s, \qquad\qquad (A2.11)$$

where:

π	= actual inflation;
π^e	= expected inflation;
$b\,(U - U_n)$	= cyclical unemployment; b = responsiveness to inflation;
s	= exogenous supply shock.

The renewed Phillips curve stipulates that inflation depends on three components: expected inflation; the deviation of unemployment from its natural rate multiplied by the responsiveness of inflation to cyclical unemployment; and exogenous supply shocks that arise from autonomous factors such as rises in oil prices or tax rates.

With expectations included, the Phillips curve is able to explain why stagflation is occurring. Hence, if workers expected inflation to occur they would anticipate it by demanding a correspondingly higher wage rise. The Phillips curve thereby shifts to the right so that employment is reduced again, while inflation lingers on the higher level (this is not shown in Figure A2.13). Exogenous supply shocks have a similar effect of shifting the Phillips curve. These supply shocks were the main reason why the fundamentals underlying the 'old' Phillips curve broke down in the 1970s and early 1980s.

Demand-pull and cost-push inflation

Two sources of inflation are thus distinguished, both of which are explained by the renewed Phillips curve. The first type constitutes *demand-pull* inflation and occurs when aggregate demand is high. It is captured by the part $b \, (U - U_v)$ in the renewed Phillips function. During expansionary tax policy, government should be on the alert for demand-pull inflation, which is often amplified as labour unions start demanding higher wages to compensate for higher prices, which further inflates product prices. A second cause of rising prices is *cost-push* inflation, whose origin lies in exogenous supply shocks as captured by s in the renewed Phillips curve. As noted, a rise in oil prices could be a source.[15] Tax increases are a second cause of exogenous supply shocks. Taxes raise wage, capital and material costs, which in turn raises product costs and prices rise.

A2.6 KEYNESIAN IMPLICATIONS OF A TAX CUT

The model and notions discussed can be used to review the macroeconomic effects of tax cuts.[16] Because government and households react in different ways, several scenarios are theoretically possible. For instance, government may react to a tax cut by reducing spending or by increasing borrowing. Households may either consume the additional disposable income or save it. As we have seen, imports also play a role. All factors affect the ultimate outcome on the economy. Six scenarios can be distinguished:

- households increase spending on goods and services, while government reduces its spending so as to leave the budget unaffected in relative terms. In this case, demand-side effects will be negligible since the rise in household spending is roughly offset by the reduction in government spending;
- households increase spending, while government retains its spending by sustaining a budget deficit. Total spending thus increases which raises output and reduces unemployment. Government should be vigilant for inflationary pressures, though;
- household saving is increased, while government reduces its spending. Aggregate demand is thereby reduced, unemployment increased and an overall deflationary effect is likely to pertain. Self-financing does not occur. Hence, the opposite of a stimulatory effect is actually produced;

---

[15] The sharp rise in oil prices at the beginning of the 21st century resulted from a mixture of higher demand and uncertainties surrounding supply.

[16] Tax increases have rarely been used in history as an explicit instrument in countercyclical fiscal policies. They remain an option in government policy.

- household saving is increased, while government maintains its spending. The deflationary effect in the above case is mitigated. The resulting budget deficit is simply financed by increased household savings (the Ricardian equivalence). In the longer run, budgetary pressures will nevertheless increase;
- households increase spending, while government reduces it equally, but instead of consuming domestically produced goods and services, households spend a larger part on imports (a real possibility in open economies with high production costs). This lowers demand faced by domestic firms, increases unemployment and has negative consequences for the trade balance; and
- households increase spending, while the government maintains its level of spending, but households spend the larger part of the increase on imports. This does not necessarily reduce economic activity even though the trade balance worsens. The budget deficit ultimately increases both inflation and interest rates.

The short-term macroeconomic effects of a tax cut are far from unequivocal. In practice, the effects are not as precisely defined as in the above scenarios, but constitute a mixture of influences. What is clear is that if government fails to foster adequate public support and confidence for the proposed measures, the effort to stimulate an economy is likely to founder.

A2.7 RICARDIAN CRITIQUE OF THE KEYNESIAN VIEW

Not everybody agrees on the stimulatory effects that emanate from a tax cut, though.[17] A main critique is that people are smart enough to realise that any tax cut must lead to future tax rises whereby the present value of future tax rises exactly equals the current tax cut. Hence, instead of consuming the additional disposable income, households will save to be able to pay higher future taxes.

This view is referred to as 'Ricardian equivalence' and was put forward by the Dutch-Portuguese economist David Ricardo (1772-1823). Ricardian equivalence assumes that people calculate the present value of the higher future taxes needed to service government debt. Households compare this to the cost of financing current increased government spending out of taxation. In present value terms the outcome should be equivalent.

For example, a taxpayer should be indifferent to paying 100 units in taxes now, or issuing public debt for the value of 100 units under the obligation to

---

[17] See also Chapter 6 in Heijdra and van der Ploeg (2002).

repay the debt in one year for 110 units (assuming an interest rate of 10 per cent), the 10 extra being interest. Rational individuals would simply increase their savings, and not consumption, by the size of the tax cut to be able to pay for higher future taxes. The taxpayer's net worth does in fact not change.

However, it is questionable if people have such forward-looking views. Many economists do not think so and believe that at least some households behave in a Keynesian fashion. Hence, (temporarily) reduced taxes raise current consumption. There is also uncertainty as to what extent households take into account the burden of deficit financing on future generations. If the current generation manages to transfer debt to future generations, this offers additional support for Keynesian theory.

It is also true that the debt claims, that is, the bonds themselves, are passed on to future generations. A high debt burden merely raises the risk premium on government debt. Typically, there would be only distributional consequences within the next generation, imposed by the current generation. However, a high debt burden may also make consumers conscious and act more rationally. For example, studies show the basic Keynesian recipe for weak demand currently to be inadequate for Japan due to an excessive government debt and rational consumer behaviour (Krueger and Prescott, 1998; Ihori et al., 2001; Perri, 2001). Japan's public debt to GDP burden exceeded 150 per cent in 2005 (see Table 1.3 in Chapter 1).

A2.8 SUMMARY

The main categories of spending that make up aggregate demand are consumption, investment, government spending and net exports. Because prices and wages are sticky in the short run, the economy can have trouble adjusting to macroeconomic demand shocks. Instead of cutting prices and wages, firms respond by reducing production and discharging workers. This causes output to fluctuate around its long-run natural level (so-called business-cycle fluctuations).

Tax and expenditure policy can be used to dampen the short-run fluctuations in output by applying expansionary or contractionary fiscal policy on, respectively, the downside or the upside of the business cycle.

The IS-LM model gives a leading interpretation of short-run Keynesian theory. The model links national income to the interest rate. The IS curve is a downward-sloping curve that represents equilibrium in the goods market. The LM curve is an upward-sloping curve that represents equilibrium in the money market. The intersection of both curves represents equilibrium in the market for goods and services and for money.

Shift in the IS curve can be related to shifts in aggregate demand, which together with aggregate supply determines equilibrium output and price level. Depending on whether tax or expenditure policy is contractionary or expansionary, aggregate demand decreases or increases so that the AD curve shifts in or outward and is steered towards the long-run natural level of output.

A central conclusion of Keynesian theory is that there is no automatic tendency for output and employment to move towards a state of full employment. A negative relationship exists between output and unemployment (formally described by Okun's law). Unemployment can in turn be associated with inflation through the renewed Phillips curve, which demonstrates that inflation arises from two main sources: demand-pull and cost-push inflation.

Finally, a main critique of Keynesian economics comes in the form of the Ricardian equivalence, which postulates that households behave rationally in response to a deficit-financed tax cut. In other words, they will anticipate higher future taxes to repay government debt and see that in net terms they are not better off. Under the Ricardian view, a tax cut has no real effects.

Appendix 3   Microeconomic topics in commodity taxation

A3.1   INTRODUCTION

The incidence of taxes and distortions that arise are analysed in a microeconomic framework. This appendix elaborates on some of the basic theory and principles, which is essential for a basic understanding of a number of the subjects discussed in the main text. To this end, the appendix will focus on consumption taxation. Many of the principles discussed may nevertheless apply likewise to taxation of labour or capital.

The appendix is structured as follows. The efficiency loss that results from imposing a *specific* or *ad valorem* tax is referred to as the 'excess burden' of taxation, or equivalently the 'deadweight loss'. To be able to appreciate its origin and magnitude, we start with an analysis of the effect of taxation in the market for a single commodity. Because such analysis considers only one commodity, keeping other things constant, it is referred to as a 'partial equilibrium analysis'. This includes three stages: familiarisation with the principles of consumer and producer surplus; consideration of the incidence of a commodity tax; and definition of the excess burden.

While such partial equilibrium analysis is useful to grasp the basic concepts, it fails to capture the interaction between markets. For example, it makes sense that if demand in the market for a certain good decreases, demand in the market for a substitute good could increase. This is why Section A3.3 considers the effect of a tax in a general equilibrium setting. Section A3.4 covers three important notions in commodity taxation: the Pigouvian tax, the Ramsey rule and the Corlett-Hague rule. The chapter concludes with a brief summary.

A3.2   PARTIAL EQUILIBRIUM ANALYSIS

To study demand, a distinction is drawn between an ordinary or uncompensated demand curve and a compensated demand curve. An *ordinary* demand curve shows the negative relationship between the price of a commodity, say good X, and its quantity demanded. Also referred to as a

Marshallian demand function, the curve expresses the empirical regularity that as the price of X falls, demand increases and vice versa. Hence, the demand curve is downward sloping, as demonstrated in Figure A3.1. [1]

The shape of the demand curve demonstrates that if the price of good X falls, a person consumes more units of X. This increases his or her utility from consumption. However, when holding the level of income fixed, not only can the person buy more of X, he or she could also change his or her consumption pattern and purchase some units of, say, good Z (for example, a more expensive qualitatively better product). A fall in the price of commodity X may thus induce the person not only to buy more units of X, but also to shift some consumption to Z.

With a fall in the price of a commodity, holding income and other prices fixed, two effects on individual demand may thus be identified. The first is an increase in the consumption of X, which is referred to as the *income* effect. The lower price of good X enables somebody to consume a larger quantity of X, as if a person's income were increased. The second effect describes the shift of consumption of good X to that of good Z. This is referred to as the *substitution* effect. Both effects are captured by an ordinary demand curve.

In contrast to the ordinary or uncompensated demand curve, the compensated demand curve eliminates the income effect from the behavioural response. This is done by compensating consumers for the effect of a price change on real incomes. Hence, by adjusting income, conceptually, simultaneous with a price rise or fall, the net effect on the demand for units of X is zero. The curve was conceived by Sir John Richard Hicks and leaves a consumer with an identical level of utility before as after the price change. The result is that the compensated demand curve reflects only the substitution effect.

So why is this seemingly technical distinction important? As we shall see, only the substitution effect is responsible for the distortion that causes an excess burden to arise, for example, by the imposition of a selective tax. The tax induces consumers to pick another less preferred consumption bundle than they would have done in the absence of the substitution effect. Hicks's compensated demand curve allows us to capture this distortion in a so-called 'deadweight loss triangle'. To see how this works, we first have to define the notions of consumer and producer surplus.

---

[1] Theoretically speaking, demand could be upward sloping. For so-called 'Giffen goods' a decrease in price causes the quantity demanded to fall. However, in real life economists have found few if any examples of such goods so they may be little more than an academic curiosity. 'Veblen goods' also display upward-sloping demand curves and relate to so-called 'conspicuous consumption' of expensive goods for the sake of displaying social status and wealth. Hence, the higher the price, the larger the quantity demanded.

Consumer and Producer Surplus

Figure A3.1 illustrates the compensated demand curve for commodity X, which can be anything from a book, or a train ticket to a litre of fuel. The demand curve describes what consumers are willing to pay for each successive unit produced. In other words, the marginal value they attach to each unit of X. In this case, somebody is willing to pay P_1 for the first unit, P_2 for the second and so on. This process continues until X_5, after which point people are unwilling to pay anything for an additional unit.

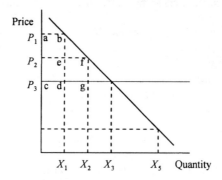

Figure A3.1   The demand curve

If we assume that the price of commodity X is exogenously set at P_3, consumers are willing to purchase 3 units of X. At this point the market is in equilibrium since the marginal benefit derived from the last unit of X (that is, as measured by the demand curve) equals the marginal cost of a unit of X (that is, the price consumers have to pay).

However, the person buying the first unit of X attaches a value of P_1 to it, namely the price he or she is actually willing to pay. Since the price is only P_3, there is an implicit gain for an amount equal to the difference between the demand curve and the actual price, or the area defined by abcd. In other words, because the consumer is willing to pay a price above the cost he or she has to incur to obtain the unit, there is a benefit from the transaction for the difference. Likewise, the person buying the second unit gains for an amount equal to the area efgd. The person buying unit X_3 is willing to pay the exact cost and thus derives no extra surplus from the transaction.

In aggregate, however, consumers benefit for an amount that corresponds to the areas abcd and efgd. This amount is referred to as the 'consumer surplus'. If the distances on the x-axis between each of the units of X traded are made infinitely small, which is a reasonable assumption in today's profuse markets for many goods and services, one can easily measure the total consumer surplus from exchange of a certain commodity as the area between the demand curve and the price line. This is shown in Figure A3.3, below.

On the opposite side of the market, a similar reasoning is responsible for the 'producer surplus'. Consider the supply curve in Figure A3.2. The curve is upward sloping, which indicates that at a higher price producers are willing to supply a greater number of commodities. The producer surplus arises because suppliers are willing to produce at a price below the actual market price of a commodity. Thus, somebody is willing to produce unit X_1 for a price of P_1. The second unit is produced for a price of P_2 and so on. If the price is again exogenously set at P_3, a total of 3 units of X are produced. Suppliers would be unwilling to produce any additional unit as marginal cost exceeds marginal revenue.

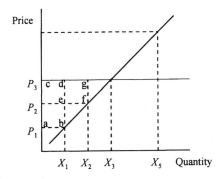

Figure A3.2   The supply curve

Because the supplier of unit X_1 incurs a cost of P_1 yet receives a purchase price of P_3, there is a benefit from the transaction by the area abcd. Unit X_2 creates a gain of dgfe and so forth. At unit X_3 marginal cost equals marginal revenue, thus no additional gain is derived.

Figure A3.3 shows the complete picture of supply and demand in equilibrium at Q and the corresponding consumer and producer surpluses. The market equilibrium is achieved by the forces of supply and demand and constitutes the state in which the price has reached the level where quantity supplied equals quantity demanded. The total economic gain from trading commodity X equals the sum of consumer and producer surplus.

The Incidence of Taxation

A tax is not necessarily borne by the person on whom the tax is legally imposed. Although government can formally impose a tax on the producer or the consumer, market functioning can shift the economic burden of a tax onto somebody other than the person it is levied from. The allocation of a tax between the individual legally responsible for remitting it and the individual on whom the economic burden really falls is called the *tax* incidence.

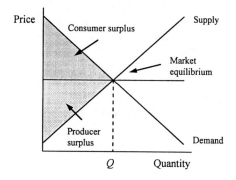

Figure A3.3   Consumer and producer surplus

For example, assume that commodity X of our previous example sells at a price of 10 units before any tax is imposed. The government now decides to introduce a commodity tax on the producer of, say, 1 unit per item sold. The price of good X may reasonably be expected to increase to 11 units. The producer would be unaffected by the tax, which is entirely borne by the consumer through a higher price. However, consumers will of course be reluctant to pay anything higher than the previous equilibrium price of 10 units. Some consumers may therefore decide to allocate their money differently and leave the market. To retain market share, the producer is thus forced to lower his/her price and thereby forgo profits.

Depending on the market-specific allocation between supply and demand, this usually leads to a midway solution whereby the producer and the consumer each bear part of the tax burden. For example, the producer receives 9.5 units and the consumer pays 10.5 units, but any other combination between 9 and 11 is perfectly possible. The example shows that there is a distinction between who is legally responsible for the tax (that is, the *legal* incidence) and who actually bears the burden of the tax (that is, the *economic* incidence).

Figure A3.4 illustrates how the tax is shifted between producer and consumer. In Figure A3.4A, the market equilibrium has initially set in at price P_0 and quantity Q_0. A tax is subsequently imposed on the producer. This is reflected by an upward shift of the supply curve from S to S' (that is, the same good becomes more expensive to market), whereby the quantity supplied falls from Q_0 to Q_1. At Q_1, the new market equilibrium sets in.

At this point there is a difference in the price paid by the consumers P_{cons} and the price received by the producers P_{prod}. The difference represents the size of the tax and is referred to as the 'tax wedge'. In our earlier example the tax wedge equalled 10 units. The total tax revenue is calculated by multiplying the wedge by the quantity of commodities sold, Q_1. Graphically, this is represented by the size of areas b and c.

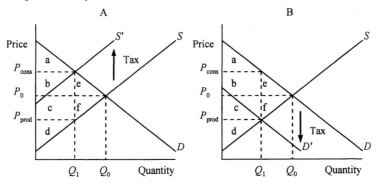

Figure A3.4   The incidence of a commodity tax

The figure also shows how the tax burden is allocated between producers and consumers. The tax paid by the producers is represented by the size of area c, hence the difference between the before-tax price P_0 and the price received after tax P_{prod}, times the quantity sold Q_1. The size of area b represents the tax paid by the consumer, which is equal to the difference between the before-tax price P_0 and the price paid after tax P_{cons}, times the quantity sold Q_1.

Figure A3.4B the alternative case is demonstrated where tax is legally imposed on the consumer. The imposition of the tax is reflected by a downward shift of the demand curve from D to D' (that is, the same good becomes more expensive to purchase, which depresses demand). As to the economic effects caused by the tax, the same reasoning applies as before. This shows that the outcome of imposing the tax either on the consumer or producer is exactly the same.

The Excess Burden of Taxation

Having seen this, it is fairly straightforward to quantify the excess burden created. With the imposition of the tax, the consumer surplus in Figure A3.4 has shrunk in size from areas a, b and e to area a (that is, the area between the demand curve and the price line P_{cons}). The producer surplus has also shrunk in size from a total of areas c, d and f to area d (that is, the area between the supply curve and the price line P_{prod}). Although this reduction presents a loss in welfare to the consumer, the loss is partly compensated by the gain to government from the tax revenue collected (that is, the size of areas b and c).

In other words, at the same time as the consumer and producer lose surplus, the government benefits in the form of tax revenue collected.

However, the sum of the reduced consumer surplus after tax of area a and the tax revenue of area b is smaller than the original surplus that was measured by areas a, b and e. An additional loss has thus been incurred. The loss is not tangible in terms of real money, but does represent a welfare loss implicit in consumption taxation. The size of the welfare loss is measured by area e. This creates a total cost to the consumer of the areas b and e. The excess burden has been created by the behavioural response induced by the tax.

The total tax burden on the producer may be established through similar reasoning. The original surplus is measured by the sum of the areas c, d and f. With the imposition of a tax the surplus is reduced to the size of area d, and the revenue collected by the government equals the wealth equivalent of area c. This leaves an excess burden the size of area f in comparison with the original surplus. This burden is borne by the producer and arises in excess of the actual cost of the tax payable to the government.

By adding up the welfare loss to the consumer and producer the total excess burden of the consumption tax is determined, namely the sum of areas c and f. It is the burden over and above the taxes payable to the government which are measured as the sum of areas b and c. This leaves a remaining consumer and producer surplus at the areas a and d. It becomes clear that the larger the tax wedge, the larger the shift from Q_0 to Q_1. The shift represents a direct reduction in output of the goods and services produced. The higher the tax rate, the larger the decline in output and the larger the excess burden.

Price Elasticities of Supply and Demand

The precise incidence of a tax and size of the excess burden depends on the sensitivity of supply and demand of a certain good to a price change. The most commonly used measure of the responsiveness of one variable to another variable is an elasticity. Hence, the 'price elasticity' is the percentage change in a variable resulting from a 1 per cent change in price of that variable.

The price elasticity of demand for a certain good is determined by equation (A3.1), where ΔQ is the change in the quantity demanded and $\Delta Q/Q$ is the percentage change in quantity demanded. Similarly, Δp is the change in price and $\Delta p/p$ is the percentage change in price. For example, if a 1 per cent price increase causes a 2 per cent decrease in quantity demanded, the elasticity of demand is $\varepsilon = -2$. The commodity is said to be *price elastic* as the percentage change in the quantity demanded is larger than the percentage change in price. In terms of equation (A3.1), the absolute value of the elasticity lies above unity ($\varepsilon > 1$). If the percentage change in the quantity demanded is smaller than the percentage change in price, the good is said to be *price inelastic* ($\varepsilon < 1$):

$$\varepsilon = \frac{\% \text{ change in quantity demanded}}{\% \text{ change in price}} = \frac{\Delta Q/Q}{\Delta p/p} \tag{A3.1}$$

The definition of the price elasticity of supply is similar to that of demand. The price elasticity of supply is determined by equation (A3.2):

$$\eta = \frac{\% \text{ change in quantity supplied}}{\% \text{ change in price}} = \frac{\Delta Q/Q}{\Delta p/p} \tag{A3.2}$$

The terms 'elastic' and 'inelastic' supply apply in a similar manner to the upward-sloping supply curve. Therefore, if supply is elastic the quantity demanded will be relatively sensitive to the change in price and vice versa.

A commodity tax under elastic and inelastic demand
Although the price elasticity varies along a downward-sloping linear demand curve (this property follows from equation (A3.1)), elastic demand is commonly represented by a flatter demand curve as a price change triggers a substantial change in the quantity demanded. If demand is inelastic, a price change causes a less than proportional change in the quantity demanded. The demand curve is typically steeper (compare Figures A3.5 and A3.6).

The more people are inclined to forgo consumption of a certain commodity in the case of a price increase, the higher the elasticity of demand. Such is often the case for goods and services with close substitutes. For example, apples have a relatively elastic demand as people can easily substitute them for some other fruit. Luxury goods and services such as televisions, cars and air travel also tend to have higher elasticities of demand.

The higher the elasticity of demand, the easier consumers are able to pass on the tax to the producer. This is illustrated in Figure A3.5A, where a unit tax is imposed on the consumer. The tax induces a downward shift of the demand curve from D to D'. The direct effect is a substantial decrease in quantity demanded from Q_0 to Q_1. Due to the high elasticity of demand, the producer is forced to bear a larger share of the burden. If he/she does not, consumers readily shift to another product. Hence, a producer who wishes to retain his/her market position absorbs a larger share of the tax. The price rise from the tax is limited as a result, though there is a significant behavioural response and excess burden.

Figure A3.5B presents the opposite situation where demand is inelastic. Goods characterised by inelastic demand include necessities such as bread, salt and healthcare, but also cigarettes which are highly addictive. With the imposition of a tax the demand curve once again shifts down from D to D'.

Although the size of the tax imposed is the same as before, the reduction in quantity demanded from Q_0 to Q_1 is smaller. Indeed, consumers are less sensitive to a price change. The producer is now better able to shift part of the tax burden. Note that the distortion from the tax, that is, the reduction in quantity demanded and thus the excess burden, is smaller. The price increase is more significant.

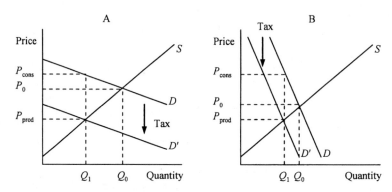

Figure A3.5   The case of elastic and inelastic demand

A commodity tax under elastic and inelastic supply

The case of elastic supply is illustrated in Figure A3.6A. The imposition of a tax on the producer induces an upward shift of the supply curve by the size of the tax (that is, the shift from S to S'). Because supply is elastic, producers are sensitive to a price change. The effect of the tax on output is therefore significant (that is, the production is cut from Q_0 to Q_1), with a considerable excess burden as the upshot. It can also be seen that the consumer bears a larger share of both the tax and the excess burden. The reason is that the producer more easily switches to producing another product if the consumer does not 'accept' a larger fraction of the tax burden. The higher the elasticity of supply, the larger this share will be. The price therefore increases relatively more.

The elasticity of supply can also differ substantially between the short and the long runs. The elasticity of supply largely depends on the producer's ability to increase or decrease production. Since a firm's production capacity is fixed in the short run, supply is less elastic. In the long run, producers are more flexible in adjusting production capacity, so they can respond better to a price change. The elasticity of supply is thus likely to rise somewhat over time.

Finally, the case of inelastic supply is illustrated in Figure A3.6B. The supply curve is steeper, which implies only a small behavioural response to the tax and a correspondingly smaller excess burden. Because supply is inelastic, the producer is forced to absorb a larger part of the tax.

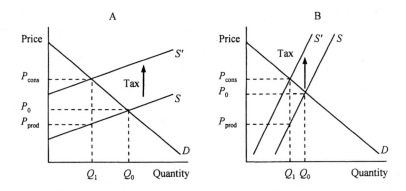

Figure A3.6   The case of elastic and inelastic supply

Summary of Effects and the Case of Perfect Elasticity

Table A3.1 sums up the impact of a commodity tax under the different market situations on the size of the excess burden, share of total tax borne by consumer and share of total tax borne by producer.

Table A3.1   Summary of tax effects in partial equilibrium

	Elastic demand	Inelastic demand	Elastic supply	Inelastic supply
Excess burden	+	-	+	-
Share consumer	-	+	+	-
Share producer	+	-	-	+

Furthermore, at both extremes, perfect elasticity implies a horizontal supply or demand curve (ε and $\eta = \infty$). This signifies the outermost case of the curves in Figures A3.5A, and A3.6A. The main consequence is that the entire burden is passed on to the producer and consumer, respectively. Under perfect inelasticity, supply and demand curves are vertical (ε and $\eta = 0$). This represents the outermost cases of the curves illustrated in Figures A3.5B and A3.6B. This time the burden is shifted entirely on to the consumer and producer, respectively.

A3.3   GENERAL EQUILIBRIUM ANALYSIS

The partial equilibrium analysis showed the implications of a consumption tax in the market for a single good or service. The supply curve and (compensated) demand curve enables one to measure the cost of a tax over and above the actual revenue collected. The approach is useful because it makes the welfare loss easily visible though the excess burden triangles.

These triangles have become known as 'Harberger triangles', named after US economist Arnold Harberger who first attempted to measure the actual size of excess burdens by this method. The triangles appear whenever the market is distorted by a tax, monopolistic behaviour or other factor that compromises the efficient allocation of resources. Formally, Harberger's analysis differs slightly from the compensated measures presented above, even though in many cases both have shown to approximate each other closely.

Harberger recognised that to fully capture the deadweight loss from a tax-induced distortion, one needs to consider more than one market. Therefore, he constructed a model where the revenue collected from a distortionary tax is returned to the consumer by a lump-sum payment. Hence, a tax would be imposed and induce a behavioural response. The revenue collected would subsequently be returned to the taxpayer in the form of a non-distortive lump-sum. Even if all revenue funds were accounted for by this payment, consumers would still be worse off after the tax. The amount by which they become worst off provides a measure of the excess burden or deadweight loss of the tax.

Here we present a simple general equilibrium analysis, which studies the interaction among two or more markets. This gives better insights into the underlying micro economic causes of tax distortions in otherwise efficient markets. Although tax effects typically extend over numerous markets, the assumption of two markets makes the analysis simpler, while it does not undermine the principles behind general equilibrium theory.

Conditions for Pareto Optimality

To measure the welfare loss from a tax-induced distortion, we start with the conditions for market efficiency. A market is considered efficient when the condition for 'Pareto efficiency' is met: 'a given economic arrangement is efficient if there can be no rearrangements which will leave someone better off without worsening the position of others'. The proposition was named after the Italian economist Vilfredo Pareto (1848-1923) who conceived it in the 19th century. The underlying rationale is that if resources in an economy are allocated inefficiently, it should be possible to make somebody better off without anybody else becoming worse off. Hence, a so-called 'Pareto improvement' is possible.

If we assume that there are two goods, X and Z, the market is Pareto efficient if the following condition is met:[2]

---

[2] Using advanced mathematics, the property can be shown to hold in the situation with multiple commodities as well. The assumption of two goods makes the analysis simpler.

$$MRS_{XZ} = MRT_{XZ} = P_X / P_Z. \tag{A3.3}$$

Equation (A3.3) states that the marginal rate of substitution of X for Z must equal the marginal rate of transformation of X for Z, which in turn is equal to the price ratio between X and Z. We shall examine this property in more detail below.

The Marginal Rate of Substitution

In choosing an optimal consumption bundle, a consumer makes a trade-off between consuming a certain amount of X, a certain amount of Z or a combination of both X and Z, given the budget constraint faced. This is illustrated graphically in Figure A3.7, where the quantity of X is located on the x-axis and the quantity of Z on the y-axis.

The *budget constraint* shows the combination of X and Z that the consumer can maximally afford to buy given relative prices P_X and P_Z and a fixed amount of income Y (assuming fixed household saving, that is, the choice between present and future consumption). The budget constraint is illustrated by line AB in Figure A3.7. At the intercept with the x-axis, the consumer can buy Y/P_X of good X; and at the intercept on the y-axis he or she can buy Y/P_Z of good Z. Between these two points, it is possible to buy any other bundle of X and Y as long as it is on or below the budget constraint. Any combination above the budget constraint cannot be obtained as income is inadequate.

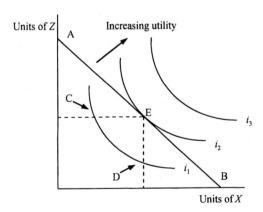

Figure A3.7 Indifference map with three indifference curves

The budget constraint of course indicates only what is possible, not what is preferred. Consumer preferences vary widely, so we need to take this into consideration. The *indifference curve* shows all bundles of X and Z that provide a consumer with an equal amount of satisfaction. Hence, each combination of X and Z on the same indifference curve gives the consumer the same utility. For example, a consumer is indifferent to receiving the bundle indicated by C, consisting of many units of Z and fewer of X, or receiving bundle D, consisting of fewer units of Z but more units of X. Each combination on the curve provides him or her with the same amount of utility.

The willingness of a consumer to actually substitute Z for X determines the exact shape of the indifference curve. This willingness differs per individual and is expressed in the slope of the indifference curve, or the marginal rate of substitution between X and Z (MRS_{XY}). The MRS defines the number of units of Z that a consumer is willing to forgo to consume an extra unit of X. By itself, there are infinitely many indifference curves that shape an individual's preferences (also called 'indifference map'). Each indifference curve shows the consumption bundles that give the consumer the same level of satisfaction.

In Figure A3.7, indifference curve i_1 is situated below the consumer's budget constraint. By choosing a consumption bundle on a higher indifference curve, that is, a next level of bundles which a consumer is indifferent to receiving, the individual is able to increase his or her utility (under the assumption that more is better). Indeed, the bundles on indifference curve i_2 imply a larger consumption than the bundles on indifference curve i_1. For this reason, a utility-maximising person will keep on increasing his/her utility by switching to a higher indifference curve until his/her budget constraint no longer permits him/her to do so. This point is reached at E where the indifference curve is tangential to the budget constraint. The consumption of a bundle on a higher indifference curve such as i_3 is not feasible as it is beyond what the consumer can afford.[3]

A utility-maximising person thus chooses the bundle of goods at point E, where the slope of the budget constraint is tangential to the slope of the indifference curve. At this point, MRS is equal to the ratio of net prices of both goods. This is described by equation (A3.4):

$$MRS_{XZ} = P_X / P_Z. \tag{A3.4}$$

The function identifies the optimal consumption choice of consumers. However, consumption needs to be matched to production, so we need to take into account output optimality as well.

---

[3] For a more elaborate treatment of the microeconomic principles underlying indifference curves see any basic or intermediate microeconomics textbook.

Marginal Rate of Transformation

The principles behind optimal consumer choice are essentially applicable in the same way to the producer output decision. A producer has to choose how to allocate his/her factors of production labour and capital between producing a combination of the goods X and Z. The trade-off between producing both goods is described by production possibilities frontier or output mix as depicted in Figure A3.8. It shows the combinations of X and Z that a producer is maximally able to produce given a certain production capacity. Depending on relative factor prices, the producer can produce any combination of X and Z in between as long as it is not above the production curve.

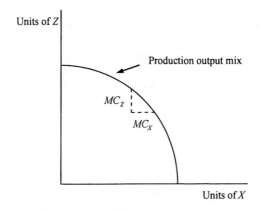

Figure A3.8   The production output mix for X and Z

The marginal rate of transformation between X and Z (MRT_{XZ}) is defined by the decrease in production of Z that is needed to produce an extra unit of X. Hence, in terms of production costs, the marginal cost of producing one incremental unit of X is measured against the incremental cost of producing one unit of Y. The MRT_{XZ} is determined by the ratio between MC_X / MC_Z, or the slope of the production output mix. The relationship is described by equation (A3.5):

$$MRT_{XZ} = MC_X / MC_Z. \tag{A3.5}$$

Since the profit-maximising firms in a competitive environment produce the quantity where marginal cost equals price P,[4] MRT_{XZ} is also determined

---

[4] Firms in perfect competition undercut prices in an effort to beat the competition. This leads to a downward spiral where prices fall until price (P) equals marginal cost (MC). Beyond this point, lowering prices leads to a net loss.

by the proportion of gross prices of X and Z (that is, prices available to the producer). This is described by equation (A3.6):

$$MRT_{XZ} = P_X / P_Z. \tag{A3.6}$$

With P equal to MC and integrating equation (A3.4) into (A3.6), the conditions for market efficiency as in equation (A3.3) are fulfilled. In this situation the consumer has chosen an optimal consumption bundle, which corresponds to an efficient output mix of the producer. Nobody can be made better off without another becoming worse off.

Introducing a General Consumption Tax

In this framework the welfare effect of a general consumption tax can be examined. Figure A3.9 shows the budget constraint AB and the indifference curve i_1 of a utility-maximising person. The government now decides to impose an *ad valorem* tax with tax rate t on both goods. Since the tax applies in the same proportion to both goods, an inward shift of the budget constraint occurs parallel to its original position. With income fixed at Y, the intercepts with the x- and y-axes are determined by, respectively, $Y / (1 + t) P_X$ and $Y / (1 + t) P_Z$.

Facing the new budget constraint A'B', the consumer is forced to consume a bundle on a lower indifference curve. Hence, he or she shifts from the consumption of bundle E to that of bundle E_1, which entails fewer goods of X and Z. So with the tax in place the person is clearly worse off than before. This is not surprising as a tax by definition imposes a cost on people. However, it remains to be seen whether an extra welfare cost has been created in addition to the tax.

Closer examination of the conditions for Pareto efficiency reveals that a general consumption tax does not induce a distortion to choice and therefore does not create an excess burden (in contrast to what might be concluded in partial equilibrium). The necessary conditions of equation (A3.3) still hold, since the ratio of the prices faced by the consumer as well as the producer after tax are the same as before tax. In other words, the slopes of the production possibilities frontier and of the indifference curve are tangential, thus MRS and MRT are equal. This means that the market allocates efficiently and that the general consumption tax has not created a distortion. Although the consumer is worse off, this is fully compensated by the increase in tax revenues for the government.

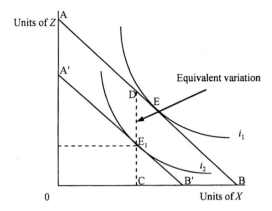

Figure A3.9   Effect of a general consumption tax and the equivalent variation

The graphical interpretation is as follows. If there were an excess burden, the loss in welfare to a consumer would go beyond the tax revenue collected. Whether this is the case can be determined by looking at the so-called 'equivalent variation', which measures the reduction in income that is needed to generate a comparable decrease in utility that the tax has generated. In other words, the hypothetical decrease in income needed to place an individual on the same indifference curve as he or she is after the imposition of the tax (that is, the wealth equivalent of the welfare loss suffered).

Utility after the tax is determined by indifference curve i_2. Because a reduction in income leads to a downward shift of the budget constraint parallel to its original position, we can conclude that the shift needed to get to the level of utility of indifference curve i_2 is measured by the distance E_1D. The decrease in income needed to attain the lower level of utility is thus equal to the vertical distance E_1D in terms of good Z.

The tax revenue is measured as follows. With the tax in force the person now consumes bundle E_1, which includes an amount of CE_1 of good Z. Without the tax he or she could have consumed CD of good Z at this point. The tax revenue collected is thus equal to the difference, that is, the vertical distance E_1D. Although measured in units of Z, the amount is easily converted into money by multiplying the difference by P_Z. As one can see, the tax revenue is equal to the equivalent variation, which implies that the imposition of the general consumption tax has not created an excess burden.

Introducing a Selective Consumption Tax

Now suppose that instead of introducing a general consumption tax, the government imposes a selective tax on good X, but not on good Z. Holding income fixed, this again changes the position of the consumer's budget constraint. Yet, this time only the price of X is affected, so the consumer is still able to buy the same amount of good Z, while the amount of good X that the person can buy has decreased to $Y / (1 + t) P_X$ (where t is the tax rate). Figure A3.10 shows that the budget constraint as a result shifts from AB to AC.

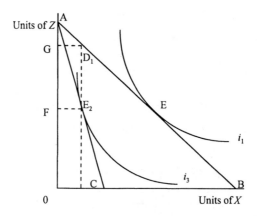

Figure A3.10   Effect of a selective consumption tax

The consumer now consumes bundle E_2 instead of E. As noted, the exact shape of the indifference curve depends on individual preferences, but the curves are drawn in a way that best illustrates the effects of a selective tax. It is possible that the curve lies somewhere else without affecting the direction of the outcome.

To see how a distortion arises this time, we shall first review the condition for Pareto efficiency. Because of the tax on good X, the MRS_{XZ} has to account for the tax, which means that consumers face a higher gross price for X. This leads to the following condition:

$$MRS_{XZ} = (1 + t) P_X / P_Z. \tag{A3.7}$$

Producers still set the production on the basis of the net prices received determined by equation (A3.6). The result is that $MRS_{XZ} \neq MRT_{XZ}$ and that the condition of Pareto efficiency is not satisfied. The market allocates inefficiently, which leads to a distortion and an excess burden.

Graphically, the excess burden can be derived by comparing the actual burden imposed by the tax to the tax revenue collected. As before, we should compare the equivalent variation to the tax revenue collected. In Figure A3.11, the budget constraint is at AC, which leads the person to consume bundle E_2. The tax revenue collected is measured by the distance E_2D_1 in terms of good Z. Namely, the individual consumes 0F of good Z while he or she could have consumed 0G without the tax. The equivalent variation is measured by E_3D in the same way as before. Since the size of the tax revenue collected E_2D_1 is smaller than the equivalent variation E_3D, an excess burden has been created by the size of E_2H (note that HD_1 is the same distance as E_3D). To explain this excess burden, we will need to look at the income and substitution effects that are associated with the imposition of a selective tax.

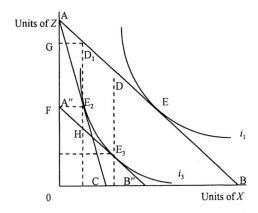

Figure A3.11   The excess burden of a selective tax

The Income and Substitution Effects

The behavioural response from the imposition of a selective tax can be split into an *income* effect and a *substitution* effect. The excess burden is quantified by differentiating between the loss in utility from the tax revenue raised and the loss in utility which results from the distortional effect of a tax. The latter effect is caused by the individual shifting consumption away from the taxed good to a non-taxed good.

Figure A3.12 combines Figures A3.9 and A3.11 which were used to analyse individually the imposition of a general and selective consumption tax in a general equilibrium framework.

The income effect in this figure measures the loss in utility because of a reduced consumption of both X and Z. This is illustrated by the case under a general consumption tax where relative prices remained unaffected and represented by the shift of the consumption of bundle E to that of bundle E_1. The tax burden is equal to the total loss of utility that was embodied in the shift from indifference curve i_1 of i_2. The utility loss was fully matched by an increase in tax revenue to the government.

The substitution effect constitutes the efficiency loss that results from a substitution of Z for X, or equivalently, the shift from consuming bundle E_3 to that of bundle E_2. The substitution effect arises solely because of the relative price change that results from a selective tax. Because of the tax, consumers are induced to switch to a different and essentially less-preferred consumption bundle. The utility loss that is created by the movement to the lower indifference curve i_3 is measured by the distance between E_2 and G in terms of good Z. The decrease in utility is not matched by additional tax revenue and therefore constitutes a welfare loss.

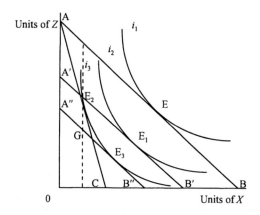

Figure A3.12   The income and substitution effect associated with a selective tax

The magnitude of the substitution effect depends on the ease with which one good is exchanged for another. This is determined by the 'elasticity of substitution'. In the extreme case of a zero elasticity of substitution, there will be no excess burden from taxation. In contrast, a higher elasticity of substitution for certain goods is associated with a larger excess burden.

A3.4   THREE NOTIONS OF OPTIMAL COMMODITY TAXATION

Pigouvian Taxation

Even if selective taxes create a distortion in choice, the market does not always allocate efficiently to start with. In fact, market failure occurs regularly. An externality is created if an activity of one individual affects the welfare of another individual. Hence, somebody experiences a cost or benefit that is external to the economic activity that causes the cost or benefit. For this reason, it is not fully reflected in prices.

For example, a *negative* externality can be the cost of pollution from production by factories of an adjacent property, the noise of passing aeroplanes or the barking of a neighbour's dog. A *positive* externality can be the benefit associated with knowledge spillovers from innovation, a communal swimming pool used by people outside the community or a lighthouse. Positive externalities are not considered in the discussion of Pigouvian taxation here.[5]

Whenever a negative externality arises, the marginal private cost of an economic activity lies below its marginal social cost. For example, a firm that pollutes accounts for the cost of the manufacturing, marketing and distribution of its products, but not for the cost incurred by people in surrounding areas of cleaning up the ensuing pollution. Hence, certain damage is inflicted that is not reflected in the cost of a product. This typically leads to oversupply of the good or service produced.

To correct such market failure, the British economist Arthur Cecil Pigou (1932) proposed the following:

'An externality can effectively be internalised by imposing a corrective tax, which should equate the marginal private cost to the marginal social cost.'

The working of the 'Pigouvian tax' is illustrated in Figure A3.13. The demand curve represents the marginal benefit to consumers and is depicted as normal. The supply curve determines a firm's production and is also depicted as normal. However, as argued the supply curve does not reflect marginal social damage that is inflicted with production. It includes only the marginal private cost incurred by the producer.

The damage accumulates with every unit produced. Hence, at zero production the marginal private cost equals the marginal social cost, as determined by the fixed cost of production. As the quantity produced increases, the respective variables diverge with every incremental unit supplied. In other words, the higher the quantity produced, the larger the externality imposed. The total cost of production is thereby represented by the higher supply curve.

The figure shows that in market equilibrium at Q_0 (that is, where the marginal benefit equals marginal private costs) there is an oversupply as compared to what is socially desirable (that is, production at Q_1 where marginal benefit equals marginal social costs). The oversupply is measured

---

[5] Whereas negative externalities can be corrected by taxes, positive externalities may be dealt with through government subsidies. Most basic or intermediate microeconomic textbooks discuss these issues in depth and can be consulted.

by the difference Q_0 and Q_1 and arises because firms do not take into account *all* the costs of production.

To correct this market failure, a unit tax should be imposed that is set equal to the marginal damage caused. In Figure A3.15 this is measured by the difference between the marginal private and social cost curves at the socially desirable level of production. Hence, the difference between points A and B. The tax raises the cost of production and reduces supply accordingly. The market now fully reflects the interests of all parties affected by production. Note that the market simply produces at the efficient level, and this does not require paying compensation to the person on whom the externality is imposed.

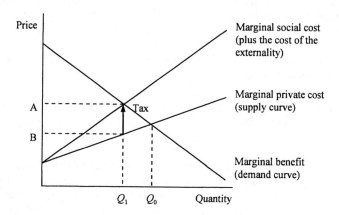

Figure A3.13   Pigouvian tax to equalise marginal private and social costs

Pigouvian taxes are widely applied in OECD economies, for example in addressing environmental problems. It may nevertheless be difficult to gauge the exact damage inflicted to establish the tax required. This is especially so if markets are large and involve many agents. The complication is not encountered under the other much used alternative of issuing firms with tradable permits to pollute under a cap and trade system. If effectively enforced, government can be sure that pollution targets are attained. The system would nevertheless also create an entirely new shadow market with other potential negative side-effects. For example, smaller firms could be forced out of the market by dominant ones acquiring more permits than necessary, or be deterred from ever entering it. A tax is then again an elegant solution.

The Ramsey Rule

A second notion in optimal commodity taxation addresses the issue of revenue-raising efficiency. The principal argument was put forward by Cambridge economist Frank Ramsey (1927), who was at that time a student of Pigou. The theory was formulated in the 'Ramsey rule' and has served as a basis in much economic research since. The rule states:

> If commodity taxes are optimally set, a small increase in taxes will cause all commodity demands to fall by the same proportions if all individuals are compensated to stay on the same indifference curve.

In order to minimise the total excess burden, tax rates should thus be set such that the percentage decrease in the quantity demanded is equal for each taxed commodity. It should be noted that at the time of the study, Ramsey was concerned only with considerations of efficiency and not of equity.

Intuitively the rule can be explained as follows. Figures A3.5 and A3.6 explained that the excess burden from a commodity tax is smaller when the elasticity of demand is low. A high elasticity of demand is associated with a large excess burden. Also, as we have seen, high tax rates involve a relatively larger excess burden than lower tax rates. From an efficiency viewpoint it is thus better to impose a low tax on many commodities, than high tax rates on just a few, provided that the same amount of revenue is to be collected.

Now assume that an equal rate of tax is imposed on all commodities. Because a tax on commodities with inelastic demands creates a relatively minor excess burden, taxes on these goods can theoretically be increased at little efficiency cost. With the additional revenue the tax rates on commodities with relatively high elasticity of demand and high excess burdens could be reduced. The same amount of revenue would thus be collected with a lower excess burden. The original result by Ramsey is not straightforwardly achieved, though, and only fully sets in when the demand for each good is independent of the price of other goods (that is, the elasticity of substitution is zero).

Given these conditions, the Ramsey rule can be reinterpreted as the 'inverse elasticity rule' (for mathematical proof see Rosen, 2005):

> In the absence of an income tax the rate on the sale of each good or service should be set inversely proportional to its elasticity of demand (holding the elasticity of supply constant).

Of course, practical application of the rule requires a complex set of different tax rates imposed on different goods. From an administrative standpoint, the Ramsey rule is therefore difficult to implement. Furthermore, as noted, the Ramsey rule observes only efficiency considerations. Goods with inelastic demand tend to include basic necessities, which are thus taxed more heavily. This would be unacceptable on equity grounds.

The Corlett-Hague Rule

An interesting extension of the Ramsey rule is the 'Corlett-Hague rule'. Although all governments tax goods and services, they cannot tax leisure. Because of this, when taxing labour the work-leisure choice is distorted, which creates an excess burden. Corlett and Hague (1953) showed that this distortion can be mitigated by taxing goods that are complementary to leisure more heavily. In other words, in the case of two or more commodities:

Goods that are complementary to leisure should be taxed more heavily than goods which are substitutes for leisure.

A tax on goods that are used in combination with leisure not only lowers demand for these goods, but because of the interdependence also lowers demand for leisure. For example, by taxing DVDs more heavily, people buy fewer of them and spend less leisure time watching television. Because goods with more inelastic demand are less substitutable for leisure than goods with a higher elasticity of demand, the Corlett-Hague rule is perfectly compatible with the Ramsey rule. That is, when a good with a high elasticity is taxed, quantity demanded will decrease significantly, which enables government to indirectly 'capture' leisure and achieve a more-efficient outcome.

A3.5 SUMMARY

A consumption tax is shifted between producers and consumers in the short run according to the elasticities of supply and demand. As a result, the economic burden of the tax is shifted more or less heavily onto the producer or consumer, irrespective of who bears legal responsibility for the tax.

Consumer surplus measures the difference between the maximum amount that a consumer would be willing to pay for a certain commodity and what he or she must actually pay. Producer surplus measures the difference between the price that a producer receives for a certain commodity and the corresponding minimum price at which he or she would be willing to supply it.

In partial equilibrium analysis the excess burden of commodity taxation can be measured by subtracting the revenue collected from producer and consumer surplus before tax. The difference constitutes the excess burden. The higher the respective elasticities of supply and demand, the larger the behavioural response and excess burden that results from a commodity tax.

General equilibrium analysis nevertheless reveals that a comprehensive consumption tax does not create a distortion of choice. Hence, no excess burden is created. A selective tax does create a distortion and welfare loss beyond the revenue collected. The size of the excess burden depends on the magnitude of the elasticity of substitution between goods.

Pigouvian taxes can be used to internalise an externality by equalising the private and social marginal returns of an economic activity. This improves welfare by increasing the cost of production so that producers have an incentive to produce no more than the socially desirable quantity. The Ramsey rule offers a theoretical solution for minimising the excess burden of commodity taxation, given a certain revenue requirement, by setting tax rates such that the percentage decrease in the quantity demanded is the same across taxed commodities. Finally, the Corlett-Hague rule calls for a higher tax on goods and services associated with leisure as an alternative for a direct tax on leisure, which is impossible to achieve in practice.

Appendix 4   The OECD classification of taxes

Below we reproduce the classification of taxes, which is used worldwide and has been developed by the OECD. It concerns an exact reproduction.

1000   *Taxes on income, profits and capital gains*
   1100   Taxes on income, profits and capital gains of individuals
       1110   On income and profits
       1120   On capital gains
   1200   Corporate taxes on income, profits and capital gains
       1210   On income and profits
       1220   On capital gains
   1300   Unallocable as between 1100 and 1200

2000   *Social security contributions*
   2100   Employees
       2110   On a payroll basis
       2120   On an income tax basis
   2200   Employers
       2210   On a payroll basis
       2220   On an income tax basis
   2300   Self-employed or non-employed
       2310   On a payroll basis
       2320   On an income tax basis
   2400   Unallocable as between 2100, 2200 and 2300
       2410   On a payroll basis
       2420   On an income tax basis

3000   *Taxes on payroll and workforce*

4000   *Taxes on property*
   4100   Recurrent taxes on immovable property
       4110   Households
       4120   Other
   4200   Recurrent taxes on net wealth
       4210   Individual
       4220   Corporate
   4300   Estate, inheritance and gift taxes
       4310   Estate and inheritance taxes
       4320   Gift taxes
   4400   Taxes on financial and capital transactions

4500 Other non-recurrent taxes on property
    4510 On net wealth
    4520 Other recurrent taxes on property
4600 Other recurrent taxes on property

5000 *Taxes on goods and services*
  5100 Taxes on production, sale, transfer, leasing and delivery of goods and rendering of services
    5110 General taxes
      5111 Value added taxes
      5112 Sales taxes
      5113 Other general taxes on goods and services
    5120 Taxes on specific goods and services
      5121 Excises
      5122 Profits of fiscal monopolies
      5123 Customs and import duties
      5124 Taxes on exports
      5125 Taxes on investment goods
      5126 Taxes on specific services
      5127 Other taxes on international trade and transactions
      5128 Other taxes on specific goods and services
    5130 Unallocable as between 5110 and 5120
  5200 Taxes on use of goods, or on permission to use goods or perform activities
    5210 Recurrent taxes
      5211 Paid by households in respect of motor vehicles
      5212 Paid by others in respect of motor vehicles
      5213 Other recurrent taxes
    5220 Non-recurrent taxes
  5300 Unallocable as between 5100 and 5200

6000 *Other taxes*
  6100 Paid solely by business
  6200 Paid by other than business or unidentifiable

Source: OECD (2005c, Annex A, p. 281) at http://www.oecd.org.

Appendix 5 Revenue statistics

Table A5.1   Personal income tax

Country	1970-74	1975-79	1980-84	1985-89	1990-94	1995-99	2000-04
Australia	9.1	11.4	12.1	13.0	11.3	12.6	12.2
	39.8	44.5	44.8	45.3	41.4	42.5	39.8
Austria	7.7	8.4	9.1	9.0	8.6	9.5	9.8
	22.0	22.4	23.1	22.2	21.1	22.0	22.7
Belgium	9.7	14.2	15.5	14.7	13.4	14.0	14.1
	27.3	34.3	36.4	33.6	31.6	31.6	31.3
Canada	10.3	10.2	11.3	12.6	14.0	13.6	12.3
	33.1	33.1	34.6	37.3	39.1	37.5	35.9
Denmark	21.4	21.3	22.6	24.3	25.1	25.9	25.4
	52.6	52.7	52.1	50.2	53.4	52.5	52.5
Finland	13.6	14.3	13.7	15.1	15.1	14.2	14.1
	40.7	37.5	36.8	36.6	33.6	30.8	31.0
France	3.5	4.2	4.9	4.7	4.9	6.2	7.6
	10.5	11.3	11.9	11.1	11.5	14.0	17.5
Germany	10.0	11.0	10.6	10.7	10.0	9.3	8.9
	29.3	30.0	28.7	28.9	27.4	25.3	24.9
Ireland	6.3	8.1	10.2	11.6	10.9	9.8	8.3
	21.9	27.4	30.7	33.0	32.0	30.7	27.9
Italy	3.2	5.1	8.3	9.5	10.5	10.7	10.5
	12.5	19.4	25.3	26.8	26.4	25.5	25.2
Japan	5.0	5.2	6.6	7.0	5.1	4.1	5.1
	23.7	23.1	24.9	24.3	26.6	20.7	19.1
Netherlands	10.1	10.8	9.7	8.6	10.4	6.6	6.4
	27.4	26.7	23.4	20.2	24.4	16.6	16.8
Norway	12.7	12.8	11.1	11.1	10.6	11.0	10.5
	33.5	31.3	26.0	25.7	25.9	26.2	24.2
Sweden	18.3	19.9	19.0	19.6	17.6	17.1	16.1
	46.3	43.1	40.0	38.6	36.1	33.8	31.5
UK	11.4	12.4	10.5	9.9	10.1	9.8	10.6
	33.3	36.4	28.4	26.5	29.2	27.6	29.4
US	9.2	9.2	10.2	9.8	9.7	11.0	10.5
	35.5	35.9	39.1	37.6	35.7	38.4	38.3
EU-15	9.0	10.3	10.9	11.1	10.7	10.5	10.4
	26.5	28.2	28.4	27.4	26.8	25.5	25.1
OECD	8.7	9.9	10.4	10.5	10.0	9.8	9.5
	29.0	30.8	30.8	29.6	28.2	26.7	25.6

Source: Electronic database OECD: Revenue Statistics.

Table A5.2   Corporate income tax

Country	1970-74	1975-79	1980-84	1985-89	1990-94	1995-99	2000-04
Australia	3.5	3.0	2.8	3.0	3.8	4.4	5.3
	15.4	11.5	10.4	10.4	14.0	14.9	17.4
Austria	1.4	1.4	1.3	1.4	1.5	1.9	2.4
	4.0	3.6	3.2	3.5	3.6	4.4	5.5
Belgium	2.7	2.6	2.2	2.6	2.3	3.3	3.5
	7.7	6.2	5.2	5.9	5.4	7.4	7.8
Canada	3.6	3.7	2.9	2.8	2.2	3.5	3.5
	11.5	11.9	9.0	8.3	6.1	9.8	10.1
Denmark	1.1	1.3	1.5	2.3	1.8	2.6	3.0
	2.7	3.3	3.4	4.7	3.9	5.2	6.1
Finland	1.5	1.7	1.5	1.4	1.3	3.4	4.3
	4.5	4.4	4.0	3.3	2.8	7.5	9.4
France	2.1	2.0	2.0	2.1	2.0	2.5	2.9
	6.3	5.3	4.9	5.1	4.7	5.7	6.6
Germany	1.7	1.9	1.9	2.1	1.4	1.5	1.2
	5.1	5.3	5.2	5.6	3.9	4.0	3.5
Ireland	1.9	1.4	1.4	1.2	2.4	3.2	3.6
	6.6	4.8	4.3	3.4	6.9	10.1	12.3
Italy	1.7	2.0	2.9	3.5	3.8	3.5	3.0
	6.7	7.5	8.7	10.0	9.6	8.4	7.3
Japan	5.3	4.7	5.4	6.6	5.1	4.1	3.5
	25.3	20.9	20.5	22.7	18.4	15.2	13.2
Netherlands	2.5	2.7	2.7	3.1	3.0	3.8	3.4
	6.8	6.7	6.4	7.3	7.2	9.7	9.0
Norway	1.1	1.9	6.6	4.2	3.5	4.4	8.8
	2.9	4.7	15.5	9.7	8.6	10.5	20.3
Sweden	1.6	1.5	1.5	2.2	1.9	2.8	3.0
	4.0	3.4	3.2	4.3	3.9	5.6	5.8
UK	2.8	2.2	3.7	4.2	2.6	3.5	3.2
	8.2	6.4	9.9	11.4	7.4	9.9	8.7
US	3.1	3.0	2.1	2.2	2.4	2.8	2.1
	11.8	11.7	8.1	8.3	8.9	9.8	7.7
EU-15	2.0	2.1	2.2	2.5	2.4	3.1	3.4
	6.5	6.0	5.8	6.5	6.3	8.0	8.6
OECD	2.3	2.3	2.4	2.6	2.6	3.1	3.4
	8.5	7.7	7.6	8.0	7.7	8.6	9.5

Source: Electronic database OECD: Revenue Statistics.

Table A5.3   Social Security Contributions

Country	1970-74	1975-79	1980-84	1985-89	1990-94	1995-99	2000-04
Australia	0.0	0.0	0.0	0.0	0.0	0.0	0.0
	0.0	0.0	0.0	0.0	0.0	0.0	0.0
Austria	8.9	10.9	12.4	13.1	13.7	14.9	14.6
	25.5	29.0	31.4	32.4	33.5	34.7	33.6
Belgium	10.7	12.4	12.9	14.6	14.9	14.5	14.3
	29.5	29.2	29.4	32.6	34.1	32.0	31.3
Canada	2.9	3.4	3.9	4.5	4.9	5.0	5.1
	9.2	10.9	12.0	13.3	13.7	13.7	14.8
Denmark	1.3	0.6	1.3	1.5	1.0	1.2	1.4
	3.0	1.4	2.9	3.1	2.1	2.3	2.9
Finland	4.2	7.9	8.2	9.3	13.4	13.2	12.1
	12.4	20.7	21.8	22.4	29.4	28.4	26.5
France	12.6	15.3	17.6	18.2	18.6	17.4	16.1
	37.4	41.2	42.8	43.2	43.9	39.5	36.9
Germany	10.7	12.4	13.1	13.7	14.0	14.7	14.3
	31.2	33.9	35.6	36.9	38.2	40.0	40.1
Ireland	2.7	4.1	4.9	5.1	5.2	4.3	4.3
	9.4	13.7	14.6	14.3	15.0	13.2	14.4
Italy	10.2	11.0	12.0	12.3	13.1	13.4	12.5
	39.5	40.5	36.1	34.0	32.0	31.4	29.2
Japan	4.8	6.7	7.9	8.3	8.0	9.1	9.7
	23.0	29.5	29.8	28.9	29.3	34.5	37.1
Netherlands	13.8	15.9	18.1	18.8	17.2	16.5	14.6
	36.2	37.7	41.7	42.7	38.6	39.9	36.7
Norway	7.8	9.6	9.2	10.4	10.5	9.7	9.6
	20.3	23.6	21.4	24.1	25.7	23.1	21.9
Sweden	6.5	11.5	13.3	13.0	13.8	13.9	14.9
	16.3	24.5	27.9	25.2	28.0	27.2	29.0
UK	5.3	6.2	6.4	6.7	6.1	6.2	6.4
	15.5	18.1	17.2	18.1	17.8	17.3	17.6
US	4.5	5.3	6.1	6.6	6.9	6.9	6.8
	17.5	20.7	23.3	25.4	25.4	24.0	25.3
EU-15	7.4	9.3	10.4	10.8	11.2	11.4	11.3
	25.5	28.7	29.1	28.5	28.9	28.6	28.4
OECD	5.7	7.1	7.5	7.8	8.7	9.1	9.3
	20.2	22.6	22.3	22.1	23.9	24.7	25.5

Source: Electronic database OECD: Revenue Statistics.

Table A5.4   General sales taxes

Country	1970-74	1975-79	1980-84	1985-89	1990-94	1995-99	2000-04
Australia	1.6	1.6	1.8	2.4	2.2	2.5	4.0
	7.1	6.3	6.7	8.4	8.2	8.3	13.0
Austria	6.7	7.7	8.1	8.4	8.2	8.1	8.0
	19.1	20.5	20.6	20.9	20.1	18.9	18.5
Belgium	7.0	7.1	7.2	7.0	6.8	6.9	7.1
	19.8	17.1	16.8	15.9	16.0	15.5	15.8
Canada	4.7	3.9	3.7	4.9	5.0	5.1	5.1
	15.1	12.5	11.3	14.4	14.1	13.9	14.9
Denmark	7.4	7.9	9.5	9.6	9.4	9.6	9.6
	18.1	19.4	21.8	19.8	20.0	19.6	19.8
Finland	6.4	6.0	6.5	8.1	8.1	8.2	8.4
	19.1	15.9	17.5	19.7	18.0	17.8	18.5
France	8.6	8.3	8.6	8.2	7.5	7.8	7.3
	25.4	22.4	20.8	19.5	17.6	17.6	16.8
Germany	5.4	5.4	6.2	5.8	6.3	6.5	6.5
	16.0	14.7	16.7	15.6	17.1	17.8	18.1
Ireland	4.2	5.0	6.2	7.3	6.8	7.0	7.1
	14.7	16.7	18.4	20.8	20.0	21.9	24.1
Italy	3.6	3.9	4.8	5.2	5.6	5.6	6.2
	14.2	15.0	14.9	14.6	14.1	13.5	14.7
Japan	0.0	0.0	0.0	0.2	1.4	2.0	2.5
	0.0	0.0	0.0	0.7	5.0	7.5	9.4
Netherlands	5.5	6.2	6.4	6.9	6.6	6.5	7.2
	15.1	15.4	15.4	16.4	15.4	16.5	19.0
Norway	8.3	8.4	7.7	8.5	7.9	8.9	8.7
	22.0	20.6	18.0	19.8	19.3	21.2	20.1
Sweden	5.2	5.9	6.4	6.9	7.8	8.9	9.1
	13.2	12.7	13.5	13.6	15.9	17.7	17.8
UK	2.5	3.2	5.3	6.0	6.5	6.7	6.8
	7.4	9.6	14.3	16.3	18.7	18.9	18.9
US	1.7	1.8	1.9	2.1	2.2	2.2	2.2
	6.4	7.0	7.2	7.9	8.0	7.8	8.1
EU-15	4.9	5.3	6.0	6.7	6.9	7.2	7.4
	16.0	15.7	16.2	17.6	17.9	18.0	18.7
OECD	4.4	4.7	5.3	5.9	6.1	6.5	6.8
	14.6	14.4	15.7	17.3	17.4	18.0	18.7

Source: Electronic database OECD: Revenue Statistics.

Table A5.5   Excises

Country	1970-74	1975-79	1980-84	1985-89	1990-94	1995-99	2000-04
Australia	12.1	12.6	14.7	11.6	9.7	8.5	8.9
	2.7	3.2	4.0	3.3	2.7	2.5	2.7
Austria	3.4	2.9	3.0	2.8	2.4	2.6	2.6
	9.8	7.8	7.5	6.8	6.0	6.0	6.0
Belgium	2.7	2.4	2.2	2.0	2.2	2.3	2.3
	7.6	5.9	5.1	4.6	5.1	5.3	5.0
Canada	2.3	2.0	3.1	2.2	2.2	1.9	1.8
	7.3	6.3	9.5	6.6	6.3	5.3	5.3
Denmark	5.7	5.6	5.2	5.8	4.6	5.4	5.0
	14.0	13.8	11.9	11.9	9.7	10.9	10.4
Finland	4.4	4.7	4.9	4.5	4.5	4.6	4.2
	13.2	12.5	13.2	11.0	10.0	10.0	9.2
France	2.7	2.4	2.4	2.6	2.6	2.9	2.7
	7.9	6.4	5.7	6.2	6.2	6.6	6.2
Germany	3.3	3.0	2.7	2.4	2.6	2.6	3.0
	9.7	8.1	7.2	6.6	7.1	7.2	8.3
Ireland	8.7	7.1	7.5	6.2	5.3	4.6	3.6
	30.2	24.1	22.7	17.7	15.7	14.5	12.1
Italy	3.3	2.4	2.0	2.4	3.1	2.8	2.4
	12.9	9.1	6.1	6.9	7.7	6.8	5.9
Japan	2.7	2.5	2.7	2.6	1.9	2.0	2.0
	12.8	11.2	10.3	9.2	6.9	7.3	7.4
Netherlands	2.6	2.4	2.2	2.3	2.6	3.1	3.2
	7.2	6.0	5.4	5.5	6.2	7.8	8.4
Norway	4.4	4.4	5.2	5.6	5.2	4.9	3.6
	11.6	10.9	12.1	12.9	12.7	11.7	8.2
Sweden	4.4	3.6	3.8	4.2	3.7	3.5	3.2
	11.1	7.9	8.1	8.3	7.5	6.9	6.3
UK	5.7	4.4	4.1	4.0	3.7	4.0	3.6
	16.6	13.0	11.1	10.6	10.8	11.2	9.9
US	2.3	1.8	1.8	1.4	1.3	1.2	1.1
	9.0	6.8	7.0	5.5	4.6	4.3	4.1
EU-15	3.6	3.3	3.5	3.5	3.5	3.6	3.3
	11.7	9.9	9.9	9.5	9.3	9.2	8.5
OECD	3.3	3.0	3.1	3.0	2.9	3.1	3.1
	11.8	10.1	10.0	9.1	8.4	8.8	8.6

Source: Electronic database OECD: Revenue Statistics.

Taxes and the Economy

Table A5.6   Taxes on property

Country	1970-74	1975-79	1980-84	1985-89	1990-94	1995-99	2000-04
Australia	2.3	2.2	2.1	2.6	2.7	2.8	2.8
	10.1	8.5	7.6	8.7	9.7	9.0	9.0
Austria	1.1	1.1	1.1	1.0	1.0	0.6	0.6
	3.3	3.0	2.8	2.5	2.5	1.4	1.3
Belgium	1.0	1.1	0.9	1.0	1.2	1.3	1.6
	2.8	2.6	2.0	2.3	2.6	2.9	3.4
Canada	3.5	3.1	3.0	3.2	3.9	3.8	3.4
	11.3	10.0	9.3	9.4	10.8	10.4	9.8
Denmark	2.4	2.4	2.1	2.3	1.9	1.7	1.8
	5.9	5.8	4.9	4.6	4.0	3.5	3.6
Finland	0.7	0.9	0.8	1.2	1.1	1.1	1.1
	2.1	2.3	2.2	3.0	2.4	2.3	2.4
France	1.5	1.8	2.1	2.6	2.9	3.1	3.1
	4.5	4.9	5.0	6.1	6.8	7.0	7.2
Germany	1.5	1.4	1.2	1.1	1.1	1.0	0.8
	4.3	3.8	3.3	3.1	2.9	2.7	2.3
Ireland	3.6	2.3	1.4	1.5	1.5	1.6	1.8
	12.3	7.8	4.3	4.2	4.5	5.0	6.0
Italy	1.4	0.9	1.0	0.9	1.6	2.2	2.4
	5.4	3.4	3.1	2.5	3.8	5.1	5.7
Japan	1.7	2.0	2.4	3.1	2.9	3.0	2.7
	8.2	8.8	8.9	10.6	10.7	11.5	11.7
Netherlands	1.1	1.3	1.5	1.6	1.7	1.9	2.1
	2.9	3.2	3.4	3.6	3.8	4.7	5.3
Norway	0.9	0.8	0.8	1.0	1.2	1.1	1.1
	2.3	2.0	1.8	2.4	2.8	2.6	2.4
Sweden	0.5	0.4	0.6	1.8	1.7	1.8	1.6
	1.3	1.0	1.2	3.5	3.5	3.5	3.2
UK	4.6	4.2	4.7	4.7	3.2	3.8	4.3
	13.4	12.3	12.5	12.6	9.2	10.6	11.7
US	3.8	3.4	2.8	2.8	3.2	3.1	3.1
	14.9	13.1	10.7	10.8	11.8	10.8	11.4
EU-15	1.7	1.5	1.4	1.6	1.7	2.0	2.0
	5.7	4.8	4.0	4.3	4.4	5.0	5.2
OECD	1.8	1.7	1.6	1.8	1.8	1.9	1.9
	7.0	6.0	5.2	5.5	5.6	5.6	5.5

Source: Electronic database OECD: Revenue Statistics.

Appendix 6   Relevant web links

Al Gore - http://www.algore04.com/
American Enterprise Institute - http://www.aei.org/
Americans for Fair Taxation - http://www.fairtax.org/
American Taxation Association - http://aaahq.org/ata/index.htm
Australian Taxation Office - http://www.ato.gov.au/
Australian Treasury - http://www.treasury.gov.au/home.asp?ContentID=521
Austrian Ministry of Finance - https://www.bmf.gv.at/
Belgian Fiscal Administrations - http://fiscus.fgov.be/interfisc/default.htm
Belgian Ministry of Finance - http://www.minfin.fgov.be/index.html
Bill Clinton Initiative - http://www.clintonfoundation.org/
Brookings Institution - http://www.brook.edu/
Bundesministerium der Finanzen - http://www.bundesfinanzministerium.de
Campaign for Tobacco-Free Kids - http://tobaccofreekids.org/
Canada Revenue Agency - http://www.cra-arc.gc.ca/menu-e.html
Canadian Department of Finance - http://www.fin.gc.ca/fin-eng.html
Canadian Tax Foundation - http://www.ctf.ca/
Cato Institute - http://www.cato.org/
Center for American Progress - http://www.americanprogress.org/
Centraal Plan Bureau - http://www.cpb.nl/
Centre of Economic Policy Research - http://www.cepr.org/default_static.htm
CESifo - http://www.cesifo.de/CESifoPortal
Citizens for Tax Justice - http://www.ctj.org/
Climate Action Network - http://www.climnet.org
Climate Institute - http://www.climate.org/climate_main.shtml
Danish Ministry of Finance - http://www.fm.dk/1024/Default.asp
Danish Ministry of Taxation - http://www.skm.dk/foreign/
Deloitte - http://www.deloitte.com
DLA Piper - http://www.dlapiper.com/Home.aspx
Doing Business, World Bank Group - http://www.doingbusiness.org/
Dutch Ministry of Finance - http://www.minfin.nl/nl/home
Dutch Tax Authorities - http://www.belastingdienst.nl/
Economist - http://www.economist.com/index.html
Ernst & Young - http://www.ey.com/global/content.nsf/International/Home
European Central Bank - http://www.ecb.int/home/html/index.en.html

European Commission, Taxation and Customs Union –
  http://ec.europa.eu/taxation_customs/taxation/index_en.htm
European Environment Agency - http://www.eea.europa.eu/
European Union - http://europa.eu
Eurostat - http://epp.eurostat.ec.europa.eu/
Fedraal Planbureau België - http://www.plan.be/nl/
Federation of Tax Administrators - http://www.taxadmin.org/
Finnish Ministry of Finance - http://www.ministryoffinance.fi/
Finnish Tax Administration - http://www.vero.fi/
Friends of the Earth - http://www.foe.org/
German Tax Authority - http://www.bzst.bund.de/
Germanwatch - http://www.germanwatch.org
Greenpeace - http://www.greenpeace.org/international/
Heritage Foundation - http://www.heritage.org/
HM Revenue & Customs - http://www.hmrc.gov.uk/
HM Treasury - http://www.hm-treasury.gov.uk/
Institute for Fiscal Studies - http://www.ifs.org.uk/
Institute for Policy Studies - http://www.ips-dc.org/
Institute for the Study of Civil Society - http://www.civitas.org.uk/
Internal Revenue Service - http://www.irs.gov/
International Bureau for Fiscal Documentation - http://www.ibfd.org/
International Energy Agency - http://www.iea.org/
International Fiscal Association - http://www.ifa.nl/index.htm
International Monetary Fund - http://www.imf.org
Irish Department of Finance - http://www.finance.gov.ie/
Irish Tax and Customs - http://www.revenue.ie/
Italian Ministry of Finance - http://www.finanze.it/
Joint Committee on Taxation - http://www.house.gov/jct/
Joint Economic Committee - http://www.house.gov/jec/
KPMG - http://www.kpmg.com/
Levy Economics Institute - http://www.levy.org/
Ministère de l'Économie - http://www.minefi.gouv.fr/
Ministry of Finance Japan (MOF) - http://www.mof.go.jp/english/index.htm
National Bureau of Economic Research - http://www.nber.org/
National Tax Administration Japan -
  http://www.nta.go.jp/category/english/index.htm
Norwegian Ministry of Finance - http://odin.dep.no/fin/english/bn.html
Norwegian Tax Authority –
  http://www.skatteetaten.no/default.aspx?epslanguage=NO
OECD - http://www.oecd.org
Österreichische Institut für Wirtschaftsforschung - http://www.wifo.ac.at/
PricewaterhouseCoopers - http://www.pwcglobal.com
Second Life - http://secondlife.com/
Sierra Club - http://www.sierraclub.org/

Statistics Norway - http://www.ssb.no/en/
Swedish Ministry of Finance - http://www.sweden.gov.se/sb/d/2062
Swedish Tax Administration - http://www.skatteverket.se/
Tax Analyst - http://www.taxanalysts.com/
Tax Links - http://www.interfisc.com/links.htm
Tax Policy Center - http://www.taxpolicycenter.org/home/
Taxation Institute of Australia - http://www.taxinstitute.com.au/
Taxman International - http://www.xs4all.nl/~edvisser/taxman/
Taxpayers' Alliance - http://www.taxpayersalliance.com/
Taxsites - http://www.taxsites.com/international.html
Taxworld - http://www.taxworld.org
US Census Bureau - http://www.census.gov/
US Department of the Treasury - http://www.ustreas.gov/
US Environmental Protection Agency - http://www.epa.gov/climatechange/
US House of Representatives - http://www.house.gov/
Whitehouse - http://www.whitehouse.gov/
Wikipedia - http://en.wikipedia.org/wiki/Main_Page
World Bank - http://www.worldbank.org/
World Economic Forum - http://www.weforum.org/en/index.htm
Worldwide Tax - http://www.worldwide-tax.com/
Yahoo Finance - http://finance.yahoo.com/
Zentrum für Europäische Wirtschaftsforschung - http://www.zew.de/

References

Åberg, Y., Hedström, P. and Kolm, A.-S. (1999), '*Social interactions and unemployment*', mimeo, Nuffield College, Oxford University and Uppsala University.

Adema W. (2001), 'Net social expenditure' (2nd edn), OECD Labour Market and Social Policy Occasional Papers, No. 52, Paris: OECD.

Adema, W. and Ladaique, M. (2005), 'Net social expenditure: more comprehensive measures of social support', OECD Social, Employment and Migration Working Papers, No. 29, Paris: OECD.

Agell, J., Englund, P. and Södersten, J. (1996), 'Tax reform of the century—the Swedish experiment', *National Tax Journal*, Vol. 49, No. 4, pp. 643-64.

Alesina, A., Glaeser, E. and Sacerdote, B. (2005), 'Work and Leisure in the US and Europe: Why So Different?', NBER Working Paper, No. 11278, Cambridge, MA: NBER.

Altig, D., Auerbach, A.J., Kotlikoff, L.J., Smetters, K.A. and Walliser, J. (2001), 'Simulating fundamental tax reform in the United States', *American Economic Review*, Vol. 91, No. 3, pp. 574-95.

Altshuler, R. (1988), 'A dynamic analysis of the research and experimentation credit', *National Tax Journal*, Vol. 41, No. 4, pp. 453-66.

Altshuler, R. and Goodspeed, T.J. (2002), 'Follow the leader? Evidence on European and U.S. tax competition', Departmental Working Papers, 2002/26, Rutgers University, New Brunswick, NJ: Department of Economics.

Andersen, M.S., Dengsøe, N. and Pedersen, A.B. (2000), '*An evaluation of the impact of green taxes in the Nordic countries*', Aarhus University: Centre for Social Research on the Environment.

Andersen, T.M. (2004), 'Challenges to the Scandinavian welfare model', *European Journal of Political Economy*, Vol. 20, No. 3, pp. 743-54.

Atkinson, A.B. (2002), 'Income inequality in OECD countries: data and explanations', CESifo Working Paper, No. 881, Munich: CESifo Group.

Atkinson, A.B. and Salverda, W. (2005), 'Top incomes in the Netherlands and the United Kingdom over the 20th century', *Journal of the European Economic Association*, Vol. 3, No. 4, pp. 883-913.

Atkinson, A.B. and Stern, N.H. (1974), 'Pigou, taxation and public goods', *Review of Economic Studies*, Vol. 41, No. 125, pp. 119-28.

Auerbach, A.J. (1985), 'The theory of excess burden and optimal taxation', in A.J. Auerbach and M. Feldstein (eds), *Handbook of Public Economics* (Vol. 1), Amsterdam: North-Holland.

Auerbach, A.J. (1991), 'Retrospective capital gains taxation', *American Economic Review*, Vol. 81, pp. 167-87.

Auerbach, A.J. (1996a), 'Measuring the impact of tax reform', *National Tax Journal*, Vol. 49, No. 4, pp. 665-73.

Auerbach, A.J., Hassett, K. and Södersten, J. (1995), 'Taxation and corporate investment: the impact of the 1991 Swedish tax reform', NBER Working Paper, No. 5189, Cambridge, MA.

Auerbach, A.J., Frenkel, J.A. and Razin, A. (1997), 'Equivalence relations in international taxation', in M.I. Blejer and T. Ter-Minassian (eds), *Macroeconomic Dimensions of Public Finance: Essays in Honour of Vito Tanzi*, London: Routledge.

Autor, D., Katz, L.F. and Kearney, M.S. (2006), 'The polarization of the U.S. labor market', NBER Working Paper, No. 11986, Cambridge, MA: NBER.

Baker and McKenzie (1999), *Survey of the Effective Tax Burden in the European Union*, Amsterdam: International Bureau of Fiscal Documentation.

Baldwin, R. and Krugman, P. (2001), 'Agglomeration, integration and tax harmonization', CEPR Discussion Paper, No 2630, London: Centre for Economic Policy Research.

Barro, R.J. (1990), 'Government spending in a simple model of endogenous growth', *Journal of Political Economy*, Vol. 98, No. 5, pp. 103-25.

Barro, R.J. and Sala-i-Martin, X. (2004), *Economic Growth* (2nd edn), Cambridge, MA: MIT Press.

Barroso, J.M. (2006), 'Moving up a gear for growth and jobs: progress on implementing the new Lisbon strategy, Seminar on 'Excellence and Partnerships for an Innovative Europe', Speech 06/569, Lisbon, 6 October.

Bartelsman, E.J. and Beetsma, R.M.W.J. (2003), 'Why pay more? Corporate tax avoidance through transfer pricing in OECD countries', *Journal of Public Economics*, Vol. 87, No. 9, pp. 2225-52.

Barton, L. and Hawksworth, J. (2003), *The Relationship between Tax, Public Spending and Economic Growth*, London: PricewaterhouseCoopers UK.

Bassanini, A., Scarpetta, S. and Hemmings, P. (2001), 'Economic growth: the role of policies and institutions: panel data from OECD countries', Economics Department Working Papers, No. 283, Paris: OECD.

Becker, G.S. (1964), *Human Capital: A Theoretical and Empirical Analysis with Special Reference to Education*, Chicago: Chicago University Press.

Becker, G.S. and Murphy, K.M. (1988), 'A theory of rational addiction', *Journal of Political Economy*, Vol. 96, No. 4, pp. 675-700.

Becker, U. and Schwartz, H. (2005), *A Critical Comparison of the Dutch, Scandinavian, Swiss, Australian and Irish Cases versus Germany and the US*, Amsterdam: Amsterdam University Press.

Bellak, C. and Leibrecht, M. (2005), 'Effective tax rates as a determinant of foreign direct investment in Central- and East European countries', SFB International Tax Coordination Working Paper, No. 7, Vienna: Vienna University of Economics.

Berwick, D.M. (2003), 'Improvement, trust, and the healthcare workforce', *Quality and Safety in Health Care*, Vol. 12, pp. 448-52.

Bettendorf, L., Gorter, J. and van der Horst, A. (2006), 'Who benefits from tax competition in the European Union?', CPB Document, No. 125, The Hague: Centraal Plan Bureau.

Bird, R.M. (1996), 'Why tax corporations?', Technical Committee on Business Taxation, Working Paper 96-2, Department of Finance: Ottawa.

Blanchflower, D.G. and Oswald, A.J. (2004), 'Well-being over time in Britain and the USA', *Journal of Public Economics*, Vol. 88, pp. 1359-86.

Blanke, J. (2006), *The Lisbon Review 2006: Measuring Europe's Progress in Reform*, Geneva: World Economic Forum.

Blasi, J.R. and Kruse, D.L. (1991), *The New Owners: The Mass Emergence of Employee Ownership in Public Companies and What It Means to American Business*, New York: HarperCollins.

Bloom, N., Griffith, R. and van Reenen, J. (2002), 'Do R&D tax credits work? Evidence from a panel of countries 1979-1997', *Journal of Public Economics*, Vol. 85, No. 1, pp. 1-31.

Blundell, R. and MaCurdy, T. (1999), 'Labour supply: a review of alternative approaches', in O. Ashenfelter and D. Card (eds), *Handbook of Labor Economics*, Vol. 3, Amsterdam: North-Holland, pp. 1559-1695.

Blundell, R, Brewer, M. and Shepherd, A. (2004), 'The impact of tax and benefit changes between April 2000 and April 2003 on patents' labour supply', *IFS Briefing Note*, No. 52, London: Institute for Fiscal Studies.

Blundell, R., Dearden, L., Meghir, C. and Sianesi, B. (1999), 'Human capital investment: the returns from education to the individual, the firm and the economy', *Fiscal Studies*, Vol. 20, No. 1, pp. 1-23.

Blundell, R., Duncan, A., McGrae, J. and Meghir, C. (2000), 'The labour market impact of the working families' tax credit', *Fiscal Studies*, Vol. 21, No. 1, pp. 75-104.

Boadway, R. and Bruce, N. (1984), 'A general proposition on the design of a neutral business tax', *Journal of Public Economics*, Vol. 24, No. 2, pp. 231-9.

Boeri, T. and Brücker, H. (2005), 'Why are Europeans so tough on migrants?', *Economic Policy*, Vol. 20, No. 44, pp. 629-704.

Bond, S.R. (2000), 'Levelling up or levelling down? Some reflections on the ACE and CBIT proposals, and the future of the corporate tax base', in S.

Cnossen (ed.), *Taxing Capital Income in the European Union: Issues and Options for Reform*, Oxford and New York: Oxford University Press.

Bond, S.R., Devereux, M.P. and Gammie, M.J. (1996), 'Tax reform to promote investment', *Oxford Review of Economic Policy*, Vol. 12, No. 2, pp. 109-17.

Bosworth, B. and Burtless, G. (1992), 'Effects of tax reform on labor supply, investment and saving', *Journal of Economic Perspectives*, Vol. 6, No. 1, pp. 3-25.

Bovenberg, A.L. (1990), 'The case for the international coordination of commodity and capital taxation', in R. Prud'homme (ed.), *Public Finance with Several Levels of Government*, The Hague: Foundation Journal Public Finance.

Bovenberg, A.L. (1999), 'Green tax reforms and the double dividend: an updated reader's guide', *International Tax and Public Finance*, Vol. 6, No. 3, pp. 421-43.

Bovenberg, A.L. (2006), 'Tax policy and labor market performance', CESifo Working Paper, No. 1035, Munich: CESifo Group.

Bovenberg, A.L. and van der Ploeg, F. (1998), 'Tax reform, structural unemployment and the environment', *Scandinavian Journal of Economics*, Vol. 100, No. 3, pp. 593-610.

Bovenberg, A.L. and Jacobs, B. (2005), 'Redistribution and education subsidies are Siamese twins', *Journal of Public Economics,* Vol. 89, Nos 11-12, pp. 2005-35.

Bradford, D.F. (1986), *Untangling the Income Tax*, Cambridge, MA: Harvard University Press.

Bradford, D.F. (1995), 'Fixing realization accounting: symmetry, consistency and correctness in the taxation of financial instruments', *New York University Tax Law Review*, Vol. 50, pp. 731-84.

Bradford, D.F. (2004), 'The X tax in the world economy', CESifo Working Paper Series, No. 1264, Munich: CESifo Group.

Breuss, F., Kaniovski, S. and Schratzenstaller, M. (2004), 'The tax reform 2004-05 – measures and macroeconomic effects, *Austrian Economic Quarterly*, Vol. 9, No. 3, pp. 127-42.

Brock, W.A. and Taylor, M.S. (2004), 'The green Solow model', NBER Working Paper, No. 10557, Cambridge, MA: NBER

Brooks, R. and Catao, L. (2000), 'The new economy and global stock returns', IMF Working Paper, No. WP/00/216, Washington, DC: IMF.

Brouwer, E., den Hertog, P., Poot, T. and Segers, J. (2002), *WBSO nader beschouwd: Onderzoek naar de effectiviteit van de WBSO*, The Hague: Ministerie van Economische Zaken, DG Innovatie.

Browning, E.K. (1976), 'The marginal cost of public funds', *Journal of Political Economy*, Vol. 84, No. 2, pp. 283-98.

Brue, S.L. and Grant, R.R. (2007), *The History of Economic Thought* (7th edn), Mason, OH: Thomson South-Western.

Buijink, W., Janssen, B. and Schols, Y. (1999), *Corporate Effective Tax Rates in the European Union*, Final report commissioned by the Ministry of Finance of the Netherlands, Maastricht: Accounting and Auditing Research and Education Centre.

Bundesministerium der Finanzen (2006), *From the 2000 tax reform to the 2008 Corporate Tax Reform – consistent and palpable reduction of direct tax burden for citizens and enterprises*, 21 November, Berlin: Bundesministerium der Finanzen.

Burda, M.C. and Wyplosz, C. (2005), *Macroeconomics: A European Text* (4th edn), Oxford: Oxford University Press.

Bye, B., Strøm, B. and Åvitsland, T. (2004), 'Welfare effects of VAT reforms: a general equilibrium analysis', Statistics Norway, Discussion Paper, No. 343, Oslo: Statistics Norway.

Cambridge Econometrics (2005), '*Modelling* the initial effects of the climate change levy', Report submitted to HM Customs and Excise by Cambridge Econometrics, Department of Applied Economics, Cambridge University and the Policy Studies Institute.

Card, D. and Robins, P.K. (1996), 'Do financial incentives encourage welfare recipients to work? Evidence from a randomized evaluation of the Self-Sufficiency Project', NBER Working Paper, No. 5701, Cambridge, MA: NBER.

Carey, D. and Rabesona, J. (2004), 'Tax ratios on labor and capital income and on consumption', in P.B. Sørensen (ed.), *Measuring the Tax Burden on Capital and Labor*, CESifo and Cambridge, MA: MIT Press.

Carlin, W. and Mayer, C. (1999), 'Finance, investment and growth', CEPR Discussion Paper, No. 2233, London: Centre for Economic Policy Research.

Cashin, P. (1995), 'Government spending, taxes, and economic growth', *IMF Staff Papers*, Vol. 42, No. 2.

Chamley, C. (1986), 'Optimal taxation of capital income in general equilibrium with infinite lives', *Econometrica*, Vol. 54, No. 3, pp. 607-22.

Chapman, B. (1997), 'Conceptual issues and the Australian experience with income contingent charges for higher education', *Economic Journal*, Vol. 107, No. 442, pp. 738-51.

Chapman, B. (2005), 'Income contingent loans for higher education: international reform', Centre for Economic Policy Research Discussion Paper, No. 491, Canberra: Australian National University.

Cherniavsky, B. (1996), 'Tax policy and job creation: specific employment incentive programs', Working Paper 96-3, Ottawa: Technical Committee on Business Taxation.

Christiansen, V. (2004), 'Norwegian income tax reforms', CESifo DICE Report, 3/2004, Munich: CESifo Group.

Clark, A.E. and Oswald, A.J. (1996), 'Satisfaction and comparison income', *Journal of Public Economics*, Vol. 61, pp. 359-81.

Cnossen, S. (1996), 'Company taxes in the European Union: criteria and options for reform', *Fiscal Studies*, Vol. 17, No. 4, pp. 67-97.

Cnossen, S. (1999), 'Fundamental tax reform in the United States', *De Economist*, Vol. 147, No. 2, pp. 229-37.

Cnossen, S. (2000), 'Taxing capital income in the Nordic countries: A model for the European Union?', in S. Cnossen (ed.), *Taxing Capital Income in the European Union: Issues and Options for Reform*, Oxford and New York: Oxford University Press.

Cnossen, S. (2001), 'Tax policy in the European Union: a review of issues and options', *FinanzArchiv*, Vol. 58, No. 4, pp. 466-558.

Cnossen, S. (2003), 'Is the VAT's sixth directive becoming an anachronism?', *European Taxation*, December.

Cnossen, S. (2004), 'Reform and coordination of corporation taxes in the European Union: an alternative agenda', *Bulletin for International Fiscal Documentation*, Vol. 58, No. 13, pp. 134-50.

Cnossen, S. (2006), 'Alcohol taxation and regulation in the European Union', CPB Discussion Paper, No. 76, The Hague: Centraal Plan Bureau.

Cnossen, S. and Bovenberg, A.L. (2001), 'Fundamental tax reform in the Netherlands', *International Tax and Public Finance*, Vol. 8, No. 4, pp. 471-84.

Cnossen, S. and Smart, M. (2005), 'Taxation of tobacco', in S. Cnossen (ed.) *Theory and Practice of Excise Taxation: Smoking, Drinking, Gambling, Polluting and Driving*, Oxford: Oxford University Press.

Code of Conduct Group (2000), 'Code of Conduct (Business Taxation)/Primarolo Group', Press release: Brussels, No. 4901/99, 29 February.

Cohen, L.R. and Noll, R.G. (1991), *The Technology Pork Barrel*, Washington, DC: Brookings Institution.

Committee on Surface Temperature Reconstructions (2006), *Surface Temperature Reconstructions for the Last 2000 Years*, Washington, DC: National Academies Press.

Corbett, J. and Jenkinson, T.J. (1997), 'How is investment financed? A study of Germany, Japan, UK and US', *The Manchester School*, Vol. 65, pp. 69-93.

Corlett, W.J. and Hague, D.C. (1953), 'Complementarity and the excess burden of taxation', *Review of Economic Studies*, Vol. 21, No. 1, pp. 21-30.

CPB (1996), *Recent Research: Tax Reform and Jobs Creation*, The Hague: Centraal Plan Bureau.

CPB (2002), *Macro Economische Verkenning (MEV) 2002*, The Hague: Centraal Plan Bureau.

CPB (2005), 'Belastingherziening 2001 en de werkgelegenheid van vrouwen', CPB Document No. 100, The Hague: Centraal Plan Bureau.

Daveri, F. and Tabellini, G. (2000), 'Unemployment, growth and taxation in industrial countries', *Economic Policy*, Vol. 15, No. 30, pp. 49-104.

Davies, J. and Whalley, J. (1989), 'Taxes and capital formation: how important is human capital', NBER Working Paper, No. 2899, Cambridge, MA: NBER.

Davis, S.J. (1992), 'Cross-country patterns of changes in relative wages', NBER Working Paper, No. 4085, Cambridge, MA: NBER.

Davis, S.J. and Henrekson, M. (2004), 'Tax effects on work activity, industry mix and shadow economy size: evidence from rich-country comparisons', NBER Working Paper, No. 10509, Cambridge, MA: NBER.

de Mooij, R.A. (2005), 'Will corporate income taxation survive?', *De Economist*, Vol. 153, No. 3, pp. 277-301.

de Mooij, R.A. and Ederveen, S. (2003), 'Taxation and foreign direct investment: a synthesis of empirical research', *International Tax and Public Finance*, Vol. 10, No. 6, pp. 673-93.

Denis, C., McMorrow, K. and Röger, W. (2004), 'An analysis of EU and US productivity developments (a total economy and industry level perspective)', European Commission: Directorate-General for Economic and Financial Affairs.

Derthick, M.A. (2002), *Up in Smoke: From Legislation to Litigation in Tobacco Politics*, Washington, DC: CQ Press.

Desai, M.A., Foley, C.F. and Hines, J.R., Jr (2001), 'Repatriation taxes and dividend distortions', *National Tax Journal*, Vol. 54, pp. 829-51.

Devereux, M.P. (1992), 'The Ruding Committee Report: an economic assessment', *Fiscal Studies*, Vol. 13, No. 2, pp. 96-107.

Devereux, M.P. and Griffith, R. (2001), 'Summary of the "Devereux and Griffith" economic model and measures of effective tax rates', Annex A of European Commission, Company Taxation in the Internal Market, COM 582 final, Brussels.

Devereux, M.P., Griffith, R. and Klemm, A. (2002), 'Corporate income tax reforms and international tax competition', *Economic Policy*, Vol. 35, pp. 451-95.

Diamond, P.A. (1998), 'Optimal income taxation: an example with a U-shaped pattern of optimal marginal tax rates', *American Economic Review*, Vol. 88, No. 1, pp 83-95.

Diamond, P.A. and Mirrlees, J.A. (1971), 'Optimal taxation and public production I: production efficiency', *American Economic Review*, Vol. 61, No. 1, pp. 8-27.

Diaw, K.M. and Gorter, J. (2002), 'The remedy may be worse than the disease: a critical account of the Code of Conduct', CBP Discussion Paper, No. 5, The Hague: Centraal Plan Bureau.

Dilnot, A.W. and Kay, J.A. (1990), 'Tax reform in the United Kingdom: the recent experience', in M.J. Boskin and C.E. McLure Jr (eds), *World Tax*

Reform: Case Studies of Developed and Developing Countries, San Francisco, CA: Institute for Contemporary Studies Press.

Disney, R. (2000), 'The impact of tax and welfare policies on employment and unemployment in OECD countries', IMF Working Paper, No. WP/00/164, Washington, DC: IMF.

Dixon, P.B. and Rimmer, M.T. (1999), 'Changes in indirect taxes in Australia: a dynamic general equilibrium analysis', *Australian Economic Review*, Vol. 32, No. 4, pp. 327-48.

Doll, R., Peto, R., Boreham, J. and Sutherland, I. (2004), 'Mortality in relation to smoking: 50 years' observations on male British doctors', *British Medical Journal*, Vol. 328, 26 June, p. 1519.

Dunning, J.H. (1981), *International Production and the Multinational Enterprise*, London: Allen & Unwin.

Dupor, B., Lochner, L., Taber, C. and Wittekind, M.B. (1996), 'Some effects of taxes on schooling and training', *American Economic Review*, Vol. 86, No. 2, pp. 340-46.

Easterly, W. and Rebello, S. (1993), 'Fiscal policy and growth: an empirical investigation', *Journal of Monetary Economics*, Vol. 32, No. 3, pp. 417-58.

Eaton, J. and Rosen, H.S. (1980), 'Taxation, human capital and uncertainty', *American Economic Review*, Vol. 70, No. 4, pp. 705-15.

Econtech (1999), '*Industry effects of tax reform*', Kingston: Econtech.

Edlund, J. (2000), 'Public attitudes towards taxation: Sweden 1981-1997', *Scandinavian Political Studies*, Vol. 23, No. 1, pp. 37-66.

Edwards, J. and Keen, M. (1996), 'Tax competition in Leviathan', *European Economic Review*, Vol. 40, No. 1, pp. 113-34.

Eisner, R., Albert, S.H. and Sullivan, M.A. (1984), 'The new incremental tax credit for R&D: incentive or disincentive?', *National Tax Journal*, Vol. 37, No. 2, pp. 171-83.

Eissa, N. and Hoynes, H. (1998), 'The earned income tax credit and the supply of labor by married couples', NBER Working Paper, No. 6856, Cambridge, MA: NBER.

Eissa, N. and Liebman, J.B. (1996), 'Labor supply response to the earned income tax credit', *Quarterly Journal of Economics*, Vol. 111, No. 2, pp. 605-37.

Engen, E.M. and Skinner, J. (1992), 'Fiscal policy and economic growth', NBER Working Paper, No. 4223, Cambridge, MA: NBER.

Engen, E.M. and Skinner, J. (1996), 'Taxation and economic growth', NBER Working Paper, No. 5826, Cambridge, MA: NBER.

Enkvist, P.A., Nauclér, T. and Rosander, J. (2007), 'A cost curve for greenhouse gas reduction', *McKinsey Quarterly*, No. 1.

EurActiv (2007), *Technologies & Climate Change*, Brussels: EurActiv.

European Commission (2000a), 'Public finances in the EMU – 2000', *European Economy*, No. 3, Directorate-General for Economic and

Financial Affairs, Luxembourg: Office for Official Publications of the European Communities.

European Commission (2000b), 'The Lisbon European council – an agenda of economic and social renewal for Europe', DOC/00/7, Brussels, 28 February.

European Commission (2001a), 'Towards an Internal Market without tax obstacles. A strategy for providing companies with a consolidated corporate tax base for their EU-wide activities', COM 582 final, Brussels.

European Commission (2001b), 'Company taxation in the Internal Market', SEC 1681 final, Brussels, 23 October.

European Commission (2002), 'Study on vehicle taxation in the member states of the European Union', Brussels, final report, January.

European Commission (2003a), 'Experimental application of a reduced rate of VAT to certain labour-intensive services', COM 309 final, Brussels, 02 June.

European Commission (2003b), 'The application of International Accounting Standards (IAS) in 2005 and the implications for the introduction of a consolidated tax base for companies' EU-wide activities', Consultation Document, February.

European Commission (2004a), 'Facing the challenge: the Lisbon strategy for growth and employment', Report from the High Level Group chaired by Wim Kok, Luxembourg: Office for Official Publications of the European Communities.

European Commission (2004b), *Structures of Taxation Systems in the EU, 1995-2004*, Luxembourg: Office for Official Publications of the European Communities.

European Commission (2005a), 'A proposal for a Code of Conduct on transfer pricing documentation for associated enterprises in the EU', COM 543 final, Brussels, 07 November.

European Commission (2005b), 'Taxation Papers. Formulary Apportionment and Group Taxation in the European Union: insights from the United States and Canada', Working Paper, No. 8, Luxembourg: Office for Official Publications of the European Communities.

European Commission (2006a), *50 years of the Treaty of Rome: Establishing the European Economic Community*, Luxembourg: Office for Official Publications of the European Communities.

European Commission (2006b), 'Structures of the taxation systems in the European Union: 1995-2004', TAXUD E4/2006/DOC/3201.

European Commission (2006c), 'State aid: Commission opens investigation into a French tax credit scheme for video game creation', Brussels: European Commission, IP/06/1602, 22 November.

European Commission (2006d), 'Company taxation: Commission proposes "Home State Taxation for SMEs"', IP/06/11, Brussels: European Commission: 19 January.

European Commission (2006e), 'Towards a more effective use of tax incentives in favour of R&D', COM 728 final, Brussels.

European Commission (2007a), 'EU-Switzerland: State aid decision on company tax regimes', Brussels: European Commission, IP/07/176.

European Commission (2007b), 'Limiting global climate change to 2 degrees celsius: the way ahead for 2020 and beyond', COM 2 final, Brussels: European Commission, 10 January.

European Communities (1975), 'Tax policy and investment in the European Community', Brussels.

European Council (1998), 'Conclusions of the Council of Economics and Finance Ministers (ECFIN)', *Official Journal of the European Communities*, 98/C 2/01.

European Parliament (2005), 'Report on the proposal for a Council directive amending Directive 77/388/EEC on the common system of value added tax, with regard to the length of time during which the minimum standard rate is to be applied', Committee on Economic and Monetary Affairs, 17 November.

Eurostat (2003), 'Environmental taxes in the European Union 1980-2001', *Statistics in Focus*, Theme 8-9/2003.

Eurostat (2007), 'Environmental taxes in the European economy 1995-2003', *Statistics in Focus*, Environment and Energy 1/2007.

Evans, W.N. and Ringel, J.S. (1999), 'Can higher cigarette taxes improve birth outcomes?', *Journal of Public Economics*, Vol. 72, No. 1, pp. 135-54.

Feige, E.L. and McGee, R.T. (1983), 'Sweden's Laffer curve: taxation and the unobserved economy', *Scandinavian Journal of Economics*, Vol. 85, No. 4, pp. 499-519.

Feldstein, M. (1995), 'The effect of marginal tax rates on taxable income: a panel study of the 1986 Tax Reform Act', *Journal of Political Economy*, Vol. 103, No. 3, pp. 551-72.

Feldstein, M. (1997), 'Employment policy in the middle Reagan years: what didn't happen and why it didn't happen', NBER Working Paper, No. 5917, Cambridge MA: NBER.

Feldstein, M. (1999), 'Tax avoidance and the deadweight loss of the income tax', *Review of Economics and Statistics*, Vol. 81, No. 4, pp. 674-80.

Feldstein, M. and Feenberg, D. (1993), 'Higher tax rates with little revenue gain: an empirical analysis of the Clinton tax plan', *Tax Notes*, 22 March.

Feldstein, M. and Feenberg, D. (1995), 'The effect of increased tax rates on taxable income and economic efficiency: a preliminary analysis of the 1993 tax rate increases', NBER Working Paper, No. 5370, Cambridge, MA: NBER.

Fölster, S. and Henrekson, M. (2001), 'Growth effects of government expenditures and taxation in rich countries', *European Economic Review*, Vol. 45, No. 8, pp. 1501-20.

Foray, D. (2004), *Economics of Knowledge*, Cambridge, MA: MIT Press.

Förster, M. and d'Ercole, M.M. (2005), 'Income distribution and poverty in the OECD countries in the second half of the 1990s', OECD Social, Employment and Migration Working Papers, No. 22, Paris: OECD.

Förster, M. and Pearson, M. (2002), 'Income distribution and poverty in the OECD area: trends and driving forces', *OECD Economic Studies*, No. 34, 2002/1.

Gemmell, N. (1997), *'Externalities to Higher Education: A Review of the New Growth Literature'*, in National Committee of Inquiry into Higher Education, *Higher Education in the Learner Society*, Norwich: HMSO.

Goode, R. (1990), 'Key issues in the reform of personal income taxes', in S. Cnossen and R.M. Bird (eds.), *The Personal Income Tax: Phoenix from the Ashes?*, Amsterdam: North-Holland.

Goolsbee, A. (1999), 'Evidence on the high-income Laffer curve from six decades of tax reform', *Brookings Papers on Economic Activity*, Vol. 1999, No. 2, pp. 1-64.

Gordon, R.H. (2000), 'Taxation of capital income vs. labour income: an overview', in S. Cnossen (ed.), *Taxing Capital Income in the European Union: Issues and Options for Reform*, Oxford and New York: Oxford University Press.

Gordon R.H. and Hines, J.R., Jr (2002), 'International taxation', NBER Working Paper, No. 8854, Cambridge, MA: NBER.

Gordon, R.H. and Mackie-Mason, J.K. (1994), 'Tax distortions to the choice of organizational form', NBER Working Paper, No. 4227, Cambridge, MA: NBER.

Gordon, R.H., Kalambokidis, L. and Slemrod, J. (2004), 'Do we *now* collect any revenue from taxing capital income?', *Journal of Public Economics*, Vol. 88, No. 5, pp. 981-1009.

Gorter, J. and de Mooij, R.A. (2001), *Capital Income Taxation in Europe: Trends and Trade-offs*, The Hague: Centraal Plan Bureau.

Gorter, J. and Parikh, A. (2000), 'How mobile is capital within the EU', CPB Research Memorandum, No. 172, The Hague: Centraal Plan Bureau.

Goulder, L.H. (1995), 'Environmental taxation and the double dividend: a reader's guide', *International Tax and Public Finance*, Vol. 2, No. 2, pp. 157-83.

Gradus, R.H.J.M. and Julsing, J.M. (2001), 'Comparing different European income tax policies making work pay', *OCFEB*, Research Memorandum 0101, Rotterdam.

Graetz, M.J. and Warren, A.C. (2006), 'Income tax discrimination and the political integration of Europe', *Yale Law Journal*, Vol. 115, No. 6, pp. 1186-1255.

Graham, J.R. (1996a), 'Proxies for the corporate marginal tax rate', *Journal of Financial Economics*, Vol. 42, No. 2, pp. 187-221.

Graham, J.R. (1996b), 'Debt and the marginal tax rate', *Journal of Financial Economics*, Vol. 41, No. 1, pp. 41-73.

Grant, R. (2004), 'Less tax or more social spending: twenty years of opinion polling', Department of Parliamentary Services, Research Paper, No. 13, Canberra: Parliamentary Library.

Grapperhaus, F.H.M. (1998), *Tax Tales: From the Second Millennium*, Amsterdam: International Bureau of Fiscal Documentation.

Grauwe, P. and Polan, M. (2003), 'Globalisation and social spending', CESifo Working Paper, No. 885, Munich: CESifo Group.

Gravelle, J.G. (2002), 'Behavioral responses to a consumption tax', in G.R. Zodrow and P. Mieszkowski (eds), *United States Tax Reform in the 21st Century*, New York: Cambridge University Press.

Gravelle, J.G. (2004), 'The Flat Tax, Value Added Tax, and National Retail Sales Tax: Overview of the Issues', CRS Report for Congress, RL 32603, Washington, DC.

Gravelle, J.G. and Kotlikoff, L.J. (1989), 'The incidence and efficiency costs of corporate taxation when corporate and noncorporate firms produce the same goods', *Journal of Political Economy*, Vol. 97, No. 4, pp. 749-81.

Greenspan, A. (2007), *The Age of Turbulence: Adventures in a New World*, New York: Penguin Press.

Griffith, R. and Klemm, A. (2004), 'What has been the tax competition experience of the last 20 years?', IFS Working Paper WP04/05, London: Institute for Fiscal Studies.

Griffith, R., Redding, S. and van Reenen, J. (2001), 'Measuring the cost-effectiveness of an R&D tax credit for the UK', *Fiscal Studies*, Vol. 22, No. 3, pp. 375-99.

Griffith, R., Sandler, D. and van Reenen, J. (1996), 'Tax incentives for R&D', *Fiscal Studies*, Vol. 16, No. 2, pp. 21-44.

Gropp, R. and Kostial, K. (2000), 'The disappearing tax base: is foreign direct investment eroding corporate income taxes?', Working Paper No. 31, Frankfurt: European Central Bank.

Gruber, J. and Mullainathan, S. (2002), 'Do cigarette taxes make smokers happier?', NBER Working Paper, No. 8872, Cambridge, MA: NBER.

Grubert, H. (1998), 'Taxes and the division of foreign operating income among royalties, interest, dividends and retained earnings', *Journal of Public Economics*, Vol. 68, No. 2, pp. 269-90.

Grubert, H. (2001), 'Tax planning by companies and tax competition by governments: is there evidence of changes in behavior?', in J.R. Hines, Jr (ed.), *International Taxation and Multinational Activity*, Chicago, IL: University of Chicago Press.

Grubert, H. and Mutti, J. (1991), 'Taxes, tariffs and transfer pricing in multinational corporate decision making', *Review of Economics and Statistics*, Vol. 73, No. 2, pp. 285-93.

Grubert, J., Randolph, W.C. and Rousslang, D.J. (1996), 'Country and multinational company responses to the Tax Reform Act of 1986', *National Tax Journal*, Vol. 49, No. 3, pp. 341-58.

Guellec, D. and Pottelsberghe, B. (2001), 'R&D and productivity growth: panel data analysis of 16 OECD countries', OECD Science, Technology and Industry Working Papers, 2001/3, Paris: OECD.

Guinet, J. and Kamata, H. (1996), 'Do tax-incentives promote innovation?', *OECD Observer*, No. 202, October/November.

Gustafsson, S. (1992), 'Separate taxation and married women's labor supply: a comparison of West Germany and Sweden', *Journal of Population Economics*, Vol. 5, No. 1, pp. 61-85.

Hall, B.H. and van Reenen, J. (2000), 'How effective are fiscal incentives for R&D? A review of the evidence', *Research Policy*, Vol. 29, No. 4, pp. 449-69.

Hall, R.E. and Jorgenson, D.W. (1967), 'Tax policy and investment behavior', *American Economic Review*, Vol. 57, No. 3, pp. 391-414.

Hall, R.E. and Rabushka, A. (1995), *The Flat Tax* (2nd edn), Stanford, CA: Hoover Institution Press.

Hamermesh, D.S. and Slemrod, J. (2005), 'The economics of workaholism: we should not have worked on this paper', NBER Working Paper, No. 11566, Cambridge, MA: NBER.

Hamilton, B. and Whalley, J. (1989), 'Reforming indirect taxes in Canada: some general equilibrium estimates', *Canadian Journal of Economics*, Vol. 22, No. 3, pp. 561-75.

Harberger, A.C. (1962), 'The incidence of the corporation income tax', *Journal of Political Economy*, Vol. 70, No. 3, pp. 215-40.

Harberger, A.C. (1964), 'The measurement of waste', *American Economic Review*, Vol. 54, pp. 58-76.

Hassett, K.A. and Hubbard, R.G. (1997), 'Tax policy and investment', in A. Auerbach (ed.), *Fiscal Policy: Lessons from Economic Research*, Cambridge, MA: MIT Press.

Hassett, K.A. and Metcalf, G.E. (1995), 'Energy tax credits and residential conservation investment: evidence from panel data', *Journal of Public Economics*, Vol. 59, No. 2, pp. 201-17.

Haveman, R. (1996), 'Reducing poverty while increasing employment: a primer on alternative strategies and a blueprint', *OECD Economic Studies*, No. 26, pp. 7-42.

Heady, C. (2004), 'The "taxing wages" approach to measuring the tax burden on labour', in P.B. Sørensen (ed.), *Measuring the Tax Burden on Capital and Labor*, Cambridge, MA: MIT Press.

Heath, A. (2006), *Flat Tax: Towards a British Model*, Stockholm: Taxpayers' Alliance and the Stockholm Network.

Heckman, J.J. (1993), 'What has been learned about labor supply in the past twenty years?', *American Economic Review*, Vol. 83, No. 2, pp. 116-21.

Heckman, J.J. (2000), 'Policies to foster human capital', *Research in Economics*, Vol. 54, No. 1, pp. 3-56.

Heckman, J.J., Lalonde, R.J. and Smith, J.A. (1999), 'The economics and econometrics of active labor market programs', in O.C. Ashenfelter and D.E. Card. (eds), *Handbook of Labor Economics*, Amsterdam: North-Holland.

Heckman, J.J., Lochner, L. and Taber, C. (1998), 'Tax policy and human-capital formation', *American Economic Review*, Vol. 88, No. 2, pp. 293-97.

Heijdra, B.J. and van der Ploeg, F. (2002), *Foundations of Modern Macroeconomics*, Oxford: Oxford University Press

Hendricks, L. (1999), 'Taxation and long-run growth', *Journal of Monetary Economics*, Vol. 43, No. 2, pp. 411-34.

Herber, B.P. and Raga, J.T. (1995), 'An international carbon tax to combat global warming: an economic and political analysis of the European Union proposal', *American Journal of Economics and Sociology*, Vol. 54, No. 3, pp. 257-68.

Hines, J.R., Jr (2002), *Applied Public Finance Meets General Equilibrium: The Research Contributions of Arnold Harberger*, Ann Arbor, MI: Office of Tax Policy Research, University of Michigan.

Hines, J.R., Jr and Rice, E.M. (1994), 'Fiscal paradise: foreign tax havens and American business', *Quarterly Journal of Economics*, Vol. 109, No. 1, pp. 149-82.

HM Treasury (2002), *Tax and the Environment: Using Economic Instruments*, London: HM Treasury.

HM Treasury (2003), *Green Book, Appraisal and Evaluation in Central Government*, London: HM Treasury.

HM Treasury (2006), *Long-Term Challenges and Opportunities for the UK: Analysis for the 2007 Comprehensive Spending Review*, London: HM Treasury.

Hodge, S.A., Beach, W.W. and Wilson, M. (1996), 'Is there a "Clinton crunch"? How the 1993 Budget Plan affected the economy', *Backgrounder*, No. 1078, Washington, DC: Heritage Foundation.

Holmøy, E. and Vennemo, H. (1995), 'A general equilibrium assessment of a suggested reform in capital income taxation', *Journal of Policy Modeling*, Vol. 17, No. 6, pp. 532-56.

Hotz, J. and Scholz, J.K. (2000), 'Not perfect, but still pretty good: the EITC and other policies to support the US low-wage labour market', *OECD Economic Studies*, No. 31, Paris: OECD.

Hutton, J.P. and Ruocco, A. (1999), 'Tax reform and employment in Europe', *International Tax and Public Finance*, Vol. 6, No. 3, pp. 263-87.

IFS Capital Taxes Group (1991), '*Equity for Companies: A Corporation Tax for the 1990s*, London: Institute for Fiscal Studies.

Ihori, T., Doi, T and Kondo, H. (2001), 'Japanese fiscal reform: fiscal reconstruction and fiscal policy', *Japan and the World Economy*, Vol. 13, No. 4, pp. 351-70.

IMF (1995), 'Unproductive public expenditures: A pragmatic approach to policy analysis', IMF Pamphlet Series, No. 48, Washington, DC: International Monetary Fund.

IMF (2002), *Government Finance Statistical Manual*, Washington, DC: International Monetary Fund.

IMF (2007a), *World Economic Outlook: Spillovers and Cycles in the Global Economy*, Washington, DC: International Monetary Fund.

IMF (2007b), *World Economic Outlook: Globalization and Inequality*, Washington, DC: International Monetary Fund.

Intergovernmental Panel on Climate Change (2007), *Climate Change 2007: The Physical Science Basis, Summary for Policymakers*, Geneva: IPCC.

International Energy Agency (2006), *World Energy Outlook 2006*, Paris: IEA.

Jacobs, B. (2004), 'The lost race between schooling and technology', *De Economist*, Vol. 152, No. 1, pp. 47-78.

Jacobs, B. (2005), 'Optimal income taxation with endogenous human capital', *Journal of Public Economic Theory*, Vol. 7, No. 2, pp. 295-315.

Jacobs, B. and de Mooij, R.A. (2002), 'Fiscaliteit en de kenniseconomie', *Openbare Uitgaven*, Vol. 34, No. 2, pp. 62-72.

Jacobs, B. and van der Ploeg, F. (2006), 'Guide to reform of higher education: a European perspective', *Economic Policy*, Vol. 21, No. 47, pp. 535-92.

Jacobs, B. and van Weinbergen, S.J.G. (2005), 'Capital market failure, adverse selection and equity financing of higher education', Tinbergen Institute Discussion Paper, TI 2005-037/3.

Jacobs, O.H. and Spengel, C. (1999), 'The effective average tax burden in the European Union and the USA. A computer-based calculation and comparison with the model of the European tax analyzer', *ZEW* Discussion Paper, No. 99-54, Centre for European Economic Research and University of Mannheim.

Jones, L.E., Manuelli, R.E. and Rossi, P.E. (1993), 'Optimal taxation in models of endogenous growth', *Journal of Political Economy*, Vol. 101, No. 3, pp. 485-517.

Jorgenson, D. and Yun, K. (1990), 'Tax reform and U.S. economic growth', *Journal of Political Economy*, Vol. 98, No. 5, pp. 151-93.

Joyeux, C. and Stockman, P. (2003), 'Een macro-economische evaluatie van de werkgeversbijdrageverminderingen in 1995-2000', Working Paper 14-03, Brussels: Federal Planning Bureau.

Judd, K.L. (1985), 'Redistributive taxation in a simple perfect foresight model', *Journal of Public Economics,* Vol. 28, No. 1, pp. 59-83.

Kaldor, N. (1977), *An Expenditure Tax*, Westport, CT: Greenwood Press.

Kanbur, R. and Keen, M. (1993), 'Jeux sans frontières: tax competition and tax coordination when countries differ in size', *American Economic Review*, Vol. 83, No. 4, pp. 877-92.

Keen, M and King, J. (2002), 'The Croatian profit tax: an ACE in practice', *Fiscal Studies*, Vol. 23, No. 3, pp. 401-18.

Keen, M. and Ligthart, J.E. (2004), 'Cross-border savings taxation in the European Union: an economic perspective', *Tax Notes International*, 9 February.

Keen, M., Kim, Y. and Versano, R. (2006), 'The "flat tax(es)": principles and evidence', IMF Working Paper, WP/06/218, Washington, DC: International Monetary Fund.

Kenkel, D.S. (1993), 'Drinking, driving and deterrence: the effect and social cost of alternative policies', *Journal of Law and Economics*, Vol. 36, No. 2, pp. 877-913.

Keynes, J.M. (1936), *The General Theory of Employment Interest, and Money*, London: Macmillan.

Killingsworth, M.R. and Heckman, J.J. (1986), 'Female labor supply: a survey', in O. Ashenfelter and R. Layard (eds), *Handbook of Labor Economics*, Vol. 1, Amsterdam: North-Holland, pp. 103-204.

King, M.A. and Fullerton, D. (1984), *The Taxation of Income from Capital*, Chicago, IL: University of Chicago Press.

King, R.G. and Rebelo, S. (1990), 'Public policy and economic growth: developing neoclassical implications', *Journal of Political Economy*, Vol. 98, No. 5, pp. 126-50.

Klemm, A. and Radealli, C. (2001), 'EU corporate tax reform', *Centre for European Policy Studies Task Force Reports*, Brussels: CEPS.

Kleven, H.J. and Kreiner, C.T. (2006), 'The marginal cost of public funds: hours of work versus labor force participation', CEPR Discussion Paper, No. 5594, London: Centre for Economic Policy Research.

Kneller, R., Bleaney, M.F. and Gemmell, N. (1999), 'Fiscal policy and growth: evidence from OECD countries', *Journal of Public Economics*, Vol. 74, No. 2, pp. 171-90.

Koester, R.B. and Kormendi, R.C. (1989), 'Taxation, aggregate activity and economic growth: cross-country evidence on some supply-side hypotheses', *Economic Inquiry*, Vol. 27, pp. 367-86.

Koga, T. (2003), 'Firm size and R&D tax incentives', *Technovation*, Vol. 23, No. 7, pp. 643-8.

Koren, S. and Stiassny, A. (1998), 'Tax and spend, or spend and tax? An international study', *Journal of Policy Modeling*, Vol. 20, No. 2, pp. 163-91.

Kovács, L. (2005), 'Tax harmonization versus tax competition in Europe', SPEECH/05/624, Brussels: European Commission.

Krueger, D. and Prescott, E.C. (1998), 'Should Japan Cut Taxes? Implications from the Neoclassical Growth Model', Federal Reserve Bank of Minneapolis.

Kutscher, C.F. (2007), *Tackling Climate Change in the US: Potential Carbon Emissions Reductions from Energy Efficiency and Renewable Energy by 2030*, New York: American Solar Energy Society.

Lammersen, L. (2002), 'Investment decisions and tax revenues under an allowance for corporate equity', ZEW Discussion Paper, No. 02-47, Mannheim: ZEW.

Layard, R. (2003), 'Income and happiness, Lionel Robbins Memorial Lectures', Centre for Economic Performance, London School of Economics.

Layard, R., Nickell, S. and Jackman, R. (2005), *Unemployment, Macroeconomic Performance and the Labour Market* (2nd edn), Oxford: Oxford University Press.

Lee, Y. and Gordon, R.H. (2005), 'Tax structure and economic growth', *Journal of Public Economics*, Vol. 89, pp. 1027-43.

Leibfritz, W., Thornton, J. and Bibbee, A. (1997), 'Taxation and economic performance', OECD Economics Department Working Papers, No. 176, Paris: OECD.

Leung, S. and Phelps, C. (1993), 'My kingdom for a drink ...? A review of estimates of the price sensitivity of alcoholic beverages', in M.E. Hilton and G. Bloss (eds), *Economics and the Prevention of Alcohol-Related Problems*, NIH Publication 93-3513, Rockville, MD: National Institutes of Health.

Levhari, D. and Weiss, Y. (1974), 'The effect of risk on the investment in human capital', *American Economic Review*, Vol. 64, No. 6, pp. 950-63.

Levine, R. (1991), 'Stock markets, growth, and tax policy', *Journal of Finance*, Vol. 46, No. 4, pp. 1445-65.

Lindert, P.H. (2004). *Growing Public: Social Spending and Economic Growth Since the Eighteenth Century*, Cambridge: Cambridge University Press.

Lindsey, L.B. (1987), 'Individual taxpayer response to tax cuts: 1982-1984. With implications for the revenue maximizing tax rate', *Journal of Public Economics*, Vol. 33, No. 2, pp. 173-206.

Lockwood, B. and Manning, A. (1993), 'Wage setting and the tax system: theory and evidence for the United Kingdom', *Journal of Public Economics*, Vol. 52, No. 1, pp. 1-29.

Lockwood, B., Sløk, T. and Tranæs, T. (2000), 'Progressive taxation and wage setting: some evidence for Denmark', *Scandinavian Journal of Economics*, Vol. 102, No. 4, pp. 707-23.

Lodin, S.O. and Gammie, M. (1999), 'The taxation of the European company', *European Taxation*, August.

Lomborg, B. (2007), *Cool It: The Sceptical Environmentalist's Guide to Global Warming*, New York: Alfred A. Knopf.

Lucas, R.E. (1988), 'On the mechanics of economic development', *Journal of Monetary Economics*, Vol. 22, pp. 3-42.

Lucas, R.E. (1990), 'Supply-side economics: an analytical review', *Oxford Economic Papers*, Vol. 42, pp. 293-316.

Luja, R.H.C. (2006), 'Stimulerende Belastingheffing', Rede uitgesproken bij aanvaarding van het ambtvan hoogleraar Comparative Tax Law, Vrijdag, 20 October.

Mankiw, N.G. (2003), *Macroeconomics* (4th edn), New York: Worth.

Mankiw, N.G., Romer, D. and Weil, D.N. (1990), 'A contribution to the empirics of economic growth', NBER Working Paper, No. 3541, Cambridge, MA: NBER.

Mankiw, N.G. and Weinzierl, M. (2004), 'Dynamic scoring: a back-of-the-envelope guide', NBER Working Paper, No. 11000, Cambridge, MA: NBER.

Mann, M.E., Bradley, R.S. and Hughes, M.K. (1998), 'Global-scale temperature patterns and climate forcing over the past six centuries', *Nature*, Vol. 392, No. 6678, pp. 779-87.

Mann, M.E., Bradley, R.S. and Hughes, M.K. (1999), 'Northern hemisphere temperatures during the past millennium: inferences, uncertainties, and limitations', *Geophysical Research Letters*, Vol. 26, No. 6, pp. 759-62.

Manning, W.G., Blumberg, L. and Moulton, L.H. (1995), 'The demand for alcohol: the differential response to price', *Journal of Health Economics*, Vol. 14, No. 2, pp. 123-48.

Mansfield, E. (1986), 'The R&D tax credit and other technology policy issues', *American Economic Review*, Vol. 76, No. 2, pp. 190-94.

Mansfield, E. and Switzer, L. (1985), 'The effect of R&D tax credits and allowances in Canada', *Research Policy*, Vol. 14, No. 2, pp. 97-107.

Markusen, J.R. (1995), 'The boundaries of multinational enterprises and the theory of international trade', *Journal of Economic Perspectives*, Vol. 9, No. 2, pp. 169-89.

Matthews, K. (2003), 'VAT evasion and VAT avoidance: is there a European Laffer curve for VAT?', *International Review of Applied Economics*, Vol. 17, No. 1, pp. 105-14.

McIntyre, R.S. (1996), *Tax Expenditures: The Hidden Entitlements*, Washington, DC: Citizens for Tax Justice.

McIntyre, S. and McKitrick, R. (2003), 'Corrections to Mann et al. (1998): proxy data base and Northern Hemispheric average temperature series', *Energy and Environment*, Vol. 14, No. 6, pp. 751-72.

McKinnon, J.D. (2002), 'IRS weighs using debt collectors to get back taxes', *Wall Street Journal*, 15 October.

Meade Committee Report (1978), *The Structure and Reform of Direct Taxation*, London: Institute for Fiscal Studies.

Mendoza, E.G., Milesi, G.M. and Asea, P. (1997), 'On the ineffectiveness of tax policy in altering long-run growth: Harberger's superneutrality conjecture', *Journal of Public Economics*, Vol. 66, pp. 99-126.

Mendoza, E.G., Razin, A. and Tesar, L.L (1994), 'Effective tax rates in macroeconomics: cross-country estimates of tax rates on factor income and consumption', *Journal of Monetary Economics*, Vol. 34, No. 3, pp. 297-323.

Messere, K. C., de Kam, C.A. and Heady, C.J. (2003), *Tax Policy: Theory and Practice in OECD Countries*, Oxford and New York: Oxford University Press

Meyer, B.D. (2002a), 'Unemployment and workers' compensation programmes: rationale, design, labour supply and income support', *Fiscal Studies*, Vol. 23, No. 1, pp. 1-49.

Meyer, B.D. (2002b), 'Labor supply at the extensive and intensive margins: the EITC, welfare and hours worked', *American Economic Review*, Vol. 92, No. 2, pp. 373-9.

Meyer, B.D. and Rosenbaum, D.T. (2001), 'Welfare, the earned income tax credit, and the labor supply of single mothers', *Quarterly Journal of Economics*, Vol. 116, No. 3, pp. 1063-114.

Michalopoulos, C., Robins, P.K. and Card, D. (1999), *When Financial Incentives Pay for Themselves: Early Findings from the Self-Sufficiency Project's Applicant Study*, Ottawa: Social Research and Demonstration Corporation.

Mincer, J. (1958), 'Investment in human capital and personal income distribution', *Journal of Political Economy*, Vol. 66, No. 4, pp. 281-302.

Mintz, J. (1996), 'Corporation tax: a survey', *Fiscal Studies*, Vol. 16, No. 4, pp. 23-68.

Mintz, J. (2003), 'Cashing out profits: international approaches to dividend taxation', *Tax Notes International*, July, p. 255.

Mirrlees, J.A. (1971), 'An exploration in the theory of optimum income taxation', *Review of Economic Studies*, Vol. 38, No. 2, pp. 175-208.

Modigliani, F. and Miller, M. (1958), 'The cost of capital, corporation finance and theory of investment', *American Economic Review*, Vol. 48, No. 3, pp. 261-97.

Moore, M.J. (1996), 'Death and tobacco taxes', *RAND Journal of Economics*, Vol. 27, No. 2, pp. 415-28.

Muscovitch, Z. (2005), 'Taxation of internet commerce', *First Monday*, Special Issue, No. 3: Internet banking, e-money, and Internet gift economies, 5 December.

Musgrave, R.A. (1983), 'Who should tax, where, and what?', in C.E. McLure (ed.), *Tax Assignment in Federal Countries*, Canberra: Australian National University.

Musgrave, R.A. and Musgrave, P.B. (1989), *Public Finance in Theory and Practice*' (5th edn), New York: McGraw-Hill.

Nadiri, M.I. (1993), 'Innovations and technological spillovers', NBER Working Paper, No. 4423, Cambridge, MA: NBER.

Nahuis, R. and de Groot, H.L.F. (2003), 'Rising skills premia: you ain't seen nothing yet?', CPB Discussion Paper, No. 20, The Hague: Centraal Plan Bureau.

Nerlove, M., Razin, A., Sadka, E. and Weizsäcker, R.K. (1993), 'Comprehensive income taxation, investments in human and physical capital, and productivity', *Journal of Public Economics*, Vol. 50, No. 3, pp. 397-406.

Nickell, S. (2003), 'Employment and taxes', CESifo Working Paper, No. 1109, Munich: CESifo Group.

Nickell, S., Nunziata, L. and Ochel, W. (2005), 'Unemployment in the OECD since the 1960s. What do we know?', *Economic Journal*, Vol. 115, No. 500, pp. 1-27.

Nicodème, G. (2001), 'Computing effective corporate tax rates: comparisons and results', ECFIN E2/358/01-EN, European Commission: Directorate-General for Economic and Financial Affairs.

Nielsen, S.B. and Sørensen, P.B. (1997), 'On the optimality of the Nordic system of dual income taxation', *Journal of Public Economics*, Vol. 63, No. 3, pp. 311-29.

Nordhaus, W. (2006), 'Critical assumptions in the Stern Review on climate change', *Science*, Vol. 317, No. 5835, pp. 201-2.

Ochel, W. (2001), 'Financial incentives to work – conceptions and results in Great Britain, Ireland and Canada', CESifo Working Paper, No. 627, Munich: CESifo Group.

OECD (1995), *The OECD's Jobs Study: Taxation, Employment and Unemployment*, Paris: OECD.

OECD (1998), *Harmful Tax Competition: An Emerging Global Issue*, Paris: OECD

OECD (2000a), 'Links between policy and growth: cross-country evidence', *OECD Economic Outlook*, Paris: OECD.

OECD (2000b), 'Tax burdens: alternative measures', OECD Tax Policy Studies, No. 2, Paris: OECD.

OECD (2000c), *Towards Global Tax Co-operation. Report to the 2000 Ministerial Council Meeting and Recommendations by the Committee on Fiscal Affairs*, Paris: OECD.

OECD (2000d), *Behavioural Responses to Environmentally Related Taxes*, Paris: OECD.

OECD (2001), *Taxation and Electronic Commerce: Implementing the Ottawa Taxation Framework Conditions*, Paris: OECD.

OECD (2003), *OECD Economic Surveys: Belgium*, Vol. 2003/1, February, Paris: OECD.

OECD (2004), 'Best practice guidelines – off budget and tax expenditures', Working Party of Senior Budget Officials, GOV/PGC/SBO(2004)6, Paris: OECD.

OECD (2005a), 'Economic Survey of Denmark', OECD Policy Brief, February.

OECD (2005b), 'E-commerce: transfer pricing and business profits taxation', *OECD Tax Policy Studies*, No. 10, Paris: OECD.

OECD (2005c), *Revenue Statistics 1965-2004 – 2005 Edition*, Paris: OECD.

OECD (2005d), *The Economic Survey of the United States 2005: Ensuring Fiscal Sustainability and Budgetary Discipline*, Paris: OECD.

OECD (2005e), 'Key Statistics. Extending Opportunities: How Social Policy Can Benefit Us All', Meeting of OECD Social Affairs Ministers, Paris, 31 March – 1 April.

OECD (2005f), *OECD Science, Technology and Industry: Scoreboard 2005*, Paris: OECD.

OECD (2005g), *Taxing Wages 2003-2004*, Paris: OECD.

OECD (2005h), *Consumption Tax Trends: VAT/GST and Excise Rates, Trends and Administration Issues*, Paris: OECD.

OECD (2005i), *Education at a Glance: OECD Indicators 2005*, Paris: OECD.

OECD (2006a), *Tax Policy Development in Denmark, Italy, Slovak Republic and Turkey*, Paris: OECD.

OECD (2006b), *International Investment Perspectives*, Paris: OECD.

OECD (2006c), *The Political Economy of Environmentally Related Taxes*, Paris: OECD.

OECD (2007), 'Economic survey of the euro area', OECD Economic Surveys, Paris: OECD.

Okun, A.M. (1983), *Economics for Policymaking*, Cambridge, MA: MIT Press.

Oswald, A.J. (1997a), 'Happiness and economic performance', *Economic Journal*, Vol. 107, No. 445, pp. 1815-31.

Oswald, A.J. (1997b), '*The missing piece of the unemployment puzzle*', Inaugural Lecture, University of Warwick, November.

Otten, J. (2007), 'Origins of executive pay and corporate governance reform codes: essays on an institutional approach to corporate governance', Doctoral thesis, Utrecht University.

Owens, J. (2006), 'Tax in a borderless world', *OECD Observer*, No. 257, October.

Padovano, F. and Galli, E. (2001), 'Tax rates and economic growth in the OECD countries (1950-1990)', *Economic Inquiry*, Vol. 39, pp. 44-57.

Papadimitriou, D.B. (2006), 'Government effects on the distribution of income: an overview', Working Paper, No. 442, Bard College: Levy Economics Institute.

Pencavel, J. (1986), '*Labor supply of men: a survey*', in O. Ashenfelter and R. Layard (eds), *Handbook of Labor Economics*, Vol. 1, Amsterdam: North-Holland, pp. 3-102

Perri, F. (2001), 'The role of fiscal policy in Japan: a quantitative study', *Japan and the World Economy*, Vol. 13, pp. 387-404.

Pevcin, P. (2004), '*Does optimal size of government spending exist?*', University of Ljubljana.

Phelps, E.S. (1994), 'Raising the employment and pay of the working poor: low-wage employment subsidies versus the welfare state', *AEA Papers and Proceedings*, Vol. 84, No. 2, May.

Phillips, A.W.H. (1958), 'Unemployment and the rate of change of money wage rates in the United Kingdom 1862-1963', *Review of Economics and Statistics*, Vol. 50, No. 1, pp. 60-7.

Pigou, A.C. (1932), *The Economics of Welfare* (4th edn), London and New York: Macmillan.

Pissarides, C.A. (1998), 'The impact of employment tax cuts on unemployment and wages: the role of unemployment benefits and tax structure', *European Economic Review*, Vol. 42, pp. 155-83.

Plasschaert, S. (1997), 'An EU tax on consolidated profits of multinational enterprises', *European Taxation*, January.

Poddar, T. and Yi, E. (2007), 'India's Rising Growth Potential', Goldman Sachs: Global Economics Paper, No. 152.

Porter, M.G. and Trengove, C. (1990), 'Tax Reform in Australia', in M.J. Boskin and C.E. McLure Jr (eds), *World Tax Reform: Case Studies of Developed and Developing Countries*, San Francisco, CA: Institute for Contemporary Studies Press.

Prescott, E.C. (2004), 'Why do Americans work so much more than Europeans?', *Federal Reserve Bank of Minneapolis Quarterly Review*, Vol. 28, No. 1, pp. 2-13.

Ramsey, F.P. (1927), 'A contribution to the theory of taxation', *Economic Journal*, Vol. 37, No. 145, pp. 47-61.

Razin, A. and Sadka, E. (1991), 'International tax competition and gains from tax harmonization', *Economic Letters*, Vol. 37, pp. 69-76.

Rebelo, S. (1991), 'Long-run policy analysis and long-run growth', *Journal of Political Economy*, Vol. 99, No. 9, pp. 500-21.

Ring, R.J. (1999), 'Consumers' share and producers' share of the general sales tax', *National Tax Journal*, Vol. 52, No. 1, pp. 79-90.

Robins, F.K. (1985), 'A comparison of the labour supply findings from the four negative income tax experiments', *Journal of Human Resources*, Vol. 20, No. 4, pp. 567-82.

Robson, P. (1998), *The Economics of International Integration* (4th edn), London: Routledge

Røed, K. and Strøm, S. (2002), 'Progressive taxes and the labour market: is the trade-off between equality and efficiency inevitable?', *Journal of Economic Surveys*, Vol. 16, No. 1, pp. 77-110.

Romer, P.M. (1986), 'Increasing returns and long-run growth', *Journal of Political Economy*, Vol. 94, No. 5, pp. 1002-37.

Rosen, C. and Young, K.M. (1991), *Understanding Employee Ownership*, Ithaca, NY: Cornell University Press.

Rosen, H.S. (2005), *Public Finance* (7th edn), Boston, MA: McGraw-Hill Irwin.

Royal Bank of Scotland (2006), 'Results of RBS/Bloomberg Survey on German VAT Hike', Edinburgh: Royal Bank of Scotland.

Ruding Committee (1992), *Report of the Committee of Independent Experts on Company Taxation*, Luxembourg: Office for Official Publications of the European Communities

Saez, E. (2001), 'Using elasticities to derive optimal income tax rates', *Review of Economic Studies*, Vol. 68, No. 1, pp. 205-29.

Saez, E. (2002), 'Optimal income transfer programs: intensive versus extensive labor supply responses', *Quarterly Journal of Economics*, Vol. 117, No. 3, pp. 1039-73.

Sapir (2006), 'Globalisation and the reform of European social models', *Journal of Common Market Studies*, Vol. 44, No. 2, pp. 369-90.

Schultz, T.W. (1963), *The Economic Value of Education*, New York: Columbia University Press.

Schweinhart, L., Barnes, H. and Weikart, D. (1993), *Significant Benefits: The High/Score Perry Pre-School Study Through Age 27*, Ypsilanti, MI: High Scope Press.

Shavell, S. and Weiss, L. (1979), 'The optimal payment of unemployment insurance benefits over time', *Journal of Political Economy*, Vol. 87, No. 6, pp. 1347-62.

Shevlin, T. (1990), 'Estimating corporate marginal tax rates with asymmetric tax treatment of gains and losses', *Journal of the American Taxation Association*, Vol. 12, pp. 51-67.

Sinn, H.-W. (1991), 'Taxation and the cost of capital: The 'old' view, the 'new' view and another view', NBER Working Paper, No. 3501, Cambridge, MA: NBER

Slemrod, J. (1990), 'Tax principles in an international economy', in M.J. Boskin and C.E. McLure Jr (eds), *World Tax Reform: Case Studies of Developed and Developing Countries*, San Francisco, CA: Institute for Contemporary Studies Press.

Smith, A. (1776 [2004]), *The Wealth of Nations*, New York: Barnes & Noble.

Smith, J.K. (1999a), 'Use of business tax incentives: part 1', *Journal of State Taxation*, Vol. 17, No. 4, pp. 1-21.

Smith, J.K. (1999b), 'Use of business tax incentives: part 2', *Journal of State Taxation*, Vol. 18, No. 1, pp. 1-23.

Smith, S. (2005), 'Economic issues in alcohol taxation', in S. Cnossen (ed.), *Theory and Practice of Excise Taxation: Smoking, Drinking, Gambling, Polluting and Driving*, Oxford: Oxford University Press.

Solow, R. (1956), 'A contribution to the theory of economic growth', *Quarterly Journal of Economics*, Vol. 70, No. 1, pp. 65–94.

Sørensen, P.B. (2002), 'The German business tax reform of 2000 – A general equilibrium analysis', *German Economic Review*, Vol. 3, No 4, pp. 347-78.

Sørensen, P.B. (2004), 'Company tax reform in the European Union', *International Tax and Public Finance*, Vol. 11, No. 1, pp. 91-115.

Spence, M. (1973), 'Job market signaling', *Quarterly Journal of Economics*, Vol. 87, No. 3, pp. 355-74.

Stern, N. (2007), *Stern Review: The Economics of Climate Change*, Cambridge: Cambridge University Press.

Sterner, T. (2007), 'Fuel taxes: an important instrument for climate policy', *Energy Policy*, Vol. 35, No. 6, pp. 3194-202.

Stiglitz, J.E. (1969), 'The effects of income, wealth, and capital gains taxation on risk-taking', *Quarterly Journal of Economics*, Vol. 83, No. 1, pp. 263-83.

Stiglitz, J.E. and Dasgupta, P. (1971), 'Differential taxation, public goods, and economic efficiency', *Review of Economic Studies*, Vol. 38, No. 2, pp. 151-74.

Stiglitz, J.E. and Weiss, A. (1981), 'Credit rationing in markets with imperfect information', *American Economic Review*, Vol. 71, No. 3, pp. 393-410.

Stockey, N.L. and Rebelo, S. (1995), 'Growth effects of flat-rate taxes', *Journal of Political Economy*, Vol. 103, No. 3, pp. 519-50.

Stuart, C.E. (1981), 'Swedish tax rates, labor supply, and tax revenues', *Journal of Political Economy*, Vol. 89, No. 5, pp. 1020-38.

Surrey, S.S. and McDaniel, P.R. (1985), *International Aspects of Tax Expenditures: A Comparative Study*, Deventer: Kluwer Law and Taxation Publishers.

Tabaksblat, M. (1993), 'Harmonization of corporate tax in the EC: the views of a multinational', *Intertax*, 1993/1.

Tang, P. and Verweij, G. (2004), 'Reducing the administrative burden in the European Union', CPB Memorandum, No. 93, The Hague: Centraal Plan Bureau.

Tax Reform Commission (2006), *Tax Matters: Reforming the Tax System*, West Molesey: Tax Reform Commission, October.

Terra, B.J.M. and Wattel, P.J. (2005), *European Tax Law* (4th edn), The Hague: Kluwer Law International.

Tiebout, C.M. (1956), 'A pure theory of local expenditures', *Journal of Political Economy*, Vol. 64, No. 5, pp. 416-24.

Trandel, G. and Snow, A. (1999), 'Progressive income taxation and the underground economy', *Economics Letters*, Vol. 62, No. 2, pp. 217-22.

Trostel, P.A. (1993), 'The effect of taxation on human capital', *Journal of Political Economy*, Vol. 101, No. 2, pp. 327-50.

UNFCCC (2007), 'Background paper on analysis of existing and planned investment and financial flows relevant to the development of effective and appropriate international response to climate change', Bonn: UNFCCC.

UNICEF (2007), 'Child poverty in perspective: an overview of child well-being in rich countries', Innocenti Report Card 7, Florence: Innocenti Research Centre.

US Department of Treasury (1992), *Integration of the Individual and Corporate Tax Systems: Taxing Business Income Once*, Washington, DC: US Government Printing Office.

US Government Accountability Office (2005), *Understanding the Tax Reform Debate: Background, Criteria, & Questions*, Washington, DC: GAO.

US Joint Committee on Taxation (1997), 'Joint Committee on Taxation tax modeling project and 1997 tax symposium papers', Washington, DC: US Government Printing Office.

US Joint Economic Committee (1998), 'Government size and economic growth', JEC Report, December.

US Joint Economic Committee (2005a), 'Individuals and the compliance cost of taxation', JEC Report, November.

US Joint Economic Committee (2005b), 'Reforming the U.S. corporate tax system to increase tax competitiveness', JEC Report, May.

Uvalic, M. (1991), 'The PEPPER Report: Promotion of Employee Participation in Profits and Enterprise Results', Luxembourg: Office for Official Publications of the European Communities.

van den Noord, P. (2000), 'The tax system in Norway: past reforms and future challenges', OECD Economics Department Working Paper, No. 244, Paris: OECD.

van der Ploeg, F. (2006a), 'Do social policies harm employment? Second-best effects of taxes and benefits on labor markets', in J. Agell and P. Sørensen (eds), *Tax Policy and Labour Market Performance*, Cambridge, MA: MIT Press.

van der Ploeg, F. (2006b), 'Conditional benefits reduce equilibrium unemployment', *Journal of Public Economic Theory*, Vol. 8, No. 4, pp. 603-10.

van der Ploeg, F. (2006c), 'The welfare state, redistribution and the economy: reciprocal altruism, consumer rivalry and second best', in F. Farina and E. Savlagia (eds), *Inequality and Economic Integration*, London: Routledge.

van der Ploeg, F. (2006d), 'Rolling back the public sector: differential effects on employment, investment, and growth', *Oxford Economic Papers*, Vol. 58, No. 1, pp. 103-22.

van Ewijk, C., Koning, M., Lever, M. and de Mooij, R.A. (2006), 'Economische effecten van aanpassing fiscale behandeling eigenwoning', Bijzondere CPB Publicatie, No. 62, The Hague: Centraal Plan Bureau.

van Loo, J., de Grip, A. and Steur, M. (2001), 'Skills obsolescence: causes and cures', *International Journal of Manpower*, Vol. 22, No. 1/2, pp. 121-37.

Vermeend, W.A.F.G. (1996), 'The Court of Justice of the European Communities and Direct Taxes: Est-ce que la justice est de ce monde?', *EC Tax Review*, Vol. 5, No. 2, pp. 2-3.

Vermeend, W.A.F.G. and van der Vaart, J. (1998), *Greening Taxes: The Dutch Model*, Deventer: Kluwer.

Volkerink, B. and de Haan, J. (2001), 'Tax ratios: a critical survey', OECD Tax Policy Studies, No. 5, Paris: OECD.

Vollebergh, H. (2007), *Impacts of Environmental Policy Instruments on Technological Change*, Paris: OECD.

Vording, H. and Meussen, G.T.K. (2004), 'VPB-tariefverlaging: waarom, hoe, voor wie?', *Weekblad Fiscaal Recht*, Afl. 6596, pp. 1507-11.

Vreymans, P. and Verhulst, E. (2005), *Growth Differentials in Europe: An Investigation into the Causes – Growth stimulating Policies*, Brussels: WorkForAll.

Wallart, N., Folmer, H. and Oates, W. (1999), *The Political Economy of Environmental Taxes: New Horizons in Environmental Economics*, Cheltenham, UK and Northampton, MA, USA: Edward Elgar.

Walsh, B. (2000), 'The role of tax policy in Ireland's economic renaissance', *Canadian Tax Journal*, Vol. 48, No. 3.

Webber, C. and Wildavsky, A. (1986), *A History of Taxation and Expenditure in the Western World*, New York: Simon & Schuster.

Weber, D. (2006), *In Search of a (New) Equilibrium between Tax Sovereignty and the Freedom of Movement within the EU*, Deventer: Kluwer.

Wegman, E.J. (2006), *Ad Hoc Committee Report on the Hockey Stick Global Climate Reconstruction*, Washington, DC: US Congressional Committee on Energy and Commerce.

Weiner, J.M. (2002), 'Formulary apportionment and the future of company taxation in the European Union', *CESifo Forum*, No. 1, Spring, pp. 10-20.

White, A.G. (2006), 'A global projection of subjective well-being: a challenge to positive psychology', *Psychtalk*, No. 56, pp. 17-20, School of Psychology, University of Leicester.

World Bank (2006a), *Global Economic Prospects 2006: Economic Implications of Remittances and Migration*, Washington, DC: World Bank.

World Bank (2006b), *Paying Taxes: The Global Picture*, Washington, DC: World Bank (with PricewaterhouseCoopers).

World Economic Forum (2005), *Global Competitiveness Report*, Geneva: World Economic Forum.

Zodrow, G.R. (1991), 'On the "traditional" and "new" views of dividend taxation', *National Tax Journal*, Vol. 44, pp. 497-509.

Zodrow, G.R. (2005), '*Capital mobility and source-based taxation of capital income*', Manuscript, Rice University, Houston, TX.

Zodrow, G.R. and Mieszkowski, P. (1986), 'Pigou, Tiebout, property taxation, and the underprovision of local public goods', *Journal of Urban Economics*, Vol. 19, No. 3, pp. 356-70.

Zodrow, G.R. and Mieszkowski, P. (eds) (2002), *United States Tax Reform in the 21st Century*, Cambridge and New York: Cambridge University Press.

Index

trends and issues, 21st century
    economic and demographic 51–8
system greening
    background 299–300
    environment and growing prosperity
        300–301
        Climate Change Performance Index
            (CCPI) 310–11, 312
        environmental Kuznets curve
            (EKC) 302
        European stance 314–15
        global temperatures and energy use,
            reversing trend 309–10
        'green Solow model' and role of
            technological innovation
            302–3
        greening as integral part of
            growth-oriented policy 301–2
        ongoing debate 305–8
        Stern Report 308–9
        USA 311, 313
        what is at stake 303–5
    measures aimed at 327–335
    tax concessions aimed at sustainable
        development, reform and 360–62
    see also environment; green taxes

Tabellini, G. 123
Taber, C. 243, 248
Tanzi, Vito 134–5
tax
    ad personam 62
    capital gains (CGT) 161, 162, 165,
        166–7
    cash-flow (CFT) 209–10
    commodity *see* consumption tax
    corporate 169–70, 181–4
    direct 61–2
    economic growth, effect on 372–3
    energy 329
    flat 133–5
    graduate 256–7
    H-R Flat 207–9
    in rem 62
    indirect 61–2
    mix, package and 347
    OECD classification 439–40
    payroll, circular flow model and 42
    poll 32
    progressive, with flat tax 134–5

property 447
retroactive 31–2
sales 42, 204–7, 445
'Tinbergen's talent' 111, 114
vehicle 214–17
wage, circular flow model and 42
withholding (WHT) 184, 277, 278,
    291
see also corporation tax; green taxes;
    income tax; second life tax;
    Value-Added Tax
tax policy
    alternatives, to stimulate labour
        market 132–7
    coordination, tax competition and 286,
        298
        banking secrecy and exchange of
            information 290
        Bolkestein Report 292–5
        EU Code of Conduct for Business
            Taxation 288–90
        EU harmonization process 291–2
        EU institutional structure 293
        models 296–7
        OECD Forum on Harmful Tax
            Practices 287–8
        Savings Directive 290–91
    equilibrium income change and,
        aggregate demand and output
        402–3
    effectiveness, R & D incentives and
        230–35
    labour market performance and 4
    lessons for 5
    short-run business-cycle fluctuations
        and, Keynesian economics
        392–5, 413
    see also fiscal policy; labour market
        performance
tax rate
    base definitions and, capital market
        investment and taxation and
        150–51
    effective 73–6, 155–6, 273–5, 297–8,
        350–51
    high marginal, drawbacks of, tax
        package and 347–8
    macro backward looking 74–5
    marginal, subsidies and 253
    micro backward looking 75–6